AMERICAN HISTORY DESK REFERENCE

TABLE OF CONTENTS

Materials selected from:
The Scholastic Encyclopedia of the Presidents and Their Times © 1994 by Scholastic Inc.
The Scholastic Encyclopedia of the United States © 1997 by Scholastic Inc.

ISBN 0-439-21602-8

The Scholastic Encyclopedia of the Presidents and Their Times was originally produced by Agincourt Press.
The Scholastic Encyclopedia of the United States was originally produced by Betsy Ryan/Bascom Communications.

10 9 8 7 6 5 4 3 2 1 0/0 01 02 03 04

Printed in the U.S.A.
First printing, September 2000

SCHOLASTIC ENCYCLOPEDIA OF THE PRESIDENTS AND THEIR TIMES

DAVID RUBEL

An Agincourt Press Book

For Julia

Editor: Sarah B. Weir
Contributing Editors: Julia Banks Rubel, Teresa Celsi, Jennifer Fleischner, Mark Hoff, Russell Shorto, Richard Smith

Design: Tilman Reitzle
Maps: Geoff Notkin, Tilman Reitzle
Photo Research: Diane Hamilton, Nora E. Malek
Production: Mike Hortens, Mark Lewis

We would like to thank Allan Shrem and Lee Schogel of the World Collectible Center for kindly allowing us access to their collection of presidential campaign memorabilia.

PHOTO CREDITS
All images are from the Library of Congress, the National Archives, and the Steele Collection, except for:
The Bettmann Archive: cover (top left, bottom left); Granger Collection: cover (bottom right); FPG International: cover (top right); Beverly R. Robinson Collection/U.S. Naval Academy Museum: 17 (bottom); World Collectible Center: 52, 116, 120, 128, 130 (bottom), 132, 136 (bottom), 140, 144, 156, 168, 172 (center, bottom), 183 (bottom), 185 (bottom), 196 (bottom), 200, 204; Levi Strauss: 66 (bottom); Alaska State Library: 79 (top); Utah Division of State History: 81 (bottom); American Heritage Center, University of Wyoming: 86 (bottom); Arizona Historical Society/Tucson: 94 (bottom); Kansas State Historical Society: 103 (bottom); Hogan Jazz Archive: 111; Sophia Smith Collection/Smith College: 131 (bottom); New York Stock Exchange Archives: 141 (bottom); Franklin Delano Roosevelt Library: 145 (top), 146 (top), 153 (top); Veterans of Foreign Wars of the United States: 153 (bottom), 179 (top), 187 (bottom); National Archives of Canada: 155; Harry S. Truman Library: 159 (bottom); Schomburg Center for Research in Black Culture: 167 (bottom), 171 (top); Soviet Life: 169 (bottom); E.C. Publications, Inc.: 171 (bottom); John Fitzgerald Kennedy Library: 172 (top), 174; U.S. Air Force: 173 (bottom); Lyndon Baines Johnson Library: 178 (top), 179 (bottom); National Aeronautics and Space Administration: 181 (bottom), 197 (bottom), 207 (bottom); New York Public Library: 182 (bottom); Jimmy Carter Library: 189 (bottom), 190; Dori Jacobson/Sophia Smith Collection/Smith College: 191 (top); Con Edison: 191 (bottom); Ronald Reagan Library: 193, 198 (bottom); Apple Computer, Inc.: 195 (bottom); National Safe Kids Campaign: 199; Earth Times: 201 (bottom); Office of George Bush: 202 (bottom); African National Congress: 203 (top); Magic Johnson Foundation: 203 (bottom); White House: 205 (top), 206, 209 (top); Tilman Reitzle: 205 (bottom); 207 (top); White House Historical Association: 212 (bottom); Rutherford Hayes Presidential Center: 215 (bottom). The Mount Rushmore cover of MAD is used with permission. © 1956, 1984 by E.C. Publications, Inc.

Library of Congress Cataloging-in-Publication Data

Rubel, David.
The Scholastic encyclopedia of the presidents and their times/David Rubel.
p. cm.
Includes index.
ISBN 0-590-49366-3
1. Presidents—United States—Encyclopedias, Juvenile. 2. United States—History—Encyclopedias, Juvenile. [1. Presidents—United States—Encyclopedias. 2. United States—History—Encyclopedias.] I. Scholastic Inc. II. Title.
E176.1.R88
973'.099—dc20 93-11810
CIP

ISBN 0-590-49366-3

Table of Contents

IN 1789, GEORGE WASHINGTON became the first president of the United States. More than forty others have followed him. The ninth president, William Henry Harrison, served less than a month. Franklin Roosevelt, the thirty-second president, served for twelve years. During Roosevelt's term, which spanned the Great Depression and World War II, the country changed a great deal. But the same can be said for almost any president. Each president's term in office is usually shaped by important events both inside and outside the United States.

This book tells the story of the United States through its presidents. It is organized by year, with one page for each year there has been a president. The year is marked at the top outside corner of each page. The book begins in 1789 and ends for now in 1997, at the beginning of President Bill Clinton's second term. The pages for each president generally correspond to the years of his administration. But not every event happened during the year of the page on which it is described. Using one page per year is just a useful way to give a sense of time as it passes.

This book also tells the story of ordinary Americans. In the outside column of each page, you can read about the political events occurring in Washington, D.C., and around the world. But on the inside, you can read features that describe events happening in the rest of the country. Words and pictures describe the arts, medicine, and the sciences as well as trends in daily life.

How to Look Up...

★A PRESIDENT – Look up the president's name in the Table of Contents and turn to the page listed.

★WHO WAS PRESIDENT DURING A PARTICULAR YEAR – Find the page corresponding to that year. At the bottom of the page, you will find the president's name and his years in office.

★PRESIDENTIAL ELECTION RESULTS – A chart listing the results of every presidential election begins on page 220.

★IMPORTANT EVENTS AND PEOPLE OTHER THAN PRESIDENTS – Look up the subject in the index at the back of the book. The index will list the numbers of the pages on which that person or event is discussed.

★PRESIDENTIAL CAMPAIGNS – To find out about a particular campaign, turn to the page corresponding to the year of the campaign in which you are interested.

★PERSONAL STATISTICS ABOUT EACH PRESIDENT – The birthdate, birthplace, death date, political party, vice president, first lady, children, and nickname of each president are listed on the first page of that president's term.

WORDS IN RED mean that a subject is discussed in greater detail elsewhere in the book. To find out where, look up the subject in the index. The most detailed entry will also be marked with red.

THE MANIFEST DESTINY MAPS (appearing on pages 1, 9, 29, 41, 73, 105, and 177) show the territorial growth of the United States, beginning with the thirteen original colonies and ending with statehood for Alaska and Hawaii in 1959. The first time each state appears on a Manifest Destiny Map, it is shown in red and labeled with the year of its admission. States already in the Union are shown in blue. Territories that have not yet been admitted as states are shown in white.

E PLURIBUS
UNUM

GEORGE WASHINGTON

1ST PRESIDENT

★

FROM 1789 TO 1797

BORN: February 22, 1732

BIRTHPLACE: Pope's Creek, Va.

DIED: December 14, 1799

PARTY: Federalist

VICE PRESIDENT: John Adams

FIRST LADY: Martha Dandridge Custis

STEPCHILDREN: John Parke Custis, Martha Parke Custis

NICKNAME: Father of His Country

The first president to appear on a postage stamp.

In the years after the American Revolution, the retired general George Washington became so popular that some people wanted to make him king. Washington, however, had no intention of becoming an American monarch. He didn't even want to be president.

Instead, he was quite content to enjoy the peaceful life of his Mount Vernon, Virginia, plantation. But the new nation that he had helped to create needed him.

When the American colonies declared their independence from Great Britain in 1776, their first task was to win the Revolutionary War. But they also had to create a new form of government. Great Britain was ruled by a king, but most Americans wanted to be governed democratically by leaders the people elected.

The first plan for such a government was set forth in the Articles of

BILL OF RIGHTS ALLOWS PASSAGE OF CONSTITUTION

THE FRAMERS OF THE Constitution were concerned that the new government they were planning might become too powerful. Americans had fought hard for their freedom, and no one wanted it taken away so soon.

The government was divided into three branches that could check and balance each other. But the Constitution did very little to protect individual rights. Critics of the Constitution vowed to fight its ratification unless individual liberties were spelled out clearly.

The first ten amendments, adopted in 1791, formed the Bill of Rights. They guaranteed to all citizens the freedoms of speech, religion, and assembly. They also protected citizens from having to testify against themselves and from having their homes searched without cause.

Most Americans trusted George Washington, but they were worried about giving any one person too much power. History has been full of modest people corrupted by power. The Bill of Rights was intended to protect the rights of every individual no matter who became president.

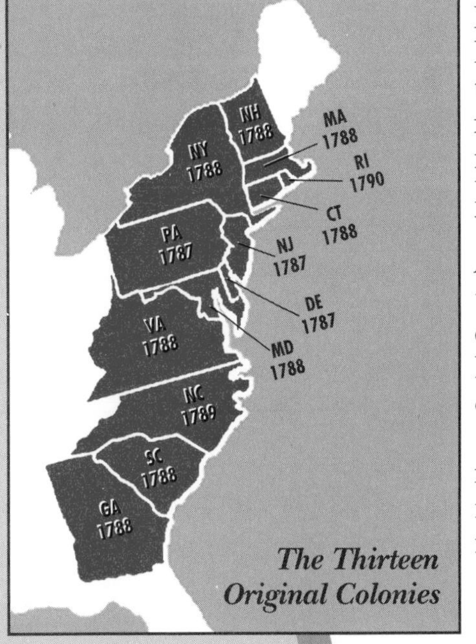

The Thirteen Original Colonies

Confederation. It included some features that linked the states together, but it lacked a strong central government with a president to run it. Individual states could still pass their own laws, issue their own money, and levy their own taxes.

The powerlessness of the federal government under the Articles of Confederation became obvious to everyone in 1786 during a revolt in Massachusetts. Farmers there rebelled because they were being jailed for their debts. The federal government could neither put down the uprising nor force the other states to help.

THE CONSTITUTIONAL CONVENTION

Because the Articles of Confederation weren't working, a national meeting was called to develop a new plan. Delegates from the states gathered in Philadelphia on May 25, 1787. George Washington presided over this group, which became known as the Constitutional Convention.

The Constitution that thirty-nine delegates signed in September set up a new federal government with three distinct branches. The legislative branch included two chambers, the House of Representatives and the Senate. The judicial branch would be headed by the Supreme Court. Finally, the executive branch would be led by the president.

CHOOSING THE FIRST PRESIDENT

Presidents have never been elected by the direct vote of the people. Instead, each state chooses a number of electors equal to its representation in Congress. These electors then vote for the president. Until 1832, electors were chosen by state legislatures. After that, electors were chosen directly by voters, except in South Carolina.

When the electoral college met for the first time in January 1789, George

The Early Years

IN 1753, GEORGE WASHINGTON WAS WORKING AS A surveyor in Virginia and serving as a major in the colonial militia. In October, Virginia's colonial governor sent the twenty-one-year-old Washington on a mission to demand that French troops leave land in the Ohio Valley claimed by Britain. The French refused, leading to the French and Indian War.

Because of his military experience during this war and his service to the Continental Congress, Washington was chosen in 1775 to command the new Continental Army. Washington experienced many more defeats than victories, but he never lost badly enough to lose the war completely. Instead, his real task was to keep the army together.

★**MYTHS ABOUT GEORGE WASHINGTON**

There are many stories that people tell about George Washington. One is that he lost all his teeth and had to wear wooden ones. In fact, he did wear false teeth. But they weren't made out of wood. Instead, he had sets made from gold, lead, and ivory. One set was even made from hippopotamus teeth.

Another myth about Washington was that, as a boy, he chopped down his father's cherry tree. When asked whether he did it, Washington supposedly said, "I cannot tell a lie. I did it." This is certainly not a true story. Rather, it was invented by Parson Mason Weems for his book *The Life and Memorable Actions of George Washington*, first published in 1800. Weems's intention was to create legends for the new country.

★THE COTTON GIN Before Eli Whitney invented the cotton gin in 1793, farmers and slaves who cleaned cotton picked the seeds out by hand. Whitney's invention saved a tremendous amount of work because it picked the seeds out mechanically. One person operating a cotton gin could clean as much cotton as fifty people working the old way.

With this new technology, southern farmers were able to expand their plantings by thousands of acres. Cotton soon became so important to the region that it was called King Cotton.

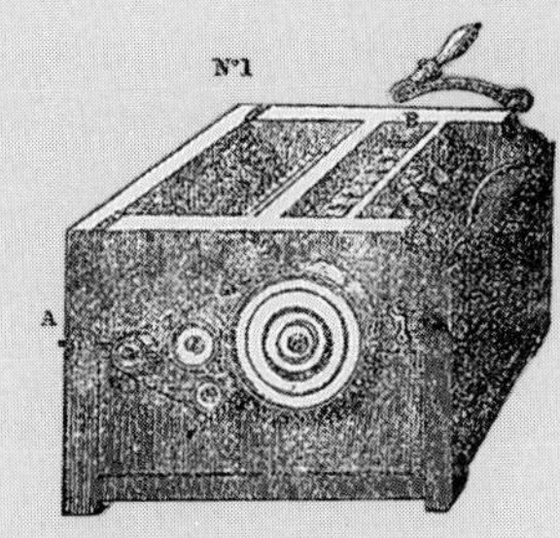

★CHIEF RED JACKET One of the most pressing problems facing Washington was trouble along the frontier. Whites who were anxious to farm the rich land in the nation's interior were settling native lands illegally. Soon enough, the Creek, Chickasaw, Cherokee, and Seminole tribes decided to fight back.

In 1792, Washington met with the Seneca chief Red Jacket, to whom he gave a silver medal as a token of respect. Red Jacket believed that the Indians would inevitably have to make peace with the powerful whites. However, later in his life, the chief fought vigorously to protect the Senecas' customs, religion, and language.

★THE FIRST LADY When George Washington became president, his wife, Martha, was wary of living a public life. As time went on, however, she grew fond of her role as the first lady. She hosted state dinners every week, and on Friday afternoons, she and Abigail Adams, the vice president's wife, held casual receptions for anyone who might want to attend. The informality of these receptions was supposed to show that the new government was not above the people. But visitors to the president's house still wore fine clothes and called Martha "Lady Washington."

Washington was the clear choice of the electors. But the retired general was still reluctant to serve, a fact that probably helped him win.

Americans continued to worry about one man having too much power. If there had to be a president, people thought, it should be someone who didn't want the job. When the vote for president was taken, Washington was the unanimous choice.

HAMILTON AND JEFFERSON

One of the president's first tasks was to appoint people to head each of the four executive departments: Foreign Affairs (later called State), War, Treasury, and Justice. For the first secretary of the treasury, Washington chose Alexander Hamilton, who had played an important role at the Constitutional Convention. Later, along with James Madison and John Jay, Hamilton had written the *Federalist Papers*, which had urged ratification of the Constitution.

Hamilton's political rival, Thomas Jefferson, became the first secretary of state. Unlike Hamilton, Jefferson feared a strong federal government. As ambassador to France, he had seen how the ruling classes there lived in luxury, while poor people dressed in rags and begged on the streets. He blamed the problems of France on its powerful central government.

Jefferson worried that a strong government in the United States might oppress people, too. From the opposite point of view, Hamilton worried that a weak federal government would accomplish nothing. Usually Washington sided with Hamilton.

At first, Washington asked each of his four department heads to meet with him separately. But this took up a lot of time and was not very effective. Eventually, the president came up with a better way. In late 1791, he instructed the secretaries to meet with him as a single group. This group became known as the cabinet.

PAYING THE STATES' DEBTS One of the most important issues faced by the cabinet during Washington's first term was the public debt owed by the states. During the Revolutionary War, most states had borrowed money from foreign and American investors to pay their soldiers. This money had to be paid back. Early in 1790, Hamilton came up with a plan. He proposed that the federal government pay off the states' debts.

Hamilton had two reasons. The first was that he wanted to establish the federal government's credit. The best way to encourage people to lend money is to show the ability to pay off a debt. Paying off the states' debts would encourage citizens and foreign governments to lend money to the federal government in the future.

The second reason was to bring the states closer together in the new union. If the debts became the responsibility of the federal government, the states would be motivated to work together to pay them off.

IMPLIED POWERS The problem with paying off the states' debts was that the Constitution had not given the federal government the power to do it. On the other hand, the Constitution had not specifically withheld that power, either. Hamilton argued that by not forbidding it, the Constitution implied the existence of such a power. Hamilton's theory has been called the doctrine of implied powers.

Jefferson thought that Hamilton's argument was dangerous. He believed the more power the government took,

Campaign ★ 1792 ★

When the Electoral College met in 1789 and again in 1792, each elector voted for two people. The person getting the most votes became president, as long as that total represented a majority. In both elections, the winner was George Washington. In 1789 and again in 1792, not a single elector cast a vote against him. Washington was the only president ever to be elected unanimously.

The person with the second highest electoral vote became vice president. In both the 1789 and 1792 elections, John Adams received the second highest total, so he became Washington's vice president.

Under the Constitution, the vice president had not much responsibility or power. His role was to break tied votes in the Senate and take over if the president resigned or died. Adams called the job the "most insignificant office that ever the invention of man contrived or his imagination conceived."

Buttons were made to honor George Washington's first inauguration on April 30, 1789. One design consisted of his initials and the words "Long Live the President." Another featured an eagle. The buttons played no role in the campaign, but they are believed to be forerunners of the campaign buttons used today.

Martha and George Washington with John and Martha Custis (left).

the less freedom the people would have. In response to Hamilton, Jefferson argued that unless the Constitution explicitly granted the power to do something, it couldn't be done. Hamilton and Jefferson's debate has continued throughout the history of the United States.

THE FIRST NATIONAL BANK Part of Hamilton's plan included the establishment of a national bank to hold federal deposits and issue paper money. Many people, especially farmers, conducted business by trading goods. When they did use money, it was in the form of gold and silver coins. Because America had only small stores of these precious metals, most people used coins that had been minted in other countries. Everything from English pounds to Russian kopecks passed from hand to hand.

The national bank met with a great deal of opposition, especially from Jefferson, who feared any concentration of governmental power. In exchange for Jefferson's acceptance of the national bank, which Congress approved in 1791, Hamilton agreed to move the nation's capital so that it would be closer to Jefferson's native Virginia.

New York City was the nation's first capital. With a population of thirty-three thousand, it was the largest city in the country. Its streets were jammed daily with city residents and country farmers who had come to sell

WAR IN EUROPE

Can the United States Stay Neutral?

THE WAR between France and Great Britain that began in 1793 had an immediate effect on the United States. Both Britain and France still held territory in North America, and the naval battles they fought off the West Indies continually disrupted U.S. shipping.

During the Revolutionary War, the Continental Congress had signed a treaty with King Louis XVI of France. In exchange for military aid, the Americans promised to defend the French West Indies against British attack.

In 1793, the French government asked for American help. But the U.S. refused, believing the treaty no longer applied because Louis XVI had been overthrown and executed.

Meanwhile, Britain, which had never fully accepted American independence, also began provoking the U.S. In 1794, the Royal Navy began boarding American ships that were suspected of carrying British deserters. During these raids, the British kidnapped not only former British sailors, but also innocent Americans. The practice was called impressment.

their goods. The wagons that clattered along the cobblestone streets made a terrible racket.

Besides these drawbacks of New York, some members of the government thought it would be wiser to move the nation's capital to a district outside the control of any one state. For the new capital, George Washington chose a site on the Potomac River between Maryland and Virginia. Each of these states donated a share of the land for the new District of Columbia within which the capital city of Washington would be built. In the meantime, Philadelphia became the temporary capital.

THE PROCLAMATION OF NEUTRALITY

America's foreign policy was first tested during Washington's second term. Soon after the French Revolution began, France declared war on Great Britain. The French had greatly aided the American cause during the American Revolution, and now they asked for help in return. Jefferson was inclined to say yes. But many officials, including Alexander Hamilton, argued against supporting France. Almost every American agreed on one point, however. No one wanted to get involved in the actual fighting.

In April 1793, knowing it would be best to stay out of a European war, Washington issued the Proclamation of Neutrality. In it, he advised the states to remain friendly with both sides. But he also warned them against smuggling weapons and other contraband, which might pull the United States into the war.

Jefferson generally supported Washington's conduct of relations with France and Britain. But he grew increasingly tired of fighting with Hamilton. In late 1793, he resigned as secretary of state.

★**THE SLAVE TRADE** The slave trade between Africa and North America began in the 1600s. By the 1790s, there were about seven hundred thousand slaves in the United States. Although the northern states all outlawed slavery between 1777 and 1804, the South became even more dependent on slave labor after the invention of the cotton gin led to more cotton planting.

Some slaves were taught skills, such as how to read and write. A few even managed to earn enough money to buy their freedom. But most slaves were beaten into obedience. Some slaveholders convinced themselves that Africans were less than human, which made it seem acceptable to treat African slaves brutally.

★**THE FRENCH REVOLUTION** By 1789, the French government was almost bankrupt. Peasants in the countryside and poor people in the cities were on the verge of rioting for food. Only the aristocracy of titled landowners remained rich.

In May 1789, the government convened an emergency meeting of the Estates-General, a special parliament made up of delegates from the clergy, the aristocracy, and the common people. Both the clergy and the aristocracy wanted to protect their privileges. But the representatives of the common people wanted to eliminate these advantages.

Alarmed by the people's demands, King Louis XVI sent twenty thousand soldiers to Versailles, where the Estates-General was meeting. News of this troop movement enraged Parisians, who responded by attacking the Bastille prison and capturing the weapons stored there. The storming of the Bastille on July 14, 1789, is considered the beginning of the French Revolution.

★**Painting in America** The most promising art students in America were usually sent to Europe for their training. The two most famous American painters of this time, Benjamin West and John Singleton Copley, both settled in London, where they followed the fashion of painting scenes from history.

In America, the most popular paintings were portraits. Most American artists painted little else until the 1840s when photography reduced the demand for them. The leading portrait painters of the time were Gilbert Stuart and Charles Willson Peale. Both men painted George Washington, who was known to be a patient subject. The most famous of these works is an unfinished portrait of Washington begun by Stuart in 1794. An etching based on this portrait appears on the dollar bill.

★**Royal Gift** Despite his achievements as a general and president, George Washington saw himself primarily as a farmer. Throughout his life, he remained interested in the breeding of animals. His specialty was breeding mules.

A mule is the offspring of a male donkey and a female horse. Washington was always trying to improve the strength of his mules.

Learning of Washington's passion, the king of Spain sent him an excellent donkey as a gift. Washington named the donkey Royal Gift and used him to breed many fine mules. He occasionally mated Royal Gift with female donkeys and sent the offspring all over the country to raise the quality of breeding stock nationwide.

★**Family Farms** Farming was the most important industry in the United States until the twentieth century. George Washington called it "the most healthy, the most useful, and the most noble employment of man." In Washington's time, most farms were small and self-sufficient, producing only a tiny surplus of crops that could be traded for manufactured goods. Women played a particularly important role on these small farms.

Girls worked with their mothers on family farms to make everything from beeswax for candles to yarn for clothing. What little extra they made they traded at the local country store for items they couldn't make themselves, such as printed cloth and sugar.

The Whiskey Rebellion

Although Washington was very successful in keeping the United States out of the war, he was much quicker to use military force at home. An important example was the Whiskey Rebellion.

In 1791, Congress ordered a tax on whiskey. This tax outraged farmers who made whiskey from their extra corn. (Otherwise, it would spoil.) Some people in the countryside even used whiskey for money.

When federal officers tried to collect the whiskey tax in western Pennsylvania, farmers there rebelled. When the governor refused to punish the farmers and collect the tax himself, the problem became a national one.

Because the Whiskey Rebellion represented a direct and immediate challenge to the authority of the national government, Washington decided to form a volunteer army to enforce the law.

In fact, the incident never posed a serious military threat. Most of the rebels turned and ran when they saw Washington's army coming. But the incident was an important test of the new government. In putting down the Whiskey Rebellion, Washington proved that the federal government had the power to enforce its laws.

Meanwhile, Washington's policy of neutrality was being tested by the British, who began to stop and search American ships that were allegedly carrying supplies to the French. Britain also began encouraging Indians to attack American settlers along the nation's northwest frontier.

In order to avoid war, the U.S. minister to Great Britain, John Jay, negotiated a new treaty with the British government. In exchange for Britain's promise to withdraw troops from the Northwest Territory, the

United States agreed to permit the inspection of its ships on the high seas. Many people criticized Jay's Treaty for bargaining away the nation's neutrality rights. But it did postpone a war that America was not prepared to fight. Washington signed the treaty and managed to get it ratified by the Senate.

THE NORTHWEST TERRITORY

Disputes between settlers and native peoples on the nation's frontier were a constant problem for Washington. At first, he tried to solve the problem militarily. He sent General Arthur St. Clair into the Northwest Territory in 1791 to build a fort there.

Washington warned St. Clair to watch for surprise attacks, but St. Clair didn't listen. His two-thousand-man army was ambushed by Indian warriors on November 4, 1791, on the site of present-day Fort Wayne, Indiana. The Americans suffered more than nine hundred casualties.

When Washington found out, he was furious. But he didn't try to cover up the blunder. Instead, he immediately informed Congress and sent General "Mad" Anthony Wayne to replace St. Clair.

Wayne was more careful. Before fighting the Indians, he spent time training his men in the methods of Indian warfare. On August 20, 1794, he engaged the tribal armies at the Battle of Fallen Timbers, where he won a decisive victory. Then, during the summer of 1795, Wayne spent six weeks negotiating a peace treaty with delegates of the Great Lakes, Mississippi River, and Ohio River tribes.

George Washington announced his retirement in his Farewell Address, which was published on September 19, 1796. In it, he warned the nation against becoming permanently allied with foreign powers.

Campaign 1796

As most people expected, Vice President John Adams announced that he would run for president in 1796. Like Washington, Adams was a member of the Federalist party, which supported a strong central government and life terms for senators.

Adams's opponent, former secretary of state Thomas Jefferson, had very different political ideas. He led a new party, the Democratic-Republicans, that favored more power for the states and limited terms for public office.

Out of personal respect for George Washington, the Democratic-Republicans had been relatively quiet during his two terms. Now that Washington was retiring, they were ready to fight.

During the American Revolution, Adams and Jefferson had been friends and colleagues. But the rough campaign of 1796, the first to be contested, turned them into enemies. The Democratic-Republicans claimed that Adams wanted to become an American king, while the Federalists condemned Jefferson as a demagogue—that is, someone who manipulates popular fears for his or her own political ends.

It was probably Washington's endorsement that won the election for Adams. Jefferson came in second, however, and became Adams's vice president. This was the only time in history that the president and vice president were members of different political parties. In 1804, the Twelfth Amendment to the Constitution changed the way the president and vice president were elected so that it wouldn't happen again.

JOHN ADAMS

2ND PRESIDENT

★

FROM 1797 TO 1801

BORN: October 30, 1735

BIRTHPLACE: Braintree, Mass.

DIED: July 4, 1826

PARTY: Federalist

VICE PRESIDENT: Thomas Jefferson

FIRST LADY: Abigail Smith

CHILDREN: Abigail, John Quincy, Susanna, Charles, Thomas

NICKNAME: Duke of Braintree

The only president to be the father of another president.

The most critical problem facing John Adams when he took office involved French raids on American shipping. U.S. neutrality in the war between Britain and France had led to a boom in trade. Both warring nations badly needed supplies from the United States, but neither wanted the other to receive any U.S. goods.

In 1794, the United States signed Jay's Treaty with Great Britain. This agreement, ratified in 1795, gave away some of the nation's neutrality. In retaliation, the French government began encouraging pirates to attack ships headed for Great Britain. As the number of seized merchant ships neared three hundred, the American public demanded war. There was even a wild rumor that the French might be planning an invasion.

Remembering the warning against foreign entanglements in Washington's Farewell Address,

ALIEN AND SEDITION ACTS PASSED BY CONGRESS

In 1798, as the United States moved closer to war with France, John Adams signed into law the Alien and Sedition Acts to protect America's security.

There were four bills: The Naturalization Act made it harder for immigrants to become U.S. citizens. The Alien and Alien Enemies acts gave the president the power, especially during wartime, to deport or imprison foreigners he considered dangerous.

Finally, the Sedition Act outlawed attacks against the government.

Jefferson saw these new laws mainly as a way for Adams to control his political rivals. The Democratic-Republicans received a lot of support from recent immigrants, and they believed Adams sought to take away these votes. The Sedition Act also limited their freedom to criticize the policies of the government.

With his opposition to the new laws, Jefferson became the first person to apply the Constitution to an actual dispute. He argued that the Sedition Act was unconstitutional because it violated the freedom of speech guaranteed by the First Amendment.

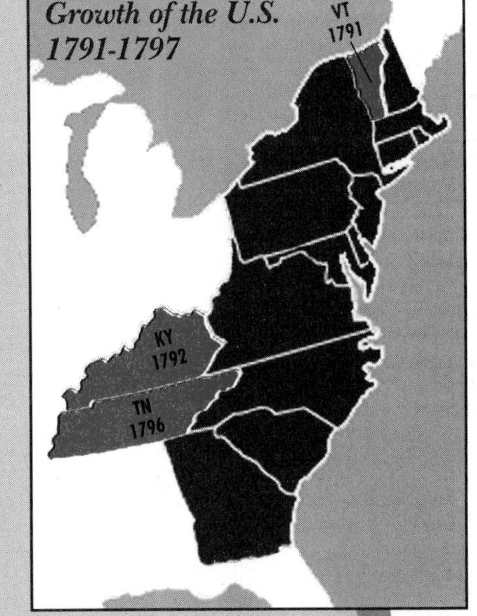

President Adams held back. Instead of fighting, he sent three diplomats to negotiate with French foreign minister Charles Talleyrand. Refusing to receive the U.S. mission himself, Talleyrand sent three aides to meet the Americans. These Frenchmen were later referred to as "X," "Y," and "Z" by Adams, who did not wish to reveal their names.

Before the Frenchmen would even listen to the Americans, they demanded a bribe of $250,000. This demand outraged Adams, who had long been famous for strictly following the law.

WAR FEVER AT HOME When news of the XYZ Affair reached the United States, the nation caught war fever. A popular slogan was "Millions for defense, but not one cent for tribute." Tribute meant the payment of bribes in order to stop the attacks.

Still, Adams would not declare war. The United States was not yet prepared to fight at sea, and it would take time to build a capable navy. In the meantime, Adams convinced Congress to stop U.S. trade with France. He also made arrangements for the powerful British navy to protect transatlantic shipping.

It was in the wartime atmosphere of 1798 that Adams obtained passage of the Alien and Sedition Acts. These laws made it hard for the Democratic-Republicans to organize opposition to the government. Jefferson's earlier, unpopular support for the French Revolution also hindered the Democratic-Republicans in their efforts to reverse Adams's policies.

Jefferson publicly accused Adams of enacting the laws in order to frustrate his political foes. He was at least partially correct. Over the next year, at least ten Democratic-Republican newspaper editors were jailed under the Sedition Act.

The Early Years

John Adams grew up on a farm in Braintree (now Quincy), Massachusetts, where he liked to spend his time hunting in the woods and playing a variety of games. Adams particularly liked flying kites, shooting marbles, and making toy boats.

After graduating from Harvard, he became a lawyer in Boston. His most famous case was argued in 1770, when he successfully defended the nine British soldiers accused in the Boston Massacre. In that pre-revolutionary incident, a resentful mob of Bostonians menaced a squad of frightened redcoats. The soldiers shot and killed five colonists despite orders not to fire.

From 1774 until 1777, Adams served as a delegate to the Continental Congress in Philadelphia. There, he nominated George Washington to be commander-in-chief of the Continental Army. He also helped Thomas Jefferson write the Declaration of Independence.

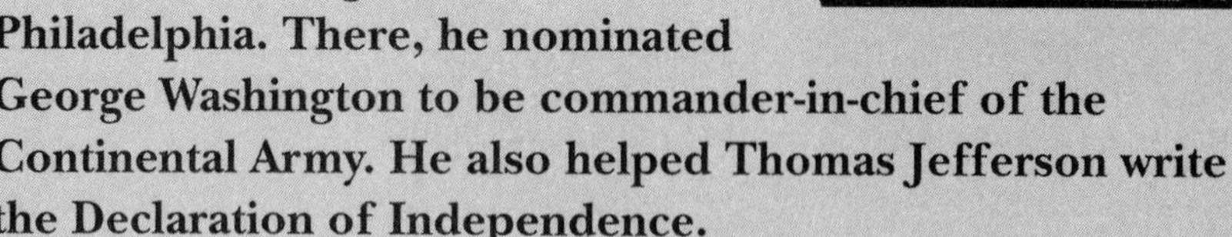

★**The First Lady** For long periods of time during the American Revolution and afterward, John Adams lived away from his Massachusetts home in Philadelphia, New York, France, and England. While he was away, his wife Abigail had to manage the family farm and raise their five children. Many of the nation's founders, including Thomas Jefferson, suffered financially because of the time they spent away from home. But Abigail Adams's shrewd handling of her husband's financial affairs kept the family prosperous.

Although she was the wife of one president and the mother of another, Abigail herself felt disappointed at the lack of opportunities she had as a woman. She regretted especially that the women of her time were denied the same education that men received. In letters she wrote to her husband, Abigail charged him to "remember the ladies" who had served the country so well during the revolution.

★**BLACK CHURCHES** Around 1800, churches began to play an important role in the lives of many African Americans in the North. Unable to attend most schools and unwelcome in politics, many black people turned to the church as a center for education and community organizing.

In the South, however, slaves were often not allowed to attend church services. Their white owners were afraid of letting them gather in large groups. Whites also worried about slaves becoming literate, and therefore discontented, through learning to read the Bible.

★**JOHNNY APPLESEED** Sometime about 1800, twenty-six-year-old John Chapman began to collect apple seeds from cider presses in western Pennsylvania. He used these seeds to grow small plants, which he planned to sell to pioneer families on the western frontier.

At that time, homesteaders were still settling the Ohio River valley. During his travels, Chapman sold or gave away thousands of apple seedlings to these people.

Although John Chapman was a real person, his exploits inspired the myth of Johnny Appleseed. Stories were told of a cheerful, generous vagabond with an upside-down pan for a hat, bare feet, and a coffee sack for a shirt. In addition to planting apple trees, Johnny Appleseed was famous for his gentleness with animals, his love for nature, and his peaceful relations with the Indians.

★**RETIREMENT** Although the end to his presidency was quite rocky, Adams enjoyed a peaceful retirement at his family home in Massachusetts. He spent most of his time reading the literature of the world in his library. Once his eyesight began to fail, his eighteen grandchildren and great-grandchildren took turns reading aloud to him. As time went on, he even renewed his friendship with Jefferson.

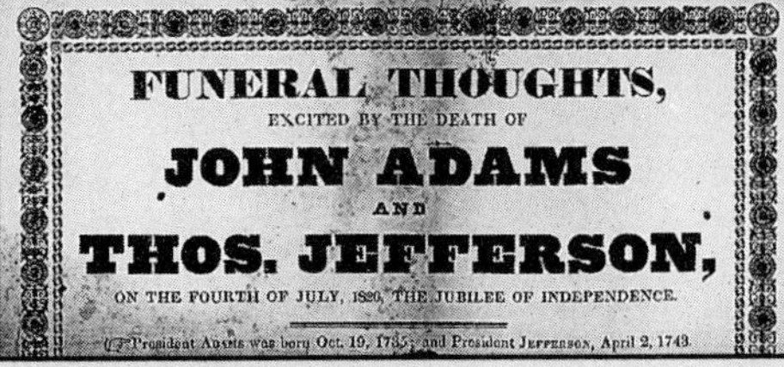

FUNERAL THOUGHTS,
EXCITED BY THE DEATH OF
JOHN ADAMS
AND
THOS. JEFFERSON,
ON THE FOURTH OF JULY, 1826, THE JUBILEE OF INDEPENDENCE.

☞ President ADAMS was born Oct. 19, 1735; and President JEFFERSON, April 2, 1743.

At the age of eighty-nine, Adams proudly watched his son John Quincy win election as the sixth president. Two years later, he was invited to participate in Boston's celebration of the fiftieth anniversary of the Declaration of Independence. Adams never made it, dying quietly in the early evening of July 4, 1826. His last words were "Jefferson still survives."

Although Adams had no way of knowing it, Jefferson had died a few hours earlier at his Monticello estate in Virginia.

To protest the Alien and Sedition Acts, Jefferson and James Madison wrote the Kentucky and Virginia Resolves, which argued that the new laws were void because they were unconstitutional. Jefferson and Madison even went so far as to insist that states had the right to reject federal laws. This argument would become much more important in the years leading up to the Civil War.

THE QUASI-WAR From the spring of 1798 through 1800, despite the official state of peace between the two nations, U.S. frigates battled the French navy. Adams hesitated to declare war because he hoped the fighting would soon stop. He thought the French were too busy in Europe to continue bothering with North America.

In September 1800, a second mission to Talleyrand negotiated an end to what had become known as the Quasi-War because it wasn't a declared war. France agreed to recognize the neutrality of U.S. shipping. In exchange, Adams agreed to increase trade with France.

This treaty helped shipbuilders and merchants in port cities along the Atlantic coast. But the new trade policy did little for citizens in the interior, most of whom were either farmers or artisans.

These people lived a self-contained life. Their work kept them cut off from the outside world. Farming left them and their families little time for education.

In contrast, the men from the east coast who ran the government were wealthy, well-educated, and out of touch with the lives and concerns of the rural farmer. One reason that Jefferson opposed life terms for senators was that he feared the creation of a class of politicians completely removed from the needs of the people.

Soon after concluding the treaty with France in the fall of 1800, John Adams and his family moved to the nation's new capital. Although ten years had passed since architects and engineers had first begun work on Washington, D.C., the city was still barely populated, rough, and muddy. The president's house wasn't finished yet, and the wing in which the Adamses lived was quite drafty. The first family stayed only a year, but during that time the damp, poorly heated house and wild, lonely city had a harmful effect on Abigail Adams's health.

Although Adams was widely popular during the Quasi-War, he lost much of that popularity during the last year of his term. People thought his government was too isolated and that it ignored their wishes. They also agreed with Jefferson that the Alien and Sedition Acts limited their personal freedom. The Federalists, too, led by Alexander Hamilton, turned against Adams because he refused to declare war on France.

THE MIDNIGHT APPOINTMENTS

Adams was not surprised when he lost the 1800 election to Jefferson. Still, the president was a stubborn, embittered man. He was determined that the policies of his Federalist administration should continue. To ensure this, he appointed a large number of judges, all Federalists, in the final days of his administration. Because they came so late in his term, they were known as the Midnight Appointments.

Adams's idea was to fill the courts with Federalists who could frustrate the plans of Jefferson and the Democratic-Republicans. Jefferson's refusal to honor these last-minute appointments led to the landmark Supreme Court case of *Marbury v. Madison.*

THE CAMPAIGN OF 1800 WAS A REPLAY OF THE 1796 election between Adams and Jefferson. Although neither candidate made public appearances or statements, the contest was a bitter one.

In the tradition of early American etiquette, both men pretended they didn't want to be president. But this false modesty didn't stop their supporters from openly insulting the opposing candidate at every opportunity. The Federalists in power even used the Sedition Act to prosecute the Democratic-Republican press.

When the electoral college met, Jefferson and Aaron Burr each received seventy-three votes, defeating the Federalist ticket of John Adams and Charles Pinckney. It had been understood during the campaign that Burr was running as the vice-presidential candidate. But after the election, Burr refused to step down. Instead, because of the tied vote, the election was thrown into the House of Representatives, which would decide the winner. After thirty-five separate votes, the House remained deadlocked.

Jefferson's old rival, Alexander Hamilton, faced a dilemma. He still had influence with the Federalist members of Congress. Using this influence, he could break the deadlock. But which candidate should he support? Hamilton disliked Jefferson personally, but he didn't trust Burr at all.

In the end, Hamilton decided that his country was more important than his personal feelings. On February 17, 1801, on the thirty-sixth ballot, he persuaded several congressmen not to vote at all. This swung the election to Jefferson, who became the third president of the United States.

THOMAS JEFFERSON

3RD PRESIDENT
★
FROM 1801 TO 1809

BORN: April 13, 1743

BIRTHPLACE: Shadwell, Va.

DIED: July 4, 1826

PARTY: Democratic-Republican

VICE PRESIDENTS: Aaron Burr, George Clinton

FIRST LADY: Martha Wayles Skelton

CHILDREN: Martha, Jane, Mary, Lucy

NICKNAME: Red Fox

Jefferson's grandson was the first baby born in the White House.

John Adams was not in Washington to see Jefferson's inauguration on March 4, 1801. Bitter at his loss, Adams snuck out of town at dawn rather than stay on to watch Jefferson take the oath of office. The transfer of power may not have been a gracious one, but it was the first time in the country's history that political power passed successfully from one party to another.

After the viciousness of the campaign, Jefferson tried to calm the nation by stressing unity and toleration in his inaugural address. To prove that he meant what he said, the president quickly asked Congress to repeal the Alien and Sedition Acts, and people jailed under these laws were soon released.

The election of 1800 was sometimes called the Revolution of 1800 because that year the

JEFFERSON BUYS FRENCH LAND

Louisiana Purchase Doubles Size of Country

The United States got the biggest bargain in history when Robert Livingston and James Monroe negotiated the massive Louisiana Purchase during the spring of 1803.

The Louisiana Territory, which covered 828,000 square miles and stretched from the Mississippi River to the Rocky Mountains, was first explored by the Spanish in the 1600s. The French later colonized the area, founding New Orleans at the mouth of the Mississippi in 1718.

Throughout the 1700s, control of the area passed back and forth between the French and the Spanish. Between 1800 and 1802, Napoleon's victories in Europe forced the Spanish to give the territory back to France. Spain had allowed U.S. ships to travel freely on the Mississippi, but Jefferson feared that the French might revoke this important privilege.

It was the job of Jefferson's envoys to secure this right of free passage and, if possible, to buy New Orleans. When the two American diplomats arrived, however, French foreign minister Charles Talleyrand surprised them by offering the entire Louisiana Territory. Was the United States interested?

Livingston and Monroe were flabbergasted. Although it exceeded their instructions, the two men soon agreed to a price of fifteen million dollars for the land, which worked out to approximately four cents an acre.

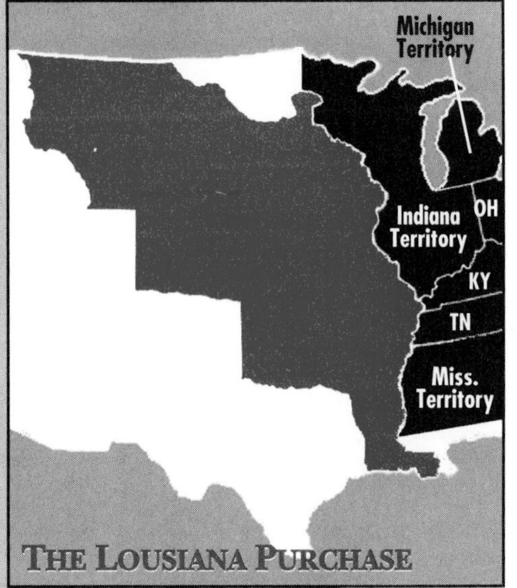

THE LOUSIANA PURCHASE

Democratic-Republicans took control of both the executive and legislative branches of government.

The Democratic-Republicans were able to win the presidency as well as comfortable majorities in both houses of Congress because the campaign had clearly shown the differences between the two parties. The Federalists believed in strong laws to protect business and property. During the campaign, they had warned that a Democratic-Republican government would lead to mob rule, as the French Revolution had.

But the country was tired of Federalist politics. Unlike most Federalists, Thomas Jefferson was more a philosopher than a politician. He was more concerned about democracy and the freedom of the individual than he was interested in the details of government.

In line with his Democratic-Republican principles, Jefferson concentrated on making the government smaller and less involved in the lives of the people. He reduced the size of the military, recalled more than half of the American diplomatic missions in Europe, and ordered a careful review of all government spending. These measures reduced the national debt by one-half.

THE BARBARY PIRATES

Jefferson's first crisis as president came in foreign affairs. The Barbary pirates were vicious buccaneers who operated out of the North African states of Morocco, Algiers, Tunis, and Tripoli. They attacked merchant ships and kidnapped sailors, imprisoning and often torturing them.

For years, the United States had been paying tribute to the leaders of the Barbary states. In exchange for these payments, the Barbary pirates agreed not to attack U.S. ships. By

The Early Years

BEGINNING IN 1762, JEFFERSON STUDIED LAW UNDER George Wythe, who also taught future Supreme Court chief justice John Marshall. Jefferson's apprenticeship ended in April 1767, when he was admitted to the bar in Virginia.

Jefferson served in the Virginia House of Burgesses from 1769 until 1774, and in the Continental Congress after that. Only thirty-three years old, Jefferson was the youngest delegate to the congress in Philadelphia, but he was nevertheless given the task of writing the Declaration of Independence.

The Continental Congress spent almost three days debating Jefferson's work, dissecting every word and phrase. Several changes were made. For instance, a passage attacking slavery was deleted. The document was finally approved on July 4, 1776.

★**MONTICELLO** Thomas Jefferson was known as a Renaissance man because he had an extraordinary range of interests. One was architecture. When the government held a competition to design the president's new home, Jefferson submitted a design anonymously. He didn't win.

Jefferson did design his own house, named Monticello, outside Charlottesville, Virginia. The first section of the house, built between 1770 and 1775, was modeled on the Italian villas designed by Andrea Palladio in the sixteenth century. Palladio's villas were in turn based on classical Roman buildings.

★**THE *CLERMONT*** On August 18, 1807, people on the banks of the Hudson River in New York saw a very strange sight. A ship, smoking as though on fire, was steadily heading up the river against the current. Even more peculiar were its sails, which were rolled up and therefore useless.

Only later did people find out that the ship, the *Clermont*, was a steamship. Its engineer, Robert Fulton, had been working on the ship's design for more than five years. Although the *Clermont* wasn't the very first steamship, it was the first commercially successful one. Fulton's boat began carrying passengers and freight in September 1807. Within two months, it turned a profit for its owners.

BANNEKER'S ALMANACK

★BENJAMIN BANNEKER Benjamin Banneker was one of the country's first important black scholars. From an early age, Banneker had a talent for mathematics and science. He was almost entirely self-taught. He learned astronomy by charting the movements of the planets in the night sky. He learned mathematics from borrowed textbooks.

President Washington appointed Banneker to the District of Columbia Commission in 1790 so that Banneker could help survey the site of the new capital. Meanwhile, between 1791 and 1802, he published a popular annual almanac. Banneker sent a copy of his first almanac to Jefferson, who was then secretary of state. He included a note asking Jefferson to use his influence to make life better for the country's blacks.

★TRIANGULAR TRADE

Although there was not nearly enough support to outlaw slavery altogether, Jefferson did manage to convince Congress to ban the slave trade. A new law that became effective on January 1, 1808, banned the importation of slaves into the United States. However, tens of thousands of slaves continued to be smuggled into the country illegally.

The slave traders had followed the same triangular route for more than a century. They carried rum from distilleries in New England to West Africa. There, the rum was traded for slaves. The slaves were usually members of rival tribes who had been captured during a war or kidnapped from their villages.

The slaves were kept shackled in the holds of ships for months. Eventually, they were taken to the West Indies, where they were traded for molasses. The molasses was then carried back to New England, where it was made into rum, completing the triangle. The slaves were sold off in the West Indies to North and South Americans.

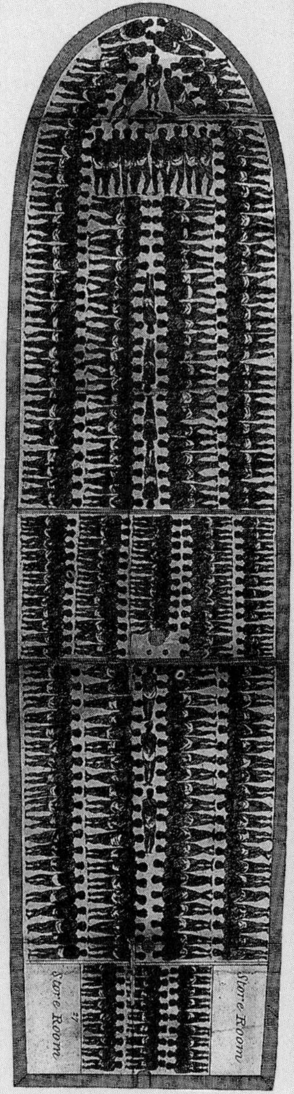

1801, nearly two million dollars had been paid in tribute.

The situation changed when the ruler of Tripoli decided that the United States wasn't paying enough money. In May 1801, he declared war on the United States, brashly cutting down the flagpole in front of the U.S. consulate in the city of Tripoli.

In response, Jefferson sent the navy to Tripoli. At first, it performed poorly. The pirates captured one ship, the *Philadelphia*, in 1803 and turned its guns against the remaining U.S. ships. It took a daring raid by Stephen Decatur, a young lieutenant, to destroy the *Philadelphia* so that its guns could not be used against the Americans.

In 1805, the U.S. fleet captured Derna, one of Tripoli's main seaports. The loss of Derna forced the ruler of Tripoli to sign a peace treaty that ended the payment of tribute forever. Pirates from the other Barbary states, however, continued to disrupt shipping for another ten years.

THE LOUISIANA PURCHASE Another foreign involvement also occupied the president's time. Napoleon's military victories in Europe had recently forced Spain to turn over many of its North American colonies to France, including control of the Mississippi River. Jefferson feared that France might now try to deny Americans the right to travel up and down the Mississippi, which would hurt trade dramatically on the western frontier.

The people settling the Mississippi River country at this time were mostly poor farming families. The only land these people could afford was on the untamed western frontier.

Families would usually travel on foot, carrying their belongings on their backs. If they were lucky, they might have a milking cow that could help them with the hauling. Once they found a place to settle, they would build a crude log cabin. The roof, usually made of mud or thatch, often leaked. The final job would be to chop down trees and turn the surrounding forest into fields that could be planted.

Believing that farmers were the key to a stable and productive country, Jefferson wanted to ensure that farmers on the western frontier could ship their goods along the Mississippi River. When a mission he sent to France was offered the entire Louisiana Territory, he was both shocked and excited. The problem was, nothing in the Constitution gave the president the power to buy land.

Throughout his years in government, Jefferson had argued against the Federalists' doctrine of implied powers. In theory, Jefferson believed that larger government meant less freedom for the people. Therefore, the best governments were small, simple, and frugal.

To authorize the purchase of the Louisiana Territory, Jefferson would have to compromise his thinking. But the offer was too good to pass up. Besides adding huge tracts of land to the young nation, the Louisiana Purchase guaranteed free passage along the Mississippi River. The irony for Jefferson was that the purchase also ensured the need for a strong central government to run the huge new country.

MARBURY V. MADISON

Back in the capital, Jefferson's ongoing battles with the Federalists led to an important Supreme Court decision. After the election of 1800 (but before the Democratic-Republicans came to power), the Federalist Congress hastily passed the Judiciary Act of 1801, creating a number of new federal judgeships.

THE ELECTION OF 1800 HAD POINTED OUT A serious flaw in the way the president and vice president were chosen. When Jefferson and Burr both received the same number of electoral votes, the stalemate nearly caused a constitutional crisis. Had it not been for Alexander Hamilton's involvement, the House of Representatives might have remained deadlocked indefinitely.

To remedy this oversight in the Constitution, the Twelfth Amendment was passed and ratified in time for the 1804 election. It changed the rules of the electoral college so that the electors now voted separately for president and vice president.

Jefferson was once again the presidential candidate of the Democratic-Republicans. But Burr, the disloyal vice president, was dropped from the ticket and replaced with Governor George Clinton of New York.

The Federalists weren't much of a factor in this election. Their candidate, Charles Pinckney of South Carolina, had run on the same ticket with John Adams in 1800. He was an experienced and qualified statesman, but Jefferson was a popular president and won easily.

Adams filled these positions at the last minute with Federalists whom he believed would frustrate Jefferson's policies. Because these Midnight Appointments were made so late, there wasn't even time to deliver the official commission to one of the new judges, William Marbury. After Jefferson took office, his secretary of state, James Madison, refused to deliver Marbury's commission. Marbury sued.

The case went all the way to the Supreme Court. In his 1803 decision, Chief Justice John Marshall declared that a section of the Judiciary Act of 1789 was unconstitutional. This action established the important principle of judicial review. Marshall's ruling demonstrated that the Supreme Court could void an act of Congress if the law in question violated the Constitution.

THE BURR CONSPIRACY In his second inaugural address, Jefferson summed up the successes of his administration and looked to the future. He announced plans to build new roads to the western lands as well as canals in the East to connect that region's major waterways. Canals promoted trade by making it easier to transport goods.

What Jefferson didn't know was that his second term would be marred by a dangerous conspiracy. A crisis abroad also contributed to the turmoil that forced him to postpone these plans.

LEOPARD ATTACKS CHESAPEAKE

Four Sailors Impressed as 21 Die

OFF VIRGINIA, June 22, 1807—The British warship *Leopard* fired today on the U.S. frigate *Chesapeake*. The British commander had demanded that the U.S. captain allow his ship to be boarded. When the *Chesapeake*'s captain refused, the *Leopard* opened fire, killing or wounding twenty-one sailors.

After disabling the *Chesapeake*, the captain of the *Leopard* sent over a boarding party, which took four sailors from the *Chesapeake*'s crew. One of these men was indeed a deserter from the Royal Navy, but the other three were U.S. citizens.

President Jefferson expressed his outrage at the continuation of the British policy of impressment, under which the Royal Navy has stopped U.S. ships on the high seas and carried away sailors by force.

As a result of the *Leopard*'s actions, state legislatures all over the country are now demanding war with Great Britain.

Aaron Burr was a jealous and bitter man. After losing the fight for the presidency in 1800, Burr was desperate to get even with Jefferson.

While Jefferson ran for reelection in 1804, Burr ran for governor of New York. In order to obtain the support of the Essex Junto, a powerful group of New England Federalists, Burr had to promise that, if he became governor, New York would secede from the union and join Massachusetts in a new Federalist country.

THE BURR-HAMILTON DUEL

Alexander Hamilton was shocked to learn of the plan. He didn't wish to see Jefferson reelected. But he couldn't stand the thought of his own state, New York, leaving the Union. When Hamilton began working against him, Burr became enraged and challenged Hamilton to a duel. On July 11, 1804, Burr shot and killed Hamilton.

Burr first fled south after being charged with Hamilton's murder. But when the charges were dropped, he returned to Washington and presided over the Senate until the end of his vice-presidential term in 1805.

Although he lost the election in New York, Burr still pursued his treasonous activities. He met with the British minister to the United States, asking him for half a million dollars and the help of the British navy in taking over the Louisiana Territory. When the British ignored him, Burr went to Louisiana anyway, where he tried to incite a rebellion by himself.

Jefferson was told of Burr's plans by General James Wilkinson, the military governor of the Louisiana Territory. Burr had recently approached Wilkinson with the idea of establishing a new empire.

In 1807, Burr was arrested for treason. Chief Justice John Marshall

★**RELIGIOUS FREEDOM** Of all Jefferson's accomplishments, he was perhaps most proud of the law guaranteeing religious freedom that he helped enact in his home state of Virginia. This law, finalized in 1786, stated that each Virginian was free to attend the church of his or her choice, or no church at all.

Some people attacked Jefferson as an atheist, although he did, in fact, believe in a single creator. Jefferson also admired the teachings of Jesus. But what he really cherished was religious tolerance. "It does me no injury," he once wrote, "for my neighbor to say there are twenty gods, or no god. It neither picks my pocket nor breaks my leg."

★**SACAJAWEA** One of the most important members of the Lewis and Clark expedition was a sixteen-year-old Shoshone girl named Sacajawea. Along with her French-Canadian husband, she joined the expedition in 1804, while Lewis and Clark were wintering in the Dakotas.

As Lewis and Clark continued west during the spring, they encountered a number of different Indian tribes. Sacajawea's ability to communicate with these native people proved to be invaluable in convincing suspicious tribes that Lewis and Clark's intentions were peaceful.

★**NOAH WEBSTER** In 1800, Noah Webster began work on a comprehensive dictionary of the English language. A famous dictionary of English had already been published by the British scholar Samuel Johnson in 1755. But Webster understood that the English language was spoken and written differently in the United States than in England.

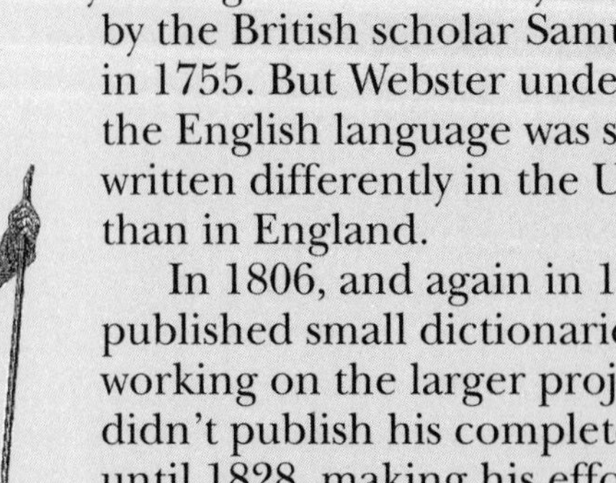

In 1806, and again in 1807, Webster published small dictionaries as he kept working on the larger project. Webster didn't publish his complete dictionary until 1828, making his effort truly the work of a lifetime. The 1828 dictionary contained more than seventy thousand words, or twelve thousand more than even Johnson's contained.

★**THE SHAKERS**
Cooperative religious communities in the United States date back to colonial times. One of the first was founded by Ann Lee, who came to America in 1774 to escape persecution in England. Her followers were a radical sect of the Quakers known as the Shaking Quakers, or simply the Shakers. They valued hard work, simplicity, thrift, and devotion to God. They also believed in and practiced equality of the sexes.

By the 1830s, there were more than six thousand Shakers living in about twenty communities, mostly in upstate New York and Massachusetts. Because Shakers did not believe in having children, their communities could only survive by recruiting new members.

★**AUDUBON'S BIRDS** The exploits of early nineteenth-century explorers, Lewis and Clark among them, helped to popularize the study of nature in the United States. One man excited by ornithology, or the study of birds, was a failed storekeeper named John James Audubon. After giving up his store on the Kentucky frontier, Audubon became the most famous nature painter in the world. Birds were Audubon's speciality. His four-volume *Birds of America*, published between 1827 and 1838, included 435 full-color illustrations. Audubon's drawings made him a sensation in London, where he would often amuse himself by walking around town dressed as an American frontiersman. For show, he would put on a fringed leather jacket and slick his hair back with bear grease.

presided at his trial. Burr was acquitted because, according to Marshall's strict interpretation of the Constitution, Burr's plotting didn't break any laws.

Although he was found innocent, Burr was completely discredited. After the trial, he left for Europe, where he tried to interest the French in conquering Canada. He finally returned to New York in 1812 under a false name and practiced law there until his death in 1836.

THE LEWIS AND CLARK EXPEDITION Even before he approved the Louisiana Purchase, President Jefferson, an amateur naturalist, had organized an expedition to explore the Louisiana Territory. To lead this survey, Jefferson chose his secretary, Meriwether Lewis.

With Jefferson's permission, Lewis wrote to William Clark, a seasoned soldier, asking Clark to join him. A month later, Lewis received a reply. Clark believed that the expedition would encounter great difficulties, but he was eager to go along.

On May 14, 1804, Lewis and Clark left St. Louis accompanied by thirty soldiers and ten civilians, including experts in botany, zoology, sign language, and navigation. After six months, they took on a fur trapper and his Shoshone wife, Sacajawea, to help them communicate with the native peoples they would encounter.

The explorers sailed up the Missouri River into what is now North Dakota. They lived on rations of salt pork and biscuits as well as wild game and fish. On November 7, 1805, the expedition reached the Pacific Ocean.

Because the Indian tribes there were in contact with trading ships, Lewis and Clark hoped to catch a ride back east to Washington. They waited for months in the hope that a ship might arrive. Eventually, they decided to make the return journey by land, arriving back in St. Louis on September 23, 1806.

Both Lewis and Clark made maps and kept journals of their trip across the continent. The journals in particular provided a huge amount of new scientific information about the American interior.

Lewis and Clark's diaries included notes about the terrain and people they encountered. The two explorers also brought back some specimens of the hundreds of plants and animals they found along the way. They even presented Jefferson with two grizzly bears, which he kept in cages on the White House lawn.

THE EMBARGO ACT

It was near the end of his second term that Jefferson faced his most dangerous foreign crisis. The trouble began in June 1807, when the British warship *Leopard* fired on the American frigate *Chesapeake*. Despite the public's demand for war, Jefferson wanted to remain reasonable. He told his minister to Great Britain to demand an apology.

When the British refused, Jefferson convinced Congress to authorize an embargo, not just against Britain but against all of Europe. He believed that withholding U.S. goods would force both France and Britain to respect U.S. neutrality. In December 1807, he signed the Embargo Act.

But the embargo was a disaster, hurting Americans much more than the British or the French. Without European buyers, many U.S. crops rotted in storage. Meanwhile, thousands of people in the shipping business, including sailors and shipbuilders, lost their jobs. A year later, Congress passed a bill repealing the embargo, which Jefferson signed on March 1, 1809, three days before leaving office.

JAMES MADISON RAN AS THE DEMOCRATIC-REPUBLICAN candidate for president in 1808. Physically, he didn't look much like a president—or rather, he didn't look the way most people thought a president should look.

Madison was just five feet, four inches tall, and he weighed barely one hundred pounds. His nose was scarred from frostbite. But Jefferson thought that his secretary of state would make a fine president, and that was good enough for the rest of the party. The Democratic-Republicans nicknamed their candidate the Great Little Madison.

Madison didn't have much opposition. The retirement of John Adams and the death of Alexander Hamilton had so devastated the Federalist party that it didn't even bother to nominate a candidate formally. Instead, the Federalists put up the same ticket they had nominated in 1804, Charles Pinckney and Rufus King. Although Federalist New England went for Pinckney, Madison carried the rest of the country easily.

Between the presidencies of John Adams and his son John Quincy Adams, the Democratic-Republicans held the White House for six consecutive terms covering twenty-four years. This string of presidents is sometimes referred to as the Jefferson Dynasty because both Madison and his successor, James Monroe, considered themselves to be pupils of Jefferson. The period is also called the Virginia Monarchy, because all three men came from Virginia.

JAMES MADISON

4TH PRESIDENT

★

FROM 1809 TO 1817

BORN: March 16, 1751

BIRTHPLACE: Port Conway, Va.

DIED: June 28, 1836

PARTY: Democratic-Republican

VICE PRESIDENTS: George Clinton, Elbridge Gerry

FIRST LADY: Dolley Dandridge Payne Todd

CHILDREN: None

NICKNAME: Father of the Constitution

The first president to wear trousers regularly (instead of knee breeches).

James Madison inherited a country in crisis. The Embargo Act had just been repealed, but its deadening economic effects were still being felt throughout the country. To make matters worse, neither France nor Britain was any closer to respecting U.S. neutrality on the high seas.

Jefferson's solution hadn't worked, and it was now up to his handpicked successor, Madison, to deal with the problem. The Embargo Act had proven that exports were crucial to the U.S. economy, and the only way to export goods to Europe was by ship. Madison's task was to find a way to protect U.S. ships without reducing trade.

WAR HAWKS RISE TO POWER

Frontier Congressmen Take Over Washington

THE MIDTERM ELECTIONS of 1810 brought a new generation of politicians to Washington. Angry with the slow pace of government, the voters had defeated nearly half the members of Congress and replaced them with young men who were very different from their stately elders.

These men took advantage of the public outrage at Britain's harassment of U.S. shipping and campaigned for war. They were nicknamed the War Hawks.

Thirty-four-year-old Henry Clay of Kentucky and John Calhoun of South Carolina, who was five years younger, were the leading War Hawks. Both men had been raised on the frontier, and their behavior reflected their upbringing. Clay and Calhoun were both rambunctious, with little of the Old World gentility that had characterized the Founding Fathers.

In addition to demanding war with Britain, the War Hawks wanted to expand the country northward by invading Canada and southward by conquering Florida and taking whatever Indian lands were available.

A DEAL WITH NAPOLEON Although Madison didn't have many options, he was also something less than a bold leader. He was shy by nature with a quiet speaking voice, and he liked to think matters through a number of times before coming to a decision. His treasury secretary once said that Madison was "slow in taking his ground, but firm when the storm rises."

Madison tried a variety of strategies. The first was to enforce the Non-Intercourse Act of 1809, which had been passed during Jefferson's final days in office. This law represented a new approach to the embargo. It lifted the trade restrictions on every nation except Britain and France and promised to lift the restrictions on these two nations as well if they promised to respect the neutrality of U.S. shipping.

The Non-Intercourse Act didn't work. Britain and France paid no attention, and trade suffered. So Madison tried a somewhat different approach. In 1810, he signed into law Macon's Bill Number Two, which offered a new deal to Britain and France: If one of them would agree to respect U.S. neutrality, trade would be cut off with the other. Napoleon was the first to agree to these terms on behalf of France, so Madison reimposed the trade embargo on Britain.

INDIAN RELATIONS Meanwhile, things were heating up along the western frontier. Ever since the Battle of Fallen Timbers in 1794, white settlers had been pushing Indians in the Ohio River valley farther and farther into the nation's interior.

Thomas Jefferson had wanted to integrate native peoples into white society by teaching them how to farm

The Early Years

JAMES MADISON WAS RAISED IN A HOUSE BUILT BY HIS grandfather within view of Virginia's Blue Ridge Mountains. As Madison grew up, there were two great traumas in his life. The first was a local smallpox epidemic. The second was the French and Indian War.

When the British general Edward Braddock was defeated by the French and their Indian allies in 1755, many Virginians feared an Indian invasion. That never happened, but the threat of one turned Madison against Indians for the rest of his life.

After serving in the Virginia House of Delegates and the Continental Congress, Madison became a delegate to the Constitutional Convention in 1787. Because of his work there, he would later be known as the Father of the Constitution.

★**THE FIRST LADY** Known for her charm and intelligence, Dolley Madison stands out as one of the nation's most extraordinary first ladies. During the War of 1812, she also proved that she could be remarkably cool in a crisis.

The first lady was in the middle of planning a dinner party for forty guests when the British closed in on Washington. The president was already safely out of town, and his wife was told to flee. But before she left, Dolley Madison packed up the Declaration of Independence, the national seal, a portrait of George Washington, and her pet parrot, sending them all ahead to safety.

★**BEAU BRUMMELL** The clothes worn by fashionable American men during the first half of the nineteenth century were examples of the Regency style that was popular in England. This style was named after its chief patron, George, the prince regent of Britain, who later became King George IV.

At the time, the most fashionable man in the world was Beau Brummell. It usually took Brummell an entire morning to dress in his long jacket, tight breeches, and elaborately ruffled scarf. His look featured country clothes that had been sharpened up for city wear. Meanwhile, fashionable women followed the French style of long, high-waisted dresses with richly embroidered hems.

★TOM MOLINEAUX One of the most popular sports during the early nineteenth century was boxing, and the best boxer in the country was a freed slave from Virginia named Tom Molineaux. While he was still in his twenties, Molineaux moved to New York, where he fought informally in amateur matches. In 1809, at the age of twenty-five, he sailed to England to box professionally.

In December 1810, Molineaux became the first American to fight an English champion. He lost to Tom Cribb in the fortieth round. The rematch, which Molineaux lost, drew a record crowd of forty thousand people.

Other popular sports at this time included horse racing, tenpin bowling, rowing, and gouging, which was a frontier sport. The point of gouging was to pluck out an opponent's eyeball. In the Ohio River valley, people grew their thumbnails especially long for this purpose.

★UNCLE SAM During the War of 1812, a merchant in Troy, New York, named Samuel Wilson supplied barrels of beef to the U.S. Army. He stamped these barrels "U.S." to show that they were government property. Because Wilson was commonly known as "Uncle Sam," and because the barrels were stamped with these initials, people began referring to the federal government as "Uncle Sam."

Cartoonists began using the symbolic figure of Uncle Sam in the early 1830s. The British humor magazine *Punch* developed the most familiar caricature of a bearded man with a top hat and striped pants. The famous political cartoonist Thomas Nast used Uncle Sam extensively during the 1870s. But the most famous Uncle Sam was drawn by James Montgomery Flagg, whose World War I recruiting poster was captioned "I Want You For the U.S. Army."

in the European fashion and how to make goods they could sell. But most whites had no intention of cooperating with Jefferson's plan, and most Indians had no interest in living as whites did.

Instead, the United States kept taking Indian land either by conquest or deception. Treaties were made and then broken. By 1810, settlers had seized more than one hundred million acres of fertile Indian land.

TECUMSEH'S CONFEDERACY

When Tecumseh, a chief of the Shawnee tribe, saw what was happening, he tried to do something about it. His strategy was to form a confederacy of all the frontier tribes from Florida to the Canadian border.

Tecumseh was clever enough to see that many settlers used alcohol to cheat Indians out of their land and control them. He realized that to fight the settlers, the Indians would have to stop drinking the rum and whiskey the settlers offered them.

On November 7, 1811, while Tecumseh was away in the south trying to enlist the Creeks in his confederacy, the U.S. army marched on his village. In the battle of Tippecanoe Creek, General William Henry Harrison beat off a dawn attack and defeated the warriors of Tecumseh's confederacy.

Tecumseh vowed to seek revenge, and he got his chance during the War of 1812. But the result turned out to be another Harrison victory. Tecumseh was killed in that battle, fighting alongside the British in Canada.

THE WAR HAWKS

A cautious man, Madison moved slowly with regard to the British. But the rest of the country had little patience for Madison's seemingly endless waiting. During the midterm elections of 1810, nearly half the members of Congress were thrown out of office. Impatient with the pace of Madison's government, the voters wanted change, so they elected a group of much younger politicians. These new congressmen were known as the War Hawks because they promised, if elected, to declare war on Britain.

Madison held firm against the War Hawks for more than a year. But in June 1812, he reluctantly bowed to their pressure and asked Congress for a declaration of war against Great Britain. Madison had few options left.

THE WAR OF 1812

Everyone knew the reasons for war: the impressment of sailors, the lack of respect for U.S. neutrality, and the continuing British agitation of Indian tribes along the northwestern frontier. But the declaration didn't come very quickly. Congress debated the war resolution for seventeen days before approving it in a rather close vote.

The opposition to the war came principally from the Federalists of New England, who were quite vocal in their opposition to what they snidely called "Mr. Madison's War." Despite the aggressive enthusiasm whipped up by the War Hawks, New England merchants wanted nothing to do with a war that would halt trade with their biggest customer, Great Britain.

To protest Madison's policy, most New Englanders boycotted the war and refused to allow their state militias to join in the fighting. Some New England merchants even flirted with treason, as they became fabulously wealthy selling supplies to both sides.

New England's opposition was just the beginning, as Madison soon discovered. As he had feared, the

CAMPAIGN 1812

THE CAMPAIGN OF 1812 WAS THE FIRST EVER HELD during a war. Despite the success of the War Hawks in 1810, opposition to the War of 1812 was strong, especially in New England.

Madison ran for reelection against former New York City mayor DeWitt Clinton, who was also a Democratic-Republican but was running independently of the party. The New England Federalists chose not to nominate their own candidate, thus ensuring that Clinton would receive their overwhelming support. Clinton also happened to be the nephew of Madison's first vice president, George Clinton, who died in April 1812.

The campaign was most notable for Clinton's outrageous habit of promising different things to different people. To people who supported the war, Clinton promised to continue the fight. To people such as the Federalists who opposed the war, he made speeches blaming the entire mess on Madison and promised to negotiate an immediate peace.

The lack of enthusiasm in the country for Madison's policies gave Clinton a chance, but the president's support in the South and the West was enough to see him through. Clinton won four New England states in addition to Delaware, New York, New Jersey, and five of Maryland's eleven votes. But Madison took the rest, winning 128 electoral votes to Clinton's 89.

War of 1812 would be much more difficult to win than it had been to declare.

Things went wrong from the start. For example, when the president called for fifty thousand army volunteers, only five thousand signed up. To make up the difference, the army began enlisting African Americans, both free blacks and slaves. Many slaves fought in the army hoping to win their freedom, but they were generally returned to slavery after the war.

THE INVASION OF CANADA

Unwilling to challenge the powerful British navy at sea, Madison instead decided to focus on a land campaign against British-held Canada. The most obvious invasion routes passed through New York and the New England states, but none of these states would permit a federal attack across its border because they opposed the war.

As a result, the first invasion of Canada was launched from Detroit in July 1812. Madison unwisely chose an aging Revolutionary War veteran, General William Hull, to lead the expedition. Hull cautiously crossed the border, but fearing Indian attacks he quickly withdrew to Detroit, which he surrendered to the lesser army of British general Isaac Brock without firing a single shot. Hull was later court-martialed for his actions.

BRITISH BURN CAPITAL

Washington in Flames

WASHINGTON, August 25, 1814—British troops entered the capital yesterday and burned most of the nation's important buildings. The first building the British set on fire was the Capitol, which was still under construction. Then they marched to the president's residence and set it aflame. As night fell, the British relaxed in empty boardinghouses and watched the city burn.

This morning, the British soldiers prepared to destroy the rest of the town, but a storm came up suddenly. The storm accomplished what the U.S. army had been unable to do. It forced the British to retreat.

The route to Washington was laid open to the British after the army failed to stop the invaders in nearby Maryland. President Madison had to flee ahead of his troops after witnessing the brief battle.

By the time the British reached the undefended capital, most of the government officials and residents had left. Only a few women remained behind, packing their belongings. The president's wife, Dolley Madison, stayed long enough to save most of the government's valuable papers.

From this poor start, things got worse. General Brock marched his troops to the Niagara River, where he began making preparations to invade New York. On October 13, 1812, a small federal regiment under Captain James E. Wool attacked Brock's forces on the Canadian side of the river.

At first, the battle went well for the Americans. Brock was killed, and the British scattered. Wool clearly had the advantage, but as he anxiously waited for reinforcements, the British regrouped, and his edge slipped away.

Just before all hope was lost, reinforcements from the New York state militia arrived on the New York side of the river. But they stopped right there. Their orders were clear: defend New York, but do not cross the river into Canada. They watched from the New York side while the British massacred Wool's men.

THE BURNING OF WASHINGTON

As James Madison took the oath of office at his second inaugural in March 1813, the country was in the midst of its greatest crisis since the American Revolution. Madison's invasion of Canada had failed miserably, and now the British were on the offensive.

The Americans enjoyed some success in the Northwest as Captain Oliver Hazard Perry won control of Lake Erie in September 1813 and General William Henry Harrison won the battle of the Thames River in Canada in October. But the British were preparing a much more effective counterpunch. At the end of 1813, they crossed the Canadian border and burned the city of Buffalo, New York. Then, during the summer of 1814, British forces swept past the weak U.S. defenses in the Chesapeake Bay and marched on

★THE WHITE HOUSE When the British invaded Washington, they burned the president's house. After the fire, only the walls of the residence remained, and these were blackened by smoke.

To cover the smoke damage, workers painted the outside walls of the reconstructed building white. The result was so eye-catching that people began referring to the president's house as the White House. In 1901, the name of the building was officially changed at the request of President Theodore Roosevelt.

★GERRYMANDERING Elbridge Gerry was Madison's second vice president and before that, governor of Massachusetts. During his term as governor, Gerry supported a bill that created a strange-looking voting district in his state. The district was drawn in such an unusual way that some people said it looked like a salamander.

The point of fashioning such an unusual district was to ensure that the Democratic-Republican party would have a voting majority there. Because of the way the district looked, people began calling this tactic "gerrymandering." The term is still used today to describe the practice of redrawing district lines to favor one party or a particular group of voters.

★FRANCIS SCOTT KEY When the British attacked Baltimore during the War of 1812, they took an influential lawyer named Francis Scott Key prisoner. Key was held aboard a British ship in the harbor, from which he could see the British bombardment of Fort McHenry.

The British kept firing at Fort McHenry through most of the night. The flashes from their cannon made the scene seem like a nightmare. Then suddenly the firing stopped. At dawn, Key strained to see which flag was flying above the fort. His joy at seeing the Stars and Stripes inspired him to write "The Star-Spangled Banner." The song became the official national anthem in 1931. It was the only piece of poetry that Key ever wrote.

★NEW ENGLAND FACTORIES In the fall of 1810, a wealthy merchant named Francis Cabot Lowell traveled from Boston to England. He told people he was going on a vacation, but Lowell actually wanted to learn more about English textile factories.

When he returned, Lowell hired an engineer named Paul Moody to help him build a new factory. The cloth-making machines that Lowell couldn't buy, he had Moody make.

In 1814, Lowell opened the first fully mechanized textile factory in the United States. He offered good wages and set up clean quarters for his workers, which made work at the factory attractive to local farm girls. The factory provided an example to other business leaders of how profitable manufacturing could be. In this way, Lowell helped change the focus of the New England economy from shipping to manufacturing.

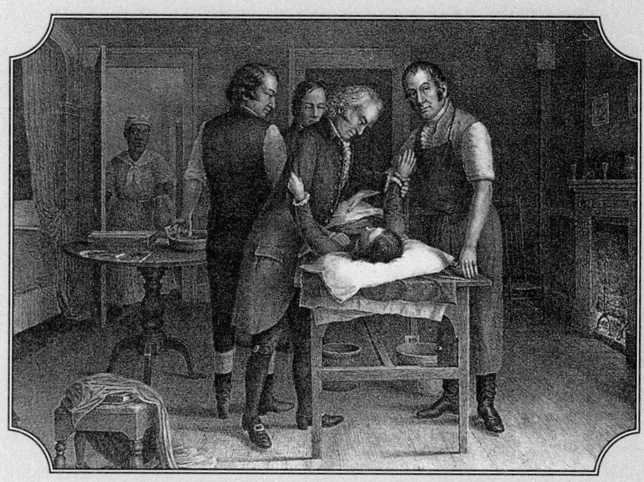

★MEDICINE American medical education during the early nineteenth century was not very good. The treatments the doctors used were based more on folk remedies than on science. Sometimes doctors would apply leeches to a patient to suck out a disease. Plants and herbs were also popular medicines, especially in rural areas.

Although many women practiced herbal medicine, most doctors were men. These men kept offices in their homes, but more often they made house calls. When necessary, they even moved in with a patient until he or she was cured.

Many Indian tribes also used herbs to treat diseases, but western Algonquins practiced a different type of therapy. Their medicine men all belonged to the Midewiwin, or Grand Medicine Society. When someone in the tribe was ill, the members of this society would seek a vision, during which spirits would instruct them in ways to cure the patient.

Washington, burning the nation's capital on August 24, 1814.

PEACE TALKS In the meantime, the British minister had informed Madison in January 1814 that his government was prepared to discuss terms for peace. Madison accepted the offer of peace talks immediately. The site would be the town of Ghent in Belgium.

The British believed that they could dictate the terms of the peace. After all, they were winning the war. As far as they were concerned, it should be the Americans who made the concessions.

The British ministers immediately presented a number of demands: They wanted the Americans to stop fishing in the waters off Newfoundland. They also wanted to move the Canadian border to provide access to the Mississippi River. And finally, they wanted to create a territory for their Indian allies in the Ohio River valley between the United States and Canada.

John Quincy Adams, the son of former president John Adams, was one of the U.S. peace commissioners in Ghent. Although he was an experienced diplomat, Adams was shocked by the British demands. He advised his fellow commissioners to return home immediately. But Henry Clay wasn't so quick to leave.

Clay was less experienced in diplomacy than Adams, but he was a better poker player. He thought the British were bluffing and that they would be willing to accept less. The Napoleonic Wars in Europe were winding down, and Great Britain had better things to do than to continue fighting a war an ocean away. Clay convinced the rest of the delegation to stay and press for better terms. The British held firm for months, but eventually they began to reduce their demands.

THE TREATY OF GHENT

When the Treaty of Ghent was finally signed in December 1814, it included none of Britain's original demands. In fact, all it did was end the fighting and restore the status quo ante bellum, which means the state of things before the war.

Neither side gained or lost any territory, and many matters were left unresolved, such as the neutrality rights of U.S. shipping. The War of 1812 did have a lasting effect, however, in that it paved the way for closer relations between the two countries. After the war, Britain showed a great deal more respect for the United States than it had ever shown before.

THE BATTLE OF NEW ORLEANS

While the Treaty of Ghent was being negotiated, however, the fighting continued. Ironically, the last battle of the War of 1812 took place on January 8, 1815, two weeks after the war had formally ended. The battle took place anyway because Ghent was a continent away from New Orleans, and it took a long time in 1815 for even important news to travel that far. Neither side knew yet that the war had ended.

The British army arrived at New Orleans in very late December. Finding the U.S. positions well fortified, they dug a few trenches and began bombarding the town. On January 8, eight thousand British soldiers attacked.

General Andrew Jackson, who led the U.S. troops, fought a brilliant defensive battle. By the end of the bloody day, the British had lost more than two thousand men. Of their four generals, one was dead, one was dying, and another was disabled. The Americans lost only twenty-one men, and Jackson became a national hero.

CAMPAIGN 1816

ONCE HE BECAME THE CANDIDATE OF THE Democratic-Republican party in 1816, Secretary of State James Monroe was practically guaranteed the presidency. Secretary of War William Crawford had a strong following in Congress that might have posed a threat to Monroe, but Crawford never mounted a serious challenge. He didn't want to risk his place in the new cabinet.

In many ways, Monroe was Madison's natural successor. As secretary of state, he had occupied the same office for Madison that Madison had filled for Jefferson. Indeed, Jefferson had served as secretary of state during the Washington administration. Moreover, Monroe was widely admired for his warm, generous personality.

Meanwhile, the Federalists didn't even bother to nominate a candidate. The failure of the Hartford Convention in 1815 had destroyed what little influence the Federalists still had. At that meeting, Federalist delegates from Connecticut, Massachusetts, and Rhode Island had discussed seceding from the union to form a new Federalist country. Although it never happened, most Americans began thinking of the Federalists as unpatriotic and possibly treasonous.

The best the Federalists could do was support Rufus King of New York, who had run for vice president in 1804 and again in 1808. A dedicated public servant, King had once been George Washington's minister to Great Britain. But King, the last Federalist candidate, was no match for Monroe. The only states that King carried were Connecticut, Delaware, and Massachusetts.

JAMES MONROE

5TH PRESIDENT

★

FROM 1817 TO 1825

BORN: April 28, 1758

BIRTHPLACE: Westmoreland County, Va.

DIED: July 4, 1831

PARTY: Democratic-Republican

VICE PRESIDENT: Daniel D. Tompkins

FIRST LADY: Elizabeth Kortright

CHILDREN: Eliza, Maria

NICKNAME: Last of the Cocked Hats

The last president to have served as an officer in the Revolutionary War.

The British burned the president's house so thoroughly during the War of 1812 that years passed before it was completely rebuilt. Even as James Monroe took the oath of office in March 1817, there remained work to be done. Rather than live in temporary housing as the Madisons had done, Monroe decided to take a grand tour of the country until the White House was ready. He wanted to have a close-up look at the country he would be governing.

Beginning his trip in Washington, D.C., Monroe traveled north as far as Portland, Maine. From there, he turned west to Detroit and then southeast back to Washington. The triangular trip took fifteen weeks, and it gave Monroe a better knowledge of the country than any president before him, with the possible exception of George Washington.

MARSHALL ISSUES LANDMARK RULINGS

WASHINGTON, December 31, 1819—The year ending today has been a remarkable one for the Supreme Court and its chief justice John Marshall. The court's rulings in two landmark cases will change the government's role in this country.

The first case, *Dartmouth College v. Woodward*, involved the charter of Dartmouth College, which the state of New Hampshire recently tried to change. Dartmouth's charter was originally granted in 1769, when New Hampshire was still a British colony.

As Marshall himself pointed out, the case was really about contracts. The chief justice explained that Dartmouth's charter was actually a contract that no one side had the right to change. The court's decision has made it clear that business contracts will be respected.

In the case of *McCulloch v. Maryland*, Marshall ruled that the state of Maryland could not tax the Second Bank of the United States because the bank was a federal institution.

Marshall's ruling stressed that states cannot restrict the federal government's constitutional powers. *McCulloch v. Maryland* also established the constitutionality of the bank itself, thus endorsing Alexander Hamilton's theory of implied powers.

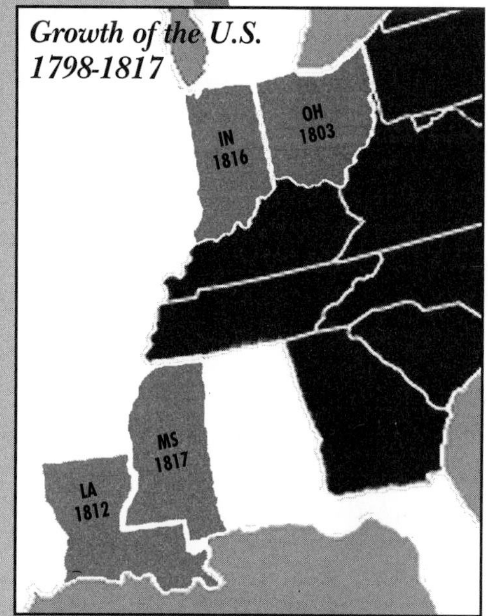

Growth of the U.S. 1798-1817

THE ERA OF GOOD FEELINGS Everywhere he went, the triumphant president was greeted with cheers from crowds lining the roadways. Even in Federalist New England, the crowds applauded this Democratic-Republican president. The *Boston Columbian Centinel* was moved to describe Monroe's joyful reception as the beginning of an "era of good feelings" for the country.

New England, which had detested James Madison, was quicker to accept Monroe because the region's economy had changed in the years during and after the War of 1812. Before the war, New England had depended almost exclusively on its trade with Great Britain. When the war cut that trade off, New Englanders were forced to find other ways to make a living.

NEW ENGLAND FACTORIES Pioneering industrialists such as Francis Cabot Lowell opened factories that helped shift the economic focus of New England from shipping to manufacturing. As a result, the region and the country became much more self-sufficient.

Factories such as Lowell's were decent places to work, unlike the grim, dirty factories of industrial England. Although the work force of young men and women typically put in twelve- and fourteen-hour days, they made good wages and were given clean, pleasant quarters in which to live. The evening lectures offered by some factories provided the only schooling most of the factory girls ever had.

But work in factories owned by less charitable people could be harsh and cruel, and soon the conditions in many factories sank to this level. Greedy owners employed entire families to work side by side on the

The Early Years

JAMES MONROE'S FATHER DIED WHEN HE WAS ABOUT sixteen years old. The system of inheritance at that time was called primogeniture. Under this system, a man's oldest son inherited all his family's property. Because James was the first-born son of five children, he inherited everything.

About the same time, Monroe enrolled at the College of William and Mary in Williamsburg, Virginia. His mind wasn't on his studies, however. Instead, like most students at William and Mary, he was caught up in the patriotic fever sweeping the colonies. In March 1776, unable to resist any longer, Monroe dropped out of college to enlist in the Continental Army.

★**WEDDING AT THE WHITE HOUSE** In 1818, James Monroe hired Samuel L. Gouverneur as a private secretary. While serving Monroe, the young man fell in love with Monroe's daughter Maria. After a two-year courtship, the couple decided to marry. The date was set for March 9, 1820.

This wedding was the first ever for a president's daughter in the White House. The ceremony was a small, private one. Only forty-two guests were invited. Everyone else had to wait until the reception five days later to congratulate the new couple.

★**JOHN JACOB ASTOR AND THE FUR TRADE** The fur trade with the Indians was for many years an important part of the North American economy. In colonial times, the most important fur trading centers were on the Great Lakes and in the Ohio River valley.

John Jacob Astor was the poor son of a German butcher. He came to this country at the age of twenty, just after the Revolutionary War. His first employer was a fur trader in New York City. Astor quickly learned the business and soon made a small fortune buying furs upstate and selling them in London.

Beaver furs were particularly valuable because hats made from them were very fashionable in Europe. In fact, so many beaver were being trapped and killed that they were soon in danger of extinction. With his fur trade profits, Astor invested in real estate. Eventually he became the richest man in the country.

★Literature in America

The new patriotism encouraged by the Era of Good Feelings helped create America's first national literature. The most important writers of the time were James Fenimore Cooper and Washington Irving.

Cooper wrote a number of stories about the frontier, called the Leatherstocking tales, in which he portrayed Indians as noble savages. His most famous book, *The Last of the Mohicans* (1826), helped popularize the American wilderness.

Irving specialized in short stories. His best known included "The Legend of Sleepy Hollow," featuring schoolmaster Ichabod Crane, and "Rip Van Winkle." Irving was the first American author to win fame in Europe.

★The Mason and Dixon Line

The Missouri Compromise made it clear that there was definitely a political division between North and South. This division was represented on most maps by the Mason and Dixon Line.

Between 1765 and 1768, two Englishmen, Charles Mason and Jeremiah Dixon, surveyed the 233-mile-long border dividing the land grants of Pennsylvania and Maryland. This border had been set by the king of England at latitude 39°43'.

In the years leading up to the Civil War, the Mason and Dixon Line came to symbolize much more than the border between two states. In the minds of most Americans, the Mason and Dixon Line was the line between freedom and slavery.

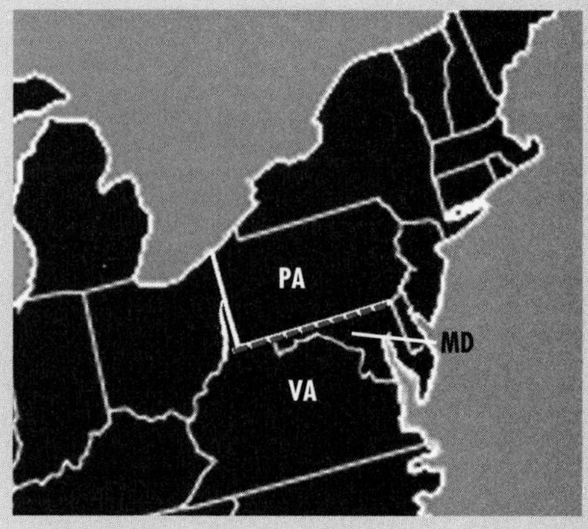

factory floor. Even the youngest children were used to carry supplies to boys and girls old enough to work the machinery.

Instead of paying cash wages, these factory owners provided their workers with run-down houses and credit at the factory store. Because they had no cash, the workers had to buy what they needed at the factory store. And because the factory store charged very high prices, the workers were always in debt.

As long as the workers owed money, they couldn't leave. And the longer they stayed, the deeper in debt they went. Eventually, they became essentially slaves to the factory owners.

The American System

On a more national scale, Congressmen Henry Clay and John Calhoun championed a series of projects designed to improve and update the country's infrastructure—that is, its roads, bridges, and canals. The bills they introduced were part of a larger plan devised by Clay called the American System.

One of these bills imposed a tariff, or tax, on manufactured goods that were imported into the country. The tariff would make European goods more expensive and thus encourage Americans to buy products made in the United States. Also, the money raised by the tariff could be used to build roads and canals in the western territories.

Monroe agreed that Calhoun's public works projects would benefit the nation. But like Madison before him, he worried that these internal improvements were not constitutional. A Jeffersonian at heart, Monroe feared that construction of roads and canals went well beyond the powers granted to the government by the Constitution.

THE CUMBERLAND ROAD

When Congress passed a bill in 1822 to extend the Cumberland Road, Monroe vetoed it because he believed road building was the responsibility of the states. It was the only bill that Monroe ever vetoed in his eight years as president.

During Monroe's administration, the country grew at an amazing rate. Much of its westward expansion took place along the route of the Cumberland Road. Beginning outside Baltimore, the Cumberland Road eventually extended through Pennsylvania, Virginia, Ohio, and Indiana before ending in Illinois. The road made it much easier for people to settle the Northwest Territory.

The first section of the road—from Cumberland, Maryland, to Wheeling in western Virginia—was built between 1811 and 1818. Before the road was extended, settlers could board steamships in Wheeling that would take them farther west along the Ohio River. In the same year that the Cumberland Road reached Wheeling, Illinois became the twenty-first state.

Although roads were less expensive to build, transportation of goods was faster and cheaper by canal. As Monroe took office, the United States had only one hundred miles of canal. By the end of his second term, that distance had jumped to one thousand miles. The canals made it economical for surplus western beef and corn to be sold in New England, where manufacturing was quickly displacing agriculture.

THE GROWTH OF REGIONALISM

Between 1816 and 1821, six new states joined the Union, making a total of twenty-four. Although they were generally welcomed, the admission of these new western and southern

CAMPAIGN 1820

THE ERA OF GOOD FEELINGS MADE JAMES MONROE one of the most popular presidents in the history of the United States. His first term was considered a great success. The peace continued, and profitable new businesses were started every day. Relations with Britain were the best they had ever been, and the Missouri Compromise had resolved the controversy between free and slave states, at least for the time being. As a result, nobody seriously wanted to replace a president who had delivered so much peace and prosperity.

Both Jefferson and Madison had served two terms, so it was expected that Monroe would serve two as well. Because the Democratic-Republicans were so sure that Monroe would be reelected, they didn't even bother to nominate him formally. What little remained of the Federalist party didn't offer any opposition, either. As a result the presidential vote in 1820 was essentially an election without a campaign.

When the electoral college met in 1820, Monroe won all the electoral votes but one. The single contrary vote was cast by New Hampshire governor William Plumer. It has been said that Plumer voted against Monroe so that George Washington would remain the only president ever elected unanimously. According to Plumer's son, however, the New Hampshire governor simply hated Monroe.

states was also unsettling for many Americans. Because new regions of the country would of course have their own concerns, those of the original states would necessarily matter less.

Northern factory owners wanted increased tariff protection for their manufactured goods. They also wanted raw materials at a cheap price. Western farmers wanted exactly the opposite. They liked to see high prices for the raw materials they grew and low prices for the manufactured goods they bought. In the South, plantation owners were concerned about a reduction in slave labor, which they thought would hurt their ability to produce cotton at a competitive price.

SLAVERY IN THE NEW STATES Each of these three regions worried about the balance of power in Congress, but the North and South were especially concerned about the issue of slavery. Many northerners wanted to abolish this brutal institution, which the South was equally determined to keep.

Both sides knew that the key votes on slavery would be cast in the West. If the new western states were admitted as slave states, then slavery would likely continue. If they were admitted as "free soil" states, which prohibited human bondage, then slavery would likely pass away in the South as well. Either way, the balance of power would soon shift decisively.

President Proclaims Monroe Doctrine

Adams' Speech Sets New Foreign Policy

WASHINGTON, December 2, 1823—President Monroe used the opportunity of his annual message to Congress today to announce a bold new foreign policy. In a speech written by Secretary of State John Quincy Adams, the president warned European nations against trying to establish any more colonies in the Americas.

Monroe also made it clear that his new doctrine does not apply to colonies already in existence.

The speech was prompted by fears that other European powers intended to help Spain recapture its lost colonies in South America. Highly publicized wars of independence have recently overthrown the Spanish colonial governments in Argentina and Colombia.

In Argentina, the fight for independence was led by José de San Martín. In Colombia, Simón Bolívar led the successful revolution against Spanish rule. Both men have since served as models for others in Central and South America who believe in the principle of self-rule.

The nation's founders had intentionally passed over the issue of slavery because it was simply too controversial. Had the Constitution tried to resolve the issue, it would never have been ratified. Instead, the fate of the slaves was left to the future.

In the thirty years since the Constitutional Convention, the cotton gin had made the South more dependent than ever on slave labor. To make sure that slavery would continue, southerners began demanding that slavery be extended to the new western states.

THE MISSOURI COMPROMISE

The issue became particularly focused when, in 1819, settlers in Missouri applied for statehood. The question on everyone's mind was: Would Missouri be admitted as a slave state or as a free state? In Washington, Congress debated whether or not the federal government had the power to ban slavery in the new states.

Southerners argued that banning slavery in Missouri would deprive slaveholders of their property—that is, their slaves. Many northerners, however, couldn't bear the thought of slavery spreading to one state and then another. Unable to resolve the issue, Congress adjourned until its next session without reaching a decision.

When Congress met again in 1820, there was a new wrinkle in the debate over Missouri's statehood. Now the territory of Maine also wanted to join the union. Being so far north, it would certainly be a free state.

A compromise was eventually worked out. Maine and Missouri would both be admitted, Maine as a free state and Missouri as a slave state. That way, the number of slave states and free states would remain equal. There would be twelve of each.

★THE CHEROKEE ALPHABET About 1809, when the Cherokee silversmith and warrior Sequoyah was in his forties, he began to work on a writing system for his tribe. The Cherokee had a spoken language but not a written one. Sequoyah believed that the increased knowledge a written language would bring might help his people remain independent of the whites.

At first, he tried using pictographs, as the ancient Egyptians had done. When these didn't work, he began adapting letters from English, Greek, and Hebrew to represent the sounds of the spoken Cherokee language. By 1821, he had created the first Cherokee alphabet.

★DISCOVERY OF SOUTH PASS In January 1824, a group of fur trappers found and crossed a wide gap in the Rocky Mountains in present-day Wyoming. Because it was the middle of the winter, the crossing was difficult. The snow was knee-deep, and the explorers had nothing to drink except for the snow they melted by the heat of their hands.

The route they discovered, later called South Pass, turned out to be the easiest way through these difficult mountains. In the 1840s, South Pass became the principal gateway to the West and was used by thousands of settlers traveling the Oregon Trail.

★EDUCATION Emma Willard was a pioneer in women's education. In 1819, she presented New York with a plan to improve education for women. The state legislature rejected her plan. Two years later, she founded the Troy Female Seminary in upstate New York.

The seminary was the first enduring college-level school for women in the United States. Few people thought that women needed or could use an advanced education. Other colleges, for example, would admit only men. But Willard wouldn't accept any such limitations, and the Troy Seminary proved she was right.

★**THE AMERICAN COLONIZATION SOCIETY** In 1817, a Presbyterian minister in New Jersey named Robert Finley founded the American Colonization Society. Its goal was to end the practice of slavery. But Finley's opposition to slavery didn't mean that he thought blacks and whites were compatible. Instead, Finley's group thought that the best solution was to resettle freed black slaves in Africa.

The American Colonization Society established Monrovia on the west coast of Africa in 1822. The colony, which became an independent republic in 1848, was supposed to be a new homeland for freed American slaves. Its name was soon changed to Liberia, but its capital kept the name Monrovia to honor James Monroe.

★**MEDICAL SCIENCE** In the early nineteenth century, medical science progressed slowly. Doctors could only guess at some of the ways the human body worked. The X-ray machine hadn't been invented yet, and there were no other ways to look inside the human body.

In 1822, a remarkable accident gave army surgeon William Beaumont an unusual opportunity. One of his patients, a French-Canadian trapper named Alexis St. Martin, had accidentally shot himself in the stomach. The shotgun blast left St. Martin with a permanent hole there.

Through this hole, Beaumont was able to observe the process of digestion as it took place. Beaumont performed various experiments on his cooperative patient and even published a book on the subject. His studies added much to human knowledge of the digestive system.

What made the deal work, however, was that southerners agreed to a northern demand that slavery be banned in the rest of the Louisiana Territory north of latitude 36°30'.

Monroe seriously considered vetoing the bill. He didn't believe that the federal government had the power to tell a state whether or not it could permit slavery. That was up to the citizens of each state. But Monroe also suspected that a veto would probably start a civil war. After three days of contemplation and consultation with his cabinet, Monroe signed the Missouri Compromise on March 6, 1820.

THE INVASION OF FLORIDA

During Monroe's administration, there was little trouble along the western frontier, but the president did face a problem in Georgia, where white settlers and Seminoles were killing each other. Seminole raiding parties that included runaway slaves were burning the farms of whites whom they believed were taking away Indian land.

Most of the Seminoles lived in Florida, which was still a colony of Spain. They made their villages in swampy, jungle-like wetlands that also attracted fugitive slaves because there were so many easy places to hide. Both the Seminoles and the Creeks liked to help escaped slaves because they shared the slaves' hatred of whites. In some villages, the blacks and Indians intermarried and raised families together.

In 1817, Monroe sent Andrew Jackson, the country's most capable general, to punish the raiders. Jackson's hatred of Indians was well known, and when forty of his men were killed in an ambush, he used the attack as an excuse to invade Florida. Jackson burned Seminole villages and hanged many tribal chiefs. Then he captured the Spanish stronghold of Pensacola, which gave him control of northern Florida.

Although Jackson didn't specifically disobey his orders, his decision to invade Florida proved embarrassing to Monroe when the Spanish minister to the United States demanded that Jackson be punished. Secretary of State John Quincy Adams defended Jackson and used Jackson's military presence as a negotiating tool with Spain.

Meeting with the Spanish minister, Adams demanded that Spain either control the inhabitants of Florida, particularly the Seminoles and fugitive slaves, or transfer the territory immediately to the United States. With General Jackson's army already in place, Spain decided to sell. For five million dollars, the United States bought all of Spain's land east of the Mississippi River as well as its claim to territory in Oregon.

THE MONROE DOCTRINE

Now that the United States controlled so much of North America, John Quincy Adams suggested to President Monroe that he use this power to warn European nations against further colonization in the Americas. On December 2, 1823, the president delivered a speech to Congress outlining what soon became known as the Monroe Doctrine.

Neither an executive order nor a law, the Monroe Doctrine was a statement of policy that has guided U.S. actions ever since. Historians have compared its importance to that of George Washington's Farewell Address and John Hay's future Open Door policy with regard to China. For the first time, the United States recognized that it had important national interests outside its geographic borders.

WITH THE PASSING AWAY OF THE FEDERALISTS, there was now just one party left in the country. The next president would surely be a Democratic-Republican. But different party members wanted the job. In the end, the election came down to a four-man race among regional candidates.

CAMPAIGN 1824

Treasury secretary William Crawford of Georgia was the early front-runner, but he suffered a stroke during the campaign that nearly destroyed his candidacy. Secretary of State John Quincy Adams had the solid backing of New England, while Speaker of the House Henry Clay found support in the West. Of the four candidates, only General Andrew Jackson of Tennessee could count on votes from all over the country.

The election of 1824 was particularly notable because it was the first time that the popular vote was considered important enough to be counted. Most of the electors chosen in 1824 were selected by the people instead of by the state legislatures. The right to vote, however, was still restricted to adult white males.

Jackson won more electoral votes than anyone else. But he didn't win a majority, so the election was thrown into the House of Representatives. With Clay's support, Adams was able to win a narrow victory on the first ballot. Adams then made Clay his secretary of state.

John Quincy Adams

6th President

★

From 1825 to 1829

Born: July 11, 1767

Birthplace: Braintree, Mass.

Died: February 23, 1848

Party: Democratic-Republican

Vice President: John C. Calhoun

First Lady: Louisa Catherine Johnson

Children: George, John, Charles, Louisa

Nickname: Old Man Eloquent

The only president to name a son George Washington.

After the House of Representatives chose John Quincy Adams to be the sixth president in February 1825, Adams's friends gave him some advice. They told him to fire all of Monroe's appointees and name his own people to federal office.

Adams's advisors were worried because many holdovers from the Monroe administration had backed Andrew Jackson during the 1824 campaign. The supporters of Andrew Jackson were furious that their candidate had lost to Adams in the House. They believed that Adams had made a corrupt bargain with Henry Clay to steal the election. Many of them vowed revenge, announcing that they would block Adams at every opportunity until Jackson could claim the presidency in 1828.

As it turned out, the advice Adams got was good, but he

THE RAILROAD IS HERE!

Work Begins on the B&O Line

BALTIMORE, July 4, 1828—Work began today on the United States' first steam-powered railroad, the Baltimore & Ohio. The first B&O line will connect Baltimore and Ellicott's Mills, Maryland, thirteen miles away.

The ceremonial first stone was laid by Charles Carroll, the last surviving signer of the Declaration of Independence, at a formal ceremony held this afternoon.

The work is expected to take about two years. After that, B&O executives plan to extend the railroad to Wheeling in western Virginia within the next twenty-five years.

The Baltimore & Ohio Railroad was chartered last year to help Baltimore compete with other cities for the profitable western trade. The Erie Canal, which opened in 1825, has funneled a great deal of this trade through New York City. Baltimore's merchants are hoping that the B&O line will do as much for their city.

refused to heed it. The new president didn't think it would be a good idea, or look right, for him to reward his own followers with powerful political appointments. Instead, his administration remained filled with people who did not wish him well.

THE AMERICAN SYSTEM

Adams was the first president to champion the government's role in making internal improvements for the benefit of trade. Both Madison and Monroe had vetoed government-financed road and canal projects because they believed them to be unconstitutional. Adams, however, wanted the government to take an active role in expanding commerce.

The president had earlier adopted the American System, developed by Secretary of State Clay while he was still in the House of Representatives. The point of the American System was to create a self-sufficient national economy. Clay believed that a factory economy in the North could provide markets for southern cotton as well as western grain and beef. In exchange, the South and West would buy northern manufactured goods.

Specifically, Clay proposed high tariffs on imported manufactured items, internal improvements, and a strong national bank. The tariffs would protect the New England factory economy, barely a decade old, from competition with cheap European goods. Meanwhile, new roads and canals in the South and West would make it cheaper for farmers to bring their crops to market. Finally, a strong bank could establish a stable national credit system so that trade within the United States could flourish.

The congressmen who fought the American System did so for a number of reasons. Some were merely blocking Adams in order to ensure the election

The Early Years

BECAUSE JOHN ADAMS WAS ONE OF THE COUNTRY'S most important diplomats, his eldest son, John Quincy, spent much of his childhood abroad. John Quincy was only ten years old when he traveled to Europe for the first time in 1778. Just three years later, he was sent to Russia with Francis Dana, another American diplomat. Dana wanted John Quincy along because the boy spoke French fluently. At that time, French was the official language of diplomacy.

In 1797, while in London, Adams met his future wife, Louisa Johnson. Although her father was American, she had been born and raised in London, which made her the only foreign-born woman to become first lady.

★***FREEDOM'S JOURNAL*** Founded in 1827, *Freedom's Journal* was the first antislavery newspaper ever published by black people. A New York City pastor, Samuel E. Cornish, edited the journal along with John Russwurm. After Russwurm moved to Liberia, Cornish continued to publish the paper under the name *Rights of All.*

★**FACTORY GIRLS** Most early American manufacturers, particularly those in New England, relied on young, unmarried women for their work force. Farmers' daughters were actively recruited to work in clothing mills, and many jumped at the opportunity to help support their families and make some extra money for themselves.

These factory girls usually worked twelve-hour days. Their pay was about $2.50 a week, which was more than a woman could earn doing any other kind of work.

★PHOTOGRAPHY John Quincy Adams was the first president to have his picture taken. The photograph was called a daguerreotype after Louis Daguerre, the Frenchman who perfected the first practical photographic process. Daguerre used a copper plate coated with silver iodide, which he first exposed to light and then to a mercury vapor. The earliest daguerreotypes had to be exposed in bright sunlight for twenty minutes or the pictures wouldn't come out.

★AFTER THE PRESIDENCY After John Quincy Adams lost the 1828 election to Andrew Jackson, most people expected him to retire. Instead, in 1830, the sixty-three-year-old Adams ran for a seat in the House of Representatives and won. He thus became the first president to serve in Congress after leaving the White House.

Adams was often in the minority on issues such as the national bank, which he favored, and the annexation of Texas, which he opposed. But he had a great success in 1844, when he helped repeal a congressional rule that suppressed petitions against slavery. To frustrate this "gag rule," Adams spent many hours reading these petitions into the official record.

In February 1848, John Quincy Adams suffered a stroke on the floor of the House. The eighty-year-old former president was carried to a nearby chamber. He died there two days later because doctors considered it too dangerous to move him.

of Jackson in 1828. Others worried that the federal government was becoming too powerful.

Although elected as a Democratic-Republican, Adams didn't share his party's view that the Constitution set very strict limits on the government. Instead, like Alexander Hamilton, he wanted to use government resources actively. In fact, the shift toward a strong federal government was well under way. Ever since the Louisiana Purchase and the War of 1812, the country's growing size and nationalism had made the role of the federal government ever more important.

This development made many states nervous for the same reason Jefferson would have been. They believed that a strong federal government was dangerous because it meant less freedom for the states. Southerners were particularly concerned because they didn't want the federal government to become more involved in the slavery issue.

Because of the opposition Adams faced within his own administration and in Congress, he was able to win passage of only two public works projects. One was an extension of the Cumberland Road into Ohio. The other was the construction of a canal between the Ohio River and the Chesapeake Bay.

THE PANAMA CONGRESS

In 1826, the new Latin American republics, which had formerly been Spanish colonies, held a congress to promote friendship within the region and discuss a unified policy toward Spain. Simón Bolívar of Colombia, who organized the event, chose Panama as the meeting place.

Mexican and Colombian ministers asked Secretary of State Clay to send two U.S. delegates. Both Clay and Adams were delighted. Although neither was sure that democratic governments could survive in Latin

America, both were anxious to offer U.S. friendship and trade.

In the Congress, opposition to the mission was strong. Southern congressmen objected because the new Latin American nations had outlawed slavery. With the help of the Jacksonians in Congress, southerners were able to delay the mission. They withheld money and confirmation of the delegates until the Panama meeting was over.

THE TARIFF OF ABOMINATIONS Throughout his presidency, Adams pressed for higher tariffs on imported manufactured goods. His proposals followed Clay's American System, which favored protection for New England manufacturing. During his last year in office, a tariff bill was finally passed by Congress, but it wasn't the bill that Adams had proposed.

In an attempt to embarrass the president, the Jacksonians in Congress had amended Adams's plan so that it raised tariffs on imported raw materials as well. The Jacksonians were sure that New England congressmen, who otherwise supported Adams, would never vote for such a bill because it would raise the prices New England factories paid for their raw materials.

They were wrong. The Tariff of 1828 passed and was signed by the president. It soon became known as the Tariff of Abominations because it was so hated. The new tariff rates dramatically raised the prices of all sorts of goods, which made the public furious.

The new law didn't embarrass Adams, but it did eliminate whatever small chance he might have had at winning reelection. Still, whatever good the Tariff of Abominations did for Andrew Jackson, it also passed along to him a crisis in the making.

CAMPAIGN 1828

GENERAL ANDREW JACKSON STARTED HIS SECOND campaign for the presidency soon after he lost his first. Throughout Adams's term, the shadow of Jackson dogged the president.

As the 1828 election approached, the Democratic-Republican party split into two camps. The Jacksonians called themselves Democrats. The Adams forces called themselves National Republicans.

Because the candidates took similar stands on the issues, the election turned on personal attacks. Adams was hammered for the "corrupt" bargain he allegedly made with Clay to win the 1824 election. Meanwhile, the National Republicans printed handbills that showed a line of coffins and accused the general of executing soldiers for minor offenses during the War of 1812.

The supporters of Adams portrayed Jackson as crude, uneducated, and always ready for a brawl. Although wealthy eastern business leaders found these traits deplorable, ordinary people on the frontier loved them. In contrast to Jackson, Adams was considered distant and unappealing.

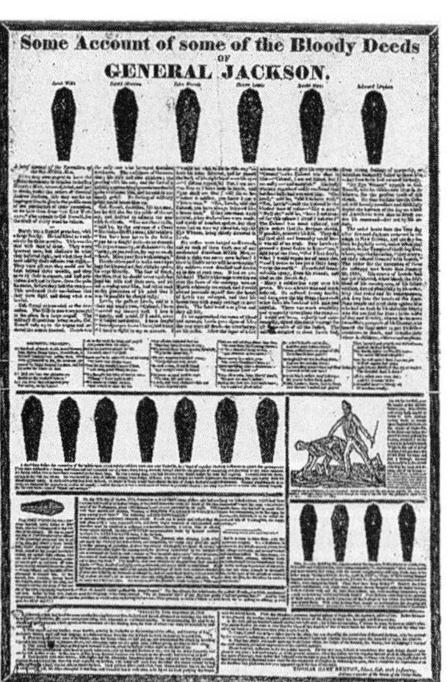
Some Account of some of the Bloody Deeds of GENERAL JACKSON.

Jackson's nickname was Old Hickory, because he was supposed to be as tough as hickory wood. To publicize his campaign, Jackson's supporters put up hickory poles all over the country. They also sponsored local picnics, parades, and barbecues. Jackson's was the first grass-roots presidential campaign in U.S. history.

Jackson later claimed that his election in 1828 was a victory for the common man. In any case, it was certainly a victory. Adams carried his base in the Northeast and nothing else.

ANDREW JACKSON

7TH PRESIDENT

★

FROM 1829 TO 1837

BORN: March 15, 1767

BIRTHPLACE: Waxhaw, S.C.

DIED: June 8, 1845

PARTY: Democrat

VICE PRESIDENTS: John C. Calhoun, Martin Van Buren

FIRST LADY: Rachel Donelson Robards

CHILDREN: None

NICKNAME: Old Hickory

The first president to ride a train.

WEBSTER, HAYNE DEBATE STATES' RIGHTS

WASHINGTON, January 27, 1830—Senator Daniel Webster of Massachusetts ended his nine-day-long debate today with Senator Robert Y. Hayne of South Carolina. The subject of their exchange was Hayne's claim that a state had the right to "nullify," or choose not to obey, a federal law.

The debate began when Hayne delivered a speech on January 19 asserting the rights of states to be free of federal interference. Hayne insisted that the Tariff of Abominations was responsible for South Carolina's current economic problems. He argued that no state should have to accept a federal law that harmed its interests.

Beginning yesterday, Webster held the attention of the Senate and the country as he delivered his response. According to Webster, no single state has the power to question laws passed by the Congress. Only the Supreme Court can do that.

The Massachusetts senator closed his remarks with the words, "Liberty and Union, now and forever, one and inseparable!"

Andrew Jackson's victory in 1828 marked a new era in U.S. politics. He was the first common man elected president. All six presidents before him had come from privileged, landed families. But Jackson was a self-made man, a poor orphan who had made a career for himself in the law and the army.

Jackson believed that ordinary Americans—the shopkeepers, farmers, and pioneers—had enough common sense to make political decisions for themselves. This idea was the cornerstone of "Jacksonian democracy," and the public loved him for it.

Jackson used his popular support whenever possible to reinforce his political strength. He also used the "spoils system." Jackson believed in the phrase, "To the victor belongs the spoils." Immediately upon taking office, he fired nearly one thousand of the

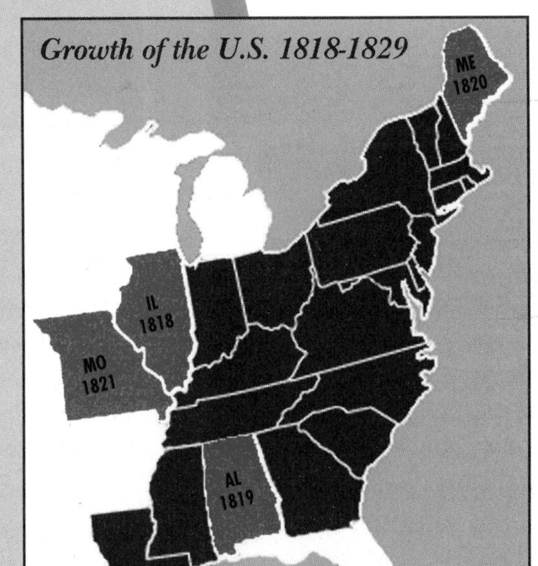

ten thousand people on the federal payroll and replaced them with his own supporters.

Because of his strategic use of the spoils system and his frequent direct appeals to the public for support, Jackson is widely considered to be the first modern president.

Jackson believed the president spoke with the voice of the people because he was the only government official (other than the vice president) elected by all the people. This attitude sometimes brought him into conflict with Congress and the Supreme Court. When that happened, he used his popular support to help him prevail.

AN INAUGURAL MESS

Because Jackson ran as their candidate, the people celebrated his inauguration as no inauguration had been celebrated before. A mob of twenty thousand well-wishers followed Jackson's carriage all the way from the Capitol to the White House. Some of them had traveled hundreds of miles to see Old Hickory, and their exuberance got the best of them.

Many followed Jackson into the White House itself—through the windows as well as the doors. They broke the presidential china, spit tobacco juice on the carpets, and stood on chairs and sofas to get a better view.

Unable to maintain order, Jackson fled through a back window and ran to a nearby hotel. Eventually, waiters drew the crowd out of the residence by serving tubs of punch on the White House lawn.

The damage was costly, but Jackson didn't really mind because the people had been acting out their joy. On the other hand, conservative Washington was scandalized, and it wouldn't be the last time. Soon after the inauguration, another scandal

The Early Years

ANDREW JACKSON'S FATHER DIED BEFORE HE WAS born, and his oldest brother died in 1779 while serving in the Continental Army. The next year, thirteen-year-old Andrew and his remaining brother, Robert, also joined the Continental Army. Andrew served as a colonel's orderly, carrying messages back and forth on horseback.

In April 1781, the brothers were captured and made to march forty miles without food or water to a prisoner-of-war camp. Robert caught smallpox there and died. Andrew's mother died the same year from a disease she caught while caring for wounded soldiers. His mother's death left Andrew alone in the world.

After studying to become a lawyer and serving as Tennessee's first U.S. representative, Jackson headed a volunteer army during the War of 1812. General Jackson won a number of victories against Britain's Indian allies before defeating the British themselves at the bloody battle of New Orleans. Jackson's successful invasion of Florida in 1818 helped John Quincy Adams negotiate the purchase of that colony from Spain.

★**THE FIRST LADY** When Andrew Jackson first wed Rachel Donelson in 1791, she was actually still married to her first husband. Both she and Jackson believed that her divorce had been finalized, but it wasn't formally granted until 1793. A few months later, Andrew and Rachel married again, this time legally.

The mistake haunted them during the 1828 campaign, when the National Republicans accused Jackson of adultery because he and Rachel had technically lived together before being legally married. The general tried to shield his wife, but Rachel eventually found out that she was being smeared in the national press.

She quickly fell ill, at least in part because of her heartache, and died less than two months after the election. She was buried in the dress that she had bought to wear at her husband's inauguration.

★**TOM THUMB** America's first steam-powered railroad locomotive was built by a wealthy inventor named Peter Cooper. He nicknamed the locomotive "Tom Thumb" because it was only twenty feet long.

Cooper demonstrated his new invention for the first time in 1830, when the Baltimore & Ohio opened its first railroad line. The locomotive reached a peak speed of fifteen miles per hour during the thirteen-mile trip and proved that train travel was practical along hilly routes.

On the return trip, Cooper and his passengers came upon a horse. A race was suggested. At first, the horse galloped into the lead. Then Tom Thumb caught up and pulled ahead. It seemed as though the locomotive would win easily, but the engine suddenly broke down, and the horse won the race.

★**UTOPIAN COMMUNITIES** One response to the horrible conditions in many U.S. factories was the cooperative community. The first of these was founded in 1825 by Robert Owen, who was already famous for pioneering labor reform at his factory in Scotland.

Owen was concerned by the wide gap between the rich and the poor. The community he founded in New Harmony, Indiana, was supposed to be a utopia, or perfect society, where all the residents worked together for the benefit of the group. Instead, many lazy and unprincipled people joined the community because they thought they could get a free ride. New Harmony failed after two years.

★***THE LIBERATOR*** In 1831, William Lloyd Garrison began publishing *The Liberator*, which would soon become the most important and hardest hitting of the abolitionist newspapers. It described the horrors of slavery in great detail and helped spark enormous growth in the northern antislavery movement.

Congressmen in Washington debated whether or not slavery should be extended to the new western states, but Garrison and his followers wanted slavery abolished everywhere, including the South, on moral grounds.

broke. This one involved Jackson's new secretary of war, John Eaton.

THE PEGGY EATON AFFAIR While he represented Tennessee in the Senate, Eaton had lived in a boardinghouse run by a woman named Peggy Timberlake, whose husband worked for the navy. When John Timberlake went away on long voyages, Eaton would often escort Mrs. Timberlake to social functions. After her husband died in 1829, Eaton married her.

Rumors circulated around town that the relationship between Eaton and his new wife was "improper." People insinuated that the couple had been involved while John Timberlake was still alive. Led by Floride Calhoun, the wife of Vice President John C. Calhoun, the wives of important government officials shunned Peggy Eaton.

Moral rules were very strict during the nineteenth century, especially with regard to women, who were believed to be pure and weak. Peggy Eaton did not fit this image. Nor did her background as a barmaid help her win the approval of Washington society.

Jackson, however, stood by her. Reminded of campaign attacks against his own wife's virtue, the president refused to listen to gossip about Peggy Eaton. Instead, he invited Mrs. Eaton to state dinners and insisted that the wives of his cabinet officers accept her.

Rather than force their wives to receive Mrs. Eaton, most of the members of President Jackson's cabinet decided to hand in their resignations.

Floride Calhoun enraged Jackson by leaving Washington rather than socialize with Peggy Eaton. On the other hand, Secretary of State Martin Van Buren's gracious acceptance of Mrs. Eaton raised his standing with the president as Vice President Calhoun's fell. During the rest of Calhoun's term, he and Jackson would grow further apart.

THE INDIAN REMOVAL ACT The most important legislation of Jackson's first term was the Indian Removal Act of 1830. For a number of years, the state of Georgia had been trying to confiscate and sell land belonging to the Cherokee Indians. The Cherokee were among five "civilized" tribes that had adopted the ways of white society in order to live peacefully among whites.

To become acceptable to whites, the Cherokee had taken up European-style farming, developed a written language, and even adopted their own constitution. But neither the government of Georgia nor President Jackson cared.

Old Hickory was well known as an Indian fighter, not as an Indian lover. The Indian Removal Act gave him the power to remove Indians from the South to lands west of the Mississippi River. During the next few years, Jackson used federal troops to force the Cherokee, Chickasaw, Choctaw, Seminole, and Creek tribes to abandon one hundred million acres of fertile land and resettle in the West.

The Cherokee asked the Supreme Court for help, arguing that the tribe was essentially a foreign nation. Chief Justice John Marshall denied their petition. Marshall did point out, however, that only the federal government had sovereignty over the Cherokee. Therefore, the state laws of Georgia did not apply to them, and no whites could settle Cherokee land without Cherokee permission. But Georgia ignored the decision, and Jackson refused to enforce it, so the forced removals continued.

THE FIRST MAJOR NATIONAL PARTY CONVENTIONS were held in 1832. Until that time, presidential candidates were generally nominated either by a group of congressmen belonging to the same party or by a state legislature.

The Democratic party met in Baltimore in May to renominate Jackson. Because of the president's fights with him, John C. Calhoun was dropped from the ticket and replaced with Martin Van Buren. Jackson clearly intended to groom Van Buren to succeed him as president.

To oppose Jackson, the National Republicans nominated Henry Clay, who attacked Jackson for his tyrannical attitudes and his use of the spoils system. National Republican cartoons portrayed the president as King Andrew I.

CAMPAIGN 1832

The most important campaign issue was Jackson's policy toward the Second Bank of the United States. The president did not try to hide his contempt for the bank. When Congress passed a bill that summer granting the national bank a new charter, Jackson vetoed it. As a temporarily bedridden Jackson told his loyal aide, "The bank, Mr. Van Buren, is trying to kill me, but I will kill it."

Jackson claimed that the bank favored the interests of the wealthy, while Clay argued that closing the bank would hurt small borrowers as well. Clay polled well in the North, but Jackson carried the South and West again and won comfortably.

REMEMBER THE ALAMO!

183 Texans Die After 13-Day Siege

SAN ANTONIO, March 6, 1836—The thirteen-day siege of the Alamo ended today when the forces of Mexican general Santa Anna stormed the outer walls of the mission. Three thousand Mexicans killed the 183 defenders of the Alamo, sparing only fifteen women and children and one black slave.

The Texan dead included colonels James Bowie and William B. Travis as well as the famous frontiersman Davy Crockett.

Estimates of Mexican dead and wounded range from one thousand to sixteen hundred men.

The Texans first captured the town of San Antonio in December of last year, beginning their ongoing war for independence. After Santa Anna's army arrived from the south on February 23, Texan general Sam Houston told the defenders of the Alamo to retreat. Writing from inside the Alamo, Travis replied, "I shall never surrender or retreat.... VICTORY OR DEATH."

THE NULLIFICATION CONTROVERSY

Although President Jackson hated the Tariff of Abominations as much as the public did, John Calhoun hated it even more. As president, Jackson worked with Congress to reduce the tariff rates, but he also took seriously his obligation to enforce the law of the land.

Calhoun thought the tariff was unconstitutional because it placed a cruel and unusual burden on his home state of South Carolina. He argued that states could "nullify," or choose not to obey, federal laws that were not in their own best interests. Calhoun's theory thus extended the states' rights theories of Jefferson.

The chief spokesman for nullification in Congress was South Carolina senator Robert Y. Hayne, who faced Daniel Webster in an important 1830 Senate debate. Afterward, people waited anxiously for Jackson to announce his position on nullification.

In April 1830, at a dinner celebrating Jefferson's birthday, Jackson made the first toast: "Our Union—it must be preserved!" Calhoun's toast was, "The Union—next to our liberty, the most dear." Obviously, Calhoun had not softened his position.

In 1832, Congress finally passed a new law reducing tariff rates, but Calhoun wasn't satisfied. Instead, he resigned the vice presidency and accepted a seat in the Senate.

Meanwhile, South Carolina decided to nullify both the 1828 and 1832 tariffs. State legislators warned that if federal troops were used to collect the tariffs, South Carolina would secede from the Union.

When Congress met again in 1833 following Jackson's comfortable reelection, nullification was the hottest issue. In nullifying the tariffs, South Carolina had brought into question the very issue of federal superiority that had been settled militarily during the Whiskey Rebellion and in the courts by the case of *McCulloch v. Maryland*.

Jackson was not about to stand for such behavior, and with the Senate's approval, he sent federal troops to the South Carolina border. In the meantime, Henry Clay shepherded a compromise tariff through Congress. Faced with the choice of a federal invasion or Clay's compromise, South Carolina backed down and began collecting the new tariff fees.

THE SECOND BANK

Having resolved the nullification crisis, Jackson now turned his attention to the Second Bank of the United States. The future of the bank had been the most important issue during his 1832 campaign against Clay.

Jackson had always hated banks, and the Second Bank in particular. Like many westerners, he blamed the conservative policies of the national bank for tightening credit and thereby slowing the economic development of the West.

The Second Bank was based in Philadelphia with branches all over the country. Its charter was due to expire in 1836, and another act of Congress would be required to keep the bank open beyond that time. But Jackson wanted to close the Second Bank even sooner. He reached out to

★THE BLACK HAWK WAR While the Cherokee tried to use the Supreme Court to stop the state of Georgia from taking their land, the Sac and Fox tribes in Illinois tried a different approach. They fought. The Black Hawk War, named after the Sac and Fox tribal leader, ended three generations of resistance to white settlement along the old Northwest frontier.

In 1832, the Illinois militia, including twenty-three-year-old Captain Abraham Lincoln, chased Black Hawk's band of warriors and their families into Wisconsin. The soldiers caught up with the Indians on the Bad Axe River. Although Black Hawk raised a white flag, the militiamen attacked anyway, shooting the women and children as well as the men.

★NAT TURNER'S REBELLION In 1831, Nat Turner began the most important, and bloodiest, slave revolt in U.S. history. A deeply religious man, he thought that a solar eclipse was a sign from God that he should free his people.

On the night of August 21, Turner killed his masters in their sleep, the first of at least fifty-one whites who would die. Then he set off with seventy-five fellow slaves for the seat of Southampton County, Virginia, where he planned to capture the armory and arm his new recruits.

But Turner's band was not nearly strong enough to face the three thousand militiamen waiting for them. Although Turner escaped, six weeks later he was captured and hanged.

Turner's rebellion terrified white southerners. Many had believed the myth that slaves were contented with their bondage and would not stage an armed revolt. Southern states quickly passed new laws to restrict the education of slaves as well as their ability to travel and gather in groups.

★DAVY CROCKETT Davy Crockett was born into a pioneer family in Tennessee. He grew up living in the wilderness of the western frontier and spent less than a hundred days in school. While in his twenties, he made a name for himself as an Indian fighter and "b'ar hunter."

Crockett served off and on in Congress from 1827 until 1835. During that time, he charmed eastern journalists with his frontier mannerisms. Soon, these men began to write books and articles about Crockett, casting him as a frontier folk hero in a coonskin cap. Some said he could leap the Ohio River and wrestle wildcats. After his death at the Alamo, Crockett lived on in dozens of books, songs, television shows, and movies.

★AMERICAN COOKING In colonial America, most cooking in the North was based on British recipes. But the food people ate was also influenced by the availability of local ingredients and by Indian cooking techniques. Pumpkin pie was one popular dish that resulted from a combination of the two cuisines.

This type of cultural exchange also took place in Texas, where local Mexicans taught white settlers how to cook with corn. In the South, cooking was influenced by West Indian and African styles brought over by the slaves. Black-eyed peas, peanuts, okra, and rice were all staples of West African cooking before they became favorites in the South.

★KITCHEN CABINET Since the administration of George Washington, presidents had met regularly with their cabinets to discuss and decide matters of government policy. But Jackson didn't like his cabinet officers very much to begin with, and he liked them even less after the Peggy Eaton Affair.

Jackson cut down the number of cabinet meetings until he stopped them altogether. Instead, he discussed politics almost every night with his closest friends at meetings held in the White House kitchen. These men—including Martin Van Buren, John Eaton, newspaper editor Amos Kendall, and William B. Lewis—came to be known as the Kitchen Cabinet.

the people and asked for their support in destroying the "monster bank."

Jackson ordered Treasury Secretary Louis McLane to withdraw all the federal deposits from the Second Bank and place them instead in state banks. When McLane refused, Jackson dismissed him and appointed William Duane, who also refused and was fired.

After a frustrating search, Jackson finally found someone who would follow his orders, Attorney General Roger B. Taney, whom Jackson would later appoint to the Supreme Court. In September 1833, Taney ordered the withdrawal of the deposits.

In response to Jackson's move, Nicholas Biddle, the president of the Second Bank, called in his bank's outstanding loans. In part this was a sensible business decision. If the Second Bank were to close, it would have to settle its affairs.

But Biddle also wanted to pressure Jackson to change his mind. By calling in the Second Bank's loans, Biddle limited the availability of credit and brought the country to the brink of a financial panic.

The pressure mounted on Jackson. But each time someone complained, the president said, "Go to Nicholas Biddle." In the end, Biddle relented, and the near-panic turned into a land boom. The state banks began lending money from the new federal deposits at bargain rates, and this in turn led to a new round of land speculation in the West.

TEXAN INDEPENDENCE During his last year in office, Jackson's attention also turned west, to Texas, which was still Mexican territory. While he longed to add Texas to the Union, he also felt bound to honor Mexico's sovereignty and was concerned that the admission of Texas as a slave state would disturb the precarious balance between North and South.

In December 1835, however, white settlers in Texas revolted against the new Mexican government of General Antonio López de Santa Anna, principally because Santa Anna had recently outlawed slavery. Raising an army, they captured the town of San Antonio, alarming Santa Anna and leading to the Mexican siege of the Alamo.

Santa Anna's victory there was short-lived, however. Six weeks later, on April 21, 1836, an army of Texans under the command of Sam Houston won both the battle of San Jacinto and independence for Texas. The Texans' battle cry was "Remember the Alamo!" On July 4, Congress agreed to recognize the new Republic of Texas, taking the first step toward making Texas part of the Union.

THE SPECIE CIRCULAR One of Jackson's last actions before leaving office was to issue the Specie Circular in July 1836. The Specie Circular declared that buyers could no longer use paper money to purchase federal land. Instead, they would have to use gold or silver. (Coins made out of precious metals were known as "specie.")

Jackson instituted this policy because of the land boom touched off by his successful campaign against the Second Bank. He was worried that all the new credit offered by the state banks was making the economy unstable. He was also concerned that speculators were buying too much land with devalued paper money instead of with hard cash.

Jackson's drastic policy reversal, from easy credit to no credit, sent land prices plunging, which in turn led to bankruptcies. By the time Jackson left office, businesses all over the country were closing their doors, and with the government still refusing paper money, the panic spread.

CAMPAIGN ★ 1836

Obeying Jackson's orders, the Democratic party nominated Vice President Martin Van Buren as its presidential candidate in 1836. Van Buren's opposition came from the Whig party, formed by Jackson's political enemies in 1834.

The Whigs were unable to decide on a single candidate, in part because they had little in common beyond their hatred of Jackson. So the party members decided to run three regional candidates. They hoped to deny Van Buren an electoral majority. If that happened, the election would be thrown into the House of Representatives.

The Whigs ran the war hero William Henry Harrison in the West, Daniel Webster in the North, and Hugh Lawson White of Tennessee in the South. Only Harrison was regarded as a serious national candidate.

Jackson's endorsement was a mixed blessing for Van Buren. The president was still personally popular, but his controversial policies, especially regarding the Second Bank, posed some problems for Van Buren.

Whenever possible, Van Buren tried to avoid the issues, especially slavery. His success depended on a coalition of Democrats from the North and South, and he didn't want to upset any of them.

Van Buren won with just over half the popular vote and a solid electoral majority. But it would be 152 years before another vice president was elected to follow the president he served.

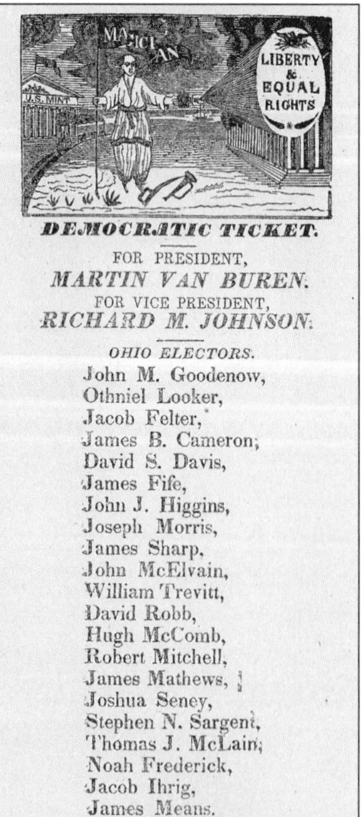

DEMOCRATIC TICKET.

FOR PRESIDENT,
MARTIN VAN BUREN.
FOR VICE PRESIDENT,
RICHARD M. JOHNSON.

OHIO ELECTORS.
John M. Goodenow,
Othniel Looker,
Jacob Felter,
James B. Cameron,
David S. Davis,
James Fife,
John J. Higgins,
Joseph Morris,
James Sharp,
John McElvain,
William Trevitt,
David Robb,
Hugh McComb,
Robert Mitchell,
James Mathews,
Joshua Seney,
Stephen N. Sargent,
Thomas J. McLain,
Noah Frederick,
Jacob Ihrig,
James Means.

MARTIN VAN BUREN

8TH PRESIDENT

★

FROM 1837 TO 1841

BORN: December 5, 1782

BIRTHPLACE: Kinderhook, N.Y.

DIED: July 24, 1862

PARTY: Democrat

VICE PRESIDENT: Richard M. Johnson

FIRST LADY: Hannah Hoes

CHILDREN: Abraham, John, Martin, Smith

NICKNAME: Little Magician

The first president not born a British subject.

Just two months after Martin Van Buren took office, the United States was hit by one of the worst depressions in the nation's history. The economic crisis that began during the summer of 1837 lasted nearly a decade. These hard times dominated Van Buren's presidency and eventually cost him reelection in 1840.

Although Van Buren received much of the blame, the crisis was largely the fault of Andrew Jackson. Jackson's policies, designed to destroy the Second Bank of the United States, had at the same time weakened the economy.

In trying to crush the Second Bank, Jackson had ordered that government funds be withdrawn from the national bank and deposited instead in state banks. These state banks, however, often used the money to make unwise loans. Their loose banking

THOUSANDS OF CHEROKEE DIE ALONG THE TRAIL OF TEARS

During 1838 and 1839, fifteen thousand Cherokee were forced to leave their homeland in Georgia and march west to government reservations in Oklahoma. This journey, during which more than one-fourth of the Cherokee died, has been called the Trail of Tears.

The Cherokee were escorted by federal troops under the command of General Winfield Scott. Along the way, government officials took what little money the Cherokee had. In return, the government provided inadequate supplies for the trip.

Despite the shortages of food and other necessities, General Scott refused to slow the pace of the march. Even the sick and the elderly were forced to keep up. This policy caused many of the deaths.

One observer wrote at the time that "such a denial of justice, and such deafness to screams for mercy, were never heard of in time of peace...since the earth was made."

practices led to a period of inflation during which prices soared.

During his last months in office, Jackson issued the Specie Circular, an executive order intended to curb this inflation and control land speculation in the West. The Specie Circular stated that paper money could no longer be used to purchase government land. Instead, buyers would have to pay for the land with specie.

During the nineteenth century, paper money was "backed" by precious metals such as gold and silver. Coins made from these valuable metals were known as "specie." Under this banking system, a one-dollar bill could be exchanged at any time for a dollar's worth of specie.

The Specie Circular forced buyers of land to exchange their paper money for gold or silver. But this created a demand for specie that the banks could not meet. Because of the inflation and the bad loans the banks had made, there was no longer enough gold and silver to back all the paper money in circulation. As a result, the value of the paper money fell.

THE PANIC OF 1837 The Panic of 1837 began when a number of banks in New York City stopped converting paper money into gold and silver. Loans also became harder to get. As a result, speculators who were denied credit stopped buying land, and land prices fell sharply.

Nearly one thousand banks around the country failed. When they did, work on the internal improvement projects the banks had been financing also stopped, throwing many people out of work. In some cities, hungry people rioted for food. Meanwhile in Washington, Van Buren wore expensive, tailored clothes, which hurt his popularity.

The Early Years

ALTHOUGH HE LATER BECAME KNOWN FOR HIS expensive tastes, Martin Van Buren did not grow up wealthy. His father was a poor farmer and tavern keeper in Kinderhook, New York, a small Dutch village on the Hudson River. The Van Burens spoke Dutch at home, and Little Mat was raised according to European customs.

After school he often helped his father in the tavern where famous politicians, including Alexander Hamilton and Aaron Burr, often stopped on their way to Albany. Young Martin loved to listen to their arguments, and he quickly developed an interest in politics that would last his entire life. He became such a crafty politician himself that he was nicknamed the Little Magician and the Red Fox of Kinderhook.

★**A DANDY PRESIDENT** A small, dapper, and refined man, Van Buren was both respected and criticized for the way he behaved and dressed. He wore a coat with a velvet collar and tight-fitting gloves made from very soft leather. He traveled through the muddy and smelly streets of Washington in a luxurious green coach driven by men in fancy uniforms. People often complained that their president behaved more like a king than a Democrat.

★**TRANSCENDENTALISM** During the 1830s, a group of writers including Ralph Waldo Emerson and Henry David Thoreau developed the philosophy of transcendentalism. Transcendentalists believed that, because people are basically good, human society can be perfected through experimentation and reform. The most important transcendentalist journal was *The Dial,* founded in 1840 and first edited by Margaret Fuller.

The transcendentalists particularly influenced American literature, but they also were active in social reform movements. Among the causes they championed were women's suffrage, public education, and better working conditions in factories.

★**FRONTIER WOMEN** The first white people to move out west were almost exclusively men. Some were cowboys, others were miners, but they were all fortune seekers who wandered through the wilderness and rarely put down roots. Not until women began moving west were the first farms settled, the first churches built, and the first towns established.

When they did arrive, women found freedom on the frontier that they could never have experienced in the established cities of the East. Life in the West was hard, and frontier women had to be tough and capable. But they did receive a certain measure of equality in return.

★**THE TELEGRAPH** Portrait painter Samuel Morse first got the idea for the telegraph in 1832. Five years later, he displayed the first working model, which introduced an electric current in a wire. Morse Code was later developed to translate letters of the alphabet into groups of long and short pulses. The telegraph provided the first means of communicating instantly over long distances.

To convince the government to fund the development of the telegraph, Morse arranged a demonstration. He had telegraph wire strung between Baltimore and Washington. Then, using equipment set up in the Supreme Court, he transmitted the message "What hath God wrought!" and received an immediate reply. Morse's device was probably more shocking to people in its time than any other invention, including the automobile, the radio, and the computer.

At first, Congress did little more than debate the country's problems. But Van Buren had a plan. He wanted to set up an independent treasury, run by the government. He felt that an independent treasury was the only way to protect federal money from irresponsible loans.

A number of congressmen opposed the president's plan because they didn't want government funds removed from the banks in their home states. It was not until 1840, the last year of Van Buren's term, that Congress finally passed the Independent Treasury Act.

THE TEXAS QUESTION In 1837, the year that Martin Van Buren became president, Washington was still a swampy, malaria-ridden town. Open sewers wound through the unpaved streets of the nation's capital. Pigs and chickens scurried about. In busy markets, slaves were bought and sold.

At his inauguration, the new president spoke directly to the issue of slavery, which he had carefully avoided during the 1836 campaign. Now Van Buren declared that he would fight attempts to abolish slavery in the South. He said that the southern states had the right to decide the matter for themselves.

What Van Buren really wanted was for the issue to go away, but it wouldn't. The president was forced to confront slavery again when Texas applied for admission to the Union shortly after winning its independence from Mexico.

If Texas were to be admitted, it would be as a slave state. There was no doubt about that. It was the Mexican government's attempt to abolish slavery in Texas that had started the rebellion there in the first place.

Admitting Texas as a slave state, however, would upset the delicate balance between slave and free states preserved by the Missouri Compromise. Despite the president's strong support of slavery in general, he decided to oppose the admission of Texas because he feared the political consequences. Van Buren worried that admitting Texas as a slave state would reopen the slavery debate.

The president's stand was unpopular in the South, of course, but it was also attacked by many others who wanted to expand the territory of the country no matter what the cost.

THE CAROLINE AFFAIR

Meanwhile, as Congress argued about Texas and the economy, the threat of war returned along the nation's northern border. The trouble began early in 1837 when Canadian rebels attacked Toronto in an effort to end British colonial rule there. When the attempt failed, the rebels retreated to Navy Island in the Niagara River, which separates the United States from Canada.

Americans supporting the Canadian rebels began ferrying them supplies from New York using the steamship *Caroline.* That December, the enraged British ordered loyal Canadian militia to attack the *Caroline* as it lay anchored off the New York shore. During the successful raid, the *Caroline* was set afire and sent over Niagara Falls. One American was killed and several injured.

Van Buren called the attack an "outrage" and sent troops to the U.S.-Canadian border. Many congressmen urged him to declare war on Britain, but Van Buren resisted the pressure and instead declared U.S. neutrality with regard to the Canadian rebellion. Despite this declaration, relations with Britain remained strained for several years.

CAMPAIGN 1840

THE 1840 ELECTION WAS DOMINATED BY THE economic depression that followed the Panic of 1837. Many people blamed Van Buren and wanted a change. To oppose the president, the Whigs put up General William Henry Harrison again.

Although Harrison's supporters assured voters that the general would end the depression, they didn't say how. Instead, they concentrated on hoopla. The Whigs' focus on staged events, campaign advertising, and campaign souvenirs, such as decorated hairbrushes and tobacco tins, made this the first modern presidential election.

The Whig campaign took on a great deal of momentum when a Democratic newspaper mocked Harrison as a bumpkin who would enjoy nothing more than a barrel of hard, or alcoholic, cider and a log cabin in which to drink it. Although Harrison actually lived in a twenty-two-room mansion, the Whigs cleverly saw the opportunity to portray him as a man of the people. To encourage this image, they used log cabins for their campaign headquarters and served hard cider in cabin-shaped mugs.

On the other extreme, rumors were spread that Van Buren was such a dandy that he ate with a golden spoon and bathed in a tub of cologne. Actually, Harrison was far wealthier than Van Buren.

The campaign was so exciting that an astounding eighty percent of eligible voters cast ballots. Van Buren kept the popular vote respectably close, but he lost the electoral vote by a wide margin, including his home state of New York.

William Henry Harrison

9th President

★

1841

Born: February 9, 1773

Birthplace: Charles City County, Va.

Died: April 4, 1841

Party: Whig

Vice President: John Tyler

First Lady: Anna Tuthill Symmes

Children: Elizabeth, John Cleves, Lucy, William, John Scott, Benjamin, Mary, Carter, Anna, James

Nickname: Old Tippecanoe

The first president to die in office.

In times of crisis, people often turn—sometimes foolishly, sometimes not—to war heroes for leadership. George Washington was such a hero. So was Andrew Jackson.

General William Henry Harrison was born on a large Virginia plantation just before the outbreak of the American Revolution. His father, Benjamin, signed the Declaration of Independence. Harrison's first career choice was medicine, but his money ran out soon after his father's death in 1791. When that happened, Harrison left medical school and joined the army as a professional soldier.

Harrison saw his first action in the Northwest Territory during the Indian wars of the 1790s. He was commended for his bravery at the Battle of Fallen Timbers in 1794.

While serving as the governor of the Indiana Territory in 1811, Harrison led an army of professional soldiers and militiamen against the village of Shawnee chief Tecumseh. His victory at Tippecanoe Creek earned him national fame and the nickname Old Tippecanoe. His 1840 campaign slogan was "Tippecanoe and Tyler, Too."

PNEUMONIA KILLS HARRISON AFTER ONE MONTH IN OFFICE

WASHINGTON, April 4, 1841—President William Henry Harrison died last night of pneumonia. A messenger has been dispatched to the home of Vice President John Tyler in Williamsburg, Virginia, to inform him of the news.

Just one month ago, the sixty-eight-year-old president gave the longest inaugural address in history, lasting nearly two hours. He delivered the speech while standing outdoors in a cold wind wearing neither a hat nor an overcoat.

Later, the president went out walking and got caught in a rainstorm. He came back to the White House drenched. The cold he caught that day later developed into the pneumonia.

Doctors applied heated suction cups to the president's skin, hoping to draw out the disease. When this and other modern treatments failed, the doctors turned in desperation to traditional Indian cures, including one therapy involving snakes.

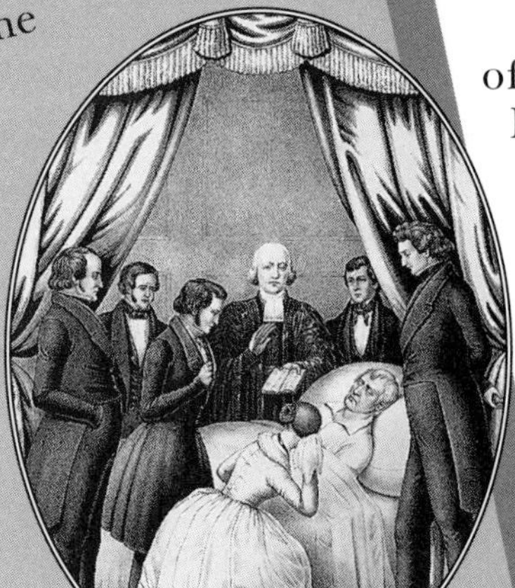

Born: March 29, 1790

Birthplace: Charles City County, Va.

Died: January 18, 1862

Party: Whig

Vice President: None

First Ladies: Letitia Christian, Julia Gardiner

Children: Mary, Robert, John, Letitia, Elizabeth, Anne, Alice, Tazewell, David, John Alexander, Julia, Lachlan, Lyon, Robert Fitzgerald, Pearl

Nickname: His Accidency

The first president to have a veto overridden.

John Tyler

10th President
★
From 1841 to 1845

Because William Henry Harrison was the first president to die in office, his death caused much confusion. Vice President John Tyler's transition to power should have been simple, but it wasn't.

Tyler didn't even know the president was sick. He was shocked when a government clerk awoke him at home in Williamsburg, Virginia, with news of Harrison's death.

Tyler's larger problem was that he had been nominated for vice president simply to balance the Whig ticket. The Whigs needed support in the South, and Tyler was a southerner. He had joined the Whig party because of his hatred for Andrew Jackson and the Democrats. But he had never really accepted the Whigs' nationalist policies. As a result, the Whig party leaders, especially Senator Henry Clay, didn't trust him.

European Immigration Wave Hits U.S.

During the 1840s, the United States experienced a massive wave of immigration from Europe. Between 1844 and 1854, nearly three million people made the Atlantic crossing. Of these immigrants, 1,300,000 were Irish and 940,000 were German.

The Irish were escaping a terrible famine in their country caused by a series of potato crop failures. Tens of thousands of people starved, but many more fled to the United States.

Because they were too poor to move farther inland, most Irish immigrants settled in the northeastern port cities in which they landed. Large Irish neighborhoods quickly grew up in New York, Boston, and Philadelphia.

German immigrants, most of whom arrived with a little more money, generally moved to the Midwest. Cities such as Milwaukee became magnets for them as well as for the Scandinavians who followed. By 1860, nearly one-third of the population of Wisconsin was foreign born.

★Edgar Allan Poe In 1841, *Graham's Magazine* published a short story by Edgar Allan Poe entitled "The Murders in the Rue Morgue." *Graham's* regularly printed works by the best known American authors—including James Fenimore Cooper, Nathaniel Hawthorne, and Henry Wadsworth Longfellow.

"The Murders in the Rue Morgue" was the first detective story ever written. It exhibited the ghoulish and gruesome style that later made Poe's work famous. His stories, poems, and essays were widely published at the time, but Poe never made much money. In 1843, his best year, he earned just three hundred dollars from his writing.

★The Oregon Trail During 1843, "Oregon fever" swept through the Mississippi Valley. A thousand settlers headed west that year to find out whether the Willamette Valley of Oregon was indeed as beautiful and fertile as people said. They followed the two-thousand-mile-long Oregon Trail.

Beginning in Independence, Missouri, the Oregon Trail passed through deserts, over mountains, and across Indian territory. Most families traveled in canvas-covered wagons called "prairie schooners" because the tops of the wagons often looked liked sails in the wind. Schooners were popular sailing ships.

Trains of fifty or so wagons set off each morning about four o'clock and kept going until dusk, stopping only to graze the animals. Even so, the trip to Oregon usually took six months, because the wagons could make only twelve miles a day over the difficult terrain.

Clay was a nationalist, which meant that he wanted to use the federal government to build a strong, unified country. His current program was a revised version of the American System he had originally developed in the years after the War of 1812.

During the month that William Henry Harrison occupied the White House, it seemed to many as though Clay was actually running the country. On most important policy matters, Harrison let the senator decide, which was exactly the way Clay had hoped it would be.

Unlike Clay, Tyler was an advocate of states' rights. He believed, as many southerners did, that strengthening the federal government threatened individual freedom. Southerners worried that a strong national government would attempt to outlaw slavery.

Clay and his followers tried to limit Tyler's power by refusing to recognize him as the new president. They referred to him as the "acting president." Although some people called him His Accidency (a pun on His Excellency, the address used for royalty), Tyler never doubted that he was president. He even returned, unopened, mail that came addressed to "Acting President Tyler."

WHIGS IN TURMOIL Tyler's first public clash with Clay came over the national bank. Clay had wanted to bring back a national bank ever since Jackson had crushed the Second Bank of the United States. Twice Clay pushed bills through Congress to charter a new Third Bank, and twice Tyler angered his own party by vetoing them.

To protest Tyler's vetoes, his entire cabinet, with the exception of Secretary of State Daniel Webster, resigned in September 1841. Webster stayed on because he was in the middle of important treaty negotiations with Britain.

Tyler quickly appointed new cabinet officers who agreed with him, but the loss of Whig support had its consequences. After the president vetoed the bank bill a second time, the Whigs disowned him. Thus, Tyler became the first president to serve without a party.

Although Tyler's domestic policies often met opposition in Congress, he had greater freedom to act when it came to foreign affairs. His administration's first success came in resolving a border fight with Canada. The agreement, negotiated by Daniel Webster and Lord Ashburton of Great Britain, granted the United States slightly more than half the disputed land along the Maine border. The Webster-Ashburton Treaty fixed the U.S.-Canadian border all the way from the Atlantic Ocean to the Rocky Mountains.

THE ANNEXATION OF TEXAS

To the south, Tyler took up the matter of Texan statehood, which had been pending since the Van Buren administration. By 1843, Texans had grown tired of waiting. They began talking with Britain about the possibility of remaining independent under British protection.

Tyler began his own secret talks with Texas, which led to a treaty rejected by the Senate in June 1844. This treaty—written by Tyler's new secretary of state, John C. Calhoun—included a section glorifying slavery that sealed its defeat.

That fall, however, James Knox Polk was elected president because he favored expansion of the nation. Polk's victory convinced Congress that the public wanted Texas to be annexed. Three days before he left office, Tyler signed a joint resolution of Congress admitting Texas to the Union.

CAMPAIGN 1844

Having thrown Tyler out of the party, the Whigs weren't about to nominate him for another term. Instead, the party chose Henry Clay, who had already run for the presidency twice before, in 1824 and again in 1832.

When the Democrats met to choose their candidate, former president Martin Van Buren won a majority of the delegate votes on the first ballot, but he never won the two-thirds necessary for nomination. As Van Buren's support waned, the convention turned to James Knox Polk, a former governor of Tennessee. This dark-horse, or long-shot, candidate was so poorly known compared to Clay that the Whigs made "Who is Polk?" their campaign slogan.

The key issues of the campaign were western expansion and the spread of slavery. Clay opposed the annexation of Texas, while Polk strongly supported that step as well as the annexation of Oregon as far north as 54°40' latitude. The Democratic slogan was "Fifty-four Forty or Fight!"

Clay's stand on Texas cost him support in the South, where voters thought he was trying to stop the spread of slavery. Clay hoped that these losses would be offset by gains in the North. But Clay, like Polk, was himself a slaveholder, which third-party abolitionist candidate James G. Birney often pointed out. Birney didn't win any electoral votes, but he did win enough popular votes in New York to tip the state—and the election—to Polk.

JAMES KNOX POLK

11TH PRESIDENT

★

FROM 1845 TO 1849

BORN: November 2, 1795

BIRTHPLACE: Mecklenburg County, N.C.

DIED: June 15, 1849

PARTY: Democrat

VICE PRESIDENT: George M. Dallas

FIRST LADY: Sarah Childress

CHILDREN: None

NICKNAME: Young Hickory

The first president to have his inauguration reported by telegraph.

During the 1840s, Americans were particularly eager to expand the territory of the United States. An almost unknown expansionist candidate, James Polk, proved the strength of this cause by defeating Henry Clay for president. After his election, Polk focused his political program on the nation's "manifest destiny" to rule the North American continent.

The phrase "manifest destiny" was first used by magazine editor John L. O'Sullivan in an 1845 article favoring the annexation of Texas. O'Sullivan used the phrase to refer to the popular belief that it was proper and inevitable for the United States government to control North America.

GOLD RUSH FEVER

MINERS HURRY TO CALIFORNIA

SAN FRANCISCO, February 28, 1849—The first ship carrying prospectors from the East arrived in port today, thirteen months after James W. Marshall discovered gold at Sutter's Fort.

These miners, nicknamed "forty-niners" after the year of their arrival, are the first of forty thousand expected to sail to California this year. As many are expected to come overland. As President Polk has pointed out, "Nearly the whole of the male population of the country [has] gone to the gold districts."

James Marshall made his discovery in January 1848 while building a sawmill for John Sutter on the American River near Sacramento. By August, when the *New York Herald* first printed news of his find in the East, there were already four thousand miners living in primitive huts on the hillside above the river.

"My eye was caught by something shining in the bottom of a ditch," Marshall wrote. "I reached my hand down and picked it up; it made my heart thump, for I was certain it was gold."

O'Sullivan wrote that it was "our manifest destiny to overspread the continent allotted by Providence for the free development of our yearly multiplying millions."

Like most of his fellow citizens, President Polk believed that it was the nation's manifest, or obvious, destiny to spread democracy from the Atlantic Ocean to the Pacific. It didn't matter that obstacles stood in the way—rivers, mountains, native peoples—because success was inevitable.

Polk believed that the United States was on a divine mission and that one day the nation would create an "empire for liberty" from New York all the way to California. He used the idea of manifest destiny to justify morally the taking of new territory. His policy was the more, the better.

THE OREGON TREATY

The annexation of Texas was completed during Tyler's last days in office, so Polk turned his immediate attention to the Oregon Territory. The southern border of Russian lands in Alaska had been set at 54°40' north latitude. The northern border of Spanish California was 42° north latitude, also known as the Forty-second Parallel. Between these two borders, from the Rocky Mountains to the Pacific, was Oregon.

Both the United States and Great Britain had longtime claims to the Oregon Territory. At first, Polk refused to negotiate with the British. After all, the Democrats' slogan during the 1844 election had been "Fifty-four Forty or Fight!"

As president, however, Polk soon agreed to a compromise. A new boundary was set at the Forty-ninth Parallel, granting to the United States present-day Oregon and Washington. Polk thus became the first president to govern a United

The Early Years

THE OLDEST OF TEN CHILDREN, JIMMY POLK WAS born on his family's farm in North Carolina. When he was ten years old, the Polks moved to central Tennessee, traveling more than five hundred miles over rough ground in a covered wagon. The family prospered there, eventually owning thousands of acres worked by more than fifty slaves.

Jimmy Polk was a sickly child, who did poorly in the rough-and-tumble games favored by boys on the frontier. He was particularly troubled by stones in his gallbladder. When he was seventeen, Polk underwent a dangerous and exceedingly painful operation to remove them. The surgeon gave him only liquor to ease the pain. It was not until the time of Polk's presidency that a doctor in Boston first used ether to put a patient to sleep during an operation.

★**THE FIRST LADY** Sarah Childress Polk was an exceptionally popular hostess in Washington because of her charm, liveliness, and intelligence. As first lady, she hosted the first Thanksgiving dinner at the White House and, being a devout Presbyterian, banned dancing and liquor at all White House events. For a woman of her time, she was unusually well educated, having attended the exclusive Moravian Female Academy in North Carolina. The president often consulted with her on policy matters.

★**AMELIA'S BLOOMERS** Women's clothing during the middle of the nineteenth century could be so confining that it sometimes felt like a cage. Underneath wide hoop skirts and stiff blouses, women wore tightly laced corsets that squeezed their waistlines down to an unnatural twenty inches. These corsets often did permanent damage to the liver and kidneys.

In 1851, a women's rights activist named Amelia Bloomer introduced a new, comfortable style of dress that featured loose-fitting trousers worn underneath a knee-length skirt. The pants quickly became known as "bloomers." Despite their practicality, bloomers so scandalized the public that women did not begin wearing trousers regularly for another century.

★The Seneca Falls Convention Many female leaders of the abolitionist movement also wanted to end the "domestic slavery" of women in the United States. In July 1848, a group of these pioneering feminists met in Seneca Falls, New York, where they founded the women's rights movement.

The delegates to the Seneca Falls convention prepared a list of ways in which women suffered discrimination and agreed to a number of resolutions for change. One of these resolutions declared that women deserved to vote, a right that nearly all nineteenth-century women were denied. Only four western states gave women the right to vote before 1900, the first of these being Wyoming in 1869.

★Frederick Douglass At the age of twenty, Frederick Douglass escaped slavery in Maryland. Seven years later, in 1845, he wrote an autobiography, which became one of the most important works of the antislavery movement. His *Narrative of the Life of Frederick Douglass, an American Slave* inspired thousands of abolitionists with its detailed description of the horrors of slavery. Later, during the Civil War, Douglass recruited blacks to serve in the Union army and advised President Abraham Lincoln on issues relating to African Americans.

States that extended from ocean to ocean.

After settling the dispute in the West, Polk's attention turned to Mexican territory in the Southwest and California, which became the focus of his expansionist policies. Polk would soon become the first president to act militarily in support of the cause of "manifest destiny."

The Mexican War

Although Texas formally joined the Union in 1845, the United States and Mexico continued to fight over Texas's southern border. Congress insisted on the Rio Grande, while the Mexicans refused to recognize Texas south of the Nueces River.

At first, Polk tried to bargain. He offered to pay Mexico for the disputed land and expressed his willingness to buy New Mexico and California as well. When the Mexicans, still angry over the annexation of Texas, refused him, Polk sent troops under General Zachary Taylor to the Rio Grande.

On April 25, 1846, Mexican troops engaged U.S. soldiers in a skirmish. In his message to Congress, Polk asked for a declaration of war because Mexican soldiers had "shed American blood upon the American soil." He got what he wanted. The vote was 40-2 in the Senate and 174-14 in the House.

The Mexican War became the central political event of the Polk presidency. His party rallied behind him, while the Whigs were divided. Those from the South and West favored the war, while northern abolitionists such as Representative Abraham Lincoln of Illinois believed the war was part of a secret plan to expand slavery into the Southwest.

The Mexican army vastly outnumbered U.S. forces in the area, but superior U.S. technology and strategy overcame this disadvantage. The revolver, invented in 1835 by Samuel Colt, proved to be a powerful weapon.

Although Colt's own business had failed in 1842, the success of his revolver during the Mexican War led to a large government contract. Colt used the money to build the world's largest private armory, where he made significant advances in the use of interchangeable parts.

The Mexican War ended in February 1848 with the signing of the Treaty of Guadalupe Hidalgo. Under its terms, Mexico ceded to the United States more than five hundred thousand square miles of territory, including New Mexico and California. In return, the U.S. paid Mexico fifteen million dollars and agreed to allow Mexicans living on the land to remain if they so chose. The Mexican Cession was the nation's largest acquisition of land since the Louisiana Purchase

RETIREMENT During the 1844 campaign, Polk had promised that, if elected, he would serve only one term as president. Although he was widely popular and could easily have won a second term, President Polk decided to keep his word. He announced that he would retire in 1849.

"I feel exceedingly relieved that I am now free from all public cares," Polk wrote in his diary on the last day of his term. "I am sure I shall be a happier man in my retirement...."

Although Polk expected to enjoy a peaceful retirement in Nashville, he fell ill during a goodwill tour of the South. Polk's condition grew progressively worse until he died just three months after the inauguration of his successor, Zachary Taylor.

BECAUSE OF POLK'S RETIREMENT, THE DEMOCRATS turned to Senator Lewis Cass of Michigan, who had sought the nomination four years earlier. The Whigs drafted General Zachary Taylor, a hero of the Mexican War.

Although the election of William Henry Harrison in 1840 had shown again that generals made popular candidates, Taylor was somewhat reluctant to accept the nomination. He had neither run for office before nor even voted in a presidential election. In the end, however, the general agreed to run and to accept the Whig platform.

The main issue of the campaign was the extension of slavery. Of particular concern was the Wilmot Proviso, a congressional bill that would have banned slavery in the territories acquired during the Mexican War. The Wilmot Proviso twice passed the House only to be defeated in the Senate.

Taylor refused to comment on the bill, but his ownership of more than one hundred slaves made his position appear clear. Cass openly opposed the measure, arguing that the decision should be left to the citizens of the territories.

Former president Martin Van Buren ran again as the candidate of the Free-Soil party. Although they were not yet willing to abolish slavery, the Free-Soilers opposed its spread and endorsed the Wilmot Proviso. Van Buren did well enough in his home state of New York to swing a very close election to Taylor, who won with less than half the popular vote. The presidential election of 1848 was the first in which the voting in every state took place on the same day.

ZACHARY TAYLOR

12TH PRESIDENT

★

FROM 1849 TO 1850

BORN: November 24, 1784

BIRTHPLACE: Orange County, Va.

DIED: July 9, 1850

PARTY: Whig

VICE PRESIDENT: Millard Fillmore

FIRST LADY: Margaret Mackall Smith

CHILDREN: Anne, Sarah, Octavia, Margaret, Mary, Richard

NICKNAME: Old Rough and Ready

Rode his horse sidesaddle into battle.

The most important issue confronting President Zachary Taylor when he took office was the extension of slavery to the territories of the Mexican Cession Southerners continued to see any limitation on slavery as a threat, while northern abolitionists refused to tolerate the spread of human bondage to any new states.

Taylor had been careful not to reveal his opinion during the campaign. Instead, he let people assume that, because he owned many slaves, he must support slavery. These same people were shocked to find out after the election that the new president intended to oppose the extension of slavery into the new territories.

Instead, Taylor proposed to Congress that two-thirds of the Mexican Cession be set aside for huge new states, New Mexico and California, and that both these states be free.

Southerners who had supported Taylor were furious at what seemed to be a change of heart. People in South Carolina were so upset that they again threatened to secede from the Union, as they had during the nullification controversy of 1833.

PRESIDENT TAYLOR DIES IN OFFICE

WASHINGTON, July 9, 1850—President Zachary Taylor died this evening in the White House from a digestive illness. During the last few days, the president's doctors had tried numerous cures, including the drug opium, but Taylor's condition steadily worsened.

Just before the end, the president said, "I am about to die. I expect the summons very soon. I have tried to discharge my duties faithfully. I regret nothing, but I am sorry that I am about to leave my friends."

Taylor began to feel sick five days ago when he spent Independence Day at the unfinished Washington Monument listening to hours of patriotic speeches in the July sun.

Returning to the White House, the president ate a bowl of cherries and drank a pitcher of milk. Later, he developed severe intestinal cramps. Taylor's doctors believe that either the cherries or the milk was contaminated with cholera, a stomach ailment caused by poor sanitation.

There was no simple solution, but statehood for California became a pressing matter once gold was found there. Because of the Gold Rush, the population of California grew from ten thousand to one hundred thousand in just a few years as a wilderness suddenly became one of the richest territories in the nation.

Moderates called for a compromise. Otherwise, the fighting over slavery might soon lead to civil war. To avoid this fearsome possibility, Senator Henry Clay proposed a set of resolutions in January 1850 that he hoped would satisfy both sides. His plan earned him the nickname The Great Compromiser.

Clay's compromise called for the admission of California as a free state, leaving the issue of slavery in the rest of the Mexican Cession to the people who lived there. Most northerners were happy to accept these points, but southerners needed a strong enticement if they were to agree.

FUGITIVE SLAVE ACT The enticement Clay offered was the Fugitive Slave Act. This notorious bill, the most controversial element of Clay's package, made it the responsibility of the federal government to return runaway slaves to their masters. At the time, escaped slaves were allowed to remain free if they could successfully reach the North.

Abolitionists were outraged by the Fugitive Slave Act. It gave southerners the right to pursue runaway slaves into the North, kidnap them, and take them back to the South without having to go through any legal process whatsoever.

While he lived, President Taylor opposed the Compromise of 1850 and made it known that he planned to veto any bill that would result in the spread of slavery. After his death, however, that decision passed to his vice president, Millard Fillmore.

Zachary Taylor was raised in Kentucky while that state was still at the edge of the western frontier. He grew up living under the constant threat of an Indian attack. Living in the wilderness, Taylor received only the most basic schooling, and he remained a poor speller all his life.

At the age of twenty-four, Taylor decided to make his career in the military. During his forty years as an army officer, he survived the War of 1812, the Black Hawk War, and the Mexican War. His victory over a much stronger Mexican army at Buena Vista in 1847 made him a national hero and an attractive candidate for president.

★**POSTAGE DUE** During the nineteenth century, presidential candidates never attended party conventions. Instead, they stayed at home and awaited the results. To notify Taylor of his nomination, the president of the Whig convention sent the general a letter. But he didn't put any postage on the envelope.

Sending mail without postage was a common practice then because it forced the recipient to pay the postage due. Taylor, however, received so many postage-due letters from admirers that he told his local post office to stop delivering them. As a result, the first notice of his nomination never arrived. Weeks later, the Whigs realized what had happened and sent another letter, postage paid.

★***UNCLE TOM'S CABIN*** In 1852, Harriet Beecher Stowe published *Uncle Tom's Cabin.* Ten thousand copies of this antislavery novel were sold in the first week, and three hundred thousand were sold in the first year after its publication.

The book helped to convince many people that slavery was indeed a terrible institution. It encouraged disobedience of the Fugitive Slave Act and stiffened opposition to the spread of slavery. But most northerners were still unwilling to abolish slavery in the South, where it was most entrenched.

Many years later, during the Civil War, President Abraham Lincoln invited Mrs. Stowe to the White House. Shaking her hand, Lincoln reportedly said, "So this is the little lady who made this big war!"

MILLARD FILLMORE

13TH PRESIDENT

★

FROM 1850 TO 1853

BORN: January 7, 1800

BIRTHPLACE: Cayuga County, N.Y.

DIED: March 8, 1874

PARTY: Whig

VICE PRESIDENT: None

FIRST LADY: Abigail Powers

CHILDREN: Millard, Mary

NICKNAME: Last of the Whigs

Established the first permanent library in the White House.

Millard Fillmore was chosen as the Whigs' vice-presidential candidate in 1848 because of his loyalty. Fillmore helped found the Whig party in western New York in the early 1830s. Later, as a congressman from the Buffalo area, he tried to prevent the split between President Tyler and the congressional Whigs. When the split came, however, Fillmore sided with the party.

Although Fillmore had a reputation for being a dull speaker and a mediocre leader, he was also known as an honorable man. He never smoked or drank, and he only gambled once in his life. At the age of fifteen, he had entered and won a turkey raffle at a New Year's Day party.

During the 1848 campaign, Fillmore was largely ignored. He didn't meet Zachary Taylor until after the election, and he was excluded from any role in shaping the cabinet.

PERRY OPENS JAPAN TO U.S. TRADE

EDO BAY, Japan, July 8, 1853—Commodore Matthew C. Perry sailed into Edo Bay today with two navy warships. Perry's mission is to force Japan, which has been isolated for two centuries, to establish diplomatic and trade relations with the United States.

The Japanese immediately ordered Perry to leave, but the commodore refused. He told the Japanese government that it must appoint a suitable official to receive the diplomatic letters he carried. Otherwise, he would deliver them by force.

Perry believes that the Japanese defenses are no match for U.S. naval power. He has long argued that only a strong show of force and a "resolute attitude" can win concessions from the Japanese.

Perry's expedition was first ordered by President Fillmore in March 1852. Since then, it has been publicized around the world. Officials in the State Department expect that, once Perry compels Japan to accept trade with the United States, other Western powers will force their way into Japanese ports.

Taylor might have found Fillmore useful in helping to promote his programs in Congress. But the president kept Fillmore so far from power that he even denied his vice president the courtesy of making political appointments in New York, Fillmore's home state. All that changed, of course, when Taylor died.

THE COMPROMISE OF 1850

President Taylor had strongly opposed the Compromise of 1850, especially those measures designed to appease the South. President Fillmore, however, supported the compromise. He thought it was the only way the nation could avoid civil war.

In September 1850, Fillmore signed the five separate bills written by Senator Henry Clay of Kentucky that together formed the compromise. By far the most controversial of these bills was the Fugitive Slave Act.

Most northerners resented this law, which gave slave owners the right to come north, kidnap blacks accused of being runaways, and take them back south without a trial or even a hearing. Abolitionist newspapers wrote often about cases of free blacks being enslaved by mistake or by unscrupulous slave hunters.

Antislavery activists tried to obstruct the law whenever possible. They offered free legal advice to escaped slaves and posted notices warning blacks of the kidnappers.

Fillmore thought that backing the Compromise of 1850 would improve his political position and perhaps earn him the 1852 Whig nomination for president. But he miscalculated. Northern Whigs refused to accept him because he had signed the Fugitive Slave Act. Denied the nomination, Fillmore retired.

Before he was made the Democratic nominee, Franklin Pierce had no intention of becoming president. The office, he had said, was "utterly repugnant to my tastes and wishes." Having retired from the Senate ten years earlier, neither he nor his wife had any desire to return to Washington, which they considered an unpleasant city.

The Democratic convention, which had been deadlocked, made Pierce its compromise choice on the forty-ninth ballot, rejecting four other candidates including Lewis Cass, James Buchanan, and Stephen Douglas. Although Pierce's name was not even mentioned before the thirty-fifth ballot, the party quickly rallied around him. "We Polked you in 1844; we'll Pierce you in 1852," the Democrats warned the Whigs.

Although Millard Fillmore was an incumbent president, he faced a tough battle for the nomination of his party. Because of his support for the Fugitive Slave Act, northern Whigs sided with yet another general, Mexican War hero and antislavery candidate Winfield Scott. Scott was nicknamed Old Fuss and Feathers because he always insisted that subordinates strictly follow military regulations.

Although Fillmore received the backing of the southern "cotton" Whigs, the northern "conscience" Whigs were able to gain the nomination for Scott on the fifty-third ballot. This division within the party, however, proved difficult for Scott to overcome during the campaign. With the backing of a united Democratic party, Pierce easily won the general election.

FRANKLIN PIERCE

14TH PRESIDENT

★

FROM 1853 TO 1857

BORN: November 23, 1804

BIRTHPLACE: Hillsborough, N.H.

DIED: October 8, 1869

PARTY: Democrat

VICE PRESIDENT: William R. King

FIRST LADY: Jane Means Appleton

CHILDREN: Franklin, Frank Robert, Benjamin

NICKNAME: Handsome Frank

Always insisted that grace be said before a meal.

Franklin Pierce was famous throughout his native New Hampshire as a brilliant courtroom lawyer. People from all over would flock to the courthouse to hear his trial speeches. Pierce was such an experienced speaker that he was able to deliver his inaugural address from memory.

In this address, Pierce stated his belief that owning slaves was a legal right guaranteed by the Constitution. However, he feared that fanatics on both sides, the proslavery South and the antislavery, abolitionist North, threatened the Union.

At his inauguration, Pierce's tone was mournful. Two months earlier, his only surviving son, Bennie, had been killed in a railroad accident. The Pierces never recovered from the loss. Two full years passed before First

TUBMAN LEADS PARENTS TO FREEDOM ALONG UNDERGROUND RAILROAD

DORCHESTER COUNTY, Maryland, June 1857—The runaway slave Harriet Tubman returned to Maryland this month to free her parents, who had remained slaves after their daughter's escape in 1849.

Tubman's journey was one of nineteen she has made to help slaves escape to the North. She has been one of the "conductors" along the Underground Railroad. The "stations" on this railroad are worked by sympathetic whites, many of them Quakers. Almost all of the conductors are black, however.

The escaped slaves move from station to station at night under the cloak of darkness. It has been estimated that more than fifty thousand slaves have traveled to freedom along the Underground Railroad. Tubman has personally led as many as three hundred people to safety.

She has been called the Moses of Her People, after the Hebrew leader who led the Jews out of bondage in ancient Egypt. Rewards for Tubman's capture have reached as high as forty thousand dollars.

Lady Jane Pierce felt comfortable appearing in public, and the White House remained a gloomy place throughout Pierce's term.

Pierce was careful to balance northern and southern interests in his cabinet. For secretary of state, the president appointed William Marcy of New York. For secretary of war, he picked a senator from Mississippi, Jefferson Davis. Pierce was so successful in his selections that he became the first president to complete his term in office without making a single change in his cabinet.

THE GADSDEN PURCHASE

During Pierce's administration, the United States continued to expand. In 1853, the U.S. minister to Mexico, James Gadsden, negotiated the ten-million-dollar purchase of land that is now in Arizona and New Mexico. The land lay in the path of a proposed new transcontinental railroad. With the addition of these 29,644 square miles, mapmakers could now draw a map of the United States showing the modern outline of the forty-eight continental states.

Pierce also wanted to acquire Cuba, the Spanish island about one hundred miles south of Florida. Secretary of State Marcy instructed the U.S. minister to Spain, Pierre Soulé, to open negotiations for the purchase of Cuba. In the meantime, at Marcy's suggestion, Soulé met in Ostend, Belgium, with the U.S. ministers to Britain and France to plan a negotiating strategy.

The result was the secret Ostend Manifesto of 1854. This document proposed offering up to $120 million for Cuba. If the Spanish refused to sell even at that price, the ministers recommended taking the island by force.

When the Ostend Manifesto was printed in the *New York Herald,* the fact that Pierce was even considering

The Early Years

FRANKLIN PIERCE GREW UP IN HILLSBOROUGH, New Hampshire, during the War of 1812. As a boy, he loved to listen to the stories of battle told by his older brothers who were serving in the army. These stories inspired Pierce to become a soldier himself.

When the Mexican War broke out in 1846, Pierce had already served a number of terms in the House and Senate. Yet despite his background, he enlisted as a private in the army's volunteer corps. Within a year, he was given a commission as a colonel in the regular army. And a month after that, he was promoted to brigadier general.

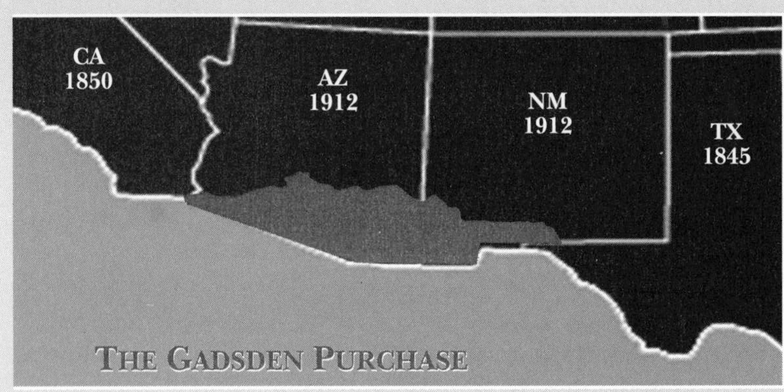

THE GADSDEN PURCHASE

★**LEVI'S** In 1850, a German immigrant named Levi Strauss traveled to San Francisco aboard a ship filled with fortune-seekers. They were just a few of the hundred thousand people drawn to California by the Gold Rush.

Strauss, who planned to open a dry goods store, brought with him a supply of blue canvas called denim. He planned to sell the material for tents, but when he got to San Francisco he found that what the miners really needed were sturdy work clothes. Strauss promptly stitched his denim into pants that later became famous as blue jeans.

★**RAILROADS** The 1850s were a boom time for railroad building in the United States. Workers laid more than twenty-one thousand miles of track. These new lines opened up the western wilderness and made the railroads the country's first billion-dollar industry.

Americans were thrilled by this display of power, speed, and national ingenuity. Writers and poets wrote in awe of the "iron horse" that snorted steam and smoke. "Railroad iron is a magician's rod," wrote Ralph Waldo Emerson. Not everyone appreciated the railroads, however. "I will not have my eyes put out and my ears spoiled by its smoke and steam and hissing," snarled Henry David Thoreau.

★**SLAVE SONGS** Slaves in the South often sang work songs and spirituals to help them get through the day. Slave owners liked to pretend that the slaves sang because they were happy.

In their songs, slaves combined elements of African and American folk songs. Some songs like "Nobody Knows the Trouble I've Seen" told the story of the slaves' difficult lives, while others told of happier times ahead. Runaway slaves often sang "Steal Away" and "O Freedom, O Freedom, O Freedom Over Me!" as they made their way north. The origins of jazz and blues lie in these moving songs.

★**WHALING** Herman Melville's *Moby Dick* told the story of an epic hunt for a great white whale. The novel was published in 1851, when the whaling industry was at its height. Whale fat, called blubber, was particularly prized for its many industrial uses.

According to the whalers, who sailed out of southern New England, the most dangerous part of the hunt was the "Nantucket sleigh ride." During this final operation, crewmen in a small boat would tie their craft to the struggling whale while a mate closed in with his harpoon for the kill.

war over Cuba caused an uproar. Northern congressmen in particular suspected that the president's hidden interest in Cuba was its slaves. Having been exposed, Pierce and Marcy were forced to abandon the Ostend Manifesto and give up their plans for Cuba.

THE KANSAS-NEBRASKA ACT

At the same time, the federal government was considering plans to build the first transcontinental railroad. Senator Stephen Douglas of Illinois was working hard to make sure that the railroad took a northerly route through his home state. He knew that wherever the railroad went, business and success would follow.

Southerners, of course, wanted the railroad to pass through their region, but they were outnumbered in Congress. To gain some more power, members of Congress from the southern states announced that they would not support a railroad through any territory that did not allow slavery.

Anxious to see the northern railroad approved, Stephen Douglas suggested a compromise that became the Kansas-Nebraska Act. Douglas's bill proposed the division of the Nebraska Territory through which the railroad would run. The residents of the two resulting territories, Kansas and Nebraska, would then decide for themselves whether or not to permit slavery.

Douglas's plan was controversial for many reasons. For one, it went against the Missouri Compromise of 1820, which had outlawed slavery north of latitude 36°30'. Both Kansas and Nebraska were north of that line. And while it was clear that Nebraska would prohibit slavery, Kansas, which bordered on slaveholding Missouri, seemed up for grabs.

BLEEDING KANSAS With Pierce's backing, the Kansas-Nebraska Act passed Congress, but it caused more problems than it solved. Fanatical abolitionists from New England poured into Kansas, hoping to win control of the territorial government. At the same time, gangs of proslavery thugs called Border Ruffians moved up from Missouri to challenge them.

During March 1855, about four thousand Missourians crossed the border and voted illegally in Kansas, electing a proslavery government. The territorial governor tried to disqualify some of the people who were elected, but President Pierce quickly ordered him back to Washington.

Feeling they had been denied a fair vote, the Free-Soilers turned to violence, and civil war broke out in Kansas. More than two hundred people were killed in the territory that became known as Bleeding Kansas.

Nor was the violence of 1856 limited to Kansas. That May, Charles Sumner of Massachusetts was attacked on the Senate floor by Representative Preston Brooks of South Carolina. Senator Sumner had earlier delivered a nasty, dramatic speech directed against supporters of slavery. When Brooks heard about the speech, he rushed onto the Senate floor and beat Sumner with a cane. Sumner collapsed on the floor, his head split open and bleeding. It took Sumner more than three years to recover.

Two days after Senator Sumner's beating, a radical abolitionist named John Brown organized a raid against his proslavery neighbors near Pottawatomie Creek, Kansas. The attack was brutal. Leading a group of seven fanatics, including his four sons, Brown broke into a number of cabins and hacked five men to death.

CAMPAIGN 1856

By the time the 1856 election came around, the country had lost confidence in Franklin Pierce. His handling of Bleeding Kansas made it clear that he could not win reelection, and Pierce himself had no interest in staying on. To replace Pierce, the Democrats chose James Buchanan. As the president's minister to Great Britain, Buchanan had avoided the many controversies that plagued Pierce's administration.

Buchanan thought slavery was immoral and even acted against it privately, but he remained acceptable to southern Democrats because he opposed interfering in the affairs of the South. His position was important because slavery wasn't simply one campaign issue. It was the only campaign issue.

Running against Buchanan was John C. Frémont of California, the first presidential candidate of the new Republican party. The Republicans had specifically come together to oppose the spread of slavery. Frémont was known as the Pathfinder of the West, because he had led surveying expeditions that helped map the growing nation.

The Republican slogan was "Free Speech, Free Press, Free Soil, Free Men, Frémont, and Victory!" The party warned that compromising with southern slaveholders increased the chances of civil war. The Democrats responded that the Republicans were too radical. They claimed that a vote for Buchanan was a vote for national stability. Although Frémont carried much of the North, the Democrats' broad national support gave Buchanan the victory.

JAMES BUCHANAN

15TH PRESIDENT
★
FROM 1857 TO 1861

BORN: April 23, 1791
BIRTHPLACE: Cove Gap, Pa.
DIED: June 1, 1868
PARTY: Democrat
VICE PRESIDENT: John C. Breckinridge
FIRST LADY: None
CHILDREN: None
NICKNAME: Ten-Cent Jimmy

The first and only bachelor president.

James Buchanan won the election of 1856 by carrying the South and taking a few key northern states. Although he was a northerner and personally opposed slavery, Buchanan nevertheless favored the interests of the South.

As Buchanan took office in 1857, the most important task facing him was the prevention of civil war. People considered the new president to be one of the most capable and experienced politicians in the country, so there was great anticipation. Everyone wondered what the Buchanan administration would do to resolve the issue of slavery, particularly with regard to its extension into the new territories.

After devouring twelve hundred gallons of ice cream, guests at Buchanan's inauguration settled down to listen to the inaugural address.

SUPREME COURT RULES IN DRED SCOTT CASE

WASHINGTON, March 6, 1857—In a 7-2 decision handed down today, the Supreme Court ruled that the slave Dred Scott cannot sue for his freedom because he is property and not a citizen. Chief Justice Roger B. Taney wrote in his opinion that Scott had "no rights which any white man was bound to respect."

The court also ruled that the Missouri Compromise of 1820 was unconstitutional, because Congress had no power to outlaw slavery in the territories. Only a state can exclude slavery from its midst, the court ruled.

People in the South were delighted by the decision, while antislavery forces in the North were outraged. "If the people obey this decision, they disobey God," one abolitionist newspaper editor wrote.

Dred Scott was a slave from Missouri who moved with his master's family to Illinois, a free state. His case, which was argued by leading antislavery lawyers, claimed that living in a free state made him free.

Buchanan stood up to his six-foot height, spread his broad shoulders apart, and announced his belief that the conflict over slavery had a clear and simple solution.

Buchanan, trained as a lawyer, was known for his devotion to reason and the law. The argument he made in his speech was both legal and logical. He pointed out that few Americans disputed the constitutionality of slavery in the southern states, where it had always existed. If these states could legally permit slavery within their borders, Buchanan reasoned, how could the federal government deny new states the same privilege? Letting new territories decide the slavery issue for themselves was therefore the proper and most reasonable course.

Just two days after Buchanan took office, the Supreme Court handed down its decision in the Dred Scott case, ruling that slaves were legally property and not citizens. The court thus confirmed Buchanan's legal view that ownership of slaves was a constitutional right that the federal government could not limit or deny.

Buchanan's argument made legal sense, but it tragically underestimated the growing opposition to slavery on moral grounds. Abolitionists believed slavery was always wrong and deserved to be outlawed everywhere.

THE KANSAS QUESTION

Meanwhile, the nation's attention remained focused on Bleeding Kansas, which was still seeking statehood. One of Buchanan's early actions as president was to appoint Robert Walker of Mississippi as the territorial governor there. Walker put the weight of the territorial government behind the proslavery forces.

At a state constitutional convention held in Lecompton in October 1857, proslavery delegates

The Early Years

JAMES BUCHANAN WAS BORN IN A LOG CABIN A FEW miles outside Mercersburg, Pennsylvania. When he was five years old, his family moved into the town of Mercersburg, where his father, an Irish immigrant, made a living as a merchant and farmer.

Buchanan attended Dickinson College, where he was considered a discipline problem. After graduation, he became a lawyer. When his fiancée died in 1819, he entered politics in earnest. Buchanan served in Congress for ten years, first as a Federalist, then as a Jacksonian Democrat. Later he became James Polk's secretary of state and Franklin Pierce's minister to Great Britain, during which time he helped write the Ostend Manifesto.

★**BACHELOR PRESIDENT** Buchanan was the only president to remain unmarried his entire life. Once, when he was twenty-eight, Buchanan had been engaged to Anne Coleman, whose father was one of the wealthiest men in Pennsylvania. After a fight, however, she broke off the engagement, and a few months later she died, possibly of suicide.

Rumors circulated that she broke off the engagement because she thought Buchanan was after her money. But Buchanan was doing quite well then as a lawyer and had about three hundred thousand dollars.

Buchanan never considered marrying again. During his term as president, his orphaned niece, Harriet Lane, served as the official White House hostess.

★**THE MODERN KITCHEN** Throughout her life, Catharine Esther Beecher lectured and wrote about the place of women in American society. She believed strongly that a woman's place was in the home. Along with her famous sister, Harriet Beecher Stowe, she wrote *The American Woman's Home.*

This manual of household advice described the sisters' design for a new type of kitchen. Their "modern" kitchen included separate areas for the sink and the stove as well as two windows for proper ventilation. The Beechers also came up with the idea for built-in cabinets and drawers. Some of their innovations are still used in kitchens today.

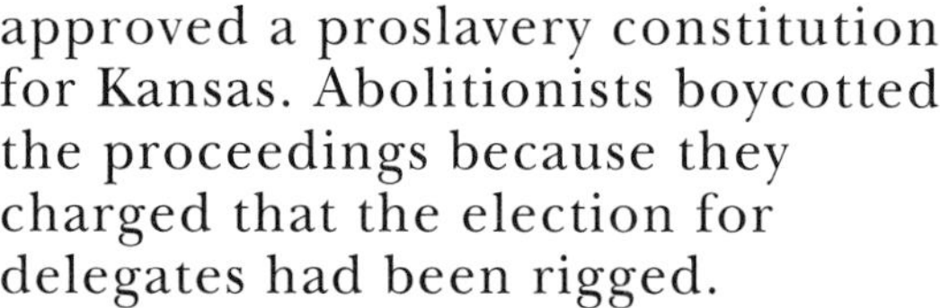

★**SOJOURNER TRUTH** In 1843, the former slave Isabella Van Wagener changed her name to Sojourner Truth and began traveling across the country. She spoke about the cause of freedom wherever she could, often in churches and on village streets.

Sojourner Truth's passionate and persuasive speeches against slavery and for the rights of women inspired thousands to give their support to these causes. In 1864, President Lincoln received her at the White House. She told Lincoln that he was the best president the country ever had but admitted that she had not heard of him before he was nominated. "I had heard of you many times before that," Lincoln told her.

★**THE PONY EXPRESS** Freight-hauler William H. Russell wanted to prove that mail could be carried promptly and profitably across the as-yet-unsettled American West. The Pony Express service that he began in April 1860 showed at least that mail could be delivered promptly.

Russell developed a relay system using lightweight teenage boys. Riding the fastest horses available, they raced from station to station. The boys changed horses six to eight times each before passing on the mail to the next rider. Using this system, Russell was able to deliver mail from St. Joseph, Missouri, to San Francisco—a distance of nearly two thousand miles—in just ten days. The Pony Express lost a huge amount of money, however, and was put out of business by the completion of the first transcontinental telegraph in October 1861.

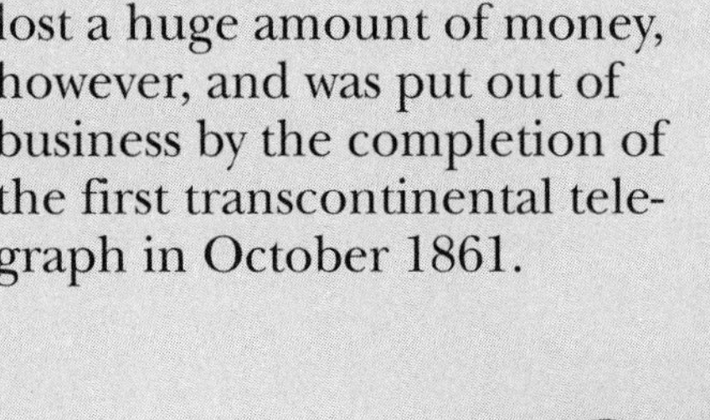

approved a proslavery constitution for Kansas. Abolitionists boycotted the proceedings because they charged that the election for delegates had been rigged.

Ignoring the boycott, Buchanan supported the Lecompton Constitution and urged Congress to admit Kansas as a slave state. Stephen Douglas of Illinois led the opposition to Buchanan in the Senate. Douglas insisted that the people of Kansas be allowed to vote up or down on the Lecompton Constitution before the Congress accepted it.

In 1858, Kansans voted in a statewide referendum and rejected the proslavery constitution by a wide margin. Buchanan didn't give up. He convinced Congress to order a second referendum. But the results were the same. By the time Kansas was finally admitted to the Union as a free state in January 1861, the nation was on the brink of civil war.

THE LINCOLN-DOUGLAS DEBATES

In 1858, Abraham Lincoln of Illinois ran for the U.S. Senate as a Republican. His opponent was the short but feisty Democratic incumbent, Stephen A. Douglas, whose nickname was the Little Giant.

Their Senate campaign, covered by the national press, featured seven eloquent debates. During one of these debates, Lincoln forced Douglas to admit that he believed a territory could outlaw slavery within its borders. This position contradicted the *Dred Scott* decision, which held that owning slaves was a constitutional right.

Douglas's answer didn't stop him from defeating Lincoln in Illinois, but it did hurt his popularity in the South. Losing southern support made it nearly impossible for him to win the Democratic nomination for president in 1860.

Despite his loss in the Senate race, Lincoln's performance in the debates earned him national fame. "A house divided against itself cannot stand," Lincoln said, using a well-known phrase from the Bible to describe the conflict between North and South over slavery.

Events in Kansas had shown that Americans on both sides were willing to shed blood over slavery. In 1859, the fanatical white abolitionist John Brown developed a daring plan. Leading a small group of raiders, he would seize the federal arsenal at Harpers Ferry, Virginia, and use the weapons he captured there to start a slave rebellion.

On October 16, 1859, Brown and twenty-one of his followers captured the arsenal but were unable to escape. The townspeople of Harpers Ferry bottled up the raiders until a company of marines led by Colonel Robert E. Lee arrived two days later. The marines captured Brown and put him on trial for treason. He was hanged on December 2.

SECESSION During the last frantic months of his failed presidency, Buchanan tried to remain friendly to the South while preserving the Union. He knew that secession, or withdrawal from the Union, was illegal, but he also feared that resisting the South would surely lead to civil war. In the end, he did nothing to stop the inevitable flow of events.

Southern states considered Lincoln's victory in the election of 1860 to be an outrage. Before Buchanan left office, seven of their number seceded from the Union. Alabama, Georgia, Florida, Louisiana, Mississippi, South Carolina, and Texas formed the Confederate States of America, electing Jefferson Davis as their president in February 1861.

THE PRESIDENTIAL CAMPAIGN OF 1860 WAS THE most fateful in U.S. history. John Brown's 1859 attempt to start a slave revolt at Harpers Ferry had brought tensions to the breaking point. The result of the upcoming election might mean the difference between war and reconciliation.

Campaign 1860

Meeting in Charleston, South Carolina, the governing Democratic party finally split over the issue of slavery. Southern Democrats were so outraged by front-runner Stephen Douglas's refusal to include a proslavery plank in the party platform that they walked out of the convention. Two months later, they held their own convention and nominated Vice President John C. Breckinridge of Kentucky to represent their views. The northern Democrats stuck with Douglas.

The young Republican party chose Abraham Lincoln over William H. Seward of New York because of Lincoln's strength in the hotly contested states of Pennsylvania and Indiana. Although the Republicans objected to the expansion of slavery, they were willing to permit slavery where it already existed. Still, the prospect of a Republican president scared southerners. They threatened to secede if Lincoln won the election.

In the South, Breckinridge competed for votes with the nominee of the new Constitutional Union party, John Bell, a moderate from Tennessee. Meanwhile, in the North, Lincoln and Douglas were the only serious candidates. When all the votes were counted, Lincoln won the presidency with nearly two-thirds of the electoral vote but only forty percent of the popular vote.

ABRAHAM LINCOLN

16TH PRESIDENT

★

FROM 1861 TO 1865

BORN: February 12, 1809

BIRTHPLACE: Hardin County, Ky.

DIED: April 15, 1865

PARTY: Republican

VICE PRESIDENTS: Hannibal Hamlin, Andrew Johnson

FIRST LADY: Mary Todd

CHILDREN: Robert, Edward, William, Thomas (Tad)

NICKNAME: Honest Abe

The first president to wear a beard while in office.

CIVIL WAR!

REBELS TAKE FORT SUMTER

CHARLESTON, S.C., April 13, 1861—Major Robert Anderson, commander of the federal troops stationed in Charleston harbor, surrendered Fort Sumter today after a thirty-four-hour bombardment by Confederate artillery. Anderson waited until he was out of ammunition and the fort was in flames before running down the U.S. flag. Remarkably, no one died during the attack, which began at 4:30 A.M. yesterday.

After taking office a month ago, President Lincoln informed the Confederacy that he intended to resupply Fort Sumter peacefully with food only. This decision placed the burden of whether or not to begin a war on the Confederate authorities. If the rebels attacked a peaceful mission bringing food, the responsibility for firing the first shot would be theirs.

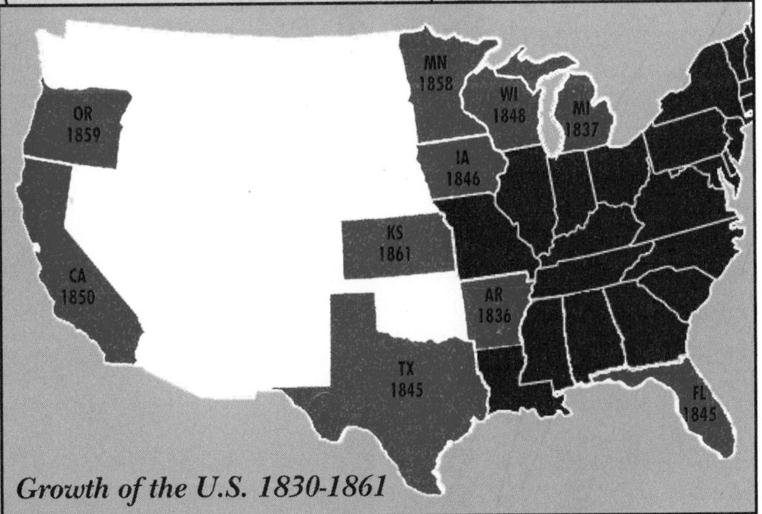

Growth of the U.S. 1830-1861

As Lincoln prepared for his March inaugural, events were already overtaking him. In the four months since his election, seven states had seceded and formed the Confederate States of America.

Before he took office, Lincoln said there would be "no bloodshed unless it is forced upon the government." But he also announced that he intended to keep control of all federal property in the South. He made it clear that his primary concern was the preservation of the Union, not the abolition of slavery.

The president responded to the Confederate attack on Fort Sumter by ordering the navy to blockade southern ports. The point of the blockade was to halt the exportation of cotton, the South's cash crop. The blockade also prevented the agricultural South from importing manufactured items such as guns and clothing, which it could not produce for itself. Meanwhile, the beginning of the war caused four more reluctant states to join the Confederacy.

Because they expected a speedy victory, most northerners supported Lincoln's war effort enthusiastically. The song "We are Coming, Father Abraham" was sung at Union army rallies that attracted thousands of recruits. At first, blacks were excluded from the army. But as the years passed, and the war took an unexpected turn for the worse, two hundred thousand blacks were eventually allowed to join the fight.

The Confederacy was no less successful in raising an army. Regional pride was particularly strong south of the Mason and Dixon Line, and volunteers flocked to enlist in the rebel army.

Fathers and sons went off to battle together as women on both sides took over family farms and businesses. Other women raised money, recruited soldiers, and served as nurses, spies, and scouts.

BULL RUN AND ANTIETAM The first real battle of the Civil War was fought in July 1861 on the banks of a creek called Bull Run in northeastern Virginia, not far from Washington, D.C.

Because the battlefield was so close to the capital, a number of congressmen rode out to Bull Run in carriages to see for themselves the defeat of the Confederacy and the end of the rebellion. Many brought picnic lunches with them.

They lost their appetites when Confederate general Thomas "Stonewall" Jackson broke the Union attack and sent the federal troops scurrying back to Washington. The battle of Bull Run taught the Union that victory would not come as easily as many people thought.

The Early Years

LINCOLN WAS BORN IN A LOG CABIN IN KENTUCKY. The cabin's one room had a dirt floor. When Abe was seven, his family moved farther west to Indiana. About Indiana, Lincoln later wrote, "It was a wild region, with many bears and other wild animals still in the woods."

Living on what was then the frontier, Lincoln had barely a year of schoolhouse education. Unlike his father, however, he did learn to read and write. Among his favorite books was Parson Weems's often-mythical biography of George Washington.

Lincoln worked as a rail-splitter turning logs into fence rails, a ferryboat captain, a clerk in a general store, and a postmaster before becoming one of the best trial lawyers in Illinois. He never lost his strong frontier accent, however. Speaking in a high voice, Lincoln would pronounce *get* as *git* and *there* as *thar*.

★THE FIRST LADY Mary Lincoln was not well-liked in Washington. Although she had been charming and witty as a young woman, her mental health, which had always been fragile, was placed under severe stress by events in the White House.

Because she came from a southern family, four of her brothers joined the Confederate army, and some congressmen accused her of being a Confederate spy. The charge upset her, but it was the death of her twelve-year-old son Willie in 1862 that finally crushed Mary Lincoln. She became noticeably disturbed and went on wild shopping sprees, buying three hundred pairs of gloves in one four-month period. Her husband's assassination sickened her further, and she was eventually admitted to an insane asylum.

★**MATHEW BRADY** Mathew Brady was the most famous photographer in the country. He specialized in portraits of famous people, especially presidents. His photographs of Lincoln are among the most memorable images of the nineteenth century.

To document the Civil War, Brady hired twenty photographers and sent them all over the country, especially to the battlefields. When pictures of the dead at Antietam first arrived at Brady's New York studio, *The New York Times* reported that "Mr. Brady has done something to bring home to us the terrible reality and earnestness of war. If he has not brought bodies and laid them on our dooryards and along the streets, he has done something very like it...."

★**HOMESTEADING** From the time of Washington, government officials assumed that public lands should be sold off to raise money. During the 1830s, however, the homesteading movement arose to demand that public lands in the West be given free to Americans willing to farm them.

In 1862, President Lincoln signed the Homestead Act, which granted 160 acres of public land free to anybody willing to farm it for at least five years. During the next forty years, homesteaders claimed more than eighty million acres of public land in the West.

Lincoln responded quickly to Bull Run. Making the first of several changes in command, he appointed George B. McClellan as commander-in-chief of the Army of the Potomac.

McClellan was a cautious general. His army was stronger and better supplied than the Confederates, but he moved slowly. During the campaign of 1861, the Confederates boldly outmaneuvered him and beat him on several occasions. In January 1862, Lincoln became worried that "delay is killing us."

During the summer of 1862, McClellan led the Peninsular Campaign against the Confederate capital of Richmond. Once again the general had a superior force, but his constant hesitation allowed Robert E. Lee to beat him back. Lee won a second victory at Bull Run in August and then marched north, crossing the border into the Union state of Maryland.

One witness called Lee's poorly supplied invasion force "the dirtiest men I ever saw, a most ragged, lean, and hungry set of wolves." At the battle of Antietam, McClellan and Lee fought to a standstill. More than twenty thousand soldiers were killed or wounded in the single day of fighting, the bloodiest day of the war. Afterward, Lee retreated back across the Potomac River. McClellan pursued the Confederates, but not quickly enough to catch them.

THE EMANCIPATION PROCLAMATION

Antietam, which could only loosely be called a Union victory, gave President Lincoln the opportunity he needed to announce his Emancipation Proclamation. This executive order formally freed the slaves in areas of rebellion—but not those in Union slave states, such as Maryland, or in areas recaptured by the Union. It also changed the government's war aim from preservation of the Union to the abolition of slavery.

After Antietam, Lincoln dismissed McClellan and replaced him with Ambrose Burnside, who protested his own appointment. Burnside turned out to be right. A month after taking command of the Union army, he suffered a disastrous defeat at Fredericksburg that prompted Lincoln to replace him immediately with Joseph Hooker.

Hooker, too, performed poorly and resigned soon after losing the battle of Chancellorsville in May 1863. Lincoln replaced Hooker with General George Meade. Meanwhile, Lee's army was marching north again, this time into Pennsylvania.

Just three days after Meade's appointment—on July 1, 1863—he and Lee met at Gettysburg. For the next seventy-two hours, their armies fought with the outcome of the war hanging in the balance. On July 3, the failure of George Pickett's charge against Union-held Cemetery Ridge sealed the Union victory. By the time Lee retreated south, he had lost more than twenty thousand men, almost a third of his entire command. The Union dead and wounded numbered twenty-three thousand.

THE GETTYSBURG ADDRESS

On November 19, Lincoln traveled to Gettysburg for the dedication of a battlefield cemetery there. The speech he gave, which became known as the Gettysburg Address, was just 272 words long. It didn't mention slavery, the battle, or even the Union army. But its remarkable language captured the reasons why the war was being fought. After Lincoln finished, the crowd burst into applause.

In March 1864, Lincoln turned over command of the Union forces to General Ulysses S. Grant. During

CAMPAIGN ★ 1864

As the campaign of 1864 got under way, Lincoln was in serious political trouble. The end of the Civil War was not yet in sight, and fear about how it would turn out hurt the president's chances for reelection. Although he was renominated without opposition, a number of Republican party leaders said publicly that he could not win the general election.

Lincoln ran in 1864 as the candidate of the National Union party. The Republicans had temporarily adopted that name in order to include within their party southern Democrats who had remained loyal to the Union. To emphasize this political marriage, Lincoln dropped Vice President Hannibal Hamlin from the ticket and replaced him with Andrew Johnson, the military governor of Tennessee and one of the leading spokesmen for the Homestead Movement.

To oppose Lincoln, the northern Democrats nominated General George B. McClellan, whom Lincoln had dismissed as commander of the Union army in 1862. McClellan blamed Lincoln for the poor performance of Union troops and called for both an immediate cease-fire and a negotiated peace treaty with the South.

In July and August, McClellan appeared to be leading the race. But Sherman's capture of Atlanta in September demonstrated that the war was now going very well for the Union. McClellan tried to back away from his call for a cease-fire, but the public's renewed confidence in Lincoln carried the president to an easy victory.

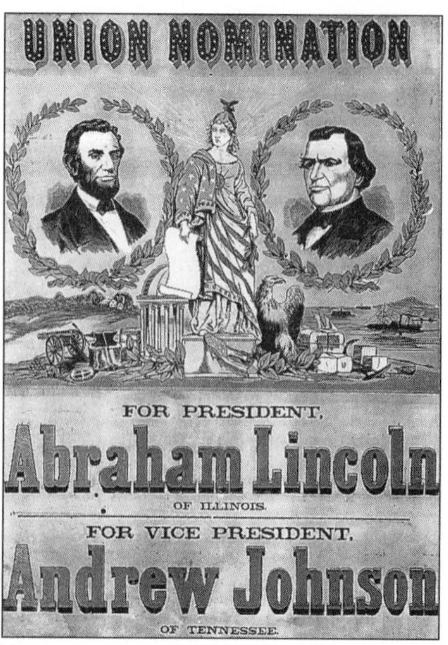

President Lincoln with his son Tad.

1862 and 1863, Grant had captured important Confederate forts in Tennessee and led Union troops in the successful siege of Vicksburg, Mississippi. Now he turned his attention to Lee and Richmond. Grant's victories had been costly, bloody ones, but Lincoln was willing to tolerate the high casualty rates. "I cannot spare this man," Lincoln said of Grant. "He fights."

THE END OF THE CIVIL WAR

Meanwhile, General William Tecumseh Sherman began his March to the Sea through Georgia. Along the way, Sherman's unstoppable army of sixty thousand soldiers destroyed the South's ability to wage war. Sherman systematically smashed railroads, factories, and plantations. Atlanta was burned.

In early 1865, Sherman's army turned north to join Grant's forces surrounding Richmond, which fell on April 3. Six days later, Robert E. Lee surrendered to Grant at Appomattox Court House, Virginia. Disease, desertion, and the Union's relentless attacks had finally brought the proud Confederacy to its knees.

LINCOLN ASSASSINATED

WASHINGTON, April 15, 1865—President Lincoln died this morning after being shot last night during a performance of the comedy *Our American Cousin* at Ford's Theater. His assassin, the actor John Wilkes Booth, escaped and is still at large.

A fanatical Confederate sympathizer, Booth arrived at the empty theater about 6:00 P.M. when he tampered with the door to the presidential box. He returned during the play's third act and, finding the president unguarded, shot him through the back of the head.

After firing his single-shot Derringer, Booth jumped down to the stage and landed awkwardly, breaking his leg. Although hobbled, he was still able to reach his horse in the alley and escape.

The dying president was carried to the bedroom of a boardinghouse across the street. Because of his six-foot, four-inch height, Lincoln was placed diagonally across the bed. When the president died just after seven o'clock this morning, Secretary of War Edwin Stanton said, "Now he belongs to the ages."

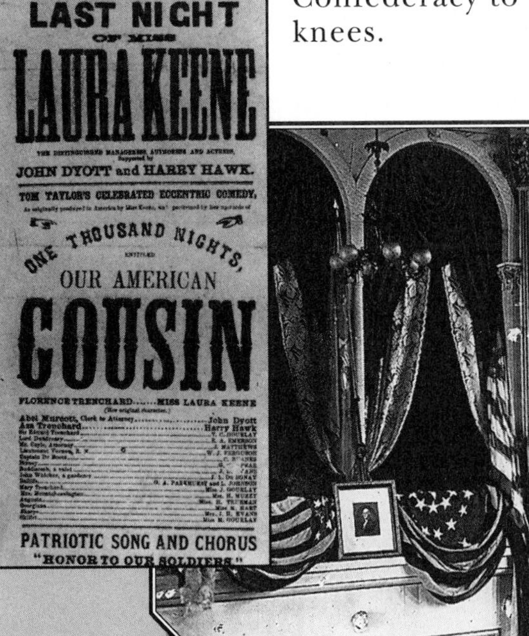

Born: December 29, 1808

Birthplace: Raleigh, N.C.

Died: July 31, 1875

Party: National Union

Vice President: None

First Lady: Eliza McCardle

Children: Martha, Charles, Mary, Robert, Andrew

Nickname: Tennessee Tailor

Andrew Johnson

17th President

★

From 1865 to 1869

His wife taught him to read and write.

The news of Abraham Lincoln's assassination shocked every American, none more so than Andrew Johnson. Less than three hours after the president's death, the one-time tailor's apprentice was sworn in as Lincoln's successor. He had been vice president for only forty-one days.

Lincoln had won the Civil War for the Union. Now it was Johnson's turn to tackle the equally enormous task of making the peace. Johnson would have to reunite a land in which neighbor had fought against neighbor, friend against friend, and brother against brother.

Johnson shared Lincoln's view that the country should forgive, forget, and welcome back the rebels. His plan was a simple one. Under the direction of temporary federal governors, each Confederate state would draft a new constitution abolishing slavery and renouncing secession. After that, the states would be free to govern themselves as before. Johnson

JOHNSON ESCAPES CONVICTION IN IMPEACHMENT TRIAL

WASHINGTON, May 16, 1868—The Senate voted today on the first of the eleven articles of impeachment brought by the House of Representatives against President Andrew Johnson. The final count was 35-19, one vote short of the two-thirds majority necessary for conviction.

President Johnson owes his acquittal to seven moderate Republican senators who chose to ignore party loyalty and instead voted with the twelve Democrats.

The House approved the impeachment articles against President Johnson on February 24. The principal charges were related to the president's dismissal of Secretary of War Edwin Stanton. Stanton's firing violated the Tenure of Office Act, which had been passed over Johnson's veto.

The House vote of 126-47 made Johnson the first president ever to suffer the indignity of impeachment. According to the Constitution, a president impeached by the House is then tried before the Senate. If convicted by the Senate, the president is removed from office.

The Early Years

Like Lincoln, Johnson began his life as one of the frontier poor. His father, Jacob, died when Andy was just three years old. Growing up without a father meant that Johnson had to work from a very early age.

When he was twelve years old, he and his brother were apprenticed to a tailor named Selby, becoming what were then known as "bound boys." They worked for room and board while they learned the trade of tailoring. Andrew Johnson received his first schooling while working for Selby, who paid people to read aloud to the apprentices as they sewed.

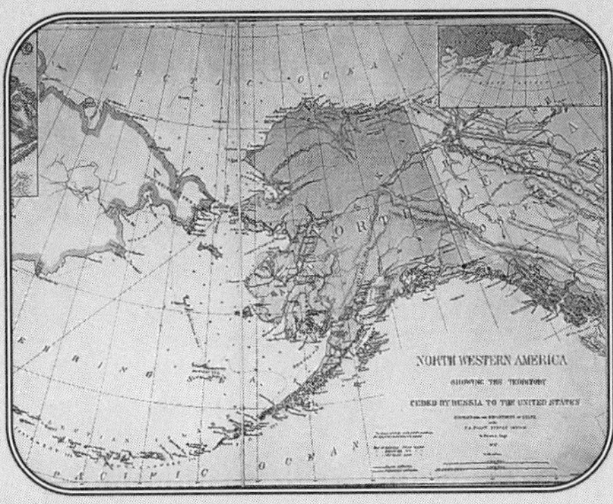

★**Seward's Folly** In 1867, Secretary of State William Seward arranged for the United States to buy Alaska from the Russians. Seward's political rivals thought he was mad to pay $7.2 million for the huge, unexplored territory, which was then an unknown quantity. For many years, while the deal still appeared foolish, people referred to Alaska as Seward's Folly. But when miners taking part in the Klondike Gold Rush found gold on Alaskan beaches, the shrewdness and foresight of Seward's purchase became clear.

★**Ku Klux Klan** Dismayed by the loss of the Civil War, and made defiant by the humiliations of Reconstruction, many white southerners formed violent vigilante groups to prevent freedmen from voting and thereby electing black candidates to public office. The most widespread of these hate groups was the Ku Klux Klan, founded in 1866 in Pulaski, Tennessee. Its members were Confederate veterans who believed that the white race was superior to all others. Often dressed in white robes and pointed hoods, klansmen rode through the night, terrorizing former slaves who tried to own property or vote.

also proposed that the citizenship of southerners be restored once they took a simple oath of allegiance to the federal government.

Johnson's plan didn't get very far. So-called Radical Republicans in the Congress wanted to punish the South for seceding. They were also worried that the Democratic party might rise again in the southern states. They still remembered the Democratic coalition that governed the country before Lincoln's election in 1860.

The Black Codes

The Civil War had ruined the southern economy and brought poverty to every level of southern society. The four million newly liberated slaves, now known as "freedmen," were the hardest hit, because they had started with the least.

The Thirteenth Amendment, ratified in December 1865, abolished slavery and liberated all those slaves not already freed by the Emancipation Proclamation. But what were the freedmen to do with their new freedom? Most owned little more than the clothes on their back. Although Congress established the Freedmen's Bureau to help former slaves find jobs and go to school, southern whites did everything they could to keep the freedmen poor and powerless.

The Black Codes were a series of measures adopted by southern states to deny African Americans the basic rights of citizenship, such as the right to vote. Radical Republicans responded by passing the Civil Rights Act of 1866, which spelled out the rights to which all Americans were entitled, regardless of the color of their skin.

Because he didn't want to anger his fellow southerners any further, Johnson vetoed the bill. But the Radical Republicans had enough votes to override Johnson's veto, and the bill became law despite the president's opposition.

During the next two years, Congress passed more laws over Johnson's veto, reorganizing the state governments of the South and forcing them to grant blacks the right to vote. Although racism continued, African Americans were able to enjoy a number of political successes.

In 1870, Hiram K. Revels of Mississippi became the first black elected to the Senate when he won the seat once occupied by Jefferson Davis. All together, between 1869 and the end of Reconstruction in 1877, sixteen blacks were elected to Congress from southern states.

IMPEACHMENT The conflict between Johnson and the Radical Republicans reached a crisis when the president fired Secretary of War Edwin M. Stanton. Like the rest of Johnson's cabinet, Stanton was a holdover from the Lincoln administration. He was also a leader of the Radical Republicans and had been working actively to undermine the tolerant Reconstruction policies of his president.

The House of Representatives responded to Johnson's dismissal of Stanton by voting to impeach the president for violating the Tenure of Office Act. This law, passed over Johnson's veto in 1867, blocked the president from removing certain government officials without the consent of the Senate.

Johnson hadn't really committed any crime, other than opposing congressmen who were determined to control the direction of Reconstruction.

Although the president survived his trial in the Senate, his political career seemed over. Denied renomination, he retired to Greenville, Tennessee.

THE NATIONAL UNION PARTY TICKET ON WHICH Lincoln and Johnson had run in 1864 didn't survive the Civil War. For the election of 1868, President Johnson returned to the Democratic party, and the Republicans took their old name back.

Having only narrowly survived impeachment, Johnson was given little chance of winning election in his own right. At the Democratic convention in July, Johnson faded early as the balloting swung to former governor Horatio Seymour of New York.

At the Republican convention, Civil War hero Ulysses S. Grant was nominated unanimously on the first ballot. Grant seemed to be the perfect choice for president. Voters naturally assumed that the brilliance and daring he had shown on southern battlefields would be easily transferred to the political battlefields of Washington. Grant's campaign theme, "Let us have peace," caught the mood of a country tired of war and the turmoil of Reconstruction.

Reconstruction was, of course, the main issue of the campaign. The Republicans planned to continue the program they had passed over Johnson's vetoes, while the Democrats favored a more lenient approach to reunification with the South.

White southerners supported Seymour overwhelmingly, but many were unable to vote, having lost their citizenship because they once swore allegiance to the Confederacy. Their former slaves could vote, however, thanks to Radical Republican laws, and these freedmen voted in huge numbers for Grant. The popular vote was close, but the general won the electoral vote by a wide margin.

Ulysses S. Grant

18th President
★
FROM 1869 TO 1877

Born: April 27, 1822

Birthplace: Point Pleasant, Ohio

Died: July 23, 1885

Party: Republican

Vice Presidents: Schuyler Colfax, Henry Wilson

First Lady: Julia Boggs Dent

Children: Frederick, Ulysses, Ellen, Jesse

Nickname: Uncle Sam

The only president to get a speeding ticket while driving a horse.

From Andrew Johnson, Grant inherited Reconstruction, an issue that dominated his first term as president. Grant also inherited a Congress with its own ideas on the subject. Because of laws enacted by the Radical Republicans, federal troops controlled nearly every aspect of civilian life in the South.

Grant understood the desire of Radical Republicans to ensure justice for blacks. But he also believed that the federal government could not force white southerners to accept a way of life they despised. These conflicting ideas put Grant in a difficult, if not impossible, position.

GOLDEN SPIKE COMPLETES TRANSCONTINENTAL RAILROAD

PROMONTORY POINT, Utah, May 10, 1869—Workers today drove a golden spike to join symbolically the Union Pacific and Central Pacific railroads into the nation's first transcontinental line. The ceremony was attended by a large number of public officials anxious to take credit for this remarkable achievement.

Congress first authorized the construction of a transcontinental railroad in 1862. Subsidies and land grants were given to two companies, the Union Pacific and the Central Pacific. The Union Pacific began laying track westward from Omaha, Nebraska, while the Central Pacific worked east from Sacramento, California.

The difficult terrain caused long delays, but the construction crews persevered. The Union Pacific, which laid 1,086 miles of track to reach Promontory Point, used crews made up mostly of Civil War veterans and Irish immigrants. The Central Pacific, which laid 689 miles of track, used primarily Chinese immigrants.

What the voters expected when they elected Grant was a decisive leader, but they didn't get one. Instead, the bold and stern general turned out to be an unsure president. Grant tended to let others make difficult policy decisions for him, and these people quickly took advantage of his gullibility and lack of leadership.

Grant himself was personally incorruptible, but many of the officials he appointed were less than honorable. As a result, Grant's administration was rocked early and often by corruption scandals.

THE GILDED AGE

The dishonesty in Washington was no worse than that in the rest of the country. Ruthless people everywhere exploited a society still weakened by the upheaval of the Civil War. Most notorious among these scoundrels were the northerners who went south and used political connections to prey on the defeated Confederacy. These men were called "carpet-baggers" because of the carpet-covered suitcases they carried. Their southern accomplices were known as "scalawags."

In the North, political "machines," such as the Tweed Ring in New York City, enriched themselves at the taxpayers' expense by corruptly dominating large groups of immigrant voters.

Simultaneously, the country's most successful industrialists made their money exploiting workers and consumers alike. These men—including Cornelius Vanderbilt, John D. Rockefeller, and Andrew Carnegie—were called "robber barons." Like Boss Tweed, they manipulated laws and lawmakers to increase their own wealth and power. Mark Twain called this period of matchless corruption, greed, and splendor the Gilded Age, and the name stuck.

The Early Years

GRANT WAS BORN IN THE OHIO COUNTRYSIDE, WHERE his father, Jesse, owned a successful leather tanning business. Jesse Grant's personality was gruff and combative, but his son was shy and sensitive. Because the boy was particularly good at handling horses, most of his chores involved their care.

When Grant was seventeen, he received an appointment to the military academy at West Point, where he was an average student. Later in his army career, he developed a drinking problem, which forced him to resign in 1854. He tried farming, real estate, and peddling firewood, but nothing worked. By Christmas 1860, he was so broke that he had to pawn his watch in order to buy presents for his family.

Grant was working at his father's leather goods store when the Civil War broke out. Because of the urgent need for experienced officers, Grant was recommissioned as a colonel and then promoted to brigadier general two months later.

★**PROFESSIONAL BASEBALL** On March 15, 1869, Harry Wright and George Ellard organized the first professional baseball team. They called their club the Cincinnati Red Stockings. Baseball had become quite popular during the Civil War, leading Wright and Ellard to believe they could make a living off the game. The ballplayers they hired barnstormed around the country, challenging local amateur clubs to games for which an admission price was charged. The success of the Red Stockings—they went undefeated during the 1869 season—paved the way for professional baseball.

★BELL'S TELEPHONE Speech specialist Alexander Graham Bell first got the idea that sound could be transmitted electrically over telegraph wires in the early 1870s. Working at night with a repair mechanic named Thomas Watson, Bell turned his idea into the telephone, for which he received U.S. Patent Number 174,465 in March 1876.

Although most people considered Bell's invention to be something of a joke, the huge Western Union Telegraph Company quickly saw its commercial possibilities and backed a rival patent. The battle over Bell's patent was the most complicated in U.S. legal history. Bell's case was so good, however, that Western Union was forced to settle.

★U.S. GRANT Jesse Grant originally named his oldest son Hiram Ulysses Grant, but young Grant hated his initials, which spelled H.U.G., so he began signing his name as Ulysses Hiram Grant. A clerical error listed him on the West Point rolls as Ulysses Simpson Grant, which Grant saw no reason to change. His West Point classmates joked that his initials stood for "Uncle Sam," and Grant was called Sam by his close friends for the rest of his life. During the Civil War, soldiers in his command took to calling him "Unconditional Surrender" Grant because of the terms he forced on his Confederate foes.

★SUSAN B. ANTHONY After the Civil War, Susan B. Anthony became an important leader in the growing women's suffrage movement. Beginning in 1868, she published a newspaper called *Revolution* in New York City. This radical weekly, edited by Elizabeth Cady Stanton, campaigned for many women's issues, including equal pay for equal work and more liberal divorce laws.

When Anthony tried to cast a ballot in the 1872 presidential election, she was arrested, convicted, and fined for voting illegally. She refused to pay the fine, but the matter was dropped. This prevented her from appealing her case all the way to the Supreme Court, which had been her plan.

BLACK FRIDAY The first of the Grant administration scandals broke in September 1869. The president had been in office a little over six months. At that time, two of the wealthiest robber barons, James Fisk and Jay Gould, tried to corner the gold market. That is, they tried to buy up enough gold to control its supply and therefore raise its price.

Their plan had one shortcoming, which was that the federal government controlled the largest supply of gold in the country. If the scheme was to work, Fisk and Gould would have to keep the government's gold off the market. They paid Grant's brother-in-law, Abel Corbin, to use his influence to do just that.

When Grant realized what was happening, he ordered Treasury Secretary George Boutwell to sell four million dollars' worth of gold from the government's reserves. The sale—which took place on September 24, 1869—ruined Fisk and Gould's plan, but it also sent the price of gold plummeting. When the fall in gold prices triggered a financial panic, Grant's reputation suffered. The day of the gold crash came to be known as Black Friday.

RECONSTRUCTION Grant tried to shake off the scandal by returning the focus of his administration to Reconstruction. Beginning in 1870, he won passage of a number of bills in Congress that gave him the power to enforce civil rights laws in the South. He used the Force Act of 1870 and the Ku Klux Klan Act of 1871 to threaten southern states with federal military action unless they stopped terrorizing blacks and denying them the right to vote. In South Carolina, for example, where the Ku Klux Klan was particularly active, Grant declared martial law and ordered mass arrests.

Until the passage of these enforcement laws, the federal government had to rely on local authorities to control the Klan. This system didn't work too well because many local policemen were themselves Klan members. Grant's enforcement of the civil rights laws temporarily broke the power of the Klan, but this period of relative safety for African Americans lasted only as long as federal troops remained in the South.

Just as the campaign of 1872 was getting under way, another scandal broke. This one involved the Union Pacific Railroad.

THE CRÉDIT MOBILIER SCANDAL By 1872, national investment in the railroads had reached nearly three billion dollars. Guaranteed federal loans and subsidies paid for much of the track work in the West, particularly along the route of the transcontinental Union Pacific Railroad.

Major stockholders in the Union Pacific formed a second company, called Crédit Mobilier of America, which they used to steal some of the federal money for themselves. They even bribed congressmen by selling them shares of stock in Crédit Mobilier at half the market price.

When the *New York Sun* broke the story of the scandal, Congress appointed a committee to investigate. Among those implicated were Vice President Schuyler Colfax and Representative James Garfield. The committee found no evidence that President Grant was involved, but many people felt the scandal was the result of his negligence.

Grant's bad fortune continued during his second term when the nation suffered one of its worst depressions. For several years, the U.S. economy had been sickly. The government was still paying off its

CAMPAIGN 1872

GRANT DIDN'T HAVE MUCH TO SHOW FOR HIS FIRST term in office. The Radical Republicans still controlled Reconstruction, and little progress had been made on economic issues. Worse still, the corruption scandals had stained his reputation. The Crédit Mobilier scandal, in particular, caused his vice president, Schuyler Colfax, to be dropped from the ticket.

Despite these problems, Grant was renominated without much of a fuss. His opponents within the party, the Liberal Republicans, didn't even bother to show up. Instead, they held their own convention and nominated New York newspaperman Horace Greeley to run against him. The disorganized Democrats also supported Greeley's candidacy because it was their only chance to oust Grant.

Greeley had made a name for himself as the editor of the *New York Tribune*. In the editorial columns of the *Tribune*, he promoted the causes of working people and denounced big business. His often-quoted advice was to "Go West, young man, and grow up with the country."

Many people considered Greeley a crackpot because of the many contradictory positions he had taken over the years. In fact, he had supported Grant in 1868 but was now critical of Grant's first term. Greeley called for an end to the corruption, reform of the civil service, full amnesty for the Confederate rebels, and the end of federal rule in the South.

Because Greeley's campaign never posed much of a threat, Grant's political backers were able to convince voters that the president was really an honest man and that the scandals were not his fault. Grant won a convincing majority in the popular vote, and Greeley died just a few weeks after the election, even before the electoral vote had been counted.

President Grant with an official of the Chinese government.

Civil War debt, while massive railroad construction projects and the 1871 Chicago Fire had drained private financial resources.

THE PANIC OF 1873 When the banking house of Jay Cooke and Company failed in September 1873, the stock market collapsed along with it. The Panic of 1873 lasted five years, put three million people out of work, and forced thousands of small companies out of business.

While the country was still reeling from the depression, Treasury Secretary William Richardson became the focus of the next Grant administration scandal. After taking over for George Boutwell in 1873, Richardson appointed his friend John D. Sanborn as special agent in charge of collecting overdue taxes.

Normally, this was a difficult and unrewarding job. But Richardson made an astonishing and illegal deal with Sanborn, allowing Sanborn to keep half the money he collected. By the time Congress got around to investigating Sanborn in 1874, he had already pocketed two hundred thousand dollars. Richardson was forced to resign, and Grant was embarrassed again.

Grant scarcely caught his breath before the next scandal broke.

CUSTER'S LAST STAND

Seventh Cavalry Massacred at Little Big Horn

MONTANA TERRITORY, June 25, 1876—General George Armstrong Custer and the men under his immediate command were all killed today when they attacked a huge Indian village on the banks of the Little Big Horn River.

Seventh Cavalry units under Major Marcus Reno and Captain Frederick Benteen survived only by retreating to a line of bluffs above the river.

Custer had been sent on a scouting mission to locate bands of hostile Sioux and Cheyenne who had left their reservations. He disobeyed orders by attacking the village, which held many thousands of Indians, including the powerful war chiefs Sitting Bull and Crazy Horse.

During the Civil War, the twenty-three-year-old Custer became the youngest general in the Union army. Afterward, like many other Civil War veterans, he continued his military career fighting Indians in the West. The Sioux called him Son of the Morning Star because of his long blond hair.

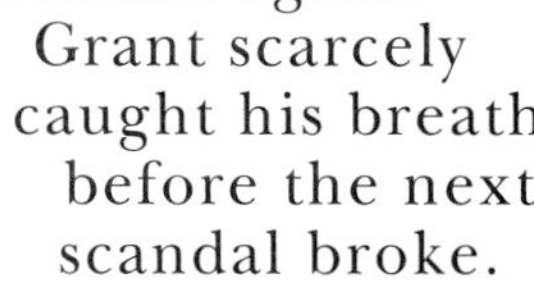

In 1875, Richardson's replacement as treasury secretary, Benjamin Bristow, uncovered a conspiracy that had been cheating the government for years. Federal officials who were supposed to be collecting liquor taxes were instead dividing the money among themselves and the distillers.

Frustrated by the unending scandals, Grant demanded quick action. He instructed the government prosecutors to arrest everyone involved. "Let no guilty man escape," Grant said. But when his own personal secretary, Orville Babcock, was implicated, the president shielded him.

While these federal officials were using their positions to get richer, the depression continued. For those who still had jobs, wages declined. In large cities, tens of thousands of homeless men and women crowded police stations for shelter. Eventually, the poor demanded a change. In the mid-1870s, thousands of low-salaried and unemployed workers staged protests in Pittsburgh, New York, Baltimore, and other cities. Often, the police and the National Guard turned out to beat the demonstrators with guns and clubs.

THE CIVIL RIGHTS ACT OF 1875 In between scandal investigations, Congress passed the Civil Rights Act of 1875. This was the last major piece of Radical Republican legislation passed during Reconstruction. It guaranteed blacks the civil rights being denied them in the South. The new law integrated hotels, theaters, and restaurants. Under its terms, owners could no longer keep African Americans out or segregate them into back rooms. The act was poorly enforced, however, and eventually declared unconstitutional by the Supreme Court in 1883.

★**THE BUTCHER OF GALENA** So many of Grant's Civil War victories were bloody ones that soldiers began calling him the Butcher of Galena. (The name referred to his hometown of Galena, Illinois.)

Yet Grant himself was highly squeamish. He became physically sick at the sight of blood and refused to eat any meat unless it was cooked until dry. Even the hint of blood in meat juices was too much for him.

The responsibility for sending tens of thousands of men to their deaths also sickened the general, who suffered regularly from severe migraine headaches. After particularly horrible battles, he would often retire to his tent and cry.

★**MARK TWAIN** Samuel Clemens grew up in Hannibal, Missouri, on the banks of the Mississippi, where he fell in love with the romance and mystery of river life. He was fascinated by the con men, thieves, and gamblers who populated the paddleboats traveling to and from New Orleans.

In 1863, Clemens began writing under the pen name Mark Twain. He borrowed it from a riverman's term for water that was barely safe for navigation. By the time he published *The Adventures of Tom Sawyer* in 1876, Twain was already famous as a humorist and lecturer. Tom Sawyer relived many of Clemens's own adventures as a child in Hannibal.

★**MAIL-ORDER CATALOGS** In August 1872, Aaron Montgomery Ward founded the first mail-order business in the United States. His first "catalog" was a single sheet of paper listing approximately 150 items. Ward's main customers were farmers in the countryside who were unable to make regular trips into town. By 1888, when Sears Roebuck began its own catalog, Montgomery Ward's sales had already topped one million dollars a year. Ward was also the originator of the money-back guarantee.

★BOOKER T. WASHINGTON Booker T. Washington was the leading African-American spokesman of the late nineteenth century and also one of the country's foremost educators. Born into slavery in Virginia, Washington was just nine years old when the Civil War ended and he was freed. Dirt poor but determined to get an education, he enrolled in 1872 at the Hampton Institute, one of the first schools for blacks in the South. He worked as a janitor there to pay his expenses.

From an early age, Washington believed that the only way for blacks to gain equality in American society was through education and economic success. In 1881, he took over a small black school in Tuskegee, Alabama, and turned it into the internationally respected Tuskegee Institute.

★THE GREAT CHICAGO FIRE For three days beginning on October 8, 1871, the city of Chicago burned. When the blaze was finally brought under control on October 10, nearly four square miles of the city, including the downtown business district, lay in ruins. The Great Fire left ninety thousand people homeless and caused two hundred million dollars' worth of damage. Legend has it that the blaze was started when a cow owned by a Mrs. O'Leary knocked over a lantern in its stall.

The final Grant administration scandal broke in 1876, when Secretary of War William Belknap was found to be taking kickbacks from traders at Indian reservations. Cheating the Indians was a long-standing government practice, but rarely did it reach as high as the president's cabinet. Belknap resigned before a Senate trial could remove him from office. A weary Grant told Congress, "Failures have been errors of judgment, not of intent."

Despite the scandals that marred his time in office, many people still wanted Grant to run for a third term. No president had ever done that before, and Grant wasn't about to become the first. He felt he had been president long enough.

The qualities that had served him so well during wartime—resolution, independence, and daring—deserted him as president. Grant entered the White House a well-meaning man pledged to peace, honesty, and civil rights. But as president, he neither resolved the key issues of Reconstruction nor set high standards for the officials he appointed.

AN INDUSTRIAL NATION

In 1803, Thomas Jefferson looked to the future and saw a nation of farmers. As late as the start of the Civil War, Jefferson's vision still held true. In 1860, the United States was still a chiefly agricultural nation. Most Americans were farmers, and farming was the nation's biggest business.

The Civil War changed all that. The need to supply a huge army with clothing, arms, and equipment sent the industrial economy of the North into high gear. When the war ended, the factories just kept going. By the end of Grant's second term, the United States had become one of the greatest industrial nations in the world. It dug more coal and iron ore, made more steel, drilled for more oil, laid more railroad track, and built more factories than any other nation on earth.

This enormous change in the country's economy had profound effects. Vast numbers of immigrants came to the United States to work in the booming cities, and the country's ethnic makeup changed dramatically. From a people of largely northern European descent, the United States became a nation of many nationalities. People began to call it a "melting pot."

Industrialization also brought a change in the nation's identity abroad. Once a distant republic, the United States now had the makings of a world power.

RETIREMENT Grant left office in 1877. After a trip around the world, he settled in Manhattan, where he invested all his money in a brokerage firm founded by his son Ulysses, Jr. Perhaps not surprisingly, this venture ended in scandal, too. Their partner, Ferdinand Ward, embezzled the firm's money, bankrupting the company and the Grants. About the same time, the former president learned that he had an advanced case of throat cancer.

Determined to provide for his family before he died, Grant set to work on his memoirs. A month before he died, he moved to Mount McGregor in the Adirondacks. Unable to speak or eat regularly, he sat on the front porch of his cottage, racing to finish his book.

Grant completed the manuscript on July 16. A week later, he died. The memoirs, published by his friend Mark Twain, sold five hundred thousand copies and restored his family's financial security.

THE ELECTION OF 1876 WAS BY FAR THE MOST controversial in U.S. history. The Republican candidate, Governor Rutherford B. Hayes of Ohio, was known as a trustworthy and reform-minded administrator. His Democratic opponent, Governor Samuel J. Tilden of New York, was even more famous as a reformer, having helped break the notorious Tweed Ring in New York City. Both men pledged to end the corruption that still plagued the Grant administration.

Because of his national reputation, the backlash against Grant, and the revival of southern Democrats, Tilden was the early favorite. But the Republicans were still the stronger national party, and Hayes made the race a close one. When the popular vote was counted, Tilden appeared to have won the election. But twenty electoral votes were in doubt.

Tilden needed only one of those votes to win the presidency. But a special election commission made up of ten congressmen and five Supreme Court justices voted 8-7 along party lines to give all the disputed votes to Hayes, who won 185-184.

Southern Democrats, believing that the election had been stolen from them, threatened to secede once again. But Tilden gracefully restrained them, and Hayes agreed to the Compromise of 1877. In order to end the crisis, Hayes promised to withdraw federal troops from the South, ending Reconstruction. He also agreed to rebuild railroads and industry there and include at least one southern Democrat in his cabinet. This remarkable back-room bargain brought some calm to U.S. politics, but it also created enormous problems for the new president.

RUTHERFORD BIRCHARD

HAYES

19TH PRESIDENT

★

FROM 1877 TO 1881

BORN: October 4, 1822

BIRTHPLACE: Delaware, Ohio

DIED: January 17, 1893

PARTY: Republican

VICE PRESIDENT: William A. Wheeler

FIRST LADY: Lucy Ware Webb

CHILDREN: Sardis, James, Rutherford, Joseph, George, Frances, Scott, Manning

NICKNAME: His Fraudulency

The first president to use a telephone in the White House.

Rutherford Hayes began his term under difficult circumstances. The Compromise of 1877 that confirmed his election as president also robbed him of the authority that usually came with the job.

Because his victory was won in the cloakrooms of Congress rather than at the polls, newspapers referred to Hayes as Rutherfraud and His Fraudulency. Out in the country, most people thought the election had been rigged. Hayes had always been an honorable and decent public servant, but he was never quite able to overcome the concessions he made in accepting the compromise.

Southern Democrats, shut out of power since the Buchanan administration, were particularly eager to embarrass Hayes. Since the Civil War, the Republicans had run "bloody shirt" campaigns against the southern Democrats. "Waving the bloody shirt" meant reminding voters that the Democrats had been the party of secession and therefore deserved the blame for the bloody war that followed.

EDISON DOES IT AGAIN!

Wizard of Menlo Park Invents Light Bulb

MENLO PARK, N.J., October 21, 1879—Thomas Edison demonstrated his newest invention today at his laboratory in Menlo Park. He calls it the light bulb.

The device consists of a vacuum-sealed glass bulb with a filament inside. When electricity passes through the filament, it glows, producing light. Edison's breakthrough came when he found the right material for the filament: scorched cotton thread.

Edison, who invented the phonograph in 1877, first became interested in electric light last year when he saw an exhibit of electric street lamps.

His announcement last fall that he would attempt to develop a cheap and practical form of electric light caused gas company stocks to tumble on Wall Street. It now seems likely that inexpensive electric light will soon replace the gas lamps used in most homes.

As part of the price for accepting Hayes as president, the southern Democrats demanded that Reconstruction end immediately. They wanted the Republican carpetbaggers out of the South along with the federal troops who supported the freedmen.

Having little choice, Hayes agreed. One of his first acts as president was to remove the last federal troops from the South, ending a decade of Radical Republican rule over the defeated Confederacy.

Although southern whites were overjoyed, their former slaves were not. The end of Reconstruction meant that political power in the South would return to those people who believed in the superiority of the white race.

By withdrawing the troops, Hayes left southern blacks at the mercy of these white supremacists. Without federal soldiers to enforce the civil rights laws, blacks were once again denied their legal right to vote. And without troops to control the Ku Klux Klan, its members resumed their nighttime missions of terror and death.

RAILROAD STRIKES Meanwhile in the North, the economy was still suffering from the lasting effects of the Panic of 1873. The railroads were in particularly bad shape. The cutthroat nature of the business, in which labor was the biggest expense, led to a series of wage cuts for railroad employees. The pay cuts announced in the spring of 1877 were the last straw for many workers.

The first spontaneous strike came in Baltimore, where firemen on the B&O Railroad walked off the job on July 16. The labor revolt then spread to Pittsburgh, where local militia called out to break the strike instead sided with the workers. Hayes finally

The Early Years

Rutherford Hayes was born at his family's home in Delaware, Ohio. The doctor's fee for the delivery was $3.50. Because his father died before he was born, Rutherford was raised by his mother, Sophia, and her bachelor brother, Sardis Birchard.

From his earliest days, Hayes dreamed of holding public office. He did well in school, graduating from Kenyon College and Harvard Law School. In 1852, at the age of thirty, Hayes married Lucy Ware Webb, a fervent abolitionist who convinced him to leave the Whigs and join the new Republican party. Beginning in 1853, Hayes devoted some of his time to defending runaway slaves.

★Lemonade Lucy A devout Methodist and a passionate believer in temperance, First Lady Lucy Hayes had an immediate impact on the White House when she banned all liquor from state functions. Because she often served lemonade instead, her critics dubbed her Lemonade Lucy. She is also remembered for conducting group hymns with the cabinet and for hosting the first White House Easter egg roll. At this annual spring event, children roll painted Easter eggs up and down the White House lawn.

★Jesse James and the James Gang Jesse James and his brother Frank were born on a farm near Centerville, Missouri. During the Civil War, they both joined bands of Confederate raiders. These rough outfits preyed on Union supply trains, especially those carrying payrolls. After the war, the James brothers took to robbing banks and civilian trains instead.

The James Gang soon became well known in the East, where stories of western adventure always sold well. Magazines filled their pages with romanticized versions of the brothers' criminal exploits. Jesse and Frank were usually portrayed as heroes who became outlaws because federal lawmen hated all former Confederates.

★THE INDIAN WARS The Civil War years were generally peaceful ones for Indian tribes on the Great Plains. Because the U.S. government thought one war was enough for the time being, federal officials negotiated a number of peace treaties with the Sioux and the Cheyenne.

One treaty signed in 1868 guaranteed the Sioux all rights to their sacred Black Hills in the Dakota Territory. General George Custer violated this treaty in 1874 when he escorted a survey team into the Black Hills looking for gold, which the expedition found. The horde of miners that followed Custer into the Black Hills provoked the Sioux to go on the warpath.

Even though the Sioux and Cheyenne were able to defeat Custer at the battle of the Little Big Horn, the Indians were no match for the U.S. army. Most were forced to return to government reservations, although a few hundred, led by Sitting Bull, escaped to Canada.

★P.T. BARNUM Phineas Taylor Barnum was probably America's greatest showman. His most famous acts were the twenty-five-inch-tall midget, General Tom Thumb, and singer Jenny Lind, whom Barnum billed as the Swedish Nightingale.

Barnum was already sixty years old when he started his first circus during the early 1870s. In 1881, he teamed up with James A. Bailey. Until that time, circuses were one-ring affairs that usually played small towns. The Barnum & Bailey Circus, however, reflected Barnum's legendary sense of spectacle. It had three rings, toured major cities, and featured nationally known acts such as the elephant Jumbo. Barnum called it "The Greatest Show on Earth."

had to send in federal troops to restore order. By August 2, after hundreds of deaths and thousands of injuries, railroad service was restored by force on all lines.

CHINESE IMMIGRATION Hayes also confronted violence born of economic despair in California, where gangs of Irish Americans were attacking Chinese immigrants.

The Chinese had come to work in California's gold mines and on its railroad construction crews. The jobs they took were the most difficult and usually paid the least—jobs that other Californians wouldn't take. By 1877, Chinese immigrants made up nearly ten percent of the state's population.

Trouble began when the gold mines went bust, railroad building tapered off, and the Chinese began competing with Irish Americans for the same jobs. The Chinese often got the jobs because they were willing to work for less. This angered the Irish, who believed they were entitled to the jobs because they had come to this country first.

The conflict came to a head in San Francisco, where Irish gangs attacked (and sometimes killed) Chinese on the street. Congress's response was to pass a law banning Chinese immigration. Hayes vetoed the bill and instead had Secretary of State William Evarts negotiate the Treaty of 1880, which limited immigration in a manner acceptable to the Chinese government.

The great success of Hayes's term was his "hard money" policy. To help finance the Civil War, the government had issued paper money called "greenbacks." The greenbacks were "soft" or "easy" money because they weren't backed by gold. That is, they could not be redeemed for gold coins, or specie.

During the Grant administration, Congress had passed the Resumption of Specie Act, which called for the government to take the greenbacks out of circulation and start redeeming paper money with gold again.

Farmers who held mortgages and other long-term debtors wanted an easy money policy that would encourage inflation. With more money in circulation, each dollar would be worth less, and their debts would be cheaper to pay off. Hayes stood firm, however, and the government resumed specie payments on schedule.

CIVIL SERVICE REFORM

Hayes's other great cause was civil service reform. Civil servants are the government's civilian employees: the bureaucrats who run everything from the mint to the post office. Under the spoils system made famous by Andrew Jackson, many of these jobs went to people whose only qualifications were their political connections.

Because he believed that government jobs shouldn't be used as political rewards, Hayes issued an executive order in June 1877 barring civil servants from taking part in political activities. He also supported the efforts of Interior Secretary Carl Schurz to develop competitive exams for hiring and promotion. But he couldn't convince Congress to act on large-scale reform.

Hayes was able to take some limited action himself. He removed a number of federal officials, including the heads of the post office in St. Louis and the customhouse in New York. Hayes said these men were misusing their public offices for political gain. One of them later became president: Chester A. Arthur, then collector of duties for the Port of New York.

CAMPAIGN 1880

When he accepted the Republican nomination in 1876, Hayes said he would serve only one term. Four years later, he hadn't changed his mind. Hayes's retirement left the race wide open. The surprise front-runner among the Republicans was former president Grant, who had decided to try for a third term after all. Opposing him were James G. Blaine of Maine and Hayes's treasury secretary, John Sherman.

Grant held the lead at the convention for thirty-five ballots, but he remained about seventy votes short of victory. On the thirty-fourth ballot, Wisconsin cast sixteen votes for a compromise candidate, Representative James Garfield of Ohio, the man who had nominated Sherman.

Garfield remained loyal to Sherman, jumping out of his seat and shouting, "I won't permit it." But two ballots later, the Blaine and Sherman forces joined together to draft him. As a gesture to the conservative Republicans, known as Stalwarts, who had supported Grant, the convention chose Chester Arthur of New York as Garfield's running mate.

To oppose Garfield, the Democrats nominated General Winfield Hancock, a Union hero and military governor during Reconstruction. The election was remarkably close. Garfield won the popular vote by just ten thousand ballots out of nine million cast. However, he got those votes where he needed them, winning the electoral college, 214-155.

Garfield had made a deal, known as the Treaty of Fifth Avenue, with New York party boss Roscoe Conkling. In exchange for Conkling's Stalwart support, Garfield agreed to consult Conkling when making federal civil service appointments in New York. As a result, the state, its thirty-five electoral votes, and the election all went to Garfield.

JAMES ABRAM GARFIELD

20TH PRESIDENT

★

1881

BORN: November 19, 1831

BIRTHPLACE: Orange, Ohio

DIED: September 19, 1881

PARTY: Republican

VICE PRESIDENT: Chester A. Arthur

FIRST LADY: Lucretia Rudolph

CHILDREN: Eliza, Harry, James, Mary, Irvin, Abram, Edward

NICKNAME: Preacher President

Juggled clubs to build up his muscles.

PRESIDENT GARFIELD DIES TEN WEEKS AFTER SHOOTING

ELBERON, N.J., September 19, 1881—President James Garfield died tonight, ten weeks after being shot by Charles Guiteau, a mentally ill office-seeker. Guiteau shot Garfield July 2 as the president walked through a Washington railroad station.

Guiteau was an obscure New York Stalwart who broke with the local party to support Garfield. After the election, he expected as a reward to be made a minister to Europe. When the State Department refused him, Guiteau decided that Garfield had to die.

At first, Garfield was treated in the White House. But once his condition stabilized, he was taken by train to the New Jersey coast, where he could escape the heat of the Washington summer. The track along his route was lined with straw to make the journey easier.

The immediate cause of Garfield's death appears to have been blood poisoning brought on by the doctors who treated him. They often failed to wash their hands and, in examining the president's gunshot wounds, used unsterile instruments, which reinfected him.

Most people didn't expect much from Garfield as president. His involvement in the Crédit Mobilier scandal and his campaign deal-making led many people to believe that his administration would be just as scandal-ridden as Grant's.

But Garfield proved them wrong during his very first week in office. When the new postmaster general uncovered evidence of wrongdoing in the post office, Garfield ordered him to pursue the investigation, no matter where it led.

Garfield also decided to take on Roscoe Conkling. Although he had promised the Republican party boss a say in appointments to government jobs, when it came time to make them Garfield ignored Conkling's wishes and made the appointments on merit alone.

During the long weeks after Garfield was shot, the president's popularity rose nearly every day. Each morning, the country waited nervously for news of his condition. A number of times it improved, but the poor state of medical science at the time eventually killed the president.

CHESTER ALAN ARTHUR

21ST PRESIDENT

★

FROM 1881 TO 1885

BORN: October 5, 1829

BIRTHPLACE: Fairfield, Vt.

DIED: November 18, 1886

PARTY: Republican

VICE PRESIDENT: None

FIRST LADY: Ellen Lewis Herndon

CHILDREN: William; Chester, Jr.; Ellen

NICKNAME: Elegant Arthur

Owned eighty pairs of pants, which he changed several times daily.

Americans hadn't expected much from James Garfield when he took office, and they expected even less from Chester Arthur when he became president upon Garfield's death. Garfield had surprised people with his turnaround on the civil service issue, but no one believed Arthur had much to offer.

Arthur had been chosen as Garfield's running mate simply to appease Roscoe Conkling and the conservative Stalwarts. No one seriously believed that Arthur would, or should, be president.

Arthur had been an important cog in Conkling's political machine. As the collector of duties for the Port of New York, he had regularly forced his employees to contribute money to Republican campaigns. Because of this practice, President Hayes had removed him from office in 1878.

Yet, in a transformation even more remarkable than Garfield's, President Arthur worked for genuine reform. When his cronies came to Washington looking for jobs, Arthur turned them

EARPS WIN GUNFIGHT AT O.K. CORRAL

TOMBSTONE, Arizona Territory, October 26, 1881—The long-standing battle between the Earps and Clantons for control of Tombstone was settled today at the O.K. Corral.

The Earps killed Billy Clanton and Tom and Frank McLaury in a shootout there. Only Ike Clanton, leader of the Clanton gang, and Billy Claiborne escaped. At stake was control of the rich silver trade, which has driven Tombstone's recent boom.

Town marshal Virgil Earp was backed up in the fight by his two brothers, Wyatt and Morgan, and also by Doc Holliday. Wyatt has been working as a gambler and guard at the Oriental Saloon. Holliday is also a gambler and gunman, who occasionally practices dentistry.

Virgil Earp insisted that he and his brothers were just enforcing the law. But townspeople, who believe the gunfight was more likely murder, are planning to fire Earp and hire a new marshal to replace him.

The Early Years

CHESTER ARTHUR'S FATHER WAS THE Reverend William Arthur, a fiery Baptist minister who served eleven different parishes in Vermont and upstate New York during his career. Because Chester moved around with his father, he didn't really settle down until he entered Union College in 1845. As a student there, Arthur took part in his share of pranks, once dumping the school bell into the Erie Canal.

Soon after moving to New York City and becoming a lawyer in 1854, Arthur agreed to represent a black woman, Lizzie Jennings, who wanted to sue a streetcar company because she had been forced to leave a whites-only car. Arthur won the case, which ended racial segregation of public transportation in New York City.

★**HOT DOGS** German immigrant Anton Feuchtwanger made his living as a sausage vendor in St. Louis. At first, he served his sausages plain. For his customers' convenience, he loaned them white gloves so that they could keep their fingers clean while they ate. The problem was that too many customers kept the white gloves instead of returning them. In 1880, Feuchtwanger decided to solve this problem by asking his brother-in-law, a baker, to make special rolls that could hold the sausages. The result was the first hot dog.

★**BUFFALO BILL** William Cody took a job as a rider for the Pony Express when he was just fourteen years old. He got his nickname eight years later in 1868, when he hunted buffalo to feed railroad crews laying track for the Union Pacific. In just eight months, he killed 4,280 buffalo.

While serving as a scout during the Indian Wars, Buffalo Bill began to realize the commercial possibilities of his frontier adventures. In 1883, he organized the first of his hugely successful Wild West shows. These traveling entertainments featured real cowboys and Indians as well as reenactments of a buffalo hunt, a stagecoach robbery, and a Pony Express ride. Cody's stars included the famous sharpshooter Annie Oakley and the legendary Sioux chief Sitting Bull.

away. "For the vice presidency, I am indebted to Mr. Conkling," Arthur once said, "but for the presidency of the United States my debt is to the Almighty." In other words, there would be no payoffs.

In 1882, Arthur proved that he meant what he said by vetoing the Rivers and Harbors Act. This bill authorized nineteen million dollars in spending for construction projects around the country.

It was an obvious example of "pork barrel" legislation, composed of unnecessary projects designed to benefit the districts of powerful congressmen. Although the veto was overridden, Arthur won praise for his attempt to stop wasteful spending.

CHINESE IMMIGRATION Arthur also vetoed a bill banning Chinese immigration for twenty years. He did, however, sign the compromise Chinese Exclusion Act of 1882, which halted immigration for ten years and kept Chinese already in the United States from becoming citizens.

This law placed the first significant restrictions on immigration to the United States. It also broke the Treaty of 1880 with China. This treaty allowed restrictions on immigration but not an outright ban. The Chinese Exclusion Act was renewed twice before being repealed in 1943.

CIVIL SERVICE REFORM In 1883, Arthur signed the most important legislation of his administration, the Pendleton Act, which reformed the civil service. Civil service reform had been an important political issue since the scandals of the Grant years. It was widely believed that the civil service was filled with politically connected people who did little or no work.

Strangely, it was President Garfield's assassination that made

real reform possible. Because Charles Guiteau had been looking for a government job when he shot the president, the public got the mistaken impression that Garfield's assassination was somehow linked to civil service corruption. Although Guiteau's motives were altogether different, people demanded immediate reform of the civil service. To everyone's surprise, Arthur enthusiastically supported the cause.

THE PENDLETON ACT

The Pendleton Act created competitive exams for government jobs. It also set up a Civil Service Commission to oversee the new merit system and banned the practice of demanding campaign contributions from federal employees.

In reforming the civil service, however, the Pendleton Act also changed the way political parties were funded—not necessarily for the better. No longer able to rely on civil service workers for income, political parties had to look elsewhere for money to run their campaigns.

Big business was the most likely source. Companies such as John D. Rockefeller's Standard Oil and Andrew Carnegie's U.S. Steel were eager to find ways to influence lawmakers. Both political parties were happy to accept their money.

By 1884, many of Arthur's critics had been won over by his handling of the presidency. But others couldn't understand his change of heart. Why, they wondered, did Arthur keep turning his back on the politicians who once bossed him around?

The answer may have been a secret known only to Arthur and his doctors. Arthur had Bright's disease, a then-fatal kidney illness. Perhaps knowing that he might die soon gave Arthur the courage he needed to do things he believed to be right.

THE DEMOCRATS HAD BEEN OUT OF POWER FOR twenty-eight years when they met in 1884 to select a presidential candidate. Desperate for a winner, the convention chose Governor Grover Cleveland of New York. Cleveland had made a name for himself by standing up to Tammany Hall, the corrupt political organization that controlled Democratic politics in New York City.

The Republicans picked James G. Blaine, who had served briefly as Garfield's secretary of state. Blaine had tried for the Republican nomination in 1876 and again in 1880 but failed both times. Arthur gave him some opposition at the convention, but the president's about-face on civil service reform had cost him his Stalwart allies without convincing reform Republicans that he could be trusted.

The campaign turned on personal attacks. The Democrats talked up the Mulligan Letters, which suggested that Blaine had taken bribes from railroads while serving in Congress. Blaine's cause was further hurt when he was seen having dinner with John Jacob Astor, Jay Gould, and other robber barons.

For their part, the Republicans unearthed the story that Cleveland, still a bachelor, had fathered a son out of wedlock ten years before. Cleveland admitted fathering the child, and the voters didn't hold it against him. To the Republican chant, "Ma, ma, where's my pa?" the Democrats replied, "Gone to the White House, ha, ha, ha!"

The election turned in New York, which Blaine lost by just a thousand votes. His close association with Protestants there cost him the support of New York's numerous Irish Catholics—and with it, the electoral votes he needed to beat Cleveland.

GROVER CLEVELAND

22ND PRESIDENT

★

FROM 1885 TO 1889

BORN: March 18, 1837

BIRTHPLACE: Caldwell, N.J.

DIED: June 24, 1908

PARTY: Democrat

VICE PRESIDENT: Thomas A. Hendricks

FIRST LADY: Frances Folsom

CHILDREN: Ruth, Esther, Marion, Richard, Francis

NICKNAME: Uncle Jumbo

The first Democrat elected president after the Civil War.

By an extremely close vote, Grover Cleveland became the first Democratic president since the Civil War. But his tiny margin of victory wasn't his only handicap. Cleveland was also little known around the country. Even in Washington, he was a stranger. His trip to the capital for the March 4, 1885, inauguration was only his second to the city. The crowd that gathered to hear him speak that day was the largest he had ever seen.

A lesser person might have been overwhelmed by the presidency, but Grover Cleveland was a man of conviction, which gave him strength. He had come to Washington to do a job, and he intended to see that job get done.

At first, Cleveland tried to do everything himself. During his

LABOR RIOT IN HAYMARKET SQUARE

CHICAGO, May 4, 1886—A workers' meeting in Haymarket Square tonight exploded into a riot when a bomb went off, killing seven policemen. The bomb thrower has not been identified.

The mass meeting had been called to protest yesterday's trouble at the McCormick Harvester Works, where police fired into a crowd of striking workers, killing four and wounding many more.

Tonight's Haymarket demonstration was organized in part by political radicals in the labor movement. "When you ask [your boss] to lessen your burdens, he sends his bloodhounds out to shoot you," one of their pamphlets read. "To arms, we call you, to arms!"

Eight radicals have been arrested for inciting murder, although only one of them was actually present in the Haymarket tonight.

Moderate union leaders are concerned that factory bosses will use popular hatred of these radicals, who are mostly foreigners, to undermine the fight for the eight-hour workday.

first months in office, he went without a secretary, even answering the White House telephone himself on occasion.

Because of his hard work and attention to detail, Cleveland usually knew more about the issues of the day than his opponents. He always did his homework. But sometimes he got so caught up in the specifics of an issue that he lost the big picture.

"HANDS-OFF" GOVERNMENT The new president was blunt and somewhat hot-tempered. He made few friends in Washington and many enemies. But he knew what he wanted, and that was a "hands-off" government. Cleveland believed that the people should support the government and not the other way around.

In 1887, for example, a severe drought hit Texas, causing terrible crop failures. The Congress passed a bill to distribute free seed there so farmers could replant. Although the bill was extremely popular, Cleveland vetoed it. He believed that people should be suspicious of government rather than look to it for handouts.

THE INTERSTATE COMMERCE ACT Because of his attitude toward government, Cleveland played almost no role in the shaping of legislation. He either signed bills or he vetoed them. One of the most important bills he signed was the Interstate Commerce Act.

For many years, railroads had been free to charge passengers and shippers whatever they liked. Often, the rates were outrageously high, and usually there was favoritism. Railroads used such practices as rebates to favor big corporations over small companies.

The Interstate Commerce Act was passed to ensure that the railroads

The Early Years

Grover Cleveland was a big, strong boy who loved fishing. In school, he was not outstanding, but he worked hard. He planned to go on to college, but his father's death in 1853 forced the sixteen-year-old Cleveland to find a job. After working for a year in New York City, he was offered a full scholarship to college if he agreed to become a Presbyterian minister, as his father had been.

Although Cleveland yearned for a formal education, he turned down the offer and decided to head west. He got as far as Buffalo, where his uncle arranged for him to study law. He eventually entered politics. His remarkable success as a reform mayor of Buffalo led to his election as governor of New York State in 1882.

★A White House Marriage Grover Cleveland became the first president to be married in the White House when he wed twenty-one-year-old Frances Folsom on June 2, 1886. Frances, the youngest first lady ever, was the daughter of the president's longtime friend and law partner Oscar Folsom. Cleveland, who was forty-nine when he married, had known Frances since her birth, but they didn't become romantically involved until she was in college.

The couple kept their engagement secret for nearly a year and revealed it just five days before their wedding. John Philip Sousa and his Marine Band played at the ceremony, which was made the focus of much attention by the press. Although the couple took a five-day honeymoon, President Cleveland worked as usual on his wedding day.

★The American Federation of Labor In 1886, Samuel Gompers organized the American Federation of Labor. The AFL was a new kind of union because its members were not workers but other unions. Until that time, organizations such as the Knights of Labor tried to win better conditions for workers through political activity. But Gompers thought political reform was a waste of time. He believed a union's strength lay in its bargaining power with big business. A strong union could force a company to pay better wages and improve working conditions. The point of the AFL, one union official explained, was "not to assist men to lift themselves out of their class, as if they were ashamed of it...but to raise the class itself in physical well-being and self-estimation."

★**GERONIMO SURRENDERS** With the flight of Sitting Bull to Canada and the death of Crazy Horse in 1877, Indian resistance to whites ended on the Great Plains. Only the Chiricahua Apaches of Arizona fought on under the leadership of the war chief Geronimo.

When Geronimo surrendered to General Nelson "Bearcat" Miles on September 4, 1886, it was the third time he had been captured by the U.S. army. Twice before, he had escaped when he feared that the soldiers planned to kill him. This time, Miles promised Geronimo that he would be able to return to his Arizona homeland after a temporary exile in Florida. But the government didn't keep its promise. Geronimo never saw Arizona again.

★**COCA-COLA** An Atlanta druggist named John Pemberton invented Coca-Cola in 1886. At first, he promoted the drink as a health tonic, but it soon became popular as a soft drink. The name Coca-Cola was chosen by Pemberton's bookkeeper, Frank Robinson, who borrowed it from the syrup's active ingredients: coca leaf and kola nut extracts.

In 1891, Pemberton sold out to Asa G. Candler, who took the drink nationwide, building bottling plants in Dallas, Philadelphia, and Los Angeles. Under Candler's leadership, sales of Coca-Cola syrup rose from 9,000 gallons in 1890 to more than 370,000 gallons in 1900. Candler, who paid Pemberton $2,300 for Coca-Cola, sold out himself in 1919 for $25,000,000.

charged "reasonable and just" rates. The Interstate Commerce Commission that it created to oversee the railroads was the first regulatory agency ever created by Congress.

INDIAN AFFAIRS In 1881, Helen Hunt Jackson published *A Century of Dishonor.* This widely read book described the federal government's cruel treatment of Indians on the frontier, and it generated an enormous emotional response. Groups devoted to defending the rights of Indians sprang up all over the country.

The goal of these groups was to help reservation Indians adopt white culture so they could be integrated into white society. Because of their prodding, Congress passed the Dawes Severalty Act in 1887. This law granted citizenship to Indians willing to renounce membership in a tribe. If they did so, they were given a small parcel of reservation land to homestead.

Although the reformers meant well, the Dawes Act was misguided because it failed to take into account the Indians' native culture. Because Indians were used to sharing their hunting grounds with others, they didn't value the concept of private property. Because they didn't understand the white meaning of ownership, they often sold their plots for a fraction of their market value. As a result, the Dawes Act did more harm than good.

PENSION BILLS Cleveland exercised his veto power often when it came to bills that he considered raids on the Treasury. Chief among these were bills introduced by congressmen to provide pensions for particular veterans of the Union army.

Cleveland believed that the government was obligated to provide pension benefits for soldiers injured in battle. But he worried that the prospect of "easy" pension money was leading to a great deal of fraud.

Corrupt lawyers often filed false claims on behalf of Union veterans who were perfectly healthy. Sometimes the Pension Bureau accepted these claims without any investigation. And even if the Pension Bureau did reject a claim, individual veterans could still request that their congressman introduce private bills forcing the Pension Bureau to pay them benefits.

In this manner, pensions were fraudulently granted to deserters, to criminals, and even to men who had never served in the army. Although his actions infuriated the veterans lobby, Cleveland read each and every one of these bills—there were hundreds—and he vetoed nearly all of them.

TARIFF REFORM Near the end of his first term, Cleveland challenged Congress to reduce U.S. tariff rates. Ever since the Lincoln administration, when rates were raised to pay for the Civil War, tariffs had been extraordinarily high. After the war, the high rates had protected developing U.S. industries, but they had also pushed up prices and created a large surplus in the Treasury.

Congressmen were eager to spend the extra money on pork barrel projects in their home states, but Cleveland wouldn't allow it. Instead, the president demanded that Congress lower tariff rates.

Reaction to Cleveland's proposal was strong. Big business enjoyed the protection from foreign competition, and labor organizations believed that high tariffs kept wages high. In fact, reaction to Cleveland's repeated call for tariff reform was so strong that his position probably cost him reelection in 1888.

CAMPAIGN 1888

By the time the Republicans met in June 1888 to nominate a presidential candidate, the united party was determined to unseat Grover Cleveland. James G. Blaine, the 1884 nominee, had stepped aside so that the party could rally behind a single candidate.

After eight ballots, the delegates nominated Benjamin Harrison, a former senator from Indiana and the grandson of President William Henry Harrison. Besides having a well-known name, Harrison came from a state whose electoral votes were considered crucial to a Republican victory. Harrison's campaign slogan was "Grandfather's Hat Fits!"

Cleveland and Harrison were both rather dull, honorable men whose campaigns matched their personalities. Cleveland made only one public appearance, while Harrison, acting under the advice of his campaign manager, stayed at home in Indianapolis, where he confined his remarks to prepared speeches before groups of people who had come to visit him.

The party platforms were remarkably similar. Both favored lower taxes, a larger navy, and statehood for the western territories. The only real difference between them had to do with tariff reform. Cleveland's insistence that tariff rates be lowered was very unpopular, and the Republicans—who favored high, protective tariffs—used the issue to hurt him.

For the fourth time in a row, the election was very close. Cleveland won the popular vote by one hundred thousand ballots but lost the electoral vote by sixty-five. Again, New York's thirty-six electoral votes, the most of any state, made the difference. Cleveland's enemies in Tammany Hall torpedoed his campaign there. Had the former governor carried New York, he would have won reelection by seven electoral votes.

BENJAMIN HARRISON

23RD PRESIDENT

★

FROM 1889 TO 1893

BORN: August 20, 1833

BIRTHPLACE: North Bend, Ohio

DIED: March 13, 1901

PARTY: Republican

VICE PRESIDENT: Levi P. Morton

FIRST LADY: Caroline Lavinia Scott

CHILDREN: Russell, Mary, Elizabeth

NICKNAME: Little Ben

The first president to use electricity in the White House.

Unlike Grover Cleveland, who could be pleasant and jovial, Benjamin Harrison was uncomfortable with people. He was highly formal, and his personality lacked warmth. Some people called him the "human iceberg."

But Harrison shared a number of important traits with Cleveland, including an attention to detail and a determined work ethic. Harrison was also personally incorruptible, which was more than could be said for his campaign manager, Matt Quay of Pennsylvania.

After winning the election, President-elect Harrison declared that "Providence has given us the victory."

Upon hearing Harrison's remark, Quay laughed, "Think of the man! He ought to know that Providence hadn't a damn thing to do with it." It was likely, Quay continued, that Harrison "would never know how close a number of men were compelled to

INDIANS MASSACRED AT WOUNDED KNEE

WOUNDED KNEE CREEK, S.D., December 29, 1890—The Seventh Cavalry today massacred more than two hundred Sioux men, women, and children who only last night had surrendered peacefully.

This morning, after the Sioux were nearly disarmed, a fight broke out over a young brave's new rifle. A shot went off, which prompted the soldiers to fire wildly into the crowd.

The Indians' clubs and knives were no match for the machine guns of General Custer's former outfit. It has been suggested that the troopers' murderous ferocity can be traced back to the regiment's defeat at the Little Big Horn.

These Sioux were the last followers of Wovoka, the holy man whose Ghost Dance religion had inspired the recent revival among the Indians. Wovoka preached that the Ghost Dance he taught would make the white man's bullets bounce off Indian warriors and bring Indian ancestors back from the dead.

approach the gates of the penitentiary to make him president." Quay's handling of the campaign left Harrison with a debt to big business that would have to be repaid sooner or later.

THE SHERMAN ANTI-TRUST ACT

During the Gilded Age, the country's largest corporations had created near-monopolies in a number of industries. In 1882, for example, John D. Rockefeller had formed the Standard Oil trust to corner the oil market legally.

In his inaugural address, Harrison warned the trusts to play by the rules of free trade or else face government discipline. When the trusts ignored his warning, Congress passed the first antitrust law in 1890.

The Sherman Anti-Trust Act, sponsored by Ohio senator John Sherman, made it a crime to restrict trade by "combination in the form of a trust or otherwise." This meant that men such as Rockefeller could no longer control, or combine, several companies in order to monopolize a particular industry.

There were a number of ways around the law, however, which were soon upheld in court. "What looks like a stone wall to a layman is a triumphal arch to a corporation lawyer," political humorist Finley Peter Dunne joked at the time.

FOREIGN POLICY

Under the leadership of Navy Secretary Benjamin F. Tracy, the Harrison administration continued the huge shipbuilding program begun during Cleveland's first term. The modernization of the navy fit in well with Harrison's plan to expand U.S. influence in Latin America and the Pacific.

Harrison favored an aggressive foreign policy and backed the first

The Early Years

BENJAMIN HARRISON WAS BORN AT THE NORTH BEND, Ohio, home of General William Henry Harrison. When he was seven, his grandfather was elected president. Benjamin's childhood was typical for a farm boy at that time. He fetched wood and water, fed the horses and cattle on the family's six-hundred-acre farm, hunted, fished, and swam.

In July 1862, after becoming a leading Republican lawyer in Indianapolis, Harrison went off to fight in the Civil War, joining the Seventieth Indiana Infantry as a second lieutenant. Rising eventually to the rank of brigadier general, Harrison fought bravely in Kentucky, Tennessee, Alabama, and Georgia.

★OLD WHISKERS President Harrison was an animal lover who always made sure his grandchildren had plenty of pets. The Harrisons had dogs, horses, and even an opossum. Their favorite pet was Old Whiskers, a goat. One day, as Old Whiskers pulled the children around the White House lawn in a cart, the gates were opened to allow the president's carriage to leave. Seizing his opportunity, Old Whiskers dashed for freedom. He took off through the gate with the children still in tow. The president couldn't believe his eyes. Nor could the residents of Washington, who watched the president of the United States race down the street, waving his cane and chasing a goat.

★POPULISM The populist movement of the 1890s had its roots in farmers' alliances such as the Grange movement of the 1870s. Granges were initially organized in the West to relieve the boredom of rural life. At first, they sponsored social activities. But they soon came to represent the farmers' political views as well.

In 1892, a number of populist groups met in St. Louis, where they formed the People's Party. Its members, mostly farmers, believed that big business had too much say in the way government was run. Wanting to reorganize things drastically, the populists called for government ownership of the railroads, an eight-hour workday, and a federal income tax.

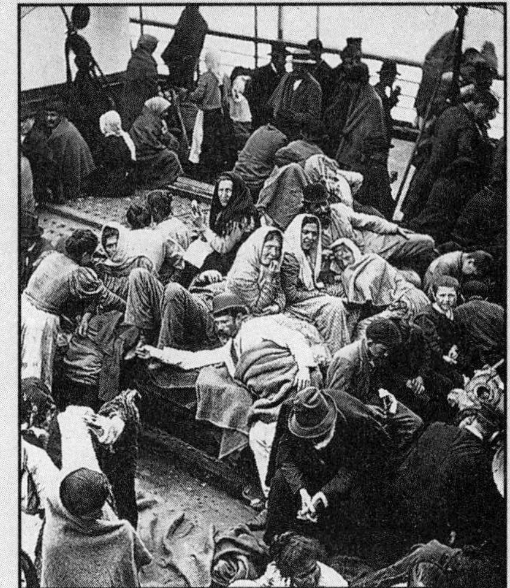

★ELLIS ISLAND By the 1890s, huge numbers of immigrants from Eastern and Central Europe were arriving in New York City every day. Overwhelmed port officials were in desperate need of a place to hold all these people until their papers could be processed.

On January 1, 1892, the federal government opened a new processing station on Ellis Island in Upper New York Bay within sight of the Statue of Liberty. For the next half-century, the red brick buildings on Ellis Island provided the first glimpse millions of immigrants, particularly Jews and Italians, got of their new home in the United States.

★CARRY A. NATION By 1890, alcoholism was becoming an increasingly severe problem in the United States. Drunkenness led to the abuse of women and children in the home as well as to absenteeism at work, not to mention frequent brawls in saloons. Women and church groups had for many years worked together unsuccessfully in the temperance movement. Their goal was to ban the sale of liquor.

The most zealous of the new wave of temperance crusaders was Carry A. Nation, who believed that her name was literally her destiny. An imposing woman who stood six feet tall and weighed 175 pounds, Nation became famous for using a hatchet to demolish saloons in Kansas. She was jailed often, but she always paid her fines using money raised from speaking tours and the sale of souvenir hatchets.

Pan-American Conference. Chaired by Secretary of State James G. Blaine, this conference increased the U.S. presence in Latin America and reduced that of Great Britain. Harrison's specific goal was to control the narrow strip of land called the Isthmus of Panama across which the United States hoped to build a canal.

Meanwhile in the Pacific, U.S. minister to Hawaii John L. Stevens landed troops to protect white business leaders who had recently rebelled against Queen Liliuokalani. After overthrowing her native government and setting up their own, the whites, mostly sugar growers, asked for immediate annexation to the United States. The president negotiated a treaty of annexation during his final weeks in office, but it was still pending before the Senate when Harrison's term ended.

THE TREASURY SURPLUS

One of the issues that Harrison faced at home was a huge Treasury surplus carried over from the Cleveland administration. Republicans and Democrats both wanted to get rid of the surplus, but they disagreed on how to do it. The Democrats wanted to lower the tariff rates and thereby take in less money, but Harrison and the Republicans wanted to spend the surplus.

The first big spending bill that Harrison signed was the Dependent and Disability Pensions Act of 1890. Harrison had been a general during the Civil War, and he had great sympathy for his fellow veterans. The Dependent and Disability Pensions Act showered money on them in the form of pensions for all Union veterans who were now unable to work for any reason. That is, their injuries did not have to be battle-related.

Meanwhile, new silver discoveries in Arizona and Nevada had created a

host of boom towns. However, the more silver the miners dug up, the less valuable the metal became, because the market could only absorb so much. To keep the price of silver up, miners lobbied the government to buy more silver with new paper money. Farmers in the South and West supported this policy because it would lead to inflation, which would make their debts cheaper to pay off.

Back East, the bankers who controlled the government's monetary policy were horrified at the thought of unlimited silver coinage. But they needed the support of the South and West to pass a new tariff bill. So the two sides agreed to a compromise.

The Sherman Silver Purchase Act committed the government to buy 4.5 million ounces of silver each month, nearly the entire output of the western mines. About the same time, the McKinley Tariff Act was passed.

THE McKINLEY TARIFF

The McKinley Tariff was the Harrison administration's payoff to big business for its support during the campaign. A highly protective measure, it raised tariff rates to forty-eight percent, their highest peacetime level ever.

But the bill, sponsored by future president William McKinley of Ohio, backfired. The point of the high tariff was to make foreign goods expensive so that Americans would be more likely to buy U.S. goods. But greedy manufacturers raised their prices to match those of the foreign goods.

Consumers were furious, and they turned their anger on the governing Republican party. A good many were voted out of office during the 1890 midterm elections, and two years later, President Harrison was tossed out, too.

CAMPAIGN 1892

THE ELECTION OF 1892 WAS A REMATCH. ALTHOUGH both candidates faced opposition within their parties, the Republicans renominated Benjamin Harrison, while the Democrats chose former president Grover Cleveland.

An early dump-Harrison movement tried to generate support for perennial candidate James G. Blaine, but the president's backers made sure he won renomination on the first ballot. Cleveland also won nomination on the first ballot, squeaking by despite vocal opposition from New York's Tammany Hall delegation and westerners who advocated the free coinage of silver, which Cleveland opposed.

The third candidate in the race was James Weaver, the nominee of the People's party, which met in Omaha. Weaver had run for president once before in 1880 as the choice of the short-lived Greenback party.

Once again, the election turned on the tariff issue, but this time the McKinley Tariff doomed the Republicans. Cleveland called attention to its upsetting effect on consumer prices and pointed out that he had favored a low tariff for years.

When the votes were counted, Cleveland won the popular vote by almost four hundred thousand, the biggest margin since Grant won reelection in 1872. Cleveland took the electoral vote, including New York's, by an even wider margin. But Weaver did remarkably well, becoming the only third party candidate between 1860 and 1912 to win at least one state. He carried four: Colorado, Idaho, Kansas, and Nevada.

Grover Cleveland

24th President

★

From 1893 to 1897

Born: March 18, 1837

Birthplace: Caldwell, N.J.

Died: June 24, 1908

Party: Democrat

Vice President: Adlai E. Stevenson

First Lady: Frances Folsom

Children: Ruth, Esther, Marion, Richard, Francis

Nickname: Uncle Jumbo

The Baby Ruth candy bar was named after Cleveland's daughter Ruth.

"Separate But Equal" Doctrine Upheld

WASHINGTON, May 18, 1896—The Supreme Court ruled today in the case of *Plessy v. Ferguson*. Its decision upheld Jim Crow laws in the South that require "separate but equal" facilities for black citizens.

The *Plessy* case hinged on an 1890 Louisiana law requiring blacks and whites to travel in separate railroad cars. When Homer Plessy refused to leave a car designated for whites only, he was arrested.

Plessy's attorneys had claimed that the Louisiana law violates their client's rights, but the Court ruled that separate accommodations are not necessarily unequal.

The Court's decision aside, the intent of the Jim Crow laws has clearly been to support white supremacy in the South. These laws, first passed at the end of Reconstruction in 1877, have segregated southern schools, parks, theaters, restaurants, and even cemeteries in addition to the railroads.

Grover Cleveland was the only president reelected after being voted out. He returned to the White House determined to lower tariff rates. But before he could do anything, the Panic of 1893 hit. The depression that followed lasted throughout Cleveland's second term.

The panic began even before Cleveland took office. In February 1893, the Philadelphia and Reading Railroad went broke, and soon others followed. By 1896, one-quarter of the nation's railroads had gone out of business.

With nearly a million workers, the railroads were the nation's biggest employers, and financing railroads was the biggest business on Wall Street. The railroad bankruptcies put hundreds of thousands of people out of work and brought Wall Street grinding to a halt.

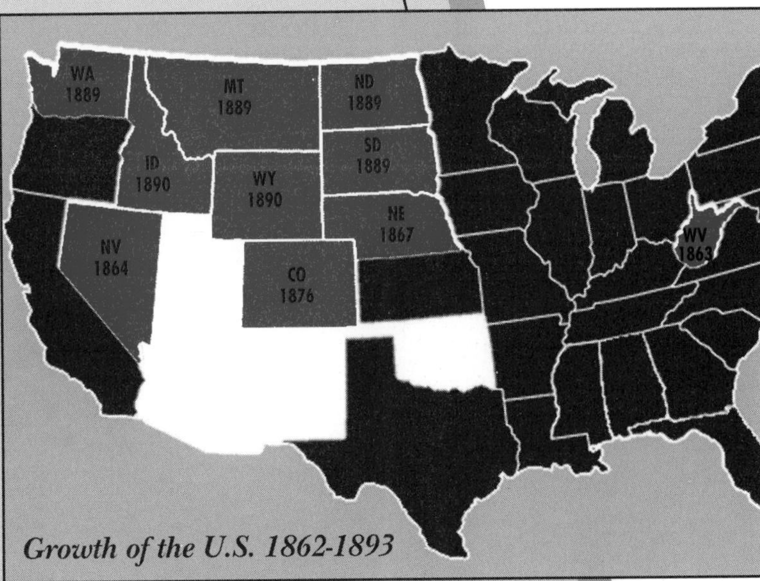

Growth of the U.S. 1862-1893

Many of the people who lost their jobs also lost their homes and became wandering hobos. Although Cleveland genuinely wanted to help these people, his belief in a "hands-off" government prevented him from proposing any relief programs. Instead, the president focused on keeping the economy above water until the storm of depression passed.

REPEAL OF THE SILVER PURCHASE ACT

The immediate crisis facing the federal government was the run on its gold reserves. Under the terms of the Sherman Silver Purchase Act, the government had to buy western silver with certificates that could be exchanged for gold. When people began using the certificates to trade their silver for gold, the government's gold supply dropped. By April 1893, the Treasury's reserves had fallen below one hundred million dollars.

Cleveland's first move was to call an emergency session of Congress to repeal the Silver Purchase Act. A terrible fight followed between conservatives, who favored the gold standard, and populists, who wanted free coinage of silver. Keeping the gold standard meant that U.S. currency would be backed by gold alone. Free coinage of silver would mean that money could be made from either silver or gold, thereby increasing the money supply.

If there were more dollars in circulation, the value of each one would go down. This prospect pleased the western and southern farmers, who didn't have much cash, but it infuriated the eastern bankers, who did.

The fight created a deep division within the Democratic party between Cleveland's "goldbugs" and the populist "silverites." The silverites were led by a dynamic young

★**SECRET SURGERY** In 1893, as Cleveland began his second term, his doctors discovered a cancerous tumor in his mouth. Believing that news of his illness might shock a nation already weakened by the Panic of 1893, Cleveland decided to have the cancer treated secretly. He quietly boarded a yacht in New York's East River, where a team of surgeons performed an hour-long operation. Working from the inside of the president's mouth so as not to leave a visible scar, they removed part of his jaw and replaced it with a rubber substitute. The operation remained a secret until one of the doctors wrote a magazine article about it in 1917.

★ **GIBSON GIRLS** Charles Dana Gibson was the highest-paid illustrator of his generation. His turn-of-the-century drawings defined the American ideal of beauty at that time. The women he drew, called Gibson girls, looked pale, dreamy, and innocent. They typically wore full, upswept hairstyles, called "pompadours," and had "hourglass" figures. Their male companions were broad-shouldered and usually clean-shaven, which started a trend. Before the appearance of the Gibson man, mustaches and beards were extremely popular.

★**BREAKFAST CEREALS** The first flaked breakfast cereal was invented by Dr. John Harvey Kellogg, the superintendent of Michigan's Battle Creek Sanitarium. The sanitarium was founded by Seventh Day Adventists, who are vegetarians. Kellogg invented cornflakes in 1895 as a healthful substitute for animal foods.

Calling his new cereal Granose, Kellogg and his brother sold ten-ounce packages for fifteen cents. About the same time, C.W. Post, a patient at the sanitarium, saw commercial possibilities in the idea of ready-to-eat breakfast cereals. In 1897, Post introduced Grape Nuts, each box of which contained his pamphlet *The Road to Wellsville.*

★**COXEY'S ARMY** In response to the depression, populist leader Jacob Coxey of Ohio proposed a half-billion-dollar public works program to help the unemployed. To rally support for this idea, he decided to lead an "army" of unemployed workers to Washington. "We will send a petition to Washington with boots on," he said.

On March 25, 1894, Coxey began the march with one hundred people. He hoped a hundred thousand more might join him, but Coxey's Army numbered just five hundred when it reached the steps of the Capitol on April 30. Police immediately arrested Coxey for trampling on the Capitol lawn, but Coxey's march heightened public awareness of the unemployment problem all over the country.

★**YELLOW JOURNALISM** In 1895, William Randolph Hearst bought the *New York Journal* and began a celebrated circulation war with Joseph Pulitzer's *New York World.* This battle over which newspaper could sell the most copies changed the newspaper business forever. Hearst and Pulitzer both tried to attract readers by playing up sensational stories, especially those relating to the rebellion in Cuba. This kind of exaggerated or unnecessarily dramatic reporting was called "yellow journalism" after a well-known comic strip, "The Yellow Kid," that was printed in the *Journal.* Hearst and Pulitzer's feverish reporting was in large part responsible for the Spanish-American War.

congressman from Nebraska named William Jennings Bryan, who held Congress spellbound with his electrifying speeches against the gold standard.

In the end, a coalition of Republicans and goldbug Democrats forced the repeal of the Silver Purchase Act. But that didn't stop the gold drain as Cleveland had expected. Now even more desperate, the president turned to Wall Street for help.

At Cleveland's request, J.P. Morgan organized a group of his fellow bankers to come to the Treasury's aid. Their loan of sixty-two million dollars in gold to the government reversed the drain and stabilized the economy. Although people's confidence in the government was restored, Morgan and his friends made a great deal of money on the loan. This led the populists to accuse Cleveland of being a puppet of Wall Street.

LABOR UNREST Meanwhile, big business used the depression as an excuse to cut workers' wages unfairly. Because the workers' quality of life was already quite low, these additional cuts merely goaded the labor movement into aggression and violence.

After the Civil War, as manufacturing industries grew larger and more powerful, companies forced workers—mostly immigrants—to accept wage cuts, longer days, and more dangerous working conditions. For most people stuck in this life of misery, unionization was the only hope.

The strikes organized by the unions usually turned violent when company bosses hired men to break up the unions by beating up the strikers. With the government, and therefore the police, on their side, the bosses usually won.

A famous example was the 1894 strike at the Pullman Palace Car

Company outside Chicago. When the Pullman Company cut wages but refused to lower rents in the company town or prices at the company store, the workers appealed for help to the American Railway Union, which Eugene V. Debs had organized only the year before.

When Pullman refused to negotiate, Debs led 120,000 workers out on strike. Although peaceful and orderly, the strike stopped nearly all the rail traffic between Chicago and the West. In fact, Debs thought he had nearly won when Cleveland's attorney general, Richard Olney, got a court injunction banning the strike. When Debs refused to obey the injunction, Olney sent in federal troops and had Debs arrested. The troops broke up the strike, and the workers were forced to return to their jobs.

Although Olney's actions temporarily ended the crisis, they also raised the level of tension between business and labor. The new labor unions, such as Samuel Gompers's American Federation of Labor, became convinced that business and government were conspiring together to enslave the working class.

THE WILSON-GORMAN TARIFF

Cleveland was so preoccupied with the economic crisis that he didn't get around to tariff reform until 1894. In that year, Representative William Wilson sponsored a bill in the House that dramatically reduced tariff rates. But the bill was reworked in the Senate by Arthur Gorman of Maryland until it barely lowered tariff rates at all. Calling the bill "party dishonor," the president refused to sign it.

Having thus failed even to reduce tariff rates, Cleveland left office as one of the most unpopular presidents of all time.

CAMPAIGN 1896

WILLIAM JENNINGS BRYAN WAS DETERMINED TO HAVE the Democratic party platform support the free coinage of silver. The platform speech he delivered to the convention, one of the most acclaimed in U.S. political history, also won him the nomination. "You shall not press down upon the brow of labor this crown of thorns; you shall not crucify mankind upon a cross of gold," Bryan said.

The Republicans nominated Governor William McKinley of Ohio on the first ballot. As a congressman, McKinley had sponsored the hated McKinley Tariff. Nevertheless, he had shown surprising strength at the 1892 Republican convention.

The campaign turned on the currency issue, which also muddied party lines. Unwilling to support either the prosilver policies of Bryan or the protective tariff advocated by McKinley, Cleveland and the goldbug Democrats backed their own candidate. Meanwhile, the Populists threw in with Bryan, who had already adopted nearly all their ideas.

The thirty-six-year-old Bryan crisscrossed the country, traveling eighteen thousand miles in three months, while McKinley stayed home and let campaign manager Mark Hanna run the election for him. Bryan had tremendous popular support in the South and West, but the Republicans controlled the East, where the money was. Raising three million dollars from leading industrialists, Hanna was able to flood the country with Republican pamphlets written in different languages so that McKinley could attract immigrant voters. By comparison, Bryan raised only five hundred thousand dollars, mostly from owners of silver mines.

Although Bryan's personal appeal was powerful, his target audience of farmers now made up less than half the population. Buoyed by the growing power of the urban manufacturing interests, McKinley won a decisive victory.

William McKinley

25th President

★

From 1897 to 1901

Born: January 29, 1843

Birthplace: Niles, Ohio

Died: September 14, 1901

Party: Republican

Vice President: Garret A. Hobart, Theodore Roosevelt

First Lady: Ida Saxton

Children: Katherine, Ida

Nickname: Wobbly Willie

Always wore a red carnation in his lapel for good luck.

REMEMBER THE MAINE!

Mysterious Explosion Sinks U.S. Ship

HAVANA, February 15, 1898—The U.S. battleship *Maine* sunk today in the harbor at Havana after an unexplained explosion punched a hole in its side. Two hundred and sixty sailors went down with the ship.

Investigators have been unable to determine the cause of the blast. The Spanish have insisted that the explosion was an accident, but unsubstantiated reports in U.S. newspapers have blamed an underwater Spanish mine.

The *Maine* had been sent to the Spanish colony of Cuba in January as a show of force to discourage the seizure of U.S. property there. The Cubans have been fighting for their independence from Spain since 1895.

Given the current war fever, the sinking of the *Maine* will almost surely lead to war with Spain.

William McKinley had a notably warm and engaging personality. It was often said of him that a person could walk into his office angry and walk out with a smile.

It helped McKinley's popularity that, like Cleveland, he was a conservative, hands-off politician. Big business was given free rein during his term, and hugely powerful trusts were allowed to develop without much restraint.

McKinley's immediate problem upon taking office was a growing budget deficit. Because the Supreme Court had recently ruled that a proposed income tax was unconstitutional, the government's revenues still came primarily from tariffs on imported goods.

Tariff rates had been the hottest issue during the last three elections. When the Democrats were in power, they lowered the rates. With Republicans such as McKinley in office, the rates went up again. The Dingley Tariff, which replaced the 1894 Wilson-Gorman Act, raised tariff rates even higher than the protective McKinley Tariff had in 1890.

At first, the public protested the Dingley Tariff because it raised prices on consumer goods, especially imported ones. But the protests didn't last long as the country soon became distracted by events taking place in Cuba.

THE CUBAN REVOLT The depression caused by the Panic of 1893 hurt Cuba's huge sugar industry badly. The Wilson-Gorman Tariff, which imposed a forty percent duty on sugar, made matters even worse. By 1895, the suffering and unemployment on the island moved the desperately poor Cubans to revolt against their Spanish colonial rulers.

The Spanish responded brutally, imprisoning the Cuban rebels in concentration camps where two hundred thousand people died of disease and starvation. Whipped into a frenzy by the grisly and often exaggerated newspaper accounts of Spanish atrocities, Americans demanded that their government do something. But Grover Cleveland, who was still president, refused to interfere, and tensions continued to mount.

When McKinley became president, he tried to avoid a fight. As a veteran of the Civil War, he knew how bloody war could be. But the sinking of the *Maine* in the harbor at Havana made war inevitable.

The Spanish maintained that the explosion had been an accident, while a U.S. investigation proved inconclusive. But the popular press kept insisting that the sinking of the *Maine* had been deliberate. McKinley couldn't resist the public sentiment in favor of war. On April 11, 1898, he sent a message to Congress urging the use of military force to pacify Cuba.

WILLIAM MCKINLEY WAS EIGHTEEN YEARS OLD when the Civil War started in April 1861. He enlisted as a private two months later and fought at Antietam, where he carried desperately needed rations to the front. For his bravery under fire, McKinley was promoted to second lieutenant. His new commanding officer was Colonel Rutherford B. Hayes, the future president. Of McKinley, Hayes once said, "Young as he was, we soon found that in the business of a soldier..., young McKinley showed unusual and unsurpassed capacity." McKinley's political career began when he helped Hayes win election as governor of Ohio in 1867.

★**THE FIRST LADY** McKinley met Ida Saxton in 1867 at a picnic in Canton, Ohio, where he had recently moved to set up a law practice. The future Mrs. McKinley was working as a cashier in her father's bank, an unusual job for a woman at that time. In fact, Ida McKinley was the first wife of a president to have worked in a profession other than teaching. Because the first lady suffered from a form of epilepsy that caused occasional seizures, McKinley insisted that she be seated beside him at state dinners. This broke a White House tradition of seating the first lady at the opposite end of the table from the president.

★**MOTION PICTURES** The first motion pictures were introduced by Thomas Edison in 1894. He called his viewers Kinetoscopes. People put coins into these machines and looked through peepholes to view short reels of film. The first "peep show" was *Fred Ott's Sneeze.* Fred Ott was an Edison factory worker who volunteered to sneeze for the camera.

Edison's mistake was that his Kinetoscopes played to only one viewer at a time. Two years later, the French brothers Auguste and Louis Lumière opened the world's first movie theater in Paris. Their Cinematographe was the first true movie projector. Unlike the Kinetoscope, it projected a movie onto a screen so that a large audience could view it.

★**The Klondike Gold Rush** Gold was first discovered along the Klondike Creek, a tributary of the Yukon River, in August 1896. But the remoteness of Canada's Yukon Territory and the onset of winter, which lasted from September until May, kept news of the Klondike strike from reaching the outside world.

The greatest gold rush in North American history began on July 16, 1897, when the news finally reached the telegraph wires. Two days later, a ship carrying two tons of Klondike gold docked in San Francisco, adding to the excitement. As the forty-niners had during the California gold rush, tens of thousands of miners hurried to northwest Canada and nearby Alaska to find their fortunes. The gold they mined expanded the money supply and helped to end the depression. It also muted populist calls for the free coinage of silver.

★**Jazz** During the late 1890s, John Philip Sousa's military marching band played the most popular music in the country. Sousa wrote highly patriotic songs such as "The Stars and Stripes Forever." In New Orleans, however, black musicians were developing a new kind of popular music. Adding complex ragtime rhythms to the brass band melodies, they created a new style of music called jazz. Early jazz bands typically used marching band instruments such as trumpets, saxophones, trombones, and drums. Some groups also used pianos, bass fiddles, and guitars.

THE SPANISH-AMERICAN WAR

Secretary of State John Hay called the Spanish-American War a "splendid little war" because it was quick and relatively painless for the United States. Only a few hundred soldiers were killed in battle, although several thousand more died from tropical diseases.

The war began in earnest on April 30, 1898, when the U.S. Pacific fleet under Commodore George Dewey sailed into Manila Bay in the Philippines. The United States had long coveted the Spanish colony, and the next day Dewey easily defeated the outdated Spanish fleet in the harbor there.

A month later, seventeen thousand soldiers left Florida for Cuba. The First Volunteer Cavalry Regiment, nicknamed the Rough Riders, was led by Theodore Roosevelt, who had just resigned as assistant secretary of the navy.

The Rough Riders were generally untrained and disorganized, but the Spanish were even more hopeless. Caught between the Rough Riders and the powerful U.S. Navy, the Spanish agreed to surrender Cuba on August 12.

In the peace talks that followed, the Cubans were granted limited independence, but the United States took possession of Puerto Rico, Guam, and the Philippines. With the annexation of Hawaii that same year, the nation was well on its way to becoming an imperial as well as a world power.

THE ANNEXATION OF HAWAII

Grover Cleveland had been so outraged by U.S. complicity in the overthrow of Queen Liliuokalani that, when he regained the presidency in 1893, he immediately withdrew the Hawaiian annexation treaty submitted by Benjamin Harrison.

Cleveland tried to restore native rule to the Hawaiian islands, but the provisional government run by the white planters refused to yield its control. When McKinley replaced Cleveland as president, U.S. policy changed again, and Hawaii was annexed in July 1898.

THE OPEN DOOR POLICY One reason for U.S. interest in the Pacific was the new and potentially huge China trade. Because China was the most populous country in Asia, and also undeveloped, U.S. businesses were anxious to establish markets there.

But the Western European powers were also interested in China, as was Japan. Despite its size, China was quite weak militarily. Secretary of State John Hay worried that the Europeans and Japan would simply divide the country into "spheres of influence," leaving nothing for the United States.

To prevent this, Hay developed the Open Door policy. He sent a series of notes in September 1899 to the European powers and Japan asking them to allow equal status for all nations trading with China.

Before the Open Door policy could be adopted, however, a group of Chinese nationalists rose up in the countryside and advanced on the capital of Peking. These people were members of a secret society known as the Righteous and Harmonious Fists. Westerners called them Boxers. Their goal was to remove all foreigners from their country.

In June 1900, the Boxers rioted in Peking. The Chinese empress decided to support them. She ordered that all foreigners in China be killed. After the German minister was murdered, most of the remaining foreigners took refuge in the British embassy. The Boxer Rebellion ended when an international rescue force captured Peking on August 14.

BY 1900, THE ECONOMY HAD TURNED AROUND completely. The depression years of the early 1890s were over, in part thanks to the Klondike gold rush. The country basked in prosperity. Knowing a popular president when they saw one, the Republicans eagerly renominated McKinley for a second term.

The only suspense surrounded the choice of a new running mate to replace Vice President Garret Hobart, who had died in office. McKinley announced that he would accept the will of the convention. Republican delegates chose Spanish-American War hero Theodore Roosevelt, then serving as governor of New York.

CAMPAIGN 1900

McKinley's opponent was once again William Jennings Bryan, the only Democratic leader with a truly national reputation. Although McKinley had beaten Bryan in 1896, the Nebraskan had kept control of his party. Winning renomination easily, he insisted that the Democrats include a free-silver plank in their 1900 party platform. His uncompromising position unnecessarily drove away gold Democrats and signaled his campaign was in trouble.

Bryan denounced McKinley for turning the United States into an imperial power by keeping the Philippine Islands after the Spanish-American War. The Republicans responded that the nation was obliged to bring "civilization" to the people who lived there.

McKinley replayed his front-porch campaign of 1896, allowing the energetic forty-one-year-old Roosevelt to campaign for him. The Republican slogan, "Four Years More of the Full Dinner Pail," emphasized the country's newfound prosperity and carried McKinley to an easy victory.

THEODORE ROOSEVELT

26TH PRESIDENT

★

FROM 1901 TO 1909

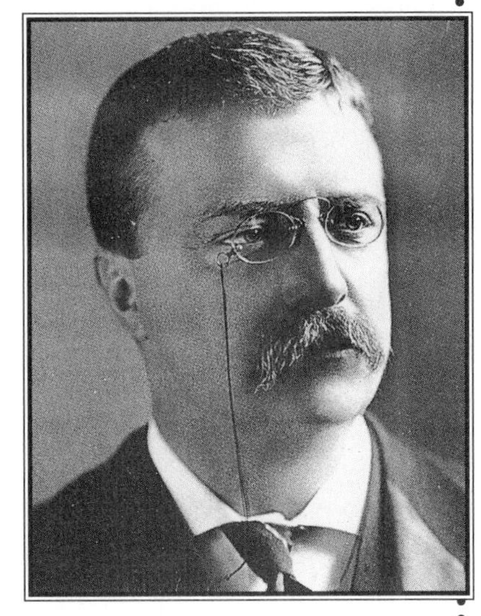

BORN: October 27, 1858

BIRTHPLACE: New York, N.Y.

DIED: January 6, 1919

PARTY: Republican

VICE PRESIDENT: Charles W. Fairbanks

FIRST LADY: Edith Kermit Carow

CHILDREN: Alice; Theodore, Jr.; Kermit; Ethel; Archibald; Quentin

NICKNAME: TR

The first president to fly in an airplane.

Although he was relatively young when he suddenly became president, Theodore Roosevelt was prepared for his new job, being both well read and well traveled. In his spare time, he read books on every conceivable subject. Sometimes he read as many as three books a night.

Yet Roosevelt was far from a shy, bookish intellectual. He loved strenuous exercise of all kinds, including horseback riding, hiking, swimming, hunting, and boxing. While he was governor of New York, he once wrestled the middleweight champion. As president, he kept in shape by boxing regularly with professional sparring partners. Every so often, he would invite political rivals to climb into the ring with him for a "friendly" round of boxing.

Roosevelt's tough image served him well as president.

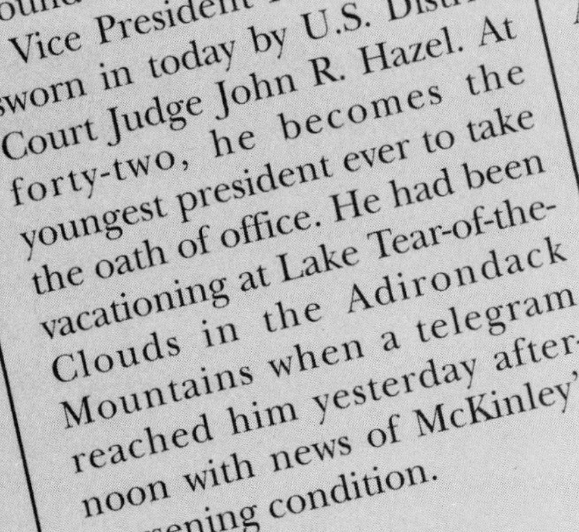

ASSASSIN'S BULLET KILLS McKINLEY

Vice President Roosevelt Succeeds Him

BUFFALO, September 14, 1901—President McKinley died shortly after two o'clock this morning, eight days after he was shot by an unemployed millworker. McKinley's death surprised his doctors, who had thought the president was recovering from the bullet wound in his abdomen.

Vice President Roosevelt was sworn in today by U.S. District Court Judge John R. Hazel. At forty-two, he becomes the youngest president ever to take the oath of office. He had been vacationing at Lake Tear-of-the-Clouds in the Adirondack Mountains when a telegram reached him yesterday afternoon with news of McKinley's worsening condition.

Roosevelt traveled all night to reach a small town where he could catch a train for Buffalo. When he arrived at the station, he found another telegram waiting for him. This one told him McKinley had died during the night.

McKinley was shot on September 6 by Leon Czolgosz, who had been waiting in line to shake the president's hand. A bandage over Czolgosz's right hand concealed the revolver he used to shoot McKinley. According to Czolgosz, "I done my duty. I don't believe one man should have so much service and another man should have none."

One of his first policy moves was also his most controversial. Soon after he took office, Roosevelt introduced "trust-busting."

TRUST-BUSTING

Trusts are companies that work together to limit competition in an industry, such as the tobacco or steel industry. The most famous trust in U.S. history was the Standard Oil trust run by John D. Rockefeller. The point of Rockefeller's trust was to fix oil prices. Rockefeller knew that if he controlled the major oil companies, he could set whatever price he wanted.

Political leaders who favored the interests of working people over those of big business were commonly called "progressives." They opposed trusts because of the unfair practices trusts used to drive small companies out of business. Progressives thought that breaking up the trusts would result in more competition and better prices for consumers.

In his first speech to Congress, Roosevelt agreed that the most ruthless trusts needed to be reformed. But there was a lot of political opposition, even within the president's own party.

THE NORTHERN SECURITIES CASE

On March 10, 1902, Roosevelt brought suit under the Sherman Anti-Trust Act against a railroad trust called the Northern Securities Company. Although his action shocked Wall Street, the antitrust suit was extremely popular with the public.

It helped Roosevelt that he understood Wall Street businessmen. He was practically one of them. His father was a wealthy merchant who served on many corporate boards of directors. As a result, Roosevelt knew most of the important business leaders in the United States.

The Early Years

TEDDY ROOSEVELT WAS A SICKLY CHILD. DURING MUCH OF his boyhood, he suffered from asthma, which prevented him from attending school. He often had to sleep sitting up in a chair or his coughing would keep him awake all night.

Many years later, in 1884, after the death of his first wife, Alice Lee, Teddy moved out west to work as a rancher in the Dakota Territory. The two years Roosevelt spent in Dakota changed his life. He left a thin, spindly man but returned with his famous barrel chest and thick neck. He married his second wife, Edith Carow, shortly after his return.

Roosevelt later said that he never would have become president if it weren't for his years in the Dakota Territory. Out west, where Roosevelt's wealth and connections meant little, he mixed with cowboys, gunslingers, drunks, and gamblers.

During the Spanish-American War in 1898, Roosevelt served as commander of a volunteer cavalry unit known as the Rough Riders. On July 1, he led a charge up San Juan Hill in Cuba. Press reports made him a national hero and helped him win election as governor of New York that same year.

★THE WRIGHT BROTHERS Orville and Wilbur Wright operated a bicycle shop in Dayton, Ohio. They first began thinking about flying machines after reading newspaper articles about German experiments with gliders. They built their first glider in 1900.

The Wright Brothers' experiments with gliders taught them about flying machines. To build a powered airplane, the Wrights would need to develop a strong propeller and a lightweight engine, neither of which existed.

They called their first powered glider *Flyer I.* Orville made the first test flight on December 17, 1903, at Kitty Hawk, North Carolina. In the first sustained flight ever, *Flyer I* stayed aloft for twelve seconds, traveling 120 feet.

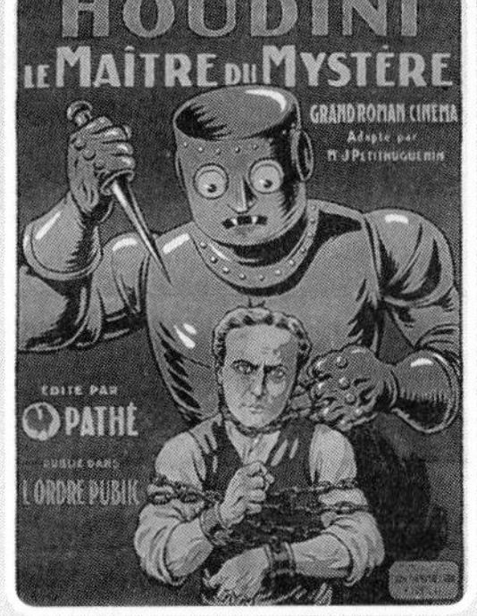

★HARRY HOUDINI Harry Houdini was the most famous escape artist of all time. Beginning in the early 1900s, he made an international reputation for himself as a magician. But he was most famous for his death-defying escapes. He would often be handcuffed, bound with ropes and chains, and placed inside a locked container, such as a trunk. Sometimes the container was even submerged in water. If Houdini didn't escape quickly, he would drown.

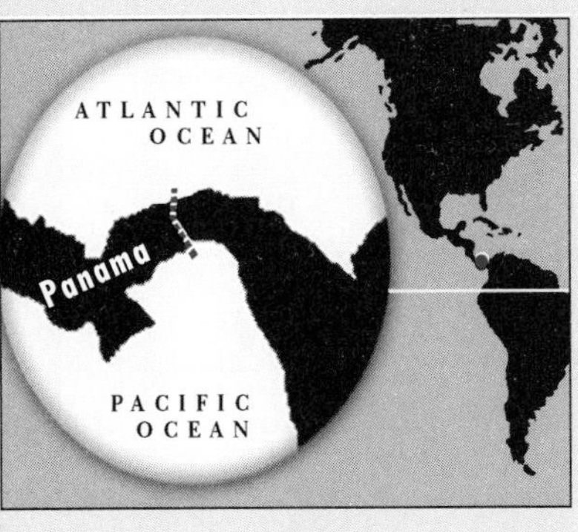

★THE PANAMA CANAL Both navigators and statesmen had long dreamed of a canal connecting the Atlantic and Pacific oceans. Without a canal, ships traveling from New York to San Francisco had to sail all the way around Cape Horn at the southern tip of South America. A canal across Central America would save seven thousand miles.

Construction of the canal began in 1904, but the work was delayed by tropical disease epidemics. A new plan by Chief Engineer John F. Stevens sped up construction. But the greatest contribution was made by Colonel William C. Gorgas, the sanitary officer. It was his work in eliminating yellow fever and malaria that made the project possible. The fifty-mile-long canal opened to shipping on August 15, 1914.

★THE TEDDY BEAR In 1902, Roosevelt went on a bear hunt in Mississippi, but the only one he found was a small black cub caught by the hunting dogs. TR refused to shoot the cub.

After hearing the story, Clifford Berryman drew a cartoon of the incident for the *Washington Post.* Two days later, Brooklyn toy maker Morris Michtom placed a copy of that cartoon in his window next to a stuffed brown bear, which he called "Teddy's Bear." The name, which stuck, was later shortened to "teddy bear."

Although Roosevelt's approach was pioneering, it also had its moderate aspects. The president didn't want to bust all the trusts, only the worst offenders. He believed that taking no action might lead Congress to take even more radical measures later on. Roosevelt called his middle path the Square Deal.

Two years passed before the Northern Securities case reached the Supreme Court, where it would finally be decided. No one really knew how the justices would rule. In earlier cases involving the Sherman Anti-Trust Act, they had ruled in favor of big business. When the ruling in the Northern Securities case came down, however, it was five to four against the trust.

The court's decision was an important victory for Roosevelt's antitrust policy. The vote was particularly close because one of the president's own appointees to the court—Justice Oliver Wendell Holmes, Jr.—voted against him. Upon hearing the news of Holmes's dissent, Roosevelt exclaimed, "I could carve a better judge out of a banana."

THE PENNSYLVANIA COAL STRIKE The most serious domestic crisis of Roosevelt's first term came in May 1902, several months after the Justice Department first filed the Northern Securities case. At that time, coal miners in Pennsylvania went on strike for better wages and safer working conditions.

During the last quarter of the nineteenth century, U.S. presidents generally sided with business owners against striking workers. But Roosevelt was a different sort of president. He sensed that times had changed and that people thought things should be different. One of his first moves was to send in federal troops. Roosevelt said the troops were being sent to protect the mine owners' property. But the soldiers were really there to protect the striking miners as well. Business owners typically ended strikes by hiring toughs to beat up striking workers. The presence of federal troops prevented that.

Next, Roosevelt invited both sides to Washington, where he helped management and labor resolve their differences peacefully. Because the strikers won many of their demands, Roosevelt's popularity soared. With his antitrust policy and now his active intervention in the Pennsylvania coal strike, Roosevelt made it clear that his administration would protect the public interest against the greed of big business.

BIG STICK DIPLOMACY On the international stage, President Roosevelt also benefited from his tough-guy image. His motto was "Speak softly and carry a big stick." As a result, his foreign policy was called Big Stick Diplomacy. The most noteworthy example of Roosevelt's approach to foreign affairs involved the Monroe Doctrine.

In 1823, President James Monroe had warned European nations against further colonization of the American continents. In 1904, Roosevelt added to the Monroe Doctrine what became known as the Roosevelt Corollary. (A corollary is a statement that logically follows from a previous statement.)

At the time, the government of the Dominican Republic was deeply in debt to several European nations. France and Italy, in particular, were threatening to take over the country if the debt wasn't promptly repaid.

In a speech to Congress, Roosevelt repeated the principle of the Monroe Doctrine: The United States would not tolerate any European intervention in the Americas.

However, with the Roosevelt Corollary, he went further. The

CAMPAIGN 1904

By 1904, when the next election came around, Teddy Roosevelt was really enjoying himself as president. The public was fascinated by his constant activity and energy, his fun-loving family, and his boundless idealism. But Roosevelt still had to convince the Republican party that he was the man to nominate.

After all, McKinley had been the nominee in 1900, and Roosevelt had become president only as the result of McKinley's assassination.

The older Republican leaders didn't like Teddy, whom they considered a young upstart. These men would have preferred to nominate Mark Hanna, the political boss and senator from Ohio who had helped McKinley rise to the presidency. When Hanna died in February, however, the nomination went to Roosevelt.

Traditionally, the Republicans favored big business, while the Democrats supported progressive candidates who advocated reform. Because Roosevelt was himself a progressive, the Democrats weren't sure what to do. In the end, they nominated a conservative candidate, Judge Alton Parker of New York, hoping to capture Republican votes.

The result was one of the greatest landslides in U.S. history. Roosevelt had expected to win, but not by such an overwhelming margin. "My dear," he told his second wife, Edith, "I am no longer a political accident."

president reserved for the United States the right to intervene in the affairs of any Latin American country that proved incapable of governing itself.

The Roosevelt Corollary was highly controversial. Critics argued that it would lead to U.S. imperialism of the kind that the Europeans practiced in Africa and Asia. In this way, the countries of Latin America would become colonies of the United States.

The president's supporters argued that the Roosevelt Corollary was simply common sense. The world was a dangerous place, and there was no nation better suited than the United States to police Latin America.

Whatever people thought, it was clear that Roosevelt was establishing U.S. leadership in the world as no president had before.

SINCLAIR'S JUNGLE EXPOSES THE MEAT INDUSTRY

Novel Leads to Passage of New Food Laws

Upton Sinclair's novel *The Jungle* was published in January 1906. In telling the story of Jurgis Rudkus, a fictional Lithuanian immigrant working in a meat packing factory, Sinclair exposed the corrupt and dangerous practices of the meat industry in the United States, and especially in Chicago.

Throughout this period, a number of crusading journalists were busy investigating corruption in U.S. industry. But it was Sinclair's novel that turned public concern into outrage. Publication of *The Jungle* led President Roosevelt to call immediately for federal regulation of food and drugs.

Two bills were quickly passed by Congress and signed by the president in June 1906. The Meat Inspection Act provided for federal inspection of meat so that consumers could be sure that the meat they bought met certain standards of freshness. Canned meats had to be accurately labeled and dated.

The second bill, the Pure Food and Drug Act, established national standards to prevent businesses from adding harmful preservatives and other hazardous ingredients to food and drugs. Never before had the federal government regulated private business so much.

THE PANAMA CANAL One of the memorable achievements of Roosevelt's first term was the Panama Canal. The president was eager to begin work on the canal before his 1904 reelection campaign. The problem was that the canal zone belonged to the nation of Colombia, which did not want to sell.

When revolution broke out in Panama in November 1903, Roosevelt supported the rebels. Once the Panamanians won their independence from Colombia, Roosevelt simply bought the canal territory from them on the same terms the Colombians had refused.

A sausage factory

Roosevelt's landslide victory in the 1904 election gave him the support he needed to pursue his progressive policies. He went to work in a whirlwind of activity. A foreign crisis, however, soon captured his attention.

THE RUSSO-JAPANESE WAR

The Russo-Japanese War began on February 8, 1904, when the Japanese launched a surprise attack on the Russian troops stationed at Port Arthur in Manchuria, which had traditionally been part of China. The Russians had recently broken a promise to withdraw from Port Arthur.

For months President Roosevelt worked behind the scenes to stop the fighting. He proposed a number of cease-fire plans, but Russia and Japan could not agree on a formula for peace. Finally, on June 11, 1905, Roosevelt negotiated a breakthrough. The two warring nations announced that they would accept the U.S. president's latest plan for peace.

Formal talks began on August 9 in Portsmouth, New Hampshire. On August 29, Russian and Japanese diplomats agreed to a treaty ending the war. Roosevelt was overjoyed, having used all his skill and influence to achieve the peace.

Russia and Japan gave Roosevelt ample credit for the Treaty of Portsmouth, and Britain, France, and Germany joined in the applause for the president's accomplishment.

In 1906, Roosevelt became the first American to win a Nobel prize when he won the Nobel Peace Prize. The Nobel prizes are awarded annually in Sweden in such areas as science, medicine, and literature.

Until Roosevelt's time, it was highly unusual for a U.S. president to be so active in world affairs. During the nineteenth century, presidents tried to stay out of European and Asian disputes as much as possible.

★THE FIRST FAMILY Journalists who covered TR said that life in the White House often resembled a circus. The president's two youngest sons, Archie and Quentin, caused most of the uproar. One of their favorite games was sliding down the central staircase on metal trays. Once Quentin rode his pony Algonquin upstairs into Archie's bedroom to cheer up his brother, who was sick.

TR's oldest child, his daughter Alice, was called Princess Alice by the press. Like the rest of her family, she loved to shock people. She would smoke in public, which was considered very bad manners for a woman. She also defied the standards set for women of the day by going to racetracks and betting on horses. She would even show off her pet snake on occasion. Alice was very popular, however, and her name became a favorite one for babies.

★THE GREAT CONSERVATIONIST Teddy Roosevelt had an especially strong love of nature. As a boy, he wanted to become a zoologist. He would later fill his Sagamore Hill home on New York's Long Island with trophies from his various hunting trips and safaris.

TR's love of nature drove him to be particularly active in the field of environmental conservation. In this work, he joined conservationists such as John Muir in California who argued that the United States must preserve its wilderness.

The country's first national park, Yellowstone in Wyoming, was established in 1872. Eighteen years later, Muir convinced the federal government to create the Yosemite and Sequoia parks in California. Roosevelt used his influence to preserve almost two hundred million acres of government land, mostly in the Northwest and Alaska.

★*HOW THE OTHER HALF LIVES* In the 1880s, Jacob Riis began using a camera to document the terrible living conditions of poor immigrants to this country. As a police reporter in New York City, he had plenty of opportunity to see how these people lived in urban tenement apartments. An immigrant himself, Riis crusaded for better conditions for the hundreds of thousands of people who sought a better life in the United States. In 1890, he published his photos in *How the Other Half Lives.* This book awakened public opinion and did much to fuel the progressive reforms of the Roosevelt, Taft, and Wilson administrations.

★MUCKRAKERS "Muckraker" was the name given to reform-minded journalists who wrote about corruption in big business. Important muckrakers included Upton Sinclair, Lincoln Steffens, and Ida Tarbell. Their articles rallied public support for progressive causes, especially government reform. Ida Tarbell's work helped bring down the Standard Oil trust.

The word "muckraker" was coined by Roosevelt, who borrowed it from *The Pilgrim's Progress* by English writer John Bunyan. Bunyan wrote about "the Man with the Muckrake... who could look no way but downward."

Roosevelt meant the name to be critical. He thought muckrakers focused too much on what was wrong with modern life and ignored what was good about it. The name quickly took on a positive meaning, however, because of the useful work the muckrakers were doing.

★THE MODEL T FORD In October 1908, Henry Ford introduced the Model T. "I will build a car for the great multitude," he said. The first Model Ts sold for $850, a fortune at the time. But Ford kept his promise. The development of assembly-line manufacturing made production more efficient, and the price of the Model T fell dramatically.

By 1927, when the car was discontinued, the price had dropped to three hundred dollars, making it widely affordable. In the meantime, Ford had sold more than fifteen million of these cars. Half the cars in the world were Model Ts.

They followed George Washington's advice to remain neutral. But as the twentieth century began, the United States was becoming a world power.

During his second term, Roosevelt became increasingly worried about the possibility of a war in Europe. Powerful European nations such as Britain and Germany were already fighting each other indirectly in colonial wars in Africa. Roosevelt feared that these conflicts might work their way back to Europe and affect the United States. For this reason, he intervened in world affairs once again.

Despite protests from Congress, Roosevelt sent U.S. representatives to a 1906 meeting held in Algeciras, Spain. The Algeciras Conference helped prevent war among Great Britain, France, and Germany over Morocco. Roosevelt's participation in the talks pointed to the end of traditional U.S. neutrality.

TAMING THE RAILROADS

Although he paid more attention to foreign policy than any president before him, Roosevelt's interest in domestic policy remained his most passionate. Roosevelt championed his progressive policies using the Square Deal slogan.

The year 1906 was particularly successful for Roosevelt. On May 18, after a long and difficult debate, the Senate passed the Hepburn Act. This law gave the president the power to regulate the prices charged by railroads on routes that passed through more than one state. It was a landmark in government efforts to control interstate business.

Progressives had long argued that the railroads, which were run by the wealthiest people in the country, charged an unfair price to move goods from one state to another. The Hepburn Act allowed Roosevelt to use the Interstate Commerce

Commission to adjust railroad shipping charges to help consumers.

AN INDUSTRIAL NATION The United States had changed tremendously since the Civil War. Factories, not farms, now dominated the nation's economy. More and more Americans moved to the cities of the Northeast and the Great Lakes to find work in the factories there. Immigrants joined them by the millions.

Working conditions in the factories were often terrible. Adults and children worked ten- and twelve-hour days for very low wages. Meanwhile, the rich business owners got richer. There was no income tax, and other taxes were extremely low.

Dirty smoke from these factories polluted many of the cities, and overcrowding made the quality of life in them even worse. Increasingly, people thought the federal government should do something about these problems.

Theodore Roosevelt was the first national leader to adopt progressive solutions to these problems. Conservatives believed in laissez-faire economics. This French phrase refers to a hands-off approach to the economy. Progressives such as Roosevelt believed that government had the right and duty to intervene in business affairs on behalf of the public.

THE PANIC OF 1907 The Panic of 1907 began when a New York bank, the Knickerbocker Trust Company, failed in October. Knickerbocker's collapse brought down a dozen more banks and even a few railroads. Roosevelt's critics blamed his prolabor policies for cutting corporate profits. The president blamed bad business practices. A recovery began the following spring of 1908.

TEDDY ROOSEVELT MADE A BIG MISTAKE IN 1904. During that campaign, he announced that "under no circumstances" would he run for president again in 1908. This was a mistake, because now that his second term was up, he wanted to stay.

Roosevelt was only forty-nine years old. He remained full of energy and ambition. But he felt bound to keep his word. So he prepared to leave.

Roosevelt's popularity was so great that he was able to choose his successor. He picked William Howard Taft, who had served in TR's cabinet as the secretary of war.

Roosevelt's strong support ensured that Taft won the nomination of the Republican party. Meanwhile, the Democrats chose William Jennings Bryan as their candidate. The defeat in 1904 of a conservative candidate, Judge Alton Parker, had convinced the Democratic party to return to its populist wing.

Bryan had run for the presidency twice before—in 1896 and 1900. The issues that he championed then and now—women's suffrage, prohibition of liquor, and the income tax—would eventually become law.

During the 1908 campaign, Bryan argued that Roosevelt's progressive policies should be extended further. He also promised to end government corruption and unfair business practices that existed despite Roosevelt's reforms. Bryan was a gifted public speaker, but Taft was nevertheless able to ride Roosevelt's popularity to victory.

WILLIAM HOWARD TAFT

27TH PRESIDENT

★

FROM 1909 TO 1913

BORN: September 15, 1857

BIRTHPLACE: Cincinnati, Ohio

DIED: March 8, 1930

PARTY: Republican

VICE PRESIDENT: James S. Sherman

FIRST LADY: Helen Herron

CHILDREN: Robert, Helen, Charles

NICKNAME: Big Bill

The first president to serve on the Supreme Court.

People voted for Taft in the 1908 election because they believed he would continue the policies of Theodore Roosevelt, who had stepped aside after his first full term. Progressives expected Taft to enforce the antitrust laws and to make sure that the country's natural resources were protected from big business. They also wanted him to protect working men, women, and children in dangerous factory jobs.

Early in Taft's administration, however, progressive support for the new president began to weaken. Part of the problem was that Roosevelt was a difficult man to follow. Taft couldn't be another TR. Yet if he did something differently, he was criticized.

For instance, President Taft began his term by appointing new cabinet officers. Of course, this meant that many members of Roosevelt's cabinet were not

TITANIC STRIKES ICEBERG

1,513 Die as Luxury Liner Sinks

OFF NEWFOUNDLAND, April 15, 1912—The British luxury liner *Titanic* hit an iceberg shortly before midnight last night. Less than three hours later, the enormous ship sank into the icy waters of the North Atlantic. More than fifteen hundred lives were lost. The *Titanic* was on its maiden, or first, voyage from England to New York City.

Another passenger liner, the *Californian*, was less than twenty miles away from the sinking *Titanic*. But its radio operator was off duty, so no one aboard heard the *Titanic*'s calls for help. Not until ninety minutes after the *Titanic* went down did another ship, the *Carpathia*, arrive to help in the rescue.

The disaster has been particularly shocking to people because the ship's owners had bragged that the *Titanic*, the largest and most elegant ship in the world, was unsinkable.

Heroes of this ill-fated maiden voyage include Isidor and Ida Straus, who gave up their spaces on a lifeboat so that younger passengers might live.

It is certain that the sinking of the *Titanic* will lead to the passage of new safety regulations for passenger ships. The *Titanic*'s lifeboats were able to hold only 1,178 of the 2,224 people aboard.

reappointed. Newspaper editorials interpreted Taft's move as an abandonment of Roosevelt's policies. Unsympathetic headlines shouted that Taft was appointing corporate lawyers who would defend the interests of big business. Taft was by nature more conservative than Roosevelt, but the criticism was still unfair. Although not many people noticed, more of Roosevelt's programs became law during the Taft administration than during Roosevelt's.

For example, Taft's record on conservation was generally as good as Roosevelt's. In some ways, it was better. Taft was the first president to protect federal lands on which oil had been found. He also protected land that contained coal, which was even more widely used at the time than oil. Both of these decisions went against the interests of big business, which wanted to exploit these lands for their energy resources.

Taft's trust-busting record was also impressive. During the four years of Taft's presidency, there were twice as many prosecutions under the Sherman Anti-Trust Act as there had been during the seven years that Roosevelt was president.

THE STANDARD OIL CASE

The most famous antitrust case during the Taft years involved the Standard Oil Company. Roosevelt had ordered that Standard Oil be investigated for its monopoly of the oil business. But the case didn't reach the Supreme Court until Taft had become president. In May 1911, the Court found that John D. Rockefeller's Standard Oil trust violated the Sherman Anti-Trust Act. The Court ordered that the trust be broken up because it unfairly restricted the oil trade.

Also on Taft's watch, Congress passed the Sixteenth and Seventeenth

The Early Years

As a boy in Ohio, Taft loved to play baseball. He was a good second baseman and could hit with power, but his extra weight made him a poor base runner. It helped him, however, when he would referee fights between his brothers.

After graduating from Yale University and the University of Cincinnati law school, Taft used his father's political connections to get a job as an assistant county prosecutor. He became a state judge in 1887. In 1892, he was promoted to the federal Circuit Court of Appeals.

In 1900, President McKinley appointed Taft commissioner of the Philippines, which the United States had just won from Spain in the Spanish-American War. It was Taft's job to establish a new government there.

★The Age of the Skyscraper As the twentieth century began, so did the age of the skyscraper. The first skyscraper in the United States was the ten-story Home Insurance Company Building in Chicago, which was built in 1885.

Skyscrapers were inspiring feats of engineering, but they were also necessary. As more and more people moved to the cities, the need for space forced people to build up rather than out. There simply wasn't enough land left to build horizontally.

The new vertical architecture was made possible by two important developments. One was the introduction of safe passenger elevators. The other was the use of steel girders in construction. Because steel is both lighter and stronger than iron, it could support taller buildings. Most of the early skyscrapers were built in New York and Chicago.

★**PRESIDENTIAL FIRSTS** During President Taft's years in office, there were an unusual number of presidential firsts. Taft bought the first cars for the White House. To house them, he had the stables converted into a garage. Taft also began the presidential tradition of throwing out the first ball on the opening day of the baseball season.

Taft was the heaviest president in U.S. history, weighing 332 pounds at his inauguration. He was so large that he once got stuck in the White House bathtub. A bathtub large enough to hold four men was installed as a replacement.

★**MODERN DANCE** Before Isadora Duncan, classical ballet was the only dance people thought of as art. As a child, however, Isadora had refused ballet lessons. Instead, she insisted on dancing more naturally, according to her own sense of movement and rhythm.

Duncan's innovative style failed in the United States, so she moved to Europe at the age of twenty-one. Since she had very little money, she sailed to England on a cattle boat. Soon, however, she became a sensation. She scandalized Europe and filled concert halls, dancing barefoot while dressed as a woodland nymph out of Greek mythology.

★**HULL HOUSE** Jane Addams was one of the most well-known social reformers of her time. She became famous for her work at Hull House, which she founded in Chicago in 1889. Hull House was the first settlement house in the United States. Its purpose was to help immigrants "settle" successfully .

Hull House tried to bridge the gap between the rich and the poor by establishing a day nursery, a boardinghouse for working girls, and an employment service. Classes in cooking and sewing were also offered.

Addams played an important role in the 1912 election, during which she supported Theodore Roosevelt and his Bull Moose (Progressive) party.

amendments, both of which were ratified in 1913. The Sixteenth Amendment made the income tax constitutional, and the Seventeenth Amendment provided for the direct election of senators. Previously, senators had been elected by state legislatures instead of by the people.

DOLLAR DIPLOMACY Taft's foreign policy was called Dollar Diplomacy because he used financial as well as military might to promote U.S. business interests overseas. Taft's particular focus was Latin America.

He encouraged U.S. bankers, for example, to invest in Honduras and Haiti. In 1912, he sent marines to Nicaragua to crush a rebellion there against a government friendly to U.S. business.

If Taft had so many important achievements in office, why was he so widely criticized? One problem was that President Taft always seemed to be doing the same thing—playing golf. Often, his golf partners were important business leaders.

Newspapers complained that the president shouldn't be playing a rich man's sport with people who had made unfair profits at the public's expense. Whether this was true or not didn't matter. People believed it.

But the more important reason was that Taft was always being compared to Roosevelt, whose explosive presence still captivated the nation. Taft's temperament was the opposite. His huge size and slow manner led many people to believe that he was not in charge of his own government.

ROOSEVELT IN AFRICA At the beginning of Taft's presidency, Roosevelt went on a widely publicized safari to Africa. TR said that he wanted to hunt wild game animals. But he really wanted to give Taft a chance to make his own mark on government.

Even in Africa, however, Roosevelt dominated the headlines. Stories reported that TR had been attacked by wild hippos, by a rhinoceros, and by an angry bull elephant. Each time, the articles told how the former president calmly rescued his safari group by bravely shooting the animals in question.

During his year-long trip, Roosevelt shot three hundred animals, including eighteen rhinos, eight elephants, nine lions, seven hippos, and six buffalo. Many of these animals were eventually stuffed and sent to the Smithsonian Institution.

TAFT'S PUBLIC IMAGE

Taft couldn't compete. Next to fascinating stories about Teddy's exploits, newspapers wrote that Taft's favorite sport was eating. For his first Thanksgiving as president, Taft received a huge Rhode Island turkey, a fifty-pound mincemeat pie from New York, and a twenty-six-pound opossum from Georgia, said to be the largest ever shot in that state. This type of publicity didn't help matters.

In 1910, Roosevelt suggested that his support of Taft might have been a mistake. This remark unleashed a storm of newspaper stories, and it deeply hurt Taft, who had considered Roosevelt a close friend and mentor. Their friendship soon became strained. Taft later said that the loss of his friendship with Roosevelt was one of the most painful events of his presidency.

For his part, Roosevelt felt that Taft had abandoned the progressives. TR had been angry when Taft dismissed some of his cabinet officers (after privately promising to keep them), but he was even more upset when Taft chose to support conservative leaders in the Republican party.

THE 1912 ELECTION WAS A MESS. THE TROUBLE BEGAN when Theodore Roosevelt decided that choosing Taft as his successor had been a mistake. To correct this error, TR decided to run again for the White House.

President Taft, of course, had no plans to step aside, so both men went after the Republican nomination. Roosevelt was the more popular among voters, but Taft was closer to the leaders who controlled the party. As a result, Taft won the nomination.

Bitterly disappointed, Roosevelt decided to start his own party. It was formally named the Progressive party, but most people called it the Bull Moose party. This nickname came from TR's often-quoted claim that he was "strong as a bull moose."

The third man in the race was the Democratic nominee, Woodrow Wilson, who was not a particularly strong candidate. It took the Democrats forty-six ballots to nominate him. But he benefited from the fact that Roosevelt and Taft split the Republican vote.

The biggest issue of the 1912 campaign was government reform. As a result, the incumbent President Taft soon fell behind. Roosevelt became particularly radical in his calls for change. He spoke often about his Square Deal. Wilson called his program the New Freedom.

The election was close, but Wilson won because of the votes that Taft took away from Roosevelt. The big loser was President Taft, who finished a distant, humiliating third. Wilson became only the second Democrat to be elected president since the Civil War. A decade later, President Harding appointed Taft chief justice of the Supreme Court.

WOODROW WILSON

28TH PRESIDENT

★

FROM 1913 TO 1921

BORN: December 29, 1856

BIRTHPLACE: Staunton, Va.

DIED: February 3, 1924

PARTY: Democrat

VICE PRESIDENT: Thomas R. Marshall

FIRST LADIES: Ellen Louise Axson, Edith Bolling Galt

CHILDREN: Margaret, Jessie, Eleanor

NICKNAME: Professor

The first president to hold a press conference.

Woodrow Wilson set the tone for his presidency in his first inaugural address. In that speech, Wilson outlined the issues facing the nation. He did so in terms of what was right and what was wrong. As the son of a Presbyterian minister, Wilson tended to view the job of chief executive as a moral responsibility.

Wilson began his term as president with tremendous energy, and the first two years of his administration were extremely productive. During that time, Congress passed some of the most progressive laws of the era. Wilson's first great accomplishment was the Underwood Tariff.

During the 1912 campaign, Wilson had promised to lower tariffs. With Wilson's encouragement, Congress passed the Underwood Tariff in 1913.

WORLD WAR I IN EUROPE

U.S. Stays Out of the Fighting

WHEN WORLD WAR I BROKE out in August 1914, many Americans took sides. Because of their close ties to Britain and France, most southerners and easterners supported the Allies. The children of German immigrants in the Midwest backed the Central Powers.

Despite these allegiances, almost everyone agreed that the United States should stay out of the fighting. It made little sense to become involved in a war an ocean away that seemed to mean so little to American life.

This policy of neutrality became harder to keep, however, when German submarines, called U-boats for short, began torpedoing U.S. ships bound for England.

Public opinion turned strongly against the Germans in 1915 after a U-boat sank the British liner *Lusitania*. Nearly twelve hundred passengers drowned, including 128 Americans. The Germans pointed out, however, that the *Lusitania* was carrying tons of rifle ammunition. So its voyage was not entirely innocent.

It cut the average tariff from forty-one to twenty-seven percent, the lowest rate since the Civil War.

THE FIRST INCOME TAX

To make up the shortfall in government revenue, the new tariff law established the first national income tax. The income tax had recently been made possible by the ratification of the Sixteenth Amendment, which changed the Constitution to make the income tax legal.

Despite the Sixteenth Amendment, the income tax was still a very controversial issue. Business groups fought against it, and many Americans resented paying the tax. The Underwood Tariff established a tax of one percent on all personal incomes above three thousand dollars a year. People making above twenty thousand dollars a year paid an additional amount as high as six percent.

Another of Wilson's achievements was the Federal Reserve Act, which reorganized a U.S. banking system badly in need of reform. The financial crisis known as the Panic of 1907 had caused many people to lose confidence in the country's banks.

The fight over the nation's banking system had been going on since the days of Alexander Hamilton and Thomas Jefferson, who fought over the First Bank of the United States. Forty years later, Andrew Jackson and Nicholas Biddle clashed over the Second Bank.

THE FEDERAL RESERVE ACT

Now, almost eighty years after that, the new Federal Reserve Act set up a network of twelve regional banks. Each reported to a board of governors appointed by the president. It was the job of the "Fed" to control the money supply, which is the amount of money available for

The Early Years

Woodrow Wilson's earliest memory was as a four-year-old boy living in Georgia. He remembered a man telling him that Lincoln had won the presidency, so there would be war between the states.

As a white child living in the South, Wilson experienced Reconstruction as a period of great injustice. Although he later pursued academic and political careers in the North, Wilson always considered himself a southerner. He believed that the South had been justified in seceding from the Union, and he also believed in the supremacy of the white race.

★**The First Ladies** A year and a half into his first term, Wilson's wife Ellen died. The president was so upset that he told an aide he hoped he would be assassinated. Ellen Wilson had been an active first lady, at one time lobbying Congress to pay for slum clearance in the District of Columbia.

About a year after Ellen died, the president became quietly engaged to a widow, Mrs. Edith Bolling Galt. When news of their engagement leaked three months later, people criticized Wilson for marrying so soon after the death of his first wife. Because of the bad publicity, Wilson offered to end the engagement, but Mrs. Galt said she would stand by him.

★**Margaret Sanger** While working as a nurse in one of Manhattan's poor immigrant neighborhoods, Margaret Sanger saw firsthand how having too many babies kept poor families poor. The lesson was a simple one: The more children women had, the more mouths there were to feed.

Having seen the consequences for herself, Sanger devoted her life to publicizing information about birth control, even though her actions were illegal at the time. The Comstock Act of 1873 had banned pamphlets about birth control, declaring them to be obscene. But Sanger ignored this restriction because she believed strongly in the right of every woman to plan the size of her family.

★**JACK JOHNSON** Jack Johnson became the first black man to win the world heavyweight boxing championship when he knocked out Tommy Burns in Sydney, Australia, on December 26, 1908. While Johnson was champion, many white boxing fans cried out for a "great white hope" to defeat the confident, arrogant boxer. They didn't believe that a black man should be champion. Johnson further outraged white America by twice marrying white women.

In his most famous fight—on July 4, 1910—Johnson beat thirty-five-year-old Jim Jeffries, a white former champion, who had been convinced to come out of retirement to put Johnson "in his place." Johnson knocked out Jeffries in fifteen rounds.

★**THE ARMORY SHOW** Modern art developed in Europe around the turn of the century. As late as World War I, however, this new style of painting was almost unknown in the United States. Among the most influential modern artists were two Frenchmen, Paul Cézanne and Henri Matisse, and Pablo Picasso, a Spaniard living in France.

Modern art was first introduced to the United States in 1913 at an exhibition held at the Sixty-ninth Regiment Armory in New York City. The exhibition's most important works were in the modern style of cubism. Cubist painters treated people and objects as though they were geometric shapes. President Herbert Hoover's favorite cartoon of himself was one done in the cubist style.

investment. During boom times, the Fed was supposed to raise interest rates, so people wouldn't borrow and spend too much money. During recessions, the Fed would lower them, so people could get the credit they needed more easily.

Wilson's early success in convincing Congress to enact his programs proved that he was a capable administrator. Very soon, however, he would also have to prove himself as a leader during two international crises. The first involved U.S. relations with Mexico.

THE MEXICAN REVOLUTION The announcement of the Roosevelt Corollary to the Monroe Doctrine had strained relations between the United States and Latin America. Countries in Central and South America resented Roosevelt's claim that the United States could intervene in their affairs whenever the U.S. government thought Latin Americans were not governing themselves properly.

When the Mexican Revolution broke out in 1911, officials in the Taft administration became worried that the fighting might spill over into Texas and the Southwest. In 1913, Mexican general Victoriano Huerta came to power and established a dictatorship. Wilson refused to recognize Huerta's government and instead continued his policy of "watchful waiting."

Despite the public pressure for an invasion of Mexico, Wilson resisted. In an important speech in Mobile, Alabama, the president announced the Mobile Doctrine, which stated that the United States would never again acquire territory by conquest.

Six months later, in April 1914, U.S. sailors in the port of Tampico, Mexico, were arrested for no reason. Although they were quickly released,

Wilson demanded a twenty-one-gun salute to the American flag as an apology. When Huerta refused, Wilson had U.S. marines occupy the Mexican city of Veracruz. Huerta resigned in July.

The man who replaced Huerta, Venustiano Carranza, didn't fare much better. The revolutionary Pancho Villa rose up against him and took control of northern Mexico. In March 1916, the worst U.S. fears came true when Villa crossed the border and attacked Columbus, New Mexico. He set fire to the town and killed seventeen people. In response, President Wilson sent General John J. Pershing, known as Black Jack, to capture Villa and his men. Crossing the border himself, Pershing followed Villa three hundred miles into Mexico, but the wily Villa managed to escape him. The chase continued until February 1917, when Wilson ordered U.S. soldiers out of Mexico. By that time, the United States was about to enter a much greater fight, the first world war.

U.S. NEUTRALITY Wilson had dedicated much of his first term to preventing U.S. involvement in World War I. He shared the public opinion that favored neutrality and did whatever he could to keep the country out of the war. Germany often made this difficult, however.

On February 4, 1915, the German government announced that it considered the waters around Great Britain to be a war zone. Therefore, all ships found in British waters—including neutral U.S. ships—would be subject to U-boat attack.

Wilson responded immediately to this violation of U.S. neutrality. He warned the Germans that continued attacks would force the United States to take military action. Wilson's threats helped convince Germany's

WILSON WON RENOMINATION EASILY AT THE Democratic convention in St. Louis, where the party unveiled its campaign slogan for the fall: "He kept us out of war."

The Democrats believed that World War I and American neutrality would be the biggest issues of the campaign. Their party platform, which listed the party's position on a number of issues, also supported new health and safety standards, a ban on child labor, and the right to vote for women.

The Republican nominee was Justic Charles Evans Hughes of the Supreme Court. The Republicans attacked Wilson for failing to protect American interests abroad. They believed that the United States should take a much tougher stance with Germany and at the same time build up its military. Hughes supported a ban on child labor, benefits for workers who were disabled on the job, and women's suffrage.

As expected, the war in Europe did dominate the election. Because Theodore Roosevelt advocated U.S. entry into the war, he supported the hawkish Republicans, and other progressives followed his lead.

As the election neared, some newspapers predicted that Hughes would win. For three days after the voting, the result was in doubt. But a late vote count in California gave Wilson a narrow victory there. With that state's thirteen electoral votes, Wilson finished with 277 to Hughes's 254. Had California gone Republican, Charles Evans Hughes would have been president.

World War I on the Home Front

Baruch, Hoover Lead Mobilization Efforts

The United States entered World War I in the late spring of 1917. But U.S. soldiers weren't ready to fight yet. The country wasn't ready, either.

To help him manage the war effort, President Wilson recruited business leaders, many of whom worked for the token salary of one dollar per year.

Wilson named Wall Street baron Bernard Baruch to head the new War Industries Board. In that position, Baruch directed U.S. heavy industry. Wilson also made mining engineer Herbert Hoover the national food administrator.

Because the war had already been going on for three years, European food supplies were running out. Hoover worked tirelessly to increase food exports to both soldiers and civilians in Europe.

But the patriotism of the war effort had its spiteful side. Propaganda against Germany led to discrimination at home against many German Americans, who were suspected of being spies and traitors.

military leadership that the U-boat attacks might bring the United States into the war on the side of the Allies. The Germans suspended the U-boat attacks in the fall of 1915.

ENTRY INTO WORLD WAR I The world was a much more interconnected place in the twentieth century than it had ever been before. Even the vast Atlantic Ocean could not insulate the United States from Europe's problems. The country was slowly but surely being dragged into the war.

While Wilson's first term was marked by the enactment of his progressive domestic policies, his second term was consumed by the country's entry into World War I. One of the reasons that most presidential scholars rate Woodrow Wilson so highly is that he proved his leadership abilities both at home and abroad.

Wilson had long believed that a neutral United States could play an important role in ending the war in Europe. In a January 1917 speech before the Senate, he called on both the Allies and the Central Powers to accept "peace without victory." But Wilson's efforts at peacemaking, while respected, were generally ignored.

The United States moved closer to war when Germany announced in January 1917 that it would resume unrestricted submarine warfare in British waters. This meant that U.S. neutrality would no longer be respected at sea. On February 3, Wilson broke off diplomatic relations

with Germany. The American public was outraged by submarine warfare, which it regarded as particularly devious and cruel. But the country was still not ready to enter the war.

All that changed on March 1, when the text of the Zimmermann Telegram was made public. This telegram from German foreign minister Arthur Zimmermann to his ambassador in Mexico had been intercepted by British intelligence agents, and a decoded copy was provided to Wilson.

In the telegram, Zimmermann proposed an alliance between Germany and Mexico. In the event that the United States entered the war, Germany offered to help Mexico reconquer its "lost territories" in Texas, New Mexico, and Arizona. After the text of the telegram was released, public opinion turned quickly in favor of war. On April 2, Wilson asked Congress to declare war on Germany. In his speech, he said, "The world must be made safe for democracy."

During much of 1917, Wilson attended to preparations for the war. He ordered General John J. Pershing to muster an American Expeditionary Force for overseas duty. He also looked to the future. He believed that making a lasting peace would be an even greater task than winning the war.

THE FOURTEEN POINTS

On January 8, 1918, Wilson gave a speech outlining the Fourteen Points upon which he thought peace should be based. These included free navigation of the seas, self-determination for colonies, and arms reduction. The last point of the president's plan called for the formation of an ambitious League of Nations, which could avoid catastrophic wars in the future by guaranteeing the rights and

★WHITE HOUSE SHEEP Edith Wilson was devoted to the war effort. During her husband's second term, she permitted a flock of sheep to graze on the White House lawn. The wool from these sheep was auctioned off to raise money for the Red Cross.

Meanwhile, she spent many nights busy at her sewing machine, which she used to make surgical clothing for Red Cross doctors. She also promoted wartime rationing by observing gasless Sundays, meatless Mondays, and wheatless Tuesdays.

★PROHIBITION During the nineteenth century, many social reformers objected to the high rate of alcohol consumption among American men. Activists sought to remove the temptation of strong drink by passing "dry" laws prohibiting its manufacture and sale.

Many business leaders favored Prohibition because they thought it would reduce absenteeism at work. Religious groups supported it because they believed drinking was sinful. Progressive groups even argued that poverty, disease, and crime were largely due to alcoholism.

The 1916 election swept a large majority of "dry" candidates into office. As a result, the Eighteenth Amendment was soon passed and ratified by the states. This amendment, combined with the Volstead Act of 1919, began the Prohibition era in America.

★THE GREAT MIGRATION The movement of southern blacks to northern cities began around 1910. During World War I, nearly half a million blacks left the rural South for urban centers such as New York, Detroit, and Chicago. By 1940, almost two millions blacks had participated in the Great Migration, which changed the racial geography of the nation.

Southern blacks were drawn to the North because of the potential for work there during the wartime and postwar boom. Many of the jobs they found were on assembly lines that had been only recently racially segregated. The need for workers, however, outweighed employer bigotry. "Prejudice vanishes when the almighty dollar is on the wrong side of the balance sheet," one black newspaper in Chicago wrote.

independence of all the world's nations.

In the spring of 1918, before the bulk of the U.S. troops arrived in Europe, the Germans launched a huge, desperate offensive. The attack failed, and by September 1918, there were more than one million Americans in France and Belgium. During the night of October 3-4, the German government sent a note to Wilson asking for a truce and peace negotiations based on the Fourteen Points.

THE PARIS PEACE TALKS Wilson's goal for years had been to promote world peace based on democratic principles. The peace talks in Paris gave him an opportunity that he couldn't pass up. Not surprisingly, but perhaps not wisely, he decided to lead the U.S. delegation to the peace talks personally.

The president was greeted enthusiastically as he toured England, France, and Italy. He was considered a hero because of his role in ending the war. In 1919, he won the Nobel Peace Prize, becoming the second U.S. president to do so. (Theodore Roosevelt had won the award in 1906 for his work in ending the Russo-Japanese War.)

Wilson stayed in Europe for more than six months while he helped negotiate the Treaty of Versailles. During his long absence, his health began to fail him. He also began to lose control of the U.S. government. When he finally returned to the United States in 1919 with his precious treaty, the Senate was far from ready to ratify it.

From Wilson's point of view, the most important section of the Treaty of Versailles was the one that established the League of Nations. But his opponents in the Senate

★CHARLIE CHAPLIN English-born Charlie Chaplin was one of the earliest American movie stars. He began his film career in 1913 making brief film comedies, called "shorts," for Mack Sennett's Keystone Company. Sennett was already famous for his slapstick Keystone Kops shorts.

While making his second film, *Kid Auto Races at Venice*, Chaplin developed his famous "tramp" character—or as Chaplin called him, "the little fellow." Within two years, Chaplin's derby hat, cane, baggy pants, and small mustache became internationally known trademarks.

★WOMEN'S SUFFRAGE Women finally won the right to vote when the Nineteenth Amendment was ratified in August 1920. Until then, only women in a few western states were permitted to cast ballots. The presidential election of 1920 was the first in which every woman who was a U.S. citizen could vote.

Women first began organizing for the right to vote during the 1840s. Although the women's suffrage movement gained momentum after the Civil War, its ultimate success can be traced to three contemporary factors: the contributions of American women during World War I, the support of President Wilson, and the confrontational tactics of Alice Paul and others. These "suffragettes" marched and picketed to demand the vote. Sometimes they were arrested and jailed.

wanted to eliminate the League of Nations from the treaty because they believed the United States should stay out of international affairs. These senators were known as "isolationists."

Republican senator Henry Cabot Lodge led a determined fight against the treaty. But Wilson was a stubborn man. Even with his health in question and his patience exhausted, he refused to compromise. He would not renegotiate the treaty.

WILSON'S STROKE

Instead, in September, Wilson went on an ill-advised nationwide speaking tour to rally support. After visiting twenty-nine cities in three weeks, he broke down physically in Pueblo, Colorado. Then, after returning to Washington, he suffered a stroke. The president recovered, but never completely.

While Wilson recuperated, he continued to make the most important governmental decisions. But he trusted his second wife, Edith, to handle the lesser details of government and to decide which matters were important enough to merit his attention. She reviewed all his papers and ran the White House in the name of the president. Wilson never offered to step down temporarily, and no one confronted him.

After Wilson refused to renegotiate the Treaty of Versailles, the Senate defeated it in March 1920. Its terms still went into effect, however, because the other Allies had already agreed to them. The terrible financial burden the treaty placed on a defeated Germany would lead to the rise of Adolf Hitler only a decade later. The League of Nations was established, but without the United States, it was never effective. The world was no safer for democracy.

Had Woodrow Wilson remained healthy, he might have run for a third term. Instead, he was forced to retire. But the 1920 election still turned on Wilson and his policies.

The Democrats nominated Governor James M. Cox of Ohio, who earnestly embraced Wilson's record. Franklin Roosevelt was picked as Cox's running mate. Roosevelt was chosen partly because of his successful record as Wilson's assistant secretary of the navy and partly because Democratic party leaders thought his famous name might win some extra votes.

The deadlocked Republican convention nominated a compromise candidate, Senator Warren G. Harding of Ohio. Harding's breakthrough came in Suite 404 of the Blackstone Hotel in Chicago, where the party bosses met secretly to work out a deal. At two o'clock in the morning, they called Harding to their "smoke-filled room" and asked him whether he had anything to hide. Harding thought for ten minutes and replied that he did not. The next day, he was nominated. Governor Calvin Coolidge of Massachusetts was chosen as his running mate.

CAMPAIGN 1920

The Republicans campaigned against Wilson's record. They claimed the president had been unprepared for the war, and they attacked his cherished League of Nations. Meanwhile, Cox urged Americans to work even harder for peace and progressive reform. He pointed to the still-unstable international situation and to the fact that one in six Americans was still illiterate. But the war-weary public was in no mood to meet his idealistic challenge. Instead, Americans embraced Harding's campaign slogan, which offered a "Return to Normalcy." The Republicans won in a landslide.

HARDING AND COOLIDGE

WARREN GAMALIEL HARDING

29TH PRESIDENT

★

FROM 1921 TO 1923

BORN: November 2, 1865

BIRTHPLACE: Corsica, Ohio

DIED: August 2, 1923

PARTY: Republican

VICE PRESIDENT: Calvin Coolidge

FIRST LADY: Florence Kling De Wolfe

CHILDREN: None

NICKNAME: Wobbly Warren

The first president to speak over the radio.

Warren Harding's "Return to Normalcy" campaign was a rejection of Woodrow Wilson's idealism. During the campaign, candidate Harding had avoided taking a position on the League of Nations. By being vague, he hoped both supporters and opponents of the League might vote for him. A month after taking office, however, President Harding announced to Congress that he would not support U.S. membership in that organization.

To help manage the executive branch, Harding proposed a new government office called the Bureau of the Budget. To run this office, he appointed Charles G. Dawes, an engineer and banker from Ohio. Dawes's job was to make a formal budget for government spending. Before the Bureau of the Budget was created, each department of the government handled its own budget. Now that process could be unified and streamlined.

Harding also signed into law two new tariffs. These replaced the 1913 Underwood Tariff and

TEAPOT DOME SCANDAL

Harding's Interior Secretary Caught in Corrupt Deal

Interior Secretary Albert Fall made a secret deal with the Mammoth Oil Company in 1922. Fall arranged for Mammoth to lease the government's Teapot Dome oil fields in Wyoming on terms that were very favorable to Mammoth. In exchange, Mammoth Oil president Harry Sinclair paid Fall a bribe of three hundred thousand dollars in cash and government bonds.

Some people asked questions when the lease was first signed, but the full story didn't come out until the release of a Senate report in October 1923. By that time, Harding was already dead, having passed away two months earlier.

The president may have learned enough before he died to know that his administration was about to unravel. That knowledge may have been a factor in his own collapse. There was no evidence in the Senate report, however, that Harding ever profited personally from any of these corrupt dealings.

raised tariff rates to an average of thirty-eight percent. Singled out for special protection were new industries that had grown up during World War I, especially the drug and chemical industries.

Harding found the role of president difficult. Despite years in the Senate, he was often confused by the complexities of legislation. For instance, one tax reform bill eluded him completely. "I can't make a damn thing out of this tax problem," Harding admitted. "I listen to one side and they seem right, and then—God!—I talk to the other side and they seem just as right, and here I am where I started."

IMMIGRATION Harding responded to the national concern about high levels of immigration by signing the Immigration Restriction Act of 1921. This law established the first general quotas, or limits, on immigration in the nation's history.

The wave of immigration from eastern and southern Europe that took place before World War I was the largest ever. Businessmen appreciated the cheap labor, but many feared that poor Europeans would bring with them dangerous ideas about socialism. Workers who had come over during previous waves of immigration feared the loss of their jobs. The Immigration Restriction Act limited immigration from each country to three percent of the number of people from that country already in the United States in 1910.

On the issue of civil rights, Harding was remarkably ahead of his time. In October 1921, he became the first president since the Civil War to deliver a speech in the South on behalf of equal rights for blacks.

Harding's biggest accomplishment came in foreign affairs. Because the victorious nations of World War I were

The Early Years

HARDING GREW UP ON A FARM IN CALEDONIA, OHIO, where his chores included milking the cows, tending to the horses, and painting the barns. In 1884, when he was not yet nineteen, Harding and two friends purchased an almost bankrupt newspaper in Marion, Ohio, for three hundred dollars. Before long, Harding became the sole owner of the *Marion Star*.

When Harding was twenty-five, he married Florence Kling De Wolfe, a thirty-year-old divorced woman with one son. Florence's father warned her not to marry Harding and at one point even threatened Harding's life. But the couple got married anyway.

Florence Harding became an excellent circulation manager. It was largely her work that built the newspaper into a business profitable enough to launch her husband's political career.

★**POKER** As a senator, Harding voted for Prohibition. But as president, he secretly stocked the White House with illegal bootleg liquor. He liked to have some on hand for his poker games, which often ran late into the night. Harding especially enjoyed playing poker with members of his cabinet. Among the regulars in what Harding called his "poker cabinet" were Secretary of War John Weeks, Attorney General Harry Daugherty, and Interior Secretary Albert Fall. Both Daugherty and Fall were key figures in Harding administration corruption scandals. During one unfortunate game, Harding gambled away a complete set of the White House china.

★**WOMEN'S WORK** The development of the typewriter gave women new opportunities in the workplace. For female high school graduates, secretarial work became an attractive alternative to traditional women's work such as teaching and nursing. It was also far less backbreaking than farm or factory work. Soon huge "pools" of neat young women clattered away at manual typewriters in city offices nationwide. By 1930, there were eleven million women in the work force, more than double the number in 1900.

★**THE ROARING TWENTIES** In a peculiar way, the outrageousness of the 1920s was caused by the restrictions of Prohibition. Because most people didn't take Prohibition seriously, business at illegal speakeasies, or bars, was always good. Once people broke one law or social taboo, it became easier to break others.

The prosperity of the 1920s produced a thrilling popular culture. Fashionable young women called "flappers" discarded their puffy prewar dresses and instead wore short ones that clung tightly to their bodies. Dancing the nights away at speakeasies, the flappers scandalized older Americans with their freedom. They were the first women to smoke cigarettes in public, and their favorite dance was the wild, flailing Charleston.

★**NEGRO LEAGUES** In the 1920s and 1930s, blacks were not allowed to play major league baseball. Instead, black players formed their own leagues. The most famous of these was the Negro National League, formed in 1920.

Teams in the Negro leagues were often as popular as major league clubs in the same town. In Chicago, for instance, the Chicago American Giants sometimes drew more fans than either the White Sox or the Cubs across town.

Perhaps the biggest Negro league star was the flamboyant pitcher Satchel Paige of the Kansas City Monarchs. Negro league games often had a carnival-like atmosphere. Sometimes Paige would dazzle the crowd by calling in his outfielders and pitching to a batter without them. He was sure that the opposing hitters couldn't hit his famous fastball.

already beginning to maneuver for power, Harding convened an international meeting on arms control. The Washington Conference for the Limitation of Armament was held in the nation's capital between November 1921 and February 1922.

The conference concluded when the United States, Great Britain, Japan, France, and Italy all agreed to limit the total size of their navies. Under the terms of this agreement, the United States and Britain were granted the largest navies. The size of the Japanese navy was capped at slightly more than half the size of the U.S. and British navies. The French and Italian fleets were limited to a little more than half the size of the Japanese fleet.

The conference also led to the Four Power Pact among the United States, Great Britain, Japan, and France. With this treaty, the four nations agreed to respect each other's territory in Asia. They also promised to resolve peacefully any disagreements among them.

TEAPOT DOME Nevertheless, by early 1923, Harding's presidency was unraveling. The rumors circulating about corruption in his administration were beginning to get louder. Senator Thomas Walsh of Montana started a formal investigation into them. His committee began collecting evidence of what became known as the Teapot Dome scandal.

Harding's problem began with the people he brought with him to Washington. The only qualification most of them had was a longtime political loyalty to the president, and they were usually more interested in private gain than public service. Because Harding was rather weak-willed, he found it difficult to refuse friends who asked for jobs. Few voters doubted Harding's own integrity, but Walsh's investigation proved that many of his appointees were crooks.

Harding Dies in Office

PRESIDENT HARDING WAS DEEPLY TROUBLED BY the growing charges of corruption in his administration. In late June 1920, just as the Senate investigation was getting under way, Harding set out on a nationwide speaking tour that he called the Voyage of Understanding. He wanted to explain his policies and assure the American people that he was an honest man.

The trip by railroad was unwise, however, because Harding was suffering from high blood pressure and heart trouble. His tiring schedule weakened him. When he reached San Francisco at the end of July, he was exhausted and had to be carried from the train. On August 2, he died unexpectedly in his room at the Palace Hotel.

After the president's death, some people claimed that Florence Harding had poisoned her husband to spare him the indignity of impeachment. Others whispered that she poisoned him because he had been unfaithful to her. (As a senator and president, Harding had two long-term affairs and fathered a child by one of these women.) The rumors were fanned by the first lady's refusal to allow an autopsy. Nothing was ever proven, however, and historians today believe Harding died of natural causes.

Campaign 1924

IN 1924, THE COUNTRY WAS PROSPEROUS AND at peace. Under normal circumstances, these two conditions would ensure the reelection of a president. But Republican party leaders were worried. They weren't sure whether voters would hold the scandals of the Harding administration against them.

Republicans were lucky that Calvin Coolidge happened to be Harding's vice president.

Coolidge's direct, upright manner enabled him to restore confidence in the government in a very short time. As a reward, he was nominated unanimously at the first national party convention broadcast on radio.

The Democratic convention, however, produced the longest deadlock in history. For more than one hundred ballots, Californian William McAdoo, the candidate of the rural South and West, battled New York governor Al Smith, who had the backing of the eastern cities. In the end, both men withdrew, and the nomination went to compromise candidate John W. Davis on the 103rd ballot.

Davis, a West Virginia lawyer, campaigned hard. But the Republican's "Keep Cool with Coolidge" campaign proved unbeatable. The independent Republican senator Robert M. LaFollette ran a strong campaign as the Progressive party candidate, winning seventeen percent of the vote. But his strength was spread much too thin. The only state he carried was his home state of Wisconsin.

CALVIN COOLIDGE

30TH PRESIDENT

★

FROM 1923 TO 1929

BORN: July 4, 1872

BIRTHPLACE: Plymouth, Vt.

DIED: January 5, 1933

PARTY: Republican

VICE PRESIDENT: Charles G. Dawes

FIRST LADY: Grace Anna Goodhue

CHILDREN: John, Calvin

NICKNAME: Silent Cal

Had an electric horse installed in his White House bedroom.

Vice President Calvin Coolidge was vacationing at his father's home in Plymouth Notch, Vermont, when President Harding died in San Francisco. The Coolidges didn't have a telephone, so a messenger had to be sent by car from a nearby town. It was after midnight when Coolidge was awakened with the news that the president had died.

The shocked vice president knelt to say a prayer. Then he went downstairs to a sitting room, where he was sworn in as president shortly before 3:00 A.M. His father, a justice of the peace, administered the oath of office at this informal ceremony. Afterward, Coolidge went back upstairs and back to sleep.

The new president had a big job ahead of him. Within months, the nation would be shaken again by news of the Teapot Dome scandal. Quickly, the phrase Teapot Dome became common shorthand for government

LUCKY LINDY LANDS SAFELY IN PARIS

PARIS, May 21, 1927—Yesterday Charles Lindbergh, a twenty-five-year-old airmail pilot, took off in his monoplane from New York. Today, he landed at Le Bourget airfield outside Paris. In the intervening 33½ hours, Lindbergh became the first person to fly solo across the Atlantic Ocean.

The nonstop flight has made Lindbergh an international hero. It has also increased public acceptance of the airplane as a mode of transportation.

For his 3,600-mile journey aboard the *Spirit of St. Louis*, Lindbergh took with him a few sandwiches and a quart of water. He also brought letters of introduction.

Lindbergh grew up in Little Falls, Minnesota, and Washington, D.C., where his father was a congressman. Consumed by a passion for flying, he dropped out of college during his second year and instead enrolled in flying school. Lindbergh traveled around the country performing as a stunt pilot before becoming an airmail pilot in 1926.

bribery and corruption. It was Coolidge's task to restore faith in the government and faith in the governing Republican party. Republican leaders were worried that the entire party would be tainted by the Harding corruption scandals.

"Silent Cal" Coolidge succeeded beyond anyone's expectations. His quiet style of governing, in contrast to the wildness of the Roaring Twenties, proved to be his greatest asset. The new president moved aggressively to root out corruption. By remaining calm, Coolidge soon convinced the public that the country's problems were over. As a result, he became a much celebrated symbol of integrity in office.

Throughout his term, people identified Calvin Coolidge with the values of old-fashioned America. The New England Puritan ethic that he lived by honored thrift, industry, dignity, morality, frugality, and faith. Coolidge's convictions stood out prominently because they contrasted so vividly with the exuberance and extravagance of the time.

THE BUSINESS OF AMERICA Coolidge believed that prosperity was closely linked to the success of the business community. "The chief business of America is business," he often said. Almost everything Coolidge did was designed to benefit business. In many ways, his conservative presidency made possible the lighthearted frolics that captured the attention of the nation.

In his 1925 inaugural address, Coolidge proposed tax cuts. He argued that reducing the tax burden on the wealthy would benefit everyone by increasing business activity. It was a very appealing policy, and it worked as long as the economy continued to grow.

The tax laws Coolidge shepherded through Congress were extremely

The Early Years

Coolidge spent his childhood in Plymouth, Vermont, where his father was a shopkeeper active in local politics. It was from his father that Calvin inherited his New England thrift and restrained nature. After college, he became a lawyer.

The event that made Coolidge nationally famous occurred during his term as governor of Massachusetts. In 1919, the police force in Boston went on strike, leading to a crime wave in that city. Coolidge sent in state troops and upheld the decision to fire the strikers. When American Federation of Labor president Samuel Gompers appealed to the governor to reconsider his decision, Coolidge sent him a characteristically terse reply. The telegram was reprinted throughout the country. "There is no right to strike against the public safety by anybody, anywhere, any time," Coolidge wrote.

★**SILENT CAL** President Coolidge was widely known as a man of few words. His nickname, Silent Cal, reflected his reserved nature. But Coolidge was also quite witty.

On one occasion at the White House, a dinner guest made a bet with a friend that she could get Coolidge to say more than two words. When she told the president about her bet, Coolidge thought for a moment. "You lose," he said.

★**RADIO** Beginning in the early 1920s, radio truly changed American life. The number of stations broadcasting programs exploded from thirty in 1922 to more than five hundred in 1923. A decade later, two-thirds of homes in the United States had radios, which was twice the number of homes with telephones.

At first, Americans resisted advertising on the radio. Commercials were only one of a number of ways that stations financed programming. During the Great Depression, however, radio commercials gained acceptance and became the norm. Soap manufacturers, for example, sponsored popular daytime dramas that became known as "soap operas."

★**WALT DISNEY** In 1928, little-known animators Walt Disney and Ub Iwerks produced the first animated cartoon with sound. Their short film, *Steamboat Willie,* starred a new character called Mickey Mouse.

From the moment that Mickey first appeared in movie theaters, people loved him. Disney, who provided the voice for Mickey, went on to make other cartoons. Mickey's huge number of fans convinced Disney that the public liked to see animals who talked and behaved like humans. To satisfy the popular demand, Disney created Donald Duck and the dogs Pluto and Goofy.

★**HARLEM RENAISSANCE** After World War I, the neighborhood of Harlem in New York City became a center for the creative outpouring of many African Americans. This was the Harlem Renaissance. Older black writers, especially James Weldon Johnson, encouraged younger writers, artists, and musicians to create works of art that described the unique experience of being black in the United States. Authors such as the poet Langston Hughes and the novelist Zora Neale Hurston were the first to write with awareness and pride about the black experience.

★**BABE RUTH** When the Boston Red Sox sold Babe Ruth to the New York Yankees in 1920, the price of $125,000 was both unheard of and a bargain. The Roaring Twenties were a golden age for sports, and no star shone brighter than the Babe's. Ruth's popularity had such a powerful effect on ticket sales that sportswriters called the new Yankee Stadium "The House That Ruth Built."

Such astounding feats as the sixty home runs he hit during the 1927 season earned the Sultan of Swat unprecedented salaries. Before the 1930 season, he signed a contract for eighty thousand dollars a year. When asked how he felt about making more money than President Hoover, the Babe said, "I had a better year," referring to the 1929 stock market crash.

favorable to business. They lowered income taxes and eliminated a number of other taxes that had been used to raise money during World War I. To a great extent, the apparent prosperity of the Roaring Twenties was a result of Coolidge's tax policy.

At first, as Coolidge had predicted, the tax cuts encouraged rich people to invest more money in business. What the frugal president hadn't expected, however, was that many more people would begin taking risks with their money in the hope of even quicker, higher returns. Such unrestrained speculation has been widely blamed for the 1929 stock market crash.

AVIATION One of Coolidge's most successful initiatives was his promotion of commercial aviation. Ever since the sensational experiments of the Wright Brothers at the turn of the century, the aviation industry had grown by great leaps, and now passenger aircraft were becoming available.

In 1926, Congress passed the Air Commerce Act. The purpose of this bill was to place commercial aviation under government regulation so the fledgling industry could be nurtured. The bill also approved the first two commercial airline routes, one north-south and the other east-west.

FARM POLICY Coolidge was also successful in defeating bills he didn't like. Twice Congress passed the McNaury-Haugen farm bill, and twice the president vetoed it. By the terms of this bill, the government would buy surplus crops from U.S. farmers at a fixed price and then sell them abroad, often at a loss. The purpose was to protect farmers from unstable crop prices.

Coolidge attacked the bill as contrary to the free-market economy that he championed. He argued that government had no business fixing crop prices and that the farmers should make do with the laws of supply and demand. According to the president's economic philosophy, crops should cost what people were willing to pay for them. Coolidge's action may have seemed sensible at the time, but it contributed greatly to the suffering of farmers during the Great Depression.

THE KELLOGG-BRIAND PACT

In foreign affairs, Coolidge followed a policy of isolationism. One exception was the treaty negotiated by Secretary of State Frank Kellogg and the French foreign minister Aristide Briand.

The countries that signed the Kellogg-Briand Pact of 1928 agreed not to use war as a tool of national policy. It was the most ambitious peacemaking effort yet. Eventually, all but five of the world's nations signed the treaty, and it was celebrated as the beginning of a new era in international relations.

However, the Kellogg-Briand Pact didn't end war because the treaty was entirely unrealistic and impractical. There was no way to enforce it and no punishment for those who broke it. The treaty did nothing, for example, to stop the growth of Nazi Germany or any of the other factors that would lead to World War II. The pact was well intentioned, but it was a complete failure.

When Coolidge's first full term came to an end in 1928, the country was still prosperous, but the president decided not to run for reelection. In a characteristically tight-lipped announcement, Coolidge said, "I do not choose to run for president in 1928." He gave no further explanation. Instead, Coolidge retired to write his autobiography, which was naturally a very short book.

When President Coolidge announced that he would not run for reelection in 1928, Secretary of Commerce Herbert Hoover became the Republican front-runner. Hoover's support—which came primarily from women, progressives, and immigrants—was strong enough to win him the Republican nomination. In his acceptance speech, Hoover said, "We shall soon with the help of God be in sight of the day when poverty will be banished from this nation."

Hoover was quiet and shy. In contrast, the Democratic candidate, Governor Alfred E. Smith of New York, was colorful and witty. He was also the first Roman Catholic to be nominated for president by a major political party.

Smith campaigned for religious tolerance, but he was largely unsuccessful. Republicans put out pamphlets, without Hoover's knowledge, claiming that Smith would be the servant of the pope in Rome. Many Protestants in the Midwest and West believed what they read.

In the northern and eastern cities, Smith attracted huge and enthusiastic crowds, but his appeal remained regional. Hoover ran a quieter campaign, emphasizing the prosperity of the Republican Coolidge administration. In November, he carried forty of the forty-eight states.

HERBERT CLARK HOOVER

31ST PRESIDENT

★

FROM 1929 TO 1933

BORN: August 10, 1874

BIRTHPLACE: West Branch, Iowa

DIED: October 20, 1964

PARTY: Republican

VICE PRESIDENT: Charles Curtis

FIRST LADY: Lou Henry

CHILDREN: Herbert, Jr.; Allan

NICKNAME: Chief

The first president to have an asteroid named for him.

At the beginning of his presidency, people thought of Hoover as a new, modern leader who could organize the government for the benefit of the people. Everyone knew of his accomplishments during World War I, when he managed the food distribution to Europe. Hoover masterfully provided more than eighteen million tons of food to starving people there. A new verb, to "hooverize," meant to conserve food for the war effort.

Hoover was also a self-made millionaire, which made him seem the right person for the times. The country was prosperous and believed that Hoover could lead it to even greater economic heights. People were not jealous of his wealth, because they knew he had been orphaned as a child and had worked hard to make his fortune. Early on, Hoover announced his hope that Americans could create a "new day" that would fulfill the country's potential, especially in the area of science.

STOCK MARKET CRASHES

"Black Tuesday" Ends Boom Years

NEW YORK, October 29, 1929—Wall Street collapsed today. Prices on the New York Stock Exchange fell disastrously in very heavy trading. In just a few hours, stock in the nation's companies lost ten billion dollars in value.

Stocks that had been selling for twenty, thirty, and forty dollars a share only a few weeks ago were dumped for pennies in the desperate rush to sell. The nosedive taken by the stock market last week was nothing compared to today's disaster.

The predictions of prominent bankers that the worst was over turned out to be tragically wrong, as did President Hoover's claim that the business of the country was "on a sound and prosperous basis." Evidently, the panic had already set in.

Experts say that the leading cause of the crash was wild and unregulated stock speculation financed by borrowing. As long as prices went up, everyone made money. But when prices started to fall a week ago, brokers called in their customers' debts.

Because these investors had all their money tied up in stocks, they had to sell in order to pay the brokers. These sales drove down the market even further until a stampede developed.

Then came the stock market crash. Hoover responded to this crisis with energy and determination. He met with business leaders and delivered many speeches designed to restore confidence in the economy. He was quite active, in fact, more so than any president before him when faced with an economic crisis. But never before had the emergency been so great.

THE GREAT DEPRESSION The crash immediately bankrupted many high rollers who had been speculating in the stock market. But its lasting effects touched everyone. The crash led to the failure of five thousand banks, wiping out the savings accounts of nine million ordinary people. During the next three years of the Great Depression, an average of one hundred thousand jobs were lost each week.

President Hoover simply failed to understand how bad things were. In March 1930, he announced that "the evidences indicate that the worst effects of the crash upon unemployment will have passed during the next sixty days." Instead, unemployment got worse.

People who were scared of losing their jobs, or had already lost them, stopped making unnecessary purchases. As a result, businesses suffered more. Then, as demand fell, even more jobs were lost.

As people's savings ran out, they became unable to repay their debts. Many lost their homes. Farmers couldn't make a living, either, because crop prices were so low. By 1930, four million people were unemployed. By 1932, twelve million people were out of work, which meant that one in four Americans had lost his or her job.

During the worst years of the Great Depression, starving people lined up for free soup and bread in towns and cities across the nation. Resorts became ghost towns.

The Early Years

HERBERT HOOVER WAS BORN IN WEST BRANCH, Iowa, which made him the first president born west of the Mississippi River. After the death of his father when he was six, Herbert was sent to live with relatives.

For eight months, he lived with an uncle on the Osage Indian reservation in Oklahoma. There, he played with Osage children and learned how to hunt with a bow and arrow. When he was nine, his mother died and he was sent to live permanently with another uncle in Oregon.

At Stanford University, Hoover studied geology. After his graduation, he got a job as a mining engineer with a company that sent him to Australia, Burma, and China. Hoover and his wife, Lou, learned Chinese so well that they often spoke the language in the White House to protect themselves against eavesdroppers.

★**FLY FISHING** Hoover was a dedicated fly fisherman. Occasionally on weekends, he liked to forget the worries of the presidency by taking fly fishing trips. He often traveled to the Rapidan River in nearby Virginia in what is now the Shenandoah National Park.

★**AL CAPONE** For organized crime, Prohibition meant good business. Making liquor illegal didn't end the demand for it, so bootleggers prospered, especially in Chicago. The biggest of the mob bosses there was Al "Scarface" Capone.

Capone ordered a great many killings. The most famous of these was the St. Valentine's Day Massacre. On February 14, 1929, members of Capone's gang disguised themselves as policemen and raided a garage run by rival gangster Bugs Moran. Capone's men lined the Moran gang up against a wall and machine-gunned them to death. Newspapers later dramatized the event, which became a symbol of the violence that engulfed Prohibition-era Chicago.

★**THE MARX BROTHERS** Americans often sought emotional relief from the Great Depression in Hollywood movies. Watching a silly comedy usually helped people forget their troubles, at least for a time. The Marx Brothers kept many Americans laughing when they might otherwise have been crying.

There were originally five Marx Brothers: Groucho, Chico, Harpo, Gummo, and Zeppo. But Gummo left the act before the brothers began making movies in the late 1920s. In those movies, Groucho, Harpo, and Chico were the central characters. Their comedy was particularly popular because it poked fun at stuffy rich people from the point of view of poor, disadvantaged outsiders.

★**THE DUST BOWL** Depression life in Oklahoma was made much worse by a severe drought that hit the region in the early 1930s. Conditions there became so bad that sometimes huge dust storms completely blocked the sun.

Hoping for a better life in California, many "Okies" headed west to work as migrant fruit pickers. John Steinbeck's novel *The Grapes of Wrath* and the songs of Woody Guthrie describe the terrible disappointments they found in California: low wages, brutal working conditions, and little hope.

Passenger trains rolled along the tracks with empty cars because no one could afford the fare.

THE SMOOT-HAWLEY TARIFF Congress's response was the Smoot-Hawley Tariff of 1930, which raised tariff rates to record levels. Hoover knew the bill was dangerous, but he signed it anyway, thinking he had no other choice. The intention of the tariff was to increase sales of U.S. products by raising the cost of imported goods.

But the new rates quickly led to an international trade war as other nations raised their tariffs as well. This drastically reduced sales of U.S. goods overseas. Overall, the worldwide depression worsened.

By 1931, most Americans thought it was obvious that the government should provide direct aid to the people. Other nations, such as Great Britain, were already making payments to the unemployed and the elderly. But the president refused to support these programs.

Hoover wanted to help people who were suffering. But he was not willing to give up his traditional American faith in individual responsibility. Hoover thought that direct aid to people would make them dependent on the government and undermine their ability to earn a living.

HOOVERVILLES Hoover himself soon came to symbolize the hardships of the Great Depression for many people. Homeless families who lived in shacks made out of discarded lumber and cardboard called their shantytowns "Hoovervilles." The newspapers that people used to cover themselves were known as "Hoover blankets." The wild rabbits they killed for food were "Hoover hogs."

A short decade before, Hoover had been hailed as the Great Humanitarian for his efforts to feed starving Europeans. By 1932, however, his reassurances that conditions would improve were greeted with jeers. No one believed him anymore, and his campaign promises of 1928 came back to haunt him. While running for president, Hoover had said, "We shall soon with the help of God be in sight of the day when poverty will be banished from this nation." Of course, things didn't work out that way.

Throughout his term, Hoover refused to allow government aid to the unemployed and the homeless. But in 1932, he did create the Reconstruction Finance Corporation. This agency loaned two billion dollars to businesses, banks, and state governments to help them through the Great Depression. Hoover believed that the money would eventually trickle down to the people who needed it. But it was much too little and much too late.

THE BONUS MARCH In May 1932, World War I veterans organized the Bonus March on Washington, D.C. In 1924, in appreciation for their service during the war, Congress had awarded them pay bonuses in the form of insurance that could be redeemed in 1945. Because of the Great Depression, the veterans wanted Congress to move up payment of these bonuses. Many veterans argued that they might not live until 1945 unless the bonuses were paid immediately.

When Congress turned them down, some members of the Bonus Army went back home. But others remained camped near the Capitol. In July, Hoover lost his patience and ordered the U.S. Army to drive away the Bonus Army. The use of tear gas and fixed bayonets against the veterans and their families was widely criticized. Once again, Hoover seemed insensitive to the suffering caused by the depression.

THE GREAT DEPRESSION DOMINATED THE 1932 campaign. The Republicans renominated President Hoover. To have given up on him would have meant admitting that the economic crisis was the fault of his Republican administration.

The Democrats nominated Franklin Roosevelt, the innovative governor of New York. Although crippled by polio in 1921, FDR had made a dramatic comeback. After his nomination, Roosevelt flew to Chicago, where he became the first presidential candidate to deliver an acceptance speech in person. Among his most wealthy and influential supporters was Joseph P. Kennedy, whose son John would later run for president himself.

Because Roosevelt was confined to a wheelchair, most people thought he would run a quiet campaign. But FDR surprised everyone with an energetic trip around the country during which he delivered more than fifty speeches.

Roosevelt promised to get the country back on its feet with public works projects and government aid to farmers. He called his program a "new deal for the forgotten man." It was no accident that FDR's New Deal sounded a lot like Teddy Roosevelt's popular Square Deal.

President Hoover insisted that Roosevelt's policies would not work and continued to warn against government aid. But the voters didn't believe the country would pull out of the Great Depression by itself. In November, Roosevelt carried forty-two of the forty-eight states.

Franklin Delano Roosevelt

32nd President

★

From 1933 to 1945

Born: January 30, 1882

Birthplace: Hyde Park, N.Y.

Died: April 12, 1945

Party: Democrat

Vice Presidents: John N. Garner, Henry A. Wallace, Harry S. Truman

First Lady: Anna Eleanor Roosevelt

Children: Anna; James; Franklin; Elliot; Franklin Delano, Jr.; John

Nickname: FDR

The first president to appear on television.

Like Lincoln, Franklin Roosevelt became president during a time of grave national crisis. The Great Depression, the worst in U.S. history, had closed banks around the country and cut industrial production in half. More than thirteen million people were out of work, and one-quarter of the nation's farmers had lost their land because banks had foreclosed on their loans.

With ordinary Americans lining up at free soup kitchens to avoid starvation, Roosevelt knew something had to be done quickly. "Action and action now" was his inaugural promise. Showing that he could be composed under pressure, Roosevelt tried to reassure people. "The only thing we have to fear is fear itself," he said.

Roosevelt's cabinet appointments reflected his plan to make changes in the way government was run. He chose

OWENS FOILS HITLER

Sprinter Wins Olympic Gold

BERLIN, Germany, August 16, 1936—The Summer Olympics ended here today with the host nation, Nazi Germany, winning the most medals. But the U.S. sprinter Jesse Owens captured headlines around the world with his four gold-medal performances.

Owens won the two sprint events and the long jump. He also ran the anchor leg for the winning sprint relay team. He tied or broke Olympic records in each of these events.

German dictator Adolf Hitler had intended to use the Berlin Olympics to show the world how completely his country had recovered from World War I. He also hoped to use the games to prove his theories that the whites of Northern Europe are by nature superior to other races.

The medals that Owens, an African American, won here have proved to the world that Hitler's theories are wrong.

liberals who were not afraid to experiment with bold reforms. The president even appointed the first female cabinet officer, Secretary of Labor Frances Perkins.

THE BANKING CRISIS

The most immediate of Roosevelt's problems was the banking crisis. Because so many banks had already failed, the public was fast losing confidence in the nation's financial institutions. Worried depositors began lining up at banks to withdraw their money. These "runs" threatened the entire banking system. On the day Roosevelt took office, nearly half the states had declared bank "holidays" to keep the remaining banks in business.

Two days later, on March 6, Roosevelt called a halt to all banking operations. Three days after that, Congress, which had been called into special session, passed the Emergency Banking Act. This law endorsed the president's action and kept the banks closed until federal auditors could examine their books.

In his first "fireside chat," Roosevelt explained the government's new banking policy, which restored much of the public's faith in the system. By the end of March, more than twelve thousand banks with ninety percent of the nation's deposits were back in business. With the unsound banks closed, the runs stopped. Roosevelt's handling of the banking crisis displayed early on his determined, energetic leadership.

The president followed this up with serious bank reform. In June 1933, Congress established the Federal Deposit Insurance Corporation to guarantee individual deposits up to five thousand dollars. As intended, the new law gave the depositors confidence that even if a bank failed, they would not lose their money.

The Early Years

As a boy, FDR enjoyed the sheltered life provided by his wealthy and well-known family. A pampered child, he wore dresses until he was five and then kilts. Not until he turned eight did Franklin wear his first pair of pants—or take his first unsupervised bath.

Following the career path of his fifth cousin Theodore Roosevelt, Franklin entered politics in 1910, winning election to the New York State Senate. Three years later, Woodrow Wilson named him assistant secretary of the navy.

In 1921, after running for vice president on the losing 1920 Democratic ticket, Roosevelt contracted polio, a disease that paralyzed his legs. He had to wear braces and use a wheelchair for the rest of his life, which made him more sensitive to the troubles of other people. After seven years of difficult physical therapy, however, he made a remarkable political comeback, winning election as governor of New York state in 1928.

★MARION POST WOLCOTT In 1938, Marion Post Wolcott took a job as a photographer with the New Deal's Farm Security Administration. This government agency hired a team of photographers during the late 1930s to compile a visual record of life in the United States. She and other FSA photographers, including Walker Evans and Dorothea Lange, traveled all over the country documenting the lives of everyday people. Roosevelt's Works Progress Administration was committed to employing other types of artists as well. The Federal Writers Project put together a state-by-state series of guidebooks, while the Federal Theater Project staged free performances, including a black version of *Macbeth* that played to more than 120,000 people.

★**FIRESIDE CHATS** Early in his first term as president, FDR began a series of informal radio speeches. He called them "fireside chats." His purpose was to explain the government's New Deal policies directly to the people.

The fireside chats reassured a worried nation. Americans listening on the radio could hear the optimism and firmness in the president's mellow voice. Speaking from the White House, Roosevelt seemed to be talking to each member of the audience personally. As a result, people came to believe that he understood their problems as no president had before.

★**HUEY LONG** One of the country's best known and most controversial politicians during the Great Depression was Huey Long, the governor of Louisiana. Long won the support of poor whites by improving rural roads and expanding government services. He paid for these programs by taxing corporations and the rich.

Nicknamed the Kingfish, Long used folksiness to hide his ruthless manner. In 1931, he resigned as governor to enter the U.S. Senate. There he developed the Share-Our-Wealth program, promising to make "every man a king." To his critics, Long was a demagogue who charmed uneducated voters with simplistic plans and impractical promises. Long planned to run for president in 1936, but in September 1935, at the height of his influence, he was assassinated in the Louisiana state capitol by the son-in-law of a politician whose career he had ruined.

★**THE *HINDENBURG*** The German airship *Hindenburg* began the first regularly scheduled transatlantic passenger service in May 1936. The 830-foot-long, hydrogen-filled zeppelin was a source of great pride for the Nazis. It carried fifty passengers in private cabins at a cruising speed of seventy-eight miles per hour.

On May 6, 1937, as the *Hindenburg* was approaching its mooring station at Lakehurst, New Jersey, the airship mysteriously burst into flames. Thirty-six people died in the explosion, which ended the brief era of lighter-than-air transport. Coincidentally, Herbert Morrison's report of the disaster was the first coast-to-coast radio broadcast.

THE HUNDRED DAYS During his first hundred days in office, Roosevelt demonstrated a concern on behalf of the government that President Hoover had not. He created a network of agencies whose sole purpose was to offer relief to the suffering public. "Only a foolish optimist can deny the dark realities of the moment," Roosevelt said. He compared the threat of the depression to the threat posed by war and suggested that he might assume powers usually granted to a president only during wartime.

Between March and May 1933, Roosevelt sent New Deal legislation to Capitol Hill piece by piece. An obedient and heavily Democratic Congress, desperate for recovery, approved nearly all of Roosevelt's requests. Mostly spending bills were passed. The New Deal's basic assumption was that government spending could "prime the pump" of business and get the economy rolling again.

THE CIVILIAN CONSERVATION CORPS Unlike Hoover, Roosevelt believed it was the federal government's responsibility to address the problems of the needy. The first New Deal program to help the unemployed was the Civilian Conservation Corps, which gave jobs to men between the ages of eighteen and twenty-five.

Recruited in the cities, these young men were put to work in rural camps built by the War Department (now the Department of Defense). They made thirty dollars a month planting trees, building dams, and doing other jobs that helped conserve the environment. Twenty-two dollars of their salary was sent home each month to their families. Between 1933 and 1941, nearly three million young men spent some time living and working in CCC camps.

The first comprehensive program for unemployment relief was the Federal Emergency Relief Administration, created in May 1933. Led by Roosevelt's trusted associate Harry Hopkins, FERA at first made cash payments directly to the unemployed. But Hopkins believed that providing people with jobs was a better way to go—both for the people, psychologically, and for the economy. Eventually, FERA spent about four billion dollars on direct relief as well as on jobs that were not supposed to compete with private business.

AGRICULTURAL PROGRAMS

Roosevelt also had to resolve a crisis in agriculture. Farmers had been suffering for years from low crop prices, which fell even further after the 1929 stock market crash. In April 1933, the *New York World-Telegram* wrote that "actual revolution already exists in the farm belt." In Iowa, farmers violently resisted when banks called in overdue mortgages and threw families out of their homes. Riots forced the governor to declare martial law in several counties.

The Agricultural Adjustment Act of May 1933 attempted to raise prices by cutting production. It authorized the government to pay farmers for taking land out of cultivation. This seemed a cruel thing to do while millions of people were starving in the cities, but Secretary of Agriculture Henry Wallace argued that farmers simply were not able to make a living any other way. "Agriculture cannot succeed in a capitalist society as a philanthropic enterprise," he said.

One of the boldest and most original of the New Deal programs was the Tennessee Valley Authority, an independent public company that Congress created to build and run dams in seven southeastern states.

No one doubted that Franklin Roosevelt would be nominated for a second term. In his acceptance speech at the Democratic convention, the president said, "There is a mysterious cycle in human events. To some generations much is given. Of other generations much is expected. This generation of Americans has a rendezvous with destiny."

The Democrats used the New Deal to portray themselves as the party of ordinary people. Farmers, workers, and the unemployed were firmly behind Roosevelt, as were blacks, who abandoned the party of Lincoln for the first time since the Civil War. Meanwhile, most Americans viewed Republicans as the party of wealthy conservatives.

Roosevelt's Republican opponent, Kansas governor Alfred M. Landon, campaigned against the New Deal, which he said undermined the American traditions of individualism and self-sufficiency. He accused the Roosevelt administration of massive waste and inefficiency in its relief programs. FDR ignored these attacks and reminded the voters that the Great Depression had started during a Republican administration.

While Landon wanted the federal government to stay out of business affairs, Roosevelt believed that it had a responsibility to protect workers by regulating the economy. Roosevelt's economic activism gave the Democrats a huge advantage.

A curious poll conducted by the *Literary Digest* using names taken at random from telephone books predicted that Landon would win by a landslide. The poll was inaccurate because, during the Great Depression, many Americans were too poor to have phones. Those who did were more likely to be well-to-do Republicans. Instead of winning in a landslide, Landon lost by more than ten million votes. His defeat was one of the worst ever suffered by the presidential nominee of a major party.

"WAR OF THE WORLDS" RADIO SHOW STARTS PANIC

NEW YORK, October 30, 1938—A radio program broadcast on CBS stations tonight has caused a nation-wide panic. The Mercury Theater of the Air's "War of the Worlds" radio play about a Martian invasion has caused thousands of people to flee their homes despite repeated announce-ments that the broadcast was only a dramatization.

The show featured simulat-ed news reports about a Martian landing at Grover's Mill, New Jersey. On a single block in nearby Newark, more than twenty families ran out into the street with wet towels over their faces because they believed the realistic reports of a gas raid.

The mastermind of this Halloween media hoax, twenty-three-year-old Orson Welles, has become an instant national celebrity. His work demonstrates the incredible power of radio, still a relatively new medium of communica-tion.

In addition to generating and selling electricity, the TVA managed reforestation and flood control programs. Many of the TVA's four hundred thousand customers were rural farmers who had never before had access to electric power.

THE NATIONAL RECOVERY ADMINISTRATION The economic cornerstone of the New Deal was the National Industrial Recovery Act passed in June 1933, which established the National Recovery Administration. The NRA's aim was to encourage business groups and trade associations to compose "codes of fair competition" for their industries. It was believed that these codes would provide a practical basis for regulating the marketplace.

In exchange for agreeing to suspend the antitrust laws so that prices and production quotas could be fixed, the government won concessions for workers. Wage scales were raised, especially among the poorest-paid workers.

The 746 different NRA codes proved to be unwieldy, however. They led to the widespread opinion among conservative business leaders that the New Deal was horrendously impractical and inefficient. Industrialists also objected to Section 7(a) of the act, which guaranteed workers the right to bargain collectively. This meant that unions could negotiate a single

contract to cover all the workers in a factory. It also led to a number of union strikes against nonunion employers.

SOCIAL SECURITY One of the most lasting of Roosevelt's innovations was the Social Security Act of August 1935. This law guaranteed support payments to people who were old, unemployed, sick, or disabled.

At the same time, Congress also passed the National Labor Relations Act, known as the Wagner Act, which made it illegal for employers to interfere with union organizers, and the Wealth Tax, which raised individual income tax rates as high as seventy-five percent for people earning over five million dollars.

What little political opposition there was to the New Deal ended in 1934 when Democrats won huge victories in the midterm congressional elections, increasing their majorities to forty-four seats in the Senate and more than two hundred in the House.

SUPREME COURT OPPOSITION The only effective opposition to President Roosevelt's programs came from the Supreme Court, which struck down many of his initiatives during 1935 and 1936. The Court ruled that the NRA codes, the Agricultural Adjustment Act, and congressional acts relating to railroad retirement, the coal industry, farm mortgages, and cities that went bankrupt were all unconstitutional.

Although the specifics of the decisions varied, the justices generally believed that Roosevelt had seized powers that rightfully belonged to Congress and the states.

Although Republican attacks on the New Deal were rejected by voters during the 1934 congressional

★**THE FIRST LADY** Shy and insecure as a young woman, Eleanor Roosevelt later blossomed into the most active and admired of first ladies. She was also the first wife of a president to make public statements on current political issues.

When both of her parents died while she was still in her teens, Eleanor was sent to an exclusive girls' school in London. When she returned to New York, she did social work in the city's slums. That same year, she met Franklin Roosevelt, her fifth cousin once removed. Once their courtship began, Eleanor helped open Franklin's eyes to the terrible conditions endured by people who lived in the poor neighborhoods where she worked. Her uncle Theodore Roosevelt gave the bride away at her 1905 wedding.

After FDR was struck down with polio in 1921 when he was thirty-nine, Eleanor encouraged him to fight the disease and return to politics. She attended political meetings for him and, as a result, became active in human rights organizations herself. In 1939, she resigned from the Daughters of the American Revolution to protest their refusal to let the black singer Marian Anderson perform in Washington's Constitution Hall. After FDR's death, President Truman made her a member of the first U.S. delegation to the United Nations.

★**ABRAHAM LINCOLN BATTALION** In 1936, a civil war began in Spain between the Nationalist rebels and the Republicans who had been elected to govern the country. Fascist Italy and Nazi Germany sent troops and tanks to support the Nationalists, while the Republicans turned to the Soviet Union for help. Although the U.S. government decided not to get involved, many Americans personally supported the Republican cause.

Soviet officials organized the International Brigades, made up of idealistic young volunteers eager to fight for democracy and freedom in Spain. One of these brigades included the Abraham Lincoln Battalion, at first made up entirely of Americans. Nearly three thousand young men, mostly students without any military training, served in the battalion. Republican sympathizer Ernest Hemingway set his popular 1940 novel *For Whom the Bell Tolls* during the Spanish Civil War, which the Nationalists won in 1939.

★**NYLON** During the 1930s, a Du Pont chemist named Wallace H. Carothers developed the first artificial fiber, later named nylon. In 1938, the first nylon toothbrushes were sold. Two years later, the first women's stockings made from this "miracle fabric" appeared in department stores across the country.

Nylon stockings quickly became the rage, helping to define a new 1940s look. The first nylons had a noticeable dark seam that ran up the underside of the leg. Like silk stockings, they were held up by garters. When the government rationed nylon during World War II—to the horror of nearly all American women—a black market quickly developed. Others simply decorated their legs with black pencil lines that looked like stocking seams.

★**AMELIA EARHART** Like Charles Lindbergh before her, Amelia Earhart performed such remarkable feats as a pilot and adventurer that she became a national hero. Earhart was the first woman to match Lindbergh's solo transatlantic flight, and she was also the first person to fly solo from Hawaii to California, an even greater distance.

During the 1930s, she used her fame to promote two cherished causes: commercial aviation and feminism. In 1937, she attempted to fly around the world with navigator Fred Noonan. Their twin-engine Lockheed Electra disappeared on July 2 during the most dangerous leg of the trip, from New Guinea to tiny Howland Island in the middle of the Pacific Ocean. Their fate remains a mystery.

campaign, Roosevelt heeded the charges that his New Deal agencies were disorganized and inefficient.

In 1935, the president proposed a reorganization of these agencies that Congress passed as the Emergency Relief Act of 1935. Most of the New Deal agencies were brought under the control of the Works Progress Administration, directed by Harry Hopkins. The WPA hired more than eight million people for public works projects before closing its doors in 1943.

PACKING THE SUPREME COURT By the time Roosevelt began his second term in 1937, government spending had brought about a limited recovery. But the president was frustrated, especially by the Supreme Court whose aging justices believed that many New Deal programs went far beyond the powers granted to the federal government by the Constitution.

To get around this roadblock, Roosevelt proposed on February 5, 1937, a plan to reorganize the Court. He wanted to appoint a new justice for every current justice over seventy years old. Because six of the justices were already past seventy, Roosevelt could appoint six more justices, bringing the total number to fifteen.

Most people agreed that something had to be done to prevent the Court from blocking reform, but Roosevelt's plan was quite controversial. The president claimed that the bill was meant to reduce each justice's workload. But it was obvious that he was trying to control the Court's decisions by creating a new majority in favor of the New Deal.

The Senate eventually rejected the plan, but in the meantime the justices got the message. While the bill was still under consideration, a previously conservative justice began voting with the Court's liberal bloc. This switch made the difference in two important 5-4 rulings supporting minimum wage laws and the Social Security Act.

AMERICA IN ISOLATION The difficulties at home made it easy for Americans to ignore events happening in the rest of the world. During the 1930s, Germany, Italy, and Japan were all turning increasingly aggressive. Germany reclaimed land it had lost during World War I, while Italy invaded Ethiopia, and Japan conquered Manchuria on the Chinese mainland. The U.S. response was generally to ignore these events. Isolationists at home believed that the Atlantic and Pacific oceans would insulate the nation from European and Asian wars.

In keeping with this isolationism, Congress enacted a series of neutrality acts beginning in August 1935 that prevented Americans from selling arms to nations at war. After World War I, many people came to believe that arms dealers were "merchants of death" who secretly conspired to start wars because wars were good business. It was thought that banning the arms trade would stop the fighting.

Unfortunately, this policy helped the aggressor nations, who had stockpiled weapons for years and were thus better prepared to fight. During the Spanish Civil War, for example, U.S. neutrality laws prevented Americans from supporting the Republican side, while the Nationalists received huge amounts of military aid from the fascist governments in Germany and Italy.

In his "quarantine" speech of October 5, 1937, Roosevelt demanded that freedom-loving nations of the world spurn aggressor nations. Ninety percent of the world's nations wanted peace, he said. The remaining ten

CAMPAIGN 1940

During the summer of 1940, Roosevelt kept his reelection plans secret. Not even the delegates to the Democratic convention knew what he intended. When Postmaster General James Farley, a trusted political ally, asked permission to launch his own campaign, the president told him to go ahead. Farley thought Roosevelt had decided to retire, but Roosevelt was really working behind the scenes to have the convention draft him.

Never before had a president run for a third term, and Roosevelt was worried that the voters might think him arrogant. By having the convention draft him, which it did, FDR could pretend that his campaign for a third term had been forced upon him by the will of the people.

To run against Roosevelt, the Republicans nominated Indiana businessman Wendell L. Willkie, who ran a power company. Willkie had been a Democrat as late as 1932, when he contributed $150 to Roosevelt's first campaign. Willkie later became a Republican after breaking with Roosevelt over the Tennessee Valley Authority, which competed with Willkie's own company.

Unlike FDR's first two campaigns, which had been dominated by economic issues, the 1940 race focused on the war in Europe and the prospect of a third term for Roosevelt. Both candidates pledged to keep the country out of the war, but those who wanted the United States to take a strong stand against Hitler tended to favor Roosevelt.

On economic issues, Willkie basically agreed with Roosevelt's New Deal policies, so he attacked Roosevelt for breaking George Washington's tradition of stepping down after two terms. Because Willkie was generally unable to distinguish himself from Roosevelt, the country decided to stick with a proven and trusted leader. Although three-quarters of the nation's newspapers endorsed Willkie, FDR's support in the cities and among the working class carried him to victory.

President Roosevelt with Joseph Stalin (left) and Winston Churchill (right).

JAPANESE ATTACK PEARL HARBOR!

Surprise Air Raid Sinks Pacific Fleet

PEARL HARBOR, Hawaii, December 7, 1941—At five minutes before eight this morning, Japanese dive bombers and torpedo planes launched a surprise attack on the U.S. naval base at Pearl Harbor.

Eight battleships were crippled in the harbor. At the nearby army air base, half the fighter planes were destroyed while they sat on the ground. In all, more than twenty-three hundred U.S. servicemen were killed during the raid.

The Japanese can now proceed with the conquest of East Asia unhindered by the U.S. Pacific Fleet, which has been seriously damaged.

President Roosevelt is expected to ask for a declaration of war when he appears before a joint session of Congress tomorrow.

percent needed to be controlled as though they were diseases.

"We are determined to keep out of war," the president said, but the world's interdependence "makes it impossible for any nation completely to isolate itself from economic and political upheavals in the rest of the world, especially when such upheavals appear to be spreading and not declining."

Roosevelt's speech created an uproar among isolationists, who believed the president was inching closer to war. Although FDR toned down his public statements after that, he remained privately determined to resist aggression.

THE GOOD NEIGHBOR POLICY Throughout his first two terms in office, Roosevelt worked hard to improve U.S. relations with Latin America. In his first inaugural address, he said that he wanted to "dedicate this nation to the policy of the good neighbor."

For many years, the United States had been a difficult neighbor indeed. During the 1920s, Harding and Coolidge sent U.S. troops into Panama, the Dominican Republic, and Honduras. When violence followed the withdrawal of U.S. troops from Nicaragua in 1925, Coolidge sent them back to meet our "moral responsibility" there.

Roosevelt promised to put an end to that sort of interference. At the Montevideo Conference of American States in 1933, Secretary of State Cordell Hull gave his support to a declaration that "no

state has the right to intervene in the internal or external affairs of another." By satisfactorily addressing this issue, the Roosevelt administration helped to ensure Latin American cooperation later in the fight against Hitler.

PREPARATIONS FOR WAR World War II began when Nazi Germany invaded Poland in September 1939 and Britain and France came to Poland's aid. Roosevelt invoked the current Neutrality Act as he was required to by law, but he made it clear whose side the United States was on. "Even a neutral cannot be asked to close his mind or his conscience," the president said.

With Great Britain threatened, Americans debated whether or not to help. Isolationists organized the America First Committee to make sure their views were heard. Prominent spokesmen such as Charles Lindbergh warned that the United States had no business intervening in European affairs. But Roosevelt quite clearly saw the threat that Hitler posed to the world. After the fall of France in June 1940, he did everything he could within the law to help the British.

On September 3, 1940, Roosevelt issued an executive order trading fifty surplus destroyers to Britain in exchange for naval bases in Newfoundland and Bermuda. The British desperately needed the destroyers to fight German submarines in the North Atlantic. Meanwhile, Congress passed the first peacetime draft in U.S. history and appropriated sixteen billion dollars for new warships and airplanes.

In a fireside chat two months after his 1940 reelection, Roosevelt declared once again his support for Britain. "All our present efforts are not enough," he said. "We must be

★FALA One of the most famous presidential pets was FDR's dog Fala. This little black Scottie went everywhere with the president. When Roosevelt and British prime minister Winston Churchill met at sea to sign the Atlantic Charter in 1941, Fala was there at his master's feet. On a voyage to Hawaii in 1944, sailors aboard the cruiser *Baltimore* lured Fala belowdecks in order to pluck tufts of his hair for souvenirs.

★JAPANESE INTERNMENT CAMPS In the months after Pearl Harbor, many Californians focused their anger on the 127,000 Japanese Americans living in this country, mostly on the West Coast. Rumors spread quickly that Japanese Americans planned to sabotage military bases there. In February 1942, President Roosevelt ordered all Japanese Americans, whether they were citizens or not, removed from the West Coast to internment camps as far away as Arkansas. This policy was urged on him in part by farming interests who proceeded to buy up—at bargain prices—the rich land that relocated families were forced to sell. No efforts were made to curb the freedom of German or Italian Americans, however.

★THE HOME FRONT After the United States' entry into World War II, the country mobilized to fight on three fronts: in Europe, in Asia, and at home. Between 1941 and 1945, fifteen million men—and for the first time, nearly two hundred thousand women—served in the armed forces. At home, however, those men left behind important jobs on the nation's assembly lines that had to be filled. A government campaign featuring a character called Rosie the Riveter encouraged women to do their part for the war effort. Their enthusiastic response allowed factories in crucial war-related industries to keep running both day and night.

★THE GEODESIC DOME R. Buckminster Fuller was a visionary architect and engineer who devoted his life to conserving the natural resources of the planet he called Spaceship Earth. During the 1940s, he developed the geodesic dome. Fuller's revolutionary geometric design was uniquely balanced so that its size was not a limiting factor. People could build geodesic domes as large as they wanted.

Fuller's domes offered many possibilities for the future. Because their strength increased with their size, geodesic domes could be built to enclose entire cities or to protect people living underwater or on other planets. One of the most famous geodesic domes would be built to house the U.S. pavilion at the 1967 world's fair, called Expo67, in Montreal.

★THE MANHATTAN PROJECT In August 1939, Albert Einstein, the most famous scientist of his time, wrote a letter to President Roosevelt on behalf of colleagues who had recently fled Nazi Germany. In his letter, Einstein warned Roosevelt that the United States should begin work on an atomic bomb unless it wanted the Germans to develop one first.

At first, Roosevelt didn't take Einstein's letter very seriously, but that changed after Pearl Harbor. The president eventually devoted two billion dollars to the research. The bomb program was code-named the Manhattan Project because most of the early work took place at Columbia University in Manhattan.

On July 16, 1945, the first atomic bomb was set off near Alamogordo in the New Mexican desert. The explosion produced a flash that lit mountains ten miles away, vaporized the bomb tower, and turned the desert sand to glass for eight hundred yards around.

the great arsenal of democracy." One week later, the president proposed the "lend-lease" program. Lend-lease provided arms to Britain immediately but deferred payment until after the war. The program was later extended to the Soviet Union after the German invasion of that country in June 1941.

In August 1941, Roosevelt met with British prime minister Winston Churchill aboard a battleship off Newfoundland. It was the beginning of an exceptionally close relationship between the two leaders. Together they drew up the Atlantic Charter, which detailed their common war aims. These included the rights of all people to choose their own form of government and to trade freely.

"DR. WIN THE WAR"

The United States finally entered the war after the Japanese attack on Pearl Harbor. Tensions between the United States and Japan had been building since the Japanese invasion of China in 1937. In 1940, Japan joined the Triple Alliance with Germany and Italy, agreeing that war against one meant war against all.

With the same energy he brought to the New Deal, Roosevelt set about retooling the country's factories for war. Diverting funds from some New Deal programs and ending others, the president began a massive defense spending program. At a press conference, Roosevelt declared that "Dr. Win the War" had replaced "Dr. New Deal."

During World War II, nearly every resource and every person in the country played some part in the war effort. The Office of Price Administration rationed many necessary commodities such as rubber, sugar, and gasoline. Roosevelt himself spent much of his time planning strategy and meeting with the Allies.

After the Allied invasion of North Africa in late 1942, Roosevelt met with Churchill at Casablanca, Morocco. The following November, the two leaders met again, this time with Soviet premier Joseph Stalin in Teheran, Iran. Together these men were known as the Big Three.

At Teheran, Roosevelt and Churchill promised Stalin that they would open a second front in Europe the following summer. Stalin eagerly awaited the Allied invasion of France because it would force the Germans to shift troops from the Russian front in the East back to the West.

D-DAY The supreme Allied commander, General Dwight D. Eisenhower, decided that the invasion of France would take place on the beaches of Normandy. The day—code-named D-Day—was June 6, 1944. The success of the D-Day invasion, the largest naval operation in history, gave the Allies a foothold in Europe, which they kept expanding until France was liberated and Germany itself threatened.

When the Big Three met for the final time in February 1945 at Yalta in the Soviet Union, the end of the war was finally in sight. By this time, Roosevelt was quite sick.

At Yalta, Stalin forced Roosevelt and Churchill to agree to allow, at least temporarily, Communist governments in Eastern Europe. Many historians have used the president's weakened condition to explain his concessions to Stalin. But others have pointed out that Roosevelt had little choice. To oppose Stalin would have required the United States to invade Eastern Europe itself.

On April 12, 1945, as the Allies converged on Berlin, Roosevelt died at his retreat in Warm Springs, Georgia. Less than a month later, on May 7, the Germans formally surrendered, ending the war in Europe.

After twelve difficult years as president, Roosevelt's health was clearly failing. Although they were certain to nominate him for a fourth term, most Democrats suspected that in choosing Roosevelt's running mate, they were choosing the next president. Because of strong opposition to incumbent vice president Henry Wallace, whom some delegates considered a socialist, Roosevelt replaced him with Senator Harry Truman of Missouri.

The Republican candidate, New York governor Thomas E. Dewey, had been the front-runner for the 1940 nomination before Wendell Willkie took it away from him. This time, Dewey won on the first ballot with 1,056 of the 1,057 votes. (The remaining vote went to General Douglas MacArthur.) Dewey had first made a name for himself during the 1930s fighting organized crime as the district attorney in New York City. As governor, he had fought corruption in the state's police department and improved conditions in its mental health facilities.

With World War II still being fought, Dewey refused to criticize Roosevelt's foreign policy. However, he did make Roosevelt's health an issue, attacking "the tired old men" in Washington who had been running the country for so long. In response to Dewey's tactic, FDR's doctor announced that the president was in excellent health. Roosevelt also campaigned in bad weather to prove that neither he nor the nation had anything to fear on that count.

Democrats claimed that Dewey, who had no foreign policy experience, was not qualified to become president during wartime. Their slogan, "Don't change horses midstream," succinctly summed up Roosevelt's appeal. In November, FDR won again, but this time by a narrower margin than in any of his three previous victories.

HARRY S. TRUMAN

33RD PRESIDENT

★

FROM 1945 TO 1953

BORN: May 8, 1884

BIRTHPLACE: Lamar, Mo.

DIED: December 26, 1972

PARTY: Democrat

VICE PRESIDENT: Alben W. Barkley

FIRST LADY: Elizabeth (Bess) Virginia Wallace

CHILDREN: Margaret

NICKNAME: Man from Independence

The first president to travel underwater in a modern submarine.

ATOMIC BOMB DROPPED ON HIROSHIMA

HIROSHIMA, Japan, August 6, 1945—The first atomic bomb ever used in warfare was dropped today on the Japanese city of Hiroshima. Of the 344,000 people living there, approximately one hundred thousand were killed instantly. Another hundred thousand died later from burns and radiation poisoning.

The ten-foot-long bomb, code-named Little Boy, was carried by the *Enola Gay*. This B-29 bomber dropped Little Boy from an altitude of thirty-two thousand feet. The bomb exploded two thousand feet above the ground, leveling more than four square miles of the city. Waves of flame engulfed the rest of Hiroshima as the river flooded, trapping wounded people too weak to move.

President Truman justified the massive civilian casualties by pointing to the hundreds of thousands of U.S. servicemen who might have died during an invasion of Japan.

On April 12, 1945, just five weeks into his vice presidency, Harry Truman was suddenly called to the White House. He met Eleanor Roosevelt in her study. The first lady put her arm around Truman's shoulder and said, "Harry, the president is dead."

Truman's first thoughts were for the president's widow. "Is there anything I can do for you?" he asked. But Mrs. Roosevelt shook her head. "Is there anything we can do for you?" she replied. "For you are the one in trouble now."

Franklin Roosevelt had been running the country for more than twelve years when he died. For Truman—or anyone else—to succeed him was a mighty task.

Roosevelt had brought the country through the Great Depression and won the war in Europe. But Japan still remained to be tamed, and communism already seemed to be threatening the stability of the postwar world.

THE POTSDAM CONFERENCE Truman began at a great disadvantage because Roosevelt had never included him in policy development meetings. Truman wasn't even briefed on the atom bomb program until after he was sworn in as president. As a result, Truman had to learn about being president in a hurry. His first important test came in July 1945 when he traveled to the Berlin suburb of Potsdam to meet Winston Churchill and Joseph Stalin.

At Potsdam, the three leaders agreed to divide postwar Germany into four zones controlled by the United States, Britain, France, and the Soviet Union. The division roughly corresponded to the troop positions at the end of the war. Although the German capital of Berlin fell entirely within the Soviet zone, it was also divided into four sectors, one for each Allied power.

THE ATOM BOMB On July 16, the day before the Potsdam conference opened, U.S. scientists conducted the first atom bomb test near Alamogordo, New Mexico. The A-bomb had been developed with the help of the British, but the Soviets knew nothing about it. After learning of the test's success, Truman decided to tell Stalin personally about the United States' new superweapon.

On July 26, the Allied leaders at Potsdam sent an ultimatum to the Japanese: "The alternative to surrender is prompt and utter destruction." But the Japanese didn't know about

The Early Years

HARRY TRUMAN HAD TO WEAR THICK GLASSES during his childhood in Independence, Missouri. Because the glasses were expensive, his mother would not allow him to play contact sports. Other boys sometimes teased him for taking piano lessons instead. "I was kind of a sissy," Truman later said.

After serving in World War I, Truman opened a men's clothing shop in Kansas City. The business failed in 1922. But that year, with the backing of local political boss Thomas Pendergast, Truman won election to the top job in the county. In 1934, also with the help of Pendergast, he won a seat in the U.S. Senate.

Although Truman was sometimes called the "senator from Pendergast," he was known to be a capable and honest public servant. The Pendergast machine was certainly corrupt, but Truman said Pendergast never asked him to do anything dishonest because "he knew I wouldn't do it if he asked it."

★JACKIE ROBINSON On April 15, 1947, twenty-eight-year-old Jackie Robinson became the first black to play in a major league baseball game. Until Robinson broke the color barrier, African Americans were forced to play in separate Negro leagues.

All through his rookie year, the Brooklyn Dodgers' new second baseman was taunted by fans and players alike, who called him "nigger" and "jungle boy." But the dignified and courageous Robinson never responded. He just played as well as he could. That year, he was named the National League's Rookie of the Year. Two years later, he won the league's Most Valuable Player award.

★**THE UNITED NATIONS** The United Nations was created at the end of World War II. Its purpose was to prevent wars, promote human rights, and aid economic development throughout the world. Delegates from fifty nations attended the conference in San Francisco at which the UN Charter was drafted and then signed in June 1945.

Twenty-five years and one world war earlier, the U.S. Senate had debated the League of Nations Covenant to the Treaty of Versailles for eight months before rejecting it. This time, the United States became the first country to join the new international organization. After just six days of debate in July, the Senate ratified the UN Charter by a vote of 89-2.

★**THE GI BILL OF RIGHTS** The GI Bill of Rights was the name soldiers gave to the Servicemen's Readjustment Act of 1944. Congress passed this bill to provide benefits for the GIs fighting World War II. It established a system of veterans' hospitals to guarantee them medical care. It also set aside money for low-interest mortgages, small business loans, and college scholarships. The money the GI Bill provided for tuition and living expenses allowed nearly ten million veterans to attend colleges and trade schools after the war. In this way, the GI Bill played an important role in retraining soldiers for jobs in the peacetime postwar economy.

★**THE BUCK STOPS HERE** Truman had a particularly feisty personality. "If you can't stand the heat, get out of the kitchen," he liked to say. He occasionally lost his temper in public and was known to use vulgar language at times. But Truman's scrappiness gave him the self-confidence he needed to make difficult decisions. A sign on his desk read, "The Buck Stops Here." It meant that he never "passed the buck," or made someone else take responsibility for a decision.

the A-bomb, so they didn't see any reason to surrender.

Truman was faced with one of the most demanding choices ever made by a president: whether or not to use the atomic bomb. If he did, he would be the first to use a weapon more deadly than anything ever created. If he didn't, hundreds of thousands of U.S. soldiers might die during the planned invasion of Japan. Although he feared its consequences, Truman decided to use the bomb.

When the August 6 attack on Hiroshima still failed to produce a Japanese surrender, Truman ordered a second bomb dropped on Nagasaki three days later. On August 10, the Japanese sued for peace, and World War II was over. As one war ended, however, another began.

THE COLD WAR

Stalin had made it clear at Yalta that the Soviet Union would accept nothing less than secure borders. To the Soviets, this meant that Communist governments would be established and maintained in Eastern Europe. Stalin believed that the industrious Germans would recover quickly, as they had after World War I, and he wanted a buffer.

However real Stalin's concerns about Germany may have been, Truman and other western leaders remained concerned about the spread of communism.

In a speech delivered in Fulton, Missouri, in March 1946, Winston Churchill said that an "iron curtain" was descending across Europe. On one side were the democracies of the West; on the other side, the Communists.

The struggle between these competing political philosophies became known as the Cold War. Although the United States and the Soviet Union never fought each other directly, they used surrogates, notably the Koreans and the Vietnamese, to fight their battles for them.

THE TRUMAN DOCTRINE

The first important conflict of the Cold War took place in the Mediterranean, where Communist rebels threatened the governments of Greece and Turkey. Many experts pointed out that, while these governments were strongly anticommunist, they also treated their people very harshly. Truman didn't really care. He believed it was more important for the United States to check the spread of Soviet influence wherever it could.

On March 13, 1947, the president explained his policy for the "containment" of communism in a speech he delivered to Congress. In order to justify his four-hundred-million-dollar aid request for Greece and Turkey, Truman argued that the United States must guarantee help to every nation fighting the Communist menace. This policy was later called the Truman Doctrine.

THE MARSHALL PLAN

In the spirit of the Truman Doctrine, Secretary of State George Marshall tackled the problem of war-ravaged Europe. Nearly three hundred thousand Americans had been killed in action during World War II, but almost none of the fighting took place on U.S. soil. Central Europe was not as fortunate. During the six years of the war, tank battles and Allied bombing reduced to rubble most of the industrial cities in Britain, France, the Soviet Union, and Germany. Four million Germans and more than eighteen million Soviets were dead.

Three months after Truman's speech on Greece and Turkey, Marshall announced his plan to rebuild Europe. He believed the only

CAMPAIGN 1948

MOST POLITICAL PROFESSIONALS WROTE TRUMAN OFF as a caretaker president even before the campaign began. Liberals within the Democratic party, including FDR's sons, tried to convince General Dwight Eisenhower to run, but Eisenhower declined. Things got worse for Truman at the convention, where Mayor Hubert Humphrey of Minneapolis led a successful fight for a strong civil rights plank in the party platform. Thirty-five southern delegates walked out in protest.

After the convention, conservative southern Democrats met in Birmingham to form the States' Rights, or Dixiecrat, party, nominating South Carolina governor Strom Thurmond for president. Meanwhile, the radical Roosevelt wing of the Democratic party, upset with Truman's tough stance on the Soviet Union, put up Henry Wallace, FDR's second vice president, as the candidate of the Progressive party. Wallace promoted peace with the Soviet Union and opposed the Marshall Plan as a disguised attempt by U.S. corporations to take over Europe.

Abandoned by members of his own party, Truman wasn't given much of a chance. New York governor Thomas E. Dewey, renominated by the Republicans after losing in 1944, sat back and waited for victory. But Truman fought hard. During a thirty-thousand-mile "whistle-stop" train campaign, he made three hundred speeches to six million people. His gutsy manner and blunt attacks on the "do-nothing Eightieth Congress" caught the attention of the country. "Give 'em hell, Harry," one man at a rally in Seattle yelled.

Truman's campaign kept this positive momentum going. Still, all the polls, and even the early returns, predicted his defeat. On Election Day, the early edition of the *Chicago Tribune* ran the headline "Dewey Defeats Truman." The president later posed with this headline after victories in California and Ohio clinched his election.

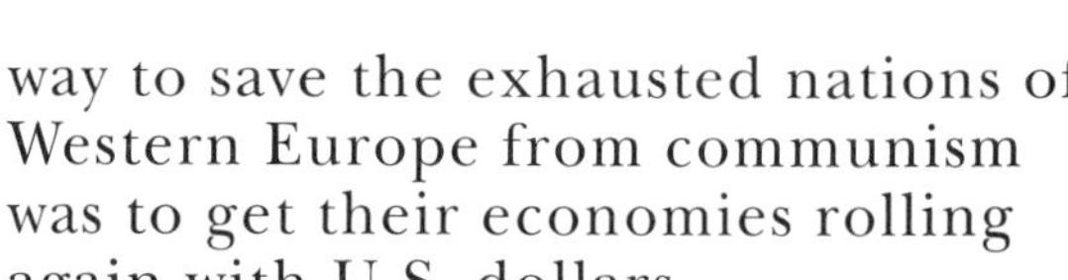

Harry, Bess, and Margaret Truman with friends.

way to save the exhausted nations of Western Europe from communism was to get their economies rolling again with U.S. dollars.

Marshall even offered to include the Soviets in his reconstruction program. "Our policy is directed not against any country or doctrine, but against hunger, poverty, desperation, and chaos," he said. A suspicious Stalin turned down the U.S. offer.

Between 1948 and 1952, Congress authorized twelve billion dollars for the Marshall Plan. Half of that went to Britain, France, and West Germany, which was created in 1949 when the three western zones were merged.

THE BERLIN AIRLIFT Meanwhile, the Soviet Union decided to test the West's resolve. It considered the Allied presence in Berlin an unnecessary annoyance. To encourage the British, French, and Americans to leave, the Soviets decided to blockade West Berlin beginning in April 1948.

Truman responded quickly and decisively by ordering an airlift to the besieged city. Using a constant shuttle of cargo planes, the United States and Great Britain were able to keep the West Berliners supplied with food, coal, and other necessities. The blockade ended in May 1949 and the successful airlift two months later.

The Berlin airlift made clear the need for a united front in Western Europe. The North Atlantic Treaty Organization, created by an

COMMUNISTS INVADE SOUTH KOREA

UN Security Council Condemns North

NEW YORK, June 25, 1950—The Communist government of North Korea launched a full-scale military invasion of South Korea today as the North Korean army crossed the Thirty-eighth Parallel border in force.

In an emergency meeting called this afternoon by President Truman, the UN Security Council voted 9-0 to hold North Korea accountable for the attack. The resolution is a prelude to sending UN troops to Korea. U.S. soldiers are expected to make up more than three-quarters of the combat troops used in this UN "police action."

As a permanent member of the Security Council, the Soviet Union had the power to veto the resolution, but the Soviet leadership continues to boycott Security Council meetings. The boycott began when the other members refused to recognize the People's Republic as the rightful government of China.

agreement signed in April 1949, provided just that. Truman's active participation in NATO finally put an end to the isolationism that had dominated U.S. foreign policy since the days of Washington.

THE FAIR DEAL Truman had a somewhat easier time with domestic issues. Of all the nations who fought in World War II, only the United States came out of the war better off economically. After years of rationing, Americans were eager to spend the money they had saved on large purchases such as cars, houses, and washing machines.

The biggest problem facing Truman was how to handle the massive demobilization of troops. At the end of the war, there were twelve million men serving in the army and navy. Within a year, nine million of them were discharged.

Truman's economic advisors worried that the discharged soldiers would have a difficult time finding new jobs now that many of their old jobs had been taken over by women and blacks. "Rosie the Riveter isn't going back to emptying slop jars," one union leader said. "Times have changed. People have become accustomed to...new ways of being treated."

The crunch was eased by two trends. Many women did indeed leave the work force to become mothers and housewives, beginning the postwar Baby Boom. Meanwhile, the country's economic boom created a great number of new jobs, particularly in home building and consumer manufacturing.

With his Fair Deal program, Truman tried to adapt Roosevelt's depression policies to postwar prosperity. Truman's top priorities were a national health care program and a civil rights bill. Both were defeated by new Republican

★**THE FIRST FAMILY** Harry Truman first met Bess Wallace in Sunday school. "I had only one sweetheart from the time I was six," Truman later said. But he and Bess didn't start dating seriously until 1913, when they were both nearly thirty. They were married in 1919.

Their daughter Margaret was an outgoing person like her mother. During her father's presidency, Margaret tried to launch a singing career. The twenty-three-year old made her debut before a national radio audience in March 1947. In 1950, the *Washington Post* music critic wrote that she "cannot sing with anything approaching professional finish." After reading the review, President Truman sent the critic an angry letter: "I have just read your lousy review.... You sound like a frustrated old man who never made a success.... I never met you, but if I do you'll need a new nose."

★**LEVITTOWN** The return of soldiers to civilian life caused a severe housing shortage after World War II. To relieve this problem, the construction firm of Levitt and Sons built a planned community on New York's Long Island that soon provided a model for suburban developers all over the country.

The secret of Levittown's success was its construction methods. Using prefabricated materials and assembly-line techniques, construction crews were able to put up as many as thirty identical houses in a single day. The homes may have lacked individuality, but they were remarkably affordable, selling for as little as seven thousand dollars each. With a GI Bill mortgage, a veteran could buy a house in Levittown for sixty-five dollars a month with no money down.

★**THE BABY BOOM** During World War II, many families put off having children. But once the war was over, there seemed little reason to wait. Between 1946 and 1960, these new parents created the Baby Boom. Because of the extraordinary size of the Baby Boom generation, its concerns and interests have always had a powerful influence on American society.

The book used to raise most of these children was *Baby and Child Care* by Dr. Benjamin Spock. This 1946 manual sold twenty-four million copies, more than any other book except the plays of Shakespeare and the Bible. It emphasized flexibility instead of the rigid schedules and discipline favored by earlier generations.

★**THE COMPUTER AGE** Besides the atom bomb, scientists made other important discoveries during World War II. At the University of Pennsylvania, J. Presper Eckert and John W. Mauchly began the computer age when they built the first all-electronic digital computer. They called their machine the Electronic Numerical Integrator and Calculator, or ENIAC for short.

The first computers, including ENIAC, used vacuum tubes to relay information. Because these tubes took up so much space, ENIAC covered fifteen hundred square feet and weighed thirty tons. The invention of the transistor in 1948 allowed scientists to replace the vacuum tubes and shrink the size of computers substantially. A transistorized version of ENIAC would have fit inside a refrigerator.

majorities in the Eightieth Congress, elected in 1946.

Much to Truman's displeasure, the Eightieth Congress did pass, over the president's veto, the Taft-Hartley Act of 1947, which rolled back many of the legal gains unions had made since the passage of the Wagner Act in 1935.

After his remarkable reelection, Truman campaigned once more for his Fair Deal programs, this time before a friendlier Democratic Congress. He got the minimum wage raised from forty to seventy-five cents an hour and won passage of the National Housing Act, which provided money for slum clearance and low-income housing. Truman had already used an executive order in July 1948 to end racial segregation in the armed forces. But the united opposition of southerners in Congress prevented him from making any further progress on the issue of civil rights.

When Truman ordered the dropping of the atom bomb in 1945, he had hoped that its use might scare other countries, especially the Soviet Union, into maintaining the peace. But the testing of a Soviet bomb in 1949 forced the president to change his thinking. Now peace depended on a stable "balance of terror" between the two superpowers.

WHO LOST CHINA? The "loss" of China that same year also hurt the Truman administration badly. The victory of Mao Zedong's Communist Red Army over the hopelessly corrupt Nationalist forces of Chiang Kai-shek had been expected by government officials. Nevertheless, it shocked ordinary citizens, who began to ask, "Who lost China?" Republicans in Congress blamed Truman's secretary of state, Dean Acheson, whom they said was "soft on communism."

THE KOREAN WAR

Communist North Korea invaded capitalist South Korea in June 1950. Given the political situation, Truman had little choice but to send troops. Although the North Koreans were able to penetrate deeply into South Korean territory, General Douglas MacArthur's brilliant landing behind enemy lines at Inchon turned the war around. By October, United Nations forces under MacArthur's command had recrossed the Thirty-eighth Parallel border into North Korea and were advancing quickly on the Yalu River, which separated North Korea from China.

As UN forces approached the Yalu, Chinese officials warned that they would not "sit back with folded hands." But MacArthur dismissed almost casually the possibility of China entering the war. With his air force controlling the sky, the general was sure that the Chinese would be slaughtered if they tried anything.

MacArthur was tragically wrong. On November 26, Chinese soldiers streamed across the border, inflicting heavy casualties and chasing U.S. and Korean troops all the way back across the Thirty-eighth Parallel. The general's command eventually regrouped, but the best he could achieve now was a stalemate.

Once the Chinese entered the war, MacArthur began asking for permission to carry the war to China. When Truman refused him, MacArthur publicly expressed his unhappiness.

As commander-in-chief of the armed forces, President Truman was not willing to tolerate any challenge to his authority. The president relieved MacArthur of his command in April 1951.

Three months later, peace talks began, but no treaty was signed with Truman in office. Despite occasional cease-fires, the fighting continued as the negotiations dragged on.

PEOPLE HAD BEEN TRYING TO CONVINCE WORLD WAR II hero Dwight D. Eisenhower to run for president ever since the German surrender. There was a problem, however: Eisenhower didn't belong to a political party. The Democrats courted him in 1948, but it turned out that Eisenhower's views were more in keeping with the Republican party.

The Republican platform called for a strong national defense and criticized the Democrats for "appeasement of communism at home and abroad." This approach played to Eisenhower's strength as a symbol of U.S. military might. "Let's face it. The only excuse for Ike's candidacy is that he's the man best qualified to deal with Stalin," one Republican strategist said. At Thomas E. Dewey's suggestion, Eisenhower picked anticommunist crusader Richard M. Nixon of California as his running mate.

Eisenhower's Democratic opponent was Governor Adlai E. Stevenson of Illinois, grandson of Grover Cleveland's vice president. Stevenson was enormously well educated and well spoken, but many voters thought he was an "egghead," or too intellectual.

Recognizing that women now made up half the voting population, the Republicans appealed directly for their votes. Stockings, nail files, makeup cases, and other women's items were printed with the slogan "I Like Ike."

For the most part, Eisenhower's campaign proceeded smoothly. The one rough spot came when *The New York Times* revealed that Nixon maintained a "slush" fund of campaign contributions, which he used to pay some of his own expenses. With Eisenhower threatening to drop him from the ticket, Nixon delivered the nationally televised "Checkers" speech on September 23. He denied using the money for personal expenses. But he did admit receiving one gift, a cocker spaniel named Checkers. "Regardless of what they say about it," Nixon declared, "we're going to keep it." Eisenhower locked up the election a few weeks later when he declared that if elected "I shall go to Korea" to get the stalled peace talks moving again.

Dwight David Eisenhower

34th President

★

From 1953 to 1961

Born: October 14, 1890

Birthplace: Denison, Texas

Died: March 28, 1969

Party: Republican

Vice President: Richard M. Nixon

First Lady: Marie (Mamie) Geneva Doud

Children: Dwight, John

Nickname: Ike

Had a putting green installed on the White House lawn.

As the Allied commander during World War II, Dwight Eisenhower developed a reputation for smooth, effective leadership. In his two terms as president, the retired general ran the government in much the same way he ran the army. That is, he appointed staff members to create and direct national policy under his supervision.

Unlike the feisty Truman, Eisenhower always seemed to be relaxed and smiling. As a result, his years in the White House were known for peace, prosperity, and blandness. Things were not as peaceful and prosperous, however, as Eisenhower's mood made them seem.

Eisenhower believed the government should remain as

SEN. McCARTHY CHARGES COMMIES IN STATE DEPT.

WHEELING, West Virginia, February 9, 1950—Speaking before a Republican women's club, Senator Joseph McCarthy of Wisconsin shocked his audience tonight when he declared that Communists are secretly working in important positions throughout the federal government.

The senator repeatedly waved a piece of paper that he claimed was a list of 205 "card-carrying Communists" currently working in the State Department. He has not yet revealed any of the names, nor has he provided any evidence to back up his sensational charges.

McCarthy's attack comes only a month after former State Department official Alger Hiss was found guilty of lying about his Communist past. For the crime of perjury, or lying under oath, Hiss was given a ten-thousand-dollar fine and five years in jail.

Time magazine editor Whittaker Chambers, himself an admitted Soviet agent, accused Hiss of spying for the Soviet Union in testimony before the House Un-American Activities Committee. Despite his conviction, Hiss still maintains his innocence.

small as possible. This attitude led him to criticize the New Deal and the Fair Deal, both of which he felt neglected traditional American individualism. Above all, however, Eisenhower was a moderate who followed "that straight road down the middle" and didn't make waves.

THE KOREAN WAR ENDS

In December 1952, Eisenhower kept his campaign promise to go to Korea, where he tried to revive the stalled peace talks. The president-elect threatened to extend the war to China and even to use small-scale atomic weapons. Still, the negotiations continued for another seven months before an armistice was signed on July 27, 1953.

The supposedly limited war in Korea cost the United States fifteen billion dollars. In an attempt to avoid paying such a high price in the future, Eisenhower and Secretary of State John Foster Dulles developed the policy of "massive retaliation." In their view, the Soviet Union would not attack the United States or any of its allies as long as the leaders in the Kremlin believed that the United States would respond with nuclear devastation.

Eisenhower was particularly motivated by his desire to cut the federal budget. He assumed that nuclear weapons provided "more bang for a buck" than conventional weapons. Therefore, he ordered severe cutbacks in army ground troops and instead invested in nuclear warheads. He also spent money on the missiles and bombers needed to deliver them. But the savings turned out to be an illusion as the cost of ever more sophisticated hardware kept defense spending high.

Meanwhile, the country remained obsessed with fears of Communist

The Early Years

DWIGHT EISENHOWER WAS RAISED IN ABILENE, Kansas, the third of six sons born to a poor family. Other boys often teased him for wearing tattered clothing and his mother's hand-me-down shoes. Young Dwight thought he would grow up to be a railroad engineer. Instead, he passed the West Point entrance exam, which earned him a free college education and a career in the army.

After graduating from the military academy, Eisenhower became a tank commander. Although he requested an overseas assignment during World War I, the army ordered him to spend the war as a training instructor. In 1932, Major Eisenhower joined the staff of Douglas MacArthur and helped the general break up the Bonus March. During World War II, General Eisenhower led the invasions of North Africa, Sicily, and Italy before President Roosevelt named him supreme Allied commander in December 1943.

★**PRESIDENTIAL RECREATION** Golf was President Eisenhower's favorite sport, and his strong interest in the game encouraged a nationwide trend. On sunny days, the president could often be found on the White House lawn practicing his chip shots. He usually scored in the eighties.

Eisenhower was also an accomplished cook. His best dishes were vegetable soup, charcoal-grilled steak, and cornmeal pancakes. He and his wife Mamie often hosted barbecues for their friends on the White House roof.

★**Hail! Hail! Rock 'n' Roll!** Memphis record producer Sam Phillips often boasted that, with "a white boy who could sing black," he could make a million dollars. On July 6, 1954, that boy recorded his first song for Phillips's Sun Records. Nineteen-year-old Elvis Presley sang in the rhythm-and-blues style that teenagers loved. The black musicians who had created rhythm-and-blues weren't played on many radio stations in the segregated South. But Elvis was different because his white skin made him acceptable. Many parents condemned Presley for the sexy way he shook his hips. They even tried to ban his records. But the campaigns against him and his rock 'n' roll music only made teenagers want more.

★**The Rosenberg Case** In July 1950, federal agents arrested Julius and Ethel Rosenberg and charged the New York couple with transmitting top-secret information to the Soviet Union. The Rosenbergs were part of an atom-bomb spy ring involving Ethel's brother, who testified against them at their trial. The Rosenbergs claimed they were innocent, but Cold War hysteria was everywhere. Julius's active membership in the Communist party hurt their case badly. The couple was sentenced to death. Despite international protests, they were executed in June 1953. Some people believed the Rosenbergs were innocent. But even among those who thought they were guilty, many considered the death penalty to have been unjust.

★**The Montgomery Bus Boycott** On December 1, 1955, in Montgomery, Alabama, a tired seamstress named Rosa Parks was told to give up her seat on a city bus to a white man. When she refused, she was arrested because in Montgomery no black person sat while a white person was standing. To protest Parks's arrest, local black ministers—led by twenty-six-year-old Martin Luther King, Jr.—organized a boycott of the bus system. For more than a year, African Americans in Montgomery used car pools, walked, and even rode horses rather than ride the segregated buses. The boycott ended when a Supreme Court decision forced the city to stop segregating black passengers in December 1956.

subversion inside the United States. President Truman had ordered a loyalty investigation of the entire government, and this bipartisan Communist witch hunt continued under Eisenhower. According to Truman's attorney general, Communists were "everywhere—in factories, offices, butcher shops, on street corners, in private business—and each carries with him the germs of death for society."

Senator Joseph McCarthy of Wisconsin quickly became famous for his crusades against the State Department, which he claimed was full of Communists. McCarthy spoke in half-truths and insinuations rather than making straightforward charges that could be proven or disproven. Often his aides would find evidence that a particular government employee had attended meetings of the Communist party during the 1930s, at a time when Communism was still considered respectable.

Although McCarthy never proved any of his outrageous charges, Eisenhower and others refrained from criticizing him. They were worried that criticizing McCarthy might make them look suspicious. People accused by Senator McCarthy, especially writers and actors, were often prevented from working because employers were also desperate not to appear disloyal. The practice of "blacklisting," or not hiring people because they were suspected of being Communists, ruined the careers of many innocent people.

THE ARMY-McCARTHY HEARINGS McCarthy's arrogance finally caught up with him in 1954. That summer, he chaired a series of nationally televised hearings about alleged Communists in the armed forces. A lawyer for the army, Joseph Welch, finally challenged the senator publicly after McCarthy tried to smear one of his young assistants. "You have done enough," Welch told McCarthy. "Have you no sense of decency, sir, at long last?"

After Welch's dignified rebuke, McCarthy's spell over Washington was broken. That December, the Senate voted to reprimand him for "conduct unbecoming a member." Since then, the term *McCarthyism* has come to mean persecution based on unproven and often unfair accusations.

FOREIGN POLICY Eisenhower generally left the nation's foreign policy in the respected care of John Foster Dulles. The secretary of state's long experience in foreign affairs, which dated back to the Wilson administration, made it difficult for others in the White House to challenge him.

Dulles's belief, which Eisenhower accepted, was that the nations of the world were either friends of the United States or friends of the Soviet Union. No single nation, in Dulles's view, could be both.

Dulles claimed to have abandoned Truman's policy of containment so that he could press for the "liberation" of "captive nations" under Communist rule. In reality, the secretary of state did nothing of the sort. When East Germany in 1953 and Hungary in 1956 tried to free themselves from Soviet domination, the United States did nothing to prevent Soviet tanks from crushing these rebellions.

In general, U.S. foreign policy remained limited to containment. In the Southeast Asian nation of South Vietnam, for example, Dulles advised his boss to support the government there in its struggle against the Communist North.

Eisenhower was particularly concerned about what might happen if South Vietnam were to fall to the Communists. "You have a row of

CAMPAIGN 1956

THE REPUBLICANS' GREATEST CONCERN DURING 1956 was Eisenhower's health. In 1955, the president had suffered what his doctors called a "moderate" heart attack, and earlier in 1956 he had undergone serious intestinal surgery. Although the president was already back at his desk after two months of rest, some people doubted his ability to serve another four years.

On the Democratic side, Adlai Stevenson decided to try for a second nomination despite his sizable defeat four years earlier. During the primaries, Stevenson was opposed by Senator Estes Kefauver of Tennessee, nationally known for his fight against government corruption. After Stevenson was renominated on the first ballot, he surprised the convention by allowing the delegates to choose his running mate. Senator John F. Kennedy of Massachusetts made a strong pitch for the second spot on the ticket, but Kefauver beat him out.

The Democrats didn't have much to work with in terms of campaign issues. Eisenhower had ended the Korean War as promised, and he had stood up to the Soviet Union. At home, the president also had performed well. Employment was up, and people all over the country felt prosperous. The only issue the Democrats really had was Eisenhower's health. But they hesitated to bring it up for fear of offending voters.

Eisenhower and Nixon were reelected easily, winning two million more votes and two more states than they had in 1952. The president's popularity, however, did not extend to other Republican candidates for office. Both the House of Representatives and the Senate remained Democratic. It was the first time since Zachary Taylor was elected in 1848 that a president had failed to carry at least one house of Congress for his party.

Mamie and Dwight Eisenhower in the Oval Office.

dominoes set up," the president said, "and you knock over the first one, and what will happen to the last one is the certainty that it will go over very quickly."

In political terms, the domino theory meant that the fall of one country to communism would always lead to the fall of others. If the chain reaction wasn't stopped in time, eventually all the "dominoes" would fall, including the United States.

THE WARREN COURT

At home, the Supreme Court was grabbing the headlines. When President Eisenhower appointed California governor Earl Warren to be the new chief justice in 1953, he thought that Warren would make an uncontroversial, middle-of-the-road justice. Instead, Warren led a revolution on the Court, particularly in the area of civil rights law.

Warren wrote his most important opinion for the 1954 case of *Brown v. Board of Education.* In this case, the Court unanimously reversed *Plessy v. Ferguson* (1896), which had upheld the "separate but equal" doctrine. Instead, Warren declared that segregating white and black students in public schools was unequal and therefore unconstitutional.

"To separate [black children] from others of similar age and qualifications solely on the basis of their race generates a feeling of inferiority...that may affect their hearts and minds in a way never to be undone," the chief justice

SOVIETS LAUNCH FIRST SATELLITE

BAIKONUR, Soviet Union, October 4, 1957—The Soviet Union began the space race today when it launched the first man-made object into orbit. The 184-pound satellite is called Sputnik, which means "fellow traveler" in Russian.

Sputnik is a steel sphere containing a radio transmitter and batteries to power the transmitter. Four whip aerials are attached to its outside casing.

Sputnik's orbit carries it over the Baikonur launch site every ninety minutes or so. The Soviet scientists have been able to track Sputnik's progress by monitoring the bleep-bleep-bleep of its radio transmitter.

The rocket that launched Sputnik into orbit was powered by the same engine that the Soviet Union uses for its new intercontinental ballistic missiles, or ICBMs.

The successful launch of Sputnik has been a blow to U.S. prestige. Many government officials also consider the Soviet lead in space to be a sign of potential U.S. military weakness.

wrote. "We conclude that in the field of public education the doctrine of 'separate but equal' has no place." Eisenhower later said that appointing Warren was "the biggest damn fool mistake I ever made."

THE CIVIL RIGHTS MOVEMENT In part because of the *Brown* decision, the civil rights movement gained great momentum during the Eisenhower years. Martin Luther King, Jr., became its most eloquent spokesperson. The Montgomery bus boycott that he led drew national attention to the fight for equal rights under the law.

Eisenhower personally objected to racial segregation, but he also believed that forcing integration was a political mistake. When he finally sent troops into Little Rock to force Central High School to admit black students, he did so because the governor of Arkansas had challenged federal authority, not because the president believed that integrating the school was desirable at that time.

SPUTNIK Because attention was so closely focused on Little Rock at the time, it came as a shock to most Americans when the Soviet Union announced the successful launch of Sputnik in October 1957. Sputnik was the first man-made object ever placed in orbit around the earth.

Enraged that the Soviets had jumped ahead of the United States in the space race, Congress passed the National Defense Education Act in September 1958. Its purpose was to develop scientific talent. The act provided money for new school laboratories and scholarships for college students. Before receiving the money, however, the students had to sign a loyalty oath swearing that they were not sympathetic to the Communist party. Many refused the

★**FEAR OF THE BOMB** Once the Soviets exploded an atomic bomb in 1949, the world was suddenly faced with the possibility of nuclear war. In the United States, where the Cold War was peaking, civil defense officials tried, often foolishly, to prepare people for nuclear attack.

Elementary school students were taught to "duck and cover" if they ever saw the bright flash that signaled the explosion of an atomic bomb. Meanwhile, parents invested in expensive underground bomb shelters to protect their families from the deadly radioactive fallout of an atomic explosion.

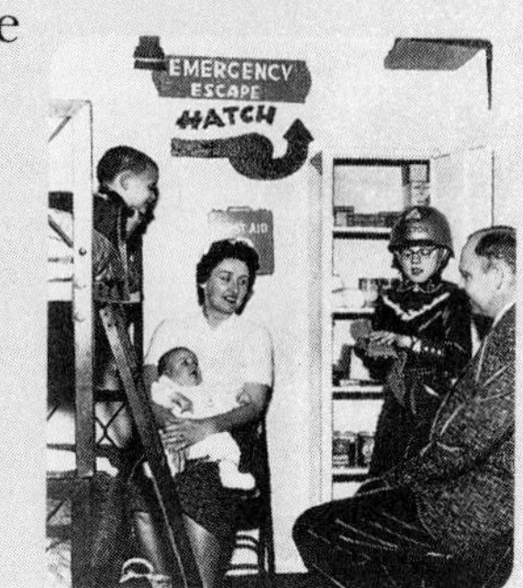

★**THE BEAT GENERATION** The Eisenhower years are best remembered for their conformity. Most people liked to do the same thing as everybody else. But other people rebelled against the safe routine of suburban life. The Beats were a group of writers, performers, and hangers-on who lived mostly in New York's Greenwich Village and San Francisco's North Beach neighborhoods. They wore black clothing (especially turtlenecks), grew beards (usually goatees), and stayed up late at night in coffeehouses listening to music (always jazz).

The most famous Beat writers were Allen Ginsberg and Jack Kerouac. Ginsberg wrote "Howl" and other works that turned poetry on its head. Kerouac wrote his novel *On the Road* during a three-week burst in 1951 on a single roll of printer's paper. The book celebrated a life of adventure unburdened by possessions or family ties.

★**THE FIRST LADY** Dwight and Mamie Eisenhower were married in 1916, when Dwight was still an army lieutenant. During their marriage, Mamie was a dutiful army wife. She adjusted quickly to life on military bases and moved twenty-eight times with her husband as he changed assignments.

As first lady during most of the 1950s, Mamie Eisenhower did what most American women did. She tried to be a good wife, mother—and in her case, grandmother. Being the wife of the president, however, required more from her than most housewives. She had to plan state dinners and supervise the White House domestic staff. She also valued her privacy and made few public appearances.

★**THE LITTLE ROCK NINE** After the Supreme Court's 1954 ruling in the *Brown* case, most school districts in the border states stopped operating separate schools for blacks and whites. In the Deep South, however, many schools refused to change. Little Rock, Arkansas, became the focus of southern resistance in September 1957 when Governor Orval Faubus used the National Guard to prevent nine black students from attending all-white Central High School. When a federal court ordered Faubus to admit them, the governor did. But he refused to protect the teenagers from the angry white mob outside the school. Faubus's actions forced President Eisenhower to send in federal troops. It was the first time since Reconstruction that federal troops had been used to defend the rights of blacks.

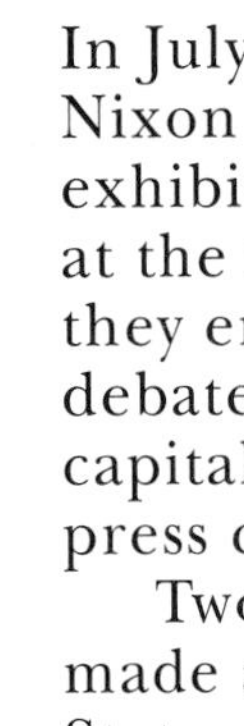

★**THE COMICS CODE** Comic books became big business during the Eisenhower years. More than a billion were sold annually. During the mid-1950s, however, parents began to complain about violence, gore, and sexuality in horror comics. To avoid legal action, comic book publishers created the Comics Code in 1954 to clean up the industry and ban the offensive stories.

William Gaines and Harvey Kurtzman were two of the most successful creators of horror comics. To beat the new code, they began printing their comic book, *Mad,* on glossy paper. The glossy paper technically turned *Mad* into a magazine, not a comic book, so the Comics Code didn't apply. *Mad* soon became famous for making fun of everything held sacred by most Americans.

money on principle rather than sign the oath.

THE KITCHEN DEBATE In an attempt to "thaw" the Cold War, Eisenhower and Soviet premier Nikita Khrushchev agreed to a series of cultural exchanges. In July 1959, Vice President Richard Nixon visited Moscow to open a U.S. exhibition there. He met Khrushchev at the model kitchen display, where they engaged in a loud, spontaneous debate about whether communism or capitalism was the better system. The press called it the "kitchen debate."

Two months later, Khrushchev made a goodwill tour of the United States. He was disappointed when security considerations prevented him from visiting Disneyland, but he had a useful visit with Eisenhower. The two leaders met at Camp David, the presidential retreat named after Eisenhower's grandson. Afterward, they agreed to continue working in "the spirit of Camp David" and made plans for a meeting in Paris the following May.

THE U-2 INCIDENT Less than two weeks before the Paris summit, the Soviet Union shot down a U.S. spy plane deep within Soviet airspace. At first the State Department issued vague denials, but Eisenhower later admitted that U-2 planes had been making secret high-altitude flights over Soviet territory for years.

Although Eisenhower promised to end the flights, he refused to apologize. An angry Khrushchev canceled the Paris meeting and Eisenhower's upcoming trip to the Soviet Union.

The early State Department denials also made Americans question their government's truthfulness. "Up until now it has been possible to say to the world that what came out of the Kremlin was deceitful and untrust-

worthy but that people could depend on what they were told by the government of the United States," the *Wall Street Journal* wrote. "Now the world may not be so sure that this country is any different from any other."

REVOLUTION IN CUBA In the meantime, an even more threatening situation was developing much closer to the United States. On New Year's Day 1959, the Cuban revolutionary leader Fidel Castro toppled the corrupt dictatorship of Fulgencio Batista. Although Batista had been a cruel leader, he still enjoyed a great deal of support in the United States because of his favorable treatment of U.S. business and gambling interests.

Castro at first sought friendship with the United States, but he soon seized foreign property, most of it belonging to U.S. corporations. It was the only way Castro felt he could end the colonial relationship that had bound Cuba since the Spanish-American War. When Eisenhower retaliated by halting trade with Cuba, Castro turned to the enemy of his enemy, the Soviet Union.

Before Eisenhower left office in 1961, he delivered a poignant farewell address, much as George Washington had. The first general to become president had pointed out the dangers of foreign entanglements, but Eisenhower warned Americans about a new danger at home: the dependence of U.S. industry on military spending.

The president called attention to the ties that had developed between the Pentagon and its military contractors. He called this relationship the "military-industrial complex" and warned that it was gaining too much influence. As the country became more involved in the war in Vietnam, Eisenhower's words began to sound wiser and even more prophetic.

WHEN JOHN F. KENNEDY ENTERED THE 1960 campaign, the experts said that the young Democratic senator from Massachusetts didn't have a chance. Because Eisenhower had been a popular Republican president, most political insiders assumed that Vice President Richard Nixon would win the election easily.

Also, Democrats worried that Kennedy's Catholic religion might hurt him. Americans had never elected a Catholic president. But Kennedy's victory in the West Virginia primary proved that he could win votes in a heavily Protestant state.

Kennedy and Nixon had similar political ideas. Both believed in a military strong enough to protect the United States from Communist attack. Both also promised to continue funding welfare programs for the poor. Throughout the summer, the race stayed close in the polls.

On September 26, Kennedy and Nixon met in the first of four debates. Although there had been presidential debates before, none had been televised nationally. Because the two candidates were so close in the polls, most people believed that the debates would decide the election.

Over one hundred million people tuned in to watch. Both men spoke well. But Nixon, who had recently been in the hospital, looked pale and uncomfortable, while Kennedy appeared tan and in charge. When Kennedy narrowly won the election six weeks later, many people thought it was due to his presidential appearance during the debates.

John Fitzgerald Kennedy

35th President

★

From 1961 to 1963

Born: May 29, 1917

Birthplace: Brookline, Mass.

Died: November 22, 1963

Party: Democrat

Vice President: Lyndon B. Johnson

First Lady: Jacqueline Lee Bouvier

Children: Caroline; John, Jr.; Patrick

Nickname: JFK

The first Boy Scout president.

The youngest man ever elected president, John F. Kennedy is best remembered for the hope he brought to the nation. In 1961, the United States was threatened by Cold War abroad and racial injustice at home. The new president admitted these problems in his inaugural address, but he also spoke with hope to a new generation ready to solve them.

In one of the most quoted inaugural addresses ever, Kennedy set forth the goals for his program called the New Frontier. He promised to work for freedom around the world and asked people at home to give something of themselves. "Ask not what your country can do for you," he said. "Ask what you can do for your country."

MISSILES IN CUBA!

WASHINGTON, October 22, 1962—President Kennedy went on television tonight and revealed spy-plane photographs of Soviet nuclear missiles currently being installed in Cuba.

After condemning the Soviet Union for lying about the missiles, the president announced a naval blockade of Cuba beginning immediately and continuing until the missiles are removed. The blockade is intended to prevent Soviet ships carrying missile parts from reaching the island.

Kennedy made it clear that the presence of nuclear missiles so close to the U.S. shore is completely unacceptable.

Before the speech, high-level sources close to the president had said that Kennedy was also considering bombing the missile bases. The president was concerned, however, that such an action would lead to a harsher Soviet military response and perhaps a nuclear war.

THE COLD WAR

Kennedy's major foreign policy concern was the Cold War with the Soviet Union. All over the world, Kennedy watched vigilantly for signs of Soviet expansionism.

When Eisenhower left office, he told Kennedy that the Central Intelligence Agency was secretly training Cuban exiles to oust Fidel Castro. Since Castro's successful 1959 revolution, Cuba had become increasingly friendly with the Soviet Union. The idea of having a Soviet ally so close to the Florida shore made most Americans, including the president, nervous. So Kennedy allowed the training to continue.

On April 17, 1961, fourteen hundred Cuban exiles landed at the Bay of Pigs. Their mission was to lead a revolt against Castro. But promised U.S. air support never arrived, and the invasion was a complete disaster. President Kennedy was forced to take the blame for a major blunder at the very beginning of his administration.

Then, in August 1961, the Soviet-backed government of East Germany built a wall dividing East Berlin from West Berlin. The United States protested, but since the wall was built entirely on the East Berlin side, it was allowed to stand.

THE CUBAN MISSILE CRISIS

Kennedy had a much more serious confrontation with the Soviet Union in October 1962 when he discovered that the Soviets were building nuclear missile bases in Cuba. The president ordered the navy to surround Cuba and dared the Soviet Union to run the blockade. Kennedy's risk paid off when Soviet premier Nikita Khrushchev agreed to remove the missiles in exchange for a U.S. promise not to invade Cuba. The Cuban Missile Crisis was the closest the world has ever come to nuclear war.

The Early Years

JOHN F. KENNEDY WAS THE SECOND OF NINE CHILDREN born into a wealthy Irish-Catholic family in Boston. His father, Joseph, was so rich that he gave each of his children one million dollars when they reached the age of twenty-one.

As a child, John (or Jack, as the family called him) was frail and sickly. He looked up to his older brother, Joe, who their father decided would one day be president. But Joe was killed during World War II.

Jack also served in the war. He was nearly killed when a Japanese destroyer rammed his gunboat, *PT-109*. But he survived the crash and won a medal for saving his crew. After the war, Jack began a career in politics, as did his brothers Bobby and Teddy.

★**THE FIRST FAMILY** As first lady, Jacqueline Kennedy set fashion trends across the United States. Her hairdo and pillbox hats inspired thousands of women to copy the Jackie Look. The young Kennedy children, Caroline and John, also kept the nation charmed.

John was often photographed hiding under his father's desk in the Oval Office during important meetings. His sister Caroline loved animals. One of her pets was a goodwill gift from the Soviet Union, a puppy named Pushinka, whose mother was the first dog to travel in space. Another was her horse, Macaroni.

★**SPACE RACE** In a speech made soon after his inauguration, JFK vowed that the United States would land a man on the moon before the end of the decade. To achieve this goal, he funded a five-billion-dollar space program.

Space was yet another arena in which the United States and the Soviet Union struggled to outdo each other. At first, the Soviets held the lead. In April 1961, cosmonaut Yuri Gagarin became the first human to orbit the planet. Three weeks later, however, a Project Mercury rocket launched U.S. astronaut Alan Shepard into space.

★**CIVIL RIGHTS** During Kennedy's years in office, the civil rights movement surged ahead in its struggle for equality. In 1960, the first sit-in protested racial discrimination at a Woolworth's lunch counter. Two years later, despite a campus riot, James Meredith became the first black to enroll at the University of Mississippi.

One of the decade's most moving moments came in August 1963 when Martin Luther King, Jr., delivered his "I Have a Dream" speech in front of 250,000 people during the March on Washington.

★**POPULAR MUSIC** Life in America during the Kennedy years was sometimes silly, sometimes troubled, but most often hopeful. During the early 1960s, the songs of the Great Dance Craze replaced those sung by the leather-jacketed rebels of the Eisenhower years. Chubby Checker had Number One hits with "The Twist" and "Pony Time." In New York's Greenwich Village, however, folk singers such as Bob Dylan and Joan Baez sang political "protest songs."

★**PEACE CORPS** President Kennedy created the Peace Corps in 1961 so that Americans could help the people of developing countries directly. Doctors, teachers, scientists, and other volunteers built hospitals, started schools, and improved farming methods all over the world. Many recent college graduates were inspired to join the Peace Corps by a growing concern for the world beyond the United States.

Meanwhile, across the globe in Vietnam, the United States was becoming involved in a different type of war. Under Kennedy, the number of military advisors in that Southeast Asian country rose from a few hundred to more than ten thousand.

Historians still argue about what Kennedy would have done in Vietnam had he lived. Some claim the president was planning to pull out all the advisors. Others say he would have sent over U.S. troops just as Lyndon Johnson later did.

CIVIL RIGHTS

At home, Kennedy's focus was on civil rights. Although the president supported equal rights for people of color, he also wanted to move slowly so that he wouldn't lose any of his political support. It took the work of activists such as Martin Luther King, Jr., to force Kennedy to act on his beliefs.

In May 1961, for example, thirteen Freedom Riders boarded a Greyhound bus in Washington, D.C. They were headed for the Deep South to protest segregated public transportation there. At nearly every stop, this mixed group of blacks and whites was attacked and beaten. Each time, Kennedy was pushed to protect them.

ASSASSINATION IN DALLAS

Almost everyone who was alive at the time remembers what they were doing when they heard the news of Kennedy's assassination in Dallas. The event still haunts many people because it symbolizes the end of an era of hope and the beginning of a period of violence.

Kennedy once described himself as "an idealist without illusions." As president, he often showed great skill at appealing to the idealism of others, especially young people. When he was killed, much of their faith in the future was shattered.

The Kennedy Assassination

Although Kennedy won the 1960 election by the slimmest of margins, he went on to become a very popular president. On November 22, 1963, about a thousand days into his presidency, Kennedy flew to Dallas to give a speech.

He and Jackie were greeted by huge cheering crowds all the way from the airport. As their open car entered Dealey Plaza, however, a number of shots were fired at Kennedy from the Texas School Book Depository building. Two hit the president, one in the throat and the other in the back of the head. Kennedy died at nearby Parkland Hospital half an hour later.

That afternoon, U.S. District Court Judge Sarah T. Hughes administered the oath of office to Vice President Lyndon Johnson aboard Air Force One, the president's airplane. Later, Lee Harvey Oswald was arrested and charged with Kennedy's murder.

Johnson soon appointed a group of respected government officials to investigate the assassination. Led by Chief Justice Earl Warren of the Supreme Court, the Warren Commission concluded that Oswald acted alone in shooting the president.

In the years since the release of the commission's report in September 1964, many people have argued that more than one assassin was involved. The truth may never be known because two days after he was arrested, Oswald was shot in the basement of the Dallas County Jail by Jack Ruby, a nightclub owner allegedly connected to organized crime.

Had Kennedy lived, he surely would have run for reelection in 1964. With JFK gone, however, the top spot on the Democratic ticket belonged to Lyndon Johnson. At the national convention in Atlantic City, Johnson was nominated by acclamation. His slogan was "All the Way With LBJ."

To run against Johnson, the Republicans picked Barry Goldwater, an extremely conservative senator from Arizona. Goldwater's policies scared many Americans. He proposed deep cuts in social programs and a large increase in the defense budget so that he could drive the Communists out of South Vietnam. Goldwater also opposed civil rights laws and wanted to make Social Security voluntary, which frightened senior citizens.

Goldwater's statements about nuclear war hurt him the most. People worried that he might actually start one. Goldwater's "In Your Heart, You Know He's Right" slogan was satirized as "In Your Heart, You Know He Might." The Johnson campaign played on these fears with a powerful television commercial that implied Goldwater would use the bomb if elected.

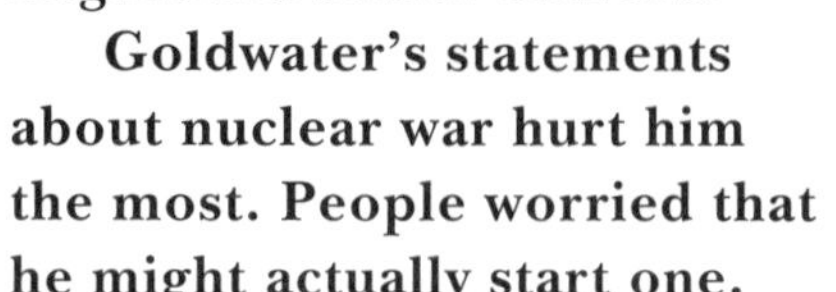

Goldwater used the president's strong stand on civil rights to hurt him badly in the Deep South. But nearly everywhere else people voted for LBJ in overwhelming numbers, and he won a resounding victory.

Lyndon Baines Johnson

36th President

★

From 1963 to 1969

Born: August 27, 1908

Birthplace: Stonewall, Texas

Died: January 22, 1973

Party: Democrat

Vice President: Hubert H. Humphrey

First Lady: Claudia Alta (Lady Bird) Taylor

Children: Lynda Bird, Luci

Nickname: LBJ

The first president sworn in by a woman.

RIOTS RAVAGE WATTS

LOS ANGELES, August 16, 1965—The rioting in Watts, a black section of Los Angeles, finally ended today after six days of burning, looting, and death. Thirty-four people have been killed, and nearly four thousand arrested. It has taken fifteen thousand police and the National Guard to restore order.

The riots began on August 11 after a patrolman arrested a black motorist for reckless driving. When the officer drew his gun, a crowd of angry neighborhood residents attacked him.

"Martin Luther King ain't my leader," one Watts youth said as he prepared to set fire to a building. "The so-called Negro leaders have no contact with us. They don't know us; they don't know how we feel or what we want any more than you do, Mr. White Man."

The damage, covering five hundred square blocks, is estimated at upwards of forty million dollars. Two hundred businesses have been destroyed, many owned by whites. The Watts neighborhood is ninety-eight percent African American.

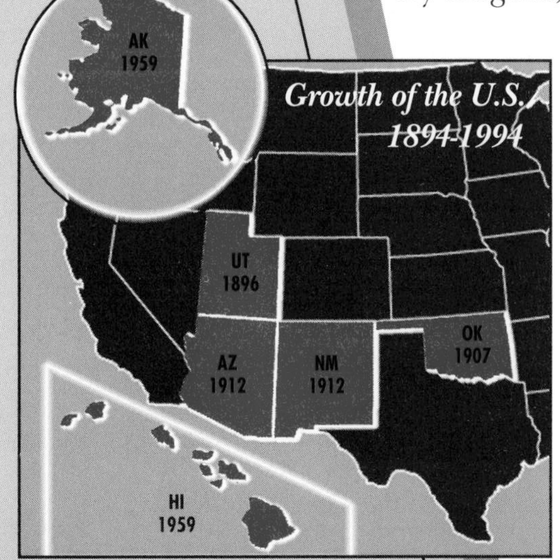

Lyndon B. Johnson had been in office only two months when he delivered his first State of the Union address. The country was still grieving deeply over the assassination of its popular young president. But John F. Kennedy's successor knew that the government had work to do.

"Unfortunately, many Americans live on the outskirts of hope, some because of their poverty and some because of their color," the new president said in his January 1964 speech. To relieve this despair, Johnson declared an unconditional "war on poverty."

As he would prove often during his presidency, Lyndon Johnson was a shrewd, down-to-earth politician who knew how to get things done. By August, with some expert arm-twisting, he had convinced Congress to approve ten antipoverty programs totaling one billion dollars. The new aid programs included a Job Corps for disadvantaged teenagers and Head Start for preschool children.

To help African Americans, Johnson pushed through the Civil Rights Act of 1964, which made it illegal for employers to discriminate on the basis of race. The new law also outlawed segregation in public places, such as hotels and restaurants, ending Jim Crow forever.

Meanwhile, the FBI continued its six-week-long search for the bodies of three civil rights workers murdered in Mississippi. Andrew Goodman, Mickey Schwerner, and James Chaney had all been taking part in the Mississippi Summer Project. The goal of the project's Freedom Summer was to organize an integrated political party to challenge the all-white state Democratic party.

After the project ended, most of the student volunteers went back to school, where many organized protests. The most compelling of these was the Free Speech Movement. This series of demonstrations at the University of California-Berkeley defended the rights of students to distribute political pamphlets on campus. But the movement also made it clear that students were not satisfied with the world as it was being run by their parents.

THE VOTING RIGHTS ACT Of all the laws passed during his administration, Lyndon Johnson was probably most proud of the Voting Rights Act of 1965. This bill outlawed literacy tests and other unfair practices that white southerners used to keep blacks from registering to vote. The Voting Rights Act made huge registration drives possible. And with more blacks registered to vote, black candidates were able to win more elections.

Prominent black mayors were elected in Cleveland, Ohio, and Gary, Indiana. And in 1966, Edward Brooke of Massachusetts became the first black senator elected since 1881.

The Early Years

Sam Ealy Johnson was a Texas state legislator, but he was also a poor farmer. The great San Francisco earthquake of 1906 had destroyed his cotton holdings. As a result, his son Lyndon was born into hardship. When he was old enough, Lyndon worked as a shoeshine boy and trapped animals to earn extra money.

From an early age, Lyndon enjoyed listening to his father talk politics. Later in life he would often repeat the advice his father gave him: "If you can't come into a roomful of people and tell right away who is for you and who is against you, you have no business in politics."

For two years after college, Johnson taught public speaking, but he quit in 1931 to work for Democratic Representative Richard Kleberg of Texas. Johnson ran for the House in 1937, winning a crowded race with only twenty-seven percent of the vote. In 1948, he won a controversial Senate race by just eighty-seven votes out of nearly one million cast.

★**BEATLEMANIA** In the months after the Kennedy assassination, grief-stricken Americans were desperate for something to lift their gloom. In February 1964, relief arrived from England. That month, the Beatles made their first U.S. appearance on the CBS Sunday night variety show hosted by Ed Sullivan. The ratings for Sullivan's show set records, and soon the Beatles had six songs in the Top Ten. Teenagers everywhere responded to the Fab Four's bouncy music, cute Liverpool accents, and mop-top hairstyles. Boys started growing their hair long, and girls rushed out to buy "mod" miniskirts popularized by British designer Mary Quant. The British Invasion that followed the Beatles included such bands as the Rolling Stones, the Animals, and the Who.

★THE MY LAI MASSACRE Every night, the television networks showed footage of the war in Vietnam, and every night Americans had to decide what to make of the brutality they witnessed. Even more horrible events were not televised. In March 1968, U.S. troops under Lieutenant William Calley massacred 347 unarmed civilians at the Vietnamese farming village of My Lai. The killings were kept secret for over a year. In April 1971, a military court sentenced Calley to life imprisonment, but he was freed after forty months. As his commander pointed out, singling out Calley was unfair. "Every unit of brigade size has its My Lai hidden someplace," he said. Guerrilla warfare made it difficult to recognize the enemy, and frightened soldiers often fired first and asked questions later.

★MALCOLM X Malcolm Little spent World War II selling drugs in Harlem and Boston. In 1946, the twenty-one-year-old hustler was arrested for burglary. In prison, he joined the Nation of Islam, a black Muslim group whose members believed that white people were devils. Malcolm changed his name to Malcolm X because "Little" was a name some white master had given his African slave ancestors.

During the early 1960s, Malcolm's fiery civil rights speeches made him famous. Unlike Martin Luther King, Jr., Malcolm preached violence as a reasonable response to violence. In 1964, however, he broke with the Nation of Islam and became a traditional Muslim, devoting himself to peace. While giving a speech in February 1965, Malcolm was shot and killed by four members of the Nation of Islam.

★HIM AND HER When Lyndon Johnson moved into the White House, he brought a pair of beagles with him. Their names were Him and Her. These two dogs soon became almost as popular as the president himself. In June 1964, they appeared on the cover of *Life* magazine.

The dogs were also a source of controversy. When Johnson was photographed picking them up by the ears, dog lovers around the country demanded an explanation and an apology. LBJ refused. "It's good for them," the president said.

A year later, President Johnson nominated Thurgood Marshall to the Supreme Court. In 1954, Marshall had argued the landmark *Brown* case before the Court. After his Senate confirmation, Marshall became the first black justice to sit on the Court.

THE GREAT SOCIETY After Lyndon Johnson's landslide victory in the 1964 election, the Great Society became the theme of his domestic program. Johnson developed Medicaid and Medicare to help poor people and the elderly pay their medical bills. He also won passage of the first serious environmental and consumer laws. These bills set standards for air and water quality as well as auto safety.

Many of the Great Society initiatives were immediate successes. But there was also a problem: The Vietnam War was eating up too much government money. As the war escalated, the president urged an increasingly reluctant Congress to fund "guns and butter." Conservatives insisted that the country could not afford both.

THE TONKIN GULF RESOLUTION In early August 1964, Johnson announced that the U.S. destroyer *Maddox* had been attacked by North Vietnamese patrol boats in international waters in the Tonkin Gulf off Vietnam. The North Vietnamese claimed that the *Maddox* had been protecting South Vietnamese raiders.

The president immediately sent Congress a resolution granting him nearly unlimited power to use U.S. military force in Vietnam. The White House staff had prepared the resolution well in advance, hoping for just such an opportunity. The Tonkin Gulf resolution passed unanimously in the House, and only two votes were cast against it in the

Senate—by Wayne Morse of Oregon and Ernest Gruening of Alaska.

In a televised speech, Johnson told the nation, "We seek no wider war." But seven months later he sent the first combat troops to Vietnam. Only thirty-five hundred Marines landed at Da Nang in March 1965, but within two years, troop levels had risen to four hundred thousand.

THE TET OFFENSIVE Johnson's military advisors promised that victory was "just around the corner." But their predictions seemed empty after January 30, 1968, when the North Vietnamese and their Viet Cong allies launched a surprise attack on major cities in the South. One Viet Cong unit even reached the grounds of the U.S. embassy in Saigon. The assault was called the Tet Offensive because it began during a cease-fire called to celebrate Tet, the Vietnamese New Year.

Although U.S. troops counter-attacked successfully, the Communists had made their point. Until the Tet Offensive, it was possible for civilians to believe that the United States might actually be winning the war. After Tet, it was obvious that victory was either impossible or a very long way off. Now, many moderate Americans joined the growing antiwar movement.

In March 1968, Senator Eugene McCarthy of Minnesota, running as a peace candidate, nearly upset President Johnson in the New Hampshire Democratic primary. Johnson's slim seven-point victory forced him to rethink running for a second full term.

On March 31, the president went on national television to announce a temporary halt to the bombing of North Vietnam so that peace talks might begin. At the end of his speech, almost as an afterthought, Lyndon Johnson revealed that he would not seek another term.

Campaign 1968

PRESIDENT JOHNSON'S MARCH 31 DECISION NOT TO run again changed everything. Quickly, Vice President Hubert Humphrey declared his candidacy. Besides Senator McCarthy, Humphrey also had to battle Senator Robert F. Kennedy, the brother of the late president. Kennedy had entered the race as a peace candidate soon after McCarthy's surprising performance in New Hampshire.

Humphrey's biggest problem was Vietnam. The war was now highly unpopular, and the continued bombing of North Vietnam made it difficult for Humphrey to distance himself from Johnson, to whom he remained loyal.

Meanwhile, Kennedy's campaign gained momentum. On June 5, Kennedy won the California primary, but that same night he was assassinated by a Palestinian immigrant named Sirhan Sirhan.

Kennedy's death assured Humphrey of the nomination, but it also deeply divided the party. At the Democratic convention in Chicago, thousands of antiwar activists demonstrated outside as the police beat journalists and protesters alike. An independent commission later called the chaos a "police riot."

Humphrey's Republican opponent, Richard Nixon, stood by as the Democrats self-destructed. During the campaign, the former vice president discussed issues only vaguely. Mostly he talked about law and order and his "secret plan" to end the war in Vietnam. Governor George Wallace of Alabama mounted a third-party campaign based on victory in Vietnam and an end to school busing to achieve integration.

Nixon left the Republican convention with a large lead. Humphrey made a strong comeback, especially after President Johnson ordered a bombing halt on October 31. But he couldn't close the huge gap in time. Although Nixon won the election by less than one percent of the popular vote, his electoral majority was comfortable. Even Wallace's forty-six electoral votes, all from the Deep South, weren't enough to stop Nixon.

RICHARD MILHOUS NIXON

37TH PRESIDENT

★

FROM 1969 TO 1974

BORN: January 9, 1913

BIRTHPLACE: Yorba Linda, Calif.

DIED: April 22, 1994

PARTY: Republican

VICE PRESIDENTS: Spiro T. Agnew, Gerald R. Ford

FIRST LADY: Thelma Catherine (Pat) Ryan

CHILDREN: Patricia, Julie

NICKNAME: Tricky Dick

The first president to resign his office.

During the late 1960s, demonstrations against the government increased both in size and vigor. A decade earlier, Americans had feared nuclear war with Communists halfway around the world. Now they worried about riots at home.

The assassination of Martin Luther King, Jr., in April 1968 shattered the nonviolent civil rights movement. Afterward, like Humpty Dumpty, the pieces couldn't be put back together again. Some people continued King's work, but others joined militant groups like the Black Panthers who demanded "black power." The antiwar movement also became more combative and more violent.

President Nixon ignored these protests because he believed he had the support of the "silent majority" of Americans. But no matter how hard he tried, he couldn't avoid the war in Vietnam.

ASTRONAUTS WALK ON THE MOON

SEA OF TRANQUILITY, July 21, 1969—The United States won the space race today when Apollo 11 astronaut Neil Armstrong became the first human being to walk on the moon. "That's one small step for man, one giant leap for mankind," Armstrong said as he climbed down from the lunar module *Eagle*.

Millions of people around the world watched both the moon landing last night and the moon walk early this morning on television. The landing redeemed the late president John F. Kennedy's pledge to land a man on the moon by the end of the decade.

During their single moon walk, Armstrong and fellow astronaut Edwin "Buzz" Aldrin planted a U.S. flag, set up three experiments, and collected rock samples from the lunar surface. They also spoke briefly with President Nixon.

The Apollo 11 crew of Armstrong, Aldrin, and Michael Collins is expected to bring back data of enormous scientific value. They will also be quarantined upon their return to ensure that they have brought no lunar diseases back with them.

During the 1968 campaign, he had boasted of a "secret plan" to end the war, but the peace talks that President Johnson had begun in Paris were going nowhere. The delegates couldn't even agree on what shape the conference table should be.

VIETNAMIZATION Nixon's secret plan turned out to be Vietnamization. The idea was to replace U.S. combat troops with South Vietnamese soldiers. Kennedy and Johnson had also thought it would be a good idea for the South Vietnamese to fight their own war. But both Democratic presidents had concluded that the result would be disastrous. Nixon went ahead anyway because it was the only way he could withdraw U.S. soldiers and still keep the war going.

To make up for the loss of combat troop strength, Nixon stepped up the bombing of North Vietnam. More bomb tonnage was dropped on North Vietnam than on Germany, Italy, and Japan during all of World War II. The president also ordered the secret bombing of nearby Cambodia, where the Viet Cong had supply bases.

NIXON IN CHINA As he tried to bring about "peace with honor" in Vietnam, Nixon looked forward to the greatest foreign policy coup of his career. All his life, Richard Nixon had fought Communists. His hostility toward them had been well known since his first political campaign.

That is why Nixon's August 1971 announcement that he would visit the People's Republic of China stunned the world. During that visit in February 1972, arranged by top aide Henry Kissinger, the president met with Communist leader Mao Zedong. Diplomatic relations were not yet restored, but Nixon's trip ensured that they soon would be.

The Early Years

RICHARD NIXON WAS BORN IN A HOUSE HIS FATHER built. Every morning before school, he helped his father truck in produce from nearby Los Angeles to sell at Nixon's Market in Whittier, California. As a student, Frank Nixon's second son was bright, serious, and quiet.

The adult Richard Nixon worked as a lawyer until 1946, when he won election to Congress. There he made a name for himself with his dogged cross-examination of alleged Soviet spy Alger Hiss. In 1950, Nixon ran for the Senate against Helen Gahagan Douglas. Referring to Douglas as the Pink Lady, Nixon distributed "pink sheets" that were supposed to show how Douglas's voting record served Communist aims. Because of this political trick, a Southern California newspaper nicknamed the new senator Tricky Dick.

★**THE ENEMIES LIST** Historians have sometimes called Nixon paranoid, meaning that he often thought people were out to get him. As proof, they point to the list of enemies Nixon ordered his staff to keep. This list included not only political opponents, but also journalists, businessmen, athletes, and movie stars. Names on the Enemies List included Bill Cosby, Jane Fonda, and quarterback Joe Namath. Nixon ordered FBI director J. Edgar Hoover to collect damaging information on some of these people using illegal wiretaps. After the Watergate hearings revealed the existence of the Enemies List, Nixon claimed that the wiretaps were justified because of "national security concerns."

★**EARTH DAY** On April 22, 1970, a number of environmental groups organized the first Earth Day. The environmental movement and its goals were still new to most people. So "teach-ins" were held on college campuses around the nation to focus public attention on such ecological issues as pollution of the air, land, and water. Since then, Earth Day activities have included beach and park cleanups as well as tree plantings.

★THE BLACK PANTHERS Bobby Seale and Huey P. Newton (right) founded the Black Panther Party for Self-Defense in Oakland, California, in 1966. The group's original purpose was to patrol black neighborhoods to protect residents there from police brutality. Soon the organization set up chapters in other cities, particularly Chicago, and became much more political. Chief spokesman Eldridge Cleaver encouraged blacks to buy guns because the Panthers believed that an armed showdown between blacks and whites was inevitable. Trouble between the police and the Panthers led to a number of shoot-outs. Newton, the Panthers' minister of defense, was later convicted of killing a police officer during one of these gun battles.

★WOODSTOCK NATION During the late 1960s, many college-age Baby Boomers developed their own distinctive styles of dress and music as well as new ways of speaking and behaving. They called their new way of living a "counterculture." Referring to themselves as "freaks" and "hippies," they gathered together at rural communes and in city neighborhoods such as San Francisco's Haight-Ashbury.

One of the most memorable countercultural events was the Woodstock Music and Art Fair held in upstate New York in August 1969. More than three hundred thousand people showed up to listen to Jimi Hendrix, the Jefferson Airplane, and many other performers. Because of the massive crowd and the lack of proper food, medical care, and sanitation, the concert site was declared a disaster area. But the show went on.

DÉTENTE In opening the door to China, long considered an enemy of the United States, Nixon played on the strained relations between the People's Republic and the Soviet Union. Although both countries were run by Communist governments, they didn't trust each other. Nixon hoped that by forging ties with China he could weaken the power and influence of the Soviet Union, which remained the United States' greatest concern.

Nixon referred to his foreign policy as "détente," which means a relaxing of strained relations or tensions. Soon after his return from China, he followed up his success there with another remarkable trip. This time, the president went to Moscow.

Nixon had been to Moscow once before, in 1959, when he and Nikita Khrushchev met in the Kitchen Debate. The highlight of this May 1972 trip was the signing of a nuclear arms control treaty. The agreement was known as the SALT treaty because it had been negotiated at the Strategic Arms Limitation Talks.

PEACE WITH HONOR Nixon's foreign policy triumphs proved that détente could work. They also did wonders for his reelection campaign. So did Henry Kissinger's announcement in October 1972, just two weeks before the election, that "peace is at hand" in Vietnam. The "breakthrough" proposal, which Kissinger and North Vietnamese negotiator Le Duc Tho had developed during secret meetings in Paris, called for an immediate cease-fire followed by a general election in the South.

After the U.S. election, however, the agreement hit a snag when each side accused the other of bargaining in bad faith. To convince the North Vietnamese to renew the talks, Nixon ordered the heaviest bombing of the war. During the "Christmas bombing" of December 1972, more than two hundred B-52 bombers flew missions around the clock over North Vietnam.

A formal peace agreement was finally signed on January 27, 1973. The South Vietnamese government retained control of Saigon, while the Viet Cong remained in place in the countryside. The United States agreed to remove all its combat troops within sixty days in return for the release of prisoners of war. Publicly Nixon claimed that he had achieved "peace with honor," but Kissinger predicted privately that South Vietnam wouldn't last eighteen months. What Kissinger didn't know was that the Nixon administration wouldn't last much longer.

THE WATERGATE BREAK-IN

On June 17, 1972, police arrested five men caught breaking into Democratic National Committee headquarters in Washington. One of the men arrested at the Watergate office building was James McCord, a former FBI agent now working for the Committee to Reelect the President. When asked about the break-in, President Nixon denied everything, insisting that no one at the White House had any knowledge of this "bizarre incident." The cover-up had begun.

At first, the scandal was limited to Nixon's reelection committee, commonly known as CREEP. But in October, Bob Woodward and Carl Bernstein began writing stories in the *Washington Post* that suggested the break-in was part of a larger Nixon campaign of "dirty tricks." Woodward and Bernstein's allegations were soon confirmed by McCord in a letter to Judge John Sirica. In his letter asking for leniency, McCord admitted that witnesses had lied. McCord later

Two important changes in the way delegates were selected made the 1972 Democratic convention a world apart from the one held in 1968. First, the party's rules were changed to include more women and minority delegates. Then, in 1971, the Twenty-sixth Amendment lowered the voting age to eighteen. These changes, along with the ongoing Vietnam War, made it possible for a liberal candidate like Senator George McGovern of South Dakota to win the Democratic nomination. McGovern promised an immediate withdrawal of U.S. troops from Vietnam. He also supported legislation banning handguns. He even proposed that the government give every person in the United States one thousand dollars.

During the primaries, Alabama governor George Wallace had challenged McGovern, winning in Maryland and Michigan. These victories proved that the conservative Wallace appealed to voters outside the South. He was especially popular with blue-collar workers who felt that the Democrats had given too much power to minority groups. Wallace's campaign was cut short when a gunman shot him at a rally. He survived but was left paralyzed below the waist. Although Wallace was now out of the race, his followers seemed unlikely to support McGovern.

Richard Nixon and Spiro Agnew easily won renomination at the Republican convention. Although the Watergate burglary had already taken place, nobody paid much attention to it. What bothered voters more was the news that McGovern's running mate, Senator Thomas Eagleton of Missouri, had once undergone electric shock therapy for depression. Although McGovern at first stood by Eagleton, he later bowed to public opinion and replaced him with former Peace Corps director Sargent Shriver.

McGovern charged that the Nixon administration was the most corrupt in U.S. history, but few people believed him. Instead they listened to Henry Kissinger announce that peace was "at hand" in Vietnam. On Election Day, Nixon's margin of victory was nearly twenty million votes. McGovern lost every state but Massachusetts.

FOUR STUDENTS KILLED AT KENT STATE

KENT, Ohio, May 4, 1970—National Guardsmen fired into an antiwar demonstration at Kent State University today, killing four students. The guardsmen were using live ammunition rather than the rubber bullets typically used for crowd control.

The noon demonstration, attended by one thousand students, was held to protest the invasion of Cambodia announced last week by President Nixon. The president's action led many students to believe that he was widening the war in Vietnam instead of ending it, as he had promised.

The National Guard was called to the campus yesterday after a demonstration on May 2 turned into a riot. That night, students burned an army-related building to the ground. This afternoon's demonstration also spun out of control when students began chanting at the armed soldiers, "Pigs off campus! We don't want your war!"

Students have held protests against the war in Vietnam since the early 1960s. But antiwar efforts have become much more vigorous since the Tet Offensive caused many Americans to reconsider whether the government has been telling the truth.

named former attorney general John Mitchell as "the overall boss."

In February 1973, the Senate established a special committee to look into "any illegal, improper, or unethical activities" that might have occurred during the 1972 campaign. During the committee's televised hearings, Senator Howard Baker of Tennessee asked nearly every witness, "What did the president know, and when did he know it?"

On July 16, presidential assistant Alexander Butterfield revealed in passing that President Nixon had been secretly recording his Oval Office conversations. The Senate committee immediately subpoenaed, or legally demanded, the tapes, as did Watergate special prosecutor Archibald Cox.

But Nixon refused to turn over the tapes. He argued that the president's executive privilege allowed him to keep his conversations private. Cox decided to fight Nixon in the federal courts.

VICE PRESIDENT FORD

One factor saving Nixon from impeachment was the reality that Vice President Spiro Agnew would succeed him. Most Democratic congressmen despised Agnew for his attacks on intellectuals as "an effete corps of impudent snobs" and reporters as "nattering nabobs of negativism." These Democrats considered the possibility of an Agnew presidency even more horrifying than the prospect of Nixon staying on.

On October 10, 1973, however, Agnew was forced to resign the vice presidency after pleading no contest to charges of

accepting bribes while governor of Maryland. Two days later, President Nixon nominated Michigan congressman Gerald Ford to be the new vice president.

Meanwhile, the tapes case, *U.S. v. Nixon,* had reached the Court of Appeals, which ordered the president to turn over the tapes.

On Saturday, October 20, Nixon tried to quash the original subpoena by ordering Attorney General Elliot Richardson to fire Cox. Richardson resigned rather than carry out Nixon's order. So did his deputy, William Ruckelshaus. Eventually Solicitor General Robert H. Bork agreed to fire Cox and terminate the office of Watergate special prosecutor.

The public response to the "Saturday night massacre" was decidedly negative. Three days later Chairman Peter Rodino announced that the House Judiciary Committee would begin impeachment hearings.

RESIGNATION Throughout the winter and spring of 1974, the subpoenas for tapes continued to be issued, and Nixon continued to avoid them. He released a few recordings and provided edited transcripts of others, but the House committee kept pressing for actual recordings of the most sensitive conversations. Finally, on July 24, 1974, the Supreme Court ruled unanimously that Nixon must turn over all the tapes. Three days later, the Judiciary Committee approved the first of three articles of impeachment against him.

On August 5, the president released transcripts of three June 23, 1972, conversations that proved he knew about and directed the cover-up. Three days later, speaking on national television, he announced his resignation. The embattled president blamed a loss of congressional support and confessed nothing.

★THE FIRST FAMILY Richard Nixon first met Pat Ryan in 1938 at auditions for a local play in Whittier. Nixon proposed that first night. "I thought he was nuts," the future Mrs. Nixon remembered. She turned him down then, but they dated for two years until she finally accepted. In the meantime, Nixon became so devoted to her that he sometimes drove her to meet other dates because she didn't have a car.

The Nixons and their daughters were an unusually close family. In 1968, Julie married David Eisenhower, grandson of the former president. Three years later, Tricia married Edward Cox in a Rose Garden ceremony. Throughout the Watergate ordeal, the president's family stood by him and reportedly urged him not to resign.

★*ROE V. WADE* AND ABORTION During the late 1960s, abortion became an important political issue, especially to the women's movement. "Pro-life" advocates believed that an unborn fetus had the right to live and that it was wrong to interfere with a pregnancy. "Pro-choice" forces believed it was a woman's right to decide whether or not to have an abortion. In states with laws against abortions, many women risked their lives having them performed illegally. In 1973, however, the Supreme Court ruled in the case of *Roe v. Wade* that every woman had a legal right to end a pregnancy during the first three months. Although the women's movement praised the decision, it was widely criticized by some religious groups as immoral and by conservative scholars as bad legal reasoning by the Court.

★WOMEN'S LIBERATION The women's liberation movement drew strength from the civil rights and antiwar protests of the 1960s. While taking part in these other movements, many women discovered that men rarely treated them as equals. They were often expected to make coffee instead of speeches and policy. Soon these women banded together to demand equal treatment. Some founded organizations like the National Organization for Women to promote issues such as day care for the children of working mothers and equal pay for equal work. Men who believed that a woman's proper place was in the home were ridiculed as "male chauvinist pigs."

Gerald Rudolph Ford

38th President

★

From 1974 to 1977

Born: July 14, 1913

Birthplace: Omaha, Neb.

Party: Republican

Vice President: Nelson A. Rockefeller

First Lady: Elizabeth Anne (Betty) Bloomer Warren

Children: Michael, John, Steven, Susan

Nickname: Mr. Nice Guy

His daughter Susan held her senior prom in the White House.

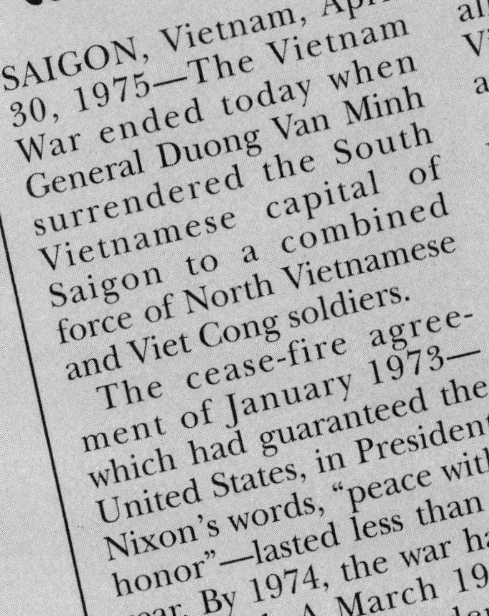

THE WAR IS OVER

Communists Capture South Vietnam

SAIGON, Vietnam, April 30, 1975—The Vietnam War ended today when General Duong Van Minh surrendered the South Vietnamese capital of Saigon to a combined force of North Vietnamese and Viet Cong soldiers.

The cease-fire agreement of January 1973—which had guaranteed the United States, in President Nixon's words, "peace with honor"—lasted less than a year. By 1974, the war had restarted. A March 1975 strategic retreat ordered by South Vietnamese president Nguyen Van Thieu quickly turned into a rout.

Sensing on April 18 that the end of the war was near, Secretary of State Henry Kissinger ordered all U.S. citizens in South Vietnam to leave immediately.

Operation Frequent Wind, which ended today when the grounds of the U.S. embassy were captured, has been the largest helicopter evacuation in history. Nearly seven thousand people, including fourteen hundred Americans, have been airlifted to U.S. ships waiting offshore.

Gerald Ford was sworn in as president on August 9, 1974, just minutes after Richard Nixon's resignation took effect. "Our long national nightmare is over," Ford said after the ceremony.

Ford had been a football star at the University of Michigan, and as a congressman from that state, he became widely known as a fair and decent man. For twenty-five years in the House of Representatives, he spoke out for Middle American values. But despite his athletic and political accomplishments, Ford also had a reputation for being mentally slow and physically awkward. It was often said jokingly that Ford couldn't walk and chew gum at the same time.

Exactly one month after taking office, President Ford pardoned Richard Nixon for any crimes Nixon may have committed during his term in office. It was Ford's belief that the country should be spared the spectacle of a former president standing trial.

Some critics suggested that a deal had been made, while others pointed out that Nixon had been pardoned while Vietnam draft resisters had not.

Ford's pardon of Nixon contributed to the low expectations people had for him. He was the first president ever to serve who had never been elected either president or vice president. Consequently, people tended to view him more as an honest caretaker than as a leader.

THE ARAB OIL EMBARGO Although the Vietnam War was finally over, its enormous cost had a lasting effect on the national economy. Under Ford, the country suffered the worst inflation and unemployment rates since the Great Depression.

Aggravating the problem was an oil embargo, which ended the era of cheap energy in the United States. In 1973, Israel and its Arab neighbors had fought the Yom Kippur War. Afterward, the Arab oil-producing nations decided to punish the United States for helping Israel by cutting off U.S. oil imports. Within a year, gasoline prices jumped seventy percent.

Ford's most publicized solution to the country's economic woes was the Whip Inflation Now campaign. Buttons were printed up with the initials WIN, but the program went nowhere. Ford later admitted that the idea was "probably too gimmicky."

When Ford became president, he promised to "heal the nation." Betty Ford took these words seriously. As first lady, she became an outspoken advocate of women's rights, supporting both liberalized abortion laws and the Equal Rights Amendment. After she developed breast cancer, she talked about her condition so that other women could learn about the importance of early detection.

Campaign 1976

Knowing that the Watergate scandal would make it difficult for Republicans to keep the White House, more than a dozen Democrats announced they would run for president in 1976. The first was Georgia governor Jimmy Carter, who entered the race in December 1974. At first, Carter didn't even show up on the public opinion polls. People often said, "Jimmy who?" But early primary victories in Iowa and New Hampshire made Carter the front-runner. At the Democratic convention, he had more than enough votes to win a first-ballot victory.

Carter had an informal manner and a big, toothy smile. He talked a lot about restoring people's faith in government. Being a Washington outsider helped him convince voters that his election could make a difference.

Although Gerald Ford was a sitting president, winning the 1976 Republican nomination was by no means a sure thing. Former California governor Ronald Reagan ran against him and won a number of important primaries. Ford barely held off Reagan, taking the nomination with 1,187 votes to Reagan's 1,070.

I'M VOTING FOR BETTY'S HUSBAND

Early in the general election campaign, opinion polls showed Carter more than thirty points ahead of Ford. During the early fall, however, the president closed the gap. By the time of the debates in early October, the election seemed too close to call. Ford probably lost the race in the second debate when he mistakenly said that Poland was free of Soviet domination.

The election attracted one of the lowest turnouts of the century. Barely half the eligible voters cast ballots. Only African Americans went to the polls in large numbers, nearly all of them pulling the lever for Carter. In the end, their support made the difference in a very tight race.

Jimmy Carter

39th President
★
from 1977 to 1981

Born: October 1, 1924

Birthplace: Plains, Ga.

Party: Democrat

Vice President: Walter F. Mondale

First Lady: Eleanor Rosalynn Smith

Children: John, James Earl III, Jeffrey, Amy

Nickname: Hot

The first president born in a hospital.

Egypt and Israel Sign Camp David Peace Accords

CAMP DAVID, Maryland, September 17, 1978—President Anwar el-Sadat of Egypt and Prime Minister Menachem Begin of Israel signed two unprecedented peace documents today after thirteen days in isolation at the presidential retreat here.

One of the Camp David accords outlines a proposed peace treaty between Egypt and Israel. The other is a framework for peace in the Middle East. Begin and Sadat have both applauded President Carter for the role he has played as host and mediator.

Before this, the last major advance in the peace process came in November 1977, when President Sadat made a courageous trip to Jerusalem to address the Israeli parliament. Sadat's trip was criticized harshly by other Arab leaders who still refuse to recognize Israel's right to exist.

Carter invited Sadat and Begin to Camp David after peace talks between the two nations had broken down. Despite Sadat's visit, Israel and Egypt have been in a formal state of war since Israel was founded in 1948. The Camp David accords are expected to bring peace soon.

Jimmy Carter came to Washington determined to change the way government worked. His informal public image helped him in that task. After promising in his inaugural address to return government to the people, the president and First Lady Rosalynn Carter walked hand in hand from the Capitol to the White House rather than ride in a limousine.

Later, when he traveled, the president often carried his own luggage. And he also insisted on using the name Jimmy Carter rather than his full name, James Earl Carter, Jr.

Gerald Ford's Whip Inflation Now campaign had focused public attention on inflation, which was six percent at the time Carter took office. In other words, prices were increasing at an average rate of six percent each year. Because earnings weren't growing as fast, people were steadily losing their buying power. Under Carter, things got

Anwar El-Sadat (left) and Menachem Begin with Jimmy Carter (center)

much worse. During his years in office, inflation doubled to twelve percent.

THE ENERGY CRISIS Carter's biggest obstacle in solving the country's economic problems was the energy crisis. Throughout Carter's term, oil prices kept going up. In 1979 alone, the Organization of Petroleum Exporting Countries, known as OPEC, doubled oil prices from fourteen to more than twenty-eight dollars a barrel. This led to a shortage of affordable gasoline. When lines at the pumps reached a mile and a half long, most states introduced gasoline rationing.

The gas shortage was a disaster for U.S. automakers. With gas prices soaring, people began to buy smaller and more fuel-efficient Japanese cars rather than the "gas guzzlers" built by U.S. companies. As many as three hundred thousand autoworkers lost their jobs. Meanwhile, Congress approved more than one billion dollars in federal loan guarantees to save one carmaker, Chrysler, from bankruptcy.

To limit dependence on foreign oil, Carter proposed an energy bill with strict rules for conservation. Carter's bill also included money for the development of new energy sources. For eighteen months, the president struggled with Congress before a watered-down version of his bill was passed in November 1978.

Carter's status as a Washington outsider helped him as a candidate, but it hurt him as president. Although he enjoyed a Democratic majority in both houses, he didn't work well with Congress, and he rarely got his way.

HUMAN RIGHTS The basis of Carter's foreign policy was the issue of human rights. The president believed it was immoral for the United States to support

The Early Years

JIMMY CARTER GREW UP NEAR PLAINS, GEORGIA, WHERE his father owned a peanut warehouse. Although the Carters were better off than most families, their farmhouse had neither electricity nor running water. Jimmy's nickname as a boy was Hot, short for Hot Shot.

After Carter graduated from the naval academy in 1946, he studied nuclear physics and served aboard one of the first nuclear submarines. He planned to make a career in the navy, but when his father died in 1953, Carter moved back to Plains, where he took over the family peanut business. He soon entered local politics, helping to ease the process of desegregation after the *Brown* decision. Carter was elected to the Georgia state senate in 1962 and to the governorship in 1970.

★**THE FIRST FAMILY** Jimmy Carter projected a down-home style to show that he was a man of the people. He dressed casually, often in sweaters. He also preferred to stay in ordinary people's homes when he traveled instead of in hotels. His youngest child, Amy, was nine years old when the Carters moved into the White House. She attended public school in Washington and often brought friends home to play in her tree house on the White House grounds. Her dog was named Grits and her cat, Misty Malarky Ying Yang.

★**PROPOSITION 13** Fed up with skyrocketing property taxes, Howard Jarvis and Paul Gann began circulating a petition in California during the late 1970s to limit those taxes. Jarvis and Gann collected over a million signatures, more than twice the number they needed to put their proposal on the ballot. California's voters then approved Proposition 13 in 1978 by a two-to-one margin. California's "tax revolt" cut property taxes by nearly sixty percent. But governmental services also had to be cut, especially those to cities and schools.

★**THE ERA** Passage of the Equal Rights Amendment, known as the ERA, was one of the chief goals of the women's movement during the 1970s. The ERA stated that "Equality of rights under the law shall not be denied or abridged...on account of sex." Women's groups saw the ERA as a way to include women's rights in the Constitution. Critics claimed that women already had equal rights under the Constitution.

The ERA passed both houses of Congress and was sent to the states for ratification in 1972. By 1978, thirty-five of the necessary thirty-eight states had approved the amendment, but the number stuck there. The ERA's leading opponent, Phyllis Schlafly, claimed that the new law threatened women's traditional family role. Schlafly finally won the battle in June 1982 when the time allowed by Congress for ratification ran out.

★**NO NUKES** During the late 1970s, people began to oppose the construction of nuclear power plants. At first, the protests were small and local. In May 1977, fifteen hundred demonstrators were arrested trying to stop construction at Seabrook in New Hampshire. However, in March 1979, a nearly disastrous accident at the Three Mile Island plant near Harrisburg, Pennsylvania, awakened the public to the possible dangers of nuclear power.

In May 1979, sixty-five thousand people went to Washington to protest nuclear power. In September, more than two hundred thousand people attended a No Nukes rally and concert in New York City. These protests halted plans to build a number of new facilities and led to improved safety at the nuclear plants that continued to operate.

governments that abused their citizens—even if those governments also opposed communism. Proving that he meant what he said, the president cut off aid to brutal military dictatorships in Argentina, Ethiopia, and Uruguay.

The United States also withdrew support from longtime ally Anastasio Somoza Debayle in Nicaragua. When Somoza's tyrannical regime was overthrown in July 1979, Carter provided immediate financial support for the new Sandinista government despite its obvious Communist sympathies.

Carter's policy in Nicaragua followed an earlier success in Central America. In September 1977, the president reached agreement with Panamanian leader Omar Torrijos Herrera on the fate of the Panama Canal. The new treaty called for turning over the canal to Panama by the end of 1999.

Conservative Republicans, notably former California governor Ronald Reagan, opposed the treaty as a giveaway, but Carter lobbied heavily from the White House. After months of debate, the Senate voted to approve the treaty. The vote was 68-32, just one vote more than the two-thirds required for ratification.

SALT II With regard to the Soviet Union, Carter continued Nixon's policy of détente The Strategic Arms Limitation Talks produced another treaty, which Carter and Soviet premier Leonid Brezhnev signed in June 1979.

Before SALT II could be ratified, however—and its prospects were not good—the Soviet Union invaded Afghanistan. Waging a war that resembled the U.S. effort in Vietnam, the Red Army spent nine years fighting unsuccessfully to defend the Soviet-backed government against Islamic rebels. In response to the invasion, President Carter cut off

U.S. grain sales and led a sixty-four-nation boycott of the Moscow Olympics held during the summer of 1980.

Carter's successes in foreign affairs, however, including his triumph at Camp David, were soon overshadowed by the hostage crisis that eventually destroyed his chances for reelection.

THE HOSTAGE CRISIS

On November 4, 1979, a mob of Islamic students attacked the U.S. embassy in Iran and took the staff hostage. Earlier that year, an Islamic revolution had toppled the U.S.-supported government of Shah Mohammad Reza Pahlavi. The student radicals demanded that the shah, then undergoing cancer treatment in New York, be returned to Iran in exchange for the release of the hostages.

President Carter did not approve of the torture the shah had used to control Iran. But neither was he willing to submit to terrorism. Instead, he tried to free the hostages through diplomatic means, all of which failed.

As the months passed, public pressure on Carter continued to grow. When nothing else seemed to work, the president approved a military rescue mission in April 1980. Unfortunately, helicopter problems forced the mission to pull out, and eight servicemen were killed when one helicopter hit a transport plane. Secretary of State Cyrus Vance, who had opposed the raid, resigned in protest, and the president's public image suffered badly.

It wasn't until January 19, 1981, his last full day in office, that Carter finally negotiated the hostages' release, ending 444 days of captivity. The former president spent the first day of his retirement welcoming the hostages back at a military hospital in West Germany.

In his campaign for reelection, President Carter was in trouble from the very beginning. Inflation was pushing down the value of money, and soaring interest rates made borrowing expensive. Meanwhile, the Iranian hostage crisis kept dragging on. All this made Carter's term in office seem a failure. During the primary campaign, Carter was challenged by Senator Edward Kennedy of Massachusetts.

The liberal wing of the Democratic party rallied to the youngest of the Kennedy brothers, but an incident from his past doomed him. In 1969, Kennedy had driven off a bridge in Chappaquiddick, Massachusetts. A female passenger died in the accident, but Kennedy didn't report it right away. Although no criminal charges were filed, many people questioned Kennedy's conduct. Carter beat Kennedy in the primaries, but the struggle weakened him and disrupted the party.

After nearly winning the Republican nomination in 1976, Ronald Reagan took it easily this time around. His strongest challenger, George Bush, withdrew before the convention. When it came time to pick a running mate, Reagan tried to work a deal with former president Gerald Ford. Being an extreme conservative, Reagan was afraid of losing the support of moderates. But the deal fell through, and Reagan picked Bush.

Republican John Anderson of Illinois dropped out early to run a third-party campaign. He combined the conservative economic policies of Reagan with the commitment to social welfare shown by Carter. Both he and Carter attacked Reagan for not caring about civil rights and for the frightening statements he made about getting tough with the Soviet Union.

None of these attacks stuck, however, because Reagan's staff shaped his image brilliantly. Voters watching on television saw not a dangerous warmonger but a strong leader. Reagan's vision was so attractive that he won in a landslide. The defining moment of the campaign came during the single televised debate when Reagan looked into the camera and asked, "Are you better off than you were four years ago?"

RONALD WILSON REAGAN

40TH PRESIDENT

★

FROM 1981 TO 1989

BORN: February 6, 1911

BIRTHPLACE: Tampico, Ill.

PARTY: Republican

VICE PRESIDENT: George Bush

FIRST LADY: Nancy Davis

CHILDREN: Maureen, Michael, Patricia, Ronald

NICKNAME: Dutch

The first president to have been divorced.

At sixty-nine, Ronald Reagan was the oldest president ever elected, but he worked hard to remain youthful. A veteran of cowboy movies, Reagan liked to play the tough guy. His image was very important to him—and to the way he governed.

Reagan owed much of his enormous personal appeal to the way he made people feel about the country. His speeches and television appearances encouraged people to believe that the nation's social and economic problems could be solved easily and painlessly. Uncomfortable with detail, the president liked to speak in folksy generalities like "a rising tide lifts all ships." He meant that good times for some Americans would bring good times for all.

Reagan always presented himself as a man of deep conviction and principle. For example, even after he was shot, he remained firmly opposed to gun control laws. By keeping his focus on the

DRIFTER SHOOTS PRESIDENT

Reagan Survives Assassination Attempt

WASHINGTON, March 30, 1981—President Reagan was shot in the chest today outside the Washington Hilton Hotel, where he had just delivered a speech. The president was rushed to a nearby hospital, where an emergency surgical team was standing by.

"I forgot to duck," Reagan joked as the doctors prepared him for surgery to remove the bullet lodged in his left lung. Despite the seventy-year-old president's age, doctors say he appears to be making a remarkable recovery.

Also injured in the attack were a policeman, a secret service agent, and presidential press secretary James Brady, who suffered permanent brain damage from a bullet wound to the head.

Reagan's would-be assassin is a twenty-five-year-old drifter named John W. Hinckley, Jr. The shooting appears to have no political motive. Instead, Hinckley claims that he shot the president as a love offering to actress Jodie Foster, whom he has never met.

big picture, Reagan was able to avoid mistakes that many new presidents tend to make. Aware that presidents with too many proposals often get nothing done, Reagan concentrated on just a few ideas. Because he had won in a landslide, Congress passed his bills without a fight.

In Reagan's view, all government spending (with the possible exception of the defense budget) was wasteful. "Government is not the solution to our problems," he said in his inaugural address, "government is the problem." Uniting Republicans and conservative Democrats into a working coalition, he lowered taxes, raised defense spending, and cut deeply into such social programs as food stamps and unemployment benefits. Reagan argued that social spending could be handled much better by the individual states.

President Reagan immediately set about reversing the liberal policies of previous administrations. Environmentalists were outraged when the Environmental Protection Agency cut the endangered species list in half and the Interior Department moved to open federal lands to private developers.

REAGANOMICS When Reagan took office, the inflation rate was over thirteen percent, and economic growth was slow. But the new president had a radical plan for fixing things. The plan was based on supply-side economics. According to this theory, increasing the amount of money in people's pockets will increase both investment and consumer spending. These, in turn, will make the economy stronger and more productive.

To begin this beneficial chain of events, Reagan proposed a major tax cut for the rich, because they were the people most likely to invest. Reagan assured the public that

As the son of a shoe salesman in Dixon, Illinois, Ronald Reagan grew up collecting butterflies and bird eggs and watching cowboy movies at the local movie theater. In high school, he was elected president of the student body and acted in school plays. At Eureka College, his grades were more often Cs than As. After college, he looked for work as a radio announcer.

Reagan moved to Hollywood in 1937 after signing an acting contract with the Warner Brothers studio. A year later, he met actress Jane Wyman during the filming of *Brother Rat.* They were married in 1940 but divorced eight years later while Reagan was president of the Screen Actors Guild. In 1952, Reagan married another actress, Nancy Davis.

Reagan began his political career as a New Deal Democrat, but his views gradually changed. He joined Democrats-for-Eisenhower in 1952 and the Republican party ten years later. In 1966, he won the governor's race in California by nearly twenty percentage points. Reagan soon gained national attention for reforming California's welfare system, balancing its budget, and ordering gas attacks on antiwar demonstrators.

★**THE GREAT COMMUNICATOR** Ronald Reagan was the first professional movie actor to become president. In *Knute Rockne—All American* (1940), he popularized the phrase "win one for the Gipper," and in *Bedtime for Bonzo* (1951), he played a college professor trying to raise a chimpanzee as a child.

Early in his career, Reagan had worked as a radio sportscaster. In those days, the briefest descriptions of out-of-town baseball games were telegraphed to radio stations, where the announcers had to make up the details. Later Reagan was a spokesperson for General Electric. Because of his ability and experience in front of a microphone, White House reporters called Reagan the Great Communicator. More so than any other president, Reagan used carefully planned television appearances to promote his policies.

★MICHAEL JACKSON *People* magazine once called Michael Jackson the most famous man in the world. His 1983 album *Thriller* set new sales records, moving more than forty million copies and winning an unprecedented eight Grammy awards. His dancing also captivated the public. In his "moonwalk" routine, Jackson appeared to be walking forward as he actually moved backward. The single, sequined glove that he wore on his right hand started a fashion trend all over the world.

★SANDRA DAY O'CONNOR During his presidential campaigns, Ronald Reagan promised to reverse the direction of the Supreme Court by appointing conservatives to replace liberal justices as they retired. The decision he most wanted the Court to reverse was *Roe v. Wade* (1973), which had legalized abortion. In 1981, Reagan made his first appointment to the Court. He picked Arizona judge Sandra Day O'Connor. She became the first woman ever to serve on the Supreme Court. Although O'Connor generally sided with the new conservative majority, she refused to support a complete reversal of *Roe v. Wade.*

★PERSONAL COMPUTERS Early computers were huge, expensive, and complicated to use. Only large businesses could afford them. Around 1980, however, companies such as IBM and Apple developed personal computers, or PCs, that ordinary people could use and afford. Apple was founded in a California garage in 1976 by two college dropouts in their twenties. Their Apple II computer, introduced in 1977, used a regular television set for a monitor and stored data on audiocassettes, but it also sold for just $1,298. IBM introduced its first PC in 1981.

economic prosperity would "trickle down" to everyone else. During the campaign, Vice President George Bush had called this plan "voodoo economics," but now he supported the president loyally.

As enacted by Congress, the Reagan tax cut added up to a twenty-five percent reduction in individual tax rates over three years. People were left with more money, but most didn't invest it. Rather, they spent it on things like videocassette recorders and aerobics classes.

Very little money trickled down to the middle class and even less to the poor. Meanwhile, the country moved deeper into the worst recession since World War II.

During the recession, high interest rates and a drop in world oil prices combined to reduce inflation to two percent. But unemployment soared from seven to nearly eleven percent in November 1982. Record numbers of people went bankrupt and lost their family farms.

BUDGET DEFICITS As many Democratic economists had predicted, the national debt ballooned. The billions saved by cutting social programs were erased by even larger increases in the defense budget. The economy didn't grow very quickly, but the budget deficit did.

President Reagan often called for a constitutional amendment to require a balanced budget. But he never submitted one himself. During his eight years in office, the national debt more than doubled. Interest payments of more than $150 billion on that debt became the third-largest item in the budget. Before Reagan, the government had never run a budget deficit higher than one hundred billion dollars. Now deficits of two hundred billion dollars and more became commonplace.

THE EVIL EMPIRE During his first term, Reagan's foreign policy focused on the Soviet Union. His attitude toward the Soviets was remarkably similar to the Cold War mentality of the 1950s. He believed that the United States, which stood for democracy and freedom, was engaged in a mortal battle against the Soviet Union, which he called "the focus of evil in the modern world."

In March 1983, the president proposed in a nationally televised speech that the United States build a space-age missile defense system that would use satellites to shoot down incoming nuclear warheads. Because Reagan's Strategic Defense Initiative would cost trillions of dollars, it became immediately controversial on Capitol Hill.

The program was dubbed Star Wars because it reminded people of special effects they had seen in science-fiction films. After the president's speech, many reputable scientists declared that the missile shield, as Reagan had described it, could not work. But the president insisted on going ahead with the project. He believed that the surest and safest way to beat the Soviets in the arms race was to outspend them.

NICARAGUA In Central America, Reagan fought another type of Cold War. During his first term, he sent large amounts of economic and military aid to the anticommunist government in El Salvador despite evidence that official "death squads" were murdering that government's political enemies.

During his second term, Reagan focused his attention on Nicaragua. After the 1979 revolution there, the remnants of the Somoza dictatorship took the name *Contras,* which means "against" in Spanish.

President Reagan was practically assured of winning reelection in 1984. The recession had bottomed out, and a sustained boom had cut unemployment in half. Also, the country was at peace.

The early Democratic front-runner was former vice president Walter Mondale. His most significant challengers were Senator Gary Hart of Colorado and the Reverend Jesse Jackson of Chicago. Hart stressed "new ideas" and attacked Mondale for his close ties to Democratic special interest groups. Jackson was the first African American to run a national primary campaign. He built a "rainbow coalition" to speak for poor and minority voters.

Mondale proved to be unstoppable, however. At the convention, he surprised most people by declaring that he would raise taxes to control the budget deficits. "Mr. Reagan will raise taxes, and so will I," Mondale said. "He won't tell you. I just did." Then came an even bigger surprise. For his running mate, Mondale chose Representative Geraldine Ferraro of New York, the first woman ever to run on a major-party ticket.

Reagan hit Mondale hard on taxes, promising to raise them only as a last resort. He also pointed out that most Americans were indeed better off than they had been four years before. Reagan's friendliness and good humor had wide appeal, as did his vision of national progress and strength. "It's morning in America," his television commercials began.

Mondale criticized Reagan's economic policies, which benefited the rich at the expense of the poor and middle class. But he stopped short of condemning Reagan directly, because he worried that voters might object to personal attacks against the popular president. On Election Day, Reagan won an even more impressive victory than in 1980, taking the electoral vote 525-13.

From bases in neighboring Honduras, they fought a guerrilla war against the new Sandinista government in Nicaragua.

In 1981, the Reagan administration cut off aid to the Sandinistas and instead began supporting the Contras, whom Reagan called "freedom fighters." By 1983, the Contras had grown into a trained army of seventy-five hundred soldiers.

After learning that the CIA had been secretly mining Nicaraguan harbors and giving lessons in political assassination, Congress passed the Boland Amendment, which prohibited further military aid to the Contras. To get around this law, administration officials assigned Lieutenant Colonel Oliver North of the National Security Council to help the Contras quietly raise money from private sources.

TERRORISM During the 1980 campaign, Reagan had repeatedly attacked Jimmy Carter for his handling of the Iranian hostage crisis. Reagan promised that he would never negotiate with terrorists. But he found that promise difficult to keep once more hostages were taken. This time, the

SPACE SHUTTLE EXPLODES

Seven Aboard Challenger Die in Crash

KENNEDY SPACE CENTER, Florida, January 28, 1986—The space shuttle *Challenger* exploded seventy-three seconds after liftoff this morning, killing all seven members of its crew.

Low temperatures preceding the launch have been blamed for the disaster. Last night was unusually cold, and this morning there were icicles on the launch tower.

It is believed that the cold caused a seal in the shuttle's booster rockets to fail. Once the seal failed, the shuttle was immediately engulfed in a fireball.

The *Challenger* crew included Christa McAuliffe, chosen from among eleven thousand applicants to become the first teacher in space. McAuliffe had prepared several lessons on space science that she planned to broadcast directly from the orbiting shuttle to U.S. classrooms.

Because of McAuliffe's participation in the mission, millions of schoolchildren were watching the launch of the *Challenger* on television when it exploded.

kidnappers were Lebanese Muslims with ties to Iran.

Lebanon was then in the middle of a civil war between Muslims and Christians, which the United States had been trying to settle. Marines had already been brought ashore into Beirut, the Lebanese capital, for peacekeeping duty. In October 1983, a van filled with explosives rammed into their barracks. The blast it created collapsed the building. Hundreds of soldiers were buried in the rubble, and 241 were killed.

Terrorist attacks weren't limited to Lebanon. In October 1985, Palestinian terrorists hijacked the Italian cruise ship *Achille Lauro.* They killed an American in a wheelchair, throwing his body overboard. Elsewhere, an April 1986 explosion at a West Berlin discotheque killed one U.S. serviceman and injured sixty others.

Charging that Libya was responsible for the discotheque bombing, Reagan ordered a raid on that country in retaliation. A squadron of F-111 bombers attacked on April 15, striking military targets as well as the living quarters of Libyan leader Muammar Qaddafi and his family.

THE GORBACHEV ERA

Meanwhile, in March 1985, an extraordinary new leader named Mikhail Gorbachev came to power in the Soviet Union. The fifty-three-year-old Gorbachev was open-minded enough to realize that his country could no longer afford to compete with the massive U.S. arms buildup. Gorbachev knew that the Soviet economy would continue to suffer unless Soviet society was itself reformed.

The two basic principles of Gorbachev's new program were *glasnost,* or openness, and *perestroika,* or restructuring. Under *glasnost,*

★**LIVE AID** In 1984, Bob Geldof produced a record featuring fellow British rock stars singing "Do They Know It's Christmas?" Proceeds from this song were donated to famine relief efforts in Ethiopia. A similar project, "We Are the World," raised money in the United States. During the summer of 1985, Geldof organized a benefit concert that would take place simultaneously in London and Philadelphia. The July 13 event, called Live Aid, was broadcast via satellite to 152 countries around the world. Performers included U2, Sting, Paul McCartney, and Madonna. The seventeen-hour show raised more than seventy million dollars for famine relief.

★**THE FIRST LADY** Nancy Reagan was one of the most controversial first ladies ever. Because she had helped her husband build his political career, many people questioned how much she still influenced him. The president obviously adored her, and White House staffers feared displeasing her.

Mrs. Reagan was criticized early in her husband's first term when she spent nearly a million dollars redecorating the White House. Later she was attacked for accepting free gowns from famous designers. Her expensive tastes in furniture and clothing seemed out of place at a time when social programs to aid the poor were being cut. During President Reagan's second term, the first lady improved her image by devoting her energies to the "Just Say No" campaign against drug use.

★**C. EVERETT KOOP** One of the most controversial figures of the Reagan administration was C. Everett Koop. The president picked Koop for the post of surgeon general because he thought the pediatrician shared his conservative values. Pro-choice groups opposed Dr. Koop's nomination for the same reason. They felt that Koop would let his personal feelings against abortion influence his judgment. But Koop's critics greatly underestimated his devotion to public service. Often during his eight years in office, the surgeon general enraged conservatives by choosing public health over politics. Koop's most controversial moment came in October 1986 when his report on the AIDS epidemic recommended that AIDS education begin in elementary schools as early as the third grade.

★**THE MORAL MAJORITY** President Reagan wanted to outlaw abortion and bring prayer back into the public schools. Although he made little progress on these issues, he spoke about them often. His greatest ally in this war of words was the Moral Majority, an ultraconservative religious group founded by Baptist minister Jerry Falwell in 1979. Falwell himself was one of a number of television evangelists who had far-reaching influence during the 1980s. Televangelism raised hundreds of millions of dollars, but it came crashing down in 1987 when television minister Jim Bakker was exposed for cheating his followers out of $150 million.

★**WALL STREET GREED** The deal-making on Wall Street was remarkably fast-paced during the Reagan years. The highest of the high-flyers was Michael Milken, who invented the "junk" bond. Milken's junk bonds used very high interest rates to lure insurance companies and banks into investing with him. The money the bondholders put up was used to buy companies. These companies were usually worth much more than the amount put up in cash, so the deals were called leveraged buy-outs, or LBOs. In 1987, Milken made an estimated $550 million. Three years later, he pleaded guilty to insider trading and went to prison.

censorship was eased so that people could express their ideas more freely. Meanwhile, *perestroika* attempted to revitalize the Communist system with a bit of capitalist private enterprise.

Although U.S.-Soviet relations were tense during Reagan's first term, Gorbachev's willingness to make peace helped wind down the Cold War. In December 1987, he and Reagan signed the Intermediate-Range Nuclear Forces agreement. For the first time, both sides actually agreed to reduce the number of nuclear warheads in their arsenals by destroying an entire class of missiles.

THE IRANIAN ARMS SALE Beginning in 1980, the Persian Gulf countries of Iran and Iraq fought an eight-year border war. The Iranians desperately needed arms because President Reagan had repeatedly asked U.S. allies not to sell them any. At the same time, however, members of Reagan's staff were secretly negotiating to sell arms to Iran. In exchange, so-called "moderates" in Iran agreed to help win the release of Americans held hostage in Lebanon.

Using a group of private dealers as middlemen, Reagan's National Security Council staff sold the arms to Iran at hugely inflated prices. In return, three hostages were released. But three more were soon taken. All the time, the arms sale was kept hidden from Congress and the public.

For a long time, the Reagan administration had been frustrated by Congress. The Boland Amendment was particularly irritating because the Contras were important to the president. To get around this law, White House officials decided to use some of the lavish profits from the Iranian arms sale to buy more weapons for the Contras.

The arms sale and the diversion of money to the Contras took place amid great secrecy. Later, the president claimed that even he didn't know what was going on. When his own staff members were asked direct questions during congressional hearings, they either gave misleading answers or lied. News of the arms sale was finally published in a small Beirut magazine in November 1986.

THE IRAN-CONTRA SCANDAL The first investigation of the scandal was conducted by Attorney General Edwin Meese. Meese's confirmation hearings had taken more than a year because Senate investigators had to look into a number of serious charges against him. A special prosecutor later concluded that Meese had probably broken the law a number of times, but that there was not enough evidence to prosecute him successfully.

Meese's early investigation of the Iran-Contra affair was badly bungled. While his aides conducted interviews in one room, Oliver North and his boss, National Security Advisor John Poindexter, shredded important documents in another. Poindexter later admitted that he had destroyed Reagan's signed authorization for the Iranian arms sale in order to save the president embarrassment. Other officials tried to protect the president by lying under oath about the order in which events took place.

During the congressional investigations and criminal trials that followed, administration officials portrayed President Reagan as a passive man, detached from details and overly willing to delegate authority to his aides. Because people knew the president liked to leave work early in the day and often got confused when he had to talk about the specifics of his policies, they tended to believe that he hadn't known what the National Security Council staff was doing.

WITH PRESIDENT REAGAN RETIRING, PRIMARY RACES in both parties were wide open. Vice President George Bush was embarrassed when he finished third among Republicans in Iowa. But he came back quickly to win New Hampshire and never looked back.

The Democratic campaign began wildly. After Colorado senator Gary Hart was forced out by a sex scandal, Governor Michael Dukakis of Massachusetts became the front-runner. With each primary, Dukakis added to his lead as his rivals dropped out one by one—except for Jesse Jackson. The Rainbow Coalition leader stayed in all the way to the convention. Jackson wanted the vice-presidential nomination, but Dukakis disagreed with some of Jackson's ultraliberal policies. Instead he picked conservative senator Lloyd Bentsen of Texas.

Bush's acceptance speech at the Republican convention called for an end to the greed of the 1980s. He said he wanted to lead a "kinder and gentler nation." However, when public opinion polls showed he was twenty points down, Bush ignored his own words and went on the offensive. His campaign was one of the most negative in history.

Avoiding serious but complicated issues, Bush attacked Dukakis for vetoing a bill that would have required schoolchildren to recite the Pledge of Allegiance. While Dukakis explained his new health insurance plan, Bush visited a flag factory. About the only thing Bush said regarding his own policies was, "Read my lips: No new taxes!" The election became a battle of media consultants, and the Democrats were unable to respond quickly or well to the attacks.

As Bush turned the word *liberal* into an insult, Dukakis's lead in the polls disappeared. The vice president's promise to carry on the Reagan Revolution carried him to victory. Bush became the first sitting vice president to be elected president since Martin Van Buren succeeded Andrew Jackson in 1836.

GEORGE HERBERT WALKER BUSH

41ST PRESIDENT

★

FROM 1989 TO 1993

BORN: June 12, 1924

BIRTHPLACE: Milton, Mass.

PARTY: Republican

VICE PRESIDENT: J. Danforth Quayle

FIRST LADY: Barbara Pierce

CHILDREN: George, Robin, John, Neil, Marvin, Dorothy

NICKNAME: Poppy

The first president to refuse publicly to eat broccoli.

UNITED NATIONS HOLDS EARTH SUMMIT

RIO DE JANEIRO, Brazil, June 14, 1992—The United Nations Earth Summit ended today as representatives of 153 nations signed treaties designed to reverse disturbing trends in the environment.

These agreements concern such issues as global warming and biodiversity. Global warming involves the greenhouse effect, which is the increase in worldwide temperature caused by man-made chemicals trapped in the atmosphere.

Biodiversity refers to the incredible variety of plant and animal species on the planet. Environmental scientists have warned that the continuing destruction of South American rain forests threatens many species that live there.

Environmental protection has become a particularly prominent issue in U.S. politics since March 24, 1989, when the oil tanker *Exxon Valdez* struck a reef off the Alaskan coast. The accident spilled ten million barrels of oil into Prince William Sound. The oil spill, the worst in the nation's history, killed thousands of birds, otters, fish, seals, and other animals.

Ronald Reagan may have fought the deciding battle, but the Cold War ended during George Bush's presidency. In a December 1988 speech to the United Nations, Soviet leader Mikhail Gorbachev declared that the Cold War was over. Then he followed up his words with some remarkable action.

Besides undertaking reform in his own country, Gorbachev reduced and then removed the Soviet troops from Eastern Europe. For the first time since World War II, East Germans, Czechs, Hungarians, and others were permitted to run their own governments. The world was no longer dominated by two superpowers challenging each other with nuclear weapons. Instead, in Bush's words, there was a "new world order."

While President Bush monitored the situation in the Soviet Union, he became more actively involved in Panama.

This strategically located Central American country was controlled in 1989 by dictator Manuel Noriega. Under the Reagan administration, the CIA had allowed Noriega to smuggle drugs because he gave them important intelligence information. As Noriega's drug trafficking and anti-American speeches became more frequent, President Bush found it difficult to ignore Noriega's illegal activities.

At first, Bush imposed economic sanctions, or penalties, and urged Noriega's rivals to stage a coup, or government takeover. When neither of these tactics worked, Bush ordered military action. Twelve thousand U.S. troops invaded Panama in December 1989. Noriega was captured and flown to Florida to stand trial on drug charges. Most Latin American countries publicly condemned the raid, but privately they expressed satisfaction with the result.

THE PERSIAN GULF WAR

A year later, Bush again considered military action. On August 2, 1990, Iraqi troops invaded the Persian Gulf nation of Kuwait. Although only a tiny country, Kuwait held about ten percent of the world's oil reserves. If Iraqi president Saddam Hussein were someday to conquer neighboring Saudi Arabia, he would control nearly half the world's oil.

President Bush immediately called the invasion "naked aggression." The United Nations Security Council imposed economic sanctions and soon gave member nations permission to enforce the sanctions using military means. Even the Soviet Union, Hussein's biggest arms supplier, stopped selling weapons to Iraq.

Six days after the invasion, President Bush began sending troops to help the Saudis defend themselves. Eventually, more than half a million

GEORGE BUSH'S FATHER WAS A WALL STREET BANKER AND later a U.S. senator from Connecticut. Prescott Bush taught his children that people of wealth and privilege should give something back to their country. On his eighteenth birthday in June 1942, George put off attending Yale University and enlisted in the navy. A year later, he earned his wings as the youngest navy pilot. During World War II, Bush flew fifty-eight combat missions against the Japanese and won the Distinguished Flying Cross.

After college, Bush turned down a job with his father's Wall Street firm. Instead, he went to Texas to learn the oil business, which eventually made him a millionaire. Running as a moderate Republican, Bush won election to the House of Representatives from Houston in 1966. Four years later, at the request of President Nixon, he ran for the Senate from Texas. When Bush lost that race, Nixon named him ambassador to the United Nations. Bush later served President Ford as the official U.S. representative to China and as director of the CIA.

★THE FIRST LADY Seventeen-year-old Barbara Pierce met her future husband at a Christmas dance in 1942. He was the first boy she ever kissed. George Bush later named his bomber plane *Barbara* after her. As first lady, Mrs. Bush immediately distanced herself from Nancy Reagan by getting involved in charitable causes. She founded an organization to help illiterate adults learn how to read, and she also spoke out for the homeless. It was often said that Barbara Bush was more popular than the president. One reason might be the bestselling *Millie's Book* she wrote from the point of view of the Bush family dog.

★**NELSON MANDELA** African National Congress leader Nelson Mandela was sent to prison in 1964 for planning to sabotage the white South African government. Mandela wanted to overthrow the South African system of apartheid. In South Africa, blacks could not vote, and whites got special treatment in every situation. During the 1980s, the United States and other nations used economic sanctions, such as halting trade, to push the white minority government into sharing power with the black majority. Although Nelson Mandela served many years at hard labor, his spirit remained unbroken. He was finally freed in February 1990 by President F.W. de Klerk, who wanted Mandela to help him negotiate a peaceful end to apartheid.

★**HIP HOP** Like most trends in popular music, including rock 'n' roll, hip hop originated in the black community. Its popularity spread quickly after MTV, the cable music television network, began airing "Yo! MTV Raps" in 1989. That show brought hip hop music, fashion, and dance styles into the mainstream. Soon baggy pants, baseball caps, gold jewelry, and hooded sweatshirts were being worn all over the country by young people who wanted to look cool. Although a handful of white performers, including Vanilla Ice, hopped onto the hip hop bandwagon, the music never lost its black urban roots.

★**MAGIC JOHNSON AND AIDS** On November 7, 1991, basketball star Earvin "Magic" Johnson told a packed news conference that he was retiring from the Los Angeles Lakers because he had become infected with the virus that causes AIDS. Magic's announcement stunned the world. Many people had refused to believe that such a skilled and popular athlete could get AIDS. For that reason, Johnson said he planned to devote the rest of his life to educating teenagers about how people become infected with AIDS. George Bush quickly appointed Johnson to the presidential AIDS commission, but he resigned in September 1992 after criticizing Bush for the president's lack of support.

U.S. soldiers took part in Operation Desert Shield. Meanwhile, the president and Secretary of State James Baker worked tirelessly to convince other nations to join a great coalition against Iraq. Great Britain, France, Egypt, and Syria all provided troops, while other nations sent planes and ships.

OPERATION DESERT STORM In November, the Security Council set a deadline of January 15, 1991, for the complete withdrawal of Iraqi troops from Kuwait. If the Iraqis did not obey, member nations could then force an Iraqi pullout. On January 12, after a lengthy debate, Congress voted to give President Bush the authority to wage war against Iraq. Seven hours after the deadline passed, Bush began Operation Desert Storm.

For nearly six weeks, coalition bombers devastated the Iraqi military. More than a hundred thousand combat missions were flown. On February 23, the ground assault began. Within one hundred hours, troops under General Norman Schwarzkopf had overwhelmed the Iraqi army, the fourth largest in the world. In the meantime, Kuwait was liberated.

After the war, Bush enjoyed enormous popularity. Not only had the United States won a convincing military victory, but it had been done as part of a worldwide coalition effort. This was the new world order that Bush had been talking about. Furthermore, the president had proven conclusively that he could handle himself well during an international crisis. But a crisis at home—that was another matter.

Throughout the Bush presidency, critics complained that the president had no goals for the country. During the 1988 campaign, Bush had vaguely promised to be the Education

President and the Environmental President. Congress waited for proposals addressing these issues, but little came from the White House. What happened instead was a banking scandal followed by a deep recession.

THE SAVINGS AND LOAN SCANDAL

During the 1980s, financial speculation grew as the Reagan administration relaxed federal regulation of the savings and loan industry. Many savings and loan owners used this new freedom to make risky loans. Others simply cheated their depositors. One of the worst owners, Charles Keating, made sizable campaign contributions to five senators in exchange for their help in warding off the few federal bank examiners still on the government payroll.

By the time the roof fell in on the savings and loan industry in 1989, hundreds of billions of dollars in government-insured deposits had disappeared. The taxpayers ended up footing the bill, and only a very few people went to jail. The Keating Five may have been the worst offenders, but most congressmen had accepted contributions from the savings and loan industry. These campaign contributions made legislators reluctant to control the problem before it got out of hand.

In late November 1990, the economic news got even worse. After four months of declining economic indicators, Federal Reserve Chairman Alan Greenspan announced that the economy was having a "meaningful downturn." A month later, unemployment reached a three-year high. At first, the president and his advisors blamed the recession on the rise in oil prices during the Persian Gulf War. They predicted growth would begin again soon, but it didn't come soon enough for Bush.

IN EARLY 1991, AFTER THE END OF THE PERSIAN GULF War, George Bush was hugely popular. His eighty-nine percent public approval rating seemed to guarantee him election to a second term. But the recession soon weakened people's confidence in his leadership.

Although there were some dramatic ups and downs during the primary season, the Democrats nominated Bill Clinton on the first ballot. The forty-six-year-old Arkansas governor claimed that he was a "new kind of Democrat," liberal on social issues and conservative on economic ones. His theme was "change." But his campaign had been dogged for months by two controversial accusations. One was that, while married, he had carried on a twelve-year affair with another woman. The other was that he had misled his draft board to avoid fighting in the Vietnam War. Although Clinton denied these charges, it sometimes seemed as though they might sink him.

Meanwhile, people turned away from Bush because he had abandoned his "Read my lips: No new taxes!" pledge. When self-made billionaire Ross Perot entered the race as an independent candidate, he focused people's attention on the budget deficit. Lecturing the public with charts and graphs, Perot said he would run the government the way he ran his own successful business. Whether voters thought he was eccentric or capable, Perot made the deficit the most important issue of the election.

Perot took nineteen percent of the popular vote, Bush thirty-eight percent, and Clinton forty-three percent. With Perot's votes, Bush would have won in a landslide. Instead, Clinton won the election with a majority in the electoral college. Less than half the voters cast ballots for Clinton, but sixty-two percent voted for change.

WILLIAM JEFFERSON CLINTON

42ND PRESIDENT

★

1993-

BORN: August 19, 1946

BIRTHPLACE: Hope, Ark.

PARTY: Democrat

VICE PRESIDENT: Albert Gore, Jr.

FIRST LADY: Hillary Rodham

CHILDREN: Chelsea

NICKNAME: Bubba

The first president to have been a Rhodes scholar.

As the first Baby Boomer president, Bill Clinton was often influenced by values he adopted during the 1960s. For example, he picked his vice president, Albert Gore, in part because of Gore's concern for the environment. Yet Clinton proved in his inaugural address that he understood traditional values as well. "It is time to break the bad habit of expecting something for nothing," he said. In other words, change would require sacrifice.

Many Americans, even those who voted against him, hoped that Clinton's election would end governmental "gridlock" between the president and Congress. For the first time in twelve years, both branches of government would be controlled by the same party. Change didn't come easily, however, and early stumbles by the Clinton team didn't help.

Clinton's first nominee for attorney general, Zoe Baird, was forced to withdraw her name after admitting that she and her husband had failed to pay social security tax for their two household

ARREST MADE IN WORLD TRADE CENTER BOMBING

NEW YORK, March 4, 1993—The FBI made the first arrest today in the World Trade Center bombing case. Agents captured Mohammed Salameh in Jersey City, New Jersey, when he attempted to collect his rental deposit on the van used in the bombing.

Salameh had told the rental company that the van had been stolen. The FBI found Salameh by tracing the vehicle using an identification number found on a piece of twisted metal at the bomb site. Salameh is a member of a Jersey City mosque attended by radical Islamic fundamentalists.

Just last week, lower Manhattan was thrown into turmoil when a huge explosion rocked the twin towers of the World Trade Center. The February 26 blast, the worst terrorist attack ever on U.S. soil, was caused by a van loaded with explosives. The van had been parked in a public garage beneath the 110-story buildings.

Five people were killed by the explosion and at least one thousand injured. The bomb left a crater in the garage seven stories deep.

employees. Still, Clinton remained committed to naming a female attorney general, and his second nominee, Florida prosecutor Janet Reno, won Senate confirmation easily. Several months later, he appointed another woman, federal judge Ruth Bader Ginsburg, to the Supreme Court.

TRADE AGREEMENTS Although he often fought with Congress during his first two years in office, Clinton did win two big victories on trade issues. In November 1993, the House passed the North American Free Trade Agreement by thirty-four votes. NAFTA created a free-trade zone linking the United States, Mexico, and Canada. A year later, Congress approved the General Agreement on Tariffs and Trade, an international treaty that took seven years to negotiate.

Another major presidential effort won passage of a thirty-billion-dollar anti-crime bill in August 1994. With health care, however, the president was less successful. A commission chaired by First Lady Hillary Rodham Clinton proposed covering all Americans and guaranteeing them a minimum package of benefits. But doctors, hospitals, and insurance companies fought these reforms, and congressmen criticized them for being too expensive. Some moderate senators offered compromises, but these were also rejected, and the gridlock on heath care continued.

THE 1994 ELECTIONS The president's party often loses seats in congressional midterm elections. But the 1994 election was unusually disastrous for the Democrats. Republicans won control of both the House and the Senate for the first time since 1955. A Republican even beat Thomas Foley, who became the first sitting speaker of the House to lose his seat in an election since 1862.

The Early Years

BILL CLINTON'S FATHER DIED IN A CAR accident before he was born. When he was seven, his mother, Virginia, remarried. Her new husband, Roger Clinton, was a car dealer and an alcoholic who sometimes beat his wife. At fourteen, Bill confronted him. "Daddy, if you're not able to stand up, I'll help you," he said, "but you must stand up to hear what I have to say. Don't ever, ever, lay your hand on my mother again."

In 1963, Bill took an American Legion trip from Arkansas to Washington, where he met President Kennedy. From that moment on, he knew he wanted a career in politics. Fifteen years later, he was elected governor of Arkansas. At thirty-two, he was the youngest governor in the country. After his first two-year term, Clinton was voted out of office for raising the state gasoline tax to pay for highway improvements. He accepted the defeat as a lesson in humility and regained the governorship in 1982.

★THE FIRST FAMILY Hillary Rodham introduced herself to Bill Clinton in law school after she noticed Clinton staring at her. In 1974, she gave up her own chance for a political career and moved to Arkansas to marry him. In Little Rock, Mrs. Clinton worked full-time as a lawyer and became active in children's issues. "If you elect Bill, you get me," she often said during the 1992 campaign. Soon after taking office, President Clinton appointed her to head his task force on health care.

Although both Clintons have supported public education, they sent their daughter Chelsea to a private school. Once when Chelsea needed permission to take some medicine, she told school officials to call her father, the president. Her mother, she said, was too busy.

★VIRTUAL REALITY Imagine being inside a video game in a world controlled by a computer. If you walk forward, the image that you see moves forward, too. If you look down, you see a graphic image of your feet. This effect is called virtual reality. During the early 1990s, great advances were made in virtual reality technology. Engineers at one space research center constructed a three-dimensional computer model of Mars, which they "explored" using head-mounted displays and data gloves to control the computer program. Meanwhile, the Pentagon developed a training center for tank commanders using virtual reality to simulate the tank battles of the Persian Gulf War.

★THE INTERNET During the mid-1990s, the number of people "surfing the Net" grew rapidly. The Internet is the "information superhighway" along which digital information travels. To take advantage of increased Internet traffic, many organizations began setting up "home pages" for people to visit electronically using their personal computers. For instance, the White House created a home page at http://www.whitehouse.gov

★SPACE Although hard times followed the *Challenger* disaster, the U.S. space program rebounded strongly in 1996. First, the National Aeronautics and Space Administration (NASA) announced in August that it had possibly found evidence that life once existed on Mars. The evidence was a potato-sized meteorite found near the South Pole in 1986. Using a powerful microscope, NASA scientists had discovered on the meteorite tiny features that looked like fossilized bacteria. A month later, the space shuttle *Atlantis* brought biologist Shannon Lucid back to earth after six months in space. Her 188-day mission aboard the Russian space station Mir broke the endurance records for an American astronaut and for a woman.

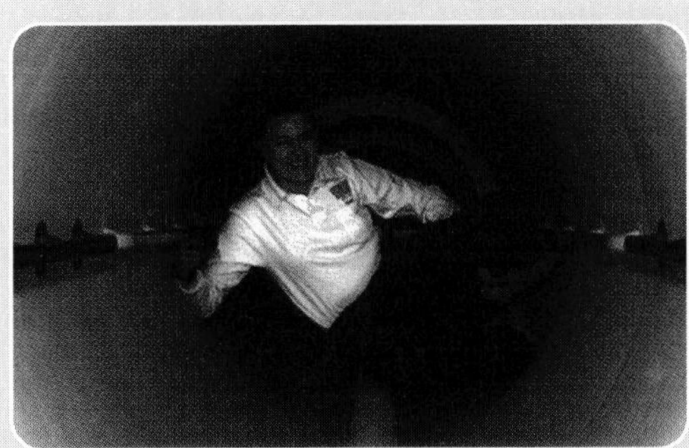

★OKLAHOMA CITY BOMBING Just after 9:00 A.M. on April 19, 1995, a bomb hidden in a rental van exploded outside the Murrah Federal Building in Oklahoma City, Oklahoma. The force of the blast collapsed most of the building, killing 168 people. The Oklahoma City bombing was the worst terrorist attack ever committed on U.S. soil.

At first, because of parallels between the Oklahoma City and World Trade Center bombings, many people assumed that the terrorists were foreigners, perhaps Islamic fundamentalists. Instead, two Americans, Timothy McVeigh and Terry Nichols, were charged in the bombing. Both men were members of the militia movement. Leaders of this extremist movement encouraged their followers to stockpile guns because they believed the government was plotting to take away their rights.

"Republicans did a good job of defining us [the Democrats] as the party of government," President Clinton said after the election, "and that [was] not a good place to be."

When it came time to govern, however, the new Republican majority in the 104th Congress ran into some unexpected problems. House speaker Newt Gingrich, in particular, learned that running the government was much more difficult than attacking it.

CONTRACT WITH AMERICA Most new Republican congressmen had backed Gingrich's Contract with America. Among the campaign promises this document had spelled out were the application of federal laws to members of Congress, the line-item veto, and an end to unfunded mandates (federal laws that require states to pay for specific federal programs). The Contract also promised swift passage of a balanced-budget amendment and legal reform.

The first three of these measures passed the House and Senate during the first hundred days of the new Congress. But the last two, like many other parts of the Contract, stalled in the Senate, where the Republicans were much less radical than those in the House.

The battle between the White House and the Congress over the budget continued for the better part of a year, reaching its climax during the fall of 1995. In late October, the House and Senate passed a bill that would have cut taxes *and* balanced the budget by 2002. It also would have cut deeply into health, education, and environmental spending.

Citing his objections to these cuts, President Clinton vetoed the bill and offered a compromise. But the Republicans turned him down. And with no budget law in place, the government began to run out of money.

GOVERNMENT SHUTDOWNS In mid-November, the budget impasse forced a partial shutdown of the federal government. Offices were closed, and eight hundred thousand workers were sent home. The shutdown lasted six days. Finally, when President Clinton accepted the Republican goal of balancing the budget within seven years, the House and Senate approved stopgap spending bills.

Yet the president and Congress continued to disagree over how to balance the budget. So, in mid-December, Congress forced another government shutdown. This one lasted three weeks.

But this time, the Republicans miscalculated. By early January 1996, a frustrated public had turned against them. Voters who had once encouraged the Republicans to dismantle the federal government now applauded President Clinton for defending programs like Medicare from a reckless Congress.

THE WAR IN BOSNIA President Clinton also encountered some difficult and risky situations in the arena of foreign policy. In the former Yugoslavia, for example, Serbs, Croats, and Muslims were fighting the bloodiest war in Europe since World War II. The Serbs wanted to carve out of the state of Bosnia an ethnically pure Serbian homeland. During four years of fighting, 250,000 people had died.

In November 1995, while the budget crisis swirled around him, President Clinton brought the warring factions together at an air force base in Dayton, Ohio. After three weeks of tense and bitter negotiations, the three parties finally agreed on a peace plan.

In his riskiest foreign policy move yet, President Clinton agreed to send

CAMPAIGN 1996

ALTHOUGH PRESIDENT Clinton's popularity fell off during his first two years in office, it rose again in the aftermath of the government shutdowns. Polls confirmed that the same voters who threw out the Democrats in 1994 didn't like the way the Republicans were acting, either.

To take advantage of the Republicans' confrontational policies, President Clinton moved noticeably to the political center. In August 1996, he staged a string of White House bill signings that emphasized his moderate policies. The bills he signed included ones that raised the minimum wage, expanded access to health insurance, and overhauled the welfare system. The president signed the welfare bill despite strong opposition from liberals within his administration who believed that removing the social safety net was unfair to poor people.

Running against Clinton was Republican nominee Bob Dole of Kansas. Before resigning in mid-June to devote himself to campaigning, Dole had been the Senate majority leader. In his acceptance speech at the Republican convention in San Diego, the seventy-three-year-old Dole talked about building a "bridge to the past," to the years immediately after World War II, when Americans felt confident and prosperous. Seizing on Dole's imagery, Clinton spoke in his own convention acceptance speech about building a bridge to the future.

In the end, as is usually the case, the election turned on how voters felt about the economy. Several character issues dogged Clinton, especially his role in an Arkansas land deal known as Whitewater. But the generally good economic news buoyed him and carried him to a decisive victory.

President Clinton delivers a radio address.

twenty thousand U.S. troops to Bosnia to help guarantee the peace. These soldiers policed Bosnia as part of a ninety-thousand-strong United Nations Implementation Force, known as IFOR. The Dayton peace plan, which preserved the unity of Bosnia, called for limited disarmament to be followed by free elections. These elections were held peacefully in September 1996.

RUSSIA UNDER YELTSIN

Meanwhile in Russia, President Boris Yeltsin spent the summer of 1996 campaigning for reelection. His chief opponent was Communist party leader Gennady Zyuganov. Since the end of the Cold War, the United States had done its best to encourage free-market reforms within the former Soviet Union. This policy included substantial economic aid and also Clinton's personal support for Yeltsin.

Although President Clinton could not appear to be too involved in the Russian election, his preference for Yeltsin was clear. When the final round of voting took place in July, Yeltsin won by a convincing margin of thirteen percentage points. However, the campaign had drained Yeltsin physically. Rumors of medical problems resurfaced, and in September 1996 it was announced that the Russian president would have to undergo surgery for an ailing heart. The operation took place in early November. According to Yeltsin's doctors, it was a complete success.

RABIN ASSASSINATED

Israeli Kills Peacemaker

TEL AVIV, Israel, November 4, 1995—Israeli prime minister Yitzhak Rabin was shot and killed today shortly after he spoke to one hundred thousand people at a peace rally in Tel Aviv.

Jewish law student Yigal Amir shot Rabin because he opposed Rabin's peace talks with the Palestinians. In September 1993, Rabin and Palestinian leader Yasir Arafat had signed a historic treaty granting Palestinians self-rule in the Gaza Strip and West Bank areas of Israel. The treaty was part of Rabin's "land for peace" strategy.

Rabin's policies, however, upset many hard-line Israelis who could not forgive Arafat for his support of terrorism in the past. Because Rabin was himself once a hard-liner, Israelis had been willing to follow him down the road to peace. Now, with Rabin dead, many doubt that the peace process can continue.

A HISTORY OF THE WHITE HOUSE

★ This is the oldest known photograph of the White House. It was taken by John Plumbe, Jr., sometime around 1846.

IN MARCH 1791, PRESIDENT GEORGE Washington personally selected some land on the Potomac River between Virginia and Maryland for the site of the nation's new capital. A year later, as plans for the District of Columbia took shape, Washington announced a national competition to design a new house for the president there. In Washington's opinion, the president's house would be one of the most important buildings constructed in the District of Columbia before the government moved there in 1800.

Washington organized this contest at the suggestion of Secretary of State Thomas Jefferson, who was himself an accomplished amateur architect. In fact, Jefferson submitted one of his own designs anonymously, but his was not chosen. Instead, the Board of Federal Commissioners selected the work of Irish immigrant James Hoban. Hoban's winning design resembled that of an English country house. (The other entries were mostly enlarged courthouses or awkward mansions.)

President Washington's personal interest in the planning of the new house was so great that after the announcement of Hoban's victory on July 17, 1792, Washington began meeting with him regularly. Although Hoban

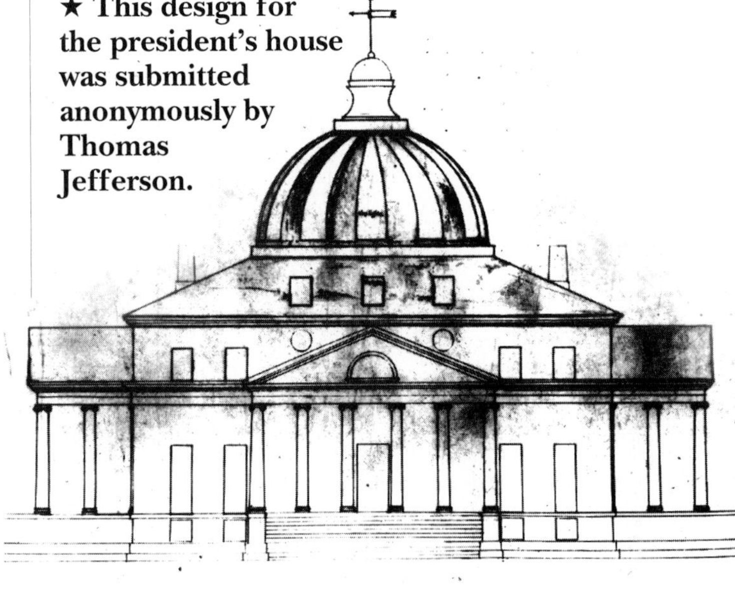

★ This design for the president's house was submitted anonymously by Thomas Jefferson.

★ **Hoban's original plans called for a mansion four times as large as the one that was built. Even so, the new house, which measured 168 feet east to west and 85 feet north to south, was larger than any house built in the United States until the 1870s.**

and Washington continued revising their plans until late 1793, work moved ahead quickly. The sandstone for the walls came on ships up the Potomac River from the Aquia Creek quarry, which also supplied stone for the U.S. Capitol. Work on the president's house was carried on each year from mid-April until mid-October, when temperatures became too cold for the mortar (used between the stones) to set properly.

Ironically, its greatest patron, George Washington, was the only president never to live in the president's house. When Washington left office in 1797, the building was still just a stone shell. A year later, the exterior walls got their first coat of whitewash. The recipe for this famous paint included salt, ground rice, glue, and lime. Almost immediately, people began calling the building the "white house." That nickname first appeared in print in a November 1810 issue of the *Baltimore Whig*. It was not until 1901, however, that President Theodore Roosevelt officially changed the name of the building from the Executive Mansion to the White House.

JUNE 1800 *President John Adams visits Washington, D.C., to inspect the public buildings under construction there. He complains that the work will not be finished before the government's arrival on November 1.*

After touring the partially completed president's house, Adams ordered the nude figures carved into the mantelpieces removed and replaced with carvings of fruit and flowers. He also asked for a bell system that he could use to summon servants. This way, he wouldn't need a servant in every room, as was then the custom in large houses.

In November, as he had suspected, the president arrived to find his new house still under construction. It smelled of plaster (mixed with horse and hog hair) and wallpaper paste (made from white flour and beer). Its floors were raw, unfinished mahogany, and the grand staircase on the north front of the house had not yet been built. Instead, wooden planks were used to span the gap from the doorway to the crude gravel road that led up to the house.

★ **Until the laundry yard was completed, Abigail Adams had her servants hang the first family's laundry in the unfinished East Room.**

★ **After the War of 1812, President James Madison ordered that the public buildings in Washington, including the White House, be rebuilt exactly as they had been before the British burned them.**

AUGUST 24 1814 *After learning of the U.S. defeat at the battle of Bladensburg, First Lady Dolley Madison flees the White House around 3:30 P.M. with the Declaration of Independence, the national seal, and her pet parrot. Invading British troops reach Washington, D.C., about 7:30 P.M.*

After burning the Capitol, Rear Admiral George Cockburn and Major General Robert Ross entered the president's house. They found the dining room table set (the Madisons had been expecting forty people for dinner) and the food already prepared in the kitchen. In Madison's dressing room on the second floor, the battle-stained British officers paused long enough to wash and change into some of Madison's clean underwear. Orders were then given to burn the house.

MARCH-MAY 1833 *Running water is installed in the White House.*

When the White House was first built, it did not have running water. Instead, water needed for the kitchen and the bathrooms was carried into the house by servants, who fetched it in buckets from two wells. These wells were located in the breezeways between the house and each of its wings. James Hoban first proposed the idea of piping running water into the White House in 1816. But Hoban's idea was rejected for being too sophisticated. In 1831, the Committee on Public Buildings finally purchased a nearby spring that could be used as a source for running water, but two more years passed before work on the project was actually begun.

The system, as designed by engineer Robert Leckie, was a deceptively simple one. Water from the spring ran downhill through iron pipes into a sand-lined fountain outside the White House. The motion of this fountain kept the water from stagnating. From the fountain, more iron pipes carried the water into the house. All that was needed to power the system was an attendant, who used a hand pump to create the necessary water pressure in the pipes.

Although many hotels and some fancy American homes already had running water, President Andrew Jackson, like most of his countrymen, was not overly impressed by the new arrangement. People during the 1830s still considered running water more of a luxury than a necessity. In fact, Leckie's system was added to the White House more for reasons of fire safety than for personal convenience.

★ Although several luxuries, including running water, were added to the White House during his administration, President Andrew Jackson worked hard to maintain his image as a man of the people. As part of his Washington's Birthday celebration in 1837, Jackson invited the public to the White House to consume a huge fourteen-hundred-pound cheese that had been given to him as a gift two years earlier. In less than two hours, the cheese was gone, but the White House smelled of it for several years afterward.

1840

President Martin Van Buren orders construction of a centralized hot-air heating system. This system replaces the many wood- and coal-burning fireplaces that have been used to heat the house.

Unlike Andrew Jackson, President Van Buren made no secret of his appreciation for the comforts of city life. His wealthy friends in New York City, for example, all had central heating in their homes. Thoughts of their good fortune made life in the drafty, chilly White House nearly unbearable for Van Buren.

To bring the White House up to date, Van Buren had workers install a large coal furnace in the basement. This new furnace was tied into a network of plaster-lined ducts that ran upstairs through the floor and walls. The hot air produced by the furnace warmed all the state rooms on the first floor. Unfortunately, it didn't reach the second-floor family rooms, which were still heated by fireplaces.

The White House heating system was operated by a fireman, whose job it was to feed coal into the furnace. During the winter, he was on duty twenty-four hours a day, but he got the summers off. A decade later, in 1853, during the administration of Franklin Pierce, Joseph Nason of Walworth & Nason, Boston, was hired to convert Van Buren's hot-air system into a more efficient hot-water system.

1848

Gaslight reaches the White House during the Polk administration.

In 1847, Congress hired the Baltimore Gas Company to build a gas plant on the Capitol grounds so that the Capitol could be lit by gaslight. Gaslight was cheaper than candles and oil lamps—and also safer, because gas lamps did not tip over and start fires. The Capitol plan was soon expanded to include the White House. Coal gas from the Capitol plant was piped to the White House along Pennsylvania Avenue, feeding streetlights along the way.

Before gaslight, the White House was lit mostly by oil lamps that burned foul-smelling lard (made from animal and vegetable fat). Candles were so expensive that they were used only on important occasions.

Most of the formal rooms in the White House had chandeliers that could be lowered on pulleys when servants needed to light or change the candles in them. In 1848, pipes and burners were attached to these chandeliers, converting them to gaslight. However, because she preferred candlelight, First Lady Sarah Polk refused to let workmen convert the chandelier in the Blue Room. At first people made fun of her for being old-fashioned, but all the teasing stopped on the night of the first gaslit state reception. No one had thought to warn the Capitol gas plant to stay open late. So when the plant shut down as usual around nine o'clock, all the lights in the White House went out—except the chandelier in the Blue Room, beneath which Mrs. Polk stood in her usual spot, bathed in candlelight.

★ **In late August, when Garfield seemed to be getting better, his doctors decided to let him leave Washington for the cool ocean breezes at Elberon, New Jersey. His cot was carried out of the White House on September 6 and placed on a wagon for the trip to the railroad station.**

MAY 10 1879 *The National Telephone Company installs the first telephone in the White House on a trial basis. It is mounted on a wall in the telegraph room.*

One problem that President Rutherford Hayes had with his new telephone was that there was almost no one to call. Because telephones were so new in 1879, very few people had them. For example, Treasury Secretary John Sherman was the only cabinet member with telephone service.

Nine months later, another invention arrived at the White House: It was the typewriter. This machine, unlike the telephone, did have an immediate impact on the way the president's staff did its work. In fact, it soon revolutionized the way the White House took care of its business on a day-to-day basis. Before Hayes's purchase of the Fairbanks & Company Improved Number Two Typewriter, his clerks, who specialized in fancy penmanship, had to write out each piece of White House correspondence by hand. Using this new machine, however, they could type out letters quickly and get a lot more done.

★ **After President Garfield's death from blood poisoning on September 19, the White House was draped in black.**

JULY 1881 *During an emergency, the White House gets the first primitive air conditioning.*

After the shooting of President James Garfield on July 2, 1881, the White House was deluged with gifts from well-wishers—everything from flowers and cards to food and clothing. Garfield's doctors, however, were particularly interested in two machines being offered by inventors. These devices were intended to help cool the wounded president, who was suffering in Washington's humid summer heat.

Both used ice to cool air, which was then piped into the president's sickroom. The problem with one machine was that the cool air moved too slowly through its pipes. The other used an innovative electric blower to move the air quickly, but the icy draft it produced made the sickroom too damp.

On the night of Friday, July 9, army doctor J. J. Woodward called Professor Simon Newcomb to the White House. Woodward wanted Newcomb, a scientist who worked for the navy, to analyze the two machines and come up with a solution to the dampness problem. Newcomb quickly developed a third, much larger machine that used several tons of ice but kept the dampness to a minimum. Working around the clock over the weekend, Newcomb built this new air conditioner with the help of R. S. Jennings, inventor of the electric-blower

★ **Tiffany's work, completed for the most part by October 1882, included a dramatic stained-glass screen that was not finished until early 1883. This screen separated the White House foyer from the hall that led to the state parlors and dining room.**

machine, and John Wesley Powell, then director of the U.S. Geological Survey. On Monday morning, Newcomb turned on the system, and it worked.

SEPTEMBER 1881

President Chester Arthur begins the most extensive work on the White House since it was rebuilt after the 1814 fire.

President Arthur, a New Yorker with elegant tastes, considered the White House worse than shabby and below the standards of even a third-rate Manhattan hotel. During a tour of the White House a few weeks after Garfield's death, he announced, "I will not live in a house like this." He insisted that the public rooms be completely redecorated before he moved in.

From late October 1881 until early December, Arthur personally supervised this redecoration. He inspected the work nightly and regularly made changes and additions. Then, shortly after moving into the White House on December 7, he let it be known that he considered the extensive work, which cost thirty thousand dollars, only temporary.

In early 1882, Arthur asked Congress for enough money to demolish and rebuild the White House, but preservationists blocked this plan. Instead, Arthur settled for another eighty thousand dollars' worth of renovation.

To perform this work, Arthur hired the most fashionable designer in New York, Louis Comfort Tiffany, son of the famous jeweler. During the early summer of 1882, Arthur moved out of the White House so that Tiffany's men could work freely. Castoff furnishings, which included Andrew Jackson's desk and James Polk's dining room chairs, were carted off in twenty-four wagonloads and sold at auction. By the time Tiffany finished his work, the White House was indeed the showplace that Arthur had wanted. "History remembers only a few things about [Chester Arthur]," wrote White House historian William Seale, but "one is that he had taste."

1891

Workmen cut into the White House walls to wire the building for electricity.

In January 1891, Senator Leland Stanford of California introduced a bill that called for a major reconstruction and expansion of the White House. The plans for this work had been personally developed by First Lady Caroline Harrison. For many years, presidents and their wives had complained about the lack of space in the White House, which had not increased in size since the time of Jefferson.

Mrs. Harrison's bold plan was turned down in March. But a few months later, she bounced back and took charge of an extensive redecoration of the White House made possible by the installation of electricity there.

As a first step, workmen scraped and washed away almost all the finish that had been applied by Tiffany at President Arthur's direction. They scrubbed the walls and ceilings until the original white plaster showed. Then electricians from the Edison General Company of New York made gouges into the walls deep enough to hold the new wiring. After the wires were installed, the walls were replastered and the redecorating began.

Normally, the new electrical wires would have been pushed through the existing gas pipes, but President Harrison did not have much faith in the new technology. He wanted the gas lights kept as a backup system in case the electricity failed. In fact, throughout their stay in the White House, the Harrisons refused to operate any of the electrical switches for fear of being shocked. Instead, servants turned the lights on and off for them.

★ **Mrs. Harrison's 1891 plan called for new east and west wings to be joined to the White House by semicircular colonnades. These wings were never built.**

APRIL 15
1902

First Lady Edith Roosevelt asks New York architect Charles F. McKim to provide some quick and easy solutions to the problem of overcrowding in the White House. McKim tells Mrs. Roosevelt that a complete renovation will be necessary to keep the president living there.

Like many New Yorkers, the Roosevelts considered Washington a second-rate city. Once it became obvious that the White House needed repair, they called in McKim, a founding partner of McKim, Mead & White, one of New York's leading architectural firms. In hiring McKim, Roosevelt bypassed the Army Corps of Engineers, which normally had control over any construction at the White House.

The most pressing problem was space. The state dining room didn't seat enough people, and eight rooms upstairs were simply not enough for the Roosevelts and their large family. On June 28, Congress appropriated $475,445 for the project, which the president declared must be finished by December 1.

One of McKim's most important changes was to move the offices of the president's staff out of the White House and into another building on the grounds, known then as the Temporary Executive Offices. Removing these offices from the second floor nearly doubled the amount of living space there. In general, McKim's mission was to preserve the historic White House while making it workable for a modern president.

MAY
1909

Needing even more office space, President William Howard Taft approves plans for an addition to the Executive Office Building. These plans include the first Oval Office.

When Charles McKim built the Temporary Executive Offices on the west side of the White House in 1902, he expected the building to be just that—temporary. However, with President Roosevelt's ever-increasing need for space, the building stayed. In fact, by the time of Taft's inauguration in 1909, Congress had appropriated forty thousand more dollars to enlarge the building. McKim had moved only staff offices out of the White House, but now the president's office would be moved to the new building as well.

Taft, who had a strong personal interest in architecture, decided not to build a second floor and instead chose to extend the building southward. According to plans drawn up by Nathan C. Wyeth, the president's new office would be oval in shape, like the Blue Room in the White House. Taft first occupied the new Oval Office in October 1909.

★ **This photograph shows the first Oval Office under construction in 1909. The Executive Office Building in which the president works is today known as the West Wing.**

1913 *With the help of landscape architect George Burnap, First Lady Ellen Wilson designs a rose garden for the area between the White House and the West Wing.*

Even in Princeton, New Jersey, a town famous for its beautiful gardens, Ellen Wilson's plantings stood out. When Mrs. Wilson moved into the White House in 1913, she surveyed the southwest garden from her dressing room window. Edith Roosevelt had planted a colonial garden, full of old-fashioned multicolored flowers. But that sort of garden didn't appeal to Mrs. Wilson, whose taste was more formal. "Come and look, children," she said, pointing out the window. "It will be our rose garden."

MARCH 14 1933 *The* New York Daily News *announces a campaign to raise money for a swimming pool in the White House. The pool will be built for President Franklin Roosevelt, whose paralysis (caused by polio) is sometimes eased by exercise in a pool. Most of the donors are schoolchildren, who pool their pennies to make twenty-five- and fifty-cent contributions.*

The White House pool, built indoors in the arcade between the main house and the West Wing, was designed by Lorenzo S. Winslow. Roosevelt liked Winslow's work so much that the president later made him the official White House architect. Because FDR loved building and remodeling, he and Winslow worked together on many more projects during the next twelve years, including a new East Wing built in 1942. Roosevelt and Winslow also took on numerous small projects. For example, they opened up the chimney in the diplomatic reception room so that FDR would no longer have to hold his fireside chats in front of a fake fireplace.

★ **This photo shows the White House on the night of December 7, 1941, after the Japanese attack on Pearl Harbor. On December 14, several government departments presented President Roosevelt with a report on how to protect the White House from enemy bombing. The suggestions rejected by Roosevelt included camouflaging the White House, painting its windows black, and setting up machine guns on the roof. However, FDR did agree to build a bomb shelter under the new East Wing.**

★ **Although President Richard Nixon was no fan of the media, during the early 1970s he ordered FDR's pool filled in so that the space could be used for a new press room.**

MAY 10

1948

Congress approves fifty thousand dollars for a structural survey of the White House, where many walls have large cracks. Just how badly the house has deteriorated becomes obvious a few months later when the leg of a piano falls through the floor in Margaret Truman's sitting room.

The moment he learned of the accident involving his daughter's piano was probably the time when President Harry Truman decided to rebuild the White House. Not surprisingly, the structural survey found that much of the building's framework was unsound. The repeated drilling into Hoban's beams for gas pipes, plumbing, and electrical wires had cut some of them completely in half.

The gutting of the White House began on December 7, 1949. Truman's plan was to raze everything but the stone walls and rebuild the interior from the ground up. As a result, all that remains today of the original White House are the same stone walls that survived the 1814 fire. The Trumans did not move back into the rebuilt White House until March 27, 1952.

Nearly half a century later, the White House remains the house that Truman rebuilt. Nine more families have lived there since the Trumans left in 1953, but none has made significant alterations.

The only noteworthy change has been the historical redecoration work begun by Mamie Eisenhower during the late 1950s and greatly expanded by Jacqueline Kennedy in 1961. These first ladies championed the idea of decorating the White House with antiques from various periods in the history of the building. On the night of February 14, 1962, Mrs. Kennedy led forty-seven million viewers on a televised tour of the White House, pointing out many of the newly acquired furnishings. It is generally agreed that her antiques program restored to the White House the sense of history that had been lost following the Truman-era reconstruction.

★ **Perhaps because he felt guilty about demolishing the inside of the White House, Truman refused to let construction crews touch the exterior stone walls. As a result, the crews had to take apart a bulldozer, piece by piece, pass it through an opening in one wall, and then reassemble it before they could dig the new basement.**

But the White House will surely not remain the way it is today. It will change again and adapt as new circumstances and tastes demand. Just as Teddy Roosevelt's desire for a larger staff forced construction of the West Wing nearly a century ago, some new presidential necessity in the future will undoubtedly force more changes. One thing will remain constant, however, and that is the White House's role as a stable, enduring symbol of the presidency.

★ **The White House today.**

★ Presidential Election Results ★

President Vice President	Term	Election	Candidates	Popular Vote	Electoral Vote
George Washington John Adams	1789-1797 1789-1797	**1789**	George Washington (Federalist) John Adams (Federalist) Others		69 34 35
		1792	George Washington (Federalist) John Adams (Federalist) George Clinton (Federalist) Others		132 77 50 5
John Adams Thomas Jefferson	1797-1801 1797-1801	**1796**	John Adams (Federalist) Thomas Jefferson (Dem.-Rep.) Thomas Pinckney (Federalist) Aaron Burr (Dem.-Rep.) Others		71 68 59 30 48
Thomas Jefferson Aaron Burr	1801-1809 1801-1805	**1800**	Thomas Jefferson (Dem.-Rep.) Aaron Burr (Dem.-Rep.) John Adams (Federalist) Charles C. Pinckney (Federalist) John Jay (Federalist)		73 73 65 64 1
George Clinton	1805-1809	**1804**	Thomas Jefferson (Dem.-Rep.) Charles C. Pinckney (Federalist)		162 14
James Madison George Clinton	1809-1817 1809-1812	**1808**	James Madison (Dem.-Rep.) Charles C. Pinckney (Federalist) George Clinton (Dem.-Rep.)		122 47 6
Elbridge Gerry	1813-1814	**1812**	James Madison (Dem.-Rep.) DeWitt Clinton (Federalist)		128 89
James Monroe Daniel D. Tompkins	1817-1825 1817-1825	**1816**	James Monroe (Dem.-Rep.) Rufus King (Federalist)		183 34
		1820	James Monroe (Dem.-Rep.) John Quincy Adams (Dem.-Rep.)		231 1

President Vice President	Term	Election	Candidates	Popular Vote	Electoral Vote
John Quincy Adams	1825-1829	**1824**	Andrew Jackson (Dem.-Rep.)	153,544	99
John C. Calhoun	1825-1829		John Quincy Adams (Dem.-Rep.)	108,740	84
			William Crawford (Dem.-Rep.)	46,618	41
			Henry Clay (Dem.-Rep.)	47,136	37
Andrew Jackson	1829-1837	**1828**	Andrew Jackson (Democrat)	647,286	178
John C. Calhoun	1829-1832		John Quincy Adams (Nat. Rep.)	508,064	83
Martin Van Buren	1833-1837	**1832**	Andrew Jackson (Democrat)	687,502	219
			Henry Clay (Nat. Rep.)	530,189	49
			John Floyd (Independent)		11
			William Wirt (Anti-Mason)		7
Martin Van Buren	1837-1841	**1836**	Martin Van Buren (Democrat)	762,678	170
Richard M. Johnson	1837-1841		William Henry Harrison (Whig)	735,561 (combined Whig vote)	73
			Hugh White (Whig)		26
			Daniel Webster (Whig)		14
			Willie P. Mangum (Whig)		11
Wm. Henry Harrison	1841	**1840**	William Henry Harrison (Whig)	1,275,016	234
John Tyler	1841		Martin Van Buren (Democrat)	1,129,102	60
John Tyler	1841-1845		Succeeded to the presidency on the death of William Henry Harrison.		
James K. Polk	1845-1849	**1844**	James Knox Polk (Democrat)	1,337,243	170
George M. Dallas	1845-1849		Henry Clay (Whig)	1,299,062	105
			James G. Birney (Liberty)	62,300	
Zachary Taylor	1849-1850	**1848**	Zachary Taylor (Whig)	1,360,099	163
Millard Fillmore	1849-1850		Lewis Cass (Democrat)	1,220,544	127
			Martin Van Buren (Free-Soil)	291,263	
Millard Fillmore	1850-1853		Succeeded to the presidency on the death of Zachary Taylor.		
Franklin Pierce	1853-1857	**1852**	Franklin Pierce (Democrat)	1,601,274	254
William R. King	1853		Winfield Scott (Whig)	1,386,580	42
			John P. Hale (Free-Soil)	155,825	
James Buchanan	1857-1861	**1856**	James Buchanan (Democrat)	1,838,169	174
John C. Breckinridge	1857-1861		John C. Frémont (Republican)	1,341,264	114
			Millard Fillmore (American)	874,534	8

President Vice President	Term	Election	Candidates	Popular Vote	Electoral Vote
Abraham Lincoln	1861-1865	**1860**	Abraham Lincoln (Republican)	1,866,452	180
Hannibal Hamlin	1861-1865		John C. Breckinridge (Democrat)	847,953	72
			John Bell (Constitutional Union)	590,631	39
			Stephen Douglas (Democrat)	1,375,157	12
Andrew Johnson	1865	**1864**	Abraham Lincoln (National Union)	2,213,635	212
			George B. McClellan (Democrat)	1,805,237	21
Andrew Johnson	1865-1869		Succeeded to the presidency on the assassination of Abraham Lincoln.		
Ulysses S. Grant	1869-1877	**1868**	Ulysses S. Grant (Republican)	3,012,833	214
Schuyler Colfax	1869-1873		Horatio Seymour (Democrat)	2,703,249	80
Henry Wilson	1873-1875	**1872**	Ulysses S. Grant (Republican)	3,597,132	286
			Horace Greeley (Democrat)	2,834,079	
Rutherford B. Hayes	1877-1881	**1876**	Rutherford B. Hayes (Republican)	4,036,298	185
William A. Wheeler	1877-1881		Samuel J. Tilden (Democrat)	4,300,590	184
James A. Garfield	1881	**1880**	James Garfield (Republican)	4,454,416	214
Chester A. Arthur	1881		Winfield S. Hancock (Democrat)	4,444,952	155
			James B. Weaver (Greenback)	308,578	
Chester A. Arthur	1881-1885		Succeeded to the presidency on the assassination of James Garfield.		
Grover Cleveland	1885-1889	**1884**	Grover Cleveland (Democrat)	4,874,986	219
Thomas A. Hendricks	1885		James G. Blaine (Republican)	4,851,981	182
			Benjamin F. Butler (Greenback)	175,370	
			John P. St. John (Prohibition)	150,369	
Benjamin Harrison	1889-1893	**1888**	Benjamin Harrison (Republican)	5,447,129	233
Levi P. Morton	1889-1893		Grover Cleveland (Democrat)	5,537,857	168
			Clinton B. Fisk (Prohibition)	249,506	
			Alson J. Streeter (Union Labor)	146,935	
Grover Cleveland	1893-1897	**1892**	Grover Cleveland (Democrat)	5,556,918	277
Adlai E. Stevenson	1893-1897		Benjamin Harrison (Republican)	5,176,108	145
			James B. Weaver (People's)	1,041,028	22
			John Bidwell (Prohibition)	264,138	

President / Vice President	Term	Election	Candidates	Popular Vote	Electoral Vote
William McKinley	1897-1901	**1896**	William McKinley (Republican)	7,104,779	271
Garret A. Hobart	1897-1899		William J. Bryan (Democrat)	6,502,925	176
Theodore Roosevelt	1901	**1900**	William McKinley (Republican)	7,207,923	292
			William J. Bryan (Democrat)	6,358,138	155
			John G. Woolley (Prohibition)	208,914	
Theodore Roosevelt	1901-1909		Succeeded to the presidency on the assassination of William McKinley.		
Charles W. Fairbanks	1905-1909	**1904**	Theodore Roosevelt (Republican)	7,623,486	336
			Alton B. Parker (Democrat)	5,077,911	140
			Eugene V. Debs (Socialist)	402,283	
			Silas C. Swallow (Prohibition)	258,536	
William H. Taft	1909-1913	**1908**	William H. Taft (Republican)	7,678,908	321
James S. Sherman	1909-1912		William J. Bryan (Democrat)	6,409,104	162
			Eugene V. Debs (Socialist)	420,793	
			Eugene W. Chafin (Prohibition)	253,840	
Woodrow Wilson	1913-1921	**1912**	Woodrow Wilson (Democrat)	6,293,454	435
Thomas R. Marshall	1913-1921		Theodore Roosevelt (Progressive)	4,119,538	88
			William H. Taft (Republican)	3,484,980	8
			Eugene V. Debs (Socialist)	900,672	
			Eugene W. Chafin (Prohibition)	206,275	
		1916	Woodrow Wilson (Democrat)	9,129,606	277
			Charles E. Hughes (Republican)	8,538,221	254
			A. L. Benson (Socialist)	585,113	
			J. Frank Hanly (Prohibition)	220,506	
Warren G. Harding	1921-1923	**1920**	Warren G. Harding (Republican)	16,152,200	404
Calvin Coolidge	1921-1923		James M. Cox (Democrat)	9,147,353	127
			Eugene V. Debs (Socialist)	919,799	
			P. P. Christenson (Farmer-Labor)	265,411	
Calvin Coolidge	1923-1929		Succeeded to the presidency on the death of Warren Harding.		
Charles G. Dawes	1925-1929	**1924**	Calvin Coolidge (Republican)	15,725,016	382
			John W. Davis (Democrat)	8,386,503	136
			Robert M. La Follette (Progressive)	4,822,856	13
Herbert C. Hoover	1929-1933	**1928**	Herbert C. Hoover (Republican)	21,392,190	444
Charles Curtis	1929-1933		Alfred E. Smith (Democrat)	15,016,443	87

President Vice President	Term	Election	Candidates	Popular Vote	Electoral Vote
Franklin D. Roosevelt	1933-1945	**1932**	Franklin D. Roosevelt (Democrat)	22,821,857	472
John N. Garner	1933-1941		Herbert C. Hoover (Republican)	15,761,845	59
			Norman M. Thomas (Socialist)	881,951	
		1936	Franklin D. Roosevelt (Democrat)	27,476,673	523
			Alfred M. Landon (Republican)	16,679,583	8
			William Lemke (Union)	892,793	
Henry A. Wallace	1941-1945	**1940**	Franklin D. Roosevelt (Democrat)	27,243,466	449
			Wendell L. Willkie (Republican)	22,304,755	82
Harry S. Truman	1945	**1944**	Franklin D. Roosevelt (Democrat)	25,602,505	432
			Thomas E. Dewey (Republican)	22,006,278	99
Harry S. Truman	1945-1953		Succeeded to the presidency on the death of Franklin D. Roosevelt.		
Alben W. Barkley	1949-1953	**1948**	Harry S. Truman (Democrat)	24,105,695	303
			Thomas E. Dewey (Republican)	21,969,170	189
			J. Strom Thurmond (States' Rights)	1,169,021	39
			Henry A. Wallace (Progressive)	1,156,103	
Dwight D. Eisenhower	1953-1961	**1952**	Dwight D. Eisenhower (Republican)	33,778,963	442
Richard M. Nixon	1953-1961		Adlai E. Stevenson (Democrat)	27,314,992	89
		1956	Dwight D. Eisenhower (Republican)	35,581,003	457
			Adlai E. Stevenson (Democrat)	25,738,765	73
John F. Kennedy	1961-1963	**1960**	John F. Kennedy (Democrat)	34,227,096	303
Lyndon B. Johnson	1961-1963		Richard M. Nixon (Republican)	34,107,646	219
Lyndon B. Johnson	1963-1969		Succeeded to the presidency on the assassination of John F. Kennedy.		
Hubert H. Humphrey	1965-1969	**1964**	Lyndon B. Johnson (Democrat)	42,825,463	486
			Barry M. Goldwater (Republican)	27,175,770	52

President Vice President	Term	Election	Candidates	Popular Vote	Electoral Vote
Richard M. Nixon Spiro T. Agnew	1969-1974 1969-1973	**1968**	Richard M. Nixon (Republican) Hubert H. Humphrey (Democrat) George C. Wallace (Amer. Ind.)	31,710,470 30,898,055 9,446,167	301 191 46
Spiro T. Agnew Gerald R. Ford	1973 1973-1974	**1972**	Richard M. Nixon (Republican) George S. McGovern (Democrat)	46,740,323 28,901,598	520 17
Gerald R. Ford Nelson A. Rockefeller	1974-1977 1974-1977		Succeeded to the presidency on the resignation of Richard M. Nixon.		
Jimmy Carter Walter F. Mondale	1977-1981 1977-1981	**1976**	Jimmy Carter (Democrat) Gerald R. Ford (Republican)	40,830,763 39,147,793	297 240
Ronald W. Reagan George H. W. Bush	1981-1989 1981-1989	**1980**	Ronald W. Reagan (Republican) Jimmy Carter (Democrat) John B. Anderson (Independent)	43,901,812 35,483,820 5,719,722	489 49
		1984	Ronald W. Reagan (Republican) Walter F. Mondale (Democrat)	54,451,521 37,565,334	525 13
George H. W. Bush J. Danforth Quayle	1989-1993 1989-1993	**1988**	George H. W. Bush (Republican) Michael S. Dukakis (Democrat)	48,881,278 41,805,374	426 111
William J. Clinton Albert Gore, Jr.	1993- 1993-	**1992**	William J. Clinton (Democrat) George H. W. Bush (Republican) H. Ross Perot (Independent)	44,908,254 39,102,343 19,741,065	370 168
		1996	William J. Clinton (Democrat) Robert Dole (Republican) H. Ross Perot (Reform)	47,401,185 39,197,469 8,085,294	379 159

Index

Red page numbers highlight the most detailed explanations of an entry.

Index

A COLLECTION OF IMPORTANT AMERICAN DOCUMENTS

TABLE OF CONTENTS

THE MAYFLOWER COMPACT

November 11, 1620

Cape Cod Harbor

The Mayflower Compact was written by the 102 men and women who traveled aboard the Mayflower in 1620. The document was written 65 days into their journey. Although 102 people helped to write the document, only 41 adult males signed it. Servants, women, and the ship's crew were not permitted to sign legal documents.

The passengers would finally land in Plymouth on December 26, 1620. Their original destination was Virginia, but they had traveled off course.

We whose names are underwritten, the loyal subjects of our dread Sovereign Lord King James, by the Grace of God of Great Britain, France and Ireland, King, Defender of the Faith, etc.

Having undertaken, for the Glory of God and advancement of the Christian Faith and Honour of our King and Country, a Voyage to plant the First Colony in the Northern Parts of Virginia, do by these presents solemnly and mutually in the presence of God and one of another, Covenant and Combine ourselves together into a Civil Body Politic, for our better ordering and preservation and furtherance of the ends aforesaid; and by virtue hereof to enact, constitute and frame such just and equal Laws, Ordinances, Acts, Constitutions and Offices, from time to time, as shall be thought most meet and convenient for the general good of the Colony, unto which we promise all due submission and obedience. In witness whereof we have hereunder subscribed our names at Cape Cod, the 11th of November, in the year of the reign of our Sovereign Lord King James, of England, France and Ireland the eighteenth, and of Scotland the fifty-fourth. Anno Domini 1620.

COMMON SENSE

Excerpts

January 10, 1776

Written by Thomas Paine

Paine argued for independence from Great Britain in his 50-page pamphlet Common Sense.

THOUGHTS ON THE PRESENT STATE OF AMERICAN AFFAIRS.

In the following pages I offer nothing more than simple facts, plain arguments, and common sense; and have no other preliminaries to settle with the reader, than that he will divest himself of prejudice and prepossession, and suffer his reason and his feelings to determine for themselves; that he will put on, or rather that he will not put off, the true character of a man, and generously enlarge his views beyond the present day.

Volumes have been written on the subject of the struggle between England and America. Men of all ranks have embarked in the controversy, from different motives, and with various designs; but all have been ineffectual, and the period of debate is closed. Arms, as the last resource, decide the contest; the appeal was the choice of the king, and the continent hath accepted the challenge. . . .

By referring the matter from argument to arms, a new æra for politics is struck; a new method of thinking hath arisen. All plans, proposals, &c. prior to the nineteenth of April, *i. e.* to the commencement of hostilities, are like the almanacks of the last year; which, though proper then, are superceded and useless now. Whatever was advanced by the advocates on either side of the question then, terminated in one and the same point, viz. a union with Great-Britain; the only difference between the parties was the method of effecting it; the one proposing force, the other friendship; but it hath so far happened that the first hath failed, and the second hath withdrawn her influence.

As much hath been said of the advantages of reconciliation, which, like an agreeable dream, hath passed away and left us as we were, it is but right, that we should examine the contrary side of the argument, and inquire into some of the many material injuries which these colonies sustain, and always will sustain, by being connected with, and dependant on Great-Britain. To examine that connexion and dependance, on the principles of nature and common sense, to see what we have to trust to, if separated, and what we are to expect, if dependant.

I have heard it asserted by some, that as America hath flourished under her former connexion with Great-Britain, that the same connexion is necessary towards her future happiness, and will always have the same effect. Nothing can be more fallacious than this kind of argument. We may as well assert that because a child has thrived upon milk, that it is never to have meat, or that the first twenty years of our lives is to become a precedent for the next twenty. But even this is admitting more than is true, for I answer roundly, that America would have flourished as much, and probably much more, had no European power had any thing to do with her. The commerce, by which she hath enriched herself are the necessaries of life, and will always have a market while eating is the custom of Europe.

But she has protected us, say some. That she hath engrossed us is true, and defended the continent at our expence as well as her own is admitted, and she would have defended Turkey from the same motive, viz. the sake of trade and dominion.

Alas, we have been long led away by ancient prejudices, and made large sacrifices to superstition. We have boasted the protection of Great-Britain, without considering, that her motive was *interest* not *attachment;* that she did not protect us from *our enemies* on *our account,* but from *her enemies* on *her own account,* from those who had no quarrel with us on any *other account,* and who will always be our enemies on the *same account.* Let Britain wave her pretensions to the continent, or the continent throw off the dependance, and we should be at peace with France and Spain were they at war with Britain. The miseries of Hanover last war ought to warn us against connexions.

It hath lately been asserted in parliament, that the colonies have no relation to each other but through the parent country, *i. e.* that Pennsylvania and the Jerseys, and so on for the rest, are sister colonies by the way of England; this is certainly a very round-about way of proving relationship, but it is the nearest and only true way of proving enemyship, if I may so call it. France and Spain never were, nor perhaps ever will be our enemies as *Americans,* but as our being the *subjects of Great-Britain.* . . .

Much hath been said of the united strength of Britain and the colonies, that in conjunction they might bid defiance to the world. But this is mere presumption; the fate of war is uncertain, neither do the expressions mean any thing; for this continent would never suffer itself to be drained of inhabitants, to support the British arms in either Asia, Africa, or Europe.

Besides, what have we to do with setting the world at defiance? Our plan is commerce, and that, well attended to, will secure us the peace and friendship of all Europe; because, it is the interest of all Europe to have America a *free port.* Her trade will always be a protection, and her barrenness of gold and silver secure her from invaders.

I challenge the warmest advocate for reconciliation, to shew, a single advantage that this continent can reap, by being connected with Great Britain. I repeat the challenge, not a single advantage is derived. Our corn will fetch its price in any market in Europe, and our imported goods must be paid for buy them where we will.

But the injuries and disadvantages we sustain by that connection, are without number; and our duty to mankind at large, as well as to ourselves, instruct us to renounce the alliance: Because, any submission to, or dependance on Great-Britain, tends directly to involve this continent in European wars and quarrels; and sets us at variance with nations, who would otherwise seek our friendship, and against whom, we have neither anger nor complaint. As Europe is our market for trade, we ought to form no partial connection with any part of it. It is the true interest of America to steer clear of European contentions, which she never can do, while by her dependance on Britain, she is made the make-weight in the scale on British politics.

Europe is too thickly planted with kingdoms to be long at peace, and whenever a war breaks out between England and any foreign power, the trade of America goes to ruin, *because of her connection with Britain.* The next war may not turn out like the last, and should it not, the advocates for reconciliation now will be wishing for separation then, because, neutrality in that case, would be a safer convoy than a man of war. Every thing that is right or natural pleads for separation. The blood of the slain, the weeping voice of nature cries, 'TIS TIME TO PART. Even the distance at which the Almighty hath placed England and America, is a strong and natural proof, that the authority of the one, over the other, was never the design of Heaven. The time likewise at which the continent was discovered, adds weight to the argument, and the manner in which it was peopled encreases the force of it. The reformation was preceded by the discovery of America, as if the Almighty graciously meant to open a sanctuary to the persecuted in future years, when home should afford neither friendship nor safety.

"REMEMBER THE LADIES"

March 31, 1776

A letter by Abigail Adams to her husband, John Adams

Abigail Adams was writing from their home in Braintree, Massachusetts.

I long to hear that you have declared an independancy—and by the way in the new Code of Laws which I suppose it will be necessary for you to make I desire you would Remember the Ladies, and be more generous and favourable to them than your ancestors. Do not put such unlimited power into the hands of the Husbands. Remember all Men would be tyrants if they could. If perticuliar care and attention is not paid to the Ladies we are determined to foment a Rebelion, and will not hold ourselves bound by any Laws in which we have no voice, or Representation.

That your Sex are Naturally Tyrannical is a Truth so thoroughly established as to admit of no dispute, but such of you as wish to be happy willingly give up the harsh title of Master for the more tender and endearing one of Friend. Why then, not put it out of the power of the vicious and the Lawless to use us with cruelty and indignity with impunity. Men of Sense in all Ages abhor those customs which treat us only as the vassals of your Sex. Regard us then as Beings placed by providence under your protection and in immitation of the Supreem Being make use of that power only for our happiness.

THE DECLARATION OF INDEPENDENCE

July 4, 1776

Philadelphia, Pennsylvania

Written by Thomas Jefferson

Approved by the Second Continental Congress

THE UNANIMOUS DECLARATION OF THE THIRTEEN UNITED STATES OF AMERICA

When in the Course of human events, it becomes necessary for one people to dissolve the political bands which have connected them with another, and to assume among the powers of the earth, the separate and equal station to which the Laws of Nature and of Nature's God entitle them, a decent respect to the opinions of mankind requires that they should declare the causes which impel them to the separation.

We hold these truths to be self-evident, that all men are created equal, that they are endowed by their Creator with certain unalienable Rights, that among these are Life, Liberty and the pursuit of Happiness.—That to secure these rights, Governments are instituted among Men, deriving their just powers from the consent of the governed, —That whenever any Form of Government becomes destructive of these ends, it is the Right of the People to alter or to abolish it, and to institute new Government, laying its foundation on such principles and organizing its powers in such form, as to them shall seem most likely to effect their Safety and Happiness. Prudence, indeed, will dictate that Governments long established should not be changed for light and transient causes; and accordingly all experience hath shewn, that mankind are more disposed to suffer, while evils are sufferable, than to right themselves by abolishing the forms to which they are accustomed. But when a long train of abuses and usurpations, pursuing invariably the same Object evinces a design to reduce them under absolute Despotism, it is their right, it is their duty, to throw off such Government, and to provide new Guards for their future security.—Such has been the patient sufferance of these Colonies; and such is now the necessity which constrains them to alter their former Systems of Government. The history of the present King of Great Britain is a history of repeated injuries and usurpations, all having in direct object the establishment of an absolute Tyranny over these States. To prove this, let Facts be submitted to a candid world.

He has refused his Assent to Laws, the most wholesome and necessary for the public good.

He has forbidden his Governors to pass Laws of immediate and pressing importance, unless suspended in their operation till his Assent should be obtained; and when so suspended, he has utterly neglected to attend to them.

He has refused to pass other Laws for the accommodation of large districts of people, unless those people would relinquish the right of Representation in the Legislature, a right inestimable to them and formidable to tyrants only.

He has called together legislative bodies at places unusual, uncomfortable, and distant from the depository of their public Records, for the sole purpose of fatiguing them into compliance with his measures.

He has dissolved Representative Houses repeatedly, for opposing with manly firmness his invasions on the rights of the people.

He has refused for a long time, after such dissolutions, to cause others to be elected; whereby the Legislative powers, incapable of Annihilation, have returned to the People at large for their exercise; the State remaining in the mean time exposed to all the dangers of invasion from without, and convulsions within.

He has endeavoured to prevent the population of these States; for that purpose obstructing the Laws for Naturalization of Foreigners; refusing to pass others to encourage their migrations hither, and raising the conditions of new Appropriations of Lands.

He has obstructed the Administration of Justice, by refusing his Assent to Laws for establishing Judiciary powers.

He has made Judges dependent on his Will alone, for the tenure of their offices, and the amount and payment of their salaries.

He has erected a multitude of New Offices, and sent hither swarms of Officers to harrass our people, and eat out their substance.

He has kept among us, in times of peace, Standing Armies without the Consent of our legislatures.

He has affected to render the Military independent of and superior to the Civil power.

He has combined with others to subject us to a jurisdiction foreign to our constitution, and unacknowledged by our laws; giving his Assent to their Acts of pretended Legislation:

For Quartering large bodies of armed troops among us:

For protecting them, by a mock Trial, from punishment for any Murders which they should commit on the Inhabitants of these States:

For cutting off our Trade with all parts of the world:

For imposing Taxes on us without our Consent:

For depriving us in many cases, of the benefits of Trial by Jury:

For transporting us beyond Seas to be tried for pretended offences:

For abolishing the free System of English Laws in a neighbouring Province, establishing therein an Arbitrary government, and enlarging its Boundaries so as to render it at once an example and fit instrument for introducing the same absolute rule into these Colonies:

For taking away our Charters, abolishing our most valuable Laws, and altering fundamentally the Forms of our Governments:

For suspending our own Legislatures, and declaring themselves invested with power to legislate for us in all cases whatsoever.

He has abdicated Government here, by declaring us out of his Protection and waging War against us.

He has plundered our seas, ravaged our Coasts, burnt our towns, and destroyed the lives of our people.

He is at this time transporting large Armies of foreign Mercenaries to compleat the works of death, desolation and tyranny, already begun with circumstances of Cruelty & perfidy scarcely paralleled in the most barbarous ages, and totally unworthy the Head of a civilized nation.

He has constrained our fellow Citizens taken Captive on the high Seas to bear Arms against their Country, to become the executioners of their friends and Brethren, or to fall themselves by their Hands.

He has excited domestic insurrections amongst us, and has endeavoured to bring on the inhabitants of our frontiers, the merciless Indian Savages, whose known rule of warfare, is an undistinguished destruction of all ages, sexes and conditions.

In every stage of these Oppressions We have Petitioned for Redress in the most humble terms: Our repeated Petitions have been answered only by repeated injury. A Prince whose character is thus marked by every act which may define a Tyrant, is unfit to be the ruler of a free people.

Nor have We been wanting in attentions to our British brethren. We have warned them from time to time of attempts by their legislature to extend an unwarrantable jurisdiction over us. We have reminded them of the circumstances of our emigration and settlement here. We have appealed to their native justice and magnanimity, and we have conjured them by the ties of our common kindred to disavow these usurpations, which, would inevitably interrupt our connections and correspondence. They too have been deaf to the voice of justice and of consanguinity. We must, therefore, acquiesce in the necessity, which denounces our Separation, and hold them, as we hold the rest of mankind, Enemies in War, in Peace Friends.

We, therefore, the Representatives of the united States of America, in General Congress, Assembled, appealing to the Supreme Judge of the world for the rectitude of our intentions, do, in the Name, and by Authority of the good People of these Colonies, solemnly publish and declare, That these United Colonies are, and of Right ought to be Free and Independent States; that they are Absolved from all Allegiance to the British Crown, and that all political connection between them and the State of Great Britain, is and ought to be totally dissolved; and that as Free and Independent States, they have full Power to levy War, conclude Peace, contract Alliances, establish Commerce, and to do all other Acts and Things which Independent States may of right do. And for the support of this Declaration, with a firm reliance on the protection of divine Providence, we mutually pledge to each other our Lives, our Fortunes and our sacred Honor.

PREAMBLE TO
THE CONSTITUTION OF THE UNITED STATES OF AMERICA

September 17, 1787

Written at the Constitutional Convention in the State House in Philadelphia, Pennsylvania

We the people of the United States, in order to form a more perfect union, establish justice, insure domestic tranquility, provide for the common defense, promote the general welfare, and secure the blessings of liberty to ourselves and our posterity, do ordain and establish this Constitution for the United States of America.

We the People

Article. 1

First page of the Constitution of the United States of America. Source: Library of Congress

THE BILL OF RIGHTS

September 25, 1789

Written by James Madison, passed by Congress, and ratified by the states

THE PREAMBLE TO THE BILL OF RIGHTS

Congress of the United States
begun and held at the City of New-York, on
Wednesday the fourth of March, one thousand seven hundred and eighty nine.

The Conventions of a number of the States, having at the time of their adopting the Constitution, expressed a desire, in order to prevent misconstruction or abuse of its powers, that further declaratory and restrictive clauses should be added: And as extending the ground of public confidence in the Government, will best ensure the beneficent ends of its institution.

Resolved by the Senate and House of Representatives of the United States of America, in Congress assembled, two thirds of both Houses concurring, that the following Articles be proposed to the Legislatures of the several States as amendments to the Constitution of the United States, all, or any of which articles, when ratified by three fourths of the said Legislatures, to be valid to all intents and purposes, as part of the said Constitution; viz.

Articles in addition to, and Amendment of the Constitution of the United States of America, proposed by Congress and ratified by the Legislatures of the several States, pursuant to the fifth Article of the original Constitution.

AMENDMENT I

Congress shall make no law respecting an establishment of religion, or prohibiting the free exercise thereof; or abridging the freedom of speech, or of the press; or the right of the people peaceably to assemble, and to petition the Government for a redress of grievances.

AMENDMENT II

A well regulated Militia, being necessary to the security of a free State, the right of the people to keep and bear Arms, shall not be infringed.

AMENDMENT III

No Soldier shall, in time of peace be quartered in any house, without the consent of the Owner, nor in time of war, but in a manner to be prescribed by law.

AMENDMENT IV

The right of the people to be secure in their persons, houses, papers, and effects, against unreasonable searches and seizures, shall not be violated, and no Warrants shall issue, but upon probable cause, supported by Oath or affirmation, and particularly describing the place to be searched, and the persons or things to be seized.

AMENDMENT V

No person shall be held to answer for a capital, or otherwise infamous crime, unless on a presentment or indictment of a Grand Jury, except in cases arising in the land or naval forces, or in the Militia, when in actual service in time of War or public danger; nor shall any person be subject for the same offence to be twice put in jeopardy of life or limb; nor shall be compelled in any criminal case to be a witness against himself, nor be deprived of life, liberty, or property, without due process of law; nor shall private property be taken for public use, without just compensation.

AMENDMENT VI

In all criminal prosecutions, the accused shall enjoy the right to a speedy and public trial, by an impartial jury of the State and district wherein the crime shall have been committed, which district shall have been previously ascertained by law, and to be informed of the nature and cause of the accusation; to be confronted with the witnesses against him; to have compulsory process for obtaining witnesses in his favor, and to have the Assistance of Counsel for his defence.

AMENDMENT VII

In suits at common law, where the value in controversy shall exceed twenty dollars, the right of trial by jury shall be preserved, and no fact tried by a jury, shall be otherwise reexamined in any Court of the United States, than according to the rules of the common law.

AMENDMENT VIII

Excessive bail shall not be required, nor excessive fines imposed, nor cruel and unusual punishments inflicted.

AMENDMENT IX

The enumeration in the Constitution, of certain rights, shall not be construed to deny or disparage others retained by the people.

AMENDMENT X

The powers not delegated to the United States by the Constitution, nor prohibited by it to the States, are reserved to the States respectively, or to the people.

THE MONROE DOCTRINE

December 2, 1823

The Monroe Doctrine was outlined in a speech made by James Monroe to Congress.

At the proposal of the Russian Imperial Government, made through the minister of the Emperor residing here, a full power and instructions have been transmitted to the minister of the United States at St. Petersburg to arrange by amicable negotiation the respective rights and interests of the two nations on the northwest coast of this continent. A similar proposal has been made by His Imperial Majesty to the Government of Great Britain, which has likewise been acceded to. The Government of the United States has been desirous by this friendly proceeding of manifesting the great value which they have invariably attached to the friendship of the Emperor and their solicitude to cultivate the best understanding with his Government. In the discussions to which this interest has given rise and in the arrangements by which they may terminate the occasion has been judged proper for asserting, as a principle in which the rights and interests of the United States are involved, that the American continents, by the free and independent condition which they have assumed and maintain, are henceforth not to be considered as subjects for future colonization by any European powers. . . .

It was stated at the commencement of the last session that a great effort was then making in Spain and Portugal to improve the condition of the people of those countries, and that it appeared to be conducted with extraordinary moderation. It need scarcely be remarked that the results have been so far very different from what was then anticipated. Of events in that quarter of the globe, with which we have so much intercourse and from which we derive our origin, we have always been anxious and interested spectators. The citizens of the United States cherish sentiments the most friendly in favor of the liberty and happiness of their fellow-men on that side of the Atlantic. In the wars of the European powers in matters relating to themselves we have never taken any part, nor does it comport with our policy to do so. It is only when our rights are invaded or seriously menaced that we resent injuries or make preparation for our defense. With the movements in this hemisphere we are of necessity more immediately connected, and by causes which must be obvious to all enlightened and impartial observers. The political system of the allied powers is essentially different in this respect from that of America. This difference proceeds from that which exists in their respective Governments; and to the defense of our own, which has been achieved by the loss of so much blood and treasure, and matured by the wisdom of their most enlightened citizens, and under which we have enjoyed unexampled felicity, this whole nation is devoted. We owe it, therefore, to candor and to the amicable relations existing between the United States and those powers to declare that we should consider any attempt on their part to extend their system to any portion of this hemisphere as dangerous to our peace and safety. With the existing colonies or dependencies of any European power we have not interfered and shall not interfere. But with the Governments who have declared their independence and maintain it, and whose independence we have, on great consideration and on just principles, acknowledged, we could not view any interposition for the purpose of oppressing them, or controlling in any other manner their destiny, by any European power in any other light than as the manifestation of an unfriendly disposition toward the United States. In the war between those new Governments and Spain we declared our neutrality at the time of their recognition, and to this we have adhered, and shall continue to adhere, provided no change shall occur which, in the judgement of the competent authorities of this Government, shall make a corresponding change on the part of the United States indispensable to their security.

The late events in Spain and Portugal shew that Europe is still unsettled. Of this important fact no stronger proof can be adduced than that the allied powers should have thought it proper, on any principle satisfactory to themselves, to have interposed by force in the internal concerns of Spain. To what extent such interposition may be carried, on the same principle, is a question in which all independent powers whose governments differ from theirs are interested, even those most remote, and surely none of them more so than the United States. Our policy in regard to Europe, which was adopted at an early stage of the wars which have so long agitated that quarter of the globe, nevertheless remains the same, which is, not to interfere in the internal concerns of any of its powers; to consider the government de facto as the legitimate government for us; to cultivate friendly relations with it, and to preserve those relations by a frank, firm, and manly policy, meeting in all instances the just claims of every power, submitting to injuries from none. But in regard to those continents circumstances are eminently and conspicuously different. It is impossible that the allied powers should extend their political system to any portion of either continent without endangering our peace and happiness; nor can anyone believe that our southern brethren, if left to themselves, would adopt it of their own accord. It is equally impossible, therefore, that we should behold such interposition in any form with indifference. If we look to the comparative strength and resources of Spain and those new Governments, and their distance from each other, it must be obvious that she can never subdue them. It is still the true policy of the United States to leave the parties to themselves, in hope that other powers will pursue the same course. . . .

THE EMANCIPATION PROCLAMATION

September 22, 1862

Issued by Abraham Lincoln

Whereas on the 22nd day of September, A.D. 1862, a proclamation was issued by the President of the United States, containing, among other things, the following, to wit:

"That on the 1st day of January, A.D. 1863, all persons held as slaves within any State or designated part of a State the people whereof shall then be in rebellion against the United States shall be then, thenceforward, and forever free; and the executive government of the United States, including the military and naval authority thereof, will recognize and maintain the freedom of such persons and will do no act or acts to repress such persons, or any of them, in any efforts they may make for their actual freedom.

"That the executive will on the 1st day of January aforesaid, by proclamation, designate the States and parts of States, if any, in which the people thereof, respectively, shall then be in rebellion against the United States; and the fact that any State or the people thereof shall on that day be in good faith represented in the Congress of the United States by members chosen thereto at elections wherein a majority of the qualified voters of such States shall have participated shall, in the absence of strong countervailing testimony, be deemed conclusive evidence that such State and the people thereof are not then in rebellion against the United States."

Now, therefore, I, Abraham Lincoln, President of the United States, by virtue of the power in me vested as Commander-In-Chief of the Army and Navy of the United States in time of actual armed rebellion against the authority and government of the United States, and as a fit and necessary war measure for supressing said rebellion, do, on this 1st day of January, A.D. 1863, and in accordance with my purpose so to do, publicly proclaimed for the full period of one hundred days from the first day above mentioned, order and designate as the States and parts of States wherein the people thereof, respectively, are this day in rebellion against the United States the following, to wit:

Arkansas, Texas, Louisiana (except the parishes of St. Bernard, Palquemines, Jefferson, St. John, St. Charles, St. James, Ascension, Assumption, Terrebone, Lafourche, St. Mary, St. Martin, and Orleans, including the city of New Orleans), Mississippi, Alabama, Florida, Georgia, South Carolina, North Carolina, and Virginia (except the forty-eight counties designated as West Virginia, and also the counties of Berkeley, Accomac, Northhampton, Elizabeth City, York,

Princess Anne, and Norfolk, including the cities of Norfolk and Portsmouth), and which excepted parts are for the present left precisely as if this proclamation were not issued.

And by virtue of the power and for the purpose aforesaid, I do order and declare that all persons held as slaves within said designated States and parts of States are, and henceforward shall be, free; and that the Executive Government of the United States, including the military and naval authorities thereof, will recognize and maintain the freedom of said persons.

And I hereby enjoin upon the people so declared to be free to abstain from all violence, unless in necessary self-defence; and I recommend to them that, in all case when allowed, they labor faithfully for reasonable wages.

And I further declare and make known that such persons of suitable condition will be received into the armed service of the United States to garrison forts, positions, stations, and other places, and to man vessels of all sorts in said service.

And upon this act, sincerely believed to be an act of justice, warranted by the Constitution upon military necessity, I invoke the considerate judgment of mankind and the gracious favor of Almighty God.

THE GETTYSBURG ADDRESS

November 19, 1863

Abraham Lincoln's speech at the dedication of a national cemetery in Gettysburg, Pennsylvania

Four-score and seven years ago, our fathers brought forth on this continent a new nation, conceived in liberty and dedicated to the proposition that all men are created equal. Now we are engaged in a great civil war, testing whether that nation or any nation so conceived and so dedicated can long endure. We are met on a great battle field of that war. We have come to dedicate a portion of that field, as a final resting place for those who here gave their lives that this nation might live. It is altogether fitting and proper that we should do this. But, in a larger sense, we can not dedicate—we can not consecrate—we can not hallow—this ground. The brave men, living and dead, who struggled here, have consecrated it, far above our poor power to add or detract. The world will little note, nor long remember, what we say here, but it can never forget what they did here. It is for us the living, rather, to be here dedicated to the unfinished work which they who fought here have thus far so nobly advanced. It is rather for us to be here dedicated to the great task remaining before us—that from these honored dead we take increased devotion to that cause for which they gave the last full measure of devotion —that we here highly resolve that these dead shall not have died in vain—that this nation, under God, shall have a new birth of freedom—and that government of the people, by the people, for the people, shall not perish from the earth.

"ARE WOMEN PERSONS?"

Excerpts

1872

Susan B. Anthony wrote this lecture in response to her arrest in November 1872 in Rochester, New York. She was charged with voting in a Presidential election.

Friends and Fellow-citizens: I stand before you to-night, under indictment for the alleged crime of having voted at the last Presidential election, without having a lawful right to vote. It shall be my work this evening to prove to you that in thus voting, I not only committed no crime, but, instead, simply exercised my citizen's right, guaranteed to me and all United States citizens by the National Constitution, beyond the power of any State to deny.

Our democratic-republican government is based on the idea of the natural right of every individual member thereof to a voice and a vote in making and executing the laws. We assert the province of government to be to secure the people in the enjoyment of their unalienable rights. We throw to the winds the old dogma that governments can give rights. Before governments were organized, no one denies that each individual possessed the right to protect his own life, liberty and property. And when 100 or 1,000,000 people enter into a free government, they do not barter away their natural rights; they simply pledge themselves to protect each other in the enjoyment of them, through prescribed judicial and legislative tribunals. They agree to abandon the methods of brute force in the adjustment of their differences, and adopt those of civilization.

Nor can you find a word in any of the grand documents left us by the fathers that assumes for government the power to create or to confer rights. The Declaration of Independence, the United States Constitution, the constitutions of the several states and the organic laws of the territories, all alike propose to protect the people in the exercise of their God-given rights. Not one of them pretends to bestow rights.

"All men are created equal, and endowed by their Creator with certain unalienable rights. Among these are life, liberty and the pursuit of happiness. That to secure these, governments are instituted among men, deriving their just powers from the consent of the governed."

Here is no shadow of government authority over rights, nor exclusion of any from their full and equal enjoyment. Here is pronounced the right of all men, and "consequently," as the Quaker preacher said, "of all women," to a voice in the government. And here, in this very first paragraph of the declaration, is the assertion of the natural right of all to the ballot; for, how can "the consent of the governed" be given, if the right to vote be denied. Again:

"That whenever any form of government becomes destructive of these ends, it is the right of the people to alter or abolish it, and to institute a new government, laying its foundations on such principles, and organizing its powers in such forms as to them shall seem most likely to effect their safety and happiness."

Surely, the right of the whole people to vote is here clearly implied. For however destructive in their happiness this government might become, a disfranchised class could neither alter nor abolish it, nor institute a new one, except by the old brute force method of insurrection and rebellion. One-half of the people of this nation to-day are utterly powerless to blot from the statute books an unjust law, or to write there a new and a just one. The women, dissatisfied as they are with this form of government, that enforces taxation without representation,—that compels them to obey laws to which they have never given their consent,—that imprisons and hangs them without a trial by a jury of their peers, that robs them, in marriage, of the custody of their own persons, wages and children,—are this half of the people left wholly at the mercy of the other half, in direct violation of the spirit and letter of the declarations of the framers of this government, every one of which was based on the immutable principle of equal rights to all. By those declarations, kings, priests, popes, aristocrats, were all alike dethroned, and placed on a common level politically, with the lowliest born subject or serf. By them, too, me, as such, were deprived of their divine right to rule, and placed on a political level with women. By the practice of those declarations all class and caste distinction will be abolished; and slave, serf, plebeian, wife, woman, all alike, bound from their subject position to the proud platform of equality.

The preamble of the federal constitution says:

"We, the people of the United States, in order to form a more perfect union, establish justice, insure domestic tranquility, provide for the common defense, promote the general welfare and secure the blessings of liberty to ourselves and our posterity, do ordain and establish this constitution for the United States of America."

It was we, the people, not we, the white male citizens, nor yet we, the male citizens; but we, the whole people, who formed this Union. And we formed it, not to give the blessings or liberty, but to secure them; not to the half of ourselves and the half of our posterity, but to the whole people—women as well as men. And it is downright mockery to talk to women of their enjoyment of the blessings of liberty while they are denied the use of the only means of securing them provided by this democratic-republican government—the ballot. . . .

But, whatever there was for a doubt, under the old regime, the adoption of the fourteenth amendment settled that question forever, in its first sentence: "All persons born or naturalized in the United States and subject to the jurisdiction thereof, are citizens of the United States and of the state wherein they reside."

And the second settles the equal status of all persons—all citizens:

"No states shall make or enforce any law which shall abridge the privileges or immunities of citizens; nor shall any state deprive any person of life, liberty or property, without due process of law, nor deny to any person within its jurisdiction the equal protection of the laws."

The only question left to be settled, now, is: Are women persons? And I hardly believe any of our opponents will have the hardihood to say they are not. Being persons, then, women are citizens, and no state has a right to make any new law, or to enforce any old law, that shall abridge their privileges or immunities. Hence, every discrimination against women in the constitutions and laws of the several states, is to-day null and void, precisely as is every one against negroes.

Is the right to vote one of the privileges or immunities of citizens? I think the disfranchised ex-rebels, and the ex-state prisoners will agree with me, that it is not only one of them, but the one without which all the others are nothing. Seek the first kingdom of the ballot, and all things else shall be given thee, is the political injunction.

Webster, Worcester and Bouvier all define citizen to be a person, in the United States, entitled to vote and hold office. . . .

And it is upon this just interpretation of the United States Constitution that our National Woman Suffrage Association which celebrates the twenty-fifth anniversary of the woman's rights movement in New York on the 6th of May next, has based all its arguments and action the past five years.

We no longer petition Legislature or Congress to give us the right to vote. We appeal to the women everywhere to exercise their too long neglected "citizen's right to vote." We appeal to the inspectors of elections everywhere to receive the votes of all United States citizens as it is their duty to do. We appeal to United States commissioners and marshals to arrest the inspectors who reject the names and votes of United States citizens, as it is their duty to do, and leave those alone who, like our eighth ward inspectors, perform their duties faithfully and well.

We ask the juries to fail to return verdicts of "guilty" against honest, law-abiding, tax-paying United States citizens for offering their votes at our elections. Or against intelligent, worthy young men, inspectors of elections, for receiving and counting such citizens' votes.

We ask the judges to render true and unprejudiced opinions of the law, and wherever there is room for a doubt to give its benefit on the side of liberty and equal rights to women, remembering that "the true rule of interpretation under our national constitution, especially since its amendments, is that anything for human rights is constitutional, everything against human right unconstitutional."

And it is on this line that we propose to fight our battle for the ballot—all peaceably, but nevertheless persistently through to complete triumph, when all United States citizens shall be recognized as equals before the law.

"I WILL FIGHT NO MORE FOREVER"

October 5, 1877

A speech made by Chief Joseph

Bear Paw Mountains, Montana

With this speech, the Nez Percé leader surrendered to United States General Nelson A. Miles.

Tell General Howard I know his Heart. What He told me before I have in my heart. I am tired of fighting, Looking Glass is dead. Too-hul-hul-sote is dead. The old men are all dead. It is the young men who say yes or no. He who led on the young men is dead. It is cold and we have no blankets. The little children are freezing to death. My people, some of them have run away to the hills, and have no blankets, no food; no one knows where they are—perhaps freezing to death. I want to have time to look for my children and see how many of them I can find. Maybe I shall find them among the dead. Hear me, my chiefs. I am tired; my heart is sick and sad. From where the sun now stands I will fight no more forever.

Chief Joseph. Source: Oregon Historical Society

"I HAVE A DREAM"

August 28, 1963

A speech made by civil rights leader, Dr. Martin Luther King, Jr.

Lincoln Memorial in Washington, D.C.

Five score years ago, a great American, in whose symbolic shadow we stand signed the Emancipation Proclamation. This momentous decree came as a great beacon light of hope to millions of Negro slaves who had been seared in the flames of withering injustice. It came as a joyous daybreak to end the long night of captivity.

But one hundred years later, we must face the tragic fact that the Negro is still not free. One hundred years later, the life of the Negro is still sadly crippled by the manacles of segregation and the chains of discrimination. One hundred years later, the Negro lives on a lonely island of poverty in the midst of a vast ocean of material prosperity. One hundred years later, the Negro is still languishing in the corners of American society and finds himself an exile in his own land. So we have come here today to dramatize an appalling condition.

In a sense we have come to our nation's capital to cash a check. When the architects of our republic wrote the magnificent words of the Constitution and the Declaration of Independence, they were signing a promissory note to which every American was to fall heir. This note was a promise that all men would be guaranteed the inalienable rights of life, liberty, and the pursuit of happiness.

It is obvious today that America has defaulted on this promissory note insofar as her citizens of color are concerned. Instead of honoring this sacred obligation, America has given the Negro people a bad check which has come back marked "insufficient funds." But we refuse to believe that the bank of justice is bankrupt. We refuse to believe that there are insufficient funds in the great vaults of opportunity of this nation. So we have come to cash this check—a check that will give us upon demand the riches of freedom and the security of justice. We have also come to this hallowed spot to remind America of the fierce urgency of now. This is no time to engage in the luxury of cooling off or to take the tranquilizing drug of gradualism. Now is the time to rise from the dark and desolate valley of segregation to the sunlit path of racial justice. Now is the time to open the doors of opportunity to all of God's children. Now is the time to lift our nation from the quicksands of racial injustice to the solid rock of brotherhood.

It would be fatal for the nation to overlook the urgency of the moment and to underestimate the determination of the Negro. This sweltering summer of the Negro's legitimate discontent will not pass until there is an invigorating autumn of freedom and equality. Nineteen sixty-three is not an end, but a beginning. Those who hope that the Negro needed to blow off steam and will now be content will have a rude awakening if the nation returns to business as usual. There will be neither rest nor tranquility in America until the Negro is granted his citizenship rights. The whirlwinds of revolt will continue to shake the foundations of our nation until the bright day of justice emerges.

But there is something that I must say to my people who stand on the warm threshold which leads into the palace of justice. In the process of gaining our rightful place we must not be guilty of wrongful deeds. Let us not seek to satisfy our thirst for freedom by drinking from the cup of bitterness and hatred.

We must forever conduct our struggle on the high plane of dignity and discipline. We must not allow our creative protest to degenerate into physical violence. Again and again we must rise to the majestic heights of meeting physical force with soul force. The marvelous new militancy which has engulfed the Negro community must not lead us to distrust of all white people, for many of our white brothers, as evidenced by their presence here today, have come to realize that their destiny is tied up with our destiny and their freedom is inextricably bound to our freedom. We cannot walk alone.

And as we walk, we must make the pledge that we shall march ahead. We cannot turn back. There are those who are asking the devotees of civil rights, "When will you be satisfied?" We can never be satisfied as long as our bodies, heavy with the fatigue of travel, cannot gain lodging in the motels of the highways and the hotels of the cities. We cannot be satisfied as long as the Negro's basic mobility is from a smaller ghetto to a larger one. We can never be satisfied as long as a Negro in Mississippi cannot vote and a Negro in New York believes he has nothing for which to vote. No, no, we are not satisfied, and we will not be satisfied until justice rolls down like waters and righteousness like a mighty stream.

I am not unmindful that some of you have come here out of great trials and tribulations. Some of you have come fresh from narrow cells. Some of you have come from areas where your quest for freedom left you battered by the storms of persecution and staggered by the winds of police brutality. You have been the veterans of creative suffering. Continue to work with the faith that unearned suffering is redemptive.

Go back to Mississippi, go back to Alabama, go back to Georgia, go back to Louisiana, go back to the slums and ghettos of our northern cities, knowing that somehow this situation can and will be changed. Let us not wallow in the valley of despair.

I say to you today, my friends, that in spite of the difficulties and frustrations of the moment, I still have a dream. It is a dream deeply rooted in the American dream.

I have a dream that one day this nation will rise up and live out the true meaning of its creed: "We hold these truths to be self-evident: that all men are created equal."

I have a dream that one day on the red hills of Georgia the sons of former slaves and the sons of former slaveowners will be able to sit down together at a table of brotherhood.

I have a dream that one day even the state of Mississippi, a desert state, sweltering with the heat of injustice and oppression, will be transformed into an oasis of freedom and justice.

I have a dream that my four children will one day live in a nation where they will not be judged by the color of their skin but by the content of their character.

I have a dream today.

I have a dream that one day the state of Alabama, whose governor's lips are presently dripping with the words of interposition and nullification, will be transformed into a situation where little black boys and black girls will be able to join hands with little white boys and white girls and walk together as sisters and brothers.

I have a dream today.

I have a dream that one day every valley shall be exalted, every hill and mountain shall be made low, the rough places will be made plain, and the crooked places will be made straight, and the glory of the Lord shall be revealed, and all flesh shall see it together.

This is our hope. This is the faith with which I return to the South. With this faith we will be able to hew out of the mountain of despair a stone of hope. With this faith we will be able to transform the jangling discords of our nation into a beautiful symphony of brotherhood. With this faith we will be able to work together, to pray together, to struggle together, to go to jail together, to stand up for freedom together, knowing that we will be free one day.

This will be the day when all of God's children will be able to sing with a new meaning, "My country, 'tis of thee, sweet land of liberty, of thee I sing. Land where my fathers died, land of the pilgrim's pride, from every mountainside, let freedom ring."

And if America is to be a great nation this must become true. So let freedom ring from the prodigious hilltops of New Hampshire. Let freedom ring from the mighty mountains of New York. Let freedom ring from the heightening Alleghenies of Pennsylvania!

Let freedom ring from the snowcapped Rockies of Colorado!

Let freedom ring from the curvaceous peaks of California!

But not only that; let freedom ring from Stone Mountain of Georgia!

Let freedom ring from Lookout Mountain of Tennessee!

Let freedom ring from every hill and every molehill of Mississippi. From every mountainside, let freedom ring.

When we let freedom ring, when we let it ring from every village and every hamlet, from every state and every city, we will be able to speed up that day when all of God's children, black men and white men, Jews and Gentiles, Protestants and Catholics, will be able to join hands and sing in the words of the old Negro spiritual, "Free at last! free at last! thank God Almighty, we are free at last!"

CIVIL RIGHTS ACT OF 1964

Excerpts

July 2, 1964

Document Number: PL 88-352

88th Congress, H.R. 7152

AN ACT

To enforce the constitutional right to vote, to confer jurisdiction upon the district courts of the United States to provide injunctive relief against discrimination in public accommodations, to authorize the Attorney General to institute suits to protect constitutional rights in public facilities and public education, to extend the Commission on Civil Rights, to prevent discrimination in federally assisted programs, to establish a Commission on Equal Employment Opportunity, and for other purposes.

Be it enacted by the Senate and House of Representatives of the United States of America in Congress assembled, That this Act may be cited as the "Civil Rights Act of 1964".

TITLE I—VOTING RIGHTS

SEC. 101. Section 2004 of the Revised Statutes (42 U.S.C. 1971), as amended by section 131 of the Civil Rights Act of 1957 (71 Stat. 637), and as further amended by section 601 of the Civil Rights Act of 1960 (74 Stat. 90), is further amended as follows:

(a) Insert "1" after "(a)" in subsection (a) and add at the end of subsection (a) the following new paragraphs:

"(2) No person acting under color of law shall—

"(A) in determining whether any individual is qualified under State law or laws to vote in any Federal election, apply any standard, practice, or procedure different from the standards, practices, or procedures applied under such law or laws to other individuals within the same county, parish, or similar political subdivision who have been found by State officials to be qualified to vote;

"(B) deny the right of any individual to vote in any Federal election because of an error or omission on any record or paper relating to any application, registration, or other act requisite to voting, if such error or omission is not material in determining whether such individual is qualified under State law to vote in such election; or

"(C) employ any literacy test as a qualification for voting in any Federal election unless (i) such test is administered to each individual and is conducted wholly in writing, and (ii) a certified copy of the test and of the answers given by the individual is furnished to him within twenty-five days of the submission of his request made within the period of time during which records and papers are required to be retained and preserved pursuant to title III of the Civil Rights Act of 1960. . . .

TITLE II—INJUNCTIVE RELIEF AGAINST DISCRIMINATION IN PLACES OF PUBLIC ACCOMMODATION

SEC. 201. (a) All persons shall be entitled to the full and equal enjoyment of the goods, services, facilities, and privileges, advantages, and accommodations of any place of public accommodation, as defined in this section, without discrimination or segregation on the ground of race, color, religion, or national origin.

(b) Each of the following establishments which serves the public is a place of public accommodation within the meaning of this title if its operations affect commerce, or if discrimination or segregation by it is supported by State action:

(1) any inn, hotel, motel, or other establishment which provides lodging to transient guests, other than an establishment located within a building which contains not more than five rooms for rent or hire and which is actually occupied by the proprietor of such establishment as his residence;

(2) any restaurant, cafeteria, lunchroom, lunch counter, soda fountain, or other facility principally engaged in selling food for consumption on the premises, including, but not limited to, any such facility located on the premises of any retail establishment; or any gasoline station;

(3) any motion picture house, theater, concert hall, sports arena, stadium or other place of exhibition or entertainment; and

(4) any establishment (A)(i) which is physically located within the premises of any establishment otherwise covered by this subsection, or (ii) within the premises of which is physically located any such covered establishment, and
(B) which holds itself out as serving patrons of such covered establishment. . . .

TITLE III—DESEGREGATION OF PUBLIC FACILITIES

SEC. 301. (a) Whenever the Attorney General receives a complaint in writing signed by an individual to the effect that he is being deprived of or threatened with the loss of his right to the equal protection of the laws, on account of his race, color, religion, or national origin, by being denied equal utilization of any public facility which is owned, operated, or managed by or on behalf of any State or subdivision thereof, other than a public school or public college as defined in section 401 of title IV hereof, and the Attorney General believes the complaint is meritorious and certifies that the signer or signers of such complaint are unable, in his judgment, to initiate and maintain appropriate legal proceedings for relief and that the institution of an action will materially further the orderly progress of desegregation in public facilities, the Attorney General is authorized to institute for or in the name of the United

States a civil action in any appropriate district court of the United States against such parties and for such relief as may be appropriate, and such court shall have and shall exercise jurisdiction of proceedings instituted pursuant to this section.

TITLE IV—DESEGREGATION OF PUBLIC EDUCATION

DEFINITIONS . . .

SURVEY AND REPORT OF EDUCATIONAL OPPORTUNITIES

SEC. 402. The Commissioner shall conduct a survey and make a report to the President and the Congress, within two years of the enactment of this title, concerning the lack of availability of equal educational opportunities for individuals by reason of race, color, religion, or national origin in public educational institutions at all levels in the United States, its territories and possessions, and the District of Columbia.

TECHNICAL ASSISTANCE

SEC. 403. The Commissioner is authorized, upon the application of any school board, State, municipality, school district, or other governmental unit legally responsible for operating a public school or schools, to render technical assistance to such applicant in the preparation, adoption, and implementation of plans for the desegregation of public schools. Such technical assistance may, among other activities, include making available to such agencies information regarding effective methods of coping with special educational problems occasioned by desegregation, and making available to such agencies personnel of the Office of Education or other persons specially equipped to advise and assist them in coping with such problems. . . .

TITLE V—COMMISSION ON CIVIL RIGHTS

SEC. 501. Section 102 of the Civil Rights Act of 1957 (42 U.S.C. 1975a; 71 Stat. 634) is amended to read as follows:

"RULES OF PROCEDURE OF THE COMMISSION HEARINGS

"SEC. 102. (a) At least thirty days prior to the commencement of any hearing, the Commission shall cause to be published in the Federal Register notice of the date on which such hearing is to commence, the place at which it is to be held and the subject of the hearing. The Chairman, or one designated by him to act as Chairman at a hearing of the Commission, shall announce in an opening statement the subject of the hearing.

"(b) A copy of the Commission's rules shall be made available to any witness before the Commission, and a witness compelled to appear before the Commission or required to produce written or other matter shall be served with a copy of the Commission's rules at the time of service of the subpoena.

"(c) Any person compelled to appear in person before the Commission shall be accorded the right to be accompanied and advised by counsel, who shall have the right to subject his client to reasonable examination, and to make objections on the record and to argue briefly the basis for such objections. The Commission shall proceed with reasonable dispatch to conclude any hearing in which it is engaged. Due regard shall be had for the convenience and necessity of witnesses. . . .

TITLE VI—NONDISCRIMINATION IN FEDERALLY ASSISTED PROGRAMS

SEC. 601. No person in the United States shall, on the ground of race, color, or national origin, be excluded from participation in, be denied the benefits of, or be subjected to discrimination under any program or activity receiving Federal financial assistance.

SEC. 602. Each Federal department and agency which is empowered to extend Federal financial assistance to any program or activity, by way of grant, loan, or contract other than a contract of insurance or guaranty, is authorized and directed to effectuate the provisions of section 601 with respect to such program or activity by issuing rules, regulations, or orders of general applicability which shall be consistent with achievement of the objectives of the statute authorizing the financial assistance in connection with which the action is taken. No such rule, regulation, or order shall become effective unless and until approved by the President. . . .

TITLE VII—EQUAL EMPLOYMENT OPPORTUNITY

DEFINITIONS . . .

DISCRIMINATION BECAUSE OF RACE, COLOR, RELIGION, SEX, OR NATIONAL ORIGIN

SEC. 703. (a) It shall be an unlawful employment practice for an employer—

(1) to fail or refuse to hire or to discharge any individual, or otherwise to discriminate against any individual with respect to his compensation, terms, conditions, or privileges of employment, because of such individual's race, color, religion, sex, or national origin; or

(2) to limit, segregate, or classify his employees in any way which would deprive or tend to deprive any individual of employment opportunities or otherwise adversely affect his status as an employee, because of such individual's race, color, religion, sex, or national origin.

TITLE VIII—REGISTRATION AND VOTING STATISTICS

SEC. 801. The Secretary of Commerce shall promptly conduct a survey to compile registration and voting statistics in such geographic areas as may be recommended by the Commission on Civil Rights. Such a survey and compilation shall, to the extent recommended by the Commission on Civil Rights, only include a count of persons of voting age by race, color, and national origin, and determination of the extent to which such persons are registered to vote, and have voted in any statewide primary or general election in which the Members of the United States House of Representatives are nominated or elected, since January 1, 1960.

TITLE IX—INTERVENTION AND PROCEDURE AFTER REMOVAL IN CIVIL RIGHTS CASES

SEC. 901. Title 28 of the United States Code, section 1447(d), is amended to read as follows:

"An order remanding a case to the State court from which it was removed is not reviewable on appeal or otherwise, except that an order remanding a case to the State court from which it was removed pursuant to section 1443 of this title shall be reviewable by appeal or otherwise."

SEC. 902. Whenever an action has been commenced in any court of the United States seeking relief from the denial of equal protection of the laws under the fourteenth amendment to the Constitution on account of race, color, religion, or national origin, the Attorney General for or in the name of the United States may intervene in such action upon timely application if the Attorney General certifies that the case is of general public importance. In such action the United States shall be entitled to the same relief as if it had instituted the action.

TITLE X—ESTABLISHMENT OF COMMUNITY RELATIONS SERVICE

SEC. 1001. (a) There is hereby established in and as a part of the Department of Commerce a Community Relations Service (hereinafter referred to as the "Service"), which shall be headed by a Director who shall be appointed by the President with the advice and consent of the Senate for a term of four years. . . .

TITLE XI—MISCELLANEOUS

SEC. 1101. In any proceeding for criminal contempt arising under title II, III, IV, V, VI, or VII of this Act, the accused, upon demand therefor, shall be entitled to a trial by jury, which shall conform as near as may be to the practice in criminal cases. Upon conviction, the accused shall not be fined more than $1,000 or imprisoned for more than six months.

This section shall not apply to contempts committed in the presence of the court, or so near thereto as to obstruct the administration of justice, nor to the misbehavior, misconduct, or disobedience of any officer of the court in respect to writs, orders, or process of the court.

No person shall be convicted of criminal contempt hereunder unless the act or omission constituting such contempt shall have been intentional, as required in other cases of criminal contempt.

Nor shall anything herein be construed to deprive courts of their power, by civil contempt proceedings, without a jury, to secure compliance with or to prevent obstruction of, as distinguished from punishment for violations of, any lawful writ, process, order, rule, decree, or command of the court in accordance with the prevailing usages of law and equity, including the power of detention.

SEC. 1102. No person should be put twice in jeopardy under the laws of the United States for the same act or omission. . . .

SEC. 1106. If any provision of this Act or the application thereof to any person or circumstances is held invalid, the remainder of the Act and the application of the provision to other persons not similarly situated or to other circumstances shall not be affected thereby.

Approved July 2, 1964.

SCHOLASTIC

ENCYCLOPEDIA OF THE UNITED STATES

JUDY BOCK AND
RACHEL KRANZ

Bascom Communications

A NOTE TO THE READER

Every best effort has been made to ensure the accuracy of this book and we have consulted the most authoritative sources during its writing.

Please be aware that you may find state areas in this book that differ from other books. The reason is that the people who measure the size of the states do so at different times of year. In the winter, surface water of a state may be frozen (and smaller in size) or liquid (and larger in size) in the spring or summer. Also, natural erosion and landfills affect measurements all the year round.

The people who measure also use different ways of totaling surface water such as lakes and rivers, and this also can lead to differences among books.

Also, the population statistics are **estimates** for the year 1995. These figures come from The Population Distribution Branch, U.S. Bureau of the Census, Consistent with Department of Commerce Press Release CB96-10.

The following have been most helpful in giving us correct information for this book: The Bureau of the Census: Geography Division • The Cartography Department of the National Geographic Society • The Department of Defense • The National Bureau of Statistics • The U.S. Geological Survey: Inquiry Group

ACKNOWLEDGMENTS

Many thanks to Betsy Ryan, president of Bascom Communications, who produced this book with intelligence and care. A great debt of gratitude is also owed to its editor at Scholastic, the peerless Carolyn Jackson. Dr. Alex Moore, Director of the Historic Society of Charleston, was gracious and generous with his time, as was Ann Grant of the Federal Museum in Arkansas.

Michael Schulman at Archive Photos is a true professional, gifted with patience and a rare sense of humor. Thanks also to the art directors: Kevin Callahan, Jonette Jakobson, Nancy Sabato, and the indefatigable David Saylor. Thanks also to Barbara Curry Walsh for her energetic assistance in photo research. And to Edward Morris, scholar and gentleman, gratitude for his constant assiduity. Thanks also to Doric Wilson.

Library of Congress Cataloging-in-Publication Data
Bock, Judy . Scholastic encyclopedia of the United States / Judy Bock, Rachel Kranz.
p. cm. Includes index.
Summary : Presents historical, geographical, and miscellaneous information about each of the fifty states.
ISBN 0-590-94747-8
1. United States—Encyclopedia, Juvenile. 2. U.S. states—Encyclopedias, Juvenile. 3. United States—Insular possessions—Encyclopedias, Juvenile. [1. United States—Encyclopedias.]
I. Kranz, Rachel. II. Title. E180.B63 1997 973'.03—dc21 96-39774 CIP AC

The *Scholastic Encyclopedia of the United States* was originally produced by Betsy Ryan/Bascom Communications.

Table of Contents

How to Use This Book

Alabama

Entrance to Bellingrath Park, Mobile

22nd state to enter the Union, December 14, 1819

The Basics

POPULATION: 4,273,084
23rd most populous state
AREA: 52,423 square miles
30th largest state
STATE CAPITAL: Montgomery
STATE BIRD: Yellowhammer (also called yellow-shafted woodpecker, flicker)
STATE FLOWER: Camellia
STATE TREE: Southern pine (also known as the longleaf yellow pine)
NICKNAMES: Yellowhammer State, Camellia State, the Heart of Dixie
STATE MOTTO: *Audemus Jura Nostra Defendere* (Latin for "We dare defend our rights")
STATE FRESHWATER FISH: Largemouth bass
STATE SALTWATER FISH: Tarpon
STATE MINERAL: Hematite (red iron ore)
STATE ROCK: Marble
STATE FOSSIL: *Basilosaurus cetoides*
STATE NUT: Pecan
STATE DANCE: Square dance
STATE DRAMA: *The Miracle Worker* by William Gibson (story of Alabama native Helen Keller)
STATE SONG: "Alabama," words by Julia S. Tutwiler, music by Edna Glockel Gussen
STATE HISTORIC PARKS: Burritt Museum and Park, Huntsville; Museum Village at Constitution Hall Park, Huntsville; Old North Hull Street Historic District, Montgomery; Pike Pioneer Museum, Troy
STATE FESTIVALS: Joe Wheeler Civil War Reenactment, Decatur (September); National Peanut Festival, Dothan (October); National Shrimp Festival, Gulf Shores (October); Tale Telling Festival, Selma (October)

2

The Basics column gives you fast facts about each state: its size, population, capital, motto, flower, tree—and much more

The **locator map** shows where each state is.

This Deep South state is filled with beauty, from the red clay soil and forests of the northern part of the state to the pine forests and rolling grasslands farther south. The Mobile Delta, just above the Gulf of Mexico, is full of swamps and bayous, while the coastline and Dauphin Island have some of the nation's most beautiful beaches. Alabama, full of variety, even has an industrial region, around Birmingham.

ROCKETS AND PLANTATIONS Most of Alabama has a hot, wet climate, barely cooled by breezes from the Gulf of Mexico. In the northern part of the state, though, are the southernmost mountains of the great Appalachians, and the weather is somewhat cooler.

Alabama was once primarily rural, but now more than 60 percent of Alabamans live in such cities as Birmingham, Mobile, Montgomery, and Huntsville.

Yet when most people think of Alabama, they picture the antebellum (pre-Civil War) mansions built by the owners of the huge Southern plantations. You can still visit such mansions in and around Mobile, Montgomery, Selma, and Monroeville. But now Alabama also has a more modern image—the Alabama Space and Rocket Center at Huntsville, where NASA scientists developed the first rocket that put people on the moon. Visitors can take a bus tour of NASA labs and visit the space museum. Children go to Space Camp here, too.

Folk dancing at Landmark Park, Dothan

MANY PEOPLES Alabama's first inhabitants were Native Americans, mainly Chickasaw, Cherokee, Creek, and Choctaw. In 1540, the Spanish explorer Hernando de Soto led an expedition through the area and defeated a Choctaw army led by Chief Tuscaloosa. The first permanent European settlement was founded by the French, who settled Mobile in 1711.

The United States took control of the area in 1813—but conflict with Native Americans was not yet over. In the 1830s the Creek Indians were moved from their land to Oklahoma, despite U.S. treaties that had said they could stay. In 1836-37 the Cherokee were also forced off their land. This forced migration of Native Americans throughout the Southeastern United States was known as the Trail of Tears. The "removals" occurred in a series of waves between 1831 and 1835.

In the nineteenth century, Alabama's economy depended on huge cotton

The center part of each page tells you the history, geography, and industry of each state. You will also see photographs of famous people who were born or who lived in the state, or festivals or interesting places to visit.

plantations, which in turn relied on the labor of African-American slaves. When President Abraham Lincoln was elected in 1860, many in the South feared that he would put an end to slavery. So in 1861 Alabama and 10 other Southern states seceded from the Union to form the Confederate States of America. For a brief time, Montgomery was the capital of this new nation, and the Confederate flag was first designed and flown there. You can still visit the "First White House of the Confederacy" near today's state Capitol building.

The Great Secession led to the Civil War, which ended in the defeat of the South and the abolition (end) of slavery. After federal troops left, supporters of the old order passed laws to keep African Americans from voting and to promote segregation—keeping black and white people as separate as possible, using separate schools, hospitals, even water fountains.

Civil Rights Memorial, Montgomery

In the 1950s the civil rights movement gained power. Its goal was to win for African Americans the same rights that white people had always taken for granted. African Americans wanted to be integrated (allowed to use the same facilities as whites). In 1953 Autherine Lucy won the right to attend the previously all-white University of Alabama. Lucy was so badly harassed, however, that she decided not to continue.

In 1955, in Montgomery, Rosa Parks refused to sit in the separate section for African Americans in the back of the bus. Her action sparked a bus boycott that lasted more than a year, which finally led to integration on buses. One of the boycott leaders was the Reverend Martin Luther King, Jr., who went on to lead many other civil rights activities.

The civil rights movement succeeded in making vast changes in Alabama. By 1984, for example, Alabamans had elected 25 black mayors. As a reminder of those earlier times, architect Maya Lin designed the Civil Rights Memorial in Montgomery. She created a 40-foot black granite wall over which water flows into a pool. Engraved on the wall is a quote from the Bible that Martin Luther King, Jr., used in one of his famous speeches, and on a nearby tablet are engraved the names of those who died in the movement for civil rights.

Helen Keller

COTTON BOLLS AND STEEL MILLS Over a hundred years ago, Alabama was called the "Cotton State." Eventually, though, cotton harvests declined, both from attacks by boll weevils (insects), and because the soil became worn out. George Washington Carver taught Alabama farmers how to rotate crops. By growing crops that added nitrogen back to the soil, farmers got better harvests and enriched the soil. They began to grow peanuts and soybeans alternately with cotton.

Alabama's many forests are used to produce timber, pulp, and paper. After the Civil War, the region of Birmingham was developed—the only big industrial city in the South. Iron and steel are still produced there. More recently, the space center in Huntsville has spurred the development of an electronics and space industry.

Fascinating Facts

FAMOUS PEOPLE BORN IN ALABAMA:
- Harper Lee, author of *To Kill a Mockingbird,* Monroeville (1926-)
- Country singer Hank Williams, Grace (1923-1951)
- Hugo L. Black, U.S. Supreme Court Justice, Harlan (1886-1971)

DID YOU KNOW THAT... William Gibson's play about Helen Keller, *The Miracle Worker*, is performed every year at "Ivy Green," Keller's home at Tuscumbia.

HOW ALABAMA GOT ITS NAME: The name was used as an Indian nation in the Creek confederacy. Then the Alabama River was named for the Indians, and the state was named for the river.

HOW ALABAMA GOT ITS STATE BIRD: The yellowhammer was chosen because its colors were the same as those worn by a company of Alabama Confederate soldiers.

ALABAMA SPORTS HALL OF FAME:
- Legendary University of Alabama football coach William "Bear" Bryant (1913-1983)
- Olympic Gold Medal track star Jesse Owens (1913-1980)
- Record-setting hitter New York/San Francisco Giants Willie Mays (1931-)
- Home run record-setter Atlanta Braves Hank Aaron (1934-)

ALABAMA HOT TIMES: Alabama is tied with Nevada for third-hottest recorded temperature in the U.S.: 122 degrees Fahrenheit in Centreville, Sept. 5, 1925.

ALABAMA IS TOPS IN...
- cast-iron and steel pipe products

ALABAMA HAD THE WORLD'S FIRST:
- electric trolley system—-Montgomery—1886

DID YOU KNOW THAT... In the 1880s, Alabama scientist George Washington Carver discovered 300 new uses for the peanut and 175 for the sweet potato, which revitalized Alabama's farm economy.

The **Fascinating Facts** column tells you state firsts, mosts, bests, and lists famous people born in the state. This column changes a little from state to state, and you'll always find a fact that you never knew before. We promise.

Alabama

The Basics

POPULATION: 4,273,084
23rd most populous state
AREA: 52,423 square miles
30th largest state
STATE CAPITAL: Montgomery
STATE BIRD: Yellowhammer (also called yellow-shafted woodpecker, flicker)
STATE FLOWER: Camellia
STATE TREE: Southern pine (also known as the longleaf yellow pine)
NICKNAMES: Yellowhammer State, Camellia State, the Heart of Dixie
STATE MOTTO: *Audemus Jura Nostra Defendere* (Latin for "We dare defend our rights")
STATE FRESHWATER FISH: Largemouth bass
STATE SALTWATER FISH: Tarpon
STATE MINERAL: Hematite (red iron ore)
STATE ROCK: Marble
STATE FOSSIL: *Basilosaurus cetoides*
STATE NUT: Pecan
STATE DANCE: Square dance
STATE DRAMA: *The Miracle Worker* by William Gibson (story of Alabama native Helen Keller)
STATE SONG: "Alabama," words by Julia S. Tutwiler, music by Edna Glockel Gussen
STATE HISTORIC PARKS: Burritt Museum and Park, Huntsville; Museum Village at Constitution Hall Park, Huntsville; Old North Hull Street Historic District, Montgomery; Pike Pioneer Museum, Troy
STATE FESTIVALS: Joe Wheeler Civil War Reenactment, Decatur (September); National Peanut Festival, Dothan (October); National Shrimp Festival, Gulf Shores (October); Tale Telling Festival, Selma (October)

Entrance to Bellingrath Park, Mobile

22nd state to enter the Union, December 14, 1819

This Deep South state is filled with beauty, from the red clay soil and forests of the northern part of the state to the pine forests and rolling grasslands farther south. The Mobile Delta, just above the Gulf of Mexico, is full of swamps and bayous, while the coastline and Dauphin Island have some of the nation's most beautiful beaches. Alabama, full of variety, even has an industrial region, around Birmingham.

ROCKETS AND PLANTATIONS Most of Alabama has a hot, wet climate, barely cooled by breezes from the Gulf of Mexico. In the northern part of the state, though, are the southernmost mountains of the great Appalachians, and the weather is somewhat cooler.

Alabama was once primarily rural, but now more than 60 percent of Alabamans live in such cities as Birmingham, Mobile, Montgomery, and Huntsville.

Yet when most people think of Alabama, they picture the antebellum (pre-Civil War) mansions built by the owners of the huge Southern plantations. You can still visit such mansions in and around Mobile, Montgomery, Selma, and Monroeville. But now Alabama also has a more modern image—the Alabama Space and Rocket Center at Huntsville, where NASA scientists developed the first rocket that put people on the moon. Visitors can take a bus tour of NASA labs and visit the space museum. Children go to Space Camp here, too.

Folk dancing at Landmark Park, Dothan

MANY PEOPLES Alabama's first inhabitants were Native Americans, mainly Chickasaw, Cherokee, Creek, and Choctaw. In 1540, the Spanish explorer Hernando de Soto led an expedition through the area and defeated a Choctaw army led by Chief Tuscaloosa. The first permanent European settlement was founded by the French, who settled Mobile in 1711.

The United States took control of the area in 1813—but conflict with Native Americans was not yet over. In the 1830s the Creek Indians were moved from their land to Oklahoma, despite U.S. treaties that had said they could stay. In 1836-37 the Cherokee were also forced off their land. This forced migration of Native Americans throughout the Southeastern United States was known as the Trail of Tears. The "removals" occurred in a series of waves between 1831 and 1835.

In the nineteenth century, Alabama's economy depended on huge cotton plantations, which in turn relied on the labor of African-American slaves. When President Abraham Lincoln was elected in 1860, many in the South feared that he would put an end to slavery. So in 1861 Alabama and 10 other Southern states seceded from the Union to form the Confederate States of America. For a brief time, Montgomery was the capital of this new nation, and the Confederate flag was first designed and flown there. You can still visit the "First White House of the Confederacy" near today's state Capitol building.

The Great Secession led to the Civil War, which ended in the defeat of the South and the abolition (end) of slavery. After federal troops left, supporters of the old order passed laws to keep African Americans from voting and to promote segregation—keeping black and white people as separate as possible, using separate schools, hospitals, even water fountains.

Civil Rights Memorial, Montgomery

In the 1950s the civil rights movement gained power. Its goal was to win for African Americans the same rights that white people had always taken for granted. African Americans wanted to be integrated (allowed to use the same facilities as whites). In 1953 Autherine Lucy won the right to attend the previously all-white University of Alabama. Lucy was so badly harassed, however, that she decided not to continue.

In 1955, in Montgomery, Rosa Parks refused to sit in the separate section for African Americans in the back of the bus. Her action sparked a bus boycott that lasted more than a year, which finally led to integration on buses. One of the boycott leaders was the Reverend Martin Luther King, Jr., who went on to lead many other civil rights activities.

The civil rights movement succeeded in making vast changes in Alabama. By 1984, for example, Alabamans had elected 25 black mayors. As a reminder of those earlier times, architect Maya Lin designed the Civil Rights Memorial in Montgomery. She created a 40-foot black granite wall over which water flows into a pool. Engraved on the wall is a quote from the Bible that Martin Luther King, Jr., used in one of his famous speeches, and on a nearby tablet are engraved the names of those who died in the movement for civil rights.

Helen Keller

COTTON BOLLS AND STEEL MILLS Over a hundred years ago, Alabama was called the "Cotton State." Eventually, though, cotton harvests declined, both from attacks by boll weevils (insects), and because the soil became worn out. George Washington Carver taught Alabama farmers how to rotate crops. By growing crops that added nitrogen back to the soil, farmers got better harvests and enriched the soil. They began to grow peanuts and soybeans alternately with cotton.

Alabama's many forests are used to produce timber, pulp, and paper. After the Civil War, the region of Birmingham was developed—the only big industrial city in the South. Iron and steel are still produced there. More recently, the space center in Huntsville has spurred the development of an electronics and space industry.

Fascinating Facts

FAMOUS PEOPLE BORN IN ALABAMA:
- Harper Lee, author of *To Kill a Mockingbird*, Monroeville (1926-)
- Country singer Hank Williams, Grace (1923-1951)
- Hugo L. Black, U.S. Supreme Court Justice, Harlan (1886-1971)

DID YOU KNOW THAT... William Gibson's play about Helen Keller, *The Miracle Worker*, is performed every year at "Ivy Green," Keller's home at Tuscumbia.

HOW ALABAMA GOT ITS NAME: The name was used as an Indian nation in the Creek confederacy. Then the Alabama River was named for the Indians, and the state was named for the river.

HOW ALABAMA GOT ITS STATE BIRD: The yellowhammer was chosen because its colors were the same as those worn by a company of Alabama Confederate soldiers.

ALABAMA SPORTS HALL OF FAME:
- Legendary University of Alabama football coach William "Bear" Bryant (1913-1983)
- Olympic Gold Medal track star Jesse Owens (1913-1980)
- Record-setting hitter New York/San Francisco Giants Willie Mays (1931-)
- Home run record-setter Atlanta Braves Hank Aaron (1934-)

ALABAMA HOT TIMES: Alabama is tied with Nevada for third-hottest recorded temperature in the U.S.: 122 degrees Fahrenheit in Centreville, Sept. 5, 1925.

ALABAMA IS TOPS IN...
- cast-iron and steel pipe products

ALABAMA HAD THE WORLD'S FIRST:
- electric trolley system—Montgomery—1886

DID YOU KNOW THAT... In the 1880s, Alabama scientist George Washington Carver discovered 300 new uses for the peanut and 175 for the sweet potato, which revitalized Alabama's farm economy.

Alaska

The Basics

POPULATION: 607,007
48th most populous state
AREA: 656,424 square miles
largest state
STATE CAPITAL: Juneau
STATE BIRD: Willow ptarmigan (pronounced *tar-mi-gan*)
STATE FLOWER: Wild forget-me-not
STATE TREE: Sitka spruce (also called yellow, tideland, western, coast, or Menzies' spruce)
NICKNAMES: The Land of the Midnight Sun, America's Last Frontier
STATE MOTTO: North to the future
STATE SPORT: Dog mushing
STATE FISH: King salmon
STATE MARINE MAMMAL: Bowhead whale
STATE MINERAL: Gold
STATE GEM: Jade
STATE SONG: "Alaska's Flag," words by Marie Drake, music by Elinor Dusenbury
STATE LANDMARK: Aniakchak, Cape Krusenstern
NATIONAL PARKS: Glacier Bay National Park, near Juneau, where 11 glaciers meet the water; Denali, near Healy; Gates of the Arctic, near Big Lake; Katmai, near King Salmer; Kenai Fjords, near Homer; Kobus Valley, near Kotzebue; Lake Clark, near Anchor Point; Wrangell-St. Elias, near Cordova
HISTORICAL PARK: Sitka National Historical Park, featuring authentic totem poles
STATE FESTIVAL: Ice Climbing Festival, Valdez (February)

Mt. McKinley National Park

49th state to enter the Union, January 3, 1959

Alaska seems to call for superlatives—most, highest, only. Alaska is the only state to include part of the Arctic. It has America's highest point—Denali, formerly Mt. McKinley; our westernmost—Cape Wrangell; and our northernmost—Point Barrow. Alaska is our largest state—twice as big as Texas—and our wildest. Thousands of acres have never been explored by Europeans. And Alaska is our coldest state: the U.S. record was set at Prospeck Creek near Barrow on January 23, 1971: 80 degrees Fahrenheit below zero.

LAND OF THE MIDNIGHT SUN Most Alaskans live along the southern coast, near the archipelago of islands that extend into the Gulf of Alaska and the Bering Sea, or on the fertile interior basin that nestles below the Alaskan Range. Farther north is the Yukon, a demanding region with winter temperatures as low as -50 degrees F, where in winter darkness or twilight lasts virtually around the clock. Farther north still is the North Slope in the Arctic Circle, a land of tundra and permafrost (permanently frozen ground). There, winter brings 67 straight days of darkness, while from mid-May through July the sun never sets.

A RUSH TO RICHES Alaska's dramatic landscape and abundant natural resources have helped to shape its history. From fur trappers to gold prospectors to wilderness buffs, thousands of people have come to Alaska seeking fortune, opportunity, and adventure.

Inuit children in traditional dress

The first Alaskans were the Inuit (Eskimo), Aleuts, Athabascans, Haida, Tlingit, and Tlairda, whose rich heritage survives today. The word Alaska comes from the Aleutian word Alaxsxaq—mainland.

Danish navigator Vitus Bering visited Alaska on behalf of the Russian czar in 1728 and took sea otter furs back home. The Russians loved the furs, and the first Alaska rush was on. Hundreds of trappers quickly depleted the sea otter population, killing or enslaving Aleuts as well. The Russian government founded the Russian-American Company in 1799 to run the fur trade and establish peaceful relations with Aleuts.

U.S. Secretary of State William Seward arranged to buy Alaska for $7.2 million in 1867. Critics called it Seward's Folly and Seward's Icebox because they believed Alaska had no value for the U.S.

They were proved wrong when, in 1897, gold was discovered in the Klondike, just across the border, in Canada. The second rush to Alaska began. In 1899 gold was discovered in Nome, and soon 10,000 gold-seekers swarmed into that region. More gold was found in Fairbanks, and near the Yellow, Iditarod, and Yukon Rivers—and each discovery brought more prospectors. But miners' camps were dismal and dangerous, and more miners went away disappointed than rich. Still, by 1910 over $100 million worth of gold had been found by a lucky few.

Alaska grew again in 1957 when oil fields were discovered in the Kenai peninsula. More oil deposits were discovered on the Alaska North Slope in 1968. To transport the oil, the Alaska government built the 800-mile-long Trans-Alaska Pipeline. Alaska has made so much money from its oil fields that it doesn't have to charge any income tax. Instead, it pays money to each person who lives there every year!

Today, many people move to Alaska to enjoy its wide open spaces and outdoor activities. The most famous is the Iditarod, an 1100-mile dogsled race held each winter. Champion racer Susan Butcher holds the Iditarod record with four victories.

A carved raven's head tops this Tlingit totem pole.

BRINGING IN A NEW ERA The second-floor visitors' gallery at the State House of Representatives is named for Elizabeth W. Peratrovich, a Tlingit (pronounced klink-it) woman who came to live in Juneau in the 1940s. There she found such signs as "No dogs, no natives" and "No Indians allowed." In 1945, she spoke before the legislature in defense of a bill that would grant full equal rights to Native Americans. Thanks to her speech, the bill passed—and, in the words of Governor Ernest Gruening, "a new era in Alaska's racial relations had begun."

WEALTH FROM THE EARTH Most of Alaska's wealth comes from its natural resources: oil, natural gas, copper, coal, and gold. Fish are also a key source of wealth, especially salmon, king crab, shrimp, and halibut. Tourism is a fast-growing industry—so much so that Alaska has more tourists than residents! The government is also a major Alaska employer, hiring people to run military bases as well as national and state parks.

Preservation of the environment is a key issue in Alaska. In 1980, Congress passed the Alaska Lands Bill, setting aside more than 104 million acres as wilderness. In 1989 the oil tanker *Exxon Valdez* ran aground in Prince William Sound, causing one of the worst oil spills in history. Environmentalists are concerned about the effects of the spill—and about how to prevent future disasters. Environmentalists also clash with developers who want to cut more timber or drill for more oil.

Fascinating Facts

THE SECOND SNOWIEST TOWN IN THE U.S.: Valdez, with a record 303.9 inches per year.

ALASKA IS TOPS IN:
- platinum
- private planes and pilots—more *per capita* (per person) than any other state
- forest acreage
- coastline—longer than all the other states combined, 6,639 miles

DID YOU KNOW THAT... Alaska's reindeer were imported from Siberia in 1891, when the near extinction of whales and walrus threatened the Inuit with starvation.

HOW NOME GOT ITS NAME: A map-maker didn't know the name of one town on his map, so he wrote "Name?" The person who was copying the map thought he wrote *Nome*—and so the town was named.

DID YOU KNOW THAT... It's too cold for houseflies to breed in Alaska.

ON KODIAK ISLAND... live Kodiak bears, the world's largest meat-eating land animals. They are ten feet tall and weigh up to a ton and a half.

DID YOU KNOW THAT... Seward only paid about two cents an acre for Alaska.

ALASKAN EXTREMES:
- Fruits and vegetables can grow two or three times their normal size because of all the extra sun they get. You can find 15-pound turnips and 90-pound cabbages.
- The state of Rhode Island could fit into Alaska 483 times. Malaspina Glacier alone is as large as Rhode Island.
- Juneau covers more ground than any other U.S. city—over 3,000 square miles, as compared to Los Angeles, with less than 500 square miles.

DID YOU KNOW THAT... The last shot of the Civil War was fired in the Bering Sea—the Confederate ship *Shenandoah* fired on a Union whaler on June 22, 1865. Neither ship knew that the war was already over!

Arizona

The Grand Canyon

48th state to enter the Union, February 14, 1912

The Basics

POPULATION: 4,428,068
21st most populous state
AREA: 114,006 square miles
6th largest state
STATE CAPITAL: Phoenix
STATE BIRD: Cactus wren
STATE FLOWER: Saguaro flower
STATE TREE: Paloverde (Green-barked Acacia)
NICKNAMES: Grand Canyon State, Apache State, Copper State, Valentine State, the Italy of America, the State Where You Can Always Expect to Enjoy the Unexpected
STATE MOTTO: *Ditat Deus* (Latin for "God enriches")
SPORTS TEAMS: Arizona Cardinals (Phoenix), football; Phoenix Suns, basketball
STATE GEM: Turquoise
STATE NECKWEAR: Bola tie
STATE SONG: "Arizona March Song," words by Margaret Rowe Clifford and music by Maurice Blumenthal
STATE LANDMARKS: Grand Canyon; Painted Desert; Petrified Forest (an ancient forest that turned to brightly colored stone about 150 million years ago); Navajo National Monument; Hubbell Trading Post (Ganado)
ARIZONA FESTIVALS: Chili Cook-Off, Kingman (May); "Helldorado" Historic Reenactment, Tombstone (October); *La Vuelta de Bisbee* Bicycle Races, Bisbee (April); Sawdust Festival Loggers' Competition, Payson (July)

Arizona is a state marked by overwhelming beauty: the Painted Desert, the Petrified Forest, mountains, plateaus, and the spectacular Grand Canyon, one of the seven natural wonders of the world. Southeast of Flagstaff, there's even a meteor crater—a hole 600 feet deep and a mile wide—left from when a giant meteor crashed into Arizona millions of years ago.

CACTUS AND CANYONS The Colorado Plateau, a flat, dry area marked by canyons and mesas, occupies the northeastern two-thirds of Arizona. The rest of the state is an arid or semi-arid region that includes the Sonoran Desert in the state's southwestern corner. Despite the name, however, only one percent of Arizona is true desert although over forty percent is desert scrub. Southeastward, near Tucson, is the Saguaro National Park, featuring fifty-foot cacti whose "arms" extend in bizarre shapes.

Geronimo, the brave leader of the Apache, led many uprisings.

Although you can see working cowboys in Arizona, some 84 percent of this state's residents live in cities and towns. Urban residents have accounted for most of Arizona's phenomenal population growth: the state has more than tripled in size since World War II, and just since 1980 its population has risen by almost 35 percent. The state's hot, dry climate has made it popular with senior citizens who come to retire in Phoenix, Tucson, Sun City, and other Arizona places in ever-increasing numbers.

GERONIMO'S LAST STAND Arizona's history begins almost two thousand years ago, with the ancient Hohokam, Mogollan, and Anasazi cultures. The best known of these is the Anasazi (a Navajo word meaning "the ancient ones"), who lived in pueblos (Spanish for village), a type of communal house that resembled modern apartment buildings, with many small rooms built into the sides of cliffs. You can still see Anasazi ruins at the Canyon de Chelly National Monument.

These ancient civilizations mysteriously disappeared around the beginning of the fifteenth century, to be replaced by other native peoples. Arizona is still home to more Native Americans, including Apache, Hualapai, Maricopa,

Papago, Pima, Southern Paiute, Yavapai, and most notably, Hopi and Navajo, than any other state.

The first Europeans came to Arizona in 1539, searching for the famous Seven Cities of Cibola, which, according to legend, were rich in gold, silver, and jewels. In 1539 the Franciscan friar Marcos de Niza arrived. He was followed in 1540 by Francisco Vasquez de Coronado. The explorers attacked and destroyed many villages—only to discover that there were no riches, after all. (If you drive on U.S. Route 66, you'll be taking Coronado's route.) In 1692, Spanish Jesuit missionaries came to convert Indians away from their own religions to Christianity.

In 1821 Arizona became part of Mexico which had recently won its own independence from Spain. Arizona was still primarily settled by Native Americans although some American trappers—Bill Williams, Pauline Weaver, and the legendary Kit Carson—established trails.

When the United States acquired Arizona in 1853, new waves of settlers moved in from Texas and the East but they were soon met with fierce resistance from the Apache, led by Mangas Coloradas, Cochise, and most famously, Geronimo. Indian resistance continued for decades. Then in 1876, the U.S. Army tried to move the Apache onto a reservation. Geronimo (1829-1909) fled with his followers and fought the U.S. Army so successfully that the federal government came to consider Geronimo its chief enemy and even offered a $25,000 reward for his capture. Much of the heaviest fighting was conducted by the Ninth and Tenth cavalries, the all-black Buffalo Soldier units stationed at Fort Bowie.

Some of the rock formations in Monument Valley rise as high as 1000 feet.

Geronimo resisted so successfully that many people came to believe that he had supernatural powers. After ten years, however, on September 4, 1886, Geronimo was captured and forced onto a reservation in Florida.

Today, Arizona's territory includes several Indian reservations operating under Indian sovereignty. Oraibi, on the Hopi Reservation, has been home to the Hopi for over 800 years—longer than any other Indian settlement in the United States.

ORANGES AND AIRPLANES Agriculture is one of Arizona's most important industries—85 percent of the state's water supply is used to irrigate crops. Arizona is among the country's leading producers of oranges and lemons, but the state's most important crop is cotton. At an average size of 4,557 acres, Arizona's farms are by far the largest in the United States. Mining has historically been a key Arizona industry as well, particularly copper mining.

One of the most important industries in Arizona is aircraft manufacturing. Electronics—stereos, telephones, and computer printers—has become an increasingly major part of the economy as well.

Fascinating Facts

ARIZONA HAD THE FIRST...

• competitive annual rodeo—begun on July 4, 1888, Prescott, Arizona

DID YOU KNOW THAT... Arizona was the last of the 48 *contiguous* (touching) states to be admitted to the Union.

HOW ARIZONA GOT ITS NAME:

Although no one knows for sure, the state's name may have come from the Spanish pronunciation of the Pima Indians' Papago dialect: *Aleh-zon* or *Arizonac*, meaning "little spring place," referring to a spring in the southern part of Arizona territory (now in Mexico). The name may also have come from an Aztec word, *Arizuma*, meaning "silver-bearing."

ARIZONA HOT SPOTS:

• The second-hottest temperature in the United States was recorded in Parker, Arizona, on July 7, 1905—127 degrees Fahrenheit.

• The sunniest city in the United States is Yuma, Arizona, which receives less than two inches of rain each year and is sunny 90 percent of the time.

• On average, the hottest U.S. city is Arizona's capital, Phoenix.

GRAND CANYON FACTS:

• 277 miles long

• 2 billion years old

• 17 miles across at its widest spot

• one mile deep—so deep that it has different climates at different levels!

FAMOUS ARIZONAN:

• Senator Barry Goldwater, born in Phoenix, 1909, Republican nominee for President in 1964

ARIZONA IS TOPS IN:

• copper production. Over fifty percent of U.S. copper comes from Arizona.

ARIZONA BRIDGES:

• London Bridge really was falling down—so it was transported from England to Arizona, where tourists can visit it.

• Arizona has the only bridge in the world built just for sheep, on the Salt River, northeast of Mesa. This unique bridge is just one sheep wide!

Arkansas

The Arlington Hotel was built in 1924.

25th state to enter the Union, June 15, 1836

The Basics

POPULATION: 2,509,793
33rd most populous state
AREA: 53,182 square miles
29th largest state
STATE CAPITAL: Little Rock
STATE BIRD: Mockingbird
STATE FLOWER: Apple blossom
STATE TREE: Pine
NICKNAMES: Land of Opportunity, Razorback State, the Natural State, the Bowie State, the Toothpick State, the Hot Water State
STATE MOTTO: *Regnat Populus* (Latin for "The people rule")
STATE INSECT: Honeybee
STATE MINERAL: Quartz crystal
STATE ROCK: Bauxite
STATE GEM: Diamond
STATE DRINK: Milk
STATE MUSICAL INSTRUMENT: Fiddle
STATE SONG: "Arkansas," words and music by Eva Ware Barnett
NATIONAL PARKS: Hot Springs, near Mountain Pine; Ouachita National Forest, near Hot Springs; Ozark National Forest, near Russellville; Buffalo National River, near Harrison; Felsenthal National Wildlife Refuge, near Crossett
STATE PARKS: Bull Shoals; Crater of Diamonds, Murfreesboro; DeGray Lake Resort, Bismarck; Petit Jean, Morrilton; Toltec Mounds Archaeological State Park, Scott
HISTORIC SITES: Arkansas Territorial Restoration, Little Rock; Mountain Village 1890, Bull Shoals; Old Washington Historic State Park, Hope; Ozark Folk Center State Park, Mountain View; Pioneer Village, Rison; Robinson Farm Museum and Heritage Centers, Valley Springs

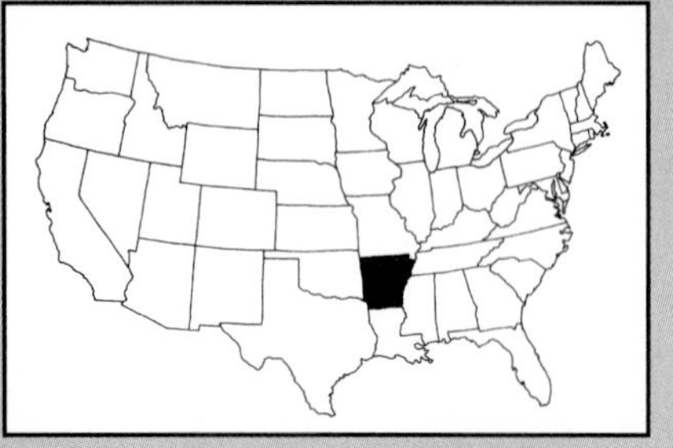

The landscape of this rural, southern state may remind you of its neighbors. To the east are cotton plantations like the ones in Alabama and Mississippi. To the southwest are Texas-style cattle ranches and grazing ranges. To the southeast are bayous, swamps, and moss-hung oak trees that look very like the Louisiana lowlands. To the north, however, Arkansas is truly unique among its neighbors for there are the Boston Mountains, part of the Ozarks, whose hills and ridges are home to Arkansas's mountain people.

DIAMONDS AND QUILTS The Ozark Folk Center in northwest Arkansas is dedicated to preserving traditional mountain culture. Visitors can explore a Victorian-era village or look at local crafts: hand-carved fiddles, straw baskets, and intricately patterned quilts. In the summer, you can see people building a pioneer settlement out of logs.

William Jefferson Clinton, our 42nd president, was born in the town of Hope.

Nearby is Blanchard Springs Caverns, one of the largest caves in the world. The surrounding area offers forested mountains and blue lakes.

In western Arkansas are the Ouachita (wah-chee-tah) Mountains, whose Hot Springs have been famous for two centuries. The earth heats spring waters from 95 to 147 degrees Fahrenheit, and many people believe the waters have healing power. The region also features an alligator farm, a working riverboat, and the Crater of Diamonds, where tourists can keep any jewels they might dig up.

A BARGAIN AT ANY PRICE When Spanish explorer Hernando de Soto visited Arkansas in 1541, he found a confederacy of native peoples: the Osage, Caddo, and Quapaw. In 1682 French explorer La Salle mapped the area and claimed it for France. (The state's name comes from the French pronunciation of the Algonquin name for the Quapaw—the Kansas, or "downstream people.")

When Thomas Jefferson was elected president in 1800, relations between the United States and France were not good. Jefferson became afraid that France would prevent American traders from shipping their goods along the Mississippi River. So in 1803, Jefferson asked to buy a small parcel of land around the river's mouth. To his surprise, the French offered instead to sell almost 800,000 square miles of territory for only $15 million. The sale, known as the Louisiana Purchase, included all of present-day Arkansas, Missouri, Iowa, North Dakota, South Dakota, Nebraska, Oklahoma, and Kansas, as well as parts of Louisiana, Wyoming, and Colorado.

FROM CIVIL WAR TO CIVIL RIGHTS When the Civil War began in 1861, Arkansas sent 60,000 soldiers to fight for the South. But 9,000 white Arkansans and 5,000 African Americans fought for the Union instead. In 1864, some Arkansas leaders even held a Unionist convention that attempted to abolish slavery in the state.

After the war, the federal government sent troops to the South to protect African Americans from those white people who thought they should not have equal rights. During this period, called Reconstruction, ex-Confederate soldiers were not allowed to vote. That made it possible for African Americans and sympathetic white people to work for equality. Many African Americans fought in the state militia against the Ku Klux Klan, an outlaw group that terrorized black people who tried to assert their rights. In 1874, however, former Confederate officers and soldiers were allowed to vote again. Soon, the Arkansas legislature was passing laws to keep black people from voting and to segregate them (keep them separate) in schools and other public places.

In 1954 the Supreme Court ruled that black and white children must be allowed to attend the same schools. On September 4, 1957, nine brave African-American students enrolled in Little Rock's all-white Central High School. Hundreds of angry white people gathered outside the school, trying to keep black students out. Arkansas's Governor Orval Faubus sent national guard troops to keep the "Little Rock Nine" from entering the building. Finally, on September 20, President Dwight Eisenhower sent federal soldiers to integrate Central High. The rest of the nation was so shocked at the image of national guardsmen aiming guns at high school students that school desegregation went more smoothly else-where. Today, almost half the students at Central High are black.

Little Rock's Old Statehouse was used for official business from 1836 to 1910.

FROM COTTON TO COAL In the state's early days, agriculture was the mainstay of the economy, especially cotton farming. Then three important discoveries changed the state's economy. Bauxite—aluminum ore—was discovered in 1887, diamonds in 1906, and oil in 1921. Now Arkansas produces these products plus coal and natural gas. Arkansas is still one of the nation's three leading cotton states, as well as a producer of cattle, corn, soybeans, and rice. One-half of the state is covered in forests, so timber is also a key Arkansas product. Nevertheless, in the 1960s, Arkansas went from being a farm state to one that relies on manufacturing.

Fascinating Facts

PRESIDENT BORN IN ARKANSAS:
- Bill Clinton (1946-), 42nd President

OTHER FAMOUS PEOPLE BORN IN ARKANSAS:
- Actress Mary Steenburgen, Newport, (1953-)
- General Douglas MacArthur, Little Rock (1880-1964)
- Baseball great Dizzy Dean, Lucas (1911-1974)

ARKANSAS IS TOPS IN:
- aluminum ore production—95 percent of U.S. ore comes from Bauxite (the name of a town, also the name of the ore itself)
- diamond mines—the Murfreesboro field is the only one in North America
- mineral springs
- mineral variety—in Magnet Cove, there are over 60 different minerals, more than in any other single region of the world
- archery bow production—Pine Bluff
- earthquakes—the 1811 quake has been called the strongest on the continent

ARKANSAS HAD THE FIRST:
- aluminum ore mine—at Bauxite—1887
- national park—Hot Springs—1932
- national river—Buffalo—1972
- woman senator—Hattie Caraway—1931

ARKANSAS IS THE ONLY STATE TO... pass a resolution on how to pronounce its name, with the last *s* silent. The state legislature decreed this in 1881.

DAVY CROCKETT SAID: "If I could rest anywhere it would be Arkansas, where the men are of the real half-horse, half-alligator breed such as grows nowhere else on the face of the universal earth."

THINGS THAT USED TO BE ILLEGAL IN ARKANSAS:
- to blindfold cows on public highways
- to file down a mule's teeth
- to set up a lunch counter on Memorial Day within a half-mile of a Confederate cemetery
- to drive an automobile without a man walking in front carrying a red flag

California

The Basics

POPULATION: 31,878,234
most populous state
AREA: 163,707 square miles
3rd largest state
STATE CAPITAL: Sacramento
STATE BIRD: California Valley quail
STATE FLOWER: Golden poppy
STATE TREE: California Redwood
NICKNAMES: The Golden State, Empire State of the West
STATE MOTTO: *Eureka!* (Greek for "I have found it!")
SPORTS TEAMS: California Angels, Los Angeles Dodgers, Oakland Athletics, San Diego Padres, San Francisco Giants, baseball; Golden State Warriors, Los Angeles Clippers, Los Angeles Lakers, Sacramento Kings, basketball; Los Angeles Rams, Los Angeles Raiders, San Francisco 49ers, San Diego Chargers, football ; Los Angeles Kings, San Jose Sharks, hockey;
STATE ANIMAL: Grizzly bear
STATE FISH: Golden trout
STATE INSECT: Dog-Face butterfly
STATE MARINE MAMMAL: Gray whale
STATE REPTILE: Desert tortoise
STATE MINERAL: Native gold
STATE ROCK: Serpentine
STATE FOSSIL: Saber-Toothed cat
STATE SONG: "I Love You, California," words by F.B. Silverwood, music by A.F. Frankenstein
STATE LANDMARK: Disneyland, Anaheim; La Brea Tar Pits, Los Angeles—bones of Ice Age animals stuck in oil
STATE NATIONAL PARKS: Yosemite; Sequoia; Kings Canyon; Inyo National Forest

Golden Gate Bridge

31st state to enter the Union, September 9, 1850

From the days of the gold rush, California has had a magical allure for people in the rest of the United States. Whether people were rushing here to prospect gold, make a movie, or just enjoy the year-round sunshine, they saw California as the land of their dreams.

FROM THE SIERRA NEVADA TO DEATH VALLEY California occupies most of the West Coast. The state is shaped by two great mountain ranges—the Coastal and the Sierra Nevada. Between them lies the fertile Central Valley. At the southern end of the Sierra Nevada is the barren Death Valley, and below that is the Mojave Desert. Along the coast, southern California is blessed with a mild, sunny climate, and beautiful beaches. Northern California has a cooler climate, stunning mountain scenery, and a dramatic rocky coastline.

Yosemite Falls are the highest waterfalls in North America.

From San Diego to Sonoma, a chain of Spanish missions stretches up the California coast. These were built in the late 1700s by people hoping to convert the Indians to Catholicism. One of the most famous missions is San Juan Capistrano, known for the swallows that travel back every spring to nest there.

A GOLDEN DESTINY Throughout its history, California has been a place to start life anew. The first Europeans to visit the area were the Spanish. They had read stories about a rich land called "California." Explorer Juan Rodriguez Cabrillo "discovered" the real California in 1542. He found none of its fabled riches, though—only the Paiute, Shoshone, Maidu, Mohave, Yuma, and some 500 other native peoples who had been living there for many years. In the late 1700s, Spanish missionaries arrived, intending to convert the Indians to Christianity. Settlers from Mexico soon followed. California became part of newly independent Mexico in 1821 and was acquired by the U.S. in 1848 after the Mexican War.

That year, gold was discovered at Sutter's Mill, and by 1849, 40,000 "forty-niners" had swarmed into the state. In one year, they found over $30 million in gold. Moses Rodgers, an African American, gained fame as one of the best mining engineers around. He used his vast earnings to free other African Americans being held as slaves in the South.

A cross-country railroad was completed in 1869, allowing farmers to come more easily to California's rich farmland, and land values rose sharply. Just in

1885, the price of an acre jumped from $350 to $10,000. In the early 1900s, moviemakers set up shop in a small town called Hollywood. Soon the very name stood for movie magic.

In 1929 America was struck by an enormous depression that put almost one-third of the country out of work. A drought hit Texas and Oklahoma, and farmers had to leave their land. Many of these displaced farmers came to California to look for work. Often they ended up living in dismal migrant labor camps. They were known, insultingly, as "Okies."

Over the years, many Japanese had become successful small farmers in California. When America went to war with Japan in 1941, some people thought these Japanese Americans would be loyal to the enemy. In 1942, the U.S. forced them into internment camps in Montana, Idaho, and other states that had no access to the ocean, so that they could not communicate with Japan. (America was also at war with Germany, but German Americans were never put in camps.) When the war was over, Japanese Americans were released—but by then, many had lost their homes, businesses, and savings. Years later, some received payment from the U. S. Congress for some of what they had lost.

California-born author, Amy Tan

After the war many Californians found jobs in the state's new aircraft factories—including the "Okies," once so scorned. The 1970s brought new glory to California as a vibrant computer industry blossomed in San Jose's Silicon Valley. Every year, its high-tech companies invent new computer products used around the world.

Also after the war, California became a land of theme parks. Knotts Berry Farm, Marineland, Sea World, and, of course, Disneyland offered tourists a new kind of day out. Disneyland, which first opened in 1955, is still the nation's most famous theme park. Its attractions include Fantasyland, full of fairy castles and storybook rides; Frontierland, which recreates the Wild West; Tomorrowland, "world of the future"; and Adventureland, where you explore jungles and haunted houses.

Redwood trees often grow 300 feet high.

SO MUCH TO DO! If California were an independent country, its economy would be the sixth largest in the world! Although only about one percent of the state's people work on farms, California leads the country in agricultural production. Airplanes and cars dominate California manufacturing, as well as high-tech industries, which employ one in every five California workers. Mining gold, silver, copper, mercury, zinc, and tungsten is also big business. With 47,000 oil wells, California ranks fourth in U.S. oil production. Of course, tourism, television, movies, and other glamour industries are key to the Golden State's economy.

Cesar Chavez, labor leader

Fascinating Facts

CALIFORNIA HAS:

- the highest point in the continental U.S.—Mount Whitney—14,494 feet
- the lowest point in the U.S.—Death Valley—282 feet below sea level
- the earth's largest living things—redwoods and sequoias—over 300 feet
- the oldest living things on earth—bristlecone pines—over 4,000 years old
- the hottest recorded temperature—134 degrees F, Death Valley, July 10, 1913

CALIFORNIA IS TOPS IN:

- fruits, vegetables, wines
- raisins, dates, figs, olives, almonds
- boron, tungsten

PRESIDENT BORN IN CALIFORNIA:

- Richard M. Nixon (1913-1994), 37th President

CALIFORNIA CITIES:

- Los Angeles (2nd largest in the nation)
- San Diego (6th largest)
- San Francisco (11th largest)
- San Jose (14th largest)

CALIFORNIA PEOPLE:

- Los Angeles has more people of Mexican ancestry than any city outside Mexico
- San Francisco's Chinatown is one of the largest Chinese communities outside Asia

CALIFORNIA'S GOVERNMENTS:

- New Albion, claimed by Sir Francis Drake for England, 1579
- Occupied by the Spanish as far north as Yerba Buena (San Francisco), 1776
- Mexican province after Mexico won independence from Spain, 1822
- California Republic, after Mexico lost the Mexican War, 1848

IT USED TO BE ILLEGAL IN CALIFORNIA:

- to shoot any game bird or animal from a car—except a whale
- for a woman to go for a drive in a housecoat
- to peel an orange in a hotel room
- to set a mousetrap without a permit

Colorado

The Continental Divide

38th state to enter the Union, August 1, 1876

The Basics

POPULATION: 3,822,676
25th most populous state
AREA: 104,100 square miles
8th largest state
STATE CAPITAL: Denver
STATE BIRD: Lark bunting
STATE FLOWER: Rocky Mountain columbine
STATE TREE: Colorado blue spruce (also called Blue spruce, Colorado spruce, Balsam, and the Prickly, White, Silver, or Parry's spruce)
NICKNAMES: The Centennial State, the Highest State, the Switzerland of America
STATE MOTTO: *Nil sine numine* (Latin for "Nothing without Providence")
STATE SPORTS TEAMS: Colorado Rockies, baseball; Denver Broncos, football; Denver Nuggets, basketball; Colorado Avalanche, hockey
STATE ANIMAL: Rocky Mountain Bighorn sheep
STATE GEM: Aquamarine
STATE COLORS: Blue and white
STATE SONG: "Where the Columbines Grow," words and music by A.J. Flynn
STATE NATIONAL PARKS: Mesa Verde; Rocky Mountain; Great Sand Dunes National Monument—mountains of sand almost 700 feet high
STATE FESTIVALS: Renaissance Festival, Larkspur (June-August); Boom Days and Burro Race, Leadville (August); *Flauschink* Ski Events, Crested Butte (April); Kinetic Conveyance Challenge, Boulder (May); National Footbag Championship, Golden (July); World's Championship Pack Burro Race, Fairplay (July)

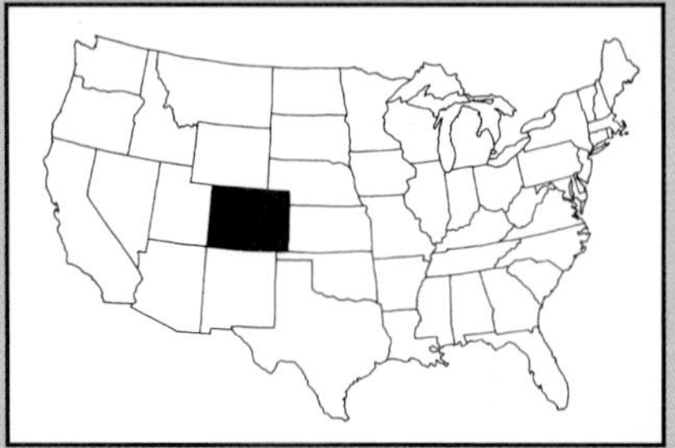

Tall, snowy mountains under a bright blue sky and sparkling sunshine… 54 of the nation's highest peaks, including Mt. Elbert, the second highest mountain in the United States—no wonder some people call Colorado the "American Switzerland!"

COWBOYS AND PIONEER WOMEN Colorado can be divided into three sections. To the east are dry, windy high plains. The central area is Colorado's Piedmont, a heartland containing 80 percent of the state's population. To the west are the Rocky Mountains, high and rugged. Through Colorado runs the Continental Divide, dividing rivers into those that run east and those that run west.

Garden of the Gods—an 8000-year-old rock formation in Colorado Springs

The capital and largest city is Denver, whose winter weather reports often begin with a rundown of skiing conditions. If you see a "D" under the date of any coin, it was made in the Denver mint.

Denver is a modern city, the commercial center of the Southwest. But you can find traces of its pioneer heritage throughout. The state Capitol building, for example, has a memorial window celebrating Aunt Clara Brown, a slave who bought her freedom in 1856 and worked her way west as a cook on a wagon train. At well over 50 years old, Brown began a new life, starting Denver's first laundry. In Denver's Black American West Museum and Heritage Center, you can learn about African-American cowboys such as Nat Love, who also started life as a slave but ended as a gunslinger on the frontier. South of Denver, black explorer Jim Beckwourth founded the frontier town of Pueblo. Beckwourth was an explorer, a fur trapper, an honorary war chief with the Crow Indians, and the man who discovered California's Beckwourth Pass.

Colorado's second city is Boulder, home of the University of Colorado. There you can take a tour of the Celestial Seasonings tea company. Colorado Springs is the home of the U.S. Olympic Center, where athletes train for the worldwide contest. It's also the site of the United States Air Force Academy and the North American Air Defense Command (NORAD).

In northwest Colorado, skiers head for Vail and Aspen. Southwest Colorado is famous for Mesa Verde, the U.S.'s largest cliff dwelling. The Anasazi, ancestors of today's Pueblo Indians, built multistoried buildings and created black-on-white pottery there between 550 and 1300.

PIKES PEAK OR BUST About four hundred years ago, Colorado was occupied by Cheyenne, Arapaho, and Ute, who chased the buffalo on Colorado's plains and lived in tipis—cone-shaped tents made of buffalo skin. The United States had acquired the territory by 1848, however, and first settled it in 1851. Between 1858 and 1891, gold and silver were discovered in Colorado, first near Denver, then at Central City, then at Leadville, and finally at Cripple Creek. Thousands of prospectors and settlers rushed into the state between the first discovery in 1858 and the last one in 1891. Pikes Peak or Bust! was their slogan, as they tried to reach Colorado's famous mountain.

Mesa Verde National Park, site of ancient Indian cliff dwellings

Slowly and reluctantly, in response to U.S. troops, the native peoples began to give up their homeland. In 1861 for example, the Cheyenne ceded a great portion of their territory to the United States. In 1864, angered by the U.S. massacre of 150 Indians at Sand Creek, the Cheyenne and the Arapaho began to fight again. But by 1867, they were defeated and forced to go to Indian Territory in Oklahoma. Likewise, in 1879, the Ute fought against U.S. encroachment, but by 1880 they had been relegated to a small reservation.

MASSACRE AT LUDLOW In 1914, another kind of massacre took place in Colorado. For many years, workers in the gold, silver, and copper mines had tried to win better wages and working conditions through their union, the Western Federation of Miners. But employers fought bitterly against these efforts, even calling in the State and National Guards to break strikes in 1903 and 1904. Ten years later, striking miners at the Colorado Fuel and Iron Corporation were horrified when the National Guard set fire to a tent colony for miners and their families at Ludlow, killing 20 people including 12 children. Over 1,000 miners took up arms in a 10-day uprising against the company, which was owned in part by John D. Rockefeller. The company called in federal troops to stop the uprising—and break the strike. Later, the miners erected a monument to those who had died.

Coyotes roam over the western United States.

AIRPLANES, AEROSPACE, AND ELECTRONICS Once agriculture was the mainstay of Colorado's economy. Even today, two-fifths of the state's land is used to graze cattle. Next, mining was king in Colorado—and uranium, gold, silver, copper, and oil are still big business. But Colorado's future lies in the aerospace, electronics, and research and development industries in and around Denver and Colorado Springs, inspired in part by the U.S. government's support for military research and nuclear power.

Fascinating Facts

COLORADO HALLS OF FAME:
- Figure Skating Hall of Fame, Colorado Springs
- Pro Rodeo Hall of Champions, Colorado Springs

DID YOU KNOW THAT... Boulder is the only city in the world that owns a glacier—Arapahoe Glacier. As the glacier melts, the city uses its water.

FAMOUS PERSON BORN IN COLORADO:
- Writer Ken Kesey, La Junta (1935-)

DID YOU KNOW THAT... Explorer Zebulon Pike was *not* the first person or the first European American to see Pikes Peak. Native Americans had known of the mountain for thousands of years; U.S. trapper James Purcell saw it in 1804.

IT USED TO BE ILLEGAL IN COLORADO:
- to watch a dogfight
- to hunt ducks from an airplane
- to throw shoes at a bridal couple

HOW COLORADO GOT ITS NAME: Colorado is Spanish for "red." The state was named for the Colorado River, which flows through canyons of red stone.

DID YOU KNOW THAT... When World War II began, Nazi dictator Adolf Hitler owned 8,960 acres of prime Colorado land.

COLORADO HAS THE NATION'S HIGHEST:
- state capital, Denver—one mile above sea level
- settlement—Climax—11,560 feet above sea level
- mean (average) altitude for a state
- automobile road—up to the top of Mount Evans, west of Denver—14,264 feet

DID YOU KNOW THAT... The song "America the Beautiful" was written by Katherine Lee Bates in 1893 after she rode up Pikes Peak in a horse-drawn wagon and got a good look at the view.

Connecticut

One of the state's covered bridges

5th state to enter the Union, January 9, 1788

The Basics

POPULATION: 3,274,238
28th most populous state
AREA: 5,544 square miles
48th largest state
STATE CAPITAL: Hartford
STATE BIRD: Robin (American robin)
STATE FLOWER: Mountain laurel
STATE TREE: White oak
NICKNAMES: The Constitution State, the Nutmeg State
STATE MOTTO: *Qui Transtulit Sustinet* (Latin for "He Who Transplanted Still Sustains")
SPORTS TEAMS: Hartford Whalers, hockey
STATE ANIMAL: Sperm whale
STATE INSECT: Praying mantis
STATE MINERAL: Garnet
STATE SHIP: *U.S.S. Nautilus*
STATE SONG: "Yankee Doodle Dandy," folk song
STATE LANDMARKS: State Capitol, Hartford; Mystic Seaport and Mystic Marinelife Aquarium, Mystic; Charter Oak Monument
NATIONAL PARKS: Weir Farm National Historic Site, Wilton, former home of artist J. Alden Weir; Salt Meadow Wildlife Refuge, Stewart B. McKinney Wildlife Refuge; Appalachian National Scenic Trail
STATE FESTIVALS: Balloons Over Bristol, Bristol (Memorial Day Weekend); Barnum Festival, Bridgeport (June-July); Powder House Day, New Haven (Spring); Shad Derby Festival, Windsor (May); Taste of Hartford, Hartford (May)

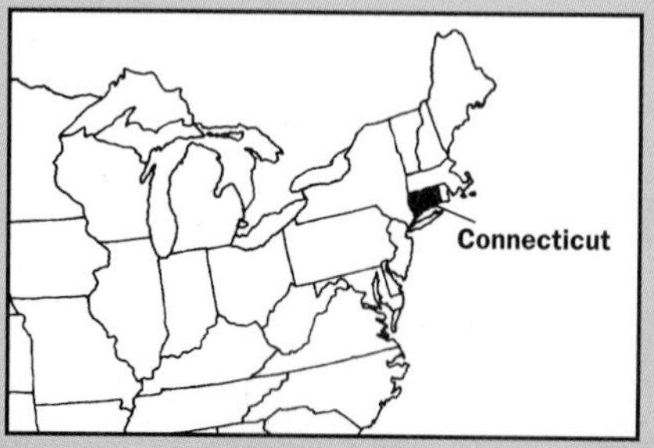

From the very beginnings of the United States, Connecticut has been a leader—in politics, in education, and in manufacturing. Today, the state has preserved its Colonial heritage—and gone on to be a leader in twentieth-century industry and finance.

VALLEYS AND SUBURBS You can divide Connecticut into four parts. To the northwest are the Western Uplands at the eastern end of the Berkshire Mountains. Below the mountains is the Connecticut Valley through which flows the Connecticut River. Farther east are the Eastern Uplands, hilly country occupied by dairy farms. And at the southern border of the state is the Long Island Sound with its inviting beaches and rocky coves.

Connecticut is an urban and suburban state, although you can also find plenty of rolling countryside dotted with small farms and scenic villages. The population is organized around two major urban areas. In the south are suburbs of New York City. Farther north, residents work at jobs in and around Hartford, the state capital.

Harriet Beecher Stowe (1811-1896) was born in Litchfield.

Other major Connecticut cities include Bridgeport, the former home of circus showman P.T. Barnum (you can visit the Barnum Museum there), and New Haven, site of Yale University. Historic sites abound in this state. In Hartford, you can visit Mark Twain's home, right next door to the house of Harriet Beecher Stowe, author of *Uncle Tom's Cabin.* Nearby is the birthplace of Noah Webster, who published the first American dictionary. Revolutionary War spy Nathan Hale once taught school in East Haddam. And at Groton is a submarine base, from which the first atomic-powered submarine, the *U.S.S. Nautilus*, was launched in 1954.

FUNDAMENTAL ORDERS Almost 150 years before the United States Constitution was signed, Connecticut residents met in Hartford to create the first constitution of a representative government. Known as the Fundamental Orders, the document declared that "the foundation of authority is in the first consent of the people." In other words, the people must agree to give authority to a government.

Connecticut residents had long prized independence. In 1636 Thomas Hooker led over a hundred settlers from Massachusetts to Connecticut to escape the harsh rule of the Puritans. The Fundamental Orders followed in 1639. In

1662 John Winthrop petitioned England's King Charles II for a charter that would make the colony almost independent of the British governor, Sir Edmund Andros. Charles agreed to Winthrop's request—but in 1687, the charter was revoked. Andros wanted to destroy the document, but the colonists were too fond of their liberty. According to legend, they hid the charter in a tree, the "Charter Oak," to guard their rights.

Yale University, New Haven, CT. One of America's oldest institutions.

Later, in 1770 Old Lyme residents had a "tea party" years before the one in Boston. They seized and burned a peddler's tea to protest the high British taxes on that product. In Lebanon, a group of citizens drafted a declaration of rights and liberties. When the Revolutionary War finally came, Connecticut furnished the United States with more soldiers and money than any other colony except Massachusetts. This state's food, clothing, and supplies were so important that George Washington called Connecticut "the Provisions State."

Square rigger at Mystic seaport

THE INSURANCE CAPITAL OF THE WORLD Early Connecticut was full of ports: New Haven, New London, and Bridgeport. Whalers sailed out of Mystic and Stonington, while Hartford linked the ocean and the Connecticut River.

Today, the sea is less important to this industrial state although the Coast Guard Academy is in Connecticut, as well as a naval submarine base. More important, however, is the massive finance industry in and around Hartford, the "Insurance Capital of the World."

Connecticut has also led in the development of modern industry. In 1798 Eli Whitney figured out that guns could be made more quickly and cheaply if some of the parts were machine-made to the same size every time. This made the parts interchangeable so that they always fit together. No longer did one worker make each gun separately. This idea was central to the system of mass production that we have today. Today, Connecticut leads the nation in production of small firearms, computers, helicopters, jet aircraft engines, submarines, ball and roller bearings, pins and needles, silverware, and thread.

Deer become a nuisance when people encroach on their land.

There is some farming in Connecticut, notably of apples, beef, eggs, milk, shrubs, flowers, and vegetables. Connecticut farmers also grow a special kind of tobacco used as the outside leaves on cigars.

Fascinating Facts

HOW CONNECTICUT WAS NAMED: The state's name comes from the Connecticut River, whose name comes from the Mohican word *quinnehtukqut*, meaning "long tidal river."

CONNECTICUT HAD THE NATION'S FIRST:
- newspaper—*Connecticut Courant*—1764 (now the *Hartford Courant*)
- law school—at Litchfield—1784
- tax-supported library—Abington—1793
- insurance company—1795
- American dictionary—first published by Noah Webster—1806
- public art museum—Wadsworth Athenaeum—1842
- use of anesthesia—Dr. Horace Wells, Hartford—1844
- commercial telephone switchboard and telephone directory—New Haven—1878
- pay telephone—Hartford—1889

CONNECTICUT INVENTIONS:
- Colt revolver—1835
- vulcanized rubber (rubber that can endure high temperatures)—Charles Goodyear—1839
- Singer sewing machine
- cotton gin

AMERICA'S FIRST... cigars, factory hats, machine-made combs, plows, tinware, friction matches, tacks... were made in Connecticut!

FAMOUS PEOPLE BORN IN CONNECTICUT:
- Revolutionary soldier Ethan Allen, Litchfield (1738-1789)
- Inventor/manufacturer Charles Goodyear, New Haven (1800-1860)
- Actress Katharine Hepburn, Hartford (1907-)

IT USED TO BE ILLEGAL IN CONNECTICUT:
- for mothers to kiss their children on Sunday
- for a man to write love letters to a woman if her mother had forbidden him to see her
- to build a dam—unless you were a beaver!

Delaware

Bombay Hook Wildlife Refuge

1st state to enter the Union, December 7, 1787

The Basics

POPULATION: 724,842
46th most populous state
AREA: 2,489 square miles
49th largest state
STATE CAPITAL: Dover
STATE BIRD: Blue hen chicken
STATE FLOWER: Peach blossom
STATE TREE: American holly (also known as holly, white holly, evergreen holly, and Boxwood)
NICKNAMES: The First State, the Diamond State, the Blue Hen State, the Peach State
STATE MOTTO: Liberty and Independence
STATE FISH: Weakfish
STATE BUG: Ladybug
STATE MINERAL: Sillimanite
STATE COLORS: Colonial blue and buff
STATE DRINK: Milk
STATE SONG: "Our Delaware," words by George B. Hynson, music by Will M. S. Brown
STATE LANDMARKS: Fort Delaware, Pea Patch Island; Odessa, featuring 200-year-old houses; Swedish log house, Wilmington, a 1638 log cabin; Winterthur Museum, Garden, and Library, outside Wilmington, a nine-story, 196-room mansion displaying two centuries of American furniture, china, and silver collected by Henry Francis du Pont; Nemours Mansion and Gardens, Wilmington, displaying luxury automobiles, antiques, and French gardens; Brandywine Zoo, Wilmington; Cypress Swamp, the U.S.'s northernmost natural stand of cypress trees
NATIONAL PARKS: Bombay Hook National Wildlife Refuge, near Smyrna; Prime Hook National Wildlife Refuge, near Milton

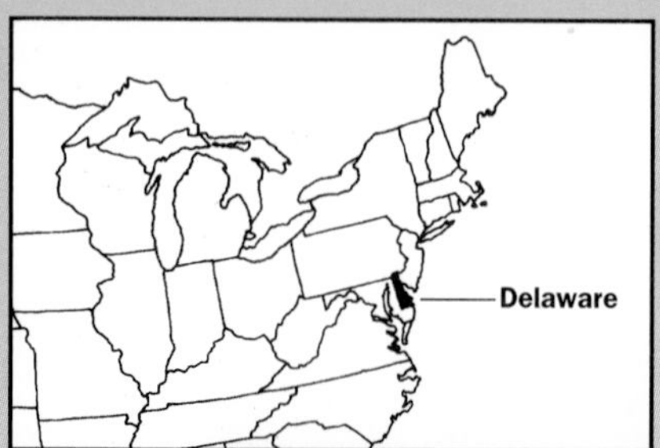

Delaware is the only colony to have been claimed by Sweden, Holland, and England. Delaware is notable for another reason: More than half of the nation's biggest companies are incorporated in Wilmington. Truly, the most important business in Delaware is business itself.

SHIPPING STATE ON THE SEABOARD Most of Delaware is a low, flat plain—farming country—although there are some rolling hills and valleys to the north. This mid-Atlantic state is strategically located along the Eastern seaboard, making it a key shipping center between New York and Washington, D.C. Its only major city, Wilmington, is conveniently situated within 10 miles of New Jersey, Pennsylvania, and Maryland.

Henry Hudson

LAND OF THE LOG CABIN Henry Hudson was probably the first European to visit Delaware when he sailed his famous ship, *Half Moon*, into Delaware Bay in 1609. He was followed in 1610 by Captain Samuel Argall of Virginia Colony. The first settlers, though, were the Dutch who in 1631 founded the town of Swaanendael near today's town of Lewes.

After the Indians drove out the Dutch, the Swedes arrived in 1638 to found Fort Christina (now part of Wilmington), named for their famous queen. The Dutchman Peter Minuit was hired by the Swedes to lead their expedition. The Swedes built the first American log cabins.

The Dutch still considered that they owned Delaware, however, and in 1656 Peter Stuyvesant brought a large fleet to enforce that claim. Then, in 1664, the English took over, making Delaware part of New York Colony. In 1673 the Dutch took the state again but returned it peacefully to the English in 1674.

Delaware's owners continued to change. In 1682 the state was given to William Penn as part of his new state, Pennsylvania. In fact, Penn's first landing in the United States was at Battery Park, New Castle, five miles south of Wilmington. Finally, in 1701 Penn gave Delaware its own separate legislature.

The people of Delaware had learned to prize their independence. Although he was dying of cancer, Delawarean Caesar Rodney made a famous ride from Dover to the Continental Congress in Philadelphia to cast the deciding vote in favor of independence. On December 7, 1787, Delaware became the first state to sign the Constitution. And during the Civil War, Delaware was one of four slave states to stick with the Union.

AMERICA'S FIRST BLACK CHURCH In the eighteenth century, there were slaves throughout the United States, north and south. And free African Americans were segregated everywhere. Even in churches, they were often required to sit in separate sections or not allowed to attend at all.

Richard Allen decided to change all that. In 1794 he founded the African Methodist Episcopal (AME) Church, the oldest and largest institution of African Americans. Allen grew up in Dover as a slave on the Stockley family plantation. There he had a religious awakening, converted his owner, and managed to buy his freedom. You can visit a marker commemorating this important man just north of the State Capitol.

BUSINESS HEADQUARTERS TO A NATION Delaware was once the center of the flour industry. Indeed, the price of wheat was set in Wilmington. In 1802, however, the Du Pont family built a gunpowder mill on the Brandywine River. This event marked the beginning of the Du Ponts' influence—and the start of Delaware's history as a manufacturing state. (At the Hagley Museum in Wilmington, you can still see the gunpowder mills, an old machine shop, and the Du Pont family mansion.)

The Delaware River was a key artery for shipping goods along the east coast, which helped bring more factories to Wilmington. In the nineteenth century, they made engines and railroad equipment. In the twentieth century, they produced machinery, ammunition, and aircraft.

Wilmington also became a major chemical center. Paints, dyes, and synthetic fabrics such as nylon and orlon are made there. These factories have brought prosperity to the state, but they may have also exposed many of Delaware's workers to toxic products, possibly leading to an unusually high rate of cancer in the state.

Delaware's orchards produce apples and peaches, while its poultry farms produce eggs and chickens. Delaware Bay yields a rich harvest of oysters, crabs, clams, and sea trout. And truck farms on Delaware's fertile plains produce soybeans, potatoes, corn, and vegetables.

The state Hall of Records in Dover

But Delaware's economy relies most of all on the corporate headquarters that are based here. The state charges no income tax or corporate tax, making it a favorable location for over 200,000 corporations. Even companies who actually do business elsewhere may officially incorporate in Delaware to take advantage of its tax laws. Banks from all over the nation have established their credit-card companies here.

Fascinating Facts

HOW DELAWARE GOT ITS NAME: Sir Thomas West, Lord de la Warr, was the first governor of the Virginia Colony. The Delaware River was named for him, and the state was named for the river. The British also used the name for the Delaware Indians, who in their own language were called the Lenni-Lenape.

DELAWARE HAD THE FIRST:

- steam railroad—out of New Castle—1831

DID YOU KNOW THAT...

- Johan Prinz, the governor of New Sweden from 1643 to 1653, weighed 400 pounds and was called the "Big Tub."
- When a ship carrying peas foundered on a sandbar, the peas grew and collected sand—forming Pea Patch Island.

FAMOUS PERSON BORN IN DELAWARE:

- Astronomer Annie Jump Cannon, Dover (1863-1941)

HOW DELAWARE GOT ITS NICKNAMES: Delaware was the "First State" to ratify the Constitution. Later, President Thomas Jefferson said Delaware was like a diamond, small but of great value—hence, "the Diamond State."

A CITY NICKNAME: Wilmington, Delaware, makes so many chemicals—the Du Pont Company is headquartered here—that it is called the Chemical Capital of the World.

DELAWARE INVENTIONS:

- nylon—This useful synthetic fabric was invented here and has become a mainstay of Delaware's textile industry.
- milling grain into flour—A Delaware mill was the first to put together all the steps in this process.

DID YOU KNOW THAT... since Delaware was the first state to ratify the Constitution, it gets to lead the parade of states every four years when the President is inaugurated.

DELAWARE IS TOPS IN:

- broiler chickens

District of Columbia

The White House was designed by James Hoban

Established December 1, 1800

The Basics

POPULATION: 543,213
AREA: 68.25 square miles
OFFICIAL BIRD: Wood thrush
OFFICIAL FLOWER: American Beauty rose
OFFICIAL TREE: Scarlet oak
NICKNAMES: The Nation's Capital, America's First City
OFFICIAL MOTTO: *Justitia Omnibus* (Latin for "Justice for all")
SPORTS TEAMS: Washington Redskins, football
STATE FLAG: based on George Washington's coat of arms
LANDMARKS: Capitol, White House, Washington Monument, Jefferson Memorial, Lincoln Memorial, Vietnam Veterans Memorial, Smithsonian Institution, National Gallery of Art, Library of Congress, U.S. Supreme Court Building, Kennedy Center, the Pentagon (home of the Department of Defense), United States Holocaust Memorial Museum, National Museum of Women in the Arts, The Shakespeare Theater.
HISTORIC SITES: Frederick Douglass National Historic Site—the abolitionist's home; Chesapeake & Ohio Canal, 19th-century waterway that carried lumber, coal, iron, and flour into Maryland; Washington Navy Yard
PARKS AND GARDENS: National Arboretum; Rock Creek Park; U.S. Botanic Garden
KEY RIVER: Potomac
D.C. FESTIVAL: Easter Egg Roll on the White House Lawn
ARTS GROUPS: National Symphony; Shakespeare Theater; Ford's Theater; Washington Opera society

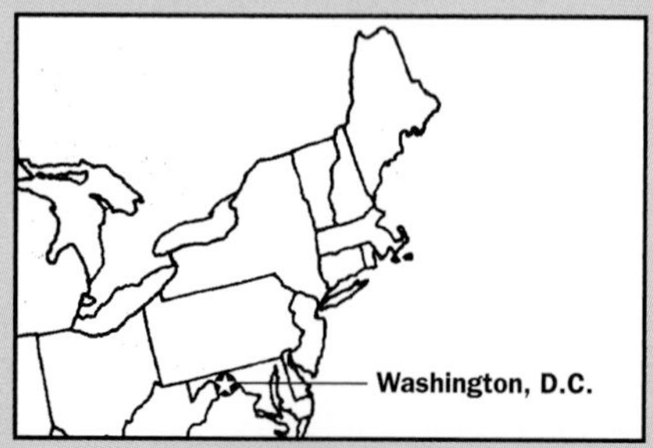

Visitors to Washington, D.C., have the chance to see United States history come to life. The historic buildings represent our nation's government, while the tradition of protest marches represents our democratic ideals.

MONUMENTS AND MUSEUMS The city of Washington and the District of Columbia are one and the same. That's why the city is often called just "D.C." or "The District." This city, which belongs to no state, is the capital of the whole United States. Here are our government buildings, along with monuments and museums that preserve our history and art. If you go to the National Archives, for example, you can see the original Declaration of Independence and Constitution.

U.S. Marine Monument depicting the flag raising on Iwo Jima during WWII. This is north of Arlington Cemetery, across the Potomac.

The Jefferson Memorial commemorates our third President, Thomas Jefferson, who wrote the Declaration. In the spring, some 3,000 Japanese cherry blossom trees bloom along the Tidal Basin at the foot of the Jefferson Memorial.

The Lincoln Memorial honors President Abraham Lincoln, who saw the nation through the Civil War. This memorial features a huge statue of Lincoln staring thoughtfully at the reflecting pool below.

Washington memorials do not only honor single individuals. Some, like the Vietnam Veterans Memorial, honor groups, such as the 58,000 Americans who were killed in Vietnam. This monument was designed by architect Maya Lin, who also designed the Civil Rights Memorial in Alabama. It consists of two black granite walls etched with the names of the dead. Nearby, the Vietnam Women's Memorial honors the women who served as nurses and soldiers.

Another highlight of Washington is the Smithsonian Institution, a huge complex of museums, including the National Air and Space Museum, the National Gallery of Art, the National Museum of Natural History, and the National Museum of American History. In these buildings, you can find everything from dinosaur bones to the evening gowns worn by first ladies at their husbands' inaugurations.

The city of Washington is laid out like a big wheel. Huge, tree-lined avenues are the spokes of the wheel, and the Capitol—where Congress meets—is the hub. That way, visitors will always remember that the main business of Washington, D.C., is to govern our country.

BUILDING THE NATION'S CAPITAL The idea of a District of Columbia began in 1783 when the Continental Congress decided that our nation needed a capital. It seemed unfair for any one state to have that honor. So Maryland and Virginia offered some of their land to create a new entity, the District of Columbia, named for Christopher Columbus.

The name Washington, of course, came from our nation's first President. In 1791 he was allowed to choose the exact site of the new capital. He also appointed French architect Pierre Charles L'Enfant to design the city and its buildings. In 1793 George Washington, a former surveyor, laid the cornerstone of the new Capitol himself.

In June 1800 the government moved from Philadelphia to Washington, even though the Capitol building wasn't yet finished. Ironically, Washington was the only President who never lived in Washington. The second President, John Adams, was the first to live in the White House.

"MARCH ON WASHINGTON" America has a long tradition of protest, and often that protest has centered on Washington. In 1894, for example, Jacob Coxey and his 500 followers, known as Coxey's Army, marched into the nation's capital to protest unemployment and demand government action to create jobs. Coxey was arrested for walking on the grass, and the protest fell apart. But in 1931 and 1932 the Great Depression brought the hardest time the United States had ever known. Hunger marchers converged on Washington, D.C., demanding social programs to help cope with their new poverty. In 1932 veterans who were not receiving their promised government bonuses actually rioted in Washington, until the U.S. Army was called in.

U.S. Supreme Court Building

Civil rights and African-American equality was the theme of the famous 1963 "March on Washington." Half a million people gathered in front of the Lincoln Memorial to hear Dr. Martin Luther King, Jr., give his now-famous speech, "I Have A Dream."

In 1969 marchers came to Washington to protest the war in Vietnam. Since then, people have marched for equal rights, freedom of choice, and Right to Life. Labor unions have marched for better treatment of working people, and gay and lesbian people have marched for their own civil rights. Other marchers have both supported and opposed equal rights for women and for gays. Still others have demonstrated for better treatment of workers and of children. In 1995 black men participated in the Million Man march to encourage increased family responsibility. Marching on Washington to make your voice heard is clearly an American tradition.

Fascinating Facts

DID YOU KNOW THAT... The United States had 36 Presidents before the people of Washington, D.C., were allowed to vote for their first President. Washington residents could not vote for President until 1964, and they couldn't elect their own Mayor until 1975. They still have no voting representative in Congress. This issue is known as *Home Rule*, and is still quite controversial in Washington.

FAMOUS PEOPLE BORN IN THE DISTRICT OF COLUMBIA:

- Actress Helen Hayes (1900-1993)
- Actress Goldie Hawn (1945-)
- Actor William Hurt (1950-)

CAPITOL FACT:

- One early plan for the Capitol called for the statue of a large rooster on top.

WASHINGTON TRAGEDIES:

- On April 14, 1865, President Abraham Lincoln was shot while attending a play at Ford's Theater.
- On September 19, 1881, President James Garfield died from an assassination attempt made at a Washington rail station.

DID YOU KNOW THAT...

- Roosevelt Island in the Potomac River at Theodore Roosevelt Memorial Bridge "grows" about 20 acres every hundred years. That's because new land forms around the brush that floats down the river and catches on the island.

WASHINGTON MONUMENT FACTS:

- 555 feet tall, obelisk-shaped
- Construction, begun in 1848, was interrupted by the Civil War—hence the color change one-third of the way up. It was completed in 1884.
- When temperature inside the monument goes up quickly, moisture condenses—and produces an indoor "rain."

IT USED TO BE ILLEGAL IN THE DISTRICT OF COLUMBIA:

- to drive a taxicab without a broom and shovel in the car
- to punch a bull in the nose

Florida

The Everglades

27th state to enter the Union, March 3, 1845

The Basics

POPULATION: 14,399,985
4th most populous state
AREA: 65,758 square miles
22nd largest state
STATE CAPITAL: Tallahassee
STATE BIRD: Mockingbird
STATE FLOWER: Orange blossom
STATE TREE: Palmetto palm
NICKNAMES: The Sunshine State, the Alligator State, the Everglades State, the Orange State
STATE MOTTO: "In God We Trust"
STATE ANIMAL: Florida panther
STATE FRESHWATER FISH: Largemouth bass
STATE SALTWATER FISH: Atlantic sailfish
STATE MARINE MAMMAL: Manatee
STATE SALTWATER MAMMAL: Porpoise
STATE STONE: Agatized coral
STATE SHELL: Horse conch
STATE GEM: Moonstone
STATE DRINK: Orange juice
STATE AIR FAIR: Central Florida Air Fair
STATE FESTIVAL: Calle Ocho-Open House 8, Miami
STATE PAGEANT: "Indian River"
STATE PLAY: "Cross and Sword"
STATE LITTER CONTROL SYMBOL: "Glenn Glitter"
STATE SONG: "Old Folks at Home" (also known as "Swanee River"), words and music by Stephen Foster
STATE LANDMARKS: John F. Kennedy Space Center at Cape Canaveral; Thomas A. Edison Home and Museum, Ft. Myers
NATIONAL PARKS: Everglades National Park; Biscayne National Park; Big Cypress National Preserve

Most of Florida is a peninsula—a long piece of land extending into the Atlantic Ocean and the Gulf of Mexico, connected to the mainland by only a tiny piece of land. Florida has the second-longest coastline in the United States (after Alaska)—4,000 miles—known for its white, sandy beaches and sparkling sapphire waters. No wonder the "Sunshine State" is such a popular spot for both tourists and retirees.

PANTHERS, CROCODILES, AND MICKEY MOUSE Florida is the southernmost state on the U.S. mainland. Over 30,000 lakes dot this humid, low-lying land. The largest lake, Okeechobee, covers 700 square miles. Florida's northern panhandle is rural, hilly country with a temperate climate, but the southern peninsula has tropical weather with very high temperatures and a long rainy season. Florida's most famous natural feature is the Everglades, one of the world's largest swamps, full of alligators, crocodiles, panthers, bobcats, and sea turtles.

Pastel-colored Victorian houses are seen all over Key West.

Off the state's southern tip, are the Florida Keys, a 31-island chain curving out into the Gulf of Mexico. The most famous islands are Key West and Key Largo whose landscape and climate resemble those of other Caribbean islands.

Florida's largest city is Miami. More than half the people in Miami are of Latino heritage, many of them from families that emigrated from Cuba during the twentieth century. Other Cuban emigrés went to Ybor City, near Tampa, creating the famous cigar-making industry there.

The city of Orlando is famous for its many theme parks: Sea World, Cypress Gardens, Disney World, and Splendid China, which re-creates many of China's most beautiful monuments and palaces. Tampa has many theme parks as well, including Busch Gardens and a Seminole Indian village where you can see people wrestling with alligators. Farther south, in Sarasota, circuses come to spend the winter, as you can learn at the Ringling Museum.

An important Florida historical site is Bethune-Cookman College in Daytona Beach. There, in 1904, Mary McLeod Bethune opened the Daytona

Playful dolphins are crowd favorites at Sea World.

Educational and Industrial Training School for Negro Girls. Although it had little money, the school's enrollment grew to 250 within its first two years, and in 1923 it merged with Cookman College, the first state school to offer higher education to African-American males. Bethune was active in civil rights and in education until she died in 1955.

African-American writer, Zora Neale Hurston was born in Eatonville, just north of Orlando. At that time—1901—Eatonville was the only incorporated black town in the nation. Hurston went on to write novels and to collect African-American folklore.

FROM ST. AUGUSTINE TO CAPE CANAVERAL The first permanent European settlement in North America was St. Augustine, founded by Spanish explorers in 1565. For the next two hundred years, the English and the Spanish fought over Florida as pirates and buccaneers raided the coast. In 1750, Creek Indians from Georgia also came into the area, where they were joined by runaway slaves and became known as the Seminoles.

When the Revolutionary War was fought in 1777, Florida was in British hands. In 1783 Florida passed back into Spanish hands. But by 1821 the United States had acquired Florida from Spain.

In 1835 the United States began a seven-year war with the Seminoles, but this was the only Indian war the United States did not win.

Seminole clothes hang from the walls of this museum.

Over a century later, Florida won world fame for its role in the space program. In 1961 Commander Alan Shepard was launched from Cape Canaveral to become the first American in space, and the next year Colonel John Glenn became the first American to orbit the earth. In 1969 Neil Armstrong left Florida to become the first person to walk on the moon. Today you can visit Spaceport USA at the John F. Kennedy Space Center in Cape Canaveral.

TOURISTS IN THE SUNSHINE STATE Tourism is probably Florida's most important industry, as more than 25 million people visit the state each year. Farming in Florida is dominated by citrus—oranges, grapefruit, and lemons. The state also produces corn, peanuts, soybeans, pecans, avocados, and flowers. Florida industry makes pulp and paper from the state's trees, and processes food, especially frozen orange juice. Electronic products are manufactured from industries clustered around Cape Canaveral.

Fascinating Facts

FLORIDA ANIMALS:

- On Lake George, near Seville, hogs swim out into the shallow waters to catch fish for dinner.
- At Hialeah Park, you can see pink flamingos eat only with their heads upside down.

FLORIDA HAS THE LONGEST... highway built over ocean waters—the Overseas Highway, running from Miami to Key West over the Florida Keys.

FLORIDA IS TOPS IN:

- cypress; turpentine; cigars; grapefruit (70% of world's crop)

FLORIDA HAD THE NATION'S FIRST:

- permanent European settlement—St. Augustine, founded by the Spanish in 1565

FLORIDA HAS THE NATION'S LARGEST:

- peninsula—over 400 miles of land between the Atlantic and the Gulf of Mexico
- cruise-ship port—Miami

DID YOU KNOW THAT... Florida's population was the nation's fastest-growing between 1980 and 1990.

HOW FLORIDA GOT ITS NAME: Spanish explorer Ponce de León landed on the Florida coast on Easter Sunday. He named the land *La Florida*, to honor the Easter feast of flowers, *Pascua Florida.*

DID YOU KNOW THAT... During the hurricane of 1926, the Miami barometer reached a record low—and hundreds of people fainted for lack of oxygen.

FLORIDA HALLS OF FAME:

- International Swimming Hall of Fame, Fort Lauderdale
- Professional Golf Association Hall of Fame, Palm Beach Gardens

IT USED IT BE ILLEGAL IN FLORIDA:

- to lure a neighbor's cook away and then hire that cook
- to stay in an election booth more than five minutes

Georgia

Forsythe Fountain, Savannah

4th state to enter the Union, January 2, 1788

The Basics

POPULATION: 7,353,225
10th most populous state
AREA 59,441 square miles
24th largest state
STATE CAPITAL: Atlanta
STATE BIRD: Brown thrasher
STATE FLOWER: Cherokee rose
STATE TREE: Live oak
NICKNAMES: The Empire State of the South, the Peach State, the Goober State, Yankee-Land of the South, the Buzzard State
STATE MOTTOES: *Agriculture and Commerce*, and *Wisdom, Justice, Moderation*
SPORTS TEAMS: Atlanta Braves, baseball; Atlanta Falcons, football; Atlanta Hawks, basketball
STATE FISH: Largemouth bass
STATE INSECT: Honeybee
STATE MARINE MAMMAL: Right whale
STATE MINERAL: Staurolite
STATE FOSSIL: Shark tooth
STATE GEM: Quartz
STATE ATLAS: *The Atlas of Georgia*
STATE SONG: "Georgia on My Mind," words by Stuart Gorrell, music by Hoagy Carmichael; originally "Georgia," words by Lottie Bell Wylie, music by Robert Loveman (changed in 1979)
STATE WALTZ: "Our Georgia," words and music by James B. Burch
STATE LANDMARK: Ocmulgee National Monument, near Macon—preserving Indian ways of life from 8000 B.C. to 1717 A.D.
STATE FESTIVALS: Appalachian Wagon Train, Chatsworth (July); Bite of the 'Boro, Statesboro (May); Okefenokee Spring Fling, Waycross (March); Tybee Jubilee, Tybee Island (September)

Georgia is an intriguing mix of old and new. In the old town of Savannah, you can still see gracious pre-Civil War mansions with their white pillars and manicured lawns. But you can also see the glass-and-steel skyscrapers of Atlanta, the new commercial center of the South.

MANY LANDSCAPES Georgia is the largest state east of the Mississippi, with a wide variety of landscapes. To the northeast are the Blue Ridge Mountains, while to the northwest are the Appalachians. Moving south, you find the fertile Appalachian Valley and below that, the Piedmont Plateau. Offshore are Jekyll, Sea and St. Simons Islands—once home to some of the richest families in the nation. And in the southeastern corner of the state is the Okefenokee Swamp, over 700 square miles of tropical wilds with 54 species of reptile (including alligators!), 49 different types of mammals, and 234 different kinds of birds.

Georgia's capital and largest city is Atlanta, a town that sprang to new life after it was burned by troops under Union General William Sherman. Today it's headquarters to the Coca-Cola corporation and to Ted Turner's communications empire, including CNN. The 1996 Summer Olympics were held in Atlanta. And Atlanta is the site of Ebenezer Baptist Church, where Martin Luther King Jr. first preached.

Savannah is Georgia's oldest city. General Sherman occupied it for more than a year at the end of his march, but it was never burned. Today it's the place to see historic homes from the 1700s, including the home of Girl Scout founder Juliette Low. Also noteworthy are Athens, home of the University of Georgia, and Augusta, site of the Master's Golf Tournament.

An alligator basking in the sun

AMERICA'S FIRST HAVEN In 1733 British General James Oglethorpe arrived in Georgia with 120 people, intending to found a colony as a haven for England's poor and oppressed. He made two rules: no drinking of alcohol, and no slaves. Georgia was the last colony created by the British in America.

Less than fifty years later, Georgia fought with its fellow colonies against the British. It soon allowed both drinking and slavery. And in 1793 Georgia resident Eli Whitney invented a machine that would make slavery even more profitable. Until then, cotton seeds had to be separated from cotton fibers by hand, a slow and expensive process. But Whitney's cotton gin could separate

500 pounds of cotton in a single day. Suddenly, cotton plantations could make huge fortunes. Plantation owners were more eager than ever to save money by using slaves to grow, tend, and pick their cotton.

Juliette Gordon Low (1860-1927)

When the election of President Lincoln seemed to threaten slavery, Georgia, like its Southern neighbors, seceded from the Union. The Civil War was extremely hard on many Georgians. Some 90 percent of Atlanta's buildings were destroyed in the 117-day siege of that city.

CARPETBAGGERS AND THE KU KLUX KLAN

After the war, Georgia still refused to recognize African-American rights. It wouldn't ratify the 14th amendment, which guaranteed equal protection under the law regardless of race, color, or creed. Nor would it ratify the 15th amendment, guaranteeing voting rights. A white terrorist group, the Ku Klux Klan, was formed to harass and kill African Americans who exercised their rights. After supporters of the Confederacy were barred from holding office, "carpetbaggers"—northerners who had come South—dominated Georgia's government. In 1870, a legislature that included African Americans and their supporters accepted the 15th Amendment, and Georgia rejoined the Union.

Nobel prize winner
Dr. Martin Luther King, Jr.

The Klan continued to operate. And when Georgia's old leaders got back into power, they continued to oppose African-Americans' rights into the twentieth century. In 1948 Governor Herman Talmadge said he'd support segregation at all costs. These racists had opposition from Ralph McGill, the editor of the Atlanta Constitution, and Mayor Ivan Allen, which is why Georgia was considered more progressive than its neighbors. And in 1966, Lester Maddox, who had closed his Atlanta restaurant rather than integrate it, was elected governor. In 1961 black students Charlayne Hunter and Hamilton Holmes had to get a court order to attend the all-white University of Georgia. Even in 1987 the Ku Klux Klan was active in the town of Cumming. But some 10,000 civil rights supporters marched to protest the Klan. Times had finally changed.

A WEALTHY LAND Georgia has one of the most prosperous economies in the South, with factories to process the food and timber that it grows in its farms and forests. Agricultural products include peanuts, corn, tobacco, sugar, pecans, and the famous Georgia peaches. Industries make peanut butter and peanut oil, and make paper from the state's forests. Atlanta is also a hub of commercial and financial activity.

Fascinating Facts

GEORGIA HAD THE FIRST:

- U.S. gold rush—-at Dahlonega—1829
- cotton gin—invented by Eli Whitney—1793
- steamship to cross the Atlantic—the *Savannah*—sailed from Atlanta, 1819
- Coca-Cola served—in an Atlanta drugstore—1887

PRESIDENT BORN IN GEORGIA:

- Jimmy Carter (1934-), 39th President

OTHER FAMOUS PEOPLE BORN IN GEORGIA:

- *Uncle Remus* author Joel Chandler Harris, Eatonton (1848-1908)
- Baseball player "Ty" Cobb, Narrows (1886-1961)
- Blues singer Gertrude "Ma" Rainey, Columbus (1886-1939)
- Writer Carson McCullers, Columbus (1917-1967)
- Baseball pioneer "Jackie" Robinson, Cairo (1919-1972)
- Civil Rights Leader Martin Luther King, Jr., Atlanta (1929-1968)
- Writer Alice Walker, Eatonton (1944-)

GEORGIA HAS THE NATION'S LARGEST:

- freshwater swamp—the Okefenokee
- urban landmark—Savannah's historic district
- isolated granite boulder—Stone Mountain, Atlanta—825 feet high, 7 billion cubic feet

HOW GEORGIA GOT ITS NAME: James Oglethorpe honored the English King George II who had given him the charter for the land.

DID YOU KNOW THAT... Although Georgia was the fourth state to ratify the Constitution, it didn't ratify the Bill of Rights until 1939.

GEORGIA IS TOPS IN:

- turpentines and resins
- peanuts and pecans
- lima beans and pimiento peppers

DID YOU KNOW THAT... In the 1740s, Mary Jones was the captain of Fort Wimberley during a Spanish attack. She and her British forces were victorious.

Hawaii

The Basics

POPULATION: 1,183,723
41st most populous state
AREA: 10,932 square miles
43rd largest state
STATE CAPITAL: Honolulu
STATE BIRD: Nene (Hawaiian goose)
STATE FLOWER: Yellow hibiscus
STATE TREE: Kukui (Candlenut)
NICKNAMES: The Aloha State, the Pineapple State, the Paradise of the Pacific, the Youngest State
STATE MOTTO: *Ua Mau ke Ea o ka Aina i ka Pono* (Hawaiian for "The life of the land is perpetuated in righteousness")
STATE COLORS: Each inhabited island has its own color: Hawaii, Red; Maui, Pink; Molokai, Green; Kahoolawe, Gray; Lanai, Yellow; Oahu, Yellow; Kauai, Purple; Nihau, White
STATE SONG: "Hawaii Ponoi," folk song
OFFICIAL LANGUAGES: English and Hawaiian
NATIONAL PARK: Hawaii Volcanoes; Haleakala
STATE FESTIVAL: Hula Festival, Honolulu (August)

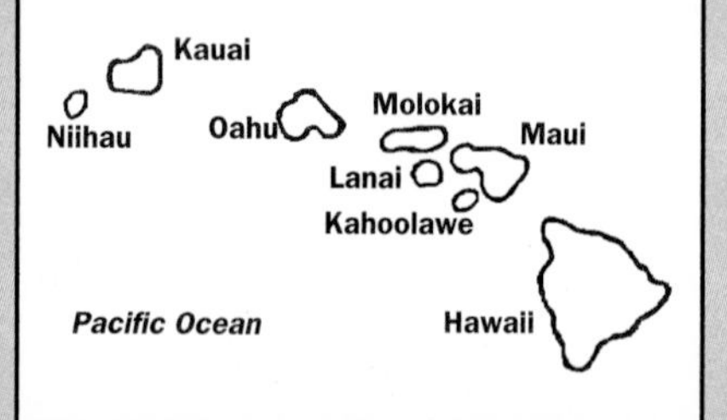

Diamond Head, on Oahu

50th state to enter the Union, August 21, 1959

Hawaii is beloved by natives and tourists for its lush tropical growth, beautiful beaches and perfect climate. The weather is so good here that the Hawaiian language has no word for "weather"!

VOLCANO ISLANDS The word "Hawaii" refers both to a single island and to a chain of 132 islands stretching over 1,500 miles across the Pacific Ocean. These islands were formed by undersea volcanoes thrusting up 15,000 feet from the ocean floor. Only the eight largest islands are inhabited.

Statue of the Hawaiian war god Kamehameha

Most people live on Oahu, the home of Hawaii's capital and largest city, Honolulu. Here you can visit the only royal palace in America, the Iolani Palace, built in 1882. Nearby is the Kawaiahao Church, built in 1842 of solid blocks of coral and used by Hawaiian royalty for coronations, weddings, and funerals. Just outside Honolulu is Waikiki Beach, as well as Diamond Head, an extinct volcano. On Diamond Head Road is a bronze tablet honoring Amelia Earhart—who in 1935 became the first pilot ever to make the 18-hour solo flight from Hawaii to North America.

The largest Hawaiian island is Hawaii itself. Here you can see cowboys herding cattle, dense rain forests, snow-covered mountains, black sand beaches, ancient temples, and the largest active volcano in the world, Mauna Loa. Here, too, is Akaka Falls, 442 feet high.

Kauai, the "Garden Island," has huge sugar plantations. It's also home to Waimea Canyon—3,600 feet deep, 2 miles wide, and 10 miles long.

PEARL HARBOR: A DAY OF INFAMY AND COURAGE At Oahu is Pearl Harbor, where a United States naval base was attacked by the Japanese on December 7, 1941, prompting the United States to enter World War II. This surprise attack revealed the heroism of Dorrie Miller, an African-American mess attendant on the battleship *Arizona.* At that time, the navy was segregated: black sailors were not even trained for combat. But when the bombing began, Miller ran up on deck and pulled an injured officer to safety. Then he took an anti-aircraft gun, which he had never been trained to use, and shot down four Japanese planes. Finally, he was ordered to abandon the ship, which sank soon after. Five months later, he was awarded the Navy Cross for "extraordinary courage." In 1988 he was awarded the Congressional Medal of Honor to commemorate his bravery.

Queen Liliuokalani, Hawaii's last monarch (1838-1917)

ONE LAND, MANY PEOPLES Hawaii today has the most diverse racial and cultural mix in the world, with some 60 different combinations of ancestry and no racial majority. About 20 percent of the population is native Hawaiian (Polynesian), 23.2 percent is Japanese, 11.3 percent is Filipino, and less than one-fourth is of European ancestry. The history of Hawaii explains how this unique cultural mix came to be.

The first settlers of the Hawaiian islands were probably the Polynesians, who between A.D. 300 and 750 arrived in their huge, double-hulled canoes. As many as 100 people rowed a single boat as these Indo-Malaysians sailed thousands of miles across the Pacific Ocean.

In 1778 Captain James Cook and his followers landed at Kauai. Cook called the land the Sandwich Islands, after his patron, the Earl of Sandwich. Because of his many injustices to the islanders, he was killed in a quarrel in 1779. Soon, though, missionaries, traders, and whalers came to Hawaii, transforming the land as their influence was felt. In the 1820s, for example, traders depleted the island's sandalwood. Hawaii's population dropped rapidly as they were exposed to unfamiliar diseases. Meanwhile, in 1810 King Kamehameha united the islands into one kingdom, recognized by the United States in 1843.

Throughout the late 1800s the United States expanded its influence in Hawaii. The first major step towards statehood came in 1875 when the U.S. won exclusive rights to Pearl Harbor. In 1893 Queen Liliuokalani was overthrown in a bloodless revolution. A republic was established in 1894 with an American, S. B. Dole, as its president. In 1898 Hawaii was annexed by the United States and in 1900 became a territory with Dole as its first governor. It did not become a state, however, until 1959.

In 1903 pineapples introduced from South America became a key crop for Hawaii. Filipino and Japanese workers were brought into the area to harvest and pack this valuable fruit. Thus Hawaii created its unique mixture of European, Asian, and South Pacific ancestry.

PINEAPPLES AND SUGAR Tourism is the biggest industry in Hawaii. Next in importance are sugar and pineapple. Recently, macadamia nuts and coffee have become significant crops as well. In the late 1980s Japanese and U.S. investors increased their investment in real estate, hoping to benefit both from tourism and from the U.S. citizens retiring here.

Costumed children perform a traditional dance.

Fascinating Facts

HAWAII IS THE ONLY STATE:
- not in North America
- made up of islands
- with two official languages, English and Hawaiian
- with a tropical climate
- ever governed by monarchs who were recognized by international law

THE EIGHT LARGEST HAWAIIAN ISLANDS: From northwest to southeast: Niihau, Kauai, Oahu, Molokai, Lanai, Maui, Kahoolawe, Hawaii

HAWAIIAN SUPERLATIVES:
- southernmost state
- wettest place on earth—Mt. Waialeale, on Kauai—460-inch average annual rainfall
- world's largest inactive volcano crater—on Maui
- world's longest island chain

HAWAII IS TOPS IN:
- canned pineapple products

THE ALOHA STATE: "Aloha" has many different meanings: *welcome, goodbye, love,* and *friendship.*

DID YOU KNOW THAT... Surfing was invented in Hawaii by kings and chieftains. Today it's a popular sport among many adults and children.

HOW HAWAII GOT ITS NAME: The islands were named by King Kamehameha I in 1819, possibly from Hawaii Loa, who according to native folklore first discovered the islands. The name may also have come from two Hawaiian words, *Hawa,* meaning "homeland," and *ii,* meaning "small."

DID YOU KNOW THAT... The Hawaiian language has only 12 letters: H, K, L, M, N, P, W, and the five vowels. Every consonant must be followed by a vowel, and each word ends with a vowel.

BIG AND SMALL: One large Hawaiian fish is called *O*. Another much smaller fish is called *Humuhumunukunukuapua'a.*

IT USED TO BE ILLEGAL IN HAWAII:
- to put pennies in your ears
- for a barber to lather a customer with a shaving brush

Idaho

Sawtooth wilderness

43rd state to enter the Union, July 3, 1890

The Basics

POPULATION: 1,189,251
40th most populous state
AREA: 83,574 square miles
14th largest state
STATE CAPITAL: Boise
STATE BIRD: Mountain bluebird
STATE FLOWER: Idaho syringa
STATE TREE: Western White Pine (also known as the White pine, the Idaho white pine, the Finger Cone pine, the Mountain pine, the Little Sugar pine, and the Mountain Weymouth pine)
NICKNAMES: The Gem State, the Gem of the Mountains, the Potato State
STATE MOTTO: *Esto perpetua* (Latin for "It is forever")
STATE HORSE: Appaloosa
STATE GEM: Star Garnet
STATE SONG: "Here We Have Idaho," lyrics by McKinley Helm and Albert J. Tompkins, music by Sallie Hume Douglas
STATE LANDMARKS: Thousand Springs (in which each spring sprouts from the side of a single cliff); Birds of Prey World Center, Boise (with the world's largest collection of living raptors); Hell's Canyon (5,500 feet deep—deeper than the Grand Canyon); Sacagawea's birthplace; Nez Percé National Historic Park, Spalding
NATIONAL PARKS: Challis National Forest; Sawtooth National Forest; Silent City of the Rocks National Reserve
STATE PARKS: Harriman State Park, including the world-famous fly-fishing stream, Henry's Fork of the Snake River; Ponderosa State Park

Idaho is a Rocky Mountain state, and no matter where you go, you're rarely out of sight of a mountain. Some people say that if you flattened all the mountains in Idaho, the state would be bigger than Texas!

WATERFALLS, TROUT STREAMS, AND THE CRATERS OF THE MOON Northern Idaho is famous for its forests—home to deer, elk, and other game. It has the greatest concentration of lakes anywhere in the country, as well as many streams that are rich in trout and salmon.

Central Idaho features one of Idaho's most famous landmarks, the Craters of the Moon. These brightly colored lava fields and craters of extinct volcanoes bear an eerie resemblance to the barren, windswept landscape of the moon, and NASA astronauts used to train here. Nearby Sun Valley is the site of America's first ski resort founded in 1935, the first place where ski chairlifts were used.

Silver City, Idaho. When the gold ran out this mining town became a ghost town.

Southern Idaho is flatter and more diverse, featuring desert, farms, and ranchland. You can still see cowboys herding cattle near such towns as Bungalow Cow Camp and Coffee Can Saddle. Snake River in southern Idaho is home to the giant white sturgeon, the biggest freshwater fish in North America. Some weigh more than 1,000 pounds, and fishermen have to use a two-horse wagon to pull them out of the water. In southwest Idaho, near the town of Twin Falls, the Snake River drops 212 feet over the Shoshone Falls, which are higher than New York's Niagara. Most people in Idaho live on or near the banks of the Snake, which provides most of the state's electrical power.

ON THE TRAIL OF LEWIS AND CLARK For thousands of years, Idaho has been home to such Indian peoples as the Kootenai, Nez Percé, Coeur d'Alene, Shoshone, and Paiute. Sometime around 1786, near the present town of Salmon, Sacagawea, a Shoshone, was born. Sacagawea eventually served as a translator for Meriwether Lewis and William Clark as they explored the Northwest Territory for the United States. Lewis and Clark passed through the northern part of the Idaho "panhandle" in 1805, much aided by the Nez Percé Indians.

The first European outpost in Idaho was the trading post established in 1809 by David Thompson of the North West Company on the eastern shore of Lake

A baby timber wolf and its mother

Pend Oreille (the lake's name comes from the French word for "earring"). In 1834 the Army constructed Fort Hall and Fort Boise (later Idaho's capital, from the French word bois, meaning "forest"). Forts and trading posts formed the basis of the Oregon Trail, which by 1845 was a well-traveled road. Travelers tended to pass through Idaho on their way to the more hospitable lands of the West Coast, however, and the first permanent settlement in Idaho was not established until June 15, 1860, when a group of Utah Mormons settled at Franklin. Idahoans now celebrate this day as Pioneer Day. As in most Western states, Indians were gradually resettled onto smaller reservations as settlers arrived.

GOLD, SILVER, AND LEAD Gold was first mined in Idaho in the 1860s. The mines relied heavily on Chinese workers. In 1870 some one-third of Idaho's 15,000 residents were Chinese, despite the anti-Chinese violence of 1866-1867 that had left almost one hundred people dead.

Union Station in Boise, Idaho

The discovery of silver in the 1880s brought in new mine workers, who responded to harsh working conditions by forming unions, such as the Western Federation of Miners. In 1892, federal troops were called in and martial law declared to break the strikes that had spread through northern Idaho. More than 600 union supporters were arrested. Martial law was established again in 1899, when hundreds more miners were imprisoned for six months.

The often bloody battles between workers and owners continued into the twentieth century. In 1906, for example, labor leader "Big Bill" Haywood was arrested for "conspiracy" after former governor Frank Steunenberg was assassinated. Famed defense lawyer Clarence Darrow successfully defended Haywood and other accused union leaders. Also active in Idaho were the "Wobblies," members of the so-called Industrial Workers of the World (IWW), of which Haywood was also a leader. The IWW organized miners, lumberjacks, and migrant farmworkers.

Today many of Idaho's mines have closed. The IWW has long since disappeared, and the unions there now are both weaker and more accepted by employers. Idaho no longer produces gold, but it still produces almost half of the nation's silver and all of the nation's antimony, which is used in making alloys (combinations of metals), storage batteries, cable sheathing, and paint pigments. It ranks second among states in the production of lead and vanadium, used in alloys. Other important Idaho products include potatoes and sugar beets. Tourism is also becoming a major industry.

Fascinating Facts

IDAHO IS TOPS IN...

- silver production (Sunshine mine, in Shoshone County, is the nation's largest)
- potatoes
- barley
- trout
- antimony

IDAHO POTATO FACTS:

- One fourth of the U.S. potato crop comes from Idaho.
- Two thirds of all U.S. *processed* potatoes come from Idaho.
- Each year, Idaho grows 27 billion potatoes—enough for every person in the United States to have 120 potatoes each.

AN IDAHO FOOTBALL CHEER: "Dice 'em, hash 'em, boil 'em, mash'em! Idaho! Idaho! Idaho!"

DID YOU KNOW THAT...

- Idaho's Malad River is the shortest river in the world.
- Idaho had one of the U.S.'s first "crime centers"—the Old West boom town of Idaho City in the 1860s. Of the 200 people buried in the pioneer cemetery there, only 28 died of natural causes.

HOW IDAHO GOT ITS NAME: Idaho is an artifical Indian word invented by George M. Willing. It's apparently based on the word *Idahi*, which the Kiowa-Apache people called the Comanches—but no one knows exactly what the word means; perhaps "fish eaters" or "mountain gem." The Shoshone phrase *Ee-dah-how*—"Sunup!" or "Behold the sun coming down the mountain"—may have been the basis for Willing's invention.

IDAHO'S POET LAUREATE... Irene Welch Grissom lived on a farm on the Snake River, near Idaho Falls. "A Pioneer Woman," one of her poems, declared
Go tell the world that women give
In an equal share with man!

IT USED TO BE ILLEGAL IN IDAHO:

- fishing for trout from a giraffe's back
- buying a chicken after dark without the permission of the sheriff
- for a man to give his sweetheart a box of candy that weighed less than 50 pounds

Illinois

Fountain at Chicago's famous Art Museum

21st state to enter the Union, December 3, 1818

The Basics

POPULATION: 11,846,544
6th most populous state
AREA: 57,918 square miles
25th largest state
STATE CAPITAL: Springfield
STATE BIRD: Cardinal (also called Red bird, Kentucky cardinal)
STATE FLOWER: Violet
STATE TREE: White oak
NICKNAMES: Land of Lincoln, the Prairie State, the Corn State, the Sucker State
SPORTS TEAMS: Chicago Cubs, Chicago White Sox, baseball; Chicago Bears, football; Chicago Bulls, basketball; Chicago Blackhawks, hockey
STATE MOTTO: "State Sovereignty—National Union"
STATE ANIMAL: White-tailed deer
STATE INSECT: Monarch butterfly
STATE MINERAL: Fluorite
STATE SONG: "Illinois," words by C. H. Chamberlain, music by Archibald Johnston
STATE LANDMARKS: Chicago Museum of Science and Industry; Field Museum of Natural History, Chicago; Lincoln Park Zoo and Brookfield Zoo, Chicago; Shedd Aquarium, Chicago; Lincoln's home and tomb, Springfield; Ulysses S. Grant's home, Galena
NATIONAL PARK: Shawnee National Forest
STATE PARK: Starved Rock State Park

"Hog Butcher for the World, Tool Maker, Stacker of Wheat," wrote poet Carl Sandburg about Illinois's largest city, Chicago, in 1914. And indeed, livestock, farm machinery, and wheat are still major products of Illinois, still processed, manufactured, and shipped through Chicago and its industrial neighbors Rockford, Peoria, East St. Louis, and Elgin. Does that make Illinois an urban or a rural state? Surprisingly, the answer is both: some 80 percent of Illinois's population lives in urban areas, while over 80 percent of the state's land is farmed.

Ulysses S. Grant lived in Galena for many years.

FROM THE GLACIERS TO SECOND CITY Most of Illinois is prairie, covered with a thick, dark blanket of fertile soil. That's the legacy of the glaciers that rolled across the state millions of years ago, leaving it flat as a pancake. There are only a few small variations. Northwest are some uplands that the glaciers missed. In the south are the rocky wooded hills of the Ozarks. And in the southernmost tip of the state, the land is part of the Gulf Coast plain.

Illinois is crisscrossed with over 500 rivers. The largest of these, the Mississippi, makes up most of the state's western border. However, in 1881 the mighty river flooded its banks and broke through a narrow peninsula that separated it from the mouth of the Kaskaskia River. As a result, the little town of Kaskaskia found itself on the west side of the river, instead of the east side.

Chicago used to be known as the Second City, because for many years it was second only to New York in population. Now Los Angeles holds that rank, but many Chicago names still include the term Second City, including a famous comedy club, where such entertainment greats as movie director Mike Nichols, screenwriter Elaine May, and much of the original cast of *Saturday Night Live* (Gilda Radner, Bill Murray, and others) got their start.

Chicago itself was founded by African-American explorer Jean Baptiste Pointe du Sable, who in the 1770s built himself a cabin and later a trading post on the marshy banks of the Checagou River. Today, Chicago is home to a rich mix of ethnicities and cultures. You'll find Eastern Europeans, Greeks, Germans, and Irish, who came here for factory and stockyard jobs in the nineteenth century. African Americans steadily emigrated from the South after slavery ended. And Asians and Latin Americans came later in the twentieth century, seeking industrial jobs like the immigrants who had come before them.

The first European settlers who came to Illinois, however, were from the American Southeast, such as the Lincoln family from Kentucky. Abraham Lincoln grew up in Illinois, worked as postmaster in New Salem, and practiced law in Springfield until he became President in 1861.

Home of Abraham Lincoln in Springfield

THE SLAVERY DEBATES Illinois first became part of the United States in 1787, as part of the Northwest Territory. By the time it became a state in 1818, slavery was a hot issue. There were already several thousand slaves within state borders, the property of settlers who had come from Kentucky and the Carolinas. In 1837 abolitionist Elijah Lovejoy actually died protecting his anti-slavery newspapers from an angry mob. Illinois didn't abolish slavery until 1848 but that didn't end the controversy. In 1853 the legislature passed a law forbidding free African Americans from entering the state. In 1858 Stephen Douglas and Abraham Lincoln had a series of seven famous debates in their race for the U.S. Senate. The pro-slavery Douglas won that election. Two years later, though, Lincoln became the president who eventually emancipated all Southern slaves. And in 1865, Illinois became the first state to ratify the 13th Amendment that finally abolished slavery throughout the United States.

AN INDUSTRIAL PIONEER Illinois has always been a pioneer in America's industrial development. In 1837 John Deere of Grand Detour invented a steel plow that could break the prairie sod. His plant at Moline still makes farm equipment. In 1847 Cyrus McCormick built a factory to make his mechanical reaper. And in 1874 Joseph Glidden opened the nation's first barbed-wire factory at De Kalb.

Today Chicago is the number one livestock marketing and meatpacking center in the nation. It is a major center for steel, printing, and manufacturing, along with its industrial neighbors. Some three-fifths of Illinois's factories are in the Chicago area.

Illinois also has some of the nation's largest coal reserves. Although burning soft or bituminous coal creates more pollution than hard coal, advances in technology may solve those problems soon.

Of course, farming remains an important part of Illinois's economy. Corn, wheat, soybeans, dairy farming, hogs, and cattle all create wealth for this midwestern state.

Wrigley Field, home of the Chicago Cubs and one of the oldest baseball parks in America

Fascinating Facts

DID YOU KNOW THAT... Chicago's O'Hare Airport is the world's busiest—it has a plane landing or taking off every 23 seconds.

ILLINOIS IS TOPS IN:
• transport—railroads carry more goods into and out of Chicago than any other city in the world.
• soybeans—Illinois produces most of the soybeans grown in the United States.

CHICAGO'S TALL BUILDINGS:
• Sears Tower—tallest in the United States—110 stories, 1,454 feet tall
• Monadnock Building—tallest building made entirely of masonry
• Tribune Tower—base includes pieces of buildings from around the world, including London's Westminster Abbey, Athens' Parthenon, and Egypt's pyramids

CHICAGO HAS THE NATION'S LARGEST:
• grain exchange
• mail-order businesses

CHICAGO HAD THE FIRST:
• skyscraper—the 10-story Home Insurance Building—1885
• air-conditioned movie theater—1919

DID YOU KNOW THAT... You can still see movies at Chicago's Biograph Theater, where gangster John Dillinger was shot by the FBI.

HOW ILLINOIS GOT ITS NAME: The French explorer La Salle named the state by trying to spell the word *Ilini* (plural, *Iliniwok*), the Illinois and Peoria Indian word for *"man"* or *"warrior."*

PRESIDENT BORN IN ILLINOIS:
• Ronald Reagan (1911-), 40th President

OTHER FAMOUS PEOPLE BORN IN ILLINOIS:
• Author Ray Bradbury, Waukegan (1920-)
• Playwright Lorraine Hansberry, Chicago (1930-1965)
• Writer/Filmmaker/TV Producer Michael Crichton, Chicago (1942-)

Indiana

INDIANAPOLIS MOTOR SPEEDWAY

Main gate at the Indianapolis Speedway

19th state to enter the Union, December 11, 1816

The Basics

POPULATION: 5,840,528
14th most populous state
AREA: 36,420 square miles
38th largest state
STATE CAPITAL: Indianapolis
STATE BIRD: Cardinal (Red bird, Kentucky Cardinal)
STATE FLOWER: Peony
STATE TREE: Tulip poplar (Tulip tree, Yellow poplar, Blue poplar, Hickory poplar, Basswood, Cucumber tree, Tulipwood, White poplar, Poplar, Old-Wive's-Shirt tree)
NICKNAME: The Hoosier State
STATE MOTTO: The Crossroads of America
SPORTS TEAMS: Indianapolis Colts, football; Indiana Pacers, basketball
STATE STONE: Limestone
STATE POEM: "Indiana" by Arthur Franklyn Mapes
STATE SONG: "On the Banks of the Wabash, Far Away," words and music by Paul Dresser
STATE LANDMARKS: Lincoln Boyhood National Memorial, Lincoln City—the farm where President Lincoln lived for 14 years as a boy; Benjamin Harrison National Historic Landmark, Indianapolis—home of the 23rd President
NATIONAL PARKS: George Rogers Clark National Historical Park, Vincennes; Indiana Dunes National Lakeshore, Porter; Hoosier National Forest,
STATE PARKS: Falls of the Ohio, New Albany, with 220 acres of fossil beds; Lincoln State Park, Lincoln City; Spring Mill, Mitchell, with a restored 1800s pioneer village; Turkey Run, Marshall; Pokagon State Park, Angola

HOOSIER HYSTERIA! That's the slogan for the basketball madness that grips Indiana every season—from the professional team of the Pacers down through the national college champs at Indiana University and Purdue, all the way to the high school teams who compete for the state championship on national television. Fans also flock to see football played by the professional Colts in Indianapolis and Notre Dame's Fighting Irish in South Bend. And of course, racing cars compete in the Indianapolis 500 every Memorial Day. This midwestern state has rich farm country and prosperous industry, but when most people think Indiana, they think sports.

GLACIER FOOTPRINTS The level, fertile farmland of Indiana makes this a typical midwestern state. The flat northern land was formed by glaciers in the last Ice Age—glaciers that also left behind a great deal of gravel and sand and formed many small lakes. Farther south along the Ohio River, you find rolling hills, mineral springs, and huge limestone caves such as the one at Wyandotte—the second largest in the United States.

The Raggedy Ann doll was created by Marcella Gruelle in Indianapolis in 1914.

If you'd like to see what life was like a hundred years ago, you might visit the Amish and Mennonite communities in Berne, Goshen, and other northern Indiana towns. Both groups emigrated from Europe in the nineteenth century to preserve their religious ways of life. They avoid such modern inventions as tractors and telephones, using their ancestors' methods to work the land and living as simply as possible.

Although 80 percent of the state is farmland, Indiana is a major manufacturing state. Principal industrial cities include Indianapolis, Gary, Fort Wayne, Evansville, and South Bend. Yet, each urban center is only minutes away from a rural way of life. West of Indianapolis, for example, is the area known as the "covered bridge capital of the world," featuring more than 30 bridges. And each winter, Parke County is dotted with "sugar shacks" as local maple trees are tapped for syrup.

TIPPECANOE AND TECUMSEH For centuries Indiana was inhabited by many native peoples, including the Illinois, Miami, and Shawnee. The area became first French, then British, then American. The British captured it for a time during the Revolutionary War but the Americans took it back in 1779.

Indians continued to oppose the Americans and in 1790-1791 the Miami chief Little Turtle defeated federal troops two times. However, in 1794 American troops under General "Mad" Anthony Wayne won a key battle at Fallen Timbers. In 1811 Tecumseh and his Shawnee were defeated by the troops of U.S. General William Henry Harrison in the Battle of Tippecanoe.

Finally, in 1812, the Miami were defeated near the town of Peru. That was the end of Indian activity in Indiana, "land of the Indians." (Later, in 1840, Harrison ran successfully for president with a running mate named John Tyler, using the slogan, "Tippecanoe and Tyler, Too!" Harrison became the only president to die after one month in office.)

A STOP ON THE UNDERGROUND RAILROAD "They must have an underground railroad running hereabouts, and Levi Coffin must be the president of it," said one disgruntled slave-hunter looking for runaways. Historians believe that's how the famous phrase was born.

From 1827 to 1847 Levi and Catharine Coffin hid slaves in the attic of their Fountain City house by day and helped them find the best route north by night. They helped some 2,000 runaway slaves escape from the South to Canada, including "Eliza," model for the character of the same name in Harriet Beecher Stowe's novel, *Uncle Tom's Cabin.* The Coffins were the models for Simeon and Rachel Halliday in the same book.

AUTOMOBILES AND VIOLINS Indiana has been a leader in U.S. manufacturing for most of this century. Before World War I, Indiana—especially South Bend—was the U.S. center for making automobiles. Gary became a steeltown in 1905 when U.S. Steel opened its largest plant there. Fort Wayne is known for machinery, Evansville for refrigeration equipment, Indianapolis for making books and chemicals, and Elkhart for producing musical instruments. Moreover, the Bedford quarries produce limestone. Mines in southwest Indiana bring forth bituminous coal, and the Indianapolis area is the longtime home of a major oil refinery.

Indiana is well placed. Shipping vessels can sail from Lake Michigan to the Atlantic or go inland on the Ohio River. Indiana is also a big farm state, leading the nation in corn, soybeans, and tomatoes; producing grain, spearmint, and peppermint; and raising hogs and cattle.

With 6,027 seats, the Elliot Hall of Music Building at Purdue University contains the largest theater in America.

Fascinating Facts

FAMOUS PEOPLE BORN IN INDIANA:

- Poet James Whitcomb Riley, Greenfield (1849-1916)
- Airplane inventor Wilbur Wright, Millville (1867-1912)
- Writer Kurt Vonnegut, Indianapolis (1922-)
- U.S. Vice President J. Danforth "Dan" Quayle, Indianapolis (1947-)

INDIANA HAD THE FIRST:

- electrically lighted city—Wabash
- first U.S. industrial union—founded by Eugene Debs at Terre Haute

INDIANA IS TOPS IN:

- production of musical instruments

DID YOU KNOW THAT:

- Indiana General Ambrose Burnside's bushy whiskers, once called "burnsides," are now called "sideburns."
- Indiana's Lost River travels 22 miles underground.

WHERE "HOOSIERS" CAME FROM:

No one knows for sure! Four theories:

- Contractor Samuel Hoosier was working on the Ohio Falls Canal at Louisville, Kentucky, in 1826. He was quicker to hire men on the Indiana side of the Ohio River—"Hoosier's Men."
- When you knocked on the door of Indiana pioneers, they'd say, "Who's here?"
- Early riverboat workers could *hush* (shut up) anyone—so they were *hushers.*
- An Indiana man beat up a bully and said, "I'm a *Hussar!*"—a type of European soldier.

INDIANA HALLS OF FAME:

- Auto Racing Hall of Fame, Indianapolis
- Indiana Football Hall of Fame, Richmond
- International Palace of Sports Hall of Fame, Warsaw
- U.S. Track and Field Hall of Fame, Angola

IT USED TO BE ILLEGAL IN INDIANA:

- to wear a mustache if you were one who "habitually kisses human beings"
- for roller-skating instructors to lead their female students astray during a lesson

Iowa

The Basics

POPULATION: 2,851,792
30th most populous state
AREA: 56,276 square miles
26th largest state
STATE CAPITAL: Des Moines
STATE BIRD: Eastern goldfinch
STATE FLOWER: Wild rose
STATE TREE: Oak (all varieties)
NICKNAMES: The Hawkeye State, the Land Where the Tall Corn Grows, the Nation's Breadbasket, the Corn State
STATE MOTTO: Our Liberties We Prize, and Our Rights We Will Maintain
STATE ROCK: Geode
STATE SONG: "The Song of Iowa," words by S.H.M. Byers set to the music of the old Christmas carol "O Tannenbaum"
UNOFFICIAL STATE SONG: "Iowa Corn Song," words and music by George Hamilton
STATE LANDMARKS: Fort Atkinson State Preserve; Herbert Hoover National Historic Site, West Branch; Homestead, Amana Colonies; South Amana, Amana Colonies
HISTORICAL PARKS: Kaslow Prairie, near Fort Dodge—preserving the unplowed, virgin prairie; Living History Farms, near Des Moines—three working farms, from the 1840s, 1900s, and the future; Heritage Village, Des Moines; Bentonsport-National Historic District, Fairfield; Kalona Historical Village, Kalona; Nelson Pioneer Farm and Craft Museum, Oskaloosa; Pella Historical Village Museum, Pella

Iowa is one of America's leading farm states **29th state to enter the Union, December 28, 1846**

When you think Iowa, think farmland. Some 97 percent of this state's land is cultivated. Only Texas and California produce more foodstuffs—yet California is three times Iowa's size, and Texas is five times bigger. This rural, farm state has another statistic to be proud of: over 99 percent of its people can read and write, a higher literacy rate than anywhere in the United States.

THE LAND WHERE THE TALL CORN GROWS Iowa's eastern border is the Mississippi River. The river lowlands are marked by bluffs and forested hills. You can see this beautiful country by driving along the Great River Road, which hugs the Mississippi all the way up the state.

Iowa's land gradually rises into flat prairie until it meets its western border, the Missouri River. In the northwest corner of the state is Iowa's resort area, the six "Iowa Great Lakes," including Spirit Lake and West and East Okoboji.

Iowa has many covered bridges.

Iowa's largest city and capital is Des Moines, known as the home of the Iowa caucuses, which begin the Presidential campaign every four years. Another principal city is Cedar Rapids, in east central Iowa. This region was home to many Czech immigrants who came in the nineteenth century to farm. To find out more about how they lived, you can visit Czech Village. Cedar Rapids also has a museum dedicated to the art of Grant Wood, who painted *American Gothic,* a famous painting that shows a stern farmer and his wife.

In the nineteenth century the Swiss philosopher Christian Metz founded a cluster of utopian colonies (colonies to serve as a model for the ideal society). People in his Amana colonies were supposed to share everything and live peacefully together. They tried to be self-supporting by making and selling furniture, woolen goods, baked goods, and wine. Although in 1932 the colonists voted to give up their communal way of life, they have become famous as the makers of home appliances, such as dishwashers and washing machines.

Another kind of communal life was practiced by the Native Americans who lived in Iowa for hundreds of thousands of years before the Europeans came. Effigy Mounds National Monument features prehistoric Native American burial mounds in animal shapes, created over 2500 years ago.

IOWA SUFFRAGISTS Two famous activists for women's rights lived in Iowa. Carrie Chapman Catt grew up in Charles City. In 1872, at age 13, she was heard to wonder aloud why women couldn't vote. When she grew up, she went on to head the National American Woman Suffrage Association. After women finally won the vote in 1920, Catt founded the League of Women Voters. She had an unusual arrangement with her second husband, George W. Catt. In a premarriage contract, they agreed that she would get two months off in the fall and two months in the spring to work for suffrage.

Amelia Bloomer spent the last forty years of her life in Council Bluffs, from 1855 to 1894. Girls and women who wear pants have Amelia Bloomer to thank. In the 1840s she invented a kind of long, loose pants for women—the first ever. At the time, they were considered scandalous.

FARMERS WORK TOGETHER Iowa farmers have often had hard times. In the 1870s they had to pay the high prices demanded by the railroads to ship their goods to market. Corn and wheat farmers had to store their goods in local grain elevators, which also charged high prices. So Iowa, Minnesota, and Illinois farmers formed the Granger Movement. ("Grange" comes from an old English word meaning "farm.") "Grangers" started low-priced cooperative grain elevators and worked together in other ways.

Still, many farmers had to borrow from banks to buy the things they needed. Then, in the 1930s, many farmers couldn't pay back their loans. So the banks took away their farms and then held auctions to sell the farms and all their equipment. Sometimes farmers turned these auctions into "penny sales." No one would bid more than a few pennies, no matter what was being sold. Neighbors would buy a family's property for a few dollars—and then give it all back. If someone tried to bid more, to keep the property for himself, neighbors would threaten to beat him up.

The Capitol building in Des Moines

After the Depression, Iowa became one of the wealthiest farm states. In times of plenty, many farmers took out government-supported loans to expand their farms or buy new equipment. Then, in the 1980s, the government's rules about the loans changed, and farmers had to pay them back more quickly. Many farmers could not afford to do this. Once again, farmers lost their land, even though they were still growing large crops or raising huge herds of hogs and cattle.

Still, Iowa continues to be first or second in producing corn for the nation, and is a leader in hogs, cattle, hay, and soybeans as well. Its industry also relates to agriculture—food processing, farm machinery, tools, and fertilizer. Des Moines is also a major insurance center, with over 50 insurance companies headquartered there.

Fascinating Facts

PRESIDENT BORN IN IOWA:
- Herbert Hoover (1874-1964), 31st President

OTHER FAMOUS PEOPLE BORN IN IOWA:
- William "Buffalo Bill" Cody, Le Clair (1846-1917)
- Artist Grant Wood, near Anamosa (1892-1942)
- Actor John Wayne, Winterset (1907-1979)

DID YOU KNOW THAT... During the Civil War Iowa had a "Greybeard Regiment," made up of men over the age of 45 (at that time the legal cutoff age for soldiers).

IOWA HAS THE NATION'S LARGEST:
- washing machine factory
- cereal mill
- popcorn processing plant

IOWA IS TOPS IN:
- corn and grain
- soybeans

IOWA DEVELOPED...
- the Delicious apple

DID YOU KNOW THAT... Farm specialist George Washington Carver studied science in Iowa. Later he went to Tuskegee Institute in Alabama to help southern farmers improve their farming.

HOW IOWA GOT ITS NAME: Iowa was named for its native Iowa Indians, who in turn took their name from the Iowa River. In their language, *Ayuxwa*, means "beautiful land." The French spelled it "Ayoua," while the British spelled it "Ioway." Many natives still pronounce it the way the British spell it, with a long *a* sound.

HOW IOWA GOT ITS NICKNAME: The unofficial nickname of the Hawkeye State was a tribute to the great Indian leader Black Hawk. He came to Iowa to die in 1838 after his release from prison for leading an uprising.

IT USED TO BE ILLEGAL IN IOWA:
- for a woman not to wear a corset

Kansas

Cornfield near Dodge City

34th state to enter the Union, January 29, 1861

The Basics

POPULATION: 2,572,150
32nd most populous state
AREA: 82,282 square miles
15th largest state
STATE CAPITAL: Topeka
STATE BIRD: Western meadowlark
STATE FLOWER: Sunflower (Helianthus)
STATE TREE: Cottonwood
NICKNAMES: The Sunflower State, the Cyclone State, the Squatter State, the Jayhawk State
STATE MOTTO: *Ad astra per aspera* (Latin for "To the stars through difficulties")
STATE ANIMAL: American buffalo
STATE REPTILE: Ornate box turtle
STATE INSECT: Honeybee
STATE SONG: "Home on the Range," words by Dr. Brewster Higley, music by Dan Kelly
STATE MARCH: "The Kansas March" by Duff E. Middleton
STATE LANDMARK: Eisenhower Library and Museum, Abilene
HISTORICAL SITES: Fort Larned National Historical Site; Hollenberg Pony Express Station, Hanover; Barton County Historical Village, Great Bend; Fort Markley and Indian Village, Seneca; Fort Scott National Historic Site; Historic Front Street, Dodge City; "Old Abilene Town"; Old Fort Bissell, Phillipsburg; Old Shawnee Town, Kansas City
STATE FESTIVALS: Buffalo Bill Cody Days, Leavenworth (September); Good Ol' Days Celebration, Fort Scott (June); International Pancake Race, Liberal (Shrove Tuesday); John Brown Jamboree, Osawatomie (June)

Kansas is famous for its cowboy history. Dodge City, for instance, was once known as "the wickedest little city in America." Rowdy cowboys and buffalo hunters drank and gambled there, kept in line by such legendary sheriffs as Bat Masterson and Wyatt Earp. You can still see cowboys herding cattle in Dodge City, but now they ride on motorcycles!

AMBER WAVES OF GRAINS Those famous words might have been written to describe the golden wheatfields of Kansas, stretching for miles across this flat, rural, Great Plains state. The eastern part of Kansas, the Osage Plains, features gently rolling hills. Then, central Kansas levels off into a region of high plains and harsh weather. Western Kansas will remind you of old cowboy movies—a remote, windy, treeless land, marked by blowing tumbleweed.

Amelia Earhart was the first person to fly from Hawaii to California.

A little-known part of Kansas history can be seen at Nicodemus. After the end of Reconstruction (the period of readjustment in the South after the Civil War), many African Americans seeking better conditions left the South and went to Kansas. Between 1875 and 1881, some 60,000 black people—the "Exodusters"—came to this state. (They were named after the biblical exodus, or journey, that Moses had led out of Egypt.) Benjamin "Pap" Singleton organized new farming colonies for the Exodusters, but most ended up in Kansas City and Topeka. But if you visit Kansas today, you can still see his surviving colony of Nicodemus.

BLEEDING KANSAS Kansas was once home to the Kansa, Osage, Wichita, Comanche, Cheyenne, Pawnee, and many other native peoples. The name Kansas comes from the French spelling of KanNze, a native word meaning "people of the south wind." These were the people discovered by Spanish explorer Coronado, who came looking for gold in 1541, and found instead a network of Indian trails. These became the Chisholm, Santa Fe, and Oregon Trails, used by thousands of pioneers crossing from East to West.

The United States bought Kansas as part of the Louisiana Purchase in 1803. Fifty years later, this western state was drawn into a huge battle begun in the East. Slave and free states were battling over what type of nation the United States should be. Should new territories joining the Union allow slavery? Formerly, the Missouri Compromise had said that for every free state let into the Union, one slave state had to be admitted, and vice versa. But when this compromise was repealed, the Kansas-Nebraska Act of 1854 let citizens of the new territory decide for themselves.

Immediately, both abolitionists and proslavery people swarmed into Kansas to help decide the issue. In 1855 the proslavery territorial legislature passed the infamous Black Laws. They gave the death penalty to anyone who helped a runaway slave and made it illegal to spread antislavery opinion. But later that year a convention in Topeka wrote an antislavery constitution. Then in 1856 the antislavery town of Lawrence was attacked. Noted abolitionist John Brown had settled in Osawatomie to defend the idea of liberty for all. He responded to the Lawrence raid with a raid of his own, executing five proslavery men near Potawatomi Creek. Open war broke out in Bleeding Kansas. One of Brown's sons was killed later that year and part of Osawatomie was burned by raiders from Kansas City. In 1859 Kansas finally approved an antislavery constitution and joined the Union as a free state in 1861.

This museum in Topeka presents artifacts from prehistoric times.

BUFFALO BILL AND THE WILD WEST The first railroad arrived in Kansas in 1860 bringing new settlers and new activity. Texas cattle could now be driven to cow towns on the railroad line—Abilene, Dodge City, and Wichita—and shipped on to the East. But the railroad owners believed that this development could not take place if Indians still lived on the land as they had for thousands of years. To push away the Indians, they decided to destroy the huge buffalo herds on which the Indians depended. Sometimes men shot the buffalo just for fun from train windows. But the railroads also hired men like William "Buffalo Bill" Cody to kill buffalo. Buffalo Bill became famous for shooting 4,280 buffalo in 18 months. Later, he went on to start America's first Wild West show: cowboys and Indians performing daredevil stunts with horses and bulls.

William F. Cody (1846-1917) worked in Kansas for the railroad.

WHEAT MILLS AND STOCKYARDS Today, Kansas City leads the nation in sorghum and wheat and is one of our major producers of beef cattle. It's also an important state for corn, soybeans, barley, alfalfa, and hogs. Its industry is centered on processing food—milling grain and packing meat. And Kansas is one of only two sources of helium in the U.S. Wichita is a major center for the construction of private aircraft.

Fascinating Facts

KANSAS IS TOPS IN:

- wheat
- airplanes—more than half the nation's civilian airplanes are built in Wichita
- gas fields—the world's largest are at Hugoton
- salt—the world's largest salt deposits are at Hutchinson
- newspapers—more *per capita* (per person) than any other state

KANSAS HAD THE NATION'S FIRST:

- woman mayor—Susanna Salter, Argonia—1887
- shopping center—Kansas City—1922

DID YOU KNOW THAT... Wyatt Earp was once said to have "amateurishly loaded all six chambers of his revolver and blasted a hole through his coat."

FAMOUS PEOPLE BORN IN KANSAS:

- Automaker Walter Chrysler, Wamego (1875-1940)
- Aviator Amelia Earhart, Atchison (1897-1937)
- Poet Edgar Lee Masters, Garnett (1869-1950)

KANSAS IN THE CIVIL WAR:

- sent the nation's highest proportion of its eligible men to fight
- suffered the most casualties in proportion to its population

DID YOU KNOW THAT... Wichita native Hattie McDaniel was the first African American to receive an Academy Award—as Best Supporting Actress for her 1939 performance in *Gone With the Wind.*

KANSAS HALL OF FAME:

- Agricultural Hall of Fame, Kansas City
- Greyhound Racing Hall of Fame, Abilene

IT USED TO BE ILLEGAL IN KANSAS:

- to exhibit the eating of snakes
- for politicians to give away cigars on election day

Kentucky

The Kentucky Derby

15th state to enter the Union, June 1, 1792

The Basics

POPULATION: 3,883,723
24th most populous state
AREA: 40,411 square miles
37th largest state
STATE CAPITAL: Frankfort
STATE BIRD: Cardinal (also called Red bird, Kentucky cardinal)
STATE FLOWER: Goldenrod
STATE TREE: Coffee tree
NICKNAMES: The Bluegrass State, the Hemp State, the Tobacco State, the Dark and Bloody Ground
STATE MOTTO: United We Stand, Divided We Fall
STATE WILD ANIMAL GAME SPECIES: Gray squirrel
STATE FISH: Bass
STATE FOSSIL: Brachiopod
STATE SHAKESPEARE FESTIVAL: Shakespeare in Central Park, Louisville
STATE TUG-OF-WAR CHAMPIONSHIP: Nelson County Fair Tug-of-War Championship Contest
STATE SONG: "My Old Kentucky Home," words and music by Stephen Foster
STATE LANDMARK: Abraham Lincoln Birthplace National Historic Site, near Bardstown
NATIONAL PARKS: Mammoth Cave, near Bowling Green; Daniel Boone National Forest; Land between the Lakes, near Golden Pond
STATE PARKS: Cumberland Falls State Park—68-foot waterfall; Old Fort Harrod State Park, Harrodsburg—from the first permanent European settlement of 1774; Fort Boonesborough State Park—reconstruction of an early Daniel Boone Fort

Kentucky was the first U.S. state west of the Appalachian Mountains. The home of the famous pioneer Daniel Boone, it's also famous for its thoroughbred race horses, a key tobacco state, and birthplace of the Louisville Slugger baseball bat.

LANDSCAPE OF THE BLUEGRASS STATE Kentucky is bordered on three sides by rivers: the Mississippi to the west, the Ohio to the north, and the Cumberland to the east. Eastern Kentucky is a maze of steep mountains, narrow ridges, and coal valleys. Central Kentucky is bluegrass country—grass covered with small blue flowers. It's a land of blue-green meadows and manicured lawns, where the rich and famous come to buy and breed horses. Western Kentucky is coal country.

Daniel Boone (1734-1820)

In the center of the state is the famous Mammoth Cave, one of the seven natural wonders of the world. This underground wonderland was first explored by an African-American slave, Stephen Bishop, who later became a guide for tourists. You can still find Bishop's name smoked into the walls of some of the caverns, deep underground.

Mammoth Cave features over 150 miles of caverns below the earth, some high enough for a twelve-story building. You can find underground lakes, rivers, a subterranean sea, even waterfalls that rush below the earth. Thousands of years ago native peoples used the entrance to the cave for shelter. The remains of a young girl buried in a grass-lined grave were found near the mouth of the cave and estimated to be 3,000 years old. In 1935 two guides found one of the most famous mummies, "Lost John," a 45-year-old man who died two miles inside the cave when a six-and-a-half-ton rock fell on him.

Birthplace of Abraham Lincoln, Hardin County

RACE COURSES AND JOCKEYS The city of Lexington is the world capital of racehorse breeding. There you can find the Kentucky Horse Park, a shrine to the Kentucky thoroughbred. Outside the shrine is a memorial honoring the state's greatest jockey, Isaac Burns Murphy (1856-1896). This African-American horseman won an amazing 44 percent of his rides and was a three-time winner of the Kentucky Derby. Although many jockeys took bribes from bettors, Murphy had a reputation for complete honesty.

Murphy's career may be less unusual than it seems, for 13 of the 14 jockeys in the first Kentucky Derby in 1875 were African Americans. Black people frequently worked as trainers and riders in Kentucky before the Civil War. With their knowledge and experience, they remained expert horsemen throughout the nineteenth century.

In Louisville you can visit Churchill Downs where the Kentucky Derby is run on the first Saturday in May. On other Saturdays you might attend "Dawn at the Downs," the daybreak training session for horses. Other Louisville attractions include an authentic steamship ride on the 1914 vessel *Belle of Louisville,* and rides in old-fashioned horse-drawn carriages. Fans of new plays will enjoy a trip to the Actors Theatre of Louisville where many new American works are developed. Or you could visit the home of Mildred and Patty Hill, the Louisville sisters who in 1893 wrote the world's most oft-sung song—"Happy Birthday To You."

Colt and his mother

DARK AND BLOODY GROUND Kentucky was once home to Cherokee, Delaware, Iroquois, Shawnee, and other Indian nations. But when the first European settlers entered the region in the late 1770s, they and the Indians fought so bitterly that Kentucky was given its first famous nickname. One of the most famous early settlers was Daniel Boone, who in 1775 led pioneers across an old Indian trail through the Cumberland Gap. Early Kentucky settlers built log cabins. Later settlers started horse farms.

This southern state had mixed feelings about slavery. In 1833, the state outlawed the importation of slaves—but this law was repealed in 1850, and Kentucky soon became an important slave center. Yet unlike its neighbors, Kentucky never seceded from the U.S. When the Civil War ended, some 45,000 Kentucky men had fought for the Confederacy—but 90,000 had fought for the Union.

TOBACCO AND COAL Tobacco used to be Kentucky's only important crop. Indeed, merchants once accepted tobacco instead of money! Now, however, soybeans, corn, and wheat are also important crops, as well as vegetables, peaches, apples, and grass seed. Horse farms too are a key part of the state's economy.

Local manufacturing derives from agriculture: meatpacking, leather tanning, farm equipment. Kentucky is a major coal mining state, and also is rich in oil, gas, clay, limestone, and cement.

Fascinating Facts

HOW KENTUCKY GOT ITS NAME: The name comes from a Cherokee word meaning "land of tomorrow," "meadow-land," or "the dark and bloody ground."

PRESIDENT BORN IN KENTUCKY:
• Abraham Lincoln (1809-1965), 16th President

DID YOU KNOW THAT... Civil War leaders Union President Abraham Lincoln and Confederate President Jefferson Davis were both born in Kentucky, less than one hundred miles apart.

OTHER FAMOUS PEOPLE BORN IN KENTUCKY:
• Temperance leader Carry Nation, Gerrard County (1846-1911)
• U.S. Supreme Court Justice Louis Brandeis, Louisville (1856-1941)
• Novelist and poet Robert Penn Warren, Guthrie (1905-1989)
• Boxer Muhammad Ali, Louisville (1942-)

CUMBERLAND FALLS, KENTUCKY, IS THE ONLY PLACE ... where you can see a "moon-bow"—a kind of rainbow visible only at night.

DID YOU KNOW THAT... Kentucky was one of four slave states that stayed in the Union during the Civil War—along with Delaware, Maryland, and Missouri.

KENTUCKY IS TOPS IN:
• pedigreed horses
• fine grass seed
• bituminous coal production

KENTUCKY HAS THE WORLD'S LARGEST:
• Braille publishing house, Louisville
• loose leaf tobacco market, Lexington

IT USED TO BE ILLEGAL IN KENTUCKY:
• for a man to buy a coat unless his wife was along to help choose
• for a wife to rearrange the furniture without her husband's permission
• for a man to marry his wife's grandmother
• for a woman to appear in a bathing suit on a highway unless she was escorted by two officers, or armed with a club
• to sleep on the floor of the Kentucky State House
• to sleep in a restaurant

Louisiana

Traditional wrought-iron balcony, New Orleans

18th state to enter the Union, April 30, 1812

The Basics

POPULATION: 4,350,579
22nd most populous state
AREA: 51,843 square miles
31st largest state
STATE CAPITAL: Baton Rouge
STATE BIRD: Brown pelican (or Eastern brown pelican)
STATE FLOWER: Magnolia
STATE TREE: Bald cypress (also called cypress, cypress tree, Southern cypress, Red cypress, Yellow cypress, Black cypress, White cypress, Gulf cypress, Swamp cypress, Deciduous cypress, Tidewater Red cypress)
NICKNAMES: Bayou State, Fisherman's Paradise, Child of the Mississippi, Sugar State, Pelican State, Creole State
STATE MOTTO: *Union, Justice, and Confidence*
SPORTS TEAM: New Orleans Saints, football
STATE DOG: Louisiana Catahoula leopard dog
STATE INSECT: Honeybee
STATE CRUSTACEAN: Crawfish
STATE REPTILE: Alligator
STATE FOSSIL: Petrified palmwood
STATE GEM: Agate
STATE FRUIT: Changes annually
STATE SONGS: "Give Me Louisiana," words and music by Doralice Fontane; "You Are My Sunshine," words and music by Jimmy H. Davis and Charles Mitchell
LOUISIANA'S STATE PLEDGE OF ALLEGIANCE: "I pledge allegiance to the flag of the state of Louisiana and to the motto for which it stands: A state, under God, united in purpose and ideals, confident that justice shall prevail for all of those abiding here."

The rowdy crowds of Mardi Gras... alligators sunning themselves in the bayous... and the busy oil wells of Baton Rouge and Shreveport. These contrasting sights are all part of Louisiana.

FROM THE BAYOU TO BOURBON STREET
For over a thousand years, rivers carried bits of soil into Louisiana, creating the rich farmland of the Mississippi Delta in the lower third of the state. Just north and west of the Delta is bayou country—a land of swamps and marshes, home to pelicans and alligators. Still farther northwest is a drier, hillier region. The entire state, however, has a subtropical climate—hot and humid, subject to tropical storms and a six-month hurricane season.

Shadows-on-the-Teche, built in 1834, is in New Iberia.

Louisiana's economy has always depended on the Mississippi River, and the state's three largest cities—New Orleans, Baton Rouge, and Shreveport—all began as shipping centers along the famous river. Levees, like little dams, keep the Mississippi from flooding, for it can rise up to five feet higher than its banks.

Louisiana's largest city, New Orleans, has many claims to fame. It's known as the birthplace of jazz. It's also known for its French quarter, or Vieux Carré (vee-YUH kah-RAY), and for Bourbon Street, renowned for its jazz and nightlife. The New Orleans Mardi Gras ("Fat Tuesday," a celebration of the Catholic holyday of Shrove Tuesday) features a huge parade with marchers dressed in colorful and outrageous costumes.

THE STATE NAMED FOR A KING For thousands of years Louisiana was home to many native peoples, including the Biloxi, Choctaw, Creek, Natchez, Opelousa, and Yazoo. Today, at Poverty Point in northwest Louisiana, you can see the embankments left by a complex civilization that flourished from about 1500 B.C. to 700 B.C.

The Spanish and French explored Louisiana in the sixteenth and seventeenth centuries. Some of their descendants married native peoples and African Americans. Now they're known as Creoles. Another people, the Cajuns, came to Louisiana from 1760 to 1790, from Acadia, a French colony in Nova Scotia, Canada, that was being taken over by the British. Their story is told in Henry

Wadsworth Longfellow's poem *Evangeline.*

For many years France, Spain, and the United States all took turns owning different parts of the Bayou State. For a short time there was even an independent Republic of Louisiana when colonists rebelled against Spain in 1768, the first North American revolution. Finally, in 1803 President Thomas Jefferson bought the western part of the state in the Louisiana Purchase and in 1810 the U.S. took the eastern part of the state from Spain. In 1812 the state of Louisiana joined the Union.

AN UNNECESSARY BATTLE On January 8, 1815 General "Stonewall" Jackson defeated the British at New Orleans in the last battle of the War of 1812. Unfortunately, neither Jackson nor the British knew that the United States and Britain had signed a treaty two weeks before! Communications were so slow that the armies hadn't heard about the peace.

Mardi Gras float—The first parade was held in 1827.

PLANTATIONS AND POPULISM Like its Southern neighbors, Louisiana used enslaved African Americans to work its huge plantations. Even free black people had a hard time during slavery. Norbert Rillieux, an African-American engineer who had been educated in France, invented a ground-breaking method for processing sugar. Thousands of plantation owners benefitted from Rillieux's invention. But Rillieux left the state when an 1854 law required all black people, slaves or free, to carry passes.

Louisiana joined the Confederacy in 1861, then rejoined the Union after the Civil War. To oppose black people's rights, many people joined the White League, a violent group that in 1874 actually fought the New Orleans city police. In 1898 the state's new rules for voting effectively kept most black people from casting a ballot.

Louisiana continued to be a poor state. From 1928 to 1932, Governor Huey Long, nicknamed Kingfish, led a movement called Populism, designed to help poor people. There have been many kinds of populist movements in the United States. Long's version was especially controversial. He did help poor and working people. For example, he provided free textbooks to public schools, which no one had ever done before. But his dictatorial methods alienated many people. In 1935, when Long was a candidate for the Democratic presidential nomination, he was assassinated. Today people still argue about the value of his work.

THE RICHES OF THE DELTA Louisiana's economy relies primarily on the oil that was discovered there in 1901. The state is also second in the production of natural gas and sulfur. Louisiana's rich delta land produces sugar, cotton, and rice, while fishing the Mississippi yields fish, oysters, and shrimp.

Its rich and colorful history, great music and food ensure the strength of Louisiana's tourism industry year after year.

Fascinating Facts

DID YOU KNOW THAT... Seven different nations have claimed Louisiana: France, Spain, Britain, the Republic of West Florida, the Republic of Louisiana, the Confederacy, the United States

LOUISIANA NAMES:

- French explorer La Salle called the state *La Louisianne*, after Louis XIV.
- Baton Rouge ("red stick" in French) was named for a red-painted tree that marked the boundary between two Indian nations.

LOUISIANA HAD THE FIRST:

- movie theater, Vitascope Hall, which opened on June 26, 1896, in New Orleans
- tabasco sauce, created in the 19th century by McIlhenny's Tabasco Company
- advice column, begun in 1894 in the *New Orleans Picayune*, by "Dorothy Dix"

FAMOUS PEOPLE BORN IN LOUISIANA:

- Folksinger Huddie "Leadbelly" Ledbetter, near Shreveport (1888-1949)
- Jazz musician (Daniel) Louis "Satchmo" Armstrong, New Orleans (1901-1971)
- Playwright Lillian Hellman, New Orleans (1905-1984)
- Gospel singer Mahalia Jackson, New Orleans (1911-1972)
- Novelist Truman Capote, New Orleans (1924-1984)

LOUISIANA IS TOPS IN...

- salt production
- wild animal skins (nutria, muskrat)
- sweet potatoes
- frogs—the town of Rayne supplies most of the country's frogs for eating and for scientific experiments

DID YOU KNOW THAT... The world's longest bridge is near New Orleans: Lake Pontchartrain Causeway, which spans 24 miles of open water.

IT USED TO BE ILLEGAL IN LOUISIANA:

- for a beauty operator to put cold cream or powder on a customer's feet
- whistling on Sunday

Maine

A lighthouse on Maine's picturesque coast

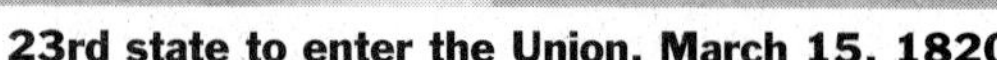

23rd state to enter the Union, March 15, 1820

The Basics

POPULATION: 1,243,316
39th most populous state
AREA: 35,387 square miles
39th largest state
STATE CAPITAL: Augusta
STATE BIRD: Chickadee (Black-capped chickadee)
STATE FLOWER: White pine cone and tassel
STATE TREE: White pine
NICKNAMES: The Pine Tree State, the Lumber State, the Border State, the Old Dirigo State
STATE MOTTO: *Dirigo* (Latin for "I direct")
STATE ANIMAL: Moose
STATE CAT: Maine coon cat
STATE FISH: Landlocked salmon
STATE INSECT: Honeybee
STATE MINERAL: Tourmaline
STATE FOSSIL: *Pertica quadrifaria*
STATE SONG: "State of Maine Song," words and music by Roger Vinton Snow
STATE LANDMARKS: Burnham Tavern, where Americans plotted the first naval battle of the Revolutionary War; Portland Head Light, built under orders of President George Washington
HISTORIC PARKS: Norlands Living History Center, Auburn; York Village, York
NATIONAL PARKS: Moosehorn; Rachel Carson National Wildlife Refuge; Acadia National Park, Mount Desert Island, Bar Harbor
STATE FESTIVALS: Maine Seafoods Festival, Rockland; Houlton Potato Feast, Houlton (August); Kenduskeag Steam Canoe Race, Bangor (April); Whatever Week, Augusta (July)

If you had a dinner of lobster, boiled potatoes, and blueberry pie, you'd be eating foods that are all specialties of the state of Maine. And if you wanted to be the first person in the United States to see the sun rise one morning, all you'd have to do was go to the top of Mount Katahdin in eastern Maine, at the northern end of the Appalachian trail.

ROCKBOUND COAST AND SNOWBOUND FORESTS Maine is the largest New England state—and the wildest. It has two main regions. Along the rockbound coast are lowlands, marked by sandy beaches, tree-lined bays, lonely lighthouses. Inland, you find the heavily forested northern end of the Appalachian mountains, featuring lakes and rivers stocked with trout and perch. In northwest Maine, the winters often bring nine feet of snow—or more. And some parts of Maine are so wild that there aren't even any roads—you have to go there by canoe or seaplane.

Buoys and lobster traps for sale in Boothbay Harbor

In northern Maine is Acadia National Park, where the mountains come right down to the sea. Nearby Bar Harbor is a famous vacation spot.

Farther south near Maine's largest city of Portland, shines the Cape Elizabeth lighthouse. It gives off 500,000 candlepower worth of light—equal to half a million candles. In Portland itself, you can visit the home of Maine native, the poet Henry Wadsworth Longfellow.

Maine was the home of many other famous writers. Sarah Orne Jewett, for example, known for her stories about Maine, was born in South Berwick. There you can see both the house she grew up in and Hamilton House, the setting for her 1901 novel, *The Tory Lover*.

Environmental writer Rachel Carson gathered material for her book, *The Edge of the Sea,* in New Harbor, at what is now the Rachel Carson Salt Pond Preserve. If you visit, you can find the creatures she wrote about: blue mussels, hermit and green crabs, periwinkles, rock algae, starfish, and sea urchins. In Wells, you can go to the Rachel Carson National Wildlife Refuge, the wetlands and woodlands that she studied so often.

Maine was also the home of Dorothea Dix, who became one of the nation's first nurses during the Civil War and who went on to crusade for better treatment of the mentally ill. If you go to Hampden you can see the Dorothea Dix Memorial Park, commemorating her birthplace.

KING PHILIP'S WAR Although Leif Eriksson and his Vikings may have visited Maine in A.D. 1000, the first European explorers who left records were the French and the English, who arrived in the 1500s and 1600s. The first permanent European settlement was founded in 1623 near Saco. At that time, over 25,000 Algonquin lived on the Maine coast.

For a time, the Europeans and the Indians lived peacefully together. After all, in Massachusetts, Chief Massasoit of the Wampanoag had helped save the Pilgrims' colony with food for the first Thanksgiving and many other types of aid. But when Massasoit died, the English settlers saw it as a chance to take all of "New England" for themselves. They attacked the Wampanoag in 1675 setting off the conflict known as King Philip's War.

Massasoit's son, Metacom, led the Wampanoag against the English in a conflict that was even bloodier than the Revolutionary War. Metacom had been given a European name, "King Philip," by the English. He had acquired guns and armor from them as well, in the days when the two nations traded peacefully together. As a result, his people were able to fight long and hard. Finally, however, the English setttlers won. Metacom was killed, and his wife and son—grandson of the chief who had saved the Pilgrims—were sold into slavery in the West Indies.

Salisbury Cove, Mt. Desert Island

REVOLUTIONARY DAYS—AND BENEDICT ARNOLD In 1629 all Maine belonged to a single English family headed by Ferdinando Gorges. In 1677 Massachusetts bought the area for $6,000, so during the Revolutionary War, Maine was part of Massachusetts. When the British tried to take Maine's tall trees for their masts, coastal people fought back fiercely. And in 1775 U.S. Colonel Benedict Arnold led his troops up through Maine to attack the British in Canada. Their route was named the Arnold Trail in his honor. (Later, he betrayed the United States so that Benedict Arnold became another word for traitor.) Maine itself finally won independence from Massachusetts in 1819. It joined the Union the year after.

There are many sea otters who swim off the coast of Maine.

CHRISTMAS TREES AND ICEBOXES Nearly 90 percent of Maine's land is forest, so lumber, paper, and pulp are Maine's chief industries. Every year nearly a million Maine firs are cut for Christmas trees. Although Maine's soil is rocky and poor, it leads the nation in potatoes and also produces sweet corn, hay, apples, and blueberries. Fishing, especially lobstering, has long been a big Maine business. One abandoned Maine business is the export of ice. Before the days of refrigerators, over three million tons of ice a year were cut from Maine's ponds and sent to other states, as well as to Europe, India, and Africa.

Fascinating Facts

DID YOU KNOW THAT... The easternmost point in the United States is West Quoddy Head.

MAINE HAD THE FIRST:
- ship built in the western hemisphere—the *Virginia*—1607
- atomic submarine, the *Swordfish*
- sawmill in the United States
- woman Republican senator, Margaret Chase Smith, elected in 1948

DID YOU KNOW THAT... The first Maine settlers brought their own lumber for house-building—and were amazed to discover Maine's rich forests.

MAINE IS TOPS IN:
- canoes
- lobsters
- potatoes
- high tides—the world's highest tides are at Passamaquoddy Bay

MAINE FOLKLORE: Barney Beal of Beal's Island was so strong, he could knock out a horse with one blow. He once beat 15 men in a tavern fight.

DID YOU KNOW THAT... The Old Gaol (Jail) in York once served the entire state—even though it had only one cell! (However, the building was enlarged in 1720.)

HOW MAINE GOT ITS NAME: No one knows for sure. Two theories:
- French explorers named it after the ancient French province of Mayne.
- The English named it, referring to the term for a *main*land as opposed to an island.

DID YOU KNOW THAT... Maine is the only state to have a state cat—the Maine coon cat.

FAMOUS PEOPLE BORN IN MAINE:
- Author Stephen King, Portland (1947-)
- U.S. Senator Margaret Chase Smith, Skowhegan (1897-1995)

IT USED TO BE ILLEGAL IN MAINE:
- to lead a bear around on a rope
- to walk the streets with untied shoelaces
- to set fire to a mule

Maryland

Statue of Tecumseh at Annapolis

7th state to enter the Union, April 28, 1788

The Basics

POPULATION: 5,071,604
19th most populous state
AREA: 12,407 square miles
42nd largest state
STATE CAPITAL: Annapolis
STATE BIRD: Northern oriole (formerly called the Baltimore oriole)
STATE FLOWER: Black-eyed Susan
STATE TREE: White oak (also known as Wye Oake, Wyle Mills)
NICKNAMES: The Old Line State, the Free State, the Pine Tree State, the Lumber State
STATE MOTTOES: *Fatti Maschii, Parole Femine* (Latin for "Manly Deeds, Womanly Words"); *Scuto Bonae Voluntatis Tuae Coronasti Nos* ("With Favor Wilt Thou Compass Us As With a Shield")
SPORTS TEAM: Baltimore Orioles, baseball
STATE SPORT: Jousting
STATE DOG: Chesapeake Bay retriever
STATE FISH: Rockfish and striped bass
STATE INSECT: Baltimore Checkerspot Butterfly
STATE SHIP: Skipjack
STATE THEATER: Center State, Baltimore
STATE SUMMER THEATER: Olney Theatre, Montgomery County
STATE SONG: "Maryland! My Maryland!", words by James Ruder Randall, set to the old tune *"Lauriger Horatius"*
STATE LANDMARKS: Fort McHenry National Monument, Baltimore; Star-Spangled Banner House (where the flag that inspired the national anthem was woven), Baltimore; U.S. Frigate *Constellation*, (oldest ship still afloat), Baltimore

If you visit Baltimore, taste the city's famous crab cakes. If you take a trip to Maryland's eastern shore, you're sure to find clams on the menu. And if you drive through Maryland's farm country, you'll see roadside stands selling corn, strawberries, and tomatoes. As you can see, the state of Maryland draws riches from both land and sea.

AN OPEN DOOR TO THE SEA This South Atlantic state includes the Allegheny Mountains to the west, the Blue Ridge Mountains and Piedmont Plateau in central Maryland, and the lowlands of the Eastern Shore around Chesapeake Bay. Yet most of the state's people live in the Baltimore-Washington, D.C. metropolitan area.

Baltimore Oriole Cal Ripken, Jr., (1960-)

Much of Maryland straddles the nation's largest bay, the Chesapeake. This bay is so deep that ocean-going vessels can sail right up to Annapolis and Baltimore. The Susquehanna River flows into the Chesapeake, linking ocean and inland.

Baltimore, Maryland's major city, was once home to the writer Edgar Allan Poe. Poe fans can visit the house where he wrote his first horror story or take a trip to Westminster Church to see his grave.

Annapolis, Maryland's capital, was once the capital of the United States. From 1783 to 1784 Congress met in the State House there. Later, in 1791 Maryland gave the United States land on which to establish the District of Columbia. The Annapolis State House, built in 1772, is still Maryland's Capitol—the oldest capitol building still in continuous use.

Annapolis is also the home of the U.S. Naval Academy, where America's first great naval hero, John Paul Jones, is buried. During the Revolutionary War, when Jones encountered the British, he uttered the famous words "I have not yet begun to fight!"

BROUGHT BY THE *ARK* AND THE *DOVE* Originally Maryland was inhabited by the Nanticoke, Piscataway, and the Powhatan Confederacy. The first European settlement arrived in 1634 on two ships named for the biblical story of Noah, the *Ark* and the *Dove.* The expedition was led by Governor Leonard Calvert whose brother, Lord Baltimore, had been granted the land by the British crown in 1632.

In 1649, Maryland became the first place to be completely tolerant of all religions with the "Act Concerning Religion." During the Revolutionary War, Maryland soldiers fought bravely in the Battle of Long Island, holding the line against the British while General Washington and the rest of the troops escaped.

For many years Baltimore was one of the centers of the U.S. slave trade. But there was also a great deal of anti-slavery activity in Maryland, especially western Maryland. The great abolitionist and social reformer Frederick Douglass was born a slave in Maryland, from which he later escaped. Likewise, Harriet Tubman grew up as a slave on a plantation in Cambridge. Tubman escaped slavery in 1849, but she returned to the South 19 times, rescuing over 300 slaves, including most of her family. She was never caught and she never lost anyone she tried to bring to freedom. During the Civil War Maryland was a "border state," one of the four Southern states that nevertheless fought with the Union.

Frederick Douglass (1817-1895)

FROM MARYLAND TO THE NORTH POLE The first man to reach the North Pole was a Maryland native. Matthew Henson was born on a Maryland farm in 1866, a time when there were few opportunities for African Americans. Yet Henson was determined to "go places." He ran off to sea at the age of 13 and eventually met Admiral Robert E. Peary, a Naval officer who took Henson with him on his 1909 expedition to the North Pole. On the last two days of the trip, Peary's toes were frozen, so he couldn't walk and had to be pulled in a sled by four Eskimo natives. Henson walked ahead, blazing a trail across the ice. He was the one to actually plant an American flag on the Pole itself. For years, Peary got all the credit for the expedition, but, in 1945, after Peary had died, Congress gave Henson a medal in recognition of his achievement.

CRAB CAKES AND TOBACCO Maryland draws riches out of the Chesapeake Bay: fish, oysters, and soft-shell crabs. Truck farms on the Eastern Shore grow corn, wheat, strawberries, and tomatoes.

Tobacco is also a key industry, and Maryland's loose-leaf tobacco auctions are the largest in the world.

Baltimore has been a shipping center since colonial times, linking Atlantic Ocean trade with western destinations along the Susquehanna. Baltimore ships transport coal from Virginia and other coal states. Ships and transportation machinery are also made in Baltimore.

Today, most of Maryland's income comes from electric and electronic products, chemicals, and steel. Government employees, living in Maryland but working in Washington, D.C., also bring income into the state. A major part of Maryland's economy is the medical research center the National Institutes of Health, located in the Washington suburb of Bethesda.

Fascinating Facts

DID YOU KNOW THAT... Maryland native Francis Scott Key was a prisoner on a British warship in 1814, as the British shelled Baltimore's Fort McHenry during the War of 1812. Key wrote "The Star-Spangled Banner" literally by the light of "the rockets' red glare."

MARYLAND HAD THE FIRST:
- passenger-carrying railroad
- telegraph message—"What hath God wrought?"—sent by telegraph inventor Samuel F.B. Morse from Washington, D.C., to Baltimore
- practical refrigerator, invented by Thomas Moore, Baltimore, 1803
- U.S. manufacture of umbrellas

FAMOUS PEOPLE BORN IN MARYLAND:
- Mathematician Benjamin Banneker, Ellicott (1731-1806)
- Writer Upton Sinclair, Baltimore (1878-1968)
- Charles Carroll, signer of the Declaration of Independence (1737-1832)
- Baseball player George Herman "Babe" Ruth, Baltimore (1895-1948)

MARYLAND HAS THE LARGEST...
- aquarium—the National Aquarium in Baltimore

HOW MARYLAND GOT ITS NICKNAMES: George Washington called it the "Old Line State" because Maryland soldiers "held the line" against the British. Maryland was called the "Free State" because in 1920 the governor refused to enforce Prohibition, a national law that made alcohol illegal.

DID YOU KNOW THAT... Maryland has the narrowest width of any state—it's only one mile wide near Hancock.

IT USED TO BE ILLEGAL IN MARYLAND:
- to mistreat an oyster

Massachusetts

Fanueil Hall in Boston

6th state to enter the Union, February 6, 1788

The Basics

POPULATION: 6,092,352
13th most populous state
AREA: 10,555 square miles
44th largest state
STATE CAPITAL: Boston
STATE BIRD: Chickadee
STATE FLOWER: Mayflower
STATE TREE: American elm
NICKNAMES: The Bay State, the Old Bay State, the Old Colony State, the Pilgrim State, the Puritan State, the Baked Bean State
STATE MOTTO: *Ense Petit Placidam Sub Libertate Quietem* ("By the sword we seek peace, but peace only under liberty")
SPORTS TEAMS: Boston Red Sox, baseball; New England Patriots, football; Boston Celtics, basketball; Boston Bruins, hockey
STATE DOG: Boston terrier
STATE FISH: Cod
STATE INSECT: Ladybug
STATE MARINE MAMMAL: Right whale
STATE MINERAL: Babingtonite
STATE ROCK: Roxbury pudding stone
STATE FOSSIL: Dinosaur track
STATE GEM: Rhodonite
STATE DRINK: Cranberry juice
STATE HEROINE: Deborah Sampson
STATE SONG: "All Hail to Massachusetts," words and music by Arthur J. Marsh
STATE FOLK SONG: "Massachusetts," words and music by Arlo Guthrie
STATE LANDMARKS: Paul Revere's House, Boston; the Witch House, Salem; Museum of Afro American History, Boston; the Whaling Museum, New Bedford; the Basketball Hall of Fame, Springfield; the Volleyball Hall of Fame, Holyoke

Massachusetts has always been a national leader. In the seventeenth century it was one of the first American colonies. In the eighteenth century it saw the first events leading to the Revolutionary War. Before the Civil War it was a leader in the Abolitionist movement, the effort to abolish (get rid of) slavery. And in the nineteenth and twentieth centuries Massachusetts was the home of many of the nation's first factories... including its first woolen mills, iron works, and shoe factories. Today Massachusetts is a first with tourists, who enjoy its beaches, its cities... and its history!

This statue of Paul Revere commemorates his "midnight ride" of April 18, 1775.

FROM THE OCEANS TO THE MOUNTAINS Massachusetts has three main geographical areas. To the east is flat coastal land, home to fishing villages and vacation resorts. Boston and its surroundings make up one of the three major metropolitan centers of the East Coast. And to the west are the Berkshire Mountains and green, hilly country dotted with small cities and college towns.

PILGRIMS AND REVOLUTIONARIES The very first residents of Massachusetts were Native Americans. In fact, the state's name actually comes from the Massachusetts Indians. The word "Massachusetts" means "near the great hill" or "the place of the great hill." In 1614 English explorer Captain John Smith identified this place as the Great Blue Hill, just south of the present-day town of Milton. Other Native American nations located within the borders of present-day Massachusetts included the Massasoit, the Samoset, and many others.

In 1620 the Pilgrims—a group of English colonists, landed at Plymouth Rock. In 1621 the Pilgrims and Native Americans held America's first Thanksgiving.

Massachusetts went on to become a thriving center for industry and trade. Although it did not depend on slave labor the way the Southern colonies did, it was a major center for the slave trade, which helped to build the fortunes of many Massachusetts millionaires. Africans were shipped into Massachusetts both from Africa itself and by way of the West Indies. Massachusetts also included a free black population made up of former slaves who had either won their freedom or who had escaped from their owners.

Ironically, it was one of these escaped slaves, Crispus Attucks, who was the first to die in America's own fight for freedom. Attucks was the leader of a group of colonists who started arguing with some British soldiers in Boston on March 5, 1770. The soldiers shot five American civilians—including Attucks—and the event became known as the Boston Massacre.

Clara Barton, founder of the American Red Cross

Massachusetts continued to be an important leader in America's battle for independence. In 1773 Boston patriots organized the Boston Tea Party, a raid on British ships in which tea was dumped into Boston Harbor to protest new taxes passed by the British parliament. Two years later, in 1775 the first battles of the Revolutionary War were fought between Minutemen and British soldiers at the Massachusetts towns of Concord and Lexington.

Many heroes of the War for Independence lived and fought in Massachusetts. One of the most fascinating was Deborah Sampson, a former indentured servant who dressed as a man and went off to fight in disguise. She served honorably from 1782 until she was discovered in 1783. Later she married, went on a lecture tour to talk about her experiences, and eventually received a full military pension for her army service.

Astronomer Maria Mitchell (1818-1889)

FROM SEA POWER TO BRAIN POWER

Massachusetts has always relied on the sea. In its early days it was a major whaling center, while Boston ship-yards built the world-famous "Yankee Clippers." Massachusetts is still home to a major fishing industry, supplying the nation with fish, scallops, lobster, and squid. And the seacoast resorts of Nantucket, Martha's Vineyard, and Cape Cod are popular East Coast vacation spots.

In the nineteenth and early twentieth centuries, rural Americans and immigrant workers—Italian, Portuguese, Irish, and Greek—built Massachusetts' textile factories. African American engineer Jan Ernst Matzeliger invented the machine that revolutionized the shoe industry.

Now those industries have moved South and overseas, while Massachusetts has moved on to electronic and computer manufacture. The Boston area, drawing on the brainpower of such universities as Harvard and Massachusetts Institute of Technology, is also a center for medical and biotechnical research. Immigrant workers—now primarily from Asia, Eastern Europe, and the Caribbean—still provide vital labor to the new economy.

Fascinating Facts

MASSACHUSETTS HAD THE FIRST ...

- college—Harvard—founded in Cambridge in 1636
- college for women—Mount Holyoke—founded in South Hadley, 1837
- public school system—founded in 1647
- large municipal public library—Boston Public Library—founded in 1852
- lighthouse—1716
- medical inoculation against smallpox in North America—1721
- printing press—1847
- subway—1897
- basketball game—1892

PRESIDENTS BORN IN MASSACHUSETTS INCLUDE:

- John Adams, (1735-1826), 2nd President
- John Quincy Adams (1767-1848), 6th President
- John F. Kennedy (1917-1963), 35th President
- George Bush (1924-), 41st President

DID YOU KNOW... that John Quincy Adams was the only President's son also to be elected President? His father was John Adams.

OTHER FAMOUS PEOPLE BORN IN MASSACHUSETTS:

- patriot of the American Revolution, diplomat, author, publisher, scientist, inventor Benjamin Frankin, Boston (1706-1790)
- essayist Ralph Waldo Emerson, born in Boston (1803-1882)
- patriot, writer, wife and mother of presidents, Abigail Adams, (1744-1818)
- novelist Nathaniel Hawthorne, born in Salem (1804-1864)
- poet Emily Dickinson, Amherst (1836-1886)
- poet e. e. cummings, Cambridge (1894-1962)
- writer and illustrator Theodor Geisel—Dr. Seuss (1904-1991)

IT USED TO BE ILLEGAL IN MASSACHUSETTS:

- to keep a dachshund as a pet dog
- to show movies that lasted more than twenty minutes
- to eat peanuts in church
- to put tomatoes in clam chowder

Michigan

Antique cars

26th state to enter the Union, January 26, 1837

The Basics

POPULATION: 9,594,350
8th most populous state
AREA: 96,705 square miles
11th largest state
STATE CAPITAL: Lansing
STATE BIRD: Robin (American robin)
STATE FLOWER: Apple blossom
STATE TREE: White pine
NICKNAMES: The Wolverine State, Great Lakes State, Lake State, Lady of the Lake, Auto State
STATE MOTTO: *Si Quaeris Peninsulam Amoenam, Circumspice* (Latin for "If you seek a pleasant peninsula, look around you")
SPORTS TEAMS: Detroit Tigers, baseball; Detroit Lions, football; Detroit Pistons, basketball; Detroit Red Wings, hockey
STATE FISH: Brook trout
STATE STONE: Petoskey stone
STATE GEM: Isle Royal greenstone (chlorastrolite)
STATE SONG: "Michigan, My Michigan," words by Giles Kavanagh, music by H. O'Reilly Clint
STATE LANDMARK: Historic Fort Wayne, Detroit
NATIONAL PARKS: Isle Royal; Pictured Rocks National Lakeshore; Sleeping Bear Dunes National Lake Shore
HISTORIC PARKS: Greenfield Village, Dearborn—built by Henry Ford, includes model of Edison's laboratory and Wright brothers' bicycle shop; Antique Auto Village, Frankenmuth, 1920s main street; Dutch Village, Holland
STATE PARK: Porcupine Mountains

You might say Michigan has a split personality. The Detroit area is one of the largest metropolitan areas in the country. Yet in rural Michigan you could drive for miles without coming to a single town. In one day, you can travel from the noise of Motor City's auto factories to the quiet woods around Lake Superior.

MACKINAC AND MOTOWN Michigan was created out of two separate peninsulas which can explain its "split personality." No land links the Upper and Lower Peninsulas and the two regions have different climates, landscapes, and economies. Yet together they make up one state—Michigan.

The Lower Peninsula is shaped like a mitten. It has a typical midwestern climate—mild and humid. And its landscape has rolling hills and flat plains. Almost all of Michigan's industry, agriculture, and population are concentrated on the Lower Peninsula. The Upper Peninsula, on the other hand has a harsh, cold, northern climate. Its mountainous, heavily forested terrain is rich in minerals, but it is a sparsely populated, rural area. Between the peninsulas are the Straits of Mackinac (pronounced mack-i-NAW, from the French). Almost half of Michigan's area is fresh water: 11,000 inland lakes and 36,000 miles of rivers. Boating and fishing are popular pastimes here.

19th century store in Greenfield Village

Michigan's largest city is Detroit, which produces over one-fourth of the nation's autos, trucks, and tractors. Nearly half of Michigan's people live in the Detroit area, which is home to over 150 ethnic groups, including almost 900,000 African Americans and 400,000 Polish Americans. The largest North American communities of Bulgarians, Belgians, and Arabs live in this state, adding to its cultural riches.

Music lovers know Detroit as the home of Motown (short for motor town), the record label and musical style made popular by Berry Gordy, Jr. When Gordy went into the music business in the late 1950s, there were many popular African-American singers and musicians, but virtually nobody of color behind the scenes. Gordy wasn't even a rich man; he was a former worker on an auto assembly line. Yet he brought to prominence such superstars as Smokey Robinson, the Four Tops, and the Temptations. Although Gordy took Motown out of the Motor City in 1971, you can visit Motown Museum at his old studio, still with his sign, Hitsville, USA.

Detroit native, Ralph Bunche (1904-1971) won the Nobel Peace Prize in 1950.

FROM FORD TO FLINT The first U.S. auto factory was the Olds Motor Works, founded in 1900 in Detroit. From this small beginning came an industry that affected the entire U.S. economy, as well as the lives of millions of workers in and out of the auto business.

When Henry Ford started the Ford Motor Company, also in Detroit, in 1903, cars were luxuries that only the rich could afford. But by 1908 Ford was offering his Model T for only $850—an affordable price for many families. Ford had discovered a revolutionary new way of making cars. Previously, workers had assembled cars in groups, which took 14 hours. Ford figured out that if you gave each worker a very small task, such as tightening one screw, and if you put car parts on automatic conveyor belts that moved quickly past workers, you could make cars more cheaply and quickly—in only 93 minutes. (Today it takes only one hour to make a car.) This assembly-line process was quickly adopted by industries nationwide, changing the way most Americans worked.

Yet this way of working was hard, often dangerous, and frequently poorly paid. Now, though, workers were all together in a single, giant factory. Looking around, they realized that they had a new kind of power—the power to stop work, or strike. On December 30, 1936, thousands of workers at the GM plant in Flint began a sit-down strike; they sat down, at their machines, and refused to work until the company improved their wages and working conditions. They also refused to leave the factory, so that no one else could come in and do their jobs.

The strike quickly spread to other factories. Outside the plants, women's auxiliaries organized demonstrations to win support for the workers and their union, the United Auto Workers. When the strike succeeded, workers in other cities and industries took up this tactic. Once again, the Michigan auto industry had been a national leader.

AUTO UPS AND DOWN Michigan is one of the nation's top six manufacturing states. For almost a century, "manufacturing" has meant "auto-making" in Michigan. When Japanese cars took some of the U.S. market, Michigan's economy suffered and millions of people lost their jobs. Even when U.S. auto production shot up between 1986 and 1990, Michigan's economy was still on shaky ground.

Michigan factories also make machine tools, appliances, light machinery, pharmaceuticals, plastics, clothing, and paper. Grand Rapids has maintained a tradition of fine furniture manufacturing since 1859.

Iron and copper mining on the Upper Peninsula is an important source of income. Oil, natural gas, and salt are key Michigan products. Agriculture, on the other hand, is a very small part of the state's economy.

Fascinating Facts

HOW MICHIGAN GOT ITS NAME:
Two theories:
- from the Chippewa words *michi gama,* meaning "great lake"
- from the Chippewa *majigan,* meaning "clearing," referring to an open area on the west side of the Lower Peninsula

MICHIGAN IS THE ONLY STATE...
- in the lower 48 states where Canada is *south* of the United States
- to have four of the five great lakes as borders—Erie, Huron, Michigan, Superior
- to be formed of two peninsulas

MICHIGAN HAD THE FIRST:
- concrete highway—1909
- university established by a state

DID YOU KNOW THAT... Michigan's shoreline is 3,121 miles—longer than the Atlantic coast from Maine to Florida.

MICHIGAN HALLS OF FAME:
- Afro-American Sports Hall of Fame, Detroit
- National Ski Hall of Fame, Ishpeming

MICHIGAN IS TOPS IN:
- car and truck production
- red tart cherries
- dry beans
- cucumbers for pickles
- baby food
- carpet sweepers
- U.S. copper reserve
- million-ton ports
- variety of trees in the U.S.

FAMOUS MICHIGAN NAMES:
- Antoine Cadillac, founded Detroit, 1701
- Pontiac, chief of the Ottawas
- Henry Ford, first Detroit automaker

PRESIDENT WHO LIVED IN MICHIGAN:
- Gerald Ford (1913-), 38th President

IT USED TO BE ILLEGAL IN MICHIGAN:
- to hitch a crocodile to a fire hydrant
- for a woman to lift her skirt more than six inches to avoid a puddle
- for a married couple not to live together

Minnesota

Minnesota winters are bitter cold

32nd state to enter the Union, May 11, 1858

The Basics

POPULATION: 4,657,758
20th most populous state
AREA: 86,943 square miles
12th largest state
STATE CAPITAL: St. Paul
STATE BIRD: Common loon
STATE FLOWER: Pink-and-white lady's slipper
STATE TREE: Norway pine (also called Red pine, Canadian red pine, Hard pine)
NICKNAMES: The North Star State, the Gopher State, Land of 10,000 Lakes, the Bread and Butter State
STATE MOTTO: *L'Etoile du Nord* (French for "The North Star")
SPORTS TEAMS: Minnesota Twins, baseball; Minnesota Vikings, football; Minnesota Timberwolves, basketball; Minnesota North Stars, hockey
STATE FISH: Walleye
STATE GRAIN: Wild rice
STATE MUSHROOM: Morel
STATE GEM: Lake Superior agate
STATE DRINK: Milk
STATE SONG: "Hail! Minnesota," words by Truman E. Rickard and Arthur E. Upson, music by Truman E. Rickard
STATE LANDMARKS: Fort Snelling, St. Paul; Grand Portage National Monument—1768 fur-trading post
NATIONAL PARK: Voyageurs,
STATE PARK: Lake Itasca State Park
STATE FESTIVALS: Defeat of Jesse James Days, Northfield (September); Eelpout Festival, Walker (February); International Rolle Bolle Tournament, Marshall (August); John Beargrease Sled Dog Marathon, Duluth (January); Laura Ingalls Wilder Pageant, Tracy (July)

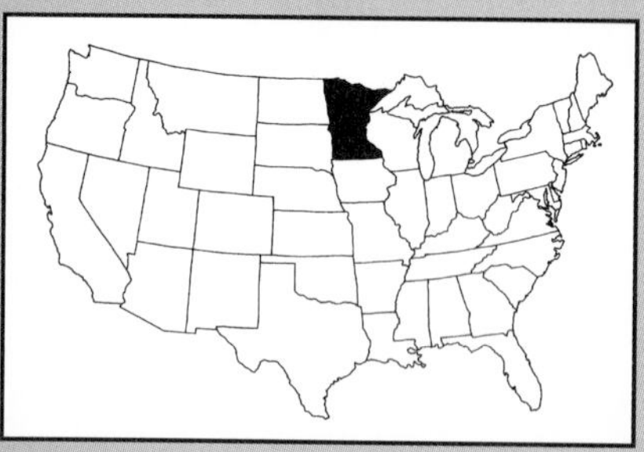

Minnesota is a land of harsh winters and hot, humid summers; of quiet, self-sufficient Scandinavians with a strong sense of community; of isolated farms and tiny prairie towns and a metropolitan area with more theater for its size than any urban area outside of New York.

LAND OF 22,000 LAKES Minnesota is our northernmost state—except for Alaska—and the winters show it. Temperatures of -40 degrees Fahrenheit—lower if you count wind chill—are not unusual.

A buffalo in Itasca State Park

Two ethnic groups have done the most to shape the state's ways. Chippewa (Ojibway) still live in northern Minnesota. Their strong relationship to the land affects Minnesotans all over the state. And Scandinavians—Danes, Swedes, Norwegians, and Finns—bring Minnesota their strong religious traditions (Lutheran and Catholic), their attachment to farm life, and their sense of civic responsibility.

Minnesota has over 22,000 lakes. With the state's many rivers, they make up over 4,000 square miles of water—almost 5 percent of the state's area. Three great river systems begin in Minnesota: the Rainy and Red Rivers run north to Hudson Bay; the St. Louis and Pigeon Rivers run east to Lake Superior and the St. Lawrence Seaway; and the Mississippi River runs south from Lake Itasca down to the Gulf of Mexico. These waterways have made Minneapolis, St. Paul, and Duluth, major centers of trade.

LITTLE TOWN ON THE PRAIRIE Northeastern Minnesota is a land of lakes and forests. Outside of Bemidji you can see the giant statues of legendary lumberjack Paul Bunyan and his blue ox, Babe. Nearby is the Iron Range, one of the world's great sources of iron ore. Northwestern Minnesota, on the other hand, is farm country. Its flat, fertile land is perfect for growing wheat, corn, soybeans, and sugar beets. Southeastern Minnesota is hilly green country, where dairy cattle graze. The southeastern town of Rochester has gained worldwide renown for the medical research done at the Mayo Clinic, started by Dr. William W. Mayo in 1855. In southwestern Minnesota is New Ulm, home of Wanda Gag, who in 1928 wrote *Millions of Cats.* Laura Ingalls Wilder grew up in the nearby town of Walnut Grove, and used it as the setting for *On the Banks of Plum Creek*, the first book in her famous *Little House* series. Further west is Pipestone, whose red rock is found in the sacred quarry of the Omaha and Yankton Indians.

The Twin Cities of Minneapolis and St. Paul are Minnesota's largest city and its capital, respectively. Here there are many professional and ameteur theaters, professional symphonies and chamber orchestras, and a growing film community. The suburb of Bloomington—Minnesota's third largest city—boasts the Mall of America. With over 400 stores, it's the largest shopping complex in the world.

INDIAN UPRISINGS AND LABOR WARS Minnesota was first explored by the French voyageurs (explorers): Pierre Esprit Radisson, Daniel Greysolon, Sieur de Lhut (Duluth), and many others who have given their names to Minnesota cities and landmarks. By 1763, however, the British had won eastern Minnesota, which, in 1783, they ceded to the United States. In 1803 President Thomas Jefferson acquired western Minnesota when he signed the Louisiana Purchase. In 1819 settlers created the first European community in Minnesota at Fort St. Anthony (now Fort Snelling, near Minneapolis).

It's no accident that the first European dwelling was a fort, far from the first; the Europeans were at odds with Minnesota's native peoples. The Ojibway and Sioux ceded more and more of their land. By 1862 the Sioux were completely dependent on U.S. government support. They were starving but a government official was supposed to have said, "Let them eat grass." This provoked the famous Sioux uprising of 1862 in which the official was found dead with his mouth stuffed with grass and 485 other white people were killed. In retaliation, U.S. troops took 2,000 prisoners and executed 37 Sioux, the largest official execution in U.S. history. The other Sioux were expelled from the state.

Laura Ingalls Wilder wrote the Little House series.

Another major uprising in Minnesota's history was the Teamsters' Strike of 1934, which provoked one of the nation's two general strikes. (A general strike is when all workers in a city go on strike. The other general strike was in San Francisco.) Four years earlier, Minnesotans had elected the first governor from a third party (neither Democrat nor Republican), the Farmer-Labor Party. The liberal tradition remained strong in Minnesota throughout the twentieth century. The state gave the nation two liberal vice-presidents, Hubert H. Humphrey and Walter Mondale.

TACONITE AND HIGH TECH Dairy products, wheat, and iron ore (taconite) are some Minnesota resources important to the state's economy. But equally important are its human resources, the men and women who work in the growing high-tech industry centered in the Twin Cities. Processed foods, office supplies, metal, paper, and printing are also important industries in this state that relies upon manufacturing.

Fascinating Facts

MINNESOTA HALL OF FAME:

• U.S. Hockey Hall of Fame, Eveleth

MINNESOTA HAS THE NATION'S LARGEST:

• unsupported marble dome—Minnesota State Capitol, built in 1905

MINNESOTA HAS THE WORLD'S LARGEST:

• human-made hole in the world—the open-pit mine at Hibbing on the Iron Range

DID YOU KNOW THAT... The Mississippi River starts in Itasca State Park—as a stream so narrow, you can actually step across the entire river!

HOW MINNESOTA GOT ITS NAME:

• from *Mnishota* in the Sioux language, meaning "sky-colored water" or "cloudy water"

HOW MINNESOTA'S CAPITAL GOT ITS NAME: Minnesota's capital was once called Pig's Eye, after the nickname of French-Canadian trader Pierre Parrant who established the city in 1840. In 1841 a Roman Catholic missionary convinced settlers to change the name to St. Paul.

MINNESOTA IS TOPS IN:

• iron ore production—50 million tons a year—60 percent of the nation's total

MINNESOTA INVENTIONS:

• flour purifier—Edmond LaCroix—1870

FAMOUS PEOPLE BORN IN MINNESOTA:

• Writer Sinclair Lewis, Sauk Centre (1885-1951)
• Writer F. Scott Fitzgerald, St. Paul (1896-1940)
• *Peanuts* Cartoonist Charles Schulz, Minneapolis (1922-)
• Writer Garrison Keillor, Anoka (1942-)
• Actress Jessica Lange, Cloquet (1949-)

DID YOU KNOW THAT... There are so many lakes in Minnesota that many share the same name; for example, there are 91 Long Lakes.

IT USED TO BE ILLEGAL IN MINNESOTA:

• to hang men's and women's underwear on a clothesline at the same time
• for a woman to appear on the street dressed as Santa Claus

Mississippi

Rosalie in Natchez, was built in 1820

20th state to enter the Union, December 10, 1817

The Basics

POPULATION: 2,716,115
31st most populous state
AREA: 48,434 square miles
32nd largest state
STATE CAPITAL: Jackson
STATE BIRD: Mockingbird
STATE FLOWER: Magnolia
STATE TREE: Southern magnolia
NICKNAMES: The Magnolia State, the Eagle State, the Border-Eagle State, the Bayou State, the Mud-Cat State
STATE MOTTO: *Virtute et armis* (Latin for "By valor and arms")
STATE WATER MAMMAL: Bottlenosed dolphin
STATE FISH: Largemouth bass
STATE INSECT: Honeybee
STATE SHELL: Oyster shell
STATE FOSSIL: Prehistoric whale
STATE DRINK: Milk
STATE SONG: "Go, Mississippi," words and music by Houston Davis
STATE PLEDGE OF ALLEGIANCE: "I salute the flag of Mississippi and the sovereign state for which it stands, with pride in her history and achievements and with confidence in her future under the guidance of Almighty God."
STATE LANDMARKS: Old Spanish Fort and Singing River, Pascagoula
HISTORICAL PARKS: Florewood River Plantation, Greenwood—shows how people lived on a cotton plantation; John Ford House, near Sandy Hook—early 1800s frontier home
STATE FESTIVAL: Anniversary of the Landing of d'Iberville, Ocean Springs (April)

If you want a glimpse of the Old South, Mississippi is the place to visit. You can still see white fields of cotton, smell magnolia blossoms, and ride steamboats up and down the Mississippi River. For a look at the New South, you can also visit Mississippi, just to see how much it has changed in the past forty years.

MISSISSIPPI MUD Have you ever had "Mississippi mud cake"? That dark, gooey, chocolatey cake is named after the rich, black mud of the Mississippi Delta, the 65-mile-wide strip along Mississippi's western border, between the Mississippi and the Yazoo Rivers. It's some of the richest farmland in the world. Moving eastward, you'll find the hilly bluffs of central Mississippi. Farther south are the Pine Hills shading into the meadowlands and coastal plains along the Gulf of Mexico. Mississippi is warm and humid, with a year-round growing season.

Ida B. Wells-Barnett (1862-1931), a distinguished journalist, was born in Holly Springs.

In the old days of flatboats and barges, goods were floated down the Mississippi—but people had to take roads to go back *up*. They used the Natchez Trace, which followed an old Indian trail. Today you can drive north on the Natchez Trace Parkway, from Natchez up to Tupelo.

Natchez is the home of more than 500 mansions built before the Civil War. Twice a year, during the Natchez Pilgrimages, costumed guides will help you tour these homes. Farther north is Jackson, the state capital and largest city. When Union General William T. Sherman occupied the state in 1863, during the Civil War, his headquarters were in Jackson.

Up at Tupelo, you can see the two-room house where Elvis Presley was born—now a major state attraction. Along the Natchez Trace, you can also see an old Choctaw village and the nation's second largest petrified forest.

THE CIVILIZED TRIBES AND THE CIVIL WAR Before the Europeans arrived in Mississippi, it was home to almost 30,000 Natchez, Choctaw, and Chickasaw. Mississippi was explored by the Spanish in the sixteenth century and settled in 1699 by the French. By 1763 the British had taken most of the state. It became American territory in 1798, though, and its people fought against the British in the War of 1812. The Choctaw fought with the Americans in the last battle of that war. But in the 1830s they and the rest of the Five Civilized Tribes were forced out of their homelands and into Indian territory in Oklahoma and

Arkansas. Thousands died on the grueling journey, known as the Trail of Tears.

Like its neighbors, Mississippi depended on African-American slaves to work its huge cotton plantations and to create lives of luxury for plantation owners. So when President Abraham Lincoln seemed about to abolish slavery, Mississippi and its neighbors seceded from the Union. The result was the Civil War, the first "modern total warfare," in which a large proportion of the population was killed. Mississippi lost 60,000 people, the greatest percentage of its population of any state.

Illinois Monument, Vicksburg National Park

FROM CIVIL WAR TO CIVIL RIGHTS Even after the Civil War was over, many Mississippians did not want to recognize African Americans as equals. In 1904 Mississippi established "separate but equal" streetcars, so that black and white passengers would not ride together. In 1958 when the African-American student Clennon King tried to enroll at the state university known as Ole Miss, he was committed to a mental hospital. In 1962 James Meredith was able to enroll in Ole Miss—but some 3,000 federal soldiers had to protect him from the violent mobs who objected and who killed two people. In 1963 civil rights leader Medgar Evers was shot in the driveway of his own home in Jackson. And in 1964 three young civil rights workers—two white, one black—were killed in Neshoba County as they tried to register black voters.

Gradually, though, the civil rights movement won political rights for black people. In fact, African Americans became important political leaders for all people in Mississippi. In 1969 Charles Evers was elected mayor of Fayette, becoming the first African-American mayor in the state's history. Today Mississippi has many black officials.

FROM AGRICULTURE TO MANUFACTURING Once cotton was king in Mississippi, along with peanuts, soybeans, sugar, corn, rice, and dairy cattle. Agriculture still contributes to the state's economy, but during the 1960s Mississippi switched from being primarily a farm state to an industrial one. Mississippi now produces petroleum, natural gas, and timber, and also makes paper, pulp, and furniture, clothes, transportation equipment, processed food, and electrical goods.

However, Mississippi has long been the poorest state in the nation, with over one-quarter of its population below the poverty level. Mississippians have the lowest personal and family income in the nation and the third highest unemployment rate. Poverty has been a hard problem to solve in Mississippi ever since cotton stopped being king.

Portrait bust of William Faulkner by Leon Koury

Fascinating Facts

DID YOU KNOW THAT...
Mississippi has a singing river, the Pascagoula, which at one point sounds "like a swarm of bees in flight."

MISSISSIPPI HAS THE WORLD'S LARGEST:
- model of a river, the Mississippi—near Jackson—210 acres; engineers use it to figure out when the river and its feeder rivers will flood

THE LAST STEAMBOAT RACE:
The *Robert E. Lee* beat the *Natchez* on the Mississippi River route from New Orleans to St. Louis in 1870.

MISSISSIPPI IS TOPS IN:
- shrimp
- oysters
- hardwood timber

MISSISSIPPI NAMES:
- Gulf Coast Indians—*Malabouchia*
- Spanish—*Rio del Espiritu Santo* (River of the Holy Spirit), *Rio Grande del Florida* (The Big River of Florida)
- French—Colbert River, St. Louis River
- Chippewa—*mici zibi*
- Algonquian—*messipi*

both of which mean "great river" or "gathering-in of all the waters"

JACKSON FACTS:
- named for General Andrew Jackson
- once the capital of the Confederacy until General Sherman's army destroyed it

FAMOUS PEOPLE BORN IN MISSISSIPPI:
- Novelist William Faulkner, New Albany (1897-1962)
- Novelist Eudora Welty, Jackson (1909-)
- Playwright Tennessee Williams, Columbus (1911-1983)
- Opera singer Leontyne Price, Laurel (1927-)
- Singer Elvis Presley, Tupelo (1935-1977)

DID YOU KNOW THAT... A mother and daughter, Maria and Miranda Youngans, ran the landmark Biloxi lighthouse for 62 years.

MISSISSIPPI IS THE STATE... where the state flower is the blossom of the state tree.

Missouri

1904 St. Louis World's Fair

24th state to enter the Union, August 10, 1821

The Basics

POPULATION: 5,358,692
16th most populous state
AREA: 69,709 square miles
21st largest state
STATE CAPITAL: Jefferson City
STATE BIRD: Bluebird (also called Eastern bluebird, Blue robin)
STATE FLOWER: Hawthorn
STATE TREE: Dogwood (also called Flowering Dogwood, Boxwood, False Box-Dogwood, New England Boxwood, Flowering Cornel, Cornel)
NICKNAMES: The Show-Me State, The Bullion State, The Cave State, The Ozark State
SPORTS TEAMS: Kansas City Royals, St. Louis Cardinals, baseball; Kansas City Chiefs, football; St. Louis Blues, hockey
STATE MOTTO: *Salus Populi Suprema Lex Est* (Latin for "The welfare of the people shall be the supreme law")
STATE MINERAL: Galena
STATE ROCK: Mozarkite
STATE SONG: "Missouri Waltz," words by J. R. Shannon, music by John Valentine Eppel
STATE LANDMARKS: Eero Saarinen's Gateway Arch, St. Louis; Mark Twain Museum and Boyhood Home, Hannibal; Fort Osage, Independence
HISTORIC PARKS: Benjamin Ranch, Kansas City; Bequette-Ribault Living History Museum; Missouri Town 1855, Blue Springs
NATIONAL PARK: Mark Twain National Forest
STATE PARKS: Lake of the Ozarks State Park; Missouri River State Trail (Katy Trail); Elephant Rocks; Johnson's Shut-Ins; Table Rock State Park

What state is the crossroads of the continental United States? Which state is halfway between the Atlantic and the Rockies, between Canada and the Gulf of Mexico? It's Missouri, the state that provided so many pioneers for America's westward expansion that it was once known as "The Mother of the West."

WHERE RIVERS MEET America's two largest rivers—the Missouri and the Mississippi—meet just north of St. Louis, Missouri's largest city. Missouri has more than 1,000 miles of navigable rivers. It has been a center for both river and railroad traffic.

The Missouri River divides the state in two. Above the Missouri it is mainly "heartland plain"—the typical midwestern landscape of rolling prairie—good land for growing corn, wheat, and soybeans. Below it is the Ozark Plateau, higher and rougher country featuring large caves and natural springs. The southeastern corner of the state, known as the Bootheel because of its distinctive shape, is part of the Mississippi River plain. Generally, Missouri has a moderate climate—but the state is visited by some 25 to 30 tornadoes a year.

Statue of Tom Sawyer in Hannibal where Mark Twain (then known as Samuel Clemens) grew up

St. Louis was made famous by the 1904 song "Meet Me In St. Louis" which referred to the first World's Fair, celebrating the hundred-year anniversary of the Louisiana Purchase. It is said that ice cream cones were invented at this fair, when a creative vendor wrapped a scoop of the frozen dessert inside a Belgian waffle. Today visitors to St. Louis can buy "concrete," a thick, solid frozen custard.

Also in St. Louis is the Scott Joplin House, home of America's most famous ragtime composer. Joplin came to St. Louis as a teenager in 1885. He went to Sedalia to study advanced harmony and music theory at George Smith College. (You can catch the Scott Joplin Festival at Sedalia during the first week of June.) There he wrote his famous "Maple Leaf Rag" in 1897. In the days before radio, new songs spread slowly—but the sheet music for Joplin's composition sold an amazing 75,000 copies in only six months. Rich and famous, Joplin bought a house in St. Louis that is now preserved as a museum.

THE WEST BEGINS On the state's western border is Kansas City, which contains the old town of Westport. Here thousands of pioneers began their journeys west on the Oregon Trail. Farther north is St. Joseph, home of the Pony Express Stables Museum. If you had read a Missouri newspaper in 1860, you might have seen the following ad: "Wanted—young, skinny, wiry fellows not over 18. Must be expert riders, willing to risk death daily. Orphans preferred. Wages $25 a week." These brave riders faced snowstorms, deserts, and bandits as they rode from St. Joseph to San Francisco in only 10 days, carrying the mail. But by 1861 the invention of the telegraph had made the service obsolete. St. Joseph is also the town where Jesse James was shot and killed by a member of his own gang.

Pony Express rider, St. Joseph

Mark Twain fans will want to visit Hannibal, where the famous author (whose real name was Samuel Clemens) grew up in a house whose picket fence looks just like the one that Tom Sawyer painted. Every year the town celebrates Tom Sawyer Day, with fence-painting contests and raft races. Near the Clemens home is the house of Laura Hawkins, Sam Clemens' boyhood sweetheart and the model for Becky Thatcher.

EXPLORERS AND GUERILLAS Missouri first entered the United States as part of the Louisiana Purchase—the territory earlier controlled by Spain and France and sold by France to the United States in 1803. The explorers Lewis and Clark left on their famous expedition from St. Louis.

In 1812 the Missouri Territory was formed—and soon became the center of a national controversy. In Congress, debate raged over whether slavery should be allowed in new territories and states. In the famous Missouri Compromise of 1820, Congress decided to admit the slave state of Missouri along with the free state of Maine. Moreover, from then on states would have to be admitted in pairs, to maintain the balance of slave and free. When this compromise was lifted in the Kansas-Nebraska Act of 1854, thousands of pro-slavery Missourians moved to Kansas territory, hoping to make it a slave state, too. In 1856 pro-slavery guerillas were active in Missouri and remained so until 1882, well after the Civil War had abolished slavery once and for all. Nevertheless, when other slave states seceded, Missouri chose to stay with the Union.

President Truman's house, Independence

BEER, LEAD, AND SOYBEANS Today, many things are manufactured in Missouri. The state leads the nation in production of beer and ale. Heavy machinery, transportation equipment, and defense aircraft are key industrial products here. Mining is also a central Missouri industry, and the state produces most of the U.S. lead supply. Besides grain and soybeans, Missouri farms are known for their livestock—hogs, turkeys, and cattle—which are slaughtered at the famous Kansas City stockyards.

Fascinating Facts

HOW MISSOURI GOT ITS NAME: It was named for the Missouri River—named for the Missouri Indians. The name comes from an Algonquin word meaning "muddy water" or "the town of large canoes."

ARCH FACTS:
- tallest monument—630 feet tall
- centerpiece of the 91-acre Jefferson National Expansion Memorial Park

MISSOURI IS TOPS IN:
- beer • mules • lead

DID YOU KNOW THAT... In 1840, the peak of buffalo hunting, the Missouri-based American Fur Company sold 67,000 buffalo pelts.

MISSOURI HAD THE FIRST:
- bridge across the Mississippi—Eads Bridge, St. Louis—1874
- school of journalism in the world—at the University of Missouri—1908
- presidential radio broadcast—by President Warren Harding at St. Louis University—1921

PRESIDENT BORN IN MISSOURI:
- Harry S Truman (1884-1972), 33rd President

OTHER FAMOUS PERSONS BORN IN MISSOURI:
- Writer Langston Hughes, Joplin (1902-1967)
- Writer Mark Twain, Hannibal (1835-1910)

HOW MISSOURI GOT ITS NICKNAME: In 1899 Missouri Congressman Willard Duncan Vandiver said in a Philadelphia speech: "...frothy eloquence neither convinces nor satisfies me. I am from Missouri. You have got to show me."

DID YOU KNOW THAT... Missouri is sometimes called "The Mother of the West" because so many of the pioneers who settled the West came from this state.

MISSOURI HALLS OF FAME:
- National Bowling Hall of Fame, St. Louis
- St. Louis Sports Hall of Fame

Montana

Glacier National Park

41st state to enter the Union, November 8, 1889

The Basics

POPULATION: 879,372
44th most populous state
AREA: 147,046 square miles
4th largest state
STATE CAPITAL: Helena
STATE BIRD: Western meadowlark
STATE FLOWER: Bitterroot
STATE TREE: Ponderosa pine
NICKNAMES: The Treasure State, the Bonanza State, Big Sky Country, Stub Toe State, Mountain State
STATE MOTTO: *Oro y Plata* (Spanish for "Gold and Silver")
STATE ANIMAL: Grizzly bear
STATE FISH: Blackspotted cutthroat trout
STATE GEM: Sapphire and Montana agate
STATE GRASS: Bluebunch grass
STATE SONG: "Montana," words by Charles C. Cohan, music by Joseph E. Howard
STATE BALLAD: "Montana Melody," words and music by Carleen and LeGrande Harvey
STATE LANDMARKS: Little Bighorn Battlefield National Monument; Big Horn Canyon; Medicine Rocks—sandstone buttes carved into strange shapes by erosion; Pompey's Pillar, a 100-foot high sandstone tower carved with Indian petroglyphs (picture-writing) and explorer William Clark's signature
NATIONAL PARK: Glacier, near Kalispell
HISTORIC PARKS: Grant-Kohrns Ranch, Deer Lodge; Nevada City, Virginia City; St. Mary's Mission, Hamilton; World Museum of Mining and Hell Roarin' Gulch, Butte

Cutting through Montana is one of the most interesting U.S. geographical features: the Continental Divide. West of the Divide, rivers flow toward the Pacific; to the east, rivers flow toward the Atlantic. Likewise, tall, rugged Rockies cover the western third of Montana, while broad, flat plains lie to the east. This rural state was born in the days of the Wild West, and its rough, beautiful terrain still has the feeling of the frontier. Montana today has more than 100 ghost towns—but every town that's still alive still has its own rodeo!

GLACIERS AND MOUNTAIN GOATS Some of the mountains in Glacier National Park are so steep and remote that they have never been climbed. You can climb some, however, as well as some of the park's 60 glaciers. The park features 200 lakes, as well as deer, elk, bears, and mountain goats.

Farther south, Flathead Lake is the largest freshwater lake west of the Mississippi. And farther west, at the National Bison Range in Dixon, you can see a herd of some 500 buffalo roaming the plains. Forests cover about a fourth of Montana's land—some 22 million acres.

Montana is an almost completely rural state—only 24 percent of its people live in such cities as Billings, Butte, Great Falls, Helena, and Missoula.

Llamas are sometimes used to herd sheep in Montana.

A MOUNTAINOUS LAND Montana's name comes from a Spanish word meaning mountainous. It was once the land of the Arapaho, Assiniboine, Blackfoot, and Shoshone. Sacagawea, Lewis and Clark's Shoshone translator, may have been born in Montana (although Idaho claims she was born there). Native peoples called Montana the "Shining Land."

In south-central Montana, near Bozeman, you can visit the Madison Buffalo Jump, or pishkun, a bluff with a cliff more than 30 feet high. Here Blackfoot used to drive herds of buffalo to their death, going to the bottom of the cliff to collect the meat, bones, and buffalo hides on which they depended. A mile-long pishkun—perhaps the largest ever discovered—is located near Great Falls.

The first European to explore the area was Pierre de la Verendrye, who also explored the Dakotas. The next major expedition was the 1805-1806 voyage of Lewis and Clark. At the State Historical Museum in Helena you can see a painting of the explorers that also portrays York, an African-American interpreter who helped develop good relations with Native Americans. York started the expedition as a slave, but when the journey ended he was given his freedom. He is also prominent in a painting behind the Speaker's desk at the State House of Representatives.

Crow Indian Fair

The Blackfoot lost their military supremacy in 1837 when they were ravaged by smallpox caught from infected blankets that U.S. soldiers and traders had deliberately given them. Ten years later the first European settlement was established at Fort Benton. In the 1850s and 1860s, more settlers came, looking for the gold and silver in Montana's mountains. Conflicts with Indians continued, as General George Custer was defeated at Little Bighorn River by Chief Sitting Bull and his Sioux and Cheyenne followers in 1876. By 1877, though, the Indians had been defeated. Four years later, railroads entered the territory. Montana, which had once been part of the territories of Louisiana, Missouri, Nebraska, Dakota, Oregon, Washington, and Idaho, would soon become a state.

PACIFIST AND SUFFRAGIST The nation's first congresswoman, Jeannette Rankin, was elected in Montana in 1916. Rankin had worked hard to win suffrage (voting rights) for women, instituted in Montana in 1914. As soon as she got to Congress, she introduced a constitutional amendment to give women the vote nationwide, a measure that finally became law in 1920. Meanwhile, Rankin supported another unpopular cause, pacifism (opposition to war). She was the only one in Congress to vote against U.S. entry into World War I and World War II. In 1968 at the age of 88, she led the Jeannette Rankin Brigade in a Washington, D.C., peace march to protest the war in Vietnam.

Logan Pass, Glacier National Park

JEWELS ON AND UNDER THE EARTH Agriculture is the mainstay of the Montana economy, particularly cattle and wheat. Montana farms also grow barley (for cattle feed) and sugar beets. Mining is a key industry, primarily for gold, silver, copper, and zinc. The only U.S. sapphires are mined in the Judith Basin in central Montana, and one of the world's largest copper mines is at Butte. Oil on the Fort Peck Reservation—on the territory of the Assiniboine and the Sioux—has generated controversy over how Montana should be developed.

Fascinating Facts

FAMOUS PEOPLE BORN IN MONTANA:

- Actor Gary Cooper, Helena (1901-1961)
- Newscaster Chet Huntley, Cardwell (1905-1993)
- Actress Myrna Loy, Radersburg (1905-1993)

DID YOU KNOW THAT... Earthquake Lake was created when a mountainside collapsed across the Madison River during the quake of August 17, 1959.

COLD AND WINDY

- The windiest city in the U.S. is Great Falls—the wind blows an average of 13.1 miles per hour all day long.
- The coldest recorded temperature in the contiguous 48 states was in Rogers Pass, -70 degrees Fahrenheit on January 20, 1954.

DID YOU KNOW THAT... The Missouri River begins in Montana.

MONTANA MYSTERY: Montana's territorial governor, Civil War hero Francis Meagher, once got on a Missouri River steamboat at Fort Benton. He went to his room—and was never seen again.

DID YOU KNOW THAT... Before Montana became a state, four brothers were born in a house near Frenchtown—but each was born in a different territory. That's because Montana was originally a part of five different territories.

MONTANA HAS THE ONLY:

- sapphire mines in the United States

MONTANA HAS THE NATION'S LARGEST:

- earth-filled or embankment dam, Fort Peck on the Missouri River

DID YOU KNOW THAT... "General" Custer was no general. Although George Custer had been a general during the Civil War, after the war he was returned to his former rank of lieutenant colonel.

Nebraska

The Basics

POPULATION: 1,652,093
37th most populous state
AREA: 77,358 square miles
16th largest state
STATE CAPITAL: Lincoln
STATE BIRD: Western meadowlark
STATE FLOWER: Late goldenrod
STATE TREE: Cottonwood (also called Eastern poplar, Carolina poplar, Eastern cottonwood, Necklace poplar, Big cottonwood, Vermont poplar, Whitewood, Cotton tree, Yellow cottonwood)
NICKNAMES: The Cornhusker State, Tree Planters' State, Antelope State, Bug-Eating State
STATE MOTTO: Equality Before the Law
STATE MAMMAL: White-tailed deer
STATE INSECT: Honeybee
STATE GRASS: Little blue stem grass
STATE ROCK: Prairie agate
STATE FOSSIL: Mammoth
STATE GEM: Blue agate
STATE SONG: "Beautiful Nebraska," words and music by Jim Fras
NATIONAL PARK: Homestead National Monument, near Beatrice—commemorates post-1862 homestead movement
STATE LANDMARKS: Agate Fossil Beds National Monument, near Scottsbluff—"stone bones" of many animals; Fort Niobrara National Wildlife Refuge—including buffalo and Texas longhorns
HISTORIC PARKS: Pioneer Village; Scout's Rest Ranch, North Platte—Buffalo Bill Cody's home and Wild West Show training grounds
STATE FESTIVALS: Applejack Festival, Nebraska City (September); Chicken Show, Wayne (July); LaVitsef Celebration, Norfolk (September)

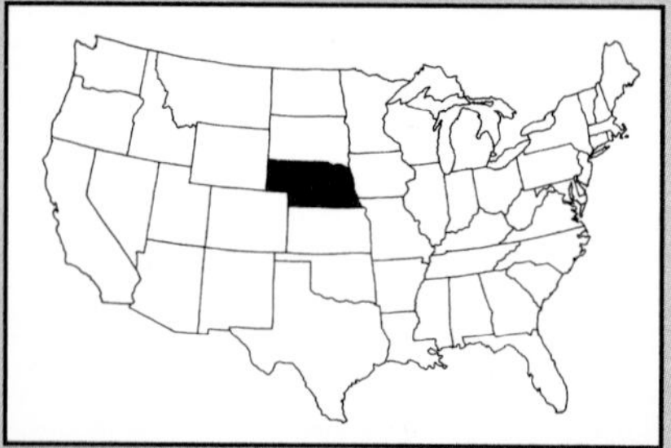

Chimney Rock, on the Oregon Trail

37th state to enter the Union, March 1, 1867

Picture a vast prairie, stretching far off into the horizon, carpeted in short grasses and brightly colored wildflowers, crisscrossed by thin, trickling streams. This is the dry, golden country of Nebraska.

GREAT PLAINS AND PRAIRIE FLOWERS The western part of Nebraska is a typical Great Plains state, marked by billowing fields of wheat. In the north central part of the state, cattle graze the far-reaching ranges, as in the northwestern Sand Hills. Eastern Nebraska features the Missouri River lowlands, whose fertile ground is given over to corn. The Platte River runs east to west across the state paralleled by the Mormon Trail and the Overland Trail once used by the Pony Express. In the 1840s thousands of settlers passed through the Platte River Valley as they used the Oregon Trail on their way west.

The Centennial Mall in Lincoln opens below the Capitol.

Once 14-foot woolly mammoths roamed these plains. Now you can see their bones at the University of Nebraska State Museum in Lincoln. Later, herds of buffalo stampeded across the flat, treeless ground. The buffalo are gone—but you can still hike through natural prairie at Nine-Mile Prairie, a nearby nature preserve.

In northwest Nebraska, Courthouse and Jail Rocks rise like sandstone towers from the rolling prairie. They were once used as landmarks by pioneers on the Oregon Trail. At Bayard, Chimney Rock, a national historic site, seems to rise up to the heavens, while Scotts Bluff was once known as Lighthouse of the Plains.

Nebraska's lovely landscape has inspired many great writers. Pulitzer Prize-winning author Willa Cather lived in Red Cloud, Nebraska, for only about six years in the 1880s, but the region became Moonstone, Black Hawk, and Frankfort in such prairie novels as *The Song of the Lark, My Antonia*, and *O Pioneers.* You can still see Cather's home and visit an historical center dedicated to her in Red Cloud. Nebraska Hall of Fame member Mari Sandoz wrote many histories of the region, including the famous *Cheyenne Autumn*, story of the 1879 rebellion of the Cheyenne people. You can visit her grave and a museum about her at Gordon.

O PIONEERS! When the 1862 Homestead Act was passed, pioneers could get 160 acres of land virtually for free, if only they were willing to stay on their

Lincoln's sunken gardens attract visitors to its fountains and paths.

"stakes" for five years. Nebraska was soon flooded with homesteaders—but there weren't enough trees to build houses for them all. So the pioneers built sod huts using huge blocks of earth from the prairie itself, held together by the roots of prairie grasses still growing in the fertile ground. Later, Nebraskans planted trees to help hold the soil in place, even creating the Nebraska National Forest at Halsey—the only national forest completely planted by the people.

The first homestead in the nation was claimed by Daniel and Agnes Freeman near Beatrice. There you can visit the Homestead National Monument to Agnes Freeman, True Pioneer Mother. Freeman lived in a one-room house, miles from any neighbor. There she raised six children, baked biscuits in a wood stove, made friends with neighboring Otoe Indians, and learned enough medicine from her doctor husband to get her own state license as a physician. One day a visiting niece asked her how she bore the loneliness. "It wasn't easy at first," Freeman answered, "but now it's my home."

Willa Cather grew up in this small Red Cloud home.

You can learn more about pioneer life at Omaha's Great Plains Black Museum. Even today, there are barely 60,000 African Americans in the five states of Nebraska, Montana, Wyoming, and the Dakotas. Yet black pioneers and cowboys are an important part of the history of the West. At this museum you can find out about Mary Fields, who ran a stagecoach stop in Cascade, Montana, or Aunt Sally Campbell, who mined gold in Deadwood, South Dakota.

THE BUSINESS OF AGRICULTURE Agriculture is the main source of income for this overwhelmingly rural state. Beef cattle graze on ranches in the west, while dairy cattle browse the Platte River Valley. The state also supports huge farms in corn, wheat, oats, rye, barley, sugarbeets, potatoes, beans, alfalfa, and sorghum. What little industry exists is based on agriculture: meatpacking, dairy processing, and agricultural machinery. Omaha is also a major insurance and telemarketing center.

Fascinating Facts

HOW NEBRASKA GOT ITS NAME: The Omahas called it *Nibthaska,* and the Otoes *Nibrathka.* Both were talking about the "flat river" that runs through the state and gave Nebraska its name. The French called the river *Platte,* which means "flat" in French, but kept the native name for the state.

HOW NEBRASKA GOT ITS NICKNAMES: The University of Nebraska football team is called the Cornhuskers. When there's a home football game, the stadium at Lincoln actually becomes "the third largest city in the state." The "bug-eating state" refers to Nebraska's many insect-eating bull bats.

PRESIDENT BORN IN NEBRASKA:
- Gerald R. Ford (1913-), 38th President

OTHER FAMOUS PEOPLE BORN IN NEBRASKA:
- Dancer Fred Astaire, Omaha (1899-1987)
- Actor Henry Fonda, Grand Island (1905-1982)
- Actor Marlon Brando, Omaha (1924-)
- Leader Malcolm X, Omaha (1925-1965)

NEBRASKA HOLIDAY: In 1872, there were very few trees in Nebraska. So newspaper publisher J. Sterling Morton asked people in his state to set aside a special tree-planting day. Arbor Day became a nationwide holiday!

NEBRASKA HAS THE NATION'S ONLY:
- *unicameral* (one-house) state legislature. That means there are no state senators, only representatives. Some people think this makes Nebraska more democratic, since its elected officials are more directly accountable to smaller numbers of people.

NEBRASKA HAD THE FIRST:
- homestead—claimed by Daniel and Agnes Freeman—near Beatrice

IT USED TO BE ILLEGAL IN NEBRASKA:
- to picnic in the same place twice within a 30-day period
- to sneeze in public
- for a mother to curl her daughter's hair without a state license

Nevada

Desert sand sculptures

36th state to enter the Union, October 31, 1864

The Basics

POPULATION: 1,603,163
38th most populous state
AREA: 110,567 square miles
7th largest state
STATE CAPITAL: Carson City
STATE BIRD: Mountain bluebird
STATE FLOWER: Sagebrush
STATE TREE: Single-leaf piñon (also called Nut pine, Pinyon, Gray pine, Nevada nut pine, and Single-leaf pinyon pine)
NICKNAMES: Silver State, Sagebrush State, Sage State, Battle Born State, Mining State
STATE MOTTO: All for our Country
STATE ANIMAL: Desert bighorn sheep
STATE FISH: Lohonta cutthroat trout
STATE METAL: Silver
STATE FOSSIL: Icthyosaur
STATE GRASS: Indian rice grass
STATE COLORS: Silver and blue
STATE SONG: "Home Means Nevada," words and music by Bertha Raffeto
NATIONAL PARK: Great Basin, near Baker, site of the Bristlecone Pines, over 2,000 years old—among the oldest living things on earth
STATE PARKS: Washoe Lake State Recreation Area, near Carson City, with views of the Sierra Nevada, known for fishing and horseback riding; Valley of Fire State Park, near Las Vegas, featuring rock formations and Pueblo petroglyphs (picture-writing)
STATE THEME PARK: Ponderosa Ranch and Western Theme Park, Crystal Bay—based on the TV series *Bonanza*

Nevada is a state with few people—but a lot of famous places. The gambling cities of Las Vegas, Reno, and Lake Tahoe are "the playground of the nation." Gigantic Hoover Dam and human-created Lake Mead are impressive sights. And the Nevada desert—dry, deserted, yet full of wildlife—is a landmark of the American West.

DESERT LAND Nevada's eerie, lovely landscape is primarily desert, for this state lies in the center of the Great Basin, a desert plateau between the Sierra Nevada and the Rocky Mountains. The 5,000-foot-high plateau is crisscrossed by valleys—most deeply, by Death Valley (mostly in California). This sparsely settled state is too dry to farm, so it has primarily been used to graze cattle, horses, and sheep.

Professional rodeo riders compete for millions of dollars in prizes.

Until recently, Las Vegas, Reno, and Lake Tahoe were the only places in the United States where widespread gambling was legal. Las Vegas, Spanish for "the meadows," is the biggest of these cities and the state's major metropolis. Although gambling was legal here by the 1930s, Las Vegas as we know it was created after World War II when the gangster Benjamin "Bugsy" Siegel decided to build a huge resort in what was then a small town. Siegel's Flamingo Hotel failed—but the idea of a gambling resort area took off and today, Las Vegas has nine of the ten largest hotels in the world.

Las Vegas offers many curious sights to the tourist: the Union Pacific train inside the Plaza Hotel; the 61-pound solid gold nugget at the Gold Nugget casino; and the one million dollars in cash displayed at Binion's Horseshoe Casino. You can also visit the Guinness World of Records Museum. The Imperial Palace Auto Collection features more than 300 antique cars, owned by such famous people as Adolf Hitler and gangster Al Capone. Las Vegas is also the site of the National Finals Rodeo.

Reno is also a key gambling city, known as the "Biggest Little City in the World." Some 24 miles away is Virginia City, an old mining town that has been preserved and restored. When gold and silver were discovered in Nevada in 1859, the rush of settlers to the state caused Virginia City to grow to 20,000 almost overnight, second only to San Francisco as a key western city. By 1863 this former mining town had luxury homes, a fancy opera house, six churches—and 110 saloons! It also had the only elevator between Chicago and the West Coast. You can visit many of these spots today.

BUILDING THE SILVER STATE Nevada was the last western state to be explored by Europeans, for it seemed to offer nothing but desert wilderness. The Mono Panamint, Utes, Western Shoshone, Washo, and Paiute lived in Nevada, but few settlers wished to do so.

One famous Washo resident was basketmaker Dat-So-La-Lee (1826-1925), whose designs have been called the most exquisite in the world. She made more than 300 baskets, each with 100,000 stitches portraying legends, sacred shapes, and Washo symbols. If you visit Carson City, you can see many of her beautiful creations in the Nevada State Museum.

Prairie dogs are often seen in the desert.

Thousands of prospectors crossed Nevada on their way to the California gold rush. By 1859 settlers came to Nevada, first for gold, then for silver. The Great Comstock Lode—named for the prospector who found it—yielded some $293 million by 1882. President Abraham Lincoln said that Nevada's riches had "made it possible for the government to…continue this terrible war for the Union." Lincoln was also eager for Nevada to become a state by 1864, so that its senators could vote for the 13th Amendment, which abolished slavery.

By the 1880s most of the old mining towns had become ghost towns. Later there were other gold and silver strikes (discoveries), but today Nevada's riches come more from tourists' pockets than from the ground.

GOLD AND GRAINS Tourism is certainly the mainstay of Nevada's economy, causing this state's population to increase more than 550 percent between 1950 and 1988. Other industries include the manufacturing of gambling equipment and mining. Nevada is first in mining U.S. gold (56 percent of all U.S. production), second in mining silver, and the only state to mine mercury.

There is also some agricultural activity, thanks to the dam. Constructed on the Colorado River in the 1930s, the Hoover Dam has made irrigation possible, so that farms can grow alfalfa, potatoes, hay, barley, and wheat. This dam, which also produces electricity, contains as much steel as the Empire State Building and enough concrete to pave a two-lane highway from Los Angeles to Miami. To build the dam, concrete had to be poured continually for two years. Lake Mead became one of the largest man-made lakes in the world when the dam was completed. It was filled by the tremendous flow of water from the Colorado River.

Hoover Dam

Most of the land in Nevada is owned not by miners or ranchers, but by the U.S. government. It was in this state that the first underground tests of atomic weapons were conducted in the 1950s, and the state is still a major site for atomic development.

Fascinating Facts

DID YOU KNOW THAT… Eighteen tunnels had to be built through the Sierra Nevada before the first railroad could cross from California into Nevada.

FISHING FOLKLORE: In northern Nevada there are both cool mountain streams and hot springs. Some fishermen claim that they can catch a fish in the cold water and then cook it in the hot water without ever taking it off the hook!

DID YOU KNOW THAT… Nevada gets less rain than any other state—about 7 1/2 inches per year.

NEVADA IS TOPS IN…

- gold—more than half of U.S. gold
- turquoise—a major world supplier
- rare opals—the world center
- open-pit copper mine—world's largest

NEVADA HAD THE FIRST… skiing in the United States, introduced in 1854 by the Norwegian John A. Thompson, who used it for his speedy mail delivery service.

DID YOU KNOW THAT… Reno, Nevada, is farther west than Los Angeles, California.

THERE ARE SO MANY TOURISTS IN NEVADA… that they outnumber the population of several other states! More than thirty million people visit the state each year.

MR. SAMUEL CLEMENS… took the pen name Mark Twain while working in Nevada from 1861-1864 on the *Territorial Enterprise,* a Virginia City newspaper. The humorist made fun of so many people, he decided to save his own name for "more serious" writing. Describing one local judge, Twain wrote, "It was impossible to print his lectures in full, as the cases had run out of capital I's."

DID YOU KNOW THAT… to meet a deadline for statehood, Nevada's whole constitution was wired to Washington for $4,303.27, the world's most expensive telegram.

IT USED TO BE ILLEGAL IN NEVADA:

- to drive a camel

New Hampshire

Colonial buildings in Harrisville

9th state to enter the Union, June 21, 1788

The Basics

POPULATION: 1,162,481
42nd most populous state
AREA: 9,351 square miles
46th largest state
STATE CAPITAL: Concord
STATE BIRD: Purple finch
STATE FLOWER: Purple lilac
STATE TREE: White birch (also known as Canoe birch, Silver birch, Paper birch, Large white birch)
NICKNAMES: The Granite State, the White Mountain State, the Switzerland of America, Mother of Rivers
STATE MOTTO: Live Free or Die
STATE ANIMAL: White-tailed deer
STATE INSECT: Ladybug
STATE REPTILE: Red-spotted newt
STATE SONG: "Old New Hampshire," words by John F. Homes, music by Maurice Hoffman; "New Hampshire, My New Hampshire," words by Julius Richelson, music by Walter P. Smith
STATE LANDMARKS: Franconia Rock, the natural profile of "The Old Man of the Mountain" (featured in Nathaniel Hawthorne's story "The Great Stone Face"), Profile Mountain, White Mountains; Franklin Pierce Homestead, Hillsboro
HISTORIC PARKS: America's Stonehenge, Salem; Canterbury Shaker Village, Concord; Six Gun City, Jefferson; Strawberry Banke, 10-acre village museum, with buildings from 1695 to 1820, Portsmouth

If you visit New Hampshire's White Mountains, you can still see the notches carved by the glaciers millions of years ago. Yet the glacial soil is too rocky to be good for farming. Though it is a rural state with forests covering 80 percent of its territory, New Hampshire depends on manufacturing for its livelihood.

LAND OF THE SMILING WATER New Hampshire divides into three regions. To the north and west are the White Mountains, the highest in New England. Central New Hampshire is full of lakes, most notably Lake Winnepesaukee, an Indian word for "Smiling Water." This region features hardwood forests and three of New Hampshire's major cities: Manchester, Nashua, and Concord. Also in central New Hampshire is Dartmouth, originally Moor's Indian Charity School and today an Ivy League college. To the southeast are New Hampshire's coastal lowlands. The 18-mile coastline is the shortest in New England, ending in Portsmouth, a busy seaport and one of New Hampshire's major cities.

Home of statesman and orator Daniel Webster, Franklin

THE STATE THAT MADE THE NATION The territory that is now New Hampshire was first inhabited by the Asmokeag, Nashua, Ossipee, Pennacook, Pequawket, Piscataqua, Squamscot, and Winnipesaukee, who gave their name to many of the state's cities and waterways. The first European in the area was probably the English sea captain Martin Pring, who in 1603 sailed up the Piscataqua River and landed near what today is Portsmouth. French explorer Samuel de Champlain followed in 1605 and after him came English captain John Smith in 1614. The first settlers, immigrants from England, established towns at Portsmouth and Dover in 1623.

Owls nest and hunt in New Hampshire's many forests. The owls also stand on one leg while sleeping.

Relations between native peoples and the new settlers were often violent. In 1627 the Indian

State House, Concord

leader Passaconaway (Child of the Bear) united 17 Indian nations into the Pennacook Confederacy, hoping to bring peace with the "palefaces." But by 1675 Indian leader King Philip began to resist the European invasion with a series of raids on farmhouses and villages. The French and Indian War led to more raids which continued until the Indians were finally defeated in 1759.

Meanwhile, English colonists—many from Massachusetts—settled along the New Hampshire coast. In 1629 Captain John Mason of the British Royal Navy was granted the land, which he named after his childhood home, England's Hampshire county.

For a time New Hampshire was part of Massachusetts, then "the Dominion of New England," but eventually it became independent. Independence was important to New Hampshirites, so much so that on January 5, 1776, they formed their own independent republic, seven months before the Declaration of Independence was signed. But until New Hampshire signed the Constitution the United States could not formally come into existence. When it became the ninth state to sign, in 1788, New Hampshire truly became "the state that made a nation."

THE FORTUNE OF AMOS FORTUNE One of New Hampshire's most famous residents was Amos Fortune, an African prince who was enslaved at an early age and brought to Massachusetts. Fortune received his freedom at age sixty—and moved to New Hampshire to begin a new life. In Jaffrey, he started a tanning business, founded a library, trained both black and white apprentices, and became a leading citizen. When he died in 1801, he left money to support the local school. The money is still used for the Amos Fortune Forum, which brings speakers to give talks each summer.

TEXTILE MILLS AND MAPLE SUGAR New Hampshire had some of America's first factories—and America's first women's strike. The women at Cocheco Manufacturing Company wanted to oppose their wage cut—from 58 cents a day to 53. They worked under harsh rules: a twelve-and-a-half-cent fine for arriving one second late and no talking at the machines. More than 300 workers paraded through the streets in December 1828—but by January 1, they had to go back to work for fear of losing their jobs.

Today New Hampshire relies less on textile mills than on high-tech industries. Many computer and software companies are attracted by the state's low taxes and have relocated from Boston. The state continues to mine granite, used in monuments and public buildings. Poultry and dairy farms sell eggs and milk to tourist hotels. And the state's hardwood forests supply maple syrup for the nation's pancakes.

Fascinating Facts

DID YOU KNOW THAT... New Hampshire granite was used to build the Library of Congress.

PRESIDENT BORN IN NEW HAMPSHIRE:
- Franklin Pierce (1804-1869), 14th President

OTHER FAMOUS PEOPLE BORN IN NEW HAMPSHIRE:
- Politician Daniel Webster, Salisbury (1782-1852)
- Mary Baker Eddy, founder of the Christian Science movement, Bow (1821-1910)

DID YOU KNOW THAT... Although the Russo-Japanese War was fought between Russia and Japan, the peace treaty ending that war was signed in Portsmouth on September 5, 1905. The conference was run by President Theodore Roosevelt.

MOUNT WASHINGTON FACTS:
- highest peak in New England—6,288 feet
- highest wind velocity in the United States—in 1934 it reached 231 miles per hour; wind averages 35.2 miles per hour
- third-snowiest place in the United States, with up to 253.5 inches per year

DID YOU KNOW THAT... New Hampshire has the largest state legislature in the country, with 400 members.

NEW HAMPSHIRE HAS THE OLDEST... continuously published paper in the United States, the New Hampshire *Gazette*, founded in 1756

NEW HAMPSHIRE HAD THE FIRST:
- machine-made watches in the world
- regular stagecoach run in the United States, between Portsmouth and Boston
- cog railway in North America—1838
- horseless carriage—built in 1869 after 13 years of work by Enos M. Clough of Sunapee—but the city fathers made him give it up because of the noise it made!

NEW HAMPSHIRE HAS THE WORLD'S LARGEST... blanket mill

New Jersey

The Basics

POPULATION: 7,987,933
9th most populous state
AREA: 8,722 square miles
47th largest state
STATE CAPITAL: Trenton
STATE BIRD: Eastern goldfinch
STATE FLOWER: Meadow violet (purple violet)
STATE TREE: Red oak and dogwood
NICKNAMES: The Garden State, Cockpit of the Revolution, the Clam State, the Camden and Amboy State, the Jersey Blue State, the Pathway of the Revolution
STATE MOTTO: Liberty and Prosperity
SPORTS TEAMS: Giants, Jets, football; New Jersey Nets, basketball; New Jersey Devils, hockey
STATE ANIMAL: Horse
STATE INSECT: Honeybee
STATE COLORS: Buff and blue
STATE SONG: "New Jersey Loyalty" (unofficial)
STATE LANDMARKS: Grover Cleveland Birthplace, Caldwell; Thomas A. Edison National Historic Site, West Orange—the inventor's workshop
NATIONAL PARK: Morristown National Historical Park—includes General George Washington's headquarters during the winter of 1779-1780 and Fort Nonsense
HISTORIC SITES: Batsto—a colonial village; Clinton Historical Museum Village, Clinton; Fosterfields Historical Farm, Morristown; Historic Allaire Village, Allaire State Park; Historic Cold Spring Village; Cape May; Historic Towne of Smithville, Absecon; Victorian Wheaton Village, Millville; Waterloo Village Restoration, Stanhope

Ships docked in Newark, one of the largest ports on the East Coast **3rd state, December 18, 1787**

This mid-Atlantic state is right in the center of the manufacturing belt that stretches from Washington, D.C., to Canada. Although it's one of our smallest states, and our most densely populated, it seems there is room for some of everything: farms and factories, superhighways and dirt roads, mountains and beaches, port cities and fishing villages. Some 90 percent of the people in this highly urban state live in cities and towns, many of which are actually suburbs of New York and Philadelphia.

Mother deer and fawn

SUNTANNING ON THE JERSEY SHORE New Jersey is almost completely bounded by water. It shares Hudson River ports with New York and Delaware River ports with Pennsylvania. Along the Atlantic coast is the famous Jersey Shore: 127 miles of sandy beaches dotted with vacation resorts and amusement parks. Young Bruce Springsteen used to perform in the Asbury Park area, and he still sings about the Jersey Shore. Farther south on the Shore is Atlantic City, a major East Coast gambling center. In nearby Ocean City, check out the Hermit Crab Race and Miss Crustacean Contest, and the Miscellaneous Suntanning Tournament, both in August.

Absecon lighthouse at Graveyard inlet

Most of southern Jersey is coastal plain, suitable for farming. Along the Hudson River, across from New York, you can see the sheer cliffs of the Palisades. New Jersey's Kittatinny Mountains—part of the Appalachians—are in the state's northwest corner. Cutting deeply across the Kittatinnies is the Delaware Water Gap.

New Jersey's towns have been home to many famous figures. The great American poet Walt Whitman lived in Camden—which is also the home of Campbell's Soup Headquarters. (See their collection of soup tureens!)

Princeton, home of Princeton University, is where physicist Albert Einstein worked. It was also the birthplace of Paul Robeson—actor, singer, and civil rights activist. Woodrow Wilson, America's president during World War I, was first a professor and then the president of Princeton University, and later the governor of New Jersey.

Mount Laurel was the birthplace of Alice Paul, who worked first for women's right to vote and then—unsuccessfully—for an Equal Rights Amendment to the Constitution that was meant to guarantee women full legal equality. Paul might have been inspired to know about the 172 women of Vineland, who in 1868 cast their ballots in a presidential election—although they would not have the legal right to do so until 1920. (The ballots were kept in a separate box and not included in the official count.) You can still see her farmhouse, Paulsdale, on Hooton Road.

Rhodes Scholar, basketball star, Senator, Bill Bradley (1943-)

In Red Bank, you can visit the T. Thomas Fortune House. In the 1880s Fortune founded the influential newspaper *New York Age.* In its pages, he argued for integrating public schools and expanding civil rights.

Perhaps the most famous place in New Jersey's history is Trenton, where General George Washington and his men crossed the ice-clogged Delaware on Christmas Night, 1776. You may have seen the famous painting *Washington Crossing the Delaware*—this is where it happened! You can still visit Trenton's Old Barracks, where Washington's men surprised the sleeping Hessians—and if you visit on Christmas, you can see the crossing reenacted at Crossing State Park.

THE GARDEN STATE GETS ITS NAME When the first Europeans arrived in New Jersey, they found a native people called the Lenni-Lanape. Early Swedish settlers bought much of the present state from these people in 1640. Dutch settlers had also come to New Jersey, and by 1655 they had forced the Swedes out. The British, in turn, took the land from the Dutch in 1664 and named the town of Elizabeth after their queen. When the colony was given to British settlers Sir John Berkeley and Sir George Cartaret, they named it after Jersey, the island in the English channel where Carteret had been born and had been lieutenant governor.

Almost 100 Revolutionary War battles were fought in New Jersey, including the Battle of Monmouth on June 28, 1778, near Freehold. The battle was waged with the help of Molly Hays, who carried water to the men as they fought. She got her famous nickname as the soldiers called for "Molly Pitcher." When her husband, an artilleryman, was shot, Molly loaded the cannon in his place and fought to the battle's end.

New Jersey's farms were of key importance in supplying soldiers with the food they needed to fight the war. New Jersey became known as the Garden State, since its gardens helped to win our independence.

A LEADER IN FARMS AND FACTORIES Farms occupy less than 20 percent of New Jersey's land, yet the fruit and vegetables grown here help feed all the city dwellers in Philadelphia and New York. New Jersey tomatoes, corn, strawberries, and peaches are especially famous. New Jersey also produces fish and shellfish—bluefish, clams, flounder, and lobster.

This industrial state is a leader in chemical production and the manufacture of medicine. Electric and electronic equipment, machinery, and printing are also important, as are New Jersey's oil refineries.

Fascinating Facts

NEW JERSEY HAD THE WORLD'S FIRST:

- professional baseball game—Hoboken—1846
- intercollegiate football game—New Brunswick—between Rutgers and Princeton
- four-lane highway—between Elizabeth and Newark
- Miss America Contest—Atlantic City—1921

NEW JERSEY INVENTIONS:

- telegraph—Samuel Morse
- lightbulb, phonograph, movie camera—Thomas A. Edison
- submarine—John P. Holland
- Standard Time—William F. Allen

PRESIDENT BORN IN NEW JERSEY:

- Grover Cleveland (1837-1908), 22nd and 24th President

OTHER FAMOUS PEOPLE BORN IN NEW JERSEY:

- Politician Aaron Burr, Newark (1756-1836)
- Author James Fenimore Cooper, Burlington (1789-1851)
- Author Stephen Crane, Newark (1871-1900)
- Poet William Carlos Williams, Rutherford (1883-1963)
- Scholar, actor, singer Paul Robeson, Princeton (1898-1976)
- Jazz great William "Count" Basie, Red Bank (1904-1984)
- Actress Meryl Streep, Summit (1949-)

NEW JERSEY IS TOPS IN:

- variety of manufactured products
- flag-making
- chemical production
- jewelry—national jewelry center is Newark

BEFORE HOLLYWOOD... New Jersey was the motion picture capital of the world until about 1916. That's because Thomas A. Edison pioneered the development of movie equipment in his laboratory at Menlo Park.

IT USED TO BE ILLEGAL IN NEW JERSEY:

- to delay or detain a homing pigeon

New Mexico

12th century Anasazi village

47th state to enter the Union, January 6, 1912

The Basics

POPULATION: 1,713,407
36th most populous state
AREA: 121,598 square miles
5th largest state
STATE CAPITAL: Santa Fe
STATE BIRD: Roadrunner (also called Chaparral bird)
STATE FLOWER: Yucca flower
STATE TREE: Piñon
NICKNAMES: Land of Enchantment, the Cactus State, the Spanish State
STATE MOTTO: *Crescit Eundo* (Latin for "It grows as it goes")
STATE ANIMAL: New Mexico black bear
STATE GRASS: Blue grama grass
STATE FOSSIL: Coelophysis
STATE GEM: Turquoise
STATE SONG: "O Fair New Mexico," words and music by Elizabeth Garrett; *Asi Es Nuevo Mejico*," words and music by Almadeo Lucero
STATE LANDMARKS: Palace of the Governors, Santa Fe; Taos Pueblo; Puye Cliff Dwellings, Santa Clara Pueblo—740-room Indian structure
NATIONAL PARKS: Carlsbad Caverns; White Sands National Monument.
STATE PARK: Valley of Fires, near Carrizozo—1,500-year-old lava flow
STATE FESTIVALS: International Balloon Fiesta, Albuquerque (October); Piñata Festival, Tucumcari (June); Whole Enchilada Fiesta, Las Cruces (October)
STATE PLEDGE OF ALLEGIANCE: In English, "I salute the flag of the state of New Mexico, the Zia Indian symbol of perfect friendship among united cultures." In Spanish, *"Saludo la bandera del estado de Nuevo Mejico, el simbolo zia de amistad perfecta, entre culturas unidas."*

New Mexico is home to many different Indian nations and pueblos, each with its own feast days, customs, and tribal governments. And New Mexico is a kind of living record of Spanish and Mexican history in the United States. Visitors to this southwestern desert state will find that it is truly a Land of Enchantment.

PUEBLO, APACHE, NAVAJO Eastern New Mexico is part of the Great Plains—flat, endless prairie. The central part of the state is occupied by the Rocky Mountains. And to the west is the Colorado Plateau, high, dry grasslands. To outsiders this land might appear harsh, if beautiful, but to the many native peoples who live here, the land is rewarding.

Cheyenne perform the Sky Dance.

There are 18 separate pueblos (Indian villages) in New Mexico, each governed by its own people, each with its own historic buildings. The Laguna pueblo consists of six villages spread over several acres. It's famous for its pottery. The Acoma pueblo is near the Enchanted Mesa, a huge monolith towering 400 feet above the plains. The Cochiti pueblo is known for its ceremonial dances and drumming, and for its storyteller dolls. The pueblo at Isleta includes an old Mission from Spanish colonial days—and nightly bingo games! At the Jemez pueblo, you can see baskets woven from yucca leaves, as well as another old Mission, of San Juan de Jemez. The largest pueblo is that of the Zuni, who are famous for their turqoise-and-silver jewelry.

Also in New Mexico is part of the Navajo reservation, home to the largest Native American group in the United States. This 16-million-acre reservation stretches into Arizona and Utah as well. And New Mexico is the site of the Jicarilla Apache and Mescalero Apache reservations.

A LAND OF LIVING HISTORY Both Indian and Spanish influences can be felt in Santa Fe, the U.S.'s oldest continuously inhabited city. The oldest house in Santa Fe was built by the Alaco Pueblo in A.D. 1200. When the Spanish came in 1540, they added adobe bricks and a fireplace.

Visiting Albuquerque, you might take one of the town's famous hot-air balloon rides. Or you can take a four-hour drive northwest and visit the Aztec Ruins National Monument, one of the largest Native American ruins on the continent. This 500-room dwelling was misnamed by the nineteenth century people who discovered it. They believed they had found Aztec ruins, not realizing that the Aztecs were active much further south, in Mexico. This was a Pueblo ruin. Not too far away, at the Petroglyph National Monument, you can see over 17,000 ancient rock drawings along a 17-mile natural wall, probably created around A.D. 1300.

Other famous landmarks in New Mexico include the artist Georgia O'Keeffe's house and studio at Abiquiú and Mabel Dodge Luhan's salon at Taos. Mabel Dodge once ran a salon (a kind of open house) in New York City, welcoming artists and writers for many evenings of conversation. Then she married the Taos Pueblo Indian Antonio Lujan (later Luhan) and moved to Taos. She continued to invite artists and writers to her new salon, including O'Keeffe and the English novelist D.H. Lawrence.

For a taste of the Old West, take a look in Lincoln at Mountain Pride, the stagecoach driven by Sadie Orchard. As you look, imagine riding in the rickety carriage over the rocky mountain roads of New Mexico. And don't miss the Carlsbad Caverns in the southeastern part of the state. Most of its 77 underground rooms aren't open to the public, but the caves that you can visit feature rock sculptures in delicate, fantastic shapes. At night, millions of bats fly out of the cave opening, like a huge column of smoke in the sky.

ALONG THE SANTA FE TRAIL The Golden Age of the Pueblo civilization was probably 950-1200. But there were still many highly developed native peoples living in New Mexico when the Spanish first arrived in the 1500s. Soon Spanish settlers brought cattle and sheep into the region and founded missions to convert the Indians to Christianity.

Ruins at Chaco Canyon National Monument

In 1680 the Pueblos drove out the Spanish. But by 1692 the Spanish had regained control. In 1821 the first caravan of Americans drove their wagons from Missouri to Santa Fe along the Santa Fe trail. Although Mexico governed New Mexico for a time, the United States eventually gained control of this land—and continued to push native peoples onto reservations. In 1886 Apache leader Geronimo led an uprising when his people were exiled to Arizona—but they were defeated.

Today native peoples still live on the lands that were set aside for them. But in New Mexico, more than any other state, Indians have managed to maintain their culture, their language, and their government.

URANIUM AND SHEEP FARMS New Mexico's sheep and cattle ranches are extremely important to the state. But its true wealth is under the ground, not on the plains. Uranium, oil, copper, zinc, potash, gold, silver, and lead are all key resources in New Mexico. And the state's natural beauty is a foundation for thriving tourism.

Fascinating Facts

NEW MEXICO HAD THE NATION'S FIRST:

- public building—Palace of the Governors, Santa Fe—1610
- road—El Camino Real—from Santa Fe to Chihuahua, Mexico
- atomic bomb—built in Los Alamos and detonated near Carrizozo—1945

DID YOU KNOW THAT... New Mexico is the only state where blue corn grows—around Albuquerque and Santa Fe.

NEW MEXICO IS TOPS IN:

- uranium
- nuclear research
- dry ice production

NEW MEXICO HAS THE WORLD'S LARGEST:

- underground room—Carlsbad Caverns
- gypsum deposit—White Sands National Monument

DID YOU KNOW THAT... Six flags have flown over New Mexico: those of Spain, the Pueblo Indians, the Republic of Mexico, the Republic of Texas, Confederacy, the United States.

NEW MEXICO HALL OF FAME:

- International Space Hall of Fame, Alamagordo

HOW NEW MEXICO GOT ITS NAME: As early as 1561, the Spanish explorers called the upper Rio Grande Valley *Nuevo Mexico. Mexico* comes from the Aztec word that means "Place of Mexitli," who was one of the Aztec gods. U.S. officials translated the name into English.

FAMOUS PEOPLE BORN IN NEW MEXICO:

- Apache leader Mangas Coloradas, southwest New Mexico (c. 1797-1863)

IT USED TO BE ILLEGAL IN NEW MEXICO:

- to have a bicycle horn with a non-harmonious sound
- to climb a building to get a free view of a ball game

New York

U.S. Military Academy at West Point

11th state to enter the Union, July 26, 1788

The Basics

POPULATION: 18,184,774
3rd most populous state
AREA: 54,471 square miles
27th largest state
STATE CAPITAL: Albany
STATE BIRD: Bluebird
STATE FLOWER: Rose
STATE TREE: Sugar maple
NICKNAMES: The Empire State, the Excelsior State, the Knickerbocker State
STATE MOTTO: *Excelsior* (Latin for "Ever upward")
SPORTS TEAMS: New York Mets, New York Yankees, baseball; Buffalo Bills, football; New York Knicks, basketball; New York Rangers, New York Islanders, Buffalo Sabres, hockey
STATE ANIMAL: American beaver
STATE FISH: Brook trout or Speckled trout
STATE INSECT: Ladybug
STATE FOSSIL: *Eurypterus remipes*
STATE GEM: Garnet
STATE BAKED GOOD: Apple muffin
STATE DRINK: Milk
STATE SONG: "I Love New York," words and music by Steve Karmen
STATE LANDMARK: U.S. Military Academy at West Point
NATIONAL PARK: Saratoga National Historical Park
STATE FESTIVALS: Alpo International Dog Sled Races, Saranac Lake (January); Fort Ticonderoga Muzzle Loading Rifle Shoot, Ticonderoga (May, September); The Hill Cumora Scottish Pageant, Palmyra (July-August); Inner Tube Regatta, Wellsville (Memorial Day weekend); Toy Festival, East (August)

New York is a state of wild contrasts. At the southeastern tip of the state is New York City, one of the largest, most diverse urban areas in the world. Stretching out into the Atlantic, Long Island, with 1,723 square miles, is the largest island on the East Coast. Further upstate is some of the nation's most beautiful countryside—dramatic mountains, peaceful orchards, lush vineyards.

FROM LEATHERSTOCKING COUNTRY TO NIAGARA FALLS Eastern New York State is dominated by mountains. The Catskills are only a few hours' drive north of New York City and were once known as The Borscht Belt—full of resort hotels catering to Jewish New Yorkers (who ate borscht and other Eastern European foods). Today most of these resorts are closed, and the Catskills are home to many craftspeople. Farther north are the Adirondacks, an older, higher mountain range, site of the luxury resorts of Lake Placid and Lake George.

Tucked in among the mountains are the Hudson and Mohawk River Valleys. Here you'll find Sunnyside, Washington Irving's estate, where he lived while writing his tales of old New York, *The Legend of Sleepy Hollow* and *Rip Van Winkle*. Here, too, are President Franklin Delano Roosevelt's home at Hyde Park, and Eleanor Roosevelt's Val-kill.

Farther west are the Appalachian Mountains, and beyond them, the Finger Lakes region—Leatherstocking country of James Fenimore Cooper. This part of New York is quintessential rural America. Cooperstown is the legendary home of America's first baseball game. Its Baseball Hall of Fame includes an exhibit on women's professional teams. The female teams began in 1943, while male players were off at war, and continued until 1954.

The World Trade Center towers over the Brooklyn Bridge.

Also in this region is Harriet Tubman's home at Auburn. From the late 1850s until the Civil War, this was Tubman's base of operations as she returned to the South to bring slaves to freedom.

Women's history was made at Seneca Falls in 1848, when a group of female abolitionists convened America's first women's rights convention. The Women's Hall of Fame is there now, in the midst of a park. Nearby, in Rochester, Susan B. Anthony wrote *History of Woman Suffrage.*

At the western end of the state is Niagara Falls. America's most famous waterfall is actually three falls in two countries: American and Bridal Veil Falls in New York and Horseshoe Falls in Ontario, Canada.

AMERICA'S LARGEST CITY New York City is the largest city in the western hemisphere and the trade capital of the world. For hundreds of years it's been home to immigrants from almost every culture and nationality on earth. In 1990 over one fifth of New York State's population was foreign-born, and nearly one fourth spoke languages other than English at home. Most of these diverse peoples were living in New York City.

Niagara Falls

Even a casual walk through the city is like taking a tour of two hundred years of American history. At the Fraunces Tavern, for example, General George Washington held a farewell dinner for the officers with whom he'd fought in the Revolutionary War. Washington chose the tavern because it was owned by his friend, Samuel Fraunces, an African American of West Indian descent who had opened the tavern in 1762. The rebellious Sons of Liberty had often met here. And when Washington became President, he made Fraunces his first Steward, in charge of getting supplies for the people entertained by the Washingtons.

New York City's Lower East Side recalls the Jews, Italians, Czechs, Poles, and Ukrainians who came to the city in the 1890s and early 1900s to work in the growing garment and construction industries. These workers started some of America's first unions. Their sons and daughters became some of our country's finest writers and artists.

Farther uptown, in Harlem, African Americans in the 1920s were also creating new art and literature, the so-called Harlem Renaissance. And for many decades thereafter, America's "classical music"—jazz—was developed in clubs throughout the city. You can still visit the homes of such artists as jazz trumpeter Louis Armstrong and poet Claude McKay.

New York continues to attract new generations of immigrants from around the world and around the nation. Both new and native New Yorkers create the city's unique energy, as well as building its industries: tourism, publishing, finance, theater, trade, and real estate.

Labor leader, Samuel Gompers (1850-1924) immigrated to America when he was 13.

UPSTATE, DOWNSTATE Rural New York is dairy country, producing cheese, butter, and milk, as well as truck vegetables, grapes, and orchard fruits. Mineral wealth comes from New York's stores of stone, gravel, and sand. Along the Hudson and Mohawk Rivers are New York's industrial cities—Albany, Troy, Schenectady, Utica, Rome, Rochester, and Buffalo. These river towns first developed when goods were being shipped from New York along the the Erie Canal to the Great Lakes. They also have their own factories, producing machinery, electrical products, chemicals, aircraft, and photographic equipment.

Fascinating Facts

NEW YORK CITY IS TOPS IN:

- book publishing—about three of every four U.S. books are published by New York companies
- hotels, museums, and tourism
- photography industry
- broadcasting stations
- banks

PRESIDENTS BORN IN NEW YORK:

- Martin van Buren (1782-1862), 8th President
- Millard Fillmore (1800-1874), 13th President
- Theodore Roosevelt (1858-1919), 26th President
- Franklin Roosevelt (1882-1945), 32nd President

OTHER FAMOUS PEOPLE BORN IN NEW YORK:

- First lady and crusader Eleanor Roosevelt, New York City (1884-1962)
- Actor Humphrey Bogart, New York City (1899-1957)
- Singer Barbra Streisand, Brooklyn (1942-)
- Actor Denzel Washington, Mount Vernon (1954-)

NEW YORK HALLS OF FAME:

- Baseball Hall of Fame, Cooperstown
- Boxing Hall of Fame, Canastota
- Hall of Fame for Great Americans, Bronx
- National Women's Hall of Fame, Seneca Falls
- Soccer Hall of Fame, Oneonta
- Speed Skating Hall of Fame, Newburgh

NEW YORK FIRSTS:

- Presidential inauguration, of George Washington—New York City—1789
- successful steamboat—*Clermont*—1807
- women's suffrage convention—Seneca Falls—1848

HOW NEW YORK GOT ITS NAME: The English wanted to honor their king's brother, the Duke of York and Albany.

IT USED TO BE ILLEGAL IN NEW YORK:

- to ring the doorbell and disturb the occupant of a house
- to arrest a dead man for a debt

North Carolina

The Basics

POPULATION: 7,322,870
11th most populous state
AREA: 53,821 square miles
28th largest state
STATE CAPITAL: Raleigh
STATE BIRD: Cardinal (Red bird, Kentucky cardinal)
STATE FLOWER: Dogwood
STATE TREE: Longleafed pine (Southern pine, Longleaf yellow pine, Pitch pine, Hard pine, Heart pine, Turpentine pine, Rosemary pine, Brown pine, Fat pine, Longstraw pine, Longleafed pitch pine)
NICKNAMES: The Tarheel State, the Old North State, the Turpentine State
STATE MOTTO: *Esse quam videri* (Latin for "To be rather than to seem")
SPORTS TEAM: Charlotte Hornets, basketball
STATE MAMMAL: Gray squirrel
STATE INSECT: Honeybee
STATE REPTILE: Eastern box turtle
STATE SALTWATER FISH: Channel bass or red drum
STATE ROCK: Granite
STATE SHELL: Scotch bonnet
STATE STONE: Emerald
STATE BEVERAGE: Milk
STATE COLORS: Red and blue
STATE SONG: "The Old North State," traditional
STATE MUSICAL TOAST: "A Toast to North Carolina"
STATE LANDMARKS: Andrew Johnson Birthplace, Raleigh; James K. Polk Birthplace, Pineville
NATIONAL PARKS: Cape Hatteras National Seashore; Cape Lookout National Seashore; Great Smoky Mountains National Park

Great Smoky Mountains

12th state to enter the Union, November 21, 1789

From Colonial times to the Civil Rights protests of the 1960s, North Carolina has played a central role in U.S. history. Mystery, intrigue, pirate battles, and heroism are all part of the North Carolina story.

SMOKY MOUNTAINS AND TOBACCO COUNTRY You can divide North Carolina into three areas. Along the coast are the Outer Banks, a long string of sandy islands running along the coast, and the dangerous waters of Cape Hatteras, Cape Lookout, and Cape Fear. This was the Graveyard of the Atlantic because of the many ships wrecked here. In the 1700s, pirates like Captain Kidd and Blackbeard (Edward Teach) buried their treasure on these islands. It's vacationland now and home to many types of sea birds.

At Kitty Hawk, the Wright Brothers first developed an airplane that could really fly. A museum shows their achievements, along with the Wright Brothers National Memorial.

Old Fire Engine Museum in New Bern

The state's heartland is the Piedmont Plateau, an industrial region of forested hills where most of the state's people live in cities: the Research Triangle of Raleigh, Durham, and Chapel Hill; and the triad of Greensboro, Winston-Salem, and High Point. This is tobacco country. You can also visit such historic sites as the 1774 Hezekiah Alexander Homesite in Charlotte, where costumed guides show you colonial customs.

Farther west are the state's Appalachian ranges: the Great Smoky Mountains (with the most-visited national park in the country, shared with Tennessee); as well as the Blue Ridge, Black, and Unaka Mountains.

MYSTERIES AND REBELLIONS The very first English colony in America was Sir Walter Raleigh's settlement at Roanoke Island, begun in 1585. The first wave of settlers faced starvation and returned to England. But in 1587 another group arrived. Virginia Dare, the first English child in North America, was born. The colony seemed secure. But when a new boat from England arrived in Roanoke three years later, they found only the word "CROATOAN" carved on a tree. The Lost Colony had disappeared.

The English settled North Carolina again in the 1650s, and in 1677 it became the site of North America's first rebellion against foreign rule. Colonists resented the royal governor's taxes on their trade, so John Culpeper led them in the uprising known as Culpeper's Rebellion. They put the governor in jail and ran the colony themselves until 1683.

Biltmore in Asheville is the largest private house in America—152 rooms.

In 1768 a group of backcountry farmers called the Regulators threatened another rebellion against British taxes. They were defeated at the 1771 Battle of Alamance Creek—which some have called the first battle of the Revolution. In 1774, the year after the Boston Tea Party, 51 Edenton women signed a petition boycotting tea; a teapot-shaped monument honors their rebellion. And in 1775, a year before the Declaration of Independence, the citizens of Mecklenberg County declared their independence from the British with the Mecklenberg Resolutions.

With such a history, it's not surprising that North Carolina was the first colony to vote for independence at the Continental Congress. North Carolina refused to ratify the Constitution, however, until the Bill of Rights guaranteed the freedom they had come to expect.

FROM SLAVERY'S WRONGS TO CIVIL RIGHTS One of the most famous tales of slavery is Harriet Ann Jacobs' *Incidents in the Life of a Slave Girl*. Jacobs was a slave in the house of Edenton plantation owner Dr. James Norcom, who "told me I was his property; that I must be subject to his will in all things." Unwilling to submit, Jacobs escaped to hide in a tiny space—"a living coffin"—under her grandmother's front porch. She stayed there nearly seven years, until she won her freedom.

Over a hundred years later, Greensboro was the site of one of the most important actions in the Civil Rights movement. On February 1, 1960, four young African-American men ordered coffee at the whites-only Woolworth lunch counter. The black students politely refused to leave until they were served—sparking a protest that spread throughout the South. It also gave birth to a new organization, the Student Nonviolent Coordinating Committee (known as SNCC, or "snick"). Thirty years later, the four men returned for an anniversary celebration of integration. They were served by the very same woman who had refused them before.

Kitty Hawk—site of the Wright Brothers first flight on December 17, 1903

TOBACCO FARMS AND TEXTILE MILLS North Carolina's economy is both agricultural and industrial—but in this state the two are closely linked. The state produces tobacco and cigarettes, cotton and textiles, lumber and paper. Only Texas has more farms than this fertile state, which also produces corn, soybeans, peanuts, and sweet potatoes, as well as chickens, hogs, and dairy products. At the Research Triangle, scientists develop electronic equipment and figure out how the latest technological discoveries can be useful to industry.

Fascinating Facts

NORTH CAROLINA IS TOPS IN:
- tobacco and cigarette production
- textiles
- softwood lumber

NORTH CAROLINA HAS THE WORLD'S LARGEST:
- cigarette factories—at Winston-Salem and Durham
- hosiery mill in Burlington

NORTH CAROLINA HAS THE WORLD'S TALLEST:
- lighthouse—Cape Hatteras—193 feet—built to protect ships from the Diamond Shoals

NORTH CAROLINA HALL OF FAME:
- PGA/World Golf Hall of Fame, Pinehurst

PRESIDENTS BORN IN NORTH CAROLINA:
- James K. Polk (1795-1849), 11th President
- Andrew Johnson (1808-1875), 17th President

OTHER FAMOUS PEOPLE BORN IN NORTH CAROLINA:
- Short story writer O. Henry, Greensboro (1862-1910)
- Author Thomas Wolfe, Asheville (1900-1938)

HOW NORTH CAROLINA GOT ITS NICKNAMES:
- The "Old North State" refers to the state's separation from South Carolina.
- "Tarheel" was an insult from Mississippi Confederate soldiers to North Carolina Confederate troops. Since the North Carolinians were chased from their position by Union soldiers, they had forgotten to "tar their heels" in order to "stick to their ground"!

IT USED TO BE ILLEGAL IN NORTH CAROLINA:
- to sing out of tune
- to drink water or milk on a train

North Dakota

Mandan Indian Village

39th or 40th state to enter the Union, November 2, 1889

The Basics

POPULATION: 643,539
47th most populous state
AREA: 70,704 square miles
19th largest state
STATE CAPITAL: Bismarck
STATE BIRD: Meadowlark
STATE FLOWER: Wild prairie rose
STATE TREE: American elm
NICKNAMES: The Sioux State, the Flickertail State, Land of the Dakotas, the Peace Garden state
STATE MOTTO: Liberty and Union Now and Forever, One and Inseparable
STATE FISH: Northern pike
STATE FOSSIL: Teredo petrified wood
STATE DRINK: Milk
STATE GRASS: Western wheat grass
STATE SONG: "North Dakota Hymn," words by James W. Foley, music by C.S. Putnam
STATE MARCH: "Spirit of the Land" by James D. Ployhar
STATE ART GALLERY: University of North Dakota Art Gallery, Grand Forks
NATIONAL HISTORIC SITES: Fort Union Trading Post; Knife River Indian Villages, near Stanton, preserving the Hidatsa and Mandan Indian earth lodges—circular mud and timber structures
NATIONAL PARKS: Theodore Roosevelt National Park, Medora; International Peace Garden, shared with Canada, established in 1941 to commemorate the longest undefended border in the world
NATIONAL TRAIL SYSTEMS: Lewis and Clark National Historic Trail; North Country National Scenic Trail
STATE FESTIVALS: Potato Bowl Weekend, Grand Forks (September); Steam Threshers Show, Carrington (September)

North Dakota's fertile prairies and sometimes deadly winters have drawn pioneers who are fond of the "wide open spaces." The land is so flat that the 19-story state capitol building in Bismarck is visible for miles. In the 1880s President Theodore Roosevelt spent three years ranching in this Great Plains state and fell in love with its beauties and its challenges. "I would never have been President," he said later, "if it had not been for my experiences in North Dakota."

FROM THE RED RIVER TO THE BADLANDS Eastern North Dakota has some of the world's best farmland, especially in the fertile Red River Valley. The rich black soil of the Central Lowlands stretches westward to Bismarck, the state capital. Western North Dakota is more arid and less hospitable to farms, particularly in the Badlands near the Montana border. Here you can see the eroded landscape carved by a river that dried up millions of years ago—cliffs, valleys, buttes, and table mesas in fantastic shapes. Here, too, you can visit Theodore Roosevelt National Park where bison, wild horses, mule deer, pronghorn antelope, and bighorn sheep still roam freely.

Four Eyes Theater, Medora

North Dakota's largest city, Fargo, has fewer than 75,000 people, and its next three principal cities—Bismarck, Grand Forks, and Minot—have fewer than 45,000 each. Although this is a rural state, over half the population lives in cities and towns.

In the nineteenth century North Dakota was settled by Norwegian immigrants who were used to farming a cold northern land. They were joined by settlers from Iceland, Germany, and Czechoslovakia. As a result, many people in the state share the same religion: some one-half of the population is Lutheran, and one-third is Catholic.

EXPLORING THE DAKOTA TERRITORY The first recorded European expedition to this state was by Pierre Gaultier de Varennes, Sieur (lord) de la Verendrye. The land he claimed for France in 1738 was already inhabited by Arapaho, Assiniboine, Cheyenne, Hidatsa, Mandan, and Sioux.

The monument to the Pioneer Family is on the state capitol grounds in Bismarck.

Most of North Dakota was bought by the United States in the Louisiana Purchase and was explored by Lewis and Clark in 1804-1806. It was at their winter quarters near Washburn, North Dakota, that they hired their Shoshone guide and translator, Sacagawea.

The Dakota territory saw few settlers until 1863 when the Homestead Act offered pioneers 160 acres of free land after five years of farming. Railroads and the U.S. government continued to offer incentives to European and U.S. settlers, despite opposition from native peoples. By 1881, however, Indians had been forced onto reservations, and North Dakota's European population skyrocketed from 37,000 in 1880 to 152,000 in 1885. By 1890 some 43 percent of the state's residents were foreign-born—one-eighth of them from Norway.

FARMERS FIGHT BACK In 1915 many North Dakota farmers were angry. They had some of the biggest and most productive farms in the country. Yet they were poor, while the grain elevators which bought their grain and the railroads that shipped it were getting rich. To fight back, farmers created the Non-Partisan League, which ran candidates in local and state elections. For a time, League-elected officials—including Governor Lynn J. Frazier—were remarkably successful. They created the only state-owned bank in the country, to make low-interest loans to farmers. They started a state-owned grain mill and grain elevator in Grand Forks, to guarantee farmers fair prices. They established social programs to benefit farmers and poor people, many of which still exist today. Although the League's effectiveness petered out by 1922, many people in North Dakota still remember the Non-Partisan League.

Lakota Sioux in traditional dress at the Whitman Ranch

BONANZA FARMS AND OIL WELLS North Dakota has more people working on farms than anywhere else in the U.S. Wheat, potatoes, sugarbeets, flax, barley, sunflowers, and soybeans are all important to this state's agricultural economy. However, family farms are in danger here as elsewhere, and more farmers have lost their land in North Dakota than in any other state.

The first lignite coal was mined here in 1884, and the first oil gushed forth in 1951. Coal and oil, as well as uranium, are still key North Dakota products.

Fascinating Facts

THE WORLD'S TALLEST STRUCTURE... is not a building but the 2,063-foot television transmission tower in Blanchard.

DID YOU KNOW THAT... The geographic center of North America is Rugby, in Pierce County, near Devils Lake.

NORTH DAKOTA FORTS:
- Fort Buford, now a state historic site, near Williston, was built in 1866. It once imprisoned Sioux leader Sitting Bull and Nez Percé Chief Joseph.
- Fort Union Trading Post, also near Williston, was built by John Jacob Astor's American Fur Company. It dominated fur trade on the upper Missouri from 1829 to 1866. John James Audubon, famous for his paintings of the birds of North America, once stayed there.

DID YOU KNOW THAT... If you were playing golf on the Portal golf course, your ball might start out in the United States—and end up in Canada!

NORTH DAKOTA IS TOPS IN:
- spring wheat • rye • flax
- barley • oats

DID YOU KNOW THAT... President Benjamin Harrison shuffled the statehood bills for North and South Dakota before signing them on the same day. So no one really knows which state is 39th and which is 40th.

FAMOUS PEOPLE BORN IN NORTH DAKOTA:
- Entertainer Lawrence Welk, Strasburg, (1903-1992)

DID YOU KNOW THAT... Underground fires have been burning in North Dakota coal beds for so long that no one knows when they started.

IT USED TO BE ILLEGAL IN NORTH DAKOTA:
- to trap birds in a cemetery
- for railroad engineers to take engines home—unless they carried a full crew!

Ohio

Rock and Roll Hall of Fame, Cleveland

17th state to enter the Union, March 1, 1803

The Basics

POPULATION: 11,172,782
7th most populous state
AREA: 44,828 square miles
34th largest state
STATE CAPITAL: Columbus
STATE BIRD: Cardinal (Red bird, Kentucky cardinal)
STATE FLOWER: Scarlet carnation
STATE TREE: Buckeye (Ohio buckeye, Fetid buckeye, Stinking buckeye, American horse chestnut)
NICKNAMES: The Buckeye State, the Mother of Modern Presidents
STATE MOTTO: With God, All Things are Possible
SPORTS TEAMS: Cincinnati Reds and Cleveland Indians, baseball; Cincinnati Bengals and Cleveland Browns, football; Cleveland Cavaliers, basketball
STATE INSECT: Ladybug
STATE FOSSIL: Trilobite
STATE GEM: Ohio flint
STATE DRINK: Tomato juice
STATE SONG: "Beautiful Ohio," words by Ballard MacDonald, music by Mary Earl
STATE LANDMARKS: Perry's Victory and International Peace Memorial, Put-in-Bay; William Howard Taft birthplace, Cincinnati
STATE HISTORIC SITES: Adena State Memorial, Chillicothe—1807 stone house; Gardens of Zoar, near New Philadelphia—1817 settlement where men and women had equal rights
STATE NATIONAL PARKS: Hopewell Culture National Historic Park, near Columbus; Cuyahoga Valley National Recreation Area

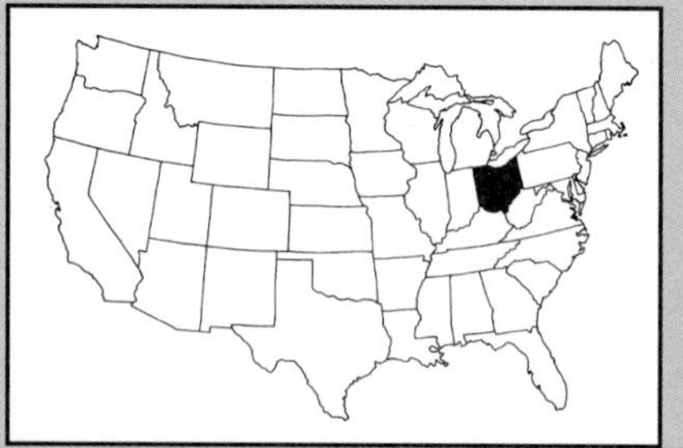

Ohio is one of our richest states—in resources, location, and people. It has rich deposits of clay, coal, and gas. It is located just west of the Appalachians, between Lake Erie and the Ohio River, giving it access to East and West, North and South, land and water. And its people benefit from the state's 43 colleges and universities—second only to Pennsylvania in the number of higher educational institutions.

PORTS AND FARMS Ohio's northern border is formed by Lake Erie, with its flat plains and its port cities of Toledo and Cleveland. Ohio's southern border is the Ohio River, with the hilly, elevated land of the Central Plains and the major city of Cincinnati. Ohio's heartland is in the heart of the Central Plains, a land of farms and small cities, as well as the state capital, Columbus. And eastern Ohio is the western end of the Allegheny Plateau, a rugged land of rivers and bluffs. No wonder the state has taken the name Ohio—"large" or "beautiful" in Iroquois.

Nobel Prize-winning author Toni Morrison was born in Lorain

BUCKEYE CITIES Some two-thirds of Ohioans live in cities, urban areas that represent the rich history of this urban state. Akron, for example, besides being the first home of the B.F. Goodrich Tire Company, was also the site of a famous convention for women's rights in 1852. There Sojourner Truth gave her famous "Ain't I a Woman?" speech.

Columbus, Ohio's largest city and state capital, is the headquarters of many big companies. Here, in 1886, Samuel Gompers helped found the American Federation of Trades and Labor, ancestor of today's AFL-CIO. And nearby, outside the town of Chillicothe, is the Hopewell Cultural National Historical Park, or Mound City, an Indian burial site used by the Hopewell Indians from about 200 B.C. to A.D. 500.

Cincinnati is the site of the Stowe House, where the young Harriet Beecher moved when she was 21. Four years later she married Calvin E. Stowe, and had five children—but she never stopped writing. In the 1830s she traveled across the Ohio River to the slave state of Kentucky. What she saw became material for her book, *Uncle Tom's Cabin.*

Cleveland was once infamous for water pollution—its Cuyahoga River actually caught fire in the 1970s because of all the toxic waste in the water, and Lake Erie was known as a "dead lake." Since then, Cleveland has made a remarkable recovery, and Lake Erie has recovered so much that you can now eat fish caught in it. Cleveland is also notable for its Art Museum and world-famous clinic.

Visitors to Dayton can take a tour of Dayton's Aviation Trail, starting at the Wright Brothers Bicycle Shop, where airplane inventors Orville and Wilbur Wright got their start. Or they can visit the Paul Laurence Dunbar House, home of the brilliant African-American poet.

The All-American Soapbox Derby is held in Akron each year.

For space buffs there is the International Women's Air and Space Museum at Centerville or the Neil Armstrong Air and Space Museum at Wapakoneta. Nature lovers can visit Kelleys Island, where millions of years ago glaciers cut deep, rippling grooves into the rocks on the Erie shore.

THE GROWTH OF AN INDUSTRIAL STATE Ohio was the first of the organized territories to be carved out of the Northwest Territory, and one of the first of those territories to try to become a state. In its key position just west of the more settled United States, Ohio was one of the first areas to experience the westward movement that followed the Revolutionary War. Gradually Ohio became the center of a network of canals, railroads, and finally, highways, which were used to bring raw materials into Ohio and carry industrial products out.

Sharp-shooter Annie Oakley (1860-1926) was born in Darke County.

Each Ohio urban center developed its own industrial specialty. Cleveland became the world's largest iron ore port. Aircraft and machinery are made in Columbus, and Cincinnati has been a port city since riverboat days. Later, jet engines were made there. Dayton was the national center for cash registers. In fact, Dayton native James Ritty invented "Ritty's incorruptible cashier" and then founded the National Cash Register company in 1879. Toledo is known for making scales and glass, while Akron is famous as one of the world's greatest rubber centers.

Ohio has rich resources of its own: limestone, sandstone, lime, salt, coal, oil, and natural gas. America's first billionaire, John D. Rockefeller, started his Standard Oil Company in Cleveland. Cleveland is also a steel town, as are many of the smaller cities around it, including Youngstown and Lorain.

Agriculture in Ohio produces corn, oats, tomatoes, grapes, tobacco, and hay. The state is second in the production of hothouse vegetables.

Fascinating Facts

OHIO FIRSTS:

- First U.S. college to enroll both men and women—Oberlin—1837
- First U.S. electric street railway—Cleveland—1884
- First professional baseball team, Cincinnati Red Stockings

PRESIDENTS BORN IN OHIO:

- Ulysses Simpson Grant (1822-1885), 18th President
- Rutherford B. Hayes (1822-1893), 19th President
- James Garfield (1831-1881), 20th President
- Benjamin Harrison (1833-1901), 23rd President
- William McKinley (1843-1901), 25th President
- William Howard Taft (1857-1930), 27th President
- Warren G. Harding (1865-1923), 29th President

FAMOUS PEOPLE BORN IN OHIO:

- General William T. Sherman, Lancaster (1820-1891)
- Inventor Thomas A. Edison, Milan (1847-1931)
- Director Steven Spielberg, Cincinnati, (1947-)

OHIO ASTRONAUTS:

- John J. Glenn, Jr., first American to orbit the earth
- Neil Armstrong, first man on the moon
- Judith Resnik, one of the first women astronauts, killed in the *Challenger* shuttle explosion

OHIO HALLS OF FAME:

- College Football Hall of Fame, Mason
- National Aviation Hall of Fame, Dayton
- Pro Football Hall of Fame, Canton
- Rock and Roll Hall of Fame, Cleveland
- Trapshooting Hall of Fame, Vandalia

OHIO IS TOPS IN:

- baseballs and footballs • pretzels
- metal toys • firefighting equipment
- machine tools • soap
- rubber products • ice cream cones
- crackerjack (candy-coated popcorn)

Oklahoma

The Basics

POPULATION: 3,300,902
27th most populous state
AREA: 69,903 square miles
20th largest state
STATE CAPITAL: Oklahoma City
STATE BIRD: Scissor-tailed flycatcher
STATE FLOWER: Mistletoe
STATE TREE: Redbud (also called Judas tree, Red Judas tree, Salad-tree, Canadian Judas tree)
NICKNAMES: The Sooner State, the Boomer State
STATE MOTTO: *Labor Omnia Vincit* (Latin for "Labor conquers all things")
STATE ANIMAL: American buffalo
STATE FISH: White bass
STATE INSECT: Honeybee
STATE REPTILE: Mountain boomer lizard
STATE ROCK: Barite rose (rose rock)
STATE COLORS: Green and white
STATE POEM: "Howdy Folks" by David Randolph Milsten
STATE SONG: "Oklahoma," words by Oscar Hammerstein II, music by Richard Rodgers
STATE FESTIVALS: World's Championship Watermelon Seed Spitting Contest; Chocolate Festival, Norman (February); Kiamichi Owa Chito Festival, Broken Bow (June); Pelican Festival, Grand Lake (September)
HALLS OF FAME: National Cowboy Hall of Fame, Oklahoma City; International Photography Hall of Fame, Oklahoma City; National Softball Hall of Fame, Oklahoma City; Rodeo Cowboy Hall of Fame, Oklahoma City; National Hall of Fame for Famous American Indians, Anadarko; National Wrestling Hall of Fame, Stillwater

Roundup on a dairy farm

46th state to enter the Union, November 16, 1907

FROM THE PANHANDLE TO THE OZARKS Oklahoma has two major climates. The state is dry along the panhandle and in the southwest. There you'll see oceans of grass and blue granite mountains. There, too, every little town has a saddle shop, a testament to the state's living cowboy heritage. In the east, on the other hand, the climate is humid and subtropical. The Ouachita Mountains can be found in the southeast, while the Ozark Mountains are in the northeast.

The largest city in northeast Oklahoma is Tulsa, "the Oil Capital of the World." Nearby is the Tallgrass Prairie Reserve, a 52,000-acre unbroken prairie of tall, waving grass; roaming herds of bison; and old cowboy bunkhouses. You can also find bison and 40 other species of wild animals roaming the Woolaroc Wildlife Preserve (visitors have to stay in their cars!). And if you want to see 1,200 wild horses running across the prairie, visit the Prairie Wild Horse Refuge.

Oklahoma City skyline

The Oklahoma City area is rich in museums and historic centers where you can see how people lived in the Old West. A cowboy monument in front of the Capitol building reminds Oklahomans of their frontier heritage.

BROKEN PROMISES ON THE TRAIL OF TEARS Before Europeans came to North America, Comanche, Osage, and other native peoples lived in Oklahoma. In 1803, when President Thomas Jefferson bought Oklahoma as part of the Louisiana Purchase, he believed that Indians could always be relegated to the western part of the new territory. Oklahoma became a place to forcefully relocate native peoples when U.S. farmers and railroads took their land. As early as 1809, the Delaware, Sac, and Fox were deported to Oklahoma. In 1830 Congress made it official, designating Oklahoma as Indian Territory.

The deportations continued. From 1831 to 1833, 20,000 Choctaw were moved to Oklahoma. Both the journey and the new life were arduous. By 1843 there were only 12,000 Choctaw left. In 1838, 15,000 Cherokee were relocated, forced to make the grueling trip along the Trail of Tears. The experience cost

4,000 Cherokee their lives. In 1842 the Seminole were defeated in Florida, and they, too, were relocated. The Creek and Chickasaw had also been moved to Oklahoma.

Once in Oklahoma, each tribe was given national sovereignty over its government, land, and schools. Many native people became farmers—some even had slaves, like farmers in the South. In 1861 when pro-slavery Southerners seceded from the Union, the Indian nations sided with the Confederacy. (When the war ended, however, African Americans were welcomed into Indian nations as equal citizens.)

Humorist Will Rogers (1879-1935) was born in Oolagah when Oklahoma was still Indian Territory.

In 1869 the U.S. Army established Fort Sill Military Reservation to insure military control over Indian nations. (In 1909 the famous Apache warrior Geronimo was killed at Fort Sill.) Throughout the 1870s, 25 more Indian nations were forced into Oklahoma, while Indian lands were gradually decreased. In 1889 Oklahoma was first opened to white settlers—who instantly swarmed in to take the free land being offered. In 1893 the Dawes Commission liquidated Indian tribal government.

Wichita grass home

Indian nations had been working together, forming their own Confederation. In 1905 they tried to form a new state, Sequoyah, but Congress rejected their plea for statehood. An Oklahoma Territory had already been established, so the Indian Territory joined with it. Together, the two territories became admitted to the nation as the state of Oklahoma, whose state seal honors the five nations. Oklahoma is still Indian country, where native culture and languages are still alive.

DUST BOWL DAYS In the 1930s the United States was shaken by a Great Depression, in which almost one-third of all workers lost their jobs. In addition, the nation was struck by drought. Oklahoma's dry soil simply blew away, creating what people called a Dust Bowl. Many white Oklahoma residents struck out for California, where they hoped to find new jobs and new lives. Many of these "Okies," however, ended up as migrant laborers, going from farm to farm as work became available. The Oklahoma-born folksinger Woody Guthrie wrote many songs about the Dust Bowl days.

BLACK GOLD AND CATTLE RANCHES The mainstay of Oklahoma's economy is oil. There's so much oil in Oklahoma, some people have found oil wells in their backyards! Natural gas and coal are also plentiful in this state. In the dry western half of the state, farmers grow wheat, hay, and rye. In the humid eastern half, sorghum, peanuts, and cotton flourish. Ranches in the west also raise cattle, sheep, horses, and turkeys. The state also manufactures machinery, plastic, and rubber.

Turner Falls in the Arbuckle Mountains

Fascinating Facts

DID YOU KNOW THAT... One of Oklahoma's oil wells pumps oil right from under the Capitol building in Oklahoma City.

HOW OKLAHOMA GOT ITS NAME: The Choctaw word *okla* means "people," while *humma* means "red." Missionary Reverend Allan Wright named this territory to which "red people" were relocated in the nineteenth century.

HOW OKLAHOMA GOT ITS NICKNAMES: On April 22, 1889, a pistol was fired to mark the day that Oklahoma Territory was opened to white settlers. Some 50,000 settlers waited for that pistol "boom" and then rushed into the area to claim *homesteads*—free land for those who would farm it for five years. These settlers were called *boomers*. Some homesteaders, however, "jumped the gun" and entered the territory *sooner.*

DID YOU KNOW THAT... In the 1920s Tulsa had more millionaires than any other U.S. city.

OKLAHOMA MINERAL WEALTH:
- first in helium
- fourth in oil and natural gas

DID YOU KNOW THAT... America's deepest hole is a 31,441-foot-deep natural gas well in Washita County.

OKLAHOMA HAD THE NATION'S FIRST:
- parking meter—Oklahoma City

FAMOUS PEOPLE BORN IN OKLAHOMA:
- Folksinger Woody Guthrie, Okemah (1912-1967)
- Novelist Ralph Ellison, Oklahoma City (1914-1994)

IT USED TO BE ILLEGAL IN OKLAHOMA:
- to get a fish drunk
- to catch whales in Oklahoma waters
- to eavesdrop

DID YOU KNOW THAT: More languages are spoken in Oklahoma than in Europe. That's because that state is home to 55 Indian nations, each with a language or dialect of its own.

Oregon

The Basics

POPULATION: 3,203,735 people
29th most populous state
AREA: 98,386 square miles
9th largest state
STATE CAPITAL: Salem
STATE BIRD: Western meadowlark
STATE FLOWER: Oregon grape
STATE TREE: Douglas fir
NICKNAMES: The Beaver State, the Web-Foot State, the Hard-Case State
STATE MOTTO: The Union; *Alis Volat Propriis* (Latin for "She flies with her own wings") is on the state seal
SPORTS TEAM: Portland Trail Blazers, basketball
STATE ANIMAL: American beaver
STATE FISH: Chinook salmon
STATE INSECT: Swallowtail butterfly
STATE ROCK: Thunderegg
STATE HOSTESS: Miss Oregon
STATE SONG: "Oregon, My Oregon," words by J.A. Buchanan, music by Henry B. Murtagh
STATE LANDMARKS: Painted Hills National Monument; John Day Fossil Beds National Monument; Fort Clatsop National Memorial, near Astoria (1805-6 winter camp of Lewis and Clark); Oregon Caves National Monument (caves on four levels); Sea Lion Caves, near Florence (home of hundreds of sea lions)
STATE HISTORIC SITE: Million Hill Village, Salem
NATIONAL PARKS: Crater Lake, near Medford; Newbery National Volcanic Monument, near Bend; Mt. Hood National Forest, near Gresham; Kalmiopsis Wilderness in Siskiyou National Forest, near Ashland

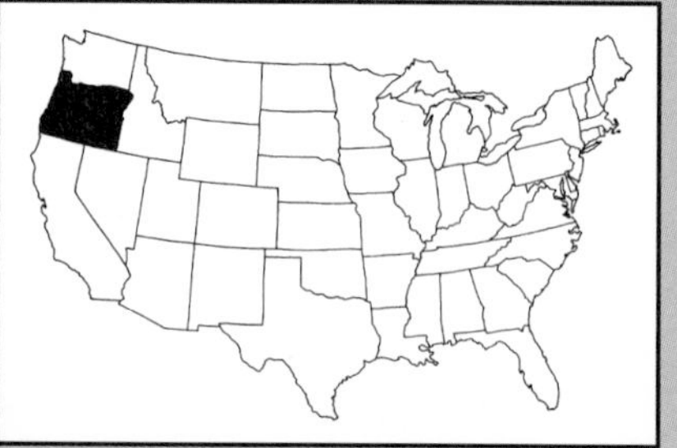

Mount Hood, near Portland

33rd state to enter the Union, February 14, 1859

Residents of Oregon tend to be mavericks—people who go their own way no matter what anybody thinks. Why else would the University of Oregon choose the "killer duck" as its mascot? Oregon's "pioneer spirit" has a more serious side, too. Long before others realized how important the environment was, Oregon passed laws to protect its land and water.

ROLL ON, COLUMBIA This Pacific Northwestern state is full of spectacular scenery: 400 miles of white sandy beaches—all public—marked by twisted rock formations, lonely lighthouses, and tiny port towns. At Gold Beach, where the Rogue River meets the ocean and temperatures are milder, you can see lilies, daffodils, and even palm trees. Cape Arago is a great place for spotting whales and sea lions, while at South Slough National Estuarine Reserve you can find bald eagles and black bears.

The Chinook used canoes like this to fish the Columbia River.

Farther inland are the Coastal Mountains, and farther still are the Cascade Mountains, so called for the many waterfalls that cascade down their rugged peaks. Most Oregonians live between these two ranges, in the Willamette Valley, which contains all of Oregon's major cities—Portland, Eugene, and Salem. East of the Cascades is the Columbia Plateau, which features a drier, harsher climate.

Oregon's northern border with Washington is formed by the mighty Columbia River. Early settlers tried to sail west on this river, but the current was too strong for their rafts and flatboats. Today that power is harnessed by the Columbia Dam, which provides one-third of the hydroelectric potential of the continental United States. Salmon swim upstream to lay and fertilize their eggs, but they can't swim through the dam. So the dam builders added fish ladders, a step-like series of pools that allow the salmon to make their way upstream.

ON THE OREGON TRAIL The land we now call Oregon was once home to over 100,000 Indians, including Shoshone, Bannock, Paiute, and Nez Percé. Conflicts began almost as soon as European explorers tried to claim the land. Then for a time the 1805-6 expedition of Lewis and Clark created more peaceful relations. (You can still visit Fort Clatsop, winter home of the explorers and their Shoshone translator, Sacagawea.)

The area that is now Oregon was claimed by Russia, Spain, and England. But the first permanent white settlement here was started in 1811 by an American corporation, John Jacob Astor's Pacific Fur Company, which called their new town Astoria. The Spanish and Russians withdrew their claim, and the British and Americans eventually agreed to share the land.

The first immigration to Oregon began in 1842 along the Oregon Trail. The trail was the major means of entering the state until the railroads came in the 1870s. When gold was discovered in the Rogue River Valley, in 1853, thousands of California miners poured into the state—and sparked a bloody war with local Indians. Within 15 years the Umatilla, Walal, Cayuse, and Paiute were defeated and sent onto reservations.

The water of Crater Lake is so clear that sunlight penetrates to a depth of 400 feet.

Battles between Indians and European Americans continued throughout the Civil War, when federal troops were busy fighting elsewhere. After the war, though, U.S. forces returned and tried to force Chief Joseph and the Nez Percé off their land. Joseph resisted, then tried to lead his people into Canada. But in 1877 they too were defeated and moved to a reservation.

THE OREGON SYSTEM In the early twentieth century, Oregon's state legislature adopted many laws that made their government more democratic. These were called the Oregon system. Although many states have such laws today, they were very unusual for their time. In 1902 Oregon approved initiative (voters can initiate putting a measure on the ballot) and referendums (legislators can put an issue on the ballot for voters to decide directly). In 1904 it established primary elections, so that voters could choose which candidates should run in the general election. The state also authorized recall, a way for voters to vote someone out of office before a regular election.

Oregon's Pacific coastline is one of the most beautiful in the world.

Later, Oregon was the first state to pass an enforceable law to protect working women and children—thanks to the hard work of crusader Caroline Gleason. In 1955 the state mandated that women should receive equal pay for equal work. And in the 1970s, the state prohibited nonrefundable bottles and cans and outlawed aerosol sprays.

TREES AND TOURISTS Some 12 million tourists visit Oregon each year to hunt, fish, and ski. Lumber is another key state industry as is the production of electricity. In recent years there has been a great deal of controversy between the lumber industry, which wants to cut down and sell Oregon's trees, and environmentalists, who want to preserve the forests and protect the species that live there.

On the coast, wild and farmed salmon and trout are caught and sold to fish canneries along the Columbia River. Although there is not much dairy farming in the state, Tillamook Valley is famous for its cheddar cheese. Western Oregon farms grow fruit and vegetables. Eastern Oregon specializes in wheat, corn, and cattle.

Fascinating Facts

OREGON IS TOPS IN:

- U.S. lumber and plywood production
- nickel—the only state to mine this product
- seeds
- filbert nuts
- peppermint oil
- blackberries, boysenberries, raspberries

OREGON DEPTHS:

- The deepest lake in the United States is Crater Lake, created when the ancient volcano Mount Mazama exploded, making a crater at the mountain's summit. The lake is nearly half a mile deep—1,932 feet.
- The Snake River canyon is the deepest in the country.

HOW OREGON GOT ITS NAME: No one knows for sure. Four theories:

- from the French-Canadian *ouragan,* "hurricane" or "storm"
- from the Columbia River, called the River of Storms *(ouragans)* by Canadian fur traders
- from the Spanish *orejon,* meaning "big-ear," applied to Indian peoples in the region
- from the Spanish *oregano,* the wild sage plant common in the area

DID YOU KNOW THAT... Oregon contains the only major city named by a coin toss. Amos Lovejoy of Boston and Francis Pettygrove of Portland, Maine, each wanted to name a city after his hometown. Pettygrove won—and the city was named Portland, Oregon.

FAMOUS PEOPLE BORN IN OREGON:

- Radical journalist John Reed, Portland (1887-1920)
- Pulitzer Prize-winning poet Phyllis McGinley, Ontario (1905-1978)
- Chemist Linus Pauling, twice honored Nobel Prize winner, Portland (1901-1994)

DID YOU KNOW THAT... The geographic center of the whole U.S.—if Guam and American Samoa are included—is in Oregon's China Cap Mountains.

IT USED TO BE ILLEGAL IN OREGON:

- for a dead person to serve on a jury

Pennsylvania

Lighted boathouses on the Schuylkill River, Philadelphia

2nd state, December 12, 1787

The Basics

POPULATION: 12,056,112
5th most populous state
AREA: 46,058 square miles
33rd largest state
STATE CAPITAL: Harrisburg
STATE BIRD: Ruffled grouse
STATE FLOWER: Mountain laurel
STATE TREE: Hemlock (Eastern hemlock, Canadian hemlock, hemlock spruce, spruce pine, New England hemlock, spruce)
NICKNAMES: The Keystone State, the Quaker State
SPORTS TEAMS: Pittsburgh Pirates, Philadelphia Phillies, baseball; Pittsburgh Steelers, Philadelphia Eagles, football; Philadelphia 76ers, basketball; Philadelphia Flyers, Pittsburgh Penguins, hockey
STATE MOTTO: Virtue, Liberty, and Independence
STATE ANIMAL: White-tailed deer
STATE DOG: Great Dane
STATE FISH: Brook trout
STATE INSECT: Firefly
STATE BEAUTIFICATION AND CONSERVATION PLANT: Penngift crownvetch
STATE FOSSIL: Trilobite
STATE DRINK: Milk
STATE COLORS: Blue and gold
STATE SLOGAN: "You've got a friend in Pennsylvania."
STATE LANDMARK: Valley Forge National Historical Park; Gettysburg
STATE FESTIVALS: Chocolate Festival, Hershey (February); St. Ubaldo Day, Scranton (Memorial Day weekend); Das Awkscht Fescht Ethnic Festival, Allentown (August); Mifflin County Goose Day Celebration, Lewiston (September)

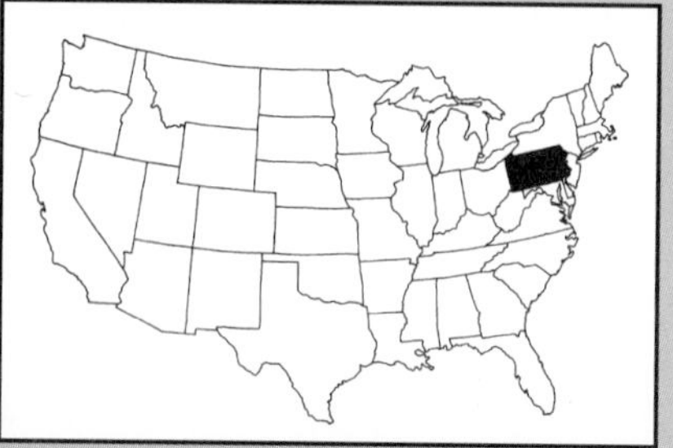

Pennsylvania was the birthplace of the nation and the home of its first government. When you think of Pennsylvania, think of historic Philadelphia, the City of Brotherly Love...Pittsburgh, the steel town... the rolling hills and Allegheny mountains of Pennsylvania's rugged countryside...and the Amish, a traditional people, driving their horse-drawn buggies down country lanes in Pennsylvania Dutch country.

APPALACHIAN HIGHLAND COUNTRY Most of this rectangular state is part of the Appalachian Highlands, a region of plateaus and valleys with two parallel mountain ranges—the Alleghenies and the Appalachians—running northeast to southwest across the state. In the southeastern corner of the state, around Philadelphia, is a small section of Atlantic coastal plain, shading into the agricultural region of the eastern Piedmont.

Dr. Benjamin Rush, noted patriot and physician

Pennsylvania is the only mid-Atlantic state that doesn't touch the ocean. But Philadelphia is a major port on the Delaware, one of Pennsylvania's four major rivers. The other key waterways in the state are the Susquehanna, the Allegheny, the Ohio, and the Monongahela.

Most Pennsylvania residents live in cities and towns, including some 1.6 million in Philadelphia, the nation's fifth-largest city (after New York, Los Angeles, Chicago, and Houston). Philadelphia is a treasure trove of historical landmarks, including Independence Hall, where the Declaration of Independence and the Constitution were signed.

Another Philadelphia landmark is the Betsy Ross House, former home of Elizabeth Griscom Ross. According to a popular myth, it was Ross, a seamstress, who made the first American flag. While no proof exists, in 1777, the marine committee of the Continental Congress did pass a resolution calling for a flag on June 14. We celebrate this as Flag Day.

The Underground Railroad stopped frequently in Philadelphia, and you can still see the house of the Quaker Samuel Johnson who not only harbored runaway slaves, but also let abolitionists use his house for meetings. Harriet Tubman once spoke there. Also in Philadelphia are the homes of Frances Ellen Watkins Harper, a nineteenth-century poet, suffragist, and crusader for civil rights; and Henry Ossawa Tanner, considered the finest African-American painter of his generation.

About 65 miles west of Philadelphia is Pennsylvania Dutch country, which is named not for the Dutch but for the German peoples who came here in the nineteenth century for religious reasons. ("Dutch" comes from the word Deutsch, which means German.) The Amish still preserve their traditional way of life, avoiding all modern conveniences, such as electricity and automobiles. They even use buttons instead of zippers.

Baseball fans might catch the Little League World Series at Williamsport. Chocolate-lovers can visit Hershey, home of the largest chocolate factory in the world. The streets of Hershey have names like Cocoa Avenue, and the streetlights are shaped like Hershey's kisses!

Singer Marian Anderson

VALLEY FORGE AND GETTYSBURG Pennsylvania was founded by William Penn, a Friend, or Quaker, who believed in freedom and equality for all. When Penn and his colonists arrived in 1682, they set about establishing peaceful relations with the Indians. They passed the first laws guaranteeing jury trials and other liberties that later became part of the U.S. Constitution. In 1774 the First Constitutional Congress was held in Philadelphia, followed by the second Congress in 1775-1776. Present at both Congresses was Pennsylvania's famous inventor and scientist, Benjamin Franklin, who would later be ambassador to France from the new United States.

Pennsylvania is also the site of Valley Forge, where General George Washington and his men passed a harsh winter before finally winning the War of Independence. And it's the only Northern state in which a critical Civil War battle took place. On July 1-3, 1863, the Battle of Gettysburg became a turning point in the war. If you visit Gettysburg you can see the battlefield. You can also visit the house of Jennie Wade, the 20-year-old woman who baked bread for the Union troops. When Confederate troops asked her to leave, she refused. She was shot on the third day of battle by a stray bullet, the only civilian to be fatally shot. Four months later, on November 19, President Lincoln gave his famous Gettysburg Address in this town.

Independence Hall

STEEL TOWNS AND DAIRY FARMS The nation's first steel mill was in Pennsylvania, and the Pittsburgh region is still our national center of steel production. The giant steel corporations have eliminated many jobs, but western Pennsylvania is still an industrial region. Cement, lime, petroleum, heavy machinery, and processed foods are other key industries for this state.

Pennsylvania farming produces eggs, cattle, and dairy products, along with buckwheat, corn, tobacco, vegetables, orchard fruits, grapes, and mushrooms. Other riches of the earth include iron ore and anthracite coal, much of which is used in local industry. Another Pennsylvania product is Christmas trees—this state is one of the leading growers.

Fascinating Facts

PENNSYLVANIA HAD THE NATION'S FIRST:

- circulating library—1731
- medical college—1765
- oil well—Titusville—1859
- fire department
- art museum—Pennsylvania Academy of the Fine Arts—1805
- natural history museum
- hospital—The Pennsylvania Hospital
- chamber of commerce
- steam locomotive on rails
- permanent commercial radio station—KDKA, Pittsburgh—1920

DID YOU KNOW THAT... Pennsylvania is actually not a state but a commonwealth. It does not have towns but boroughs.

PENNSYLVANIA IS TOPS IN:

- hard coal or anthracite—all the nation's hard coal is mined here
- pig iron
- steel

HOW PENNSYLVANIA GOT ITS NAME: Colony founder William Penn wanted to call the land Sylvania, Latin for woods or woodland. King Charles II, who granted Penn the land, insisted on calling it *Penn's* woods—Pennsylvania.

PRESIDENT BORN IN PENNSYLVANIA:

- James Buchanan (1791-1868), 15th President

OTHER FAMOUS PEOPLE BORN IN PENNSYLVANIA:

- Writer Louisa May Alcott, Germantown (1832-1888)
- Writer Stephen Vincent Benét, Bethlehem (1898-1943)
- Singer Marian Anderson, Philadelphia (1902-1993)
- Actor Bill Cosby, Philadelphia (1937-)

DID YOU KNOW THAT... The carp crowd so closely together in Lake Pymantuning that ducks can walk across their backs.

IT USED TO BE ILLEGAL IN PENNSYLVANIA:

- to talk loudly at picnics

Rhode Island

Williams Memorial overlooks the Capitol

13th state to enter the Union, May 29, 1790

The Basics

POPULATION: 990,225
43rd most populous state
AREA: 1,545 square miles
Smallest state
STATE CAPITAL: Providence
STATE BIRD: Rhode Island Red (a chicken)
STATE FLOWER: Violet
STATE TREE: Red Maple
NICKNAMES: Little Rhody, the Smallest State, Ocean State, Land of Roger Williams, the Plantation State
STATE MOTTO: Hope
STATE MINERAL: Bowenite
STATE ROCK: Cumberlandite
STATE COLORS: Blue, white, and gold
STATE SONG: "Rhode Island," words and music by T. Clarke Brown
STATE AMERICAN FOLK ART SYMBOL: Charles I. D. Loof Carousel
STATE LANDMARKS: Old Colony House, headquarters of Colonial and state governments, 1739, Newport; Touro Synagogue, oldest U.S. synagogue, 1763, Newport; Trinity Church, 1724, Newport; Redwood Library, oldest U.S. library in continuous use, 1748, Newport; Capitol Building, with the largest unsupported dome in the United States, Providence; First Baptist Church, 1639, oldest church in America, Providence
STATE HISTORIC MUSEUM: Slater Mill, Pawtucket, one of the first textile mills in North America, founded in 1793, now a museum
STATE FESTIVAL: Hot-Air Balloon Festival, Kingston (July or August)

Rhode Island is one of the six New England states. The original Rhode Island, also called Aquidneck Island, is the largest island in the Narragansett Bay. But today's state of Rhode Island also includes the land that surrounds that bay, as well as Connecticut Island, Prudence Island, and Block Island.

SANDBARS AND SALT MARSH The Narragansett Bay cuts up from Rhode Island Sound as far north as Providence, the state's capital and largest city. West of the bay is flat, rocky soil, not good for farming.

Mainland Rhode Island's coastline is rocky and marked by sandbars, sometimes blending into salt marsh. But the island beaches are broad and sandy, making this a popular area for swimming and sailing.

MANY PEOPLES, MANY LANGUAGES Although only about a million people live in Rhode Island, the state is remarkable for its diversity. In the state's early days, Narragansett and Wampanoag lived there. In Colonial times, French Huguenots (an outcast Protestant minority), English Quakers, and Portuguese Sephardic Jews came to Rhode Island in search of the colony's famed religious freedom. In the 1820s, laborers came to work in Rhode Island's new industries: primarily Irish Catholics, but also French Canadians, Portuguese, Cape Verdeans, Italians, and Poles. Later they were joined by Ukrainians, Lithuanians, Armenians, Syrians, Greeks, and Germans. Most recently, immigrants came from the Portuguese islands, Latin America, and Southeast Asia, as well as from the U.S. South. In 1990 almost 10 percent of all Rhode Islanders were foreign-born, with one-fourth of those coming from Portugal. A full 17 percent spoke some language other than English at home, including Portuguese, Spanish, French, Italian, Polish, Mon-Khmer (Cambodian), German, Chinese, Thai (Laotian), and Armenian.

John Carter Brown House, built in 1786, Providence

IN SEARCH OF RELIGIOUS FREEDOM The founder of Rhode Island was Roger Williams, who came with his followers from Massachusetts in 1636. Williams's group had been expelled by the Puritans, in part for religious differences, in part because they criticized their fellow English for taking land from the Indians.

Williams made peaceful arrangements with the Indians in his region, and in 1639 he and his followers founded the First Baptist Church.

Newport State House

Another free thinker who came to Rhode Island was Anne Hutchinson, and her husband, who founded the town of Pocasset (now Portsmouth). The state's tradition of religious freedom attracted Quakers, Jews, Seventh Day Adventists, and others who could not worship freely elsewhere.

Williams had had good relations with the Indians he knew, but by 1652 Wampanoag leader King Philip had started a war with the European colonists, trying to regain the lands his people had lost. Philip was captured and killed in 1676, ending Indian power in the region.

Princess Red Wing at Tomaquag Indian Museum

Rhode Island passed the first law against slavery in North America on May 18, 1652, and for actually abolishing slavery in 1784. This was especially striking because much of Rhode Island's early economy was based on the infamous "triangle trade." Rhode Island merchants would trade rum for slaves in Africa, trade slaves for molasses in the West Indies, and then make rum out of molasses back in Rhode Island.

Rhode Islanders greatly prized independence, and they were the first to resist British taxation in 1769. When the British ship *Gaspee* came to collect taxes in 1772, Rhode Islanders actually set it on fire. On March 2, 1775, Providence residents had their own "tea party," throwing tea from British ships into Narragansett Bay. One Providence man actually crossed out the word "tea" in every sign in the city! On May 4, 1776—two months before the other 12 colonies—Rhode Island declared its indpendence from the British, calling itself the "first free republic in the New World." It was the last colony to join the new United States, however, waiting until the Bill of Rights was added before it would ratify the Constitution.

Touro Synagogue, the oldest in the U.S., was founded in 1763.

THE COSTUME JEWELRY CAPITAL OF THE WORLD The U.S. industrial revolution began in Rhode Island with the textile mills of Samuel Slater and Moses Brown. Half the state's economy once relied on textiles. Now costume jewelry and electronics are more important industries. Rhode Island also produces machinery, rubber and plastic goods, and silverware.

Although Rhode Island is a small state with poor farmland, it is famous for developing the Rhode Island Red, a chicken that lays lots of eggs. The state is considered the birthplace of the modern poultry industry and eggs are still big business in Rhode Island.

Fascinating Facts

THE SMALLEST AND THE LARGEST: Rhode Island is the smallest state in the Union—only 48 miles long and 37 miles wide. But it has the longest official name: "The State of Rhode Island and Providence Plantations." You could fit 220 Rhode Islands into Texas and 483 Rhode Islands into Alaska. But this state has more people per square mile than any state except New Jersey.

DID YOU KNOW THAT... From 1663 to 1854, Rhode Island had five capitals at once: Newport, East Greenwich, Bristol, South Kingstown, and Providence. From 1854 to 1900, Newport and Providence were both capitals. Finally, in 1900, Providence became the only capital.

RHODE ISLAND HAD THE FIRST:
- spinning jenny—1790—used in the first U.S. cotton mill, at Pawtucket
- U.S. power loom—1814—at Peacedale
- torpedo boat—1855—Bristol

RHODE ISLAND INVENTION:
- steam engines for mills, invented by George Corliss of Providence, 1848

RHODE ISLAND HALL OF FAME:
International Tennis Hall of Fame, Newport

FAMOUS PEOPLE BORN IN RHODE ISLAND:
- General Nathanael Greene, George Washington's second in command, Warwick (1742-1786)
- Painter Gilbert Stuart, foremost portrait painter of George Washington, North Kingstown (1755-1828)
- Composer George Michael Cohan, who wrote "I'm a Yankee Doodle Dandy," Providence (1878-1942)

HOW RHODE ISLAND GOT ITS NAME:
Some people believe that the Italian explorer Giovanni da Verrazano was comparing nearby Block Island to the Mediterranean island of Rhodes in 1524. Others believe that the Dutch explorer Adriaen Block called it *roodt eylandt*, meaning "red island," for its red clay soil.

South Carolina

Traditional street in Charleston

8th state to enter the Union, May 23, 1788

The Basics

POPULATION: 3,698,746
26th most populous state
AREA: 32,008 square miles
40th largest state
STATE CAPITAL: Columbia
STATE BIRD: Carolina wren
STATE FLOWER: Yellow jasmine
STATE TREE: Palmetto (also called Sabal palmetto, Cabbage palm, Cabbage palmetto, Tree palmetto, Bank's palmetto)
NICKNAMES: The Palmetto State, the Rice State, the Swamp State, Keystone of the South Atlantic Seaboard, the Iodine State
STATE MOTTO: *Animis Opibusque Parati* (Latin for "Prepared in mind and resources") and *Dum Spiro Spero* (Latin for "While I breathe, I hope")
STATE ANIMAL: White-tailed deer
STATE FISH: Striped bass
STATE STONE: Blue granite
STATE SHELL: Lettered olive
STATE GEM: Amethyst
STATE FRUIT: Peach
STATE DRINK: Milk
STATE DANCE: The Shag
STATE SONGS: "Carolina," words by Henry Timrod, music by Anne Custis Burgess; "Carolina on My Mind," traditional
STATE LANDMARKS: Andrew Jackson State Park, near Lancaster—birthplace of the President; President Woodrow Wilson's boyhood home, Columbia
HISTORIC PARK: Historic District, Cheraw
STATE FESTIVAL: Spoleto USA, Charleston (May-June)
STATE PLEDGE: "I salute the flag of South Carolina and pledge to the Palmetto State love, loyalty, and faith."

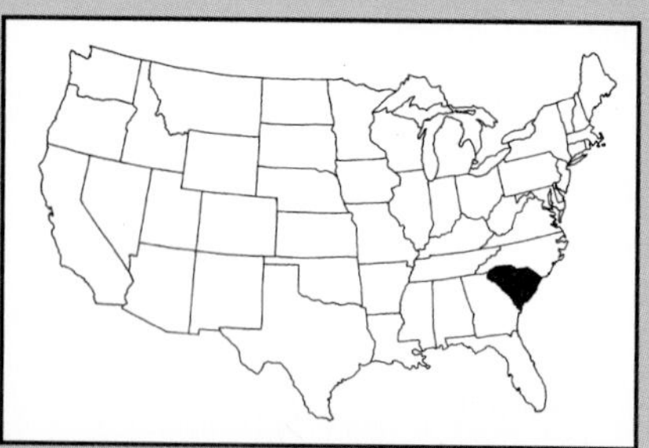

South Carolina's warm, humid climate and its miles of sandy beaches have made it one of America's top vacation spots. On the Grand Strand, from the state's northeast border to Georgetown, South Carolina offers a lively family resort area featuring golf, camping, malls, and live entertainment. The aristocratic Low Country—including the barrier islands of Hilton Head, Edisto, and Fripp—offers a more exclusive and genteel vacation area. No wonder tourism is a key industry here!

AT THE HEART OF PLANTATION COUNTRY South Carolina's coastal lowlands, with their marshy ground and subtropical climate, extend inland for up to 150 miles. Most of the state, however, is the Piedmont plain, a hilly country that rises gradually westward until, at the extreme western end of the state, you reach the Blue Ridge range of the Appalachians.

House on Tradd Street, one of the oldest streets in America

South Carolina's most distinctive city is Charleston. Although this gracious city was badly damaged during the Civil War, many of its eighteenth- and nineteenth-century mansions have been restored, and many of its lovely cypress and magnolia gardens are open to the public. At the Charleston City Hall you can see a portrait of the young George Washington, before false teeth changed the shape of his face—and without his white wig! Charleston is also the site of the Old Slave Mart Museum, located in an old warehouse used to house slaves who were about to be auctioned. From Colonial times until 1930, South Carolina had more black residents than white, because local plantations had held so many African-American slaves to till huge fields of indigo, rice, and cotton. Charleston was also one of the most active slave-trading ports, receiving ships directly from Gambia and the Gold Coast.

WINNING THE WAR OF INDEPENDENCE North and South Carolina weren't separated until 1712, and the two states share a heritage of independence. In 1719, South Carolinians overthrew the king-appointed Lords Proprietors that governed them and elected their own governor instead. During the Revolutionary War, backwoods guerillas as well as trained soldiers fought the British. Francis Morgan, the Swamp Fox, founded one of the most famous guerilla bands. The first decisive American victory, at Fort Moultrie, was won in South Carolina, as was the Battle of King's Mountain, the turning point of the war.

Aerial view of Charleston

REBELLIONS AND SECESSION South Carolina has had a long history of slave rebellions, starting in Stono River in 1739. At that time the Spanish were occupying Florida. They sent a message north saying that slaves who reached St. Augustine would be given freedom. A slave leader, Cato, organized 100 people to break into a weapons storehouse and begin a trek southward to liberty. His band killed 21 people—and was caught within five hours. Some 44 rebels were executed—and the colony passed a law making it illegal to teach slaves to read.

Another African-American leader, the minister Denmark Vesey, planned a general black uprising and the seizing of Charleston for mid-July 1822—but he never lived that long. A thousand slaves and four white men were involved in the plan, and one of the slaves betrayed the plan to the authorities. Vesey and 34 others were hanged on July 2, and the state passed a law restricting the number of black people allowed to gather at one time. Since Vesey had been a free man, the state also made it nearly impossible for slaves to purchase their freedom.

Epworth House (1717) in Beaufort

White citizens of South Carolina were also rebellious. They strongly supported slavery and feared that when President Abraham Lincoln was elected, slavery would become illegal. So in 1860, they were the first state to secede from the Union. And on April 12, 1861, South Carolinians fired the first shot of the Civil War on Fort Sumter in Charleston Harbor.

TEXTILES AND TOURISM South Carolina takes second place only to North Carolina as a producer of textiles. Wool, rayon, nylon, orlon—and cotton from homegrown plants—are all produced in this state. In recent years, however, industry has grown to include the manufacture of chemicals, plastics, and rubber. BMW, the German auto maker, has one of its largest plants here.

South Carolina also depends on tourism, particularly to beautiful, historic Charleston, and in the resort areas of Hilton Head Island and Myrtle Beach. Tobacco, soybeans, corn, peaches, and lumber are also major products, as well as furniture made from local wood.

Fascinating Facts

SOUTH CAROLINA REVOLUTIONARY WAR FACTS:

- More Revolutionary War battles were fought in South Carolina than in any other state. Some 137 battles were fought here, 103 without help from other colonies.
- The first battle of the Revolutionary War was won by a band of patriots in a fort built of palmetto logs, Fort Moultrie on Sullivan's Island, giving South Carolina its nickname.

CHARLESTON HAD THE NATION'S FIRST:

- public library—1698
- theater—Dock Street Theatre—1736
- museum—Charleston Museum—1773
- opera performed in America—1735
- play—written and performed by English actor Tony Aston in 1703
- landscaped gardens—Middleton Place gardens—carved out of wilderness by Henry Middleton, President of the First Continental Congress—1741

SOUTH CAROLINA HAD THE NATION'S FIRST:

- steam railroad
- cotton mill
- European settlement—San Miguel de Guadalupe—founded at Winyah Bay by Spanish Captain Lucas Vasquez de Ayllon—1526

SOUTH CAROLINA HAS THE WORLD'S LARGEST:

- pigeon farm—Sumter

PRESIDENT BORN IN SOUTH CAROLINA:

- Andrew Jackson (1767-1845), 7th President

SOUTH CAROLINA HALL OF FAME:

NMPA Stock Car Hall of Fame, Darlington

IT USED TO BE ILLEGAL IN SOUTH CAROLINA:

- to file down a mule's teeth
- to go to church without carrying a gun
- to act in an obnoxious manner on the campus of a girls' school without the permission of the principal

South Dakota

The Basics

POPULATION: 732,405
45th most populous state
AREA: 77,121 square miles
17th largest state
STATE CAPITAL: Pierre
STATE BIRD: Ring-necked pheasant
STATE FLOWER: American pasqueflower
STATE TREE: Black Hills spruce
NICKNAMES: The Sunshine State, the Coyote State, the Artesian State
STATE MOTTO: Under God the People Rule
STATE ANIMAL: Coyote
STATE FISH: Walleye
STATE INSECT: Honeybee
STATE GRASS: Western wheat grass
STATE MINERAL: Rose quartz
STATE STONE: Fairborn agate
STATE FOSSIL: Triceratops
STATE GEM: Fairburn agate
STATE COLORS: Blue and gold
STATE GREETING: *"How Kola"* (Souix greeting that means "Hello, friend."
STATE SONG: "Hail! South Dakota," words and music by Deecort Hammitt
STATE LANDMARKS: Badlands National Park; Black Hills National Forest (shared with Wyoming); Crazy Horse Memorial—a statue of the Dakota leader carved into a mountain; Jewel Cave National Monument—a cave of beautiful crystals; Mount Rushmore National Memorial—the heads of Washington, Jefferson, Lincoln, and Theodore Roosevelt carved into a mountain; Custer State Park, where the bison still roam

Mt. Rushmore

39th or 40th state to enter the Union, November 2, 1889

South Dakota is a land rich in both nature and culture. It has some of the most extraordinary geographical features in the United States. And it has a rich heritage of Indian nations who still speak their languages, practice their religion, and keep their traditions alive.

THE BADLANDS AND THE BLACK HILLS South Dakota is a flat prairie state. To the southwest lie the Badlands—colored rocks in strange shapes, the result of millions of years of the earth's erosion. To the west are the Black Hills, sacred to the Dakota people and prized by other Americans for their rich stores of gold and oil. Most of the rest of South Dakota is either farmland or grazing land that supports huge ranches of cattle and sheep. The geographic center of the United States is near the small South Dakota town of Castle Rock.

Millions of years of erosion have produced the spectacular landscape of Badlands National Park.

INDIAN WARS, PAST AND PRESENT For thousands of years the region now known as South Dakota was inhabited by the Dakota, a vast nation including many different peoples, among them the Oglala, the Lakota, and the Teton. Dakota means "friend" or "ally." Ojibwa, however, referred to the nation as Sioux from an insult meaning Snake People. The name became common among other Native Americans.

The first Europeans came to South Dakota in 1743. French explorers Louis-Joseph and Francois Verendrye were looking for a route to the Pacific. French fur traders came soon after. President Thomas Jefferson bought the state as part of the Louisiana Purchase in 1803, and in 1804-1806 Lewis and Clark explored the area with the help of their translator and guide, the Shoshone Indian Sacagawea. (Although Sacagawea's final resting place is unknown, there is a monument in Mobridge claiming that "Sakakawea" died there.)

Gradually farmers and ranchers began to settle the land that the Dakota still regarded as their nation. U.S. Army troops moved in, so that the first permanent settlement was Fort Pierre (later it became Pierre, South Dakota's capital city).

After the Civil War the newly reunited United States was tired of fighting. The U.S. and Dakota made peace with an 1868 treaty that placed the region

State Capitol in Pierre

under Indian rule. Then, in 1874 gold was discovered in the Black Hills and U.S. troops again tried to seize the land. The Sioux fought back but were finally defeated after the 1890 uprising at Wounded Knee. They were relocated onto reservations throughout the state, where many Sioux continue to live today.

The Sioux people, however, have never forgotten the many injustices of the United States government. Many are still working through the United Nations and the U.S. courts to win recognition for the 1868 treaty. Others began a lawsuit in the U.S. Court system in 1922, trying to set economic compensation. Demonstrations erupted in the 1970s, including a second uprising at Wounded Knee. In 1979, $105 million was awarded as compensation for lost land, but many issues have been left unaddressed. Indian political activity continues today for treaty rights as well as for preserving the Dakota language and culture.

DANCE HALLS ON THE PRAIRIE If you visit South Dakota today you can still see the traces of this state's Wild West heritage. In Deadwood, for example, Main Street is lined with replicas of the saloons and dance halls that made this gold rush boomtown famous throughout the 1870s. Here Wild Bill Hickock was shot during a poker game. Here, too, "Poker Alice" Tubbs—who gambled her way across the mining camps of the West—used to smoke her big cigars while winning thousands of dollars at cards.

Another famous South Dakota landmark can be found in De Smet. This town is the original "little town on the prairie" featured in six of the Laura Ingalls Wilder series. Laura's parents were the first white family to settle in the area, in 1879, and you can still visit some of the houses where the Ingalls lived.

Sioux Indians at Sitting Bull Crystal Cave

RICHES ON AND UNDER THE EARTH Before the Europeans arrived, the Plains Indians of South Dakota survived by killing the buffalo and bison that abounded in the region. When the railroads wanted to move into the state in the 1870s, they hired hunters like "Buffalo Bill" Cody to kill the buffalo so that South Dakota became a land of farms and ranches. Cattle and sheep are still important products in South Dakota today. The state also produces wheat, corn, and other grains.

South Dakota is primarily an agricultural, rural state. Most of its manufacturing is food processing, in very small factories with fewer than 50 workers. However, tourism, and, recently, telemarketing are also important industries.

Fascinating Facts

MOUNT RUSHMORE FACT:
- The largest sculptures in the world are these presidents' heads. They average 60 feet tall—six stories—and Lincoln's mouth is 22 feet wide.

FAMOUS SOUTH DAKOTANS:
- Crazy Horse, leader of the Oglala Sioux nation. In 1876 he and fellow leaders Sitting Bull and Gall defeated General George Custer at the Battle of Little Bighorn, but eventually had to surrender. He was stabbed to death trying to escape from prison in 1877.
- Sitting Bull, another Dakota leader. He and his followers fled to Canada after defeating Custer. Later he appeared in Buffalo Bill's Wild West Show and was killed while allegedly resisting arrest in 1890.
- Calamity Jane, a frontierswoman whose real name was Martha Jane Cannary. She got her name by saying that to offend her was to "court calamity" (ask for a disaster).
- Wild Bill Hickok (James Butler Hickok), American frontier marshal who fought outlaws in Kansas.
- Senator George McGovern, the 1972 Democratic Presidential candidate.

DID YOU KNOW THAT... South Dakota was once home to tiny three-toed horses and saber-toothed tigers. Their fossilized bones were discovered in the White River Badlands and can now be seen in museums around the world. Scientists also think the ancient camel originated here.

SOUTH DAKOTA IS TOPS IN...
- geese
- gold mines—the largest working gold mine in the Americas is the Homestake Mine in Lead (rhymes with "fed"), South Dakota. It has produced more gold than any other single mine in the world.

DID YOU KNOW THAT... South Dakota and North Dakota are the only two states to enter the Union on the same day.

IT USED TO BE ILLEGAL IN SOUTH DAKOTA:
- for an 80-year-old woman to stop in the street to talk to a young married man.

Tennessee

Lookout Mountain

16th state to enter the Union, June 1, 1796

The Basics

POPULATION: 5,319,654
17th most populous state
AREA: 42,146 square miles
36th largest state
STATE CAPITAL: Nashville
STATE BIRD: Mockingbird
STATE FLOWER: Iris
STATE WILDFLOWER: Passionflower
STATE TREE: Tulip poplar
NICKNAMES: The Volunteer State, Big Bend State, Mother of Southwestern Statesmen, Hog State, Hominy State
STATE MOTTO: Agriculture and Commerce
STATE WILD ANIMAL: Raccoon
STATE INSECTS: Firefly, ladybug
STATE ROCK: Limestone
STATE GEM: Tennessee pearl
STATE RAILROAD MUSEUM: Tennessee Valley Railroad Museum
STATE FINE ART: Porcelain painting
STATE FOLK DANCE: Square dance
STATE SONGS: "My Homeland, Tennessee," words and music by Nell Grayson Taylor and Roy Lamont; "When It's Iris Time in Tennessee," words and music by Willa Mae Waid; "My Tennessee," words and music by Francis Hannah Traum; "The Tennesee Waltz," words and music by Redd Stewart and Pee Wee King; "Rocky Top," words and music by Boudleaux and Felice Bryant
STATE POEM: "Oh Tennessee, My Tennessee," by Admiral William Lawrence
STATE LANDMARKS: The Hermitage, east of Nashville—home of President Andrew Jackson; Home of President James K. Polk, Columbia; Home and Tailor Shop of President Andrew Johnson, Greenville
STATE NATIONAL PARKS: Great Smoky Mountains National Park, near Gatlinburg; Chickamauga-Chattanooga military park

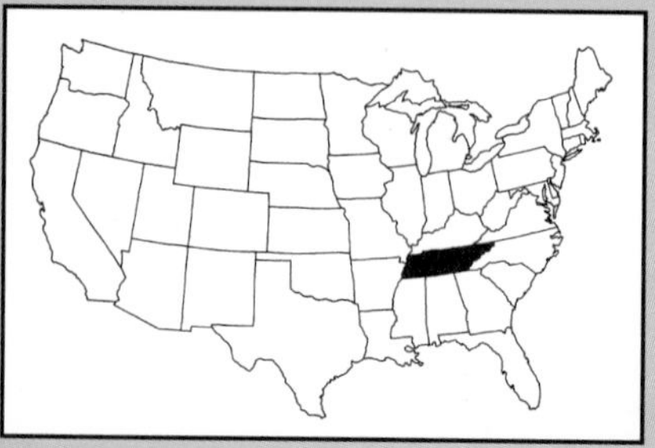

When you think Tennessee, think music. The Grand Ole Opry in Nashville; Beale Street in Memphis, birthplace of the blues; Memphis's Sun Studio, birthplace of rock and roll, where Elvis Presley, Jerry Lee Lewis, B.B. King, and Roy Orbison launched their careers—these historic sites contribute to a living Tennessee heritage of American music.

THREE STARS—THREE STATES The three stars on Tennessee's flag refer to the three parts of the state. In east Tennessee are the Great Smoky Mountains, with hills so steep that farmers have to harvest their crops on sleds. Here, too, is the Tennessee River Valley, between the Blue Ridge and Cumberland Mountains. East Tennessee's Chattanooga is located at the meeting point of three ancient Indian trails. The city's "Blue Goose Hollow" is the birthplace of blues singer Bessie Smith. As a little girl, she sang outside her broken-down shack, until she was discovered in 1912 by the great Ma Rainey.

Elvis Presley, rock star (1935-1977)

Central Tennessee is the land of the Cumberland foothills, a rolling, hilly country where sheep, cattle, and horses graze. This is the "bluegrass basin" and the home of the famous Tennessee walking horse. In central Tennessee is Nashville, where the longest-running radio show in the country is still broadcast live each week from the Grand Ole Opry.

West Tennessee is bounded by the Tennessee and Mississippi Rivers. Its level, fertile land is planted with cotton fields. Memphis, the state's largest city, looks out over the Mississippi.

Near Memphis you can visit the Chucalissa Archaeological Museum, a reconstruction of a Native American village that stood on the banks of the Mississippi from 1000 to 1500. At the C.H. Nash Museum, you can see contemporary Choctaw craftspeople making jewelry, weapons, and pottery.

STRUGGLES OF A STATE Tennessee had to struggle more than most to become a state. In 1663 it was part of the Carolina colony. But in 1772 settlers on the Watauga River formed the Watauga Association to be free of the British Royal Colony and create "a homespun government." Nonetheless, in 1777, they were annexed as North Carolina's Washington County.

Tennessee's patriots would not give up. In 1784 the pioneers between the mountains and the Mississippi formed the State of Franklin (named for Ben

Tennessee walking horse

Franklin) and applied to the Continental Congress for entry into the Union. Neither the Congress nor North Carolina would recognize the "Franklinites," but they had their own governor and legislature until 1788 when they joined North Carolina once again. In 1789 North Carolina ceded the land to the federal government, which created the "Territory of the United States South of the Ohio River." Finally, in 1796, Tennessee had enough people to become a state.

Unlike most other Southern states, Tennessee was sharply divided on the issue of slavery. It was the last state to secede from the Union in 1861, largely because East Tennessee was antislavery and pro-Union. During the Civil War some 186,000 men from Tennessee signed up as Confederate soldiers—but over 30,000 fought for the Union. Tennessee was the only state to free slaves by popular vote, on February 25, 1865, and it was the first state to rejoin the Union in 1866.

DEATH OF A LEADER In February 1968 the Memphis garbage collectors—almost all African American—had had enough. They refused to continue working for low pay, in unsafe conditions, and subject to racial insults from white supervisors. But Memphis city government refused to budge. The strike had gone on for weeks when civil rights leader Martin Luther King, Jr., was invited down to help. On April 3, King marched with the strikers, wearing a badge with the slogan of the strike: "I am a man." That night he spoke to cheering crowds. The next day he was assassinated by James Earl Ray while standing on the balcony of the Lorraine Motel. Riots broke out nationwide after his death. The motel was turned into a museum to honor Dr. King.

COTTON AND COUNTRY MUSIC For years, Tennessee was a major cotton state. Gradually, though, the soil wore out, and floods washed away the topsoil. Tennessee's economy suffered. Then, in 1933, the Tennessee Valley Authority, a government agency, built dams throughout the valley, bringing hydroelectric power and economic revitalization to the region. Now Tennessee has a growing industrial sector, manufacturing chemicals and machinery. Cottonseed oil is made in Memphis, where cotton is still traded. Soybeans, wheat, and tobacco have become more important crops, however. Tourism is another key industry, as is music recording and publishing.

Fascinating Facts

HOW TENNESSEE GOT ITS NAME: The Cherokee Indians called two villages on what is now the Little Tennesse River *Tanasi.* No one now knows what the word means, but it was used to name both the river and the region.

HOW TENNESSEE GOT ITS NICKNAMES: Tennessee volunteer troops fought bravely under Tennessee native Andrew Jackson in the Battle of New Orleans in the War of 1812—so the state became "The Volunteer State." "The Big Bend State" refers to the Tennessee River; "the Mother of Southwestern Statesmen" refers to the two American presidents who lived there.

THEY LIVED IN TENNESSEE:
- Andrew Jackson (1767-1845), 7th President
- Andrew Johnson (1808-1875), 17th President

DAVY CROCKETT:
- born in Great Smoky Mountains, 1786
- soldier and Indian scout
- elected to Congress three times
- motto: "Be sure you're right, then go ahead."

DID YOU KNOW THAT... The state's biggest lake, Reelfoot, near Tiptonville, was formed by an earthquake in 1811.

TENNESSEE HAS THE WORLD'S LARGEST:
- cotton market—Memphis
- underground lake—the Lost Sea, in Craighead Cavern

TENNESSEE IS TOPS IN:
- U.S. alumimun production
- greatest variety of birds in the U.S.

IT USED TO BE ILLEGAL IN TENNESSEE:
- for a motorist to drive unless he or she had warned the public one week in advance with a notice in the newspapers
- to take a fish off another person's hook

Texas

The Basics

POPULATION: 19,128,261
2nd most populous state
AREA: 268,601 square miles
2nd largest state
STATE CAPITAL: Austin
STATE BIRD: Mockingbird
STATE FLOWER: Bluebonnet
STATE TREE: Pecan
NICKNAMES: The Lone Star State, the Beef State, the Banner State
STATE MOTTO: Friendship
SPORTS TEAMS: Houston Astros, Texas Rangers, baseball; Dallas Cowboys, Houston Oilers, football; Dallas Mavericks, Houston Rockets, San Antonio Spurs, basketball
STATE DISH: Chili
STATE GEM: Topaz
STATE GRASS: Sideoats grama
STATE STONE: Petrified pinewood
STATE SONG: "Texas, Our Texas," words and music by William J. Marsh and Gladys Yoakum Wright
STATE LANDMARK: Alamo
NATIONAL PARKS: Big Bend, near Alpine; Guadalupe Mountains, near El Paso; Padre Island National Seashore, near Corpus Christi—untouched since Indian times; Aransas National Wildlife Refuge, near Tivoli—winter ground of whooping cranes
STATE PLEDGE OF ALLEGIANCE: "Honor the Texas Flag; I pledge allegiance to thee, Texas, one and indivisible."
TEXAS FESTIVALS: Goat Cookoff and Goat Roping, Sonora (May); Great Mosquito Festival, Brazosport (July); Rattlesnake Roundup, Big Spring (March)

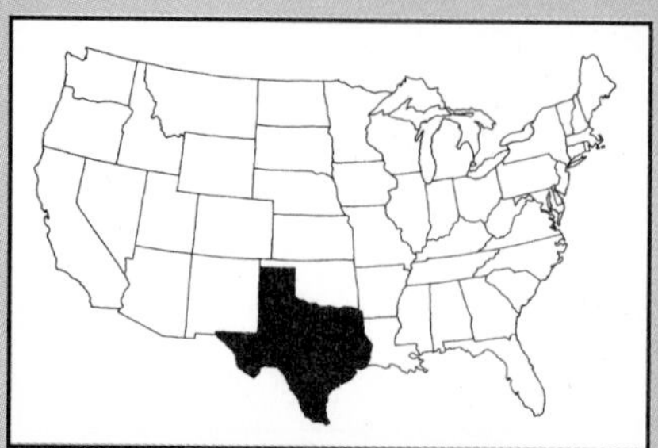

The Alamo

28th state to enter the Union, December 29, 1845

When you think Texas, think BIG! You could fit 220 Rhode Islands into Texas, which is second only to Alaska in size. Texas is so big that it has different climates—subtropical along the Gulf Coast, cold as an Illinois winter up north. In fact, Texas is so big, it's the only state with permission to turn itself into five states if its people choose!

FROM BEAUMONT TO EL PASO Eastern Texas is more like the South than the West: piney woods, rolling hills, and vast fields of cotton. In this region is Beaumont, home of the Babe Didrikson Memorial Museum. Didrikson (later Zaharias), a Beaumont native, was a 1932 Olympic Gold medalist who became one of the world's outstanding golfers. Although she died in 1956 of cancer, at age 45, she remains an inspiration to women athletes.

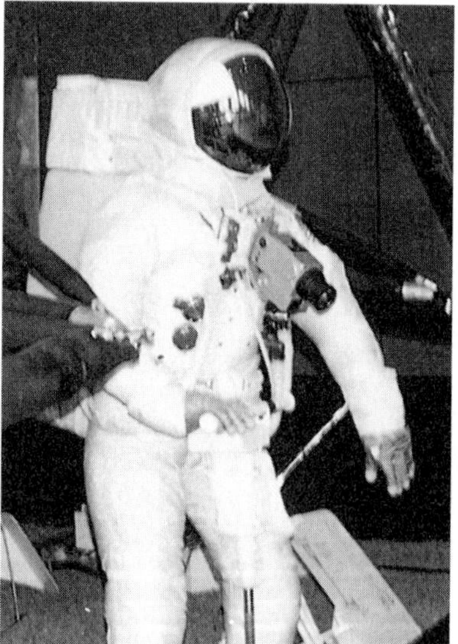

Spacesuit at Johnson Space Center

Houston is in the fertile crescent of the Gulf Coast plain, watered by many rivers and by complex irrigation systems. Here, grapefruit, pecans, and peanuts grow. Houston is Texas's largest city. Its mix of new buildings and boarded-up homes reflects the boom and then the bust in the 1980s oil market. Houston is also known for its famous covered Astrodome and for NASA's Johnson Space Center.

Farther northwest is hill country, which turns into the Great Plains, a deserted, windswept area. And west of the Pecos River, all the way to El Paso, is desert, marked by tumbleweed and sagebrush.

The famous cities Dallas and Fort Worth are in northeast Texas. Dallas is in the heart of oil and cotton country. It's glitzy and ritzy, although folks tend to go to bed early and go to church on Sunday. Fort Worth is more down-to-earth, though Dallasites call it a "cow town." It's true that Fort Worth is Texas's cattle capital, with an Old West history second to none. Just southeast of here was the hideout of Butch Cassidy (Robert Leroy Parker) and the Sundance Kid (Harry Longbaugh). The two used to come into the rowdy section of Fort Worth, known as "Hell's Half Acre."

If you want to see rural Texas, though, you'd better visit Big Bend National Park, where millions of years of erosion have carved out deep canyons and weird rock formations. Here are black bears, mountain lions, coyotes, javelinas, and jackrabbits, along with over 430 species of birds. Nearby is the Rio Grande, the

Congresswoman Barbara Jordan (1936-1995)

"big river" that many see as the heart of Texas. For 800 miles this river forms the border between the United States and Mexico.

REMEMBER THE ALAMO This southwestern state has been shaped by its Wild West heritage, and by its mix of Chicano, African-American, and Anglo cultures. First to enter the state were the Spanish explorers—Fernando Vasquez de Coronado, Hernando de Soto, and others—who were looking for the golden cities they mistakenly believed had been built here. The first permanent European settlement was at Ysleta, in 1682. By 1731 the Spanish had erected dozens of missions and forts. They wanted to subdue the Indians militarily, and they wanted to convert them to Christianity.

In 1821 Mexico won its own independence from Spain. Although there were already U.S. citizens living in Texas, Mexico claimed the land and even tried to stop immigration in 1830, fearing that too many Anglos would change the area's culture and political loyalties. In fact, American colonists did revolt. In the Texas Revolution of 1835, they took San Antonio. In 1836, 187 Texas volunteers holed up in a fort known as the Alamo, resisting for 13 days the siege of Mexico's dictator, Santa Anna. Everyone at the Alamo was killed, including Davy Crockett and Jim Bowie (five survivors were killed as prisoners later). But Texas leader Sam Houston rallied his troops with the cry, "Remember the Alamo!" and went on to win independence for Texas.

Tigua Indian drummer in El Paso

From 1836 to 1845 Texas was its own independent Republic. During this time, it drove the Cherokee people into Mexico and expelled other native peoples. Finally Texas became part of the United States.

Then, in 1861, states that supported slavery seceded from the Union. Texas seceded too and joined the Confederacy. Not until 1870 was Texas to belong to the United States, once and for all.

BLACK GOLD In 1901 the famous Spindletop gusher, near Beaumont, exploded through the earth. This amazing oil well produced a record 100,000 barrels of petroleum each day. The oil industry has been good to Texas, creating a group of millionaires and a boom economy. Natural gas, coal, salt, sulfur, and other minerals are also important to Texas. Cotton is the state's main cash crop. Cattle are another key product. In 1902 the Chicago packing companies of Swift and Armour set up stockyards in Fort Worth—and shipped the meat in brand-new refrigerator cars.

The space program has brought new industry to Texas. The Johnson Space Center in Houston monitors and controls U.S. manned space flights. Aerospace equipment is manufactured in Dallas.

Fascinating Facts

HOW TEXAS GOT ITS NAME: The Caddo Indian word *Texas* or *Teysha* means "Hello, friend." The name is also spelled *Texias, Tejas*, and *Teysas.*

DID YOU KNOW THAT... Texas has had six national flags flying over it: those of Spain, France, Mexico, the Republic of Texas, the Confederacy, and the United States. (That's where the original Six Flags amuseument park got its name!)

TEXAS HALLS OF FAME:
- National Cowgirl Hall of Fame, Hereford
- Texas Rangers Hall of Fame, Waco

TEXAS FIRST:
- First woman to manage a circus—Mollie Bailey, Mollie A. Bailey Show—late 1800s

TEXAS IS TOPS IN:
- amount of farmland farmed
- sheep and cattle
- rice, cotton, spinach
- oil (almost half of U.S. production)
- natural gas (almost half of U.S. production)
- salt, magnesium, sulfur, helium
- asphalt
- kinds of wildflowers and reptiles
- drive-in theaters

TEXAS HAS THE BIGGEST:
- ranch—King Ranch—bigger than Rhode Island!
- state capitol building
- state fair—Dallas—October
- rose-growing center—near Tyler
- battle monument—Houston
- urban bat colony—Austin

TEXAS HAD THE NATION'S MOST:
- rainfall—43 inches at Alvin, July 25-26, 1979

PRESIDENTS BORN IN TEXAS:
- Dwight D. Eisenhower (1890-1969), 34th President
- Lyndon B. Johnson (1908-1973), 36th President

Utah

The Basics

POPULATION: 2,000,494 people
34th most populous state
AREA: 84,904 square miles
13th largest state
STATE CAPITAL: Salt Lake City
STATE BIRD: California gull
STATE FLOWER: Sego lily
STATE TREE: Blue spruce (also called Colorado blue spruce, balsam, Colorado spruce, Prickly spruce, White spruce, Silver spruce, Parry's spruce)
NICKNAMES: The Beehive State, the Mormon State, the Land of the Saints, the Salt Lake State
STATE MOTTO: Industry
SPORTS TEAM: Utah Jazz, basketball
STATE EMBLEM: Beehive
STATE ANIMAL: Elk
STATE FISH: Rainbow trout
STATE INSECT: Honeybee
STATE GEM: Topaz
STATE SONG: "Utah, We Love Thee," words and music by Evan Stephens
STATE LANDMARK: Golden Spike National Historic Site, Promontory—where railroad tracks from east and west met in 1869
NATIONAL PARKS: Bryce Canyon, Zion, Arches, Canyonlands, Capitol Reefs
NATIONAL MONUMENTS: Dinosaur National Monument, Jensen; Timpanogos Cave, American Fork; Natural Bridges National Monument, Lake Power
STATE PARKS: Goblin Valley State Park, Green River—wind-eroded sandstone "goblins"; This Is The Place State Park, Salt Lake City, recreates 1850s township of early Mormons
STATE FESTIVAL: Deseret Vagabond Days, Kanab (July)

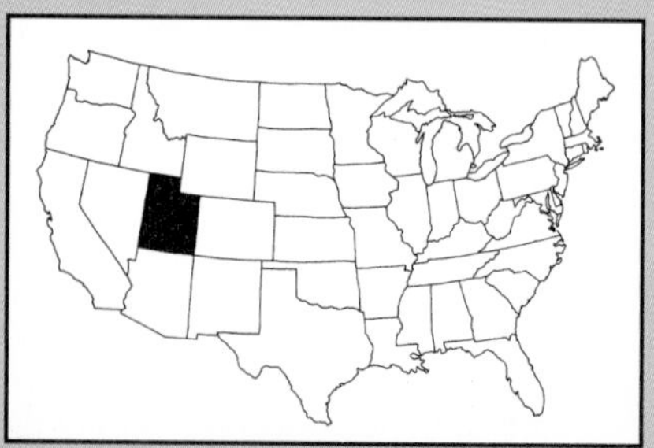

Bryce Canyon

45th state to enter the Union, January 4, 1896

Utah has a beauty unlike that of any other state. Where else could you find a desert with seagulls and pelicans, or a collection of weird, brilliantly colored sandstone shapes rising out of the dusty ground? This western, rural, Rocky Mountains state is known for its luxury ski resorts and for the influence of its Mormon founders.

ROCKY MOUNTAIN DESERT Southern Utah is famous for the spectacular red deserts of the Colorado Plateau, along with strangely colored canyons, bizarrely shaped rock formations, and petrified forests. The landscape has been etched by Ice Age glaciers and the erosion from flash floods.

There are many dinosaur fossils at Dinosaur National Monument near Vernal.

In northeastern Utah are the Wasatch and Uinta Mountains. And to the west is the Great Salt Lake Desert, with the famous lake that was once an inland sea. Water flows into the lake but has nowhere to drain. So it just evaporates, leaving salt and minerals behind.

Utah was once home to many native peoples. An 83-room Anasazi village is now the site of Anasazi State Park in southern Utah. The dwellings were probably built between A.D. 1129 and 1169 by people from the Kayenta Anasazi region of northeastern Arizona. Anasazi and Fremont rock art can also be seen in several Utah state parks.

THIS IS THE PLACE So said Mormon leader Brigham Young, who with a party of 143 men and three women, arrived at what is now Salt Lake City in 1847. The Mormons had left their prosperous communities in Ohio, Missouri, and Illinois for a place where they would be left alone to practice their religion. Young chose Utah because he thought no one else would want it.

Of course, many native peoples lived in Utah. When Young arrived, he found Paiutes, Shoshones, Gosiute, and Ute. Navajo arrived in the 1860s. But by 1868 Indians had been forced off their land onto reservations.

Meanwhile, the Mormons were facing the difficult task of growing food in the hot, dry climate. They developed a complex system of irrigation channels that made the desert bloom and led Utah to be known as "the cradle of American irrigation." Mormons feared starvation when a swarm of crickets threatened to eat the entire crop of 1847—but in 1848 a flock of seagulls miraculously appeared to eat the insects and save the crops. That's why Utah now has the world's only monument to a bird.

State Capitol, Salt Lake City

In 1849 thousands of prospectors were heading to California for the gold rush. Mormons prospered as they supplied these pioneers on their journey. From 1855 to 1860, 8,000 Mormons arrived in Utah from Europe. Over 3,000 had walked from the railroad station in Iowa to Salt Lake City, pushing their possessions on handcarts. They founded towns in Utah, Idaho, and Nevada—including Las Vegas!

Utah kept applying for statehood, but the Mormon practice of polygamy—one husband having many wives—was frowned on by Congress. In 1857, 2,500 Army troops entered the state to install a governor to replace Brigham Young. Mormons responded with the Utah War, killing 120 emigrants on their way to California. In 1858, the area won amnesty—but not statehood. In the 1880s and 1890s, over 1,000 Mormons were fined or imprisoned as the government continued to oppose polygamy. Finally Mormons themselves outlawed this practice, and after 46 years of being a territory, Utah's seventh application for statehood was accepted.

In the twentieth century the Mormons—officially, the Church of Jesus Christ of Latter-Day Saints—refused to ordain African Americans as priests. Yet at least three black pioneers were among Brigham Young's original party, and several black converts came to the area over the years. At least one African-American man, Elijah Abel, served as a priest until his death in 1884. In 1978 Joseph Freeman, Jr. was ordained as the first modern African-American Mormon priest.

The Mormon Tabernacle

TABERNACLES AND BEEHIVES Visitors to Salt Lake City can see many historical and religious monuments that are still in use today: the Salt Lake Tabernacle, home of the Mormon Tabernacle Choir; the six-spired Salt Lake Temple; and the Beehive House, where Brigham Young lived with his many wives and children. Next door was Lion House, where another seven wives resided. (The rest were dispersed around the state.) In the same neighborhood was the home of Ann Eliza Webb Young, who made history in 1873 by moving out of her cottage into a hotel and demanding a divorce from Young. She became a nationwide crusader against polygamy.

RICHES UNDER THE EARTH Copper and coal are key Utah products, as well as gold, silver, lead, zinc, uranium, magnesium, molybdenum, and petroleum. Soft western woods—fir, pine, and spruce—support Utah's timber and paper industries. Manufacturing in the state is primarily making metals and food processing. There is some high-tech industry near Provo, and the West's largest steel plant is near that town. Tourism, centered in the ski resort at Park City, is also an important Utah industry.

Fascinating Facts

HOW UTAH GOT ITS NAME: The Mormons first proposed the name *Deseret,* "land of the honeybee," but Congress rejected that name. The actual name was chosen through misunderstanding: White Mountain Apaches referred to the Navajo as *Yuttahih,* "one who is higher up." Europeans thought they were referring to the Utes, who lived higher up in the mountains than the Navajo, so the state became known as Utah.

DID YOU KNOW THAT... Zion Narrows Canyon is so deep and so narrow that even in bright daylight, you can see stars from the bottom of the canyon.

GREAT SALT LAKE FACTS:

- The water in the lake is more than four times as salty as any ocean.
- The only water saltier than this lake's is that of the Dead Sea.
- When fur trapper and scout James Bridger became the first white man to see the lake, he thought he'd found the Pacific Ocean.
- In 1983 record rain and snow brought flooding to Utah, and the lake rose ten feet in two years. By the decade's end, though, the lake level had fallen again.

DID YOU KNOW THAT... Utah has the only major east-west mountain range in the United States—the Uintas.

UTAH HALL OF FAME:

- Hollywood Stuntmen's Hall of Fame, Moab

DID YOU KNOW THAT... Bear River is the continent's longest river that *doesn't* reach the sea.

UTAH HAD THE NATION'S FIRST:

- solar cell power plant—Natural Bridges Monument——June 7, 1980

IT USED TO BE ILLEGAL IN UTAH:

- for a person to wear shoes with heels higher than one and one-half inches
- for two dancing partners to dance so close that daylight could not be seen between them

Vermont

Dairy farm in Williamstown

14th state to enter the Union, March 4, 1791

The Basics

POPULATION: 588,654
49th most populous state
AREA: 9,615 square miles
45th largest state
STATE CAPITAL: Montpelier
STATE BIRD: Hermit thrush
STATE FLOWER: Red clover
STATE TREE: Sugar maple (also called Hard maple, Rock maple, Black maple)
NICKNAMES: The Green Mountain State
STATE MOTTO: Freedom and Unity
STATE ANIMAL: Morgan horse
STATE COLD-WATER FISH: Brook trout
STATE WARM-WATER FISH: Walleye pike
STATE INSECT: Honeybee
STATE SOIL: Tunbridge soil series
STATE DRINK: Milk
STATE SONG: "Hail, Vermont!" words and music by Josephine Hovey Perry
STATE LANDMARKS: Calvin Coolidge Historic Site, Plymouth Notch; Chester Alan Arthur Historic Site, near Fairfield
NATIONAL PARK: Green Mountain National Forest
HISTORIC PARKS: Candle Mill Village, Arlington; Shelburne Museum, Shelburne—37 early American buildings and a side-wheeler steamship; Peter Matteson Tavern, Shaftsbury—200-year-old stagecoach tavern; Green Mountain Railroad, Bellows Falls—26-mile scenic train ride; Hyde log cabin, built in 1738, on Grand Isle
STATE FESTIVALS: Bay Day, St. Albans (July 4 weekend); Wurstfest, Stratton Mountain (Labor Day weekend); Vermont Maple Festival, Franklin County (April)

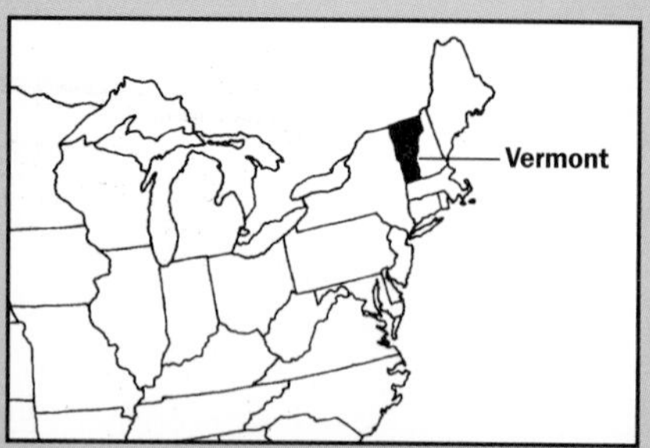

Nature-lovers have many reasons to enjoy Vermont. This rural state is famous for its brilliant fall foliage, its green mountains, its miles of ski trails, and its 400 lakes.

GREEN MOUNTAINS AND POETRY Vermont is the most sparsely populated state east of the Mississippi. Only 23 percent of its people live in cities. It's our most rural state, with the smallest state capital. Although Vermont is the only New England state with no seacoast, it is bounded by two major bodies of water—Lake Champlain and the Connecticut River.

The Green Mountains—part of the Appalachians—run down the state from Canada to Massachusetts. These mountains are among the oldest in the nation, nearly half a billion years old. A few hundred million years ago the tallest mountain, Mt. Mansfield, was 12,000 feet high. Now, thanks to erosion, it's only 4,393 feet.

Although Vermont's cities are small, they are rich in history and culture. Bennington, for example, is the home of Bennington College and was once the home of the abolitionist William Lloyd Garrison. Garrison published his famous newspaper, *The Liberator*, in Massachusetts, but he got his start in Vermont publishing *The Journal of the Time,* which you can see in the Bennington Museum.

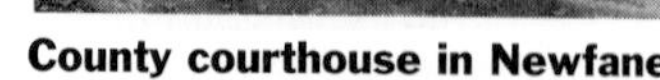
County courthouse in Newfane

Middlebury is the site of Middlebury College as well as the former home of poet laureate Robert Frost, who spent 23 summers at his farm in the area. Visitors can walk along the Robert Frost Wayside Trail, reading bits of Frost's nature poetry posted along the way. Vermont seems to attract famous writers. Russian Nobel Prize-winning novelist Alexander Solzhenitsyn settled there after emigrating from the Soviet Union in the 1970s. He returned to his native land only after the fall of Communism. Other well-known Vermont cities include Burlington, Rutland, Barre, and the famous ski resort of Stowe.

THE GREEN MOUNTAIN BOYS When French explorer Samuel de Champlain first set foot in Vermont in 1609, it was peopled by the Abenaki, Mohican, Pennacook, and Iroquois. Champlain claimed the land for France and named Lake Champlain after himself.

Over one hundred years later, British soldiers established the first permanent

European settlement at Fort Drummer (now Brattleboro). Despite attacks from the French and the Indians, the English retained control of the territory. However, two American colonies both claimed Vermont's land. In 1741 England's King George II granted the land to New Hampshire, but in 1764 King George III granted much the same land to New York. In 1770 Vermonter Ethan Allen founded the Green Mountain Boys to chase New York settlers away. In May 1775 he and his "boys" won further fame by taking Fort Ticonderoga from the British during the Revolutionary War.

Poultney Historical Society

When the 13 colonies signed the Declaration of Independence in 1776, Vermont was not among them because neither New York nor New Hampshire considered it a separate colony. In 1777, however, Vermont declared its own independence from the British as a separate nation called New Connecticut. Finally, in 1790, the competing land claims were resolved. In 1791 Vermont became the first state *after* the original 13 colonies to join the Union.

A DEMOCRATIC TRADITION From the beginning, Vermont stood for democracy and equal rights for all. In 1777 its "national" constitution declared that slavery was illegal—the first North American government to do so. Moreover, Vermont was the first government to call for "universal suffrage"—voting rights for all. (Up to this time, states would only permit property owners to vote.) Of course, "universal" suffrage did not include voting rights for Indians, African Americans, or women, but the measure was quite radical for its time.

18th century round barn in Irasburg

The basic unit of Vermont government is the town meeting. When an important issue comes up, all the townspeople assemble at town hall, discuss the issue, and come to a decision together. The New England town meeting is a democratic ideal that has inspired people around the world.

MARBLE AND MAPLE SYRUP Although Vermont's soil is poor, farming is more important here than in other New England states. Dairy farms and apple orchards are most suitable for the state's hilly land. Of course, Vermont's most famous agricultural product is maple syrup.

Vermont's lush forests cover 70 percent of the state, providing lumber and supporting wood-processing and paper industries as well. Vermont's quarries have made it a leader in granite, marble, slate, talc, and asbestos. (You can see Vermont granite in the United Nations building in New York.) The state has many factories near its small cities, making tools, machinery, electronic equipment, measuring instruments, stuffed toys, and quilts. Rutland and St. Johnsbury make scales, while Brattleboro is famous for making organ pipes.

Fascinating Facts

HOW VERMONT GOT ITS NAME: In 1647 Samuel de Champlain named the region *Verd Mont*, or "Green Mountain." *Verd* is the old spelling of the French word for green.) The name took its present form in 1777, when the area was an independent nation, New Connecticut. Vermont became the official name in 1790.

DID YOU KNOW THAT: The people of Vermont were so enraged at the Nazis that in 1941 they declared war on Germany—two months before the United States did!

PRESIDENTS BORN IN VERMONT:
- Chester Alan Arthur (1829-1886), 21st President
- Calvin Coolidge (1872-1933), 30th President

VERMONT HAS THE WORLD'S LARGEST:
- granite quarry, near Barre

VERMONT HAD THE NATION'S FIRST:
- marble quarry—Manchester—1785
- canal—Bellows Falls—1802
- ski tow—Woodstock—1933
- patent issued in the United States

VERMONT IS TOPS IN:
- maple syrup

VERMONT HAS THE ONLY:
- breed of horse produced in the U.S., the Morgan horse, developed in the late 1700s by schoolteacher Justin Morgan

DID YOU KNOW THAT... British author Rudyard Kipling wrote *The Jungle Book* and *Captains Courageous* in Brattleboro, where he lived for four years.

DID YOU KNOW THAT... At the Haskell Opera House at Derby Line, the audience sits in the U.S. but the singers are in Canada. Once, a U.S. police officer had to sit in the audience and watch a wanted criminal perform on stage.

IT USED TO BE ILLEGAL IN VERMONT:
- to paint a horse

Virginia

Mt. Vernon, home of George Washington

10th state to enter the Union, June 25, 1788

The Basics

POPULATION: 6,675,451
12th most populous state
AREA: 42,777 square miles
35th largest state
STATE CAPITAL: Richmond
STATE BIRD: Cardinal (also called Red bird, Kentucky cardinal)
STATE FLOWER: Dogwood flower
STATE TREE: Dogwood (also called Flowering dogwood, Boxwood, False box-dogwood and New England boxwood.
NICKNAMES: The Old Dominion, the Mother of Presidents, the Mother of States, the Mother of Statesmen, the Cavalier State
STATE MOTTO: *Sic semper tyrannis* (Latin for "Thus always to tyrants")
STATE DOG: American foxhound
STATE SHELL: Oyster shell
STATE DRINK: Milk
STATE SONG EMERITUS: "Carry Me Back to Old Virginia," words and music by James B. Bland
STATE LANDMARKS: Monticello, home of Thomas Jefferson; Mount Vernon, home of George Washington; Yorktown, where the English surrendered to George Washington; Robert E. Lee's birthplace, Stratford Hall, near Montross, and his grave at Lexington; Arlington National Cemetery
HISTORIC SITES: Jamestown, replicas of 1607 fort and ships; Williamsburg, replica of 200-year-old colonial village
NATIONAL PARK: Shenandoah
STATE FESTIVALS: Chili Cookoff, Roanoke (May); Pony Penning, Chincoteague (July); Pork, Peanut and Pine Festival, Surry (July); Virginia Poultry Festival, Harrisonburg (May)

If you had to pick just one state whose history was intertwined with the early history of the United States, that state would be Virginia. Four of the first five American presidents were born in Virginia. The decisive battle of the Revolutionary War was fought at Yorktown. The ending of the Civil War—Confederate General Robert E. Lee's surrender to Union commander Ulysses S. Grant—took place in the Virginia town of Appomattox. To tour Virginia is to take a tour of our nation's history.

FROM TIDEWATER TO THE APPALACHIANS This rural mid-Atlantic state can be divided into three sections. Its eastern Atlantic coast is a low-lying area where several rivers—the Potomac, Rappahannock, York, and James—empty into the Chesapeake Bay. This Tidewater region was once covered by ocean. Farther west, the central Piedmont region is a fertile land of rolling hills. And still farther west are the Appalachian mountains, the Blue Ridge Range, and the Shenandoah Valley.

1791 lighthouse at Cape Henry

In Tidewater is the so-called Historic Triangle: Williamsburg, Jamestown, and Yorktown. All year long at Williamsburg, costumed interpreters and craftspeople re-create a colonial village, down to the authentic taverns serving foods of the times. Near Jamestown, the first permanent English settlement, you can see another living history re-creation, and in the harbor you can see replicas of the ships that first brought the colonists to America: the *Godspeed, Discovery,* and *Susan Constant.* At the Yorktown Victory Center you can see a re-created Continental Army encampment and a working tobacco farm.

In northern Virginia is the most visited house museum in the nation: Mount Vernon, the home of George Washington. In the Piedmont region is Monticello, Thomas Jefferson's estate, full of such Jeffersonian inventions as a two-pen contraption for copying letters as he wrote them. Just outside Washington, D.C. is the Arlington National Cemetery, final resting place of thousands of American soldiers. It is also the site of the Tomb of the Unknown Soldier and the eternal flame lit in memory of President John F. Kennedy.

POCAHONTAS AND JOHN SMITH Sir Walter Raleigh was the first European to colonize Virginia—which he named after his sovereign, Elizabeth, known as the "Virgin Queen." In 1607 the first English colonists established themselves at Jamestown, but they faced hard times in this unknown land. Pocahontas, daughter of the Indian emperor Powhatan, was only ten when the English arrived. She taught them how to grow tobacco, corn, and peanuts and helped to save the life of their leader, John Smith. Later she married another settler, John Rolfe, and went to England with him.

Tomb of the Unknown Soldier in Arlington Cemetery

TWO TRADITIONS Virginia is a land of both democratic and aristocratic traditions. In 1619, for example, Virginians formed the House of Burgesses, the first democratically elected legislature in the world. Yet in the same year, people in this southern state began to own slaves.

Throughout the Revolutionary years Virginia was a leader in the fight for independence. It was at the Virginia Convention of 1775 that Virginia politician Patrick Henry cried "Give me liberty, or give me death!" Virginia's Thomas Jefferson wrote the Declaration of Independence; the state's James Madison wrote the Constitution. Virginia's own bill of rights was the model for the national document. And of course, Virginia's George Washington first led American armies to victory and then became the nation's first president.

In 1861 Virginia became a leader of another nation: the Confederacy. Richmond was the Confederacy's final capital, while native son Robert E. Lee was the Confederacy's commander in chief.

African Americans in Virginia also followed two traditions: rebellion and compromise. Nat Turner, a Virginia slave, led an 1831 uprising in Southampton County that lasted for three days. While he and his 60 followers failed to end slavery, they did shatter the myth that slaves were happy with their lot. Another famous Virginian, Booker T. Washington, had a very different approach to improving the lives of African Americans. Washington was born into slavery on a tobacco farm near Roanoke. In the years after the Civil War he rose to become one of the most influential black politicians this country has ever known. Washington believed that African Americans should improve themselves by working as skilled laborers. That way, they could gradually acquire the money and respectability that would win them acceptance into American society. Washington's ideas were controversial among both black and white people of his time. A living history museum now marks his birthplace.

Robert E. Lee at age 33

SHIPYARDS AND DAIRY FARMS Manufacturing is a key part of Virginia's economy, mainly shipbuilding, although the state also produces paper, clothing, chemicals, light machinery, and processed stone. Dairy products, chickens, turkeys, and hogs are also important, as are tobacco, wheat, orchard fruits, peanuts, and fish from the Chesapeake Bay. Suburbs of Washington, D.C., are Virginia's most populated area, and a great deal of income comes into the state from people employed in our nation's capital.

Fascinating Facts

PRESIDENTS BORN IN VIRGINIA:

- George Washington (1732-1799), 1st President
- Thomas Jefferson (1743-1826), 3rd President
- James Madison (1751-1836), 4th President
- James Monroe (1758-1831), 5th President
- William Henry Harrison (1773-1841), 9th President
- John Tyler (1790-1850), 10th President
- Zachary Taylor (1784-1850), 12th President
- Woodrow Wilson (1856-1924), 28th President

OTHER FAMOUS PEOPLE BORN IN VIRGINIA:

- Explorer Meriwether Lewis, Albemarle County (1774-1809)
- Writer Willa Cather, Winchester (1873-1947)

VIRGINIA HAS THE WORLD'S LARGEST:

- naval station—Norfolk Naval Station
- Naval Air Station

VIRGINIA HAD THE NATION'S FIRST:

- manufacturing—a glass factory—1608
- democratically elected legislature—the House of Burgesses—1619
- canal—7 miles between Richmond and Westham—1790
- reaper—1831

VIRGINIA HAS THE NATION'S OLDEST CONTINUOUS:

- daily newspaper—the Alexandria *Gazette*
- sporting event—the annual jousting tournament near Staunton

DID YOU KNOW THAT...

All or part of Illinois, Indiana, Kentucky, Michigan, Minnesota, Ohio, West Virginia, and Wisconsin were once carved out of the original Virginia colony....Before the Revolutionary war, in Virginia you could pay your taxes in tobacco!

IT USED TO BE ILLEGAL IN VIRGINIA:

- to have a bathtub in the house

Washington

The Basics

POPULATION: 5,532,939
15th most populous state
AREA: 71,302 square miles
18th largest state
STATE CAPITAL: Olympia
STATE BIRD: Willow goldfinch
STATE FLOWER: Pink rhododendron (Coast rhododendron, Rhododendron)
STATE TREE: Western hemlock (West coast hemlock, Pacific hemlock, Hemlock spruce, California hemlock spruce, Western hemlock fir, Prince Albert's fir, Alaskan pine)
NICKNAMES: The Evergreen State, the Chinook State
STATE MOTTO: *Alki* (an Indian word for "By and by")
SPORTS TEAMS: Seattle Mariners, baseball; Seattle Seahawks, football; Seattle SuperSonics, basketball
STATE FISH: Steelhead trout
STATE GEM: Petrified wood
STATE DANCE: Square dance
STATE SONG: "Washington, My Home," words and music by Helen Davis
STATE LANDMARKS: Gingko Petrified Forest, near Ephrata; Grand Coulee Dam
NATIONAL PARKS: Mount Rainier, near Enumclaw; North Cascades, near Bellingham; Olympic, near Port Angeles; Columbia River National Scenic Area; Dungeness National Wildlife Refuge
HISTORIC PARKS: Fort Vancouver National Historic Site—1825 fur trading post; Klondike Gold Rush National Historical Park/Pioneer Park, Seattle
STATE PARK: Leadbetter Point State Park, Ilwaco has over 100 species of birds.

Mt. Rainier National Park

42nd state to enter the Union, November 11, 1889

Washington residents are particularly proud of their state's beauty: its rugged Alpine scenery, its glistening evergreen forests, and its sparkling lakes and rivers. Its largest city, Seattle, used to be a simple port town. However, in recent years it has become a sophisticated coastal city, particularly well-known for its elaborate coffee drinks. Its first gourmet coffee shop, Starbucks, opened in 1981. The 607-foot-high Space Needle has been a symbol of the city since it was constructed for the 1962 World's Fair.

WASHINGTON'S SPLIT PERSONALITY The Cascade Mountains run north to south, from Canada to Oregon, splitting Washington into two parts. West of the Cascades are coastal lowlands and evergreen forests. Northwest is the Olympic Peninsula, marked by the Olympic Mountains and the climate of a temperate rain forest. Further south is Puget Sound, the most populous part of the state and site of Washington's three principal cities: Seattle, Tacoma, and Olympia.

State Capitol at Olympia

Western Washington is quite damp with ocean moisture. But the Cascades trap the moisture in their high peaks. So east of the Cascades is a semi-desert region in which you can't see a tree for miles.

Washington is a favorite state of those who like to hunt, fish, and ski. The Columbia and Snake Rivers offer more than 40 types of fish. The Olympic Peninsula features the Hoh Rain Forest, the Sol Duc Hot Springs, and the spectacular views from Hurricane Ridge, a mile above sea level. An even more isolated spot is Long Beach Peninsula, where the Columbia River and the Pacific Ocean meet. Nearby is Oysterville, a town that prospered in 1854 when the shellfish abounded. Now the oysters have been fished to extinction and most townspeople have moved away, leaving their homes to be washed away by the tides. A small village still remains, though.

LOOKING FOR BOUNDARIES The borders of the Washington Territory changed several times between the first European explorers of the 1770s and Washington's entry into the Union in 1889. Both British explorer Captain George Vancouver and U.S. Captain Robert Gray tried to claim the land in 1792—while Cayuse, Colville, Nez Percé, Okanogan, Spokane, Yakima, Chinook, and Puyallup peoples were still living there.

Settlement was slow, as settlers feared attack by local native peoples. When gold was discovered in 1855, attempts were made to resettle Washington's western Indians but they bitterly resisted. Finally, in 1858 a confederacy of Yakima, Spokane, Coeur d'Alene, Nez Percé, and Palouse was defeated by federal troops and local militia. Washington's Indians were forced onto reservations.

Seattle skyline

Meanwhile, in 1848 the Oregon Territory had been formed, including Oregon, Washington, and parts of Idaho. In 1853 the Washington Territory was formed, leaving out Oregon but including parts of Idaho and Montana, and expanding in 1859 to Wyoming as well. This territory was to have been named the Territory of Columbia, after the river. But the U.S. already had a District of Columbia, so the name Washington was chosen, to honor the nation's first president. Finally, in 1863 Idaho Territory was formed, and Washington got its present boundaries.

GEORGE WASHINGTON AND GEORGE BUSH No, those names don't refer to two presidents. The George Washington Park in Centralia honors a former slave who escaped from Virginia, resisted the racial restrictions of slave-holding Missouri, and joined a wagon train on the Oregon Trail in 1850. Washington thrived in the lumber business and founded the town of Centerville, now called Centralia. When he died in 1905 the town shut down for a day of mourning.

Ferry on Puget Sound

George Bush was born free but he, too, resented Missouri's racial restrictions. He came to the Oregon Territory in 1844—only to discover that African Americans were not allowed to own property there. He was so disgusted that he crossed into Washington, where he prospered as a farmer near Tumwater. Exhibits in the Henderson House Museum tell his story.

RICH RESOURCES Washington is blessed with abundant natural resources. But it has been a logging state for so many years now that environmentalists worry that the forests will become exhausted. Logging companies argue that if they cut down fewer trees, the economy will suffer. The argument continues—and so does the extensive logging.

Salmon, halibut, and other ocean fish are an important Washington resource. Seattle is one of the largest salmon markets in the world, selling fish from both Washington and Alaska. Farms in western Washington raise beef and dairy cattle, wheat, fruit, and vegetables.

Seattle's aircraft industry, particularly Boeing, has had financial challenges in recent years but a merger with Rockwell International bodes well for the area. And Microsoft, the computer software giant, has created many jobs in the state.

Fascinating Facts

HOW WASHINGTON GOT ITS MOTTO:
When settlers landed at Alki Point—now Seattle—they called it "New York Alki." That meant that *Alki*—"by and by"—they hoped their town would someday be the New York of the West Coast.

WASHINGTON IS TOPS IN:
- apple production—world leader
- hops, rhubarb, edible peas, cherries
- vegetable seeds

WASHINGTON HAD THE FIRST:
- female symphony conductor in America, possibly in the world—Mary Davenport Engberg, who conducted the 85-member symphony orchestra in Bellingham in 1914
- Native American woman novelist, Mourning Dove, an Okanogan who wrote *Cogewea, the Half Breed* and *Coyote Stories*

THE SNOWIEST TOWN IN THE U.S.:
- Stampede Pass—431.9 inches/year

THE CLOUDIEST TOWN IN THE U.S.:
- Quillayute—241 cloudy days a year

DID YOU KNOW THAT... La Push is the westernmost town in the continental U.S. and Cape Alava the westernmost point.

HYDROELECTRIC FACTS:
- Washington furnishes 30 percent of our hydroelectric power.
- The Grand Coulee is the nation's largest concrete dam, completed in 1942.
- It has enough concrete to pave a four-lane highway from Seattle to New York.

THE LARGEST ORGANISM is a 1,500-acre fungus growing south of Mt. Adams.

IT USED TO BE ILLEGAL IN WASHINGTON:
- to hunt ducks from a rowboat unless you were sitting up and visible from the waist up

West Virginia

Coal miners are important to the state's economy

35th state to enter the Union, June 20, 1863

The Basics

POPULATION: 1,825,754
35th most populous state
AREA: 24,231 square miles
41st largest state
STATE CAPITAL: Charleston
STATE BIRD: Cardinal (Red bird, Kentucky cardinal)
STATE FLOWER: Big rhododendron
STATE TREE: Sugar maple (Hard maple, Rock maple, Black maple)
NICKNAMES: The Mountain State, the Switzerland of America, the Panhandle State
STATE MOTTO: *Montani Semper Liberi* (Latin for "Mountaineers are always free")
STATE ANIMAL: Black bear
STATE FISH: Brook trout
STATE FRUIT: Apple
STATE SONGS: "This Is My West Virginia," words and music by Iris Bell; "West Virginia, My Home Sweet Home," words and music by Julian G. Hearne; "The West Virginia Hills," words by David King, music by H.E. Engle
STATE LANDMARK: Harpers Ferry National Historical Park
NATIONAL PARK: Monongahela National Forest
HISTORIC PARKS: Beckley Exhibition Mine—with 1890s coal-car ride through mine; Cass Scenic Railroad—with old logging train ride to mountaintop; Watters Smith Memorial Park, near Clarksburg—200-year-old pioneer farm; West Virginia State Farm Museum, Point Pleasant
STATE FESTIVALS: Apple Butter Festival, Berkeley Springs (Columbus Day weekend); Webster Springs Wood-chopping Festival, Webster Springs (May)

West Virginia has given the nation two famous folk songs. "John Brown's Body" (whose tune was later used in "The Battle Hymn of the Republic") tells of the abolitionist who seized the arsenal at Harpers Ferry. "John Henry" describes the legendary railroad worker who died drilling a tunnel through a West Virginia mountain. Rugged individualism, mountainous terrain, and folk music still shape this historic state.

PANHANDLES AND PLATEAUS West Virginia has the most irregular boundaries of any state in the Union. That's because it was created from another state—Virginia—without that state's consent. As a result, and also to resolve old boundary disputes, West Virginia has two panhandles, extending north and east. Most of the state is mountain country, dominated by the Appalachians. The Allegheny Plateau occupies the western two-thirds of the state, with the Appalachian Valley as the eastern third.

Most of West Virginia is too rocky for farming. The only level ground is bound in the valleys of the Ohio and Kanawha Rivers. So this rural state is highly industrial, relying on manufacturing and mining. Yet West Virginia has lovely unspoiled scenery, including 200 natural springs. One of them, Berkeley Springs, was George Washington's favorite vacation spot.

GRAVE CREEK MOUND: A LOST CIVILIZATION The world's tallest burial mound is in West Virginia—the Grave Creek Mound on the bank of the Ohio River. The earthen mound is about 62 feet high and 240 feet in diameter. It was built by the Adena people over a hundred-year period, from 200 to 100 B.C. Originally the mound was surrounded by a moat some 910 feet long, 4 feet deep, and 40 feet wide. The earth taken from the moat was used to build the mound. Although the Adena people had neither wheels nor horses, they managed the amazing engineering feat of using three million basketloads of earth to build a one-million-cubic-foot structure.

The Greenbriar Hotel

JOHN BROWN'S INSURRECTION John Brown was a white man who believed that black and white people were equal, and he hated slavery with a passion. By 1859 he was tired of trying to abolish slavery by legal means. He wanted to set off a revolt in which African-American slaves would rise up and end slavery by force. So on October 16, 1859, Brown and his team of 21 men—including five African Americans—seized the armory (weapons storehouse) at Harpers Ferry. Federal troops quickly moved to West Virginia (then still a part of Virginia) to put down the uprising. Instead of sparking a nationwide rebellion, Brown lost two of his sons and was later executed himself. Some abolitionists supported him. Others, like Frederick Douglass, were opposed. Slavery finally came to an end during the Civil War, with the Emancipation Proclamation of 1863.

Today you can visit the Harpers Ferry National Historic Park, where costumed guides demonstrate Colonial skills on the city's old cobblestone streets. The John Brown Wax Museum depicts the famous raid.

A DOUBLE SECESSION Until 1861 West Virginia was part of Virginia. But east and west had always been distinct cultures. East Virginia was an aristocratic agricultural region that depended on slavery to farm its large plantations. West Virginia was mountain country, occupied by workers who mined salt, cut timber, dug for coal—and opposed slavery. When Virginia wanted to secede from the Union in 1861, legislators from the west voted against it. So the west seceded from Virginia, called itself Kanawha, and asked to be readmitted to the Union. The first Union soldier killed in the Civil War was Baily Thornsberry Brown, of the 2nd West Virginia Volunteers. Some 36,530 West Virginians fought for the Union—although another 7,000 became Confederate soldiers. West Virginia was hotly contested territory during the War Between the States. One town, Romney, actually changed hands 56 times!

The arsenal at Harpers Ferry was built in 1740.

COAL COUNTRY More than half of West Virginia rests on rich seams of bituminous (soft) coal, and the state's economic history is full of stories of mine explosions, union battles, and, finally, mine closings. Of all the states, West Virginia lost the highest percentage of its population between 1980 and 1990. In 1985 it had the highest unemployment rate in the nation—showing how the once prosperous mines had declined.

Coal is still important to West Virginia's economy, as are natural gas, salt, clay, sand, and gravel. The manufacture of chemicals, rubber, metals, ceramics, glass, food products, and machinery are key elements as well. Although the Shenandoah Valley is an important apple-producing area, agriculture is far less important in this industrial state.

Fascinating Facts

DID YOU KNOW THAT... The West Virginia northern panhandle is so narrow that the city of Weirton stretches from border to border—one city is the width of the whole state!

WEST VIRGINIA CURIOSITIES:

- The "bug factory" of entomologist (insect scientist) Romeo D. Erdie, where millions of model insects are made. The bugs are used for everything from exterminator ads to fine jewelry.

WEST VIRGINIA IS TOPS IN:

- overseas shipment of coal
- mining of bituminous coal and metallurgical coke

DID YOU KNOW THAT... Shepherdstown was on George Washington's list for the choice of a national capital.

THE FIRST WOMAN JOURNALIST... To interview a president was Ann Royall. She stole John Quincy Adams' clothes while he was swimming and wouldn't return them until he agreed to talk to her.

WEST VIRGINIA ELEVATION FACTS:

- In terms of average height of land above sea level, West Virginia is the "highest" state east of the Rockies.
- Bluefield, 2,558 feet above sea level, is the highest city east of Denver.

HOW WEST VIRGINIA GOT ITS CAPITAL: Reportedly, when voters were being asked to choose between Charleston and Wheeling, the former capital, a touring circus stopped at Charleston. Voters from across the state went to see the circus—and to vote for Charleston!

WEST VIRGINIA HAD THE NATION'S FIRST...

- Mother's Day celebration—May 10, 1908—Andrews Methodist Church, Grafton
- sales tax—July 1, 1921

IT USED TO BE ILLEGAL IN WEST VIRGINIA:

- to sneeze on a train

Wisconsin

Super Bowl Champion Green Bay Packers

30th state to enter the Union, May 29, 1848

The Basics

POPULATION: 5,159,795
18th most populous state
AREA: 65,499 square miles
23rd largest state
STATE CAPITAL: Madison
STATE BIRD: Robin (American robin)
STATE FLOWER: Wood violet
STATE TREE: Sugar maple (also called Hard maple, Rock maple, Black maple)
NICKNAMES: The Badger State, the Copper State
STATE MOTTO: Forward
SPORTS TEAMS: Milwaukee Brewers, baseball; Green Bay Packers, football; Milwaukee Bucks, basketball
STATE ANIMAL: Badger
STATE DOMESTIC ANIMAL: Dairy cow
STATE WILDLIFE ANIMAL: White-tailed deer
STATE FISH: Musekellunge or Muskie
STATE INSECT: Honeybee
STATE MINERAL: Galena
STATE ROCK: Red granite
STATE SOIL: Antigo silt loam
STATE SONG: "On, Wisconsin," words and music by William T. Purdy
STATE LANDMARKS: Wisconsin Dells—rocks cut into strange shapes by the Wisconsin River.
STATE HISTORIC SITES: Cave of the Mounds, near Blue Mounds; Circus World Museum, Baraboo—where the Ringling Brothers began; Stonefield Village, near Cassville—1890s crossroad village; Galloway House and Village, Fond du Lac; Historical Society Log Village and Museum, Reedsburg; Historyland, Hayward; Old Falls Village, Menominee Falls;
STATE PARK: Heritage Hill, Green Bay

Ice fishing on a frozen, northern lake...Dairy cattle grazing in a lush green pasture...Families riding the Wisconsin Ducks down the peaceful river at Wisconsin Dells... Hunters stalking deer in the deep north woods...Beer being bottled at the giant Milwaukee breweries....These are just some images of Wisconsin, in the heart of the Midwest.

GLACIER COUNTRY Wisconsin is almost completely surrounded by water: Lake Michigan to the east; the Menominee River to the northeast; Lake Superior to the north; and the St. Croix and Mississippi Rivers to the west. There's a lot of water in Wisconsin, too: 10,000 smaller rivers and streams, and over 8,500 lakes. You can boat and fish on ice in the winter, or just boat and fish on water in the summer.

Ojibwa perform a traditional dance.

You can still see the traces left by glaciers in Wisconsin millions of years ago. The northern part of the state has a granite bed and tends to be flat, forested land—glaciers flattened it as they slid southwards. The southeastern part of the state, on the other hand, features rolling hills and choppy ridges. That's where the glacier tore up the land.

Wisconsin is primarily a rural state, but its major cities—Milwaukee, Madison, Green Bay, and Racine—are modern urban areas. They tend to combine a modern, glass-and-steel downtown area with neighborhoods of gracious nineteenth-century homes. Milwaukee is known for its many breweries, and for its summer of festivals by the lake. Madison is the state capital and is home to the University of Wisconsin.

WORLD LEADER FROM WISCONSIN One of Wisconsin's most famous residents was Golda Meir, whose family emigrated to Milwaukee from Kiev in the Russian Empire when she was only eight years old. Meir became a socialist and a Zionist—someone who believed in establishing a Jewish nation. From 1969 to 1974 she served as the prime minister of the Jewish state of Israel—a job she began at the age of seventy! The Milwaukee school she attended was renamed the Golda Meir School in her honor. On a 1969 visit, she told students, "It was here I first experienced a lack of prejudice."

HOMELAND Wisconsin got its name from the Chippewa word for the Wisconsin River, spelled Ouisconsin or Mesconsing in early reports. The word may be translated as grassy place, gathering of the waters, wild rice country, or homeland. Before the Europeans came, Wisconsin was home to many native peoples, including the Winnebago, Dakota, and Menominee. French explorers and fur traders first came to Wisconsin in the early 1600s. In the late 1600s new Indian peoples came to the state: Chippewa, Sac, Fox, Ottawa, Kickapoo, Miami, Illinois, and Potawatomie. For a while they lived peacefully with the Europeans, but during the French and Indian Wars there were conflicts.

One of 50 restored buildings on 576 acres in the Southern Kettle Moraine State Forest

In 1832 Chief Black Hawk fled Illinois and came to Wisconsin at the end of the Black Hawk War. At the Battle of Bad Axe, Black Hawk's people were defeated, and they were massacred as they tried to escape across the Mississippi. As in other states, Indians were gradually either driven out of Wisconsin or relocated onto reservations.

IMMIGRANTS AND PROGRESSIVES After Wisconsin became a state in 1848, many immigrants came to farm its fertile fields and pastures. Throughout the state you can find historical parks commemorating these early residents. In Southern Kettle Moraine State Forest, farm and village buildings have been gathered from across the state and restored to show German, Norwegian, Danish, and Finnish settlements. Near Madison you can visit Little Norway, as well as the Swiss Historical Village in New Glarus. This international heritage still shapes the state's culture today.

Hamlin Garland wrote about rural Wisconsin in the 19th century.

Another strong Wisconsin heritage is that of Governor Robert La Follette, part of the Progressive movement to take power away from big business and run government honestly. After La Follette's term, Wisconsin became a leader in social programs to help workers and their families, providing the first workers' compensation and pensions (1911); teachers' pensions (1911); mothers' pensions (1913); minimum wage (1913); old age pensions (1931); and unemployment insurance (1932).

CHEESE AND TREES Wisconsin is the leading dairy state, providing 40 percent of the nation's cheese and 20 percent of our butter. However, manufacturing is actually a bigger part of the state's economy. Wisconsin's forests cover almost half the state, providing the resources for the state paper industry. Factories near Lake Michigan also make tractors, auto engines, hardware, furniture, and beer.

Fascinating Facts

DID YOU KNOW THAT...
When French explorer Jean Nicolet sailed into Lake Michigan in 1634, he believed he'd found China—so he came ashore in Chinese robes on the banks of Green Bay.

WISCONSIN HAD THE NATION'S FIRST:
- kindergarten—organized by Margarethe Schurz, Watertown—1856
- typewriter—invented by Christopher Sholes, Milwaukee, 1868
- hydroelectric plant—Appleton—1882
- state income tax—1911
- statewide bicycle trail

WISCONSIN IS TOPS IN:
- milk, cheese, butter
- paper
- mink
- beer

DID YOU KNOW THAT... The Ringling Brothers' first show—even before they had their famous circus—was given in Wisconsin in 1882.

WISCONSIN HALL OF FAME:
- Green Bay Packers Hall of Fame, Green Bay

FAMOUS PEOPLE BORN IN WISCONSIN:
- Author Laura Ingalls Wilder, Lake Pepin (1867-1957)
- Architect Frank Lloyd Wright, Richland Center (1867-1959)
- Artist Georgia O'Keeffe, Sun Prairie (1887-1986)
- Author Thornton Wilder, Madison (1897-1975)
- Actor Spencer Tracy, Milwaukee (1900-1967)

DID YOU KNOW THAT: Pioneer Wisconsin had so few people that Justice of the Peace Pat Kelly sometimes had to use trees as witnesses.

THINGS THAT USED TO BE ILLEGAL IN WISCONSIN:
- to sell artificially colored margarine
- to sell a meal costing 25 cents or more without including a small piece of cheese

Wyoming

Grand Tetons National Park

44th state to enter the Union, July 10, 1890

The Basics

POPULATION: 481,400
least populous state
AREA: 97,818 square miles
10th largest state
STATE CAPITAL: Cheyenne
STATE BIRD: Western meadowlark
STATE FLOWER: Indian paintbrush
STATE TREE: Plains cottonwood (also called the Cottonwood, Plains poplar)
NICKNAMES: The Equality State, Big Wyoming, the Cowboy State
STATE MOTTO: Equal Rights
STATE GEM: Jade
STATE SONG: "Wyoming," words by Charles E. Winter, music by George E. Knapp
STATE LANDMARK: Hell's Half Acre, central Wyoming,—320-acre depression filled with pits and caverns
HISTORIC SITES: Fort Laramie National Historic Site—a fort that helped win the West, still with 21 buildings; Fort Bridger—key stop on the Oregon Trail; Riverton Museum, Riverton; South Pass City, Lander—a gold camp near the Oregon trail; Wyoming Territorial Prison Park, Laramie—where outlaw Butch Cassidy once was in jail
HISTORICAL MUSEUMS: Buffalo Bill Historical Center, Cody; Plains Indian Museum, Cody; Winchester Museum, Cody; Wyoming Pioneer Museum, Douglas
NATIONAL PARKS: Grand Teton, near Jackson; Yellowstone, near Cody
STATE FESTIVAL: Frontier Days, Cheyenne—a rodeo that has been held each July since 1897; prizes are awarded for roping, bronco-riding, and *bulldogging* (throwing steers)

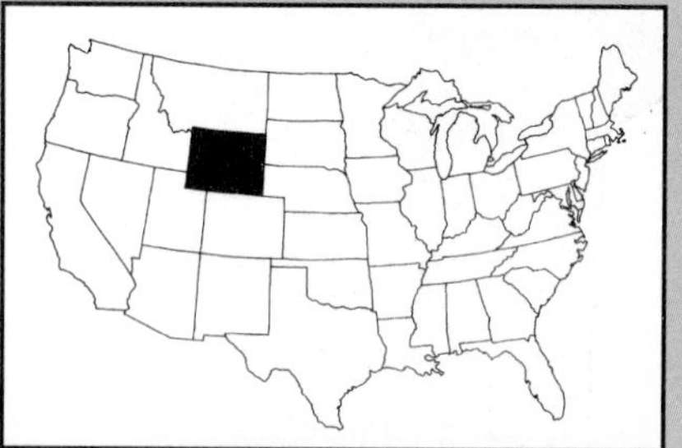

Wyoming is a land of fire and ice: from the hot springs of Yellowstone Park to the snowcapped Rockies. The western frontier of Wyoming is a solid wall of mountains, made up of more than a dozen ranges, including the Grand Tetons. Eastern Wyoming is part of the Great Plains: flat, rolling prairies marked by buttes (pronounced byoots), or towers of rock. This is an overwhelmingly rural state, whose principal cities—Casper, Cheyenne, and Laramie—have only about 50,000 people or less.

YELLOWSTONE FANTASIES When John Colter reported the first descriptions of what is now Yellowstone Park in a St. Louis newspaper in 1810, readers thought he was telling tall tales. How else to explain his fantastic stories of fuming mud pots, geysers, and waterfalls? We now know that Yellowstone's hot spots are caused by molten rock collected near the earth's surface, which heats snow and rainwater to boiling.

Old Faithful is heated by molten rock beneath the earth's crust.

Yellowstone National Park still offers many fascinating sights. The Grand Canyon of the Yellowstone is 24 miles long and 1,200 feet deep, its red and ochre stone a brilliant contrast to the emerald forest above. True to its name, the geyser called Old Faithful erupts about once an hour, while the Steamboat Geyser shoots water 300 feet into the air. Elk, bison, and other wildlife roam the park, to visitors' delight.

COWBOYS AND CATTLE WARS Wyoming is the only state to be formed out of the four principal U.S annexations: the Louisiana Purchase in 1803, the annexation of Texas in 1845, the cession of Oregon by the British in 1846, and the land taken at the end of the Mexican War in 1848. Before U.S. possession, Wyoming belonged to the Arapaho, Cheyenne, and Shoshone.

In the 1850s Wyoming was a place that settlers passed through to get to the California gold rush: more than 60,000 people crossed the state in 1850 alone. After the railroad was completed in 1869, however, ranchers, farmers, and coal miners began to come to the area. Wyoming was known for its Wild West rough-and-tumble cowboy atmosphere.

Wars with the Shoshone and Arapaho were finally settled by forcing them onto reservations in eastern Wyoming. Later the reservations were made smaller as more settlers came looking for land.

Like its neighbor Idaho, Wyoming depended on Chinese immigrants to work its mines, and like Idaho, it had a violent, often bloody labor history. In 1885, for example, 85 Chinese coal miners were killed and hundreds more chased out of town near Rock Spring. Federal troops were brought in to restore order—and remained for 14 years.

Tower Falls in Yellowstone National Park

In 1892 another conflict shook the state: the Johnson County Cattle War. "Nesters"—big ranchers and farmers—hired gunmen to shoot "rustlers"—the small ranchers and homesteaders who they believed were stealing their cattle. From 1897 to 1901 the conflict was between sheep and cattle ranchers fighting over which animal would be allowed to graze Wyoming's plains. Some 16 men and 10,000 sheep were killed by the cattle owners before the sheep ranchers finally won: six million Wyoming sheep outnumbered cattle by 7 to 1, and Wyoming led the nation in wool production.

WYOMING WOMEN CLAIM THEIR RIGHTS Wyoming has certainly lived up to its motto of "Equal Rights" where women are concerned. In 1869 before it was even a state, it became the first U.S. location where women could vote. The first U.S. woman to hold public office was Wyoming Justice of the Peace Esther Hobart Morris, appointed in 1870. In that year U.S. women were first allowed to serve on juries, in Laramie. The world's first female forewoman of a jury was Louise Spinner Graf, chosen in 1950. The first U.S. woman elected to state office was State Superintendent of Public Instruction Estelle Reel. The first U.S. woman governor was Nellie Tayloe Ross, elected in 1924.

Wyoming women were often active in politics. In 1920 an all-woman ticket ran for Jackson city government, and won by 2 to 1 against an all-male ticket. In 1921 the women ran for re-election—and won by 3 to 1.

COAL, OIL, AND COWS Almost half Wyoming's land is owned by the U.S. government, which then leases it out for grazing, mining, and logging. More than 80 percent of state land is used for cattle. Wyoming also remains a national leader in producing sheep and wool.

Mining is the state's main business. Years ago, the Cheyenne dipped twigs in puddles of oil and lit them as torches. Now Wyoming produces a great deal of oil, natural gas, iron ore, and uranium. It has the nation's largest coal reserves and is second in coal production.

State Capitol at Cheyenne

Fascinating Facts

WYOMING HAD THE FIRST:

- national park—Yellowstone—1872
- national monument—Devils Tower—1906
- national forest—Shoshone
- dude ranch (ranch for tourists to visit)—Eaton Brothers, near Dayton
- "yellow pages"—Cheyenne—1883

DEVILS TOWER FACTS:

- a stone stump rising 865 feet above the Belle Fourche River
- featured in the movie *Close Encounters of the Third Kind*

HOW WYOMING GOT ITS NAME: The state was named for the Wyoming Valley in Pennsylvania, which in turn got its name from two words in the Delaware Indian language: *mecheweami-ing,* meaning "mountains and valleys alternating"; in Algonquin, it means "large prairie place."

DID YOU KNOW THAT... The Indian name for Bull Lake was "the lake that roars"—from the wind rubbing against the ice.

WYOMING HAS THE WORLD'S LARGEST:

- hot springs, at Hot Springs State Park, Thermopolis
- elk (wapiti) herd, at the Jackson Elk Refuge
- pronghorn antelope population—the state has about 10,000 more antelope than people!

DID YOU KNOW THAT... Medicine Wheel is a prehistoric stone construction about 2000 years old, in the shape of a huge wheel with 28 spokes. Scholars believe it may have been a kind of calendar.

DID YOU KNOW THAT... When telephone poles were first erected in Wyoming, buffalo used to use them for scratching posts. You might see as many as 30 buffalo waiting their turn for each pole.

IT USED TO BE ILLEGAL IN WYOMING:

- to take a picture of a rabbit from January through April—unless you had a license.

American Samoa

Samoan village

U.S. acquired the right to govern, 1899

The Basics

POPULATION: 55,223
AREA: 77 square miles
AREA OF TUTUILA AND AUNU'U: 53 square miles
AREA OF TA'U: 17 square miles
AREA OF OFU AND OLOSEGA: 5 square miles
AREA OF SWAINS ISLAND: Nearly 2 square miles
CAPITAL: Pago Pago, island of Tutuila
FLOWER: Paogo (Ula-fala)
PLANT: Ava
MOTTO: *Samoa Muamua le Atua* (Polynesian for "In Samoa, God is first")
SONG: "Amerika Samoa"
HIGHEST POINT: 3,160 feet—Lata Mountain
LOWEST POINT: Sea level

Samoan boys use Japanese fishing floats to store water.

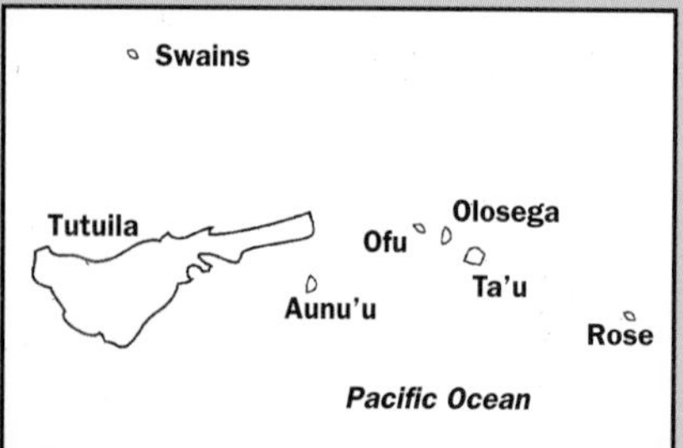

Picture a group of seven islands scattered across the Pacific, 2,300 miles southwest of Hawaii. This is American Samoa, the jewel of the South Pacific.

SEVEN ISLANDS Six of American Samoa's islands are part of the Samoan chain. They are divided among three groups: Tutuila and Aunu'u; Ofu, Olosega, and Ta'u (the Manu'a group); and Rose. The seventh island, Swains Island, is 200 miles north of the rest.

Swains Island is unusual in that it has been the property of the Jennings family ever since 1856, when the American Eli Jennings and his Samoan wife settled there.

This typical Polynesian hut is woven with leaves of palm.

The largest and most important of the American Samoan islands, however, is Tutuila. This is the island that includes Pago Pago, the territory's capital, with its beautiful harbor and port facilities. The novel *Rain* by Somerset Maugham was set in Pago Pago. There are no other cities in the territory.

Only about one-third of the total territory can be used for farmland. That's because the islands aren't made of earth and stone, like the United States continental mainland. Instead, Rose and Swains Islands are made of coral—the accumulation of centuries of reefs built up from the bottom of the sea. The other islands are the remains of extinct volcanoes, mountainous, with some fertile soil in the valleys or along the coast.

These tropical islands have a warm, wet climate. Temperatures are neither too hot nor too cold, ranging from 70 degrees to 90 degrees Fahrenheit. However, rainfall averages over 200 inches a year.

A POLYNESIAN PEOPLE Most of the people living in American Samoa are Polynesians, a South Pacific native people. Their primary language is Samoan, although most also speak English.

Because, years ago, Christian missionaries went to Samoa to convert people from their native religions to Christianity, most American Samoans are now Christian. But traditional culture is still very strong in Samoa. Most people still wear their traditional garment, the lavalava. They still hollow out tree trunks to make fautasi, longboats, sometimes as much as forty feet long, propelled by many oars. They still share their traditional dance, the siva, with the many tourists that come to the islands.

And most American Samoans still live in villages, with daily life focused around the family. Each family group—which might include aunts, uncles, and cousins—is headed by a family chief. The chief controls the entire family's property, is responsible for the sick and aged, and represents the family in the village council.

Gradually, however, traditional ways are being affected by modern life. In the 1960s the United States began an economic development program in the region, bringing factories and industrial development to Pago Pago. Many people left their villages to live in the city. Their thatch-roofed fale (houses) were torn down and hurricane-proof concrete buildings were put up instead. Children from ages 6 to 18 were required to attend school, where they might be taught by television. No one knows how these changes will finally affect traditional life.

Many American Samoan villages are built around lagoons.

AMERICANS AND GERMANS The first Polynesians probably came to Samoa some 2,000 years ago, migrating from eastern Melanesia. They were joined in 1722 by the Dutch explorer Jacob Roggeveen. Over the years the United States, Britain, and France all wanted to trade with the island, and to make use of its land and waters. Finally, in 1878, the United States put forth the strongest claim by establishing a naval station at Pago Pago. In 1899 the United States, Great Britain, and Germany agreed that the United States had the right to govern the islands that are now called American Samoa. From 1900 to 1951 American Samoa was governed by the U.S. Navy. From 1951 to the present it has been governed by the U.S. Department of the Interior, which until 1978 even appointed the island's governor. Now, however, Samoans elect their own governor. They also elect one member to the U.S. House of Representatives who is allowed to vote in committees but not on the House floor.

This Tiki god is carved of mahogany.

The face of this Polynesian War God is carved to resemble a wild, tusked boar.

COCOA AND CRAFTS The leading industry in Samoa is tuna canning. In fact, over 96 percent of exports are fish products. But Samoa is also known for its cocoa—considered the world's best. And Samoan crafts are world-famous. Samoans make tapa cloth by pounding the bark of paper mulberry trees. They weave baskets and laufala floor mats from palm leaves. Other exports include tropical products such as copra, breadfruit, yams, coconuts, bananas, oranges, and pineapples. And, of course, tourism is an important part of the islands' economy.

Fascinating Facts

DID YOU KNOW THAT... American Samoa is the most southerly region governed by the United States.

AMERICAN SAMOAN POLITICS:
- elect a governor, who holds the most governmental power
- two-house legislature: a Senate with 18 members chosen by county councils to serve two- to four-year terms; a House of Representatives with 20 members elected by the people to serve two-year terms
- voting age: 18

DID YOU KNOW THAT... Residents of American Samoa are U.S. nationals but not citizens. That means they may freely enter the United States, work there, and enjoy all the privileges of residency—but they may not vote, serve on a jury, or exercise any other citizen's right.

AMERICA IN SAMOA:
- 1899— agreement between Great Britain, Germany, and the U.S. to give the U.S. sovereignty over eastern Samoan islands
- 1900 — local chiefs ceded Tutuila and Aunu'u to the U.S.
- 1904—chiefs ceded Manu'a group and Rose.
- 1925—Swains Island was annexed.

DID YOU KNOW THAT... Only about 100 people live on Swains Island.

AMERICAN SAMOAN GEOGRAPHY:
- about 70 percent of the land is bush and mountains

DID YOU KNOW THAT... Western Samoa—the part that does not belong to American Samoa—includes the larger Samoan islands. It used to be under New Zealand's rule and a United Nations Trusteeship until it won its independence on January 1, 1962.

WHERE DO SAMOANS LIVE?
- 55,223 live in Samoa
- 20,000 live in Hawaii
- 65,000 live in California and Washington

Guam

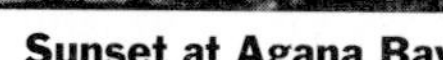

Sunset at Agana Bay

Ceded to the United States in 1898

The Basics

POPULATION: 133,152
AREA: 209 square miles
CAPITAL: Agana
BIRD: Toto (fruit dove)
FLOWER: Puti Tai nobio (Bougainvillea)
TREE: Ifit (Intsiabijuga)
NICKNAME: Where America's Day Begins
SONG: "Stand Ye Guamians"
WIDTH, NORTH TO SOUTH: About 4 to 8.5 miles
LENGTH, EAST TO WEST: About 30 miles
HIGHEST POINT: 1,332 feet—Mt. Lamlam
LOWEST POINT: Sea level

Old Spanish Gate at Agana

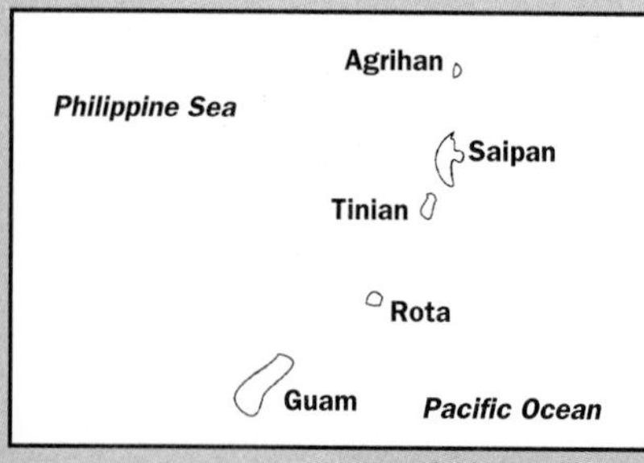

Guam's key feature is a U. S. Naval Air Base. Although Guam is far from the continental United States, it is actually U. S. territory. So the U.S. soldiers stationed on Guam can actually consider themselves right at home on the small island in the middle of the Pacific Ocean.

WHERE AMERICA'S DAY BEGINS Guam is a self-governing organized unincorporated U.S. territory. That means that the people in Guam elect their own leaders but don't have the power to affect the national U.S. government. Guam's people are U.S. citizens, but they cannot vote for president.

Water buffalo at Fort Santa Soledad

Guam is the southern-most of a string of Pacific islands called the Marianas, about 1,500 miles east of the Philippines and 3,700 miles west of Hawaii. It's also the largest of the Marianas. Like them, it has a warm, pleasant tropical climate and a landscape dotted with palm trees and brightly colored tropical blooms.

If you walked along a beach in Guam, you'd see stony coral reefs rising from the ocean. If you traveled inland you'd find mountains, and on the southern half of the island you'd find hills that were formed by volcanoes millions of years ago. Guam's northern half used to be heavily forested, but much of this land has been cleared for farms and airfields. Throughout the island, coconut groves thrive, cultivated for their sweet fruit.

Guamanians are a multiracial, multicultural people. Many are Chamorros, descended from the Indonesian and Spanish settlers who came to Guam a few hundred years ago. Others are descended from American, Italian, French, British, Japanese, Chinese, Filipino, and Mexican settlers. Because the U.S. military base is such a big part of the island's economy, about one-third of the people on the island are military personnel and their dependents. Before the United States became an important presence on the island, Chamorro was the main language. Now most people speak English. Some 95 percent of Guamanians are Roman Catholic, reflecting their Spanish heritage.

FROM MAGELLAN'S EXPEDITION TO WORLD WAR II The first Europeans to land on Guam were explorer Ferdinand Magellan and his followers, who arrived there in 1521. Forty years later Spain claimed the island for itself. Guam remained under Spanish rule for over three hundred years, until Spain lost the Spanish-American War in 1898. Then Spain gave up many of its Pacific and Caribbean possessions to the United States. One of these was Guam, which was then administered by the U.S. Navy.

Beached Japanese barge near Inarajan

Because Guam was U.S. territory, it was a logical target for Japan during World War II. The Japanese attacked Guam on December 7, 1941 (U.S. date) and captured it on December 10th. It took the United States three years to regain the island: U.S. forces landed on Guam on July 21, 1944, and recaptured it completely on August 15, 1944.

On August 1, 1950, Guam was declared a territory. The U.S. Department of the Interior became responsible for the land, rather than the Navy, and Guamanians became U.S. citizens and were allowed to elect their own legislature. However, until 1970 the U.S. President appointed the island's governor. Now the governor is elected.

Guam continued to have military importance for the United States. In 1954 the U.S. Air Force Strategic Air Command made Guam its Pacific headquarters.

TROPICAL FRUITS Farmers on Guam raise corn, cattle, and hogs. They also grow many tropical fruits and vegetables: cabbages, eggplants, cucumbers, long beans, tomatoes, bananas, coconuts, watermelons, yams, canteloupes, papayas, maize, and sweet potatoes. The island has traditionally relied on agriculture, but over the years some industry has developed including construction, light manufacturing, banking, and tourism. Factories on Guam make textiles and process foods.

The U.S. military base is also a major part of the economy. Some 7,200 people on Guam are employed by the U.S. government. And close to a quarter of Guam's workers are employed in service industries, many of which are set up to serve residents of the base.

Tropical fruits and vegetables are grown on farms like this one.

Fascinating Facts

DID YOU KNOW THAT... Guam is the most easterly region governed by the United States. That's why its nickname is "Where America's Day Begins"—because the sun rises over Guam before anywhere else in America.

GUAMIAN GOVERNMENT:
- elected governor and lieutenant governor to four-year terms
- unicameral (one-house) legislature, with 21 members elected to two-year terms

GUAM'S CLIMATE:
- 72 to 88 degrees Fahrenheit
- 90 inches average rain per year
- frequent typhoons

DID YOU KNOW THAT... In 1962 a typhoon destroyed 95 percent of Guam's buildings.

GUAM'S TOWNS AND CITIES:
- largest city—Tamuning
- major port—Apra Harbor
- other major cities—Mongmong, Agana Heights
- towns of less than 3,000 people—Agana (the capital), Agat, Barrigada, Dededo, Santa Rita, Sinajana, Toto, Yona

DID YOU KNOW THAT... Heavy fighting between U.S. and Japanese troops had virtually destroyed Agana, which had to be rebuilt after World War II had ended.

GUAM'S PEOPLE:
- Chamorro—43%
- Filipino—28%
- Chinese, Japanese, Korean, and other Asian—18%
- European/North American—10%

DID YOU KNOW THAT... About 52 percent of the residents of Guam were born outside the island. Of these, some 48 percent were born in Asia, while 40 percent—primarily military personnel and their dependents—were born in the United States.

Puerto Rico

Estado Libre Asociado de Puerto Rico

Fishermen in San Juan

Became a commonwealth on July 25, 1952

The Basics

OFFICIAL NAME: Commmonwealth of Puerto Rico; *Estado Libre Asociado de Puerto Rico*
POPULATION: 3,622,063
AREA: 3,435 square miles
CAPITAL: San Juan
BIRD: Reinita
FLOWER: Maga
TREE: Ceiba
MOTTO: *Joannes Est Nomen Eujus* (Latin for "John is his name"
FLAG: Five horizontal stripes, alternating red and white, with a blue triangle at the left, bearing a five-pointed white star.
SEAL: A central medallion with a lamb, symbol of St. John (San Juan) holding a white banner and resting on the New Testament's Book of Revelation, just above the commonwealth's motto. Above the lamb are the crowned letters *F* and *I*, for Spain's King Ferdinand and Queen Isabella. Around the border of the seal are symbols of the Kingdom of Spain.
SONG: La Borinqueña
LANDMARKS: El Morro Fortress, San Juan
NATIONAL PARKS: El Yunque Rain Forest
WILDLIFE REFUGE: Caribbean Islands Refuge
FESTIVALS: Kings' Day, January 6; Birthday of educator and writer Eugenio Maria de Hostos (January 11); San Juan Carnival (February); Emancipation Day—the abolition of slavery in 1873 (March 22); Birthday of Puerto Rican patriot Jose de Diego (April 16); Tropical Flower Show, San Juan (April); Eve of San Juan Bautista Day (June 23); Birthday of patriot Luis Munoz Rivera (July 17)

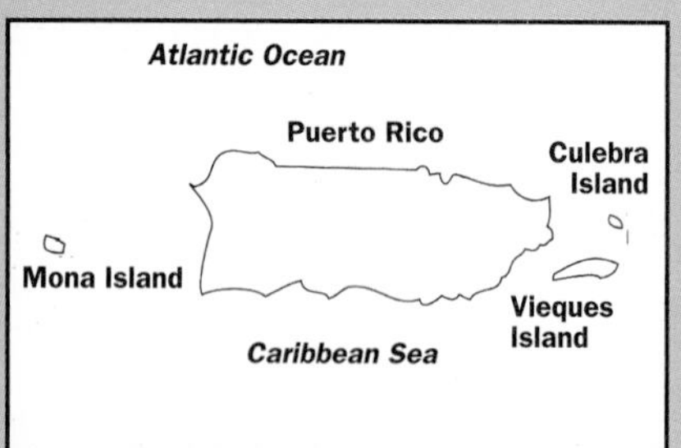

Puerto Rico is so small that you can drive virtually anywhere in less than a day. Yet, the island hosts a wide variety of beautiful landscapes mountains, beaches, rain forests. No wonder Puertoriqueños love th homeland so much!

TROPICAL BEACHES AND SPANISH FORTS The spine of Puerto Rico is the Cordillera Central, a 3,000-foot-high mountain range running through the center of the island. The range slopes steeply to the dry southeastern part of the island, and more gently to the humid, rainy northern half. The island is bordered with sandy white beaches along the warm Caribbean.

Puerto Rico's tropical climate is generally pleasant. The temperature ranges from 60 to 98 degrees Fahrenheit, with a mean temperature of 77. The warm, rainy weather makes for a long growing season, but only one-third of the island is suitable for farming. The rest is too mountainous or marshy.

Two-thirds of Puerto Rico's residents live in cities, primarily San Juan, Bayamon, Ponce, Carolina, Caguas, and Mayaguez. San Juan is by far the largest. The city is a striking mix of Spanish colonial architecture and modern luxury hotels. One of its most famous buildings is the El Morro Fortress, built by the Spaniards between 1539 and 1787 to guard the Bay of San Juan. The University of Puerto Rico, founded in 1903, has a beautifully ornamented administration building. It's also the site of lively demonstrations by students and by its unionized clerical workers.

Rain forest near Santurcé

Puerto Rico is famous for its sandy beaches, especially Luquillo Beach on the northeast corner of the island. Phosphorescent Bay, at La Parguera on the southwest coast, literally glows in the dark. That's because tiny living organisms in the water called plankton actually give off light. At El Yunque's rain forest, you can see wild parrots and wild orchids.

SUGARCANE AND OPERATION BOOTSTRAP Puerto Rico's first inhabitants were the Taino, who spoke Arawak. They were "discovered" by Christopher Columbus on November 19, 1493, during his second visit to the western hemisphere. Columbus claimed the land for Spain, and in 1508 the Spanish began to settle there. In 1515 the first sugarcane was brought from the Dominican Republic. And in 1518 the first African slaves were brought to work on the sugarcane plantations.

Like slaves in North America, slaves in Puerto Rico were cruelly treated. And, as in North America, the colonizers drove native peoples out of their lands. By 1550 Taino who had not been killed or enslaved by the Spanish had fled into the mountains. Although the French, English, and Dutch each challenged Spain's claim, Puerto Rico remained in Spanish hands until 1898.

Statue of Christopher Columbus in San Juan

In that year, U.S. troops landed in Puerto Rico as part of the Spanish-American War, which was fought mainly on the land of Spain's colonies. When Spain was defeated, the United States acquired Puerto Rico, along with the Philippines, Cuba, and other Spanish colonies.

Even though slavery had been abolished in 1873, workers continued to be poorly treated on the sugar plantations. By 1920 almost three-fourths of Puerto Rico's population depended on sugarcane for its livelihood. Later tobacco, mining of iron ore, and tourism became important island industries as well. And in the 1940s the United States started Operation Bootstrap, designed to lure U.S companies to build factories on the island, by offering them attractive tax breaks.

INDEPENDENCE, STATEHOOD, OR STATUS QUO? Puerto Ricans have been debating the best political system for their country since the first Spanish colonists arrived 400 years ago. Now there are three main opinions in Puerto Rico. Some people believe that Puerto Rico should become the 51st state, losing its identity as a nation but gaining in political influence in America. Others think that Puerto Rico's commonwealth status—with U.S. financial support but without political participation—is best. Still others want Puerto Rico to be fully independent, and they have fought for independence for many years.

Morro Castle, San Juan

FROM SUGARCANE TO TOURISM Like most Caribbean nations, Puerto Rico has had trouble achieving economic independence. That's because it produces raw materials—sugarcane, coffee, and bananas—while the more profitable work of processing materials and selling industrial goods is done by companies whose headquarters are on the U.S. mainland. As a result, the profits are taken out of Puerto Rico, even when the work is done there. There is some native Puerto Rican industry—pharmaceuticals, petrochemicals, machinery, clothing, and textiles. Tourism is also important to the economy.

One of the saddest things for many Puerto Ricans is the lack of jobs on their island. This means that they must go to the United States for work. As a result, some 2.7 million Puerto Ricans live in the continental United States. Of these, a million live in New York City. There, Nuyorican culture has developed, which in turn shapes the Puerto Rican culture on the island itself.

Fascinating Facts

PUERTO RICO'S MANY NAMES:

- The original Taino Indian name for the island was *Borinquen*.
- In 1493 Christopher Columbus called the island *San Juan* (St. John).
- Ponce de Leon renamed the capital city of Caparra *Puerto Rico,* "rich port," in 1511.
- Later, the island became known as Puerto Rico, and the capital city, San Juan.

PUERTO RICO AND THE U.S.:

- self-governing commonwealth
- residents are American citizens
- residents can vote in primaries, but not in general elections for president
- residents elect a nonvoting Resident Commissioner to Congress
- residents do not pay income tax on income earned in Puerto Rico

PUERTO RICO'S POLITICS:

- a Commonwealth Legislature with 27 senators and 51 representatives
- 78 municipalities elect their own mayors and city governments

SAN JUAN FACTS:

- estimated 1993 population—433,372
- founded in 1508 by Juan Ponce de Leon, who called it Caparra
- oldest city in any U.S. territory or state

DID YOU KNOW THAT... Although the tiny island of Puerto Rico has nearly 1,300 streams and 50 rivers, none of them is navigable.

EL YUNQUE FACTS:

- name means "the anvil"
- a mountain with a rain forest on its slopes
- the only national park that is a rain forest, home to 240 native species of trees, some of which grow nowhere else
- home to many species of birds
- unlike other rain forests, has no alligators or monkeys

U.S. Virgin Islands

Harbor at Charlotte Amalie

Inhabitants became American nationals in 1927

The Basics

TOTAL POPULATION: 114,000
MAIN ISLANDS: St. John, St. Thomas, St. Croix
POPULATION OF ST. CROIX: 61,000
POPULATION OF ST. THOMAS: 50,000
POPULATION OF ST. JOHN: 3,000
AREA: 128 square miles
AREA OF ST. CROIX: 82 square miles
AREA OF ST. THOMAS: 27 square miles
AREA OF ST. JOHN: 19 square miles
CAPITAL: Charlotte Amalie, St. Thomas
BIRD: Yellow breast
FLOWER: Yellow elder or yellow trumpet (Ginger Thomas)
FLAG: A golden American eagle with a U.S. shield on its breast, against a white field. The eagle holds blue arrows in its left talon, symbolizing war, and a sprig of green laurel in its right talon, symbolizing peace. The blue letters *V* and *I* are to the left and right of the eagle.
SEAL: The U.S. coat of arms, with the American eagle and the U.S. shield in the center of the seal. The words "Government of the Virgin Islands of the United States" surrounds the coat of arms.
SONG: "Virgin Islands March"
HIGHEST POINT: Crown Mountain, St. Thomas—1,556 feet
LOWEST POINT: Sea level
NATIONAL PARK: Virgin Islands National Park
FESTIVAL: Carnival, St. Thomas (April)

Atlantic Ocean
St. Thomas
St. John
St. Croix
Caribbean Sea

The name Virgin Islands refers to two groups of small islands between the Caribbean Sea and the Atlantic Ocean, east of Puerto Rico. One group—St. Croix, St. John, and St. Thomas—belongs to the United States and is known as the United States Virgin Islands. The other group—Anegada, Jost van Dyke, Tortola, and Virgin Gorda Islands, along with surrounding small islets—is the British Virgin Islands.

ISLAND PARADISE The United States Virgin Islands are rugged and hilly, except for the largest island, St. Croix, which is sandy and flat. When you picture the islands, think small. Their total size, only 133 square miles, would fit nine times into Rhode Island, the mainland's tiniest state. Yet they offer 117 miles of coastline—beautiful beaches along the sapphire-blue Caribbean.

The Virgin Islands were once entirely covered by the sea. Fossils of ancient animals can still be found on island shores. Once, volcanoes pushed the islands up from the ocean floor. If you walk along an island beach, you can see tiny islets jutting up from the water, like little rocks. Imagine them millions of years ago, being thrust up from the ocean by a huge, boiling volcano. Then look at them again, cool and peaceful in the island surf, some covered with green plant life.

Palm Passage on St. Thomas

Tropical flowers and trees grow all over these lovely islands. All year round you can see the scarlet, pink, and white blooms of the bougainvillea, canaria, flame tree, and hibiscus. The delightful tropical climate ranges from 70 to 90 degrees Fahrenheit, averaging a balmy 78 degrees Fahrenheit. You're likely to find good weather all year long, although there are sometimes heavy rains in the spring and fall.

The largest island of the group is St. Croix (pronounced saynh kroy), French for "holy cross." In Spanish it's called Santa Cruz, as Christopher Columbus named it. St. Croix has about two-thirds of the islands' area and is home to the cities Christiansted and Frederiksted.

St. John has villages at Cruz Bay and Coral Bay, but about three-fourths of its land is occupied by Virgin Islands National Park. St. Thomas is known for its central range of hills, from which you can see the ocean. It's also home to the islands' capital, Charlotte Amalie.

A NEW CARIBBEAN LAND The United States Virgin Islands were once home to native peoples such as the Siboney Indians, the Carib, and the Arawak from South America. The Arawak created an important invention—the hammock. These were the peoples whom Christopher Columbus found when he reached the Virgin Islands in 1493.

Mending a fishing trap

The Carib did not take kindly to the European invaders, and they fought fiercely with Columbus' crew at Sugar Bay on St. Croix. Throughout the 1500s the Caribs tried hard to defend their land from the Europeans. But in the mid-1500s King Charles I of Spain sent soldiers to kill all the Indians so that Spain could take their lands. By the 1600s when the British and Danes began to approach the islands, the native people had all been killed or chased off.

In 1607 a group of English settlers stopped at the islands, but they continued on their way to the colony at Jamestown, Virginia. For years, pirates used the island to bury their treasure. Throughout the 1600s, 1700s, and 1800s, the islands were claimed by Holland, Spain, France, England, and Denmark. (You can see the Danish influence in the "sted" endings of the names of St. Croix's towns.)

Children's parade on St. Thomas

Finally, in 1917, the United States bought its portion of the Virgin Islands from Denmark, to keep them from being taken by the Germans during World War I. In 1927 Virgin Islanders became American nationals. They were allowed a limited form of self-government in 1936 and somewhat expanded rights in 1954. Today the Virgin Islands elects a governor, lieutenant governor, and parliament to run the islands, as well as a nonvoting member to the U.S. House of Representatives.

TOURISM, RUM, AND OIL When native people lived on the islands, they fished the sea and ate the fruits and vegetables they could grow or pick wild. But the islands don't have the resources to support a modern economy.

Thus, the major industry is tourism, with a large number of visitors coming from the United States. There are some other industries too. Residents of St. John make charcoal and pick bay leaves, which are made into bay rum. Oil refineries on St. Croix produce petroleum. Other manufacturing includes watchmaking, aluminum production, textiles, electronics, and perfumes. Most goods are exported to the United States.

Fascinating Facts

VIRGIN ISLANDS POLITICS:

- administered by the U.S. Department of the Interior
- constitution—the Revised Organic Act of the Virgin Islands, passed by the U.S. Congress in 1954
- elects a governor for a four-year term with a limit of two consecutive terms
- territorial legislature—one house with 15 senators elected to two-year terms
- St. Croix elects 7 senators; St. Thomas and St. John together elect 7 senators; one senator is elected at large
- judicial system—U.S. District Court of the Virgin Islands, with the judge appointed by the U.S. president with the advice and consent of the U.S. Senate
- municipal court judges—appointed by the governor, with the advice and consent of the territorial legislature

VIRGIN ISLANDS WEATHER:

- average rainfall: 40 to 60 inches of rain each year
- average rainfall at higher elevations: 50 to 60 inches each year

VIRGIN ISLANDS TOURISM:

- more than one million tourists each year
- $10 million worth of business

VIRGIN ISLANDS AGRICULTURE:

- eggs
- beef and dairy cattle
- hogs
- pigs
- sheep
- cucumbers, peppers, tomatoes
- fruits and nuts
- grain sorghum for livestock feed

DID YOU KNOW THAT... During the 1700s landowners began developing huge sugarcane plantations on the islands. These are no longer profitable, although sugarcane is an important crop elsewhere in the Caribbean. However, you can still visit the ruins of large farms like the Princess Plantation on St. Croix.

The United States of America

New Hampshire
Maine
Vermont
Michigan
Minnesota
Massachusetts
Wisconsin
New York
Rhode Island
Connecticut
Pennsylvania
New Jersey
Iowa
Ohio
Indiana
Delaware
Illinois
West Virginia
Maryland
Virginia
Missouri
Kentucky
Washington, D.C.
North Carolina
Tennessee
Oklahoma
South Carolina
Arkansas
Mississippi
Alabama
Georgia
Florida
Louisiana

Places to Visit

ALABAMA

If you would like to learn more about **Helen Keller**, who lived a full and remarkable life in spite of being deaf, mute, and blind, then visit her birthplace, "Ivy Green," at 300 West North Common Street, Tuscumbia.

The poet, educator and reformer who changed many children's lives, **Julia Tutwiler,** is honored with a memorial in her name at the Department of Archives and History at Washington Avenue in Montgomery.

ALASKA

If you're interested in outdoor sports and dogs, then visit the **Anchorage Sled Dog Racing Association,** which hosts races on winter weekends. Or see the world-famous **Iditarod**, the 1,049-mile-long dog-sled race held in March. **The Fur Rendezvous** is the site of dogsled races held in Anchorage in mid-February. For helpful information on all three, contact the Anchorage Convention and Visitors Bureau at 524 West 4th Avenue in Anchorage, AK 99501.

Alaskan native boy in traditional clothes

The Anchorage Museum of History and Art is a treasure trove of native arts and crafts at West 7th Avenue and A Street in Anchorage.

Kodiak, the largest island in the United States is home to the Kodiak brown bear, the largest land mammal in North America.

Contact Southwest Alaska Municipal Conference at 3300 Arctic Boulevard (Suite 203) Anchorage, AK 99503.

ARIZONA

The **Grand Canyon,** the largest land gorge in the world, is 277 miles long, 17 miles wide at its broadest point, and 1 mile deep. It is in **Grand Canyon National Park,** the site of many panoramic views such as **The Watchtower** at the South Rim or **Point Imperial**—at 8,803 feet, the highest viewpoint in the canyon. Because of its remote location and heavy snowfalls, the North Rim of the Grand Canyon is closed from October to April. If you want to get "up close," the National Park Service sponsors several hikes along the many trails in and around this geological phenomenon. Contact the National Park Service at Box 129 Grand Canyon.

If you're curious about Native American life, visit **Quechan Indian Reservation**. For more information, contact the Quechan Tribal Council at P.O. Box 1352, Yuma, AZ 85364.

ARKANSAS

How are diamonds "made"? Find out at the only working diamond mine in North America at the **Crater of Diamonds State Park** in Murfreesboro.

History comes to life at **Ozark Folk Center State Park**, where the Ozark Mountain way of life is preserved and carried on through presentations of traditional dancing and singing, along with demonstrations of folk arts and crafts. This unique park is in Mountain View.

You can also explore the past at **Quapaw Quarter**, a completely restored nineteenth-century neighborhood that includes homes, churches, and some of the state's oldest buildings. It's at 1321 Scott Street, Little Rock.

CALIFORNIA

California has some of the most beautiful—and varied—scenery in the world. **U.S. 1**, an interstate highway, runs along the 400-mile-long coastline. The highway is bordered by forests: the world's tallest tree—a 365-foot-high redwood—is in Humboldt County. And **Point Reyes National Seashore** attracts many seals, birds, and migrating whales.

You can also travel the two-mile-long **"Path of History"** in **Monterey State Historic Park.** The starting point of this self-guided coastal tour is **The Custom House**, built by Mexico in 1817, and believed to be the oldest government building west of the Rockies. Contact

A beautiful Japanese garden in Golden Gate Park, San Francisco

the California Division of Tourism in Sacramento for information about these sights.

Hancock Park is the home of one of the world's greatest museums, the **Los Angeles County Museum of Art** at 5905 Wilshire Boulevard. **Hancock Park** is built on top of the **La Brea Tar Pits**, from which more than 100 tons of fossils have been removed.

The Tech Museum of Innovation in San Carlo is devoted entirely to the computer; you can visit in person at 145 West San Carlos Street, or on the **Internet** at http://www.thetech.org

Yosemite Falls, in **Yosemite National Park** rise 2,425 feet, making them the highest falls in North America. The park also offers hiking, backpacking, and camping surrounded by glacial granite peaks and clear, blue lakes.

California is home to many celebrities, but some of its "forgotten" natives claim distinction born of real-life achievement. If you would like to find out about one of them, visit the home of **Harriet Chalmers Adams**, an anthropologist (someone who studies the origins and relationships between humans and their social and cultural environments) who travelled more than 100,000 miles to explore dangerous, remote jungles and native tribes during the 1890s. It's at 605 North Eldorado Avenue, Stockton.

COLORADO

In the town of Golden, you can find out more about a famous, real-life cowboy at **The Buffalo Bill Grave and Museum** at the top of Lookout Mountain. The trip up gives you a spectacular panoramic view of Denver. To get there, take Route 5 off I-70.

St. James United Methodist Church has a **Monument to Clara Brown,** the Virginia-born slave whose hard work and faith were responsible for the founding of this pioneer church in 1872. It is at Eureka Street in Central City.

Rocky Mountain National Park in Estes Park has some of the most spectacular mountains, lakes, and wildlife in the United States. It covers 250,000 acres and offers hiking, camping, fishing and scenic drives through its wilderness.

The **Garden of the Gods** offers picnic sites and opportunities for hiking among 1,350 acres of windswept rock formations and exotic plant life. Visit them at Off Ridge Road, north of U.S. 24, Colorado Springs.

CONNECTICUT

The Peabody Museum of Natural History in New Haven is the largest of its kind in New England, and includes dinosaur fossils, birds, and meteorites. It also has exhibits of early Native American life in the area.

The **Mystic Marine Life Aquarium** in Mystic has more than 6,000 specimens and 50 live exhibits of sea life. It also presents live dolphin and sea lion shows every hour.

Did you ever wonder where your dictionary got its start? Well, it was with Noah Webster in 1806, and you can learn more about him by visiting the **Noah Webster House and Museum** in Hartford.

Hartford is also the home of the country's first public art museum, **The Wadsworth Athenaeum** (founded in 1842), which includes more than 40,000 works that span 5,000 years of art.

Emma Hart Willard began the first endowed school for girls in 1821. If you are curious about this rebel with a cause, visit her birthplace at Norton Rd. and Lower Lane in Berlin.

Mark Twain's house in Hartford, Connecticut

DELAWARE

With 175 rooms and acres of gardens, **Winterthur Museum, Garden and Library** features American art and antiques from 1640-1860. Take Route 52 in Winterthur.

New Castle, where William Penn first lived in 1682, is a completely restored colonial town of 200-year-old homes and a **Courthouse** that was the state capital during the Revolution.

Rehobeth Beach is a beautiful place to explore Delaware's largest shoreline area. With a busy boardwalk and acres of white beach, it's one of the Atlantic coast's most picturesque scenes.

DISTRICT OF COLUMBIA

Black history comes alive when you visit the **Frederick Douglass National Historic Site,** Cedar Hill. With its restored house and nine acres of land, this was the last home of the great abolitionist, who lived there from 1878 until his death in 1895. (1411 W Street, S.E.)

The **Lincoln Memorial** honoring our 16th president is one of the great public monuments in the United States. With its marble columns, long reflecting pool, and imposing statue of Abraham Lincoln by sculptor Daniel Chester French, the memorial is equally beautiful by night or day. It has been the site of numerous public demonstrations since its completion in 1914. The memorial is at the west end of the Mall.

Jazz pianist and composer "Duke" Ellington (1899-1974)

The Smithsonian Institution, which includes seven museums, features a variety of items ranging from Dorothy's red slippers from *The Wizard of Oz* to Charles Lindbergh's plane, *The Spirit of St. Louis*, which he flew solo across the Atlantic in 1927.

Designed by young architect, Maya Lin, the **Vietnam Veterans Memorial** in polished black granite is a somber reminder of the high price of war. Its companion, the **Vietnam Women's Memorial**, designed by Glenna Goodacre, stands nearby at 23rd St. and Constitution Ave., N.W.

Home to presidents since John Adams lived there from 1797 through 1801, **The White House** has survived fire and war, destruction and restoration. There are daily tours of its public rooms and gardens.

FLORIDA

If you're interested in ecology, **The Florida Everglades** includes the country's largest sub-tropical wilderness (with more than 1.4 million acres). Half-land, half-water, you can visit this national park in Homestead, just south of Miami.

Thomas Edison's Winter Home is the place to go to learn more about the legendary inventor—the record player and microphone are only two of hundreds of his inventions. The home includes Edison's laboratory and a museum with his inventions. 2350 McGregor Blvd. Ft. Myers, FL

Zora Neale Hurston Memorial Park is dedicated to the distinguished African-American writer whose novels have been widely praised by critics. The park is at 11 People Street in the Eatonville Municipal Complex.

In the Cocoa Beach area, **Spaceport U.S.A.** at the Kennedy Space Center presents the wonders of space travel through filmed presentations and bus tours of spacecraft hangars and rocket launch sites. Call 1-800-432-2153 for more information.

GEORGIA

The **Juliette Gordon Low Birthplace/Girl Scout National Center** is the home of the founder of the Girl Scouts of America. This beautiful old house at 142 Bull Street was the first registered National Historic Landmark in Savannah.

The **Martin Luther King, Jr. National Historic District** begins at King Center, 449 Auburn Avenue in Atlanta. The spirit of the 1960s Civil Rights movement is commemorated in a museum and library. And an eternal flame burns at the tomb of Dr. King, illuminating the words "Free at Last Free At Last Thank God Almighty I'm Free at Last."

British actress Fanny Kemble (1809-1893) published a controversial journal after living on her slaveholder husband's Georgia plantation.

Because 32nd President Franklin Delano Roosevelt was physically challenged by polio, he often came to Warm Springs for his health. In addition to a simple home he called **"The Little White House,"** he established a health center for others with the disease. For more information call 1-800-847-4842 (the Georgia Department of Industry, Trade and Tourism).

HAWAII

If you are interested in volcanoes, the Hawaiian islands are a great place to see them up close. **Hawaii Volcanoes National Park** covers 344 acres on the the big island of Hawaii, and features many attractions related to Mount Kilauea, the world's most active volcano.

On the island of Maui, **Haleakala National Park** begins at 7,000 feet, and continues to 9,800 where rangers can tell you fascinating information about volcanoes. You'll also get a 360-degree view of other islands in the Hawaiian chain.

The *USS Arizona* Memorial honors the memory of all those killed during the Japanese attack on Pearl Harbor on December 7, 1941. 1,102 crewmen on the *Arizona* drowned when their ship sank. The memorial is twenty minutes west of downtown Honolulu off the island of Oahu.

Craters of the Moon National Monument

IDAHO

Lunar astronauts trained at **Craters of the Moon National Monument,** which covers 83 square miles and is home to lava flows, caves, and volcanic cones. Write Box 29 in Arco, 83213.

Only seven miles south of Boise you'll find the **World Center for Birds of Prey,** home to live falcons and other birds of prey.

ILLINOIS

Jane Addams's Hull House Museum at 800 South Halstead Street in Chicago commemorates the life and work of the dedicated crusader for children and immigrants.

The **Art Institute of Chicago** is one of the world's finest museums. It features five-thousand-year-old Asian art, plus paintings and sculpture from the Middle Ages to the present. The Thorne miniature rooms illustrate every historic style of the interiors of homes. 111 South Michigan Avenue, Chicago.

The Field Museum of Natural History is packed with fascinating exhibits such as "Life Over Time," which traces the evolution of life on earth from DNA to dinosaurs. You can find more about ancient Egypt, view a multimedia presentation of Africa, and learn about all kinds of animals from a microscopic head louse to a 40-foot killer squid.

A "WANTED" poster offering a $100,000 reward for Lincoln's assassin.

The **Ulysses S. Grant Home** looks just as it did back in 1865 when residents of the town of Galena presented it to Grant in honor of his service to the Union. (500 Bouthillier Street.)

The capital of Springfield has many historic sites dedicated to Abraham Lincoln: the **Lincoln Home Historic Site** at 426 S. 7th Street; **Lincoln Tomb State Historic Site** located in Oak Ridge Cemetery; the **Lincoln-Herndon Law Offices** at 6th and Adams Streets provide a look at Lincoln's life and career before he was elected president.

INDIANA

The **George Rogers Clark National Historical Park** commemorates Clark's battle to take Fort Sackville from the British during the Revolutionary War. It is located in 300-year-old Vincennes, Indiana's oldest community.

For anyone who likes racecars and wants to know more about the world famous Indy 500, a visit to the **Indianapolis Motor Speedway Hall of Fame Museum at** 4790 West 16th Street in Indianapolis is a must.

IOWA

The Amana Colonies include 500 restored buildings that have been designated a National Historic Landmark. **The Museum of Amana History** presents documents and artifacts relating to the nineteenth-century settlement of the area by German/Swiss immigrants. Call 1-800-245-5465.

The Davenport Municipal Museum has a large collection of Grant Wood paintings and memorabilia for those who would like to find out more about the man who painted the famous *American Gothic*.

Take a trip back in time to an eighteenth-century Iowa Indian village, nineteenth-century working farms, and an 1875 town. It's all at **Living History Farms**, a 600-acre open-air museum in Urbandale.

KANSAS

The **Amelia Earhart Birthplace** is the first home of the great aviator, and contains memorabilia of her life. (223 North Terrace in Atchison.)

Although born in Denison, Texas, Dwight D. Eisenhower moved to Kansas with his family when he was two years old. **The Eisenhower Center** complex includes his boyhood home, a museum and library dedicated to the 34th president of the U.S. You can learn more about his life from his youth through his success as a World War II general to his popular presidency. The center is at S. Buckeye St. at 4th Street in Abilene.

The **Kansas Cosmosphere and Space Center** in Hutchinson houses more than $100 million worth of exhibits that explain the history of space exploration. It also has a planetarium. Call 1-800-397-0330.

KENTUCKY

Early American history comes alive at **Fort Boonesborough State Park** in Bluegrass. This reconstruction of one of Daniel Boone's early forts also includes a museum and demonstrations of pioneer crafts. 1-800-255-7275.

White Hall State Historic Site in Richmond is the home of nineteenth-century abolitionist Cassius Marcellus Clay, for whom boxer Muhammed Ali was named at birth.

LOUISIANA

The site of the **Battle of New Orleans** honors the memory of General Andrew Jackson and his soldiers who won a decisive battle against the British on January 8, 1815. Call 1-800-334-8626.

Horses dot the landscape all over Bluegrass country in Kentucky.

The **Louisana Children's Museum** features hands-on exhibits and activities. It's at 428 Julia Street in New Orleans.

Melrose Plantation on Route 119 in Natchitoches is the site of African House, a museum that shows the art of internationally acclaimed African-American painter Clementine Hunter.

MAINE

Acadia National Park has beautiful stretches of shoreline and the highest mountains along the East Coast. It offers hiking, biking, camping, and boating.

The **Acadian Whale Watcher** takes you out to see the great whales that swim off the coast of Maine.

You can find out what it is like to be a lobster catcher, shopkeeper or computer expert when you visit the **Children's Museum of Maine** in Portland.

MARYLAND

The **Banneker-Douglass Museum** honors the lives and work of scientist Benjamin Banneker and abolitionist Frederick Douglass. (84 Franklin Street in Annapolis.)

The **Clara Barton National Historic Site** was the home of the Civil War nurse and founder of the American Red Cross. (5801 Oxford Road in Glen Echo.)

Fort McHenry National Monument and Historic Shrine in Baltimore harbor is the site of a naval victory over the British during the War of 1812. The battle inspired Francis Scott Key to write "The Star-Spangled Banner."

MASSACHUSETTS

The **African Meeting House** was built in 1806, making it the oldest standing African-American church building in the United States. (8 Smith Street in Boston.)

The **Emily Dickinson Homestead** at 280 Main Street in Amherst looks exactly the way it did when the popular poet lived there in the nineteenth century.

A good way to get acquainted with the historic city of Boston is to take a walk on the three-mile-long **Freedom Trail** that winds past sixteen of the city's most important sites. Call 1-800-888-5515.

MICHIGAN

The **Henry Ford Museum and Greenfield Village** in Dearborn is America's largest indoor-outdoor museum. Its exhibits show how the United States changed from a rural to an industrial society in areas such as communication, transportation, domestic life, agriculture and industry. The complex also has 80 historic buildings including one of Thomas Edison's laboratories. At 20900 Oakwood Boulevard.

Michigan's Upper Peninsula is home to wildlife such as this elk.

The Sojourner Truth Grave in Oak Hill Cemetery is the burial place of the great nineteenth-century African-American speaker and abolitionist. It is located at South Avenue and Oak Hill Drive in Battle Creek.

More than 100 years old, the **Grand Hotel** on Mackinac Island is a Victorian masterpiece that features the world's longest porch.

MINNESOTA

The birthplace of the present-day Twin Cities is commemorated at **Fort Snelling State Park,** where you can see the historic fort built in 1819 at the junction of the Mississippi and Minnesota rivers. The park is just south of downtown St. Paul, at Route 5 and Post Road.

Henry Wadsworth Longfellow's famous *Song of Hiawatha* was inspired by Minnehaha Falls. "This is the forest primeval," wrote the poet. Now it's **Minnehaha Park,** on the Mississippi River, just outside of Minneapolis. Above the waterfall is a statue of Hiawatha and Minnehaha. You can walk, jog, bike, or roller-skate for 15 miles along Minnehaha Parkway, on the banks of Minnehaha Creek.

For visitors who like the wilderness, a trip to the **Boundary Waters Canoe Area** in northeastern Minnesota offers over 1,000 rural lakes surrounded by dense forests. To rent a canoe, or just to find out more about the area, contact the Ely Chamber of Commerce, 1600 Sheridan Street, Ely, MN, 55731, or 1-800-777-7281.

Nearby, the **Vermilion Interpretive Center,** 1900 E. Camp Street, has exhibits on Minnesota's famous iron range, the fur trade, and Native Americans.

MISSISSIPPI

The lovely old town of Natchez survived the Civil War almost untouched, so today it's one of the best places to visit the plantation homes and townhouses built by rich cotton merchants in the early nineteenth century. In 1932, the women of Natchez started offering tours of these homes—many of which are privately owned and still in use, and can be seen only twice a year, for three weeks in October and four weeks in March and April. For a historic tour, contact the **Pilgrimage Tour Headquarters,** 220 State St., Natchez, MS, 39121, or call 1-800-647-6742. You can also get a **carriage tour** of downtown Natchez.

In June, visitors to Biloxi can see the **Blessing of the Shrimp Fleet.** For information about this historic ritual, contact the Biloxi Chamber of Commerce, 39501.

MISSOURI

Branson is the new country-music capital of the United States, growing so fast that some believe it may rival Nashville. Branson is home to such halls as the Roy Clark Celebrity Theatre and the Cristy Lane Theatre. If you drive along Route 76, you'll encounter miniature-golf courses, bumper cars, souvenir shops, and other amusements.

Just east of Kansas City is the **Harry S Truman Library and Museum** (U.S. 24 and Delaware Street) and the **Truman Home** (219 N. Delaware Street), both located in Independence, the former home of the U.S. President. The President and First Lady Bess Truman spent their summers here while Truman was president.

George Washington Carver, the famous African-American botanist who discovered many new uses of the peanut, was born about 70 miles west of Springfield. Today, the **George Washington Carver National Monument**, off Route V, marks his birthplace.

Fans of Laura Ingalls Wilder's "Little House" books will want to visit the **Laura Ingalls Wilder Home** (Route A) in Mansfield, about 40 miles east of Springfield on Route 60. This is where the author lived while writing her famous series. Here you can see some of her handwritten manuscripts—written in pencil on school notebooks—as well as the original version of Pa's fiddle.

Another famous author lived in Missouri—Samuel Clemens, better known as Mark Twain. You can visit the author's boyhood home, now the **Mark Twain Home and Museum**, 208 Hill Street, Hannibal. Not too far away, at Route 79, is the **Mark Twain Cave,** the model for the one where Becky Thatcher and Tom Sawyer get lost in *The Adventures of Tom Sawyer.* For more information about the cave, contact the Hannibal Visitors and Convention Bureau, 320 Broadway, Box 624, Hannibal, MO 63401.

MONTANA

One of the most awesome sights to be found anywhere in the United States is the real glacier to be found at **Glacier National Park.** Contact National Park Service, West Glacier, MT 59936. This park preserves more than one million acres of mountains, waterfalls, and lakes, populated with elk, deer, wolves, and other Rocky Mountain wildlife. The 50-mile **Going-to-the-Sun Road** runs through the park; you can travel it by car, on horseback, or in a guided bus tour.

NEBRASKA

The Pulitzer-Prize-winning author Willa Cather lived in Red Cloud, where you can find the **Willa Cather Historical Center.** At 326 N. Webster Street. Five miles to the south is the **Cather Memorial Prairie,** a 610-acre area dedicated to preserving the plains that the author loved so much.

If you drive along the Great Platte River Road (take I-80 west from Omaha and Lincoln), you'll encounter the **Stuhr Museum of the Prairie Pioneer** in Grand Island (at the junction of U.S. 34 and U.S. 281). Here you'll find artifacts of American Indians and of the Old West, including a 60-building "Railroad Town" that features a restored farmhouse and people wearing old-fashioned costumes. The Railroad Town is closed from mid-October through April, so call to make sure it's open when you go.

NEVADA

Valley of Fire State Park offers dramatic landscapes on Route 169, in Overton, just 55 miles northeast of Lake Mead. There you can see many colorful sandstone formations as well as the petroglyphs (picture writing on rocks) of the ancient Anasazi Indians.

About 25 miles east of Las Vegas is the impressive **Hoover Dam** (Route 93, just east of Boulder City), built in the 1930s on the wild waters of the Colorado River. You can visit the 727-foot-high structure every day except Christmas.

NEW HAMPSHIRE

The poet **Robert Frost** lived in Franconia, where you can visit his home on Ridge Road. See the landscape that inspired such great works as "The Road Less Traveled."

Visit **Canterbury Shaker Village,** south of Lake Winnipesaukee, for a look at the history of this nineteenth-century community whose crafts and simple way of life are famous to this day.

The highest mountain in New England is **Mount Washington,** in the **White Mountains** of northern New Hampshire. The 750,000-acre White Mountain National Forest is a wilderness area that stretches all the way up to the Canadian border.

NEW JERSEY

The famous Revolutionary War heroine, "Molly Pitcher," got her nickname at **Molly Pitcher's Spring,** now on Wemrock Street off Route 522 in Freehold. Here Mary Hays carried water to the thirsty fighting troops, who created her nickname by calling out "Molly, pitcher!" whenever they wanted water.

Science lovers won't want to miss the **Liberty Science Center** at **Liberty State Park** in Jersey City (at Exit 14B off the New Jersey Turnpike). The center features three floors of hands-on exhibits plus a huge Omnimax theater with an 88-foot-wide domed screen.

People who think of New Jersey as an urban state will be glad to visit the **Pinelands National Reserve** for a taste of the wild side of the Garden State. You can find hundreds of creeks and streams suitable for canoeing in this 1.1-million-acre park near Chatsworth, the nation's first national reserve.

NEW MEXICO

Carlsbad Caverns National Park has one of the world's largest cave systems, with 77 caves, some as deep as 750 feet, others big enough to hold 14 Houston Astrodomes. The park can be entered at 3225 National Parks Highway.

A yucca plant in White Sands National Monument, New Mexico

In Santa Fe, the **Wheelwright Museum of the American Indian** (704 Camino Lejo) is housed in a building in the form of a traditional Navajo hogan. Inside, you can see the arts and crafts of many different native cultures.

NEW YORK

Do you like dinosaurs? Are you interested in wolves and bison? Do you want to find out more about Native Americans, Inuit, and many other cultures? Then you shouldn't miss a visit to the **American Museum of Natural History,** home to over 30 million artifacts and located at Central Park West and 77th Street in New York City.

Overlooking the Hudson River, Sunnyside was the home of writer Washington Irving (1783-1859).

For a look at the history of women's rights, stop by the **Susan B. Anthony House** at 17 Madison Street, Rochester, home of America's most famous crusader for women's right to vote.

The largest urban zoo in the United States is the **International Wildlife Conservation Park,** or the "Bronx Zoo" for short. Located at Fordham Road and the Bronx River Parkway in the Bronx, New York City, the conservation park features tram rides through simulated wilderness areas where you can see lions, tigers, bears, and more exotic animals roaming outside of cages.

Baseball fans will surely want to see the **National Baseball Hall of Fame** on Main Street in Cooperstown. There you'll find displays, paintings, and audiovisual presentations that tell about baseball's heroes and recount the history of the game.

Harriet Tubman, herself an escaped slave, made many trips to free other Southern slaves. During the Civil War, she served as scout and spy for the Union. When the war finally put an end to slavery, she settled in Auburn, where you can now visit the **Harriet Tubman Home** (180 South Street, Route 34).

NORTH CAROLINA

Discovery Place is a fascinating hands-on science museum at 301 N. Tryon Street in Charlotte. There you'll find aquariums, an indoor rain forest, a planetarium, a touch tank, and a huge Omnimax theater.

On December 17, 1903, Wilbur and Orville Wright made the first airplane flight, in their plane, the *Flyer.* You can see a replica of this famous aircraft at the **Wright Brothers National Memorial** in Kill Devil Hills (U.S. 158 Bypass).

NORTH DAKOTA

In the state capital of Bismarck, the **North Dakota Heritage Center** exhibits Native American and pioneer artifacts as well as natural history displays. Visit the center at 612 East Boulevard.

President Theodore Roosevelt always credited North Dakota's rough country with helping him to regain his health. Now you can visit the **Theodore Roosevelt National Park** (Box 7, Medora, ND 58645), which is divided into two halves, with 50 miles of Badlands running in between. Scenic drives through the park ask drivers to slow down in order to protect the bison, wild horses, mule deer, pronghorn antelope, and bighorn sheep that still live in this area. You might start your tour seven miles east of Medora on I-94, at the **Painted Canyon Overlook and Visitors Center**, where picnic tables offer tourists both a great view and a chance to eat. One segment of the park includes Roosevelt's **Elkhorn Ranch.**

OHIO

One of the first nationally recognized African-American poets, Paul Laurence Dunbar, was born in Dayton, where today you can visit the **Paul Laurence Dunbar House** at 219 North Summit Avenue. Dunbar's most famous line (later picked up by Maya Angelou for her autobiography) was "I know why the caged bird sings."

Paul Laurence Dunbar (1872-1906)

At the **Mound City Group National Monuments,** some 24 prehistoric Indian burial mounds have been preserved.

Neil Armstrong, the first man on the moon, is honored at the **Neil Armstrong Air and Space Museum** off 1-75 between Cincinnati and Toledo, in Armstrong's home town of Wapakoneta. If you want to feel what a space trip might be like, take exit 111. (The museum is closed from December through February.)

OKLAHOMA

Along Route 123 in northeastern Oklahoma is **Woolaroc**, a drive-through wildlife preserve where bison and 40 other animal species roam—so obey the rules and stay inside your car! At the center of the preserve is a museum packed with Native American art as well as artifacts from pioneer days. (For information, write Woolaroc, Box 1647, Bartlesville, OK 74005.)

Just north of the state capital, Oklahoma City, is the **National Cowboy Hall of Fame and Western Heritage Center**, home to paintings, sculpture, and other artifacts of cowboy life, as well as a re-created frontier town that features a sod house, saloon, and mine. Kachina dolls, used to teach Hopi children about sacred spirits of the dead, can be seen at this museum, at 1700 N.E. 63rd Street.

OREGON

Have you ever seen a 6,800-year-old lake? You'll get your chance at **Crater Lake National Park** (Box 7, Crater Lake, OR 97604), where you can see the result of the volcano that destroyed Mount Mazama. The empty cauldron of the former mountain soon filled up with rain and snow, creating a sapphire-blue lake so clear that sunlight reaches down into the water for 400 feet.

Crater Lake is one of the most beautiful bodies of water in the United States.

At Washington State Park in Portland, see the **Statue of Sacagawea**, a monument to the young Native American woman who served as a translator on the historic Lewis and Clark expedition through the Northwest Territory.

PENNSYLVANIA

Today, most people have heard about the dangers to the environment. But 30 years ago, the concepts of pollution and ecology were still unfamiliar ideas. Rachel Carson's book *Silent Spring* began the modern movement to save the environment. You can see the natural landscape that inspired this important author at the **Rachel Carson Homestead,** 613 Marion Avenue, Springdale.

The turning point of the Civil War was the Battle of Gettysburg, commemorated today at **Gettysburg National Military Park** (97 Taneytown Road). Stand on the ground where so many soldiers fought and died, and learn more about this historic battle from the markers and plaques that honor this site.

The **Frances Ellen Watkins Harper House** (1006 Bainbridge Street, Philadelphia) was once home to the nineteenth-century lecturer and crusader for African-American rights. Harper's most famous book, the novel *Iola Leroy,* painted an optimistic picture of what African-Americans might achieve once the Civil War had ended slavery.

RHODE ISLAND

Through the eighteenth and nineteenth centuries, America's aristocrats went to the seaside community of Newport to build lovely mansions and enjoy the summer weather. **Hunter House** (54 Washington Street), built in 1748, remains a stunning example of colonial architecture.

Also in Newport, **Touro Synagogue** still stands. Dedicated in 1763, this is the oldest surviving synagoge in the United States.

SOUTH CAROLINA

The first shot of the Civil War was fired at Fort Sumter. This famous moment is commemorated at the **Fort Sumter National Monument** in Charleston Harbor, Charleston.

In Columbia, the **South Carolina State Museum** (301 Gervais Street) is housed in a renovated textile mill, honoring

The Corn Palace in Mitchell, South Dakota was built in 1892.

the industry that created the state's wealth. The museum includes exhibits of archaeology, fine arts, science and technology. Check out the gift shop for some unusual souvenirs.

SOUTH DAKOTA

Over 1.3 million acres of western South Dakota is preserved in the **Black Hills National Forest,** an area that the Sioux considered sacred ground. To reach this fascinating part of the country, take Rural Route 2. For more information, write Box 200, Custer, SD 57730.

For more on the Indian point of view, visit the **Sioux Indian Museum** (515 West Boulevard), which exhibits artifacts from Sioux and other American Indian peoples.

You might also visit the **National Hall of Fame for Famous American Indians,** on U.S. 62 East near Anadarko.

Back in the Black Hills National Forest, 21 miles southwest of Rapid City on U.S. 16, is **Mt. Rushmore National Memorial** (Box 268, Keystone, SD 57701), the granite cliff where the giant faces of Presidents George Washington, Thomas Jefferson, Abraham Lincoln, and Theodore Roosevelt are carved. Sculptor Gutzon Borglum worked on the monument for more than 14 years, and even then the work had to be completed by his son, Lincoln. From June to mid-September, a dramatic lighting ceremony at dusk shows off the carving to its best advantage.

TENNESSEE

What do Elvis Presley and Dolly Parton have in common? They both recorded famous hits at the legendary **RCA Studio B** in Nashville. You can visit this historic studio when you buy a ticket to the **Country Music Hall of Fame and Museum** (4 Music Square E.).

Check out a different type of music in Memphis at the **W.C. Handy Memphis Home and Museum** (352 Beale Street). Handy is considered the creator of modern jazz.

If Handy was king of the blues, another Memphis resident, Elvis Presley, was king of rock and roll. You can visit Presley's famous estate, **Graceland,** 12 miles southeast of downtown Memphis. If you want to visit, make a reservation (1-800-238-2000); tours include a trip through the mansion, automobile museum, and burial site, along with a view of Elvis's two private jets and a piano covered in gold.

If you prefer presidents to rock stars, don't miss the home of U.S. President Andrew Jackson, **The Hermitage,** 4580 Rachel's Lane, Hermitage. (Rachel was the name of the President's wife.)

TEXAS

The unofficial state motto is "Remember the Alamo," commemorating the famous battle between Texans and Mexicans at the fort in San Antonio. You can visit **The Alamo** at Alamo Plaza, where you can learn more about the 189 volunteers who died in the historic battle in 1836, including famed U.S. pioneers Davy Crockett and James Bowie.

Davy Crockett is also honored at **David Crockett National Forest,** Ratcliff Lake, 1240 East Loop 304, Crockett. In the piney woods of east Texas, you can find places to hike, canoe, camp, and picnic.

In Big Bend, over 800,000 acres of canyons, desert, woodlands, mountains, and lakes are preserved in **Big Bend National Park** on U.S. 385. This wildlife area is the state's major national attraction, as it reveals millions of years of erosion that have created a junglelike floodplain, the Chihuahuan Desert, and the Chisos Mountains, home to black bears, mountain lions, coyotes, deer, jackrabbits, and over 430 species of birds, including the roadrunner.

UTAH

Picture a stone cathedral spire, a deep canyon, or a colorful stretch of desert. These are only some of the unique geographical features you might find in **Canyonlands National Park,** south of Moab (Route 313, Moab, UT 84532). This park is divided into three distinct areas, each with its own visitor center.

Dinosaur National Monument features the prehistoric remains of the earth's ancient beasts. For more information, write Box 128, Jensen, UT 84035.

If choir music appeals to you, you shouldn't miss a concert at the world-famous **Mormon Tabernacle** at Temple Square in Salt Lake City. Besides dramatic concerts on Thursdays and Saturdays, the Tabernacle buildings and grounds introduce visitors to the Mormon religion, including exhibits and art with religious themes.

VERMONT

Anyone who likes eating ice cream should make a point of touring **Ben and Jerry's Ice Cream Factory,** Route 100, one mile north of I-89 in Stowe. Tours take you through the entire ice-cream-making process, from receiving the milk to adding the mix-ins, with free samples at the end. The factory also includes a gift shop, playground, and, of course, concession stands serving ice cream.

One of the Revolutionary War's earliest heroes was Ethan Allen, leader of Vermont's Green Mountain Boys. The **Bennington Battle Monument** at 15 Monument Avenue honors these fighting men.

Have you ever wondered what an early American farm was like? You might find out at **Shelburne Museum,** a complex of 35 buildings that houses one of the largest Americana collections in the United States. The drive to the museum—located on U.S. 7 just outside of Burlington—offers some lovely views.

VIRGINIA

Monticello is the magnificent mansion that President Thomas Jefferson designed to overlook the majestic countryside. Like all southern plantations, Monticello was built and maintained by slave labor. Today, you can visit Monticello by taking Route 53 out of Charlottesville.

Carter's Grove Plantation, Virginia

The man who wrote *Up from Slavery* is honored at the **Booker T. Washington National Monument,** marking the birth of the great African-American educator and statesman. Take Route 3 out of Hardy, or, for more information, write Box 310, Highway 122, Hardy, VA 24011.

In Jamestown, near the Old Church Tower, you can find the **Pocohantas Statue,** dedicated to the memory of the young Native American woman who, in 1607, helped save the first British colonists from starvation. Jamestown includes many other references to the proud history of this early colony.

A later period in U.S. history is commemorated in Staunton at the **Museum of American Frontier Culture** (230 Frontier Drive). The building has been restored to re-create early American farm life, showing the animals and crops that would have been raised on eighteenth-century farms.

WASHINGTON

About 85 miles southeast of Seattle is **Mt. Rainier National Park,** a 400-square-mile wilderness area whose visitor center offers a 360-degree view of the famous mountain. For more information, write the Superintendent's Office, Tahoma Woods, Star Route, Ashford, WA 98304.

Throughout the Pacific Northwest are tributes to Lewis, Clark, and Sacagawea, explorers of the Northwest Territory in the early 1800s. Near Iwalco, a small fishing community of about 600 people, you can find the **Lewis and Clark Interpretive Center,** which documents the 8,000-mile round-trip journey, starting in Wood River, Illinois, and turning around at the mouth of the Columbia River.

WEST VIRGINIA

One of America's many unsung female heroes was Agnes Jane Reeves Greer (1880-1972)—inventor, business-woman, and architect. You can visit **Greer Mansion** at Cheat Lake in Morgantown to learn more about this remarkable woman.

Years before the beginning of the Civil War, abolitionist John Brown and a small band of antislavery activists staged his famous raid on Harpers Ferry. This

The majestic Grand Teton mountains in Wyoming

action is commemorated at **Harpers Ferry National Historical Park** (Box 65, Harpers Ferry, WV 25425), where the Potomac and Shenandoah rivers join.

WISCONSIN

Years before Golda Meir became the prime minister of Israel, she was a public school teacher. Visit the **Golda Meir School**, named in her honor, located in Milwaukee at 1555 North Martin Luther King, Jr., Drive.

Ella Wheeler Wilcox was once one of the country's most famous poets. You can learn more about this writer at the **Ella Wheeler Wilcox Birthplace** at County Trunk A at Scharine Road in Johnstown.

One of the U.S.'s best-loved family resort areas is **Wisconsin Dells**, located between Milwaukee and Madison. For nearly 15 miles along U.S. 12 (south of I-90/94), you can see huge eroded rock formations that were created over thousands of years, as the Wisconsin River bit into the earth's soft limestone. Almost three million visitors come to the Dells each year to enjoy the area's water parks, miniature golf courses, theme parks, and other amusements.

WYOMING

Wyoming is the land of national parks, most notably **Yellowstone,** which in this state you can reach through Mammoth. The first reports of this amazing national park—reported in St. Louis newspapers in 1810—were considered tall tales. Now, of course, we know that there are indeed giant elk, steaming mud pots, spurting geysers, and dramatic waterfalls in this beautiful national park, which in 1872 became the country's first.

Grand Teton National Park is also an exciting place to visit, offering lakes, mountains, and views of moose and bison along the Snake River. Contact The National Park Service, Drawer 170, Moose, WY 83012.

In Cody, the **Buffalo Bill Historical Center** (720 Sheridan Avenue) includes a number of museums with a western theme: **Plains Indian Museum, Cody Firearms Museum,** the **Buffalo Bill Museum,** and the **Whitney Gallery of Western Art.**

PUERTO RICO

The **Walled City of San Juan** includes Puerto Rican family treausres from the sixteenth and seventeenth centuries.

The **El Yunque** is a dramatic national park, where visitors can see many tropical plants, flowers, and animals.

U.S. VIRGIN ISLANDS

The **Christiansted Historic District** is probably the most interesting place to visit in this American possession, located at Harbor and West Streets, Christiansted, St. Croix.

Bibliography

These fiction and nonfiction books can tell you more about life in each state or territory.

ALABAMA

Alabama Bandits, Bushwhackers, Outlaws, Crooks, Devils, and Characters. Carole Marsh. The title says it all.

A Christmas Memory, Truman Capote. The author remembers a beloved aunt from his childhood.

Helen Keller's Teacher, Margaret Davidson. The true story of Anne Sullivan Macy who became Helen Keller's teacher and lifelong friend.

To Kill a Mockingbird, Harper Lee. In this classic story, a child tries to come to terms with racism and the fight for justice in a small town in the 1900s.

ALASKA

Call of the Wild, Jack London. In this story, a dog starts his life as a civilized pet but ends up a wild wolf in northern Alaska.

Julie of the Wolves, Jean Craighead George. Thirteen-year-old Julie is lost in the Alaskan wilderness—but gradually she is accepted by a pack of Arctic wolves that teach her to survive.

Racing the Iditarod Trail, Ruth Crisman. All about Alaska's most famous dog race.

Thunderfeet, Alaska's Dinosaurs and Other Prehistoric Critters, Shelley R. Gill. They're long gone but interesting to imagine.

ARIZONA

Anpao: An American Indian Odyssey, Jamake Highwater. A brave young man undertakes a quest that takes him across the face of the ancient world.

The Call of the Canyon, Zane Grey. This classic Western includes many beautiful descriptions of the Arizona landscape.

The Enemy Gods, Oliver LaFarge. The author paints an authentic portrait of Navajo life.

ARKANSAS

The Enduring Hills, Janice Holt Giles. This novel takes place in Arkansas's Ozark Mountains and tells about life and customs there.

True Grit, Charles Portis. A Yell County farm girl goes to Fort Smith and persuades a U.S. Marshal to help her track down her father's killer.

CALIFORNIA

California Blue, David Klass. John and his father get into an environmental tug-of-war after John discovers a new sub-species of butterfly.

Child of the Owl, Laurence Yep. When Case goes to live with her grandmother in San Francisco's Chinatown, she learns about her Chinese heritage.

The Great American Gold Rush, Rhoda Blumberg. How the discovery of gold at Sutter's Mill changed California forever.

Island of the Blue Dolphins, Scott O'Dell. An Indian girl left by her tribe survives alone for 18 years on a bleak island off the coast of California. Based on a true story.

Local News, Gary Soto. Thirteen wonderful stories about Mexican-American teens living in California.

Manzanar, John Armor and Peter Wright. A nonfiction account of the California internment of Japanese-Americans during World War II. Photos by Ansel Adams.

COLORADO

The Mountain Lion, Jean Stafford. A brother and sister have an unhappy youth until they escape to a Colorado ranch.

Tales, Trails, and Tommyknockers. Myriam Friggins. Stories from Colorado's past.

CONNECTICUT

Country Place, Ann Petry. This African-American author grew up in Old Saybrook and set this novel in the town of Lenox.

A Connecticut Yankee in King Arthur's Court, Mark Twain. A classic humorous tale of time travel.

DELAWARE

Delaware Timeline: A Chronology of Delaware History, Mystery, Trivia, Legend, Lore and More.

Voices of the River: Adventures on the Delaware River. Illustrated by Jan Cheripko.

DISTRICT OF COLUMBIA

First Children, Growing up in the White House, Katherine Leiner. Fascinating accounts of the lives of young people who have called the White House "home."

How the White House Really Works, George Sullivan. Home, office, museum and tourist attraction—how the White House operates. A fascinating behind-the-scenes look at America's "home."

FLORIDA

Jonah's Gourd Vine, Zora Neale Hurston. An Alabama cotton picker becomes a preacher in a small Florida town.

Strawberry Girl, Lois Lenski. Adventures of a girls in the Florida lake country.

The Yearling. Marjorie Kinnan Rawlings. Jody and his pet fawn are inseperable as they grow up in the Florida Everglades.

GEORGIA

Cold Sassy Tree, Olive Ann Burns. It's 1906, and things turn topsy-turvy when 14-year-old Will Tweedy's grandmother dies and his grandfather remarries.

Kidding Around Atlanta: A Young Person's Guide to the City. Anne Pedersen. What you might want to see and do in one of the South's most popular cities.

When Birds Could Talk and Bats Could Sing, Virginia Hamilton. A retelling of African-American folktales collected in the 1880s by journalist Martha Young. Illustrated by Barry Moser.

HAWAII

The Day Pearl Harbor Was Bombed: A Photohistory of World War II, George Sullivan. This arresting account is done is magazine format.

At the Gateways of the Day, Padraic Colum. The author adapted these stories from Hawaiian folklore.

Mark Twain's Letters from Hawaii, edited by A. Grove Day. These 25 travel letters from the famous American author detail a four-month visit to Hawaii in 1866.

'Olelo No'eau: Hawaiian Proverbs and Political Sayings, Mary Kawena Pukui. Reading these proverbs is a great way to get a feeling for the way Hawaiians look at things.

IDAHO

Stomp Ranch Pioneer, Nelle P. Davis (Idaho Yesterdays Series). A deeply moving novel about a pioneer woman farmer.

In Tragic Life, Vardis Fisher. This is the first of four autobiographical novels set in Idaho about a boy from a Morman pioneer background.

ILLINOIS

Across Five Aprils, Irene Hunt. On a southern Illinois farm during the Civil War, Jethro is loyal to the Union and his beloved brother is a Rebel.

Dandelion Wine, Ray Bradbury. This classic fantasy novel is set in a small Illinois town.

The Great Fire, Jim Murphy. Vivid, first-hand accounts of the 1871 Chicago fire make this nonfiction gripping.

INDIANA

Except for Me and Thee, Jessamyn West. The details of life in rural Indiana come alive in this novel about a Quaker family during Reconstruction.

Girl of the Limberlost, Gene Stratton Porter. The writer's detailed account of Indiana wildlife in this novel make the place come alive.

Jokelore: Humorous Folktales from Indiana, Ronald Baker. This collection of funny stories gives the flavor of Indiana life and sensibilities.

IOWA

Charlie Young Bear, Catherine Von Ahnen. Iowa's Mesqkuakie Indians receive payment for their lands in the 1950s.

True Tales from Iowa's Past, O. J. Fargo. Short nonfiction chapters about Iowa history.

Iowa Past to Present, People and the Prairie, Dorothy Schweider. A young people's history.

High on the Hog, Kimberly Olson Fakih. Trapp spends a rewarding summer on her great-grandparents' Iowa farm before moving to New York City.

An Occasional Cow, Polly Horvath. A New York City kid finds summer in Iowa a lot more exciting than she imagined.

KANSAS

Folklore from Kansas: Customs, Beliefs, and Superstitions, William E. Koch. A collection of ghost stories and folktales from Kansas.

The Learning Tree, Gordon Parks. A novel based on the author's own life tells of a black child growing up in a small town in the 1920s.

Lost Star: The Story of Amelia Earhart, Patricia Lauber. An award-winning biography of a Kansas native and America's most famous female aviator.

KENTUCKY

Cloud-Walking, Marie Campbell. A collection of the tales of mountain people.

The Court Martial of Daniel Boone, Allan W. Eckert. An historical novel based on the events of 1778.

Mountain Path, Harriette Simpson Arnow. A rural school teacher reaches out to the children in her community in this semi-autobiographical novel about the Cumberland region.

Singing Family of the Cumberlands, Jean Ritchie. This memoir of a folk musician born in the Cumberlands in 1922 includes traditional songs and is illustrated by Maurice Sendak.

LOUISIANA

The Autobiography of Miss Jane Pittman, Ernest Gaines. The fictional memoirs of a 100-year-old ex-slave about her life on a Louisiana plantation.

Creole Folk Tales, Hewitt L. Ballowe. These tales give the flavor of life in Louisiana's Mississippi Delta.

Other Voices, Other Rooms, Truman Capote. An old plantation is the setting for this novel about an adolescent's self-discovery.

Sounder, Bill and Vera Cleaver. Heartwarming novel about an African-American boy, his imprisoned father, and their dog.

MAINE

Especially Maine: The Natural World of Henry Beston, Henry Beston. A naturalist tells about the state that he loves and has observed for many years.

The Edge of the Sea, Rachel Carson. A beautiful and perceptive book by a Pulitzer prize-winning writer.

Folklore and the Sea, Horace Beck. This book of maritime legends includes many set in Maine.

Rebecca of Sunnybrook Farm, Kate Douglas Wiggin. High-spirited Rebecca grows up in Maine at the turn of the century.

The Maine Woods, Henry David Thoreau. The nineteenth-century author recalls trips to Mount Katahdin, Moosehead Lake, and the West Branch of the the Penobscot.

MARYLAND

Awesome Chesapeake, David O. Bell. The bay around which much of Maryland's history and economy are grounded is brought to life.

Maryland: Its Past and its Present. The interesting history of the nation's seventh state.

Jacob Have I Loved, Katherine Paterson. The sibling rivalry of twins, Louise and Caroline, who live on an island in the Chesapeake where their father harvests oysters and crabs, is the theme of this novel.

MASSACHUSETTS

April Morning, Howard Fast. Fifteen-year-old Adam Cooper becomes a man on the day of the Revolutionary Battle of Lexington.

Johnny Tremain, Esther Forbes. Johnny goes from being an arrogant young apprentice to a dedicated helper of the colonists in this Revolutionary War tale.

Little Women, Louisa May Alcott. The four March girls must learn to find their own identities in this story about a Massachusetts family during the Civil War.

Nightbirds on Nantucket, Joan Aiken. An English girl lost at sea is rescued by a New England whaling vessel and taken back to Nantucket where a hilarious mystery unfolds.

Samuel Eaton's Day, Kate Waters. A vivid photo recreation of a Pilgrim boy's daily life on Plimouth Plantation.

MICHIGAN

The Dollmaker, Harriette S. Arnow. During World War II, a gentle mountain woman brings her family to Detroit where she tries to hold on to her mountain customs and values.

Michigan's Past and the Nation's Future, Bruce Catton. The author explores Michigan's history in this contemporary book about the Wolverine State.

We'll Race You Henry: A Story About Henry Ford, Barbara Mitchell. This partly fictionalized biography focuses on race cars.

MINNESOTA

Lake Wobegon Days, Garrison Keillor. These playful stories are a fictionalized version of the popular radio talk show host's own childhood in Minnesota.

We Made It Through the Winter: A Memoir of a Northern Minnesota Boyhood, Walter O'Meara. Surviving the frigid Minnesota winter was an even greater challenge one hundred years ago when O'Meara was a boy.

MISSISSIPPI

Collected Stories, Eudora Welty. One of Mississippi's finest writers, born in Jackson, tells classic tales of small town and rural life.

A Treasury of Mississippi Folklore, B.A. Botkin. A rich collection of myths, legends and stories.

MISSOURI

The Adventures of Tom Sawyer, Mark Twain. Tom Sawyer enjoys the free and easy life of a boy in Hannibal, Missouri, in the middle of the nineteenth century.

Flood: Wrestling with the Mississippi, Patricia Lauber. What happens when a rain-swollen river overrides its banks? And how can people who live along it protect themselves?

Hilly Billy, Rose Wilder Lane. Laura Ingalls Wilder's daughter wrote this description of the customs and speech of the Ozark Mountains.

MONTANA

The Big Sky, Alfred B. Gutherie. A boy runs away from home to join the Blackfoot in the Teton Mountains in the 1820s.

A River Runs Through It and Other Stories, Norman Maclean. This autobiographical narrative of growing up in rural Montana centers on trout fishing in the Blackfoot River.

Sweetgrass, Jan Hudson. This award-winning novel shows how a 15-year-old Blackfoot girl proves herself in a terrible year for her tribe.

NEBRASKA

The Buffalo Wallow, Charles Tenney Jackson. The author recalls his boyhood in a prairie sodhouse in the 1890s.

Prairie Songs, Pam Conrad. A beautiful, illustrated novel of how one family thrives on the harsh prairie life.

Signs, Omens and Portents in Nebraska Folklore, Margaret Cannell and Emma L. Snap. Ghost stories and legends from the state are collected in this volume.

NEVADA

Between Two Worlds, Candice Ransom. The true story of a nineteenth-century Paiute woman's struggle to resist removal of her people to a Washington state reservation.

Roughing It, Mark Twain. The 25-year-old author remembers life in Virginia City as a journalist.

NEW HAMPSHIRE

The Isles of Shoals in Lore and Legend, Lyman Rutledge. This volume collects folklore about one of New Hampshire's most beautiful spots.

An Old Town by the Sea, Thomas Bailey Aldrich. This nonfiction account of Portsmouth draws on the author's childhood memories of that city, where he lived in the middle of the nineteenth century.

NEW JERSEY

The Chinaberry Tree, Jessie Redmon Fauset. This novel by one of the few women writers of the Harlem Renaissance explores life in a small black community.

The Folklore and Folklife of New Jersey, David S. Cohen. This is a contemporary collection of New Jersey folklore, compiled in 1983.

A New Jersey Reader, Henry Charlton Beck. This anthology of stories includes both fiction and historical material in its portrait of New Jersey's history and folklore.

NEW MEXICO

Book of the Hopi, Frank Waters. This nonfiction work tells of Hopi folklore, history, and customs.

Cuentos: Tales from the Hispanic Southwest, José Griego y Maestas and Rudolfa A. Anaya. This is a bilingual collection of tales collected from Spanish-speaking families in northern New Mexico and southern Colorado.

The House at Otowi Bridge: The Story of Edith Warner and Los Alamos, Peggy P. Church. This story of a woman who lived at Los Alamos at the time of the creation of the atomic bomb also conveys the way the nuclear project affected the region.

House Made of Dawn, N. Scott Momaday. A contemporary Indian attempts to recover the mystical tradition of his ancestors in this groundbreaking novel.

Indeh: An Apache Odyssey, Eve Ball. The oral history of the Apaches tells of their life in the land that became New Mexico.

Journey to the People, Ann N. Clark. A teacher and writer who won the 1953 Newbery Award remembers her life in New Mexico.

NEW YORK

Behind the Lines, Isabelle Holland. A young Irish maid gets caught up in the New York City race riots during the Civil War.

The Contender, Robert Lipsyte. Alfred, a black dropout, enters the Harlem Training Center for Boxers, hoping to become a contender for the championship.

Nilda, Nicholasa Mohr. Nilda, who lives with her large, affectionate family in Spanish Harlem, begins the painful process of growing up.

The Rifleman, John Brick. The life of Timothy Murphy, upstate hero of the Revolution, is the basis for this historical novel.

Remember the Ladies: The First Women's Rights Convention, Norma Johnson. A clearly written account of the event with many photos and interesting facts.

The Sketch Book, Washington Irving. This volume of essays and German folktales includes "Rip Van Winkle" and "The Legend of Sleepy Hollow."

Trimmed Lamp, and Other Stories of the Four Million, O. Henry (William Sydney Porter). These New York short stories feature O. Henry's classic "surprise ending" as they portray the lives of working men and women in early 20th-century New York.

We Shall Not Be Moved, Joan Dash. A compelling, nonfiction account of the 1909 strike by teenage girls working in the shirtwaist factories of New York.

NORTH CAROLINA

The Land Breakers, John Ehle. This novel tells of pioneer life beyond the Blue Ridge in the eighteenth and nineteenth centuries.

My Folks Don't Want Me to Talk about Slavery: Twenty-one Oral Histories of Former North Carolina Slaves, Belinda Hurmence (editor). This collection of oral histories presents new insight into slavery and the Civil War.

The Ragged Ones, Burke Davis. This historical novel of the Revolution is noted for its realism and accuracy.

Rough Weather Makes Good Timber: Carolinians Recall, Patsy M. Ginns. In 1977, the author collected these stories and proverbs from North Carolina residents.

The Swamp Fox, Noel Gerson. General Francis Marion, the "Swamp Fox," is the subject of this historical novel.

Where the Lilies Bloom, Vera Cleaver and Bill Cleaver. In this lyrical novel, 14-year-old Mary Call promises her dying father that she will keep the family together.

NORTH DAKOTA

American Daughter, Eta Bell Thompson. This is the autobiography of an African-American woman who moved with her farming family to the small town of Driscoll in 1914.

Badlands and Bronco Trails, Lewis F. Crawford. The story of Ben Conner, a pioneer in the days after the Civil War.

Dakota Diaspora: Memoirs of a Jewish Homesteader, Sophie Trupin. The author remembers life in one of the few Jewish immigrant communities of North Dakota.

Dust Bowl Diary, Ann Amie Low. The author remembers

life on a stock farm in southeastern North Dakota in the late 1920s.

Hunting Adventures in the West, Theodore Roosevelt. The author, who became a U.S. President, worked on a ranch in North Dakota in the 1880s, and wrote this memoir of his favorite hunting trips.

OHIO

Arilla Sun Down, Virginia Hamilton. A seventh grader from a small Ohio town, Arilla Mooning Running Adams, comes from an interracial background, part black, part Indian.

Ballads and Songs from Ohio, Mary O. Eddy (compiler). The author compiled versions of 25 English and Scottish popular ballads and almost 300 European and Native American folksongs.

The Bent Twig, Dorothy Canfield Fisher. This novel about the family of a college professor is based on the author's experience of Columbus in the late nineteenth century.

The Second Bend in the River, Ann Rinaldi. The daughter of settlers in 1798 befriends Native American chief, Tecumseh.

Leafy Rivers, Jessamyn West. This historical novel is set in Ohio Territory around 1800.

OKLAHOMA

Bound for Glory, Woody Guthrie. The songwriter and singer tells the story of his life from his upbringing in Okemah through his involvement with social protest in the 1930s and 1940s.

A Girl from Yamhill: A Memoir, Beverly Cleary. The popular author tells the story of her life.

Sequoyah, Grant Foreman. The biography of the Cherokee leader recounts how he invented a way of writing down his language.

The Way to Rainy Mountain, N. Scott Momaday. The author, a Native American novelist, created this account of the folklore, history, and present life of the Kiowa Indians of the Wichita Mountains.

The Will Rogers Book, ed. Paul M. Love. Rogers was a popular, homespun philosopher in the 1920s and 1930s. Some of his work is collected in this volume.

OREGON

Across the Wide and Lonesome Prairie, Kristiana Gregory. The Oregon Trail Diary of Hattie Campbell. A fictional account inspired by historic events.

Big Sam, Sam Churchill. A lumberjack recalls his life at the beginning of the 20th century.

Oregon Folklore, Suzi Jones (editor). These folktales include ghost stories, love stories, and legends.

PENNSYLVANIA

Fabulous Valley, Cornelia Parker. This novel tells of the 1859 discovery of oil in Pennsylvania.

Gettysburg, Stephen Longstreet. This historical novel describes there actions of ordinary townspeople to the great battle.

The Killer Angels, Michael Shaara. This Pulitzer Prize-winning novel tells of the Battle of Gettysburg from the point of view of officers on both sides.

The Patch Boys, Jay Parini. This novel tells of coming of age in an Italian-Polish mining community in 1925.

Spellbound: Growing Up in God's Country, David McKain. The author recalls growing up in a small town in the Alleghenies in the 1940s and 1950s.

RHODE ISLAND

I Seek a City, Gilbert Rees. This fictional autobiography of Roger Williams tells of his quest for religious freedom.

Our Own Kind, Edward McSorley. An Irish immigrant family struggles to survive in South Providence in the early twentieth century in this historical novel.

Saltbound: A Block Island Winter, Chilton Williamson, Jr. The beauties of Block Island are chronicled by this Rhode Island resident.

SOUTH CAROLINA

The Day Fort Sumter Was Fired On: A Photo History of the Civil War, Jim Haskins. Tells the effects of this military event on women, slaves, and children as well as the men who fought there.

Folk Song in South Carolina, Charles W. Joyner. One of the best ways to learn about a people is through their songs, as this volume demonstrates.

Jesse Jackson, A Biography, Patricia McKissack. A lively and even-handed story of the life of this South Carolina presidential candidate.

Scarlet Sister Mary, Julia Peterkin. The author was an owner and manager of a plantation near Fort Motte. She wrote several novels, like this Pulitzer Prize-winner, about the lives and folklore of the Gullah people.

A Short Walk, Alice Childress. This historical novel tells of an African-American woman who gets involved in Marcus Garvey's campaign for returning to Africa.

SOUTH DAKOTA

Bury My Heart at Wounded Knee: An Indian History of the American West, Dee Brown. The Sioux Massacre of the nineteenth century is the point of departure for this historical narrative about American Indians.

Dakota Dream, James Bennett. After dreaming of a life away from orphanages and foster homes, a boy escapes to a Sioux reservation.

Land of the Spotted Eagle, Luther Standing Bear. In this 1933 memoir, a Dakota chief writes about his people and the land they inhabit.

Little House Series: By the Shores of Silver Lake, The Long Winter, Little Town on the Prairie, These Happy Golden Years, Laura Ingalls Wilder. Novels from the famous Little House series set in Smet, South Dakota, where the author grew up.

TENNESSEE

Chariot in the Sky: A Story of the Fisk Jubilee Singers, Arna Bontemps. This 19th-century historical narrative tells the story of the internationally renowned Fisk Jubilee Singers.

The Hawk's Done Gone and Other Stories, ed., by Mildred Haun. This collection draws on the lives of the East Tennessee mountain people.

TEXAS

Make Way for Sam Houston, Jean Fritz. This biography captures the spirit of this larger-than-life hero.

Old Yeller, Fred Gipson. In this classic story, a boy and his dog have many adventures in the Texas hill country.

UTAH

Saints of Sage and Saddle: Folklore Among the Mormons, Austin E. Fife and Alta Fife. The Mormons were the first European Americans to settle in Utah. These are their stories.

Wind in the Rock, Ann Zinger. This essay describes the natural beauty of five southern Utah canyons.

Why the North Star Stands Still and Other Indian Legends, William R. Palmer. The author collected these tales of the native peoples of Utah.

VERMONT

Understood Betsy, Dorothy Canfield Fisher. A popular classic about Elizabeth Ann and the fearful new life she meets in the wilds of Vermont.

Hill Song: A Country Journal, Lee P. Huntington. The author shares the beauties and challenges of each of the Vermont seasons.

VIRGINIA

Grandfather Tales: American English Folktales, ed., Richard Chase. These stories were collected from North Carolina, Virginia, and Kentucky, reflecting the English heritage of all three states.

The Double Life of Pocahontas, Jean Fritz. A biography of the Indian girl who befriended white settlers in seventeenth-century Virginia.

When Will This Cruel War Be Over? Barry Denenberg. The fictional Civil War diary of Emma Simpson.

A Picture of Freedom, Patricia McKissack. The fictional diary of Clotee, a slave girl on Belmont Plantation in 1859.

Thomas Jefferson: The Man With a Vision, Ruth Crisman. This biography recounts the many achievements of our fourth president: statesman, writer, musician and architect.

WASHINGTON

Great Son, Edna Ferber. This novel chronicles four generations of a Seattle family from 1851 to 1940.

Haboo: Native American Stories from Puget Sound, Vi Hilbert. This collection of Indian folklore was compiled in 1985.

WEST VIRGINIA

The Telltale Lilac Bush and Other West Virginia Ghost Stories, Ruth Ann Music. West Virginia mountain people told the author these scary tales.

Up from Slavery: An Autobiography, Booker T. Washington. One of America's most influential African-American leaders tells of his early life in Malden, where he worked in a saltworks, in a coal mine, and as a domestic servant.

WISCONSIN

Caddie Woodlawn, Carol Ryrie Brink. This delightful novel about a red-haired tomboy and her brothers in early Wisconsin won the Newbery Award in 1936.

Little House in the Big Wood, Laura Ingalls Wilder. This timeless classic tells the story of a log-cabin family in Wisconsin in the 1800s. Illustrated by Garth Williams.

Rascal, Sterling North. The author relates his boyhood adventures with a pet raccoon in rural Wisconsin.

WYOMING

Bendigo Shafter, Louis L'Amour. Set in Wyoming, this Western novel was written by one of America's most popular authors.

My Friend Flicka, Mary O'Hara. In this beloved classic novel, Ken is delighted when he gets his own horse, Flicka, on his Wyoming ranch.

One Day at Teton Marsh, Sally Carrigher. The author describes the ecology and wild life of a pond near Jackson Hole.

Shane, Jack Shaefer. This classic Western recounts the struggle between farmers and ranchers in the 1890s.

PUERTO RICO

Puerto Rico in Pictures. The life and history, culture and geography of this rich land.

The Three Wishes: A Collection of Puerto Rican Folk Tales, Ricardo Alegría. Puerto Rican stories and legends give readers the flavor of life on the island.

Index

D

E

F

G

U

V

W

Y

PHOTO CREDITS

All photos courtesy of Archive Photos with the exception of the following: p. 47 Ralph Bunche, p. 50 Ida B. Wells-Barnett, p. 72 Toni Morrison, p. 79 Marion Anderson, p. 89 Barbara Jordan, p. 121 Paul Laurence Dunbar, all courtesy of The Schomburg Center for the Study of Black Culture, a division of the New York Public Library, Astor, Lenox and Tilden Foundations; p. 2 Folk Dancers courtesy of the Alabama Bureau of Tourism; p. 8 President William Jefferson Clinton, p. 16 Henry Hudson, p. 30 Raggedy Ann doll, p. 42 Cal Ripken Jr., p. 48 snow scene, p. 49 Laura Ingalls Wilder, p. 58 desert scene, p. 63 Bill Bradley, p. 98 coal miners, p. 100 Green Bay Packers, all courtesy of Scholastic Inc.